SPSS FOR MACINTOSH MADE SIMPLE

SPSS FOR MACINTOSH
MADE SIMPLE

Colin D. Gray

Paul R. Kinnear

Department of Psychology,

University of Aberdeen

This book is not sponsored or approved by SPSS, and any errors are in no way the responsibility of SPSS.
SPSS is a registered trademark and the other product names are trademarks of SPSS Inc.
SPSS Screen Images © SPSS Inc.
For further information, contact:
SPSS UK Ltd, First Floor St Andrew's House, West Street, Woking, Surrey, GU21 1EB, UK

Windows is a registered trademark of Microsoft Corporation.
For further information, contact:
Microsoft Corporation, One Microsoft Way, Redmond, WA 98052-6399, USA

Apple, the Apple logo, Macintosh, PowerBook are trademarks of Apple Computer Inc.,
registered in the United States and other countries.
For further information, contact:
Apple Computer Inc., 1 Infinite Loop, Cupertino, CA 95014-2084, USA

Copyright © 1998 by Psychology Press Ltd, a member of the Taylor & Francis group
All rights reserved. No part of this publication may be reproduced, stored in a retrieval system, or transmitted in any form or by any means, electronic, mechanical, photocopying, recording or otherwise, without permission in writing from the publisher.

Reprinted 1998

Psychology Press Ltd, Publishers
27 Church Road
Hove
East Sussex
BN3 2FA
UK

British Library Cataloguing-in-Publication Data

A catalogue record for this book is available from the British Library

ISBN: 0-86377-742-2

Printed and bound in the UK by TJ International, Padstow, from camera-ready copy provided by the authors

CONTENTS

PREFACE   ix

CHAPTER 1   THE MACINTOSH PERSONAL COMPUTER   *1*

1.1   INTRODUCTION *2*
- 1.1.1   To The Reader *2*
- 1.1.2   Computers in general *2*
- 1.1.3   Memory *3*
- 1.1.4   Programs, programming and packages *4*
- 1.1.5   Operating systems and interfaces *4*
- 1.1.6   Files and folders *5*
- 1.1.7   Changing from MACOS: Windows conventions for file names *5*

1.2   THE MACINTOSH KEYBOARD *5*
- 1.2.1   Arrangement of the keys on a Mac keyboard *6*
- 1.2.2   A glossary of keys for future reference *7*

1.3   BEGINNING AND ENDING A SESSION ON THE MAC *9*
- 1.3.1   Booting up *10*
- 1.3.2   Using a machine in a network: Logging in and logging out *10*

CHAPTER 2   BASIC MACINTOSH OPERATIONS FOR SPSS *11*

2.1   THE GRAPHICAL USER INTERFACE (GUI) *12*
- 2.1.1   What happens when you turn on the Mac *12*
- 2.1.2   The desktop *12*
- 2.1.3   The screen pointer: Handling the mouse *13*

2.2   THE MENU BAR *14*
- 2.2.1   Getting help: the Guide menu *15*
- 2.2.2   The Application Menu *15*
- 2.2.3   How new folders and files are created *16*
- 2.2.4   The disk icons and the Wastebasket *16*

2.3   THE MACINTOSH HARD DISK WINDOW *17*
- 2.3.1   Opening the window *18*
- 2.3.2   Controlling the window display: The View menu *18*
- 2.3.3   Viewing the contents of the Macintosh HD window *19*

Contents

   2.3.4 Opening a file: The Memory Control Panel *20*

2.4 SOME USEFUL OPERATIONS WITH THE FILE MENU *22*

   2.4.1 The Find ... command *23*

   2.4.2 Short cuts: Using key combinations *24*

   2.4.3 Creating an alias *25*

2.5 THE APPLE MENU *26*

   2.5.1 A look at the Apple menu *26*

   2.5.2 Customising the Apple menu: The Apple Menu Items folder *27*

2.6 BEGINNING SPSS FOR MACINTOSH *28*

   2.6.1 The Data Editor window *28*

   2.6.2 Resuming work on a saved data set: A short-cut *31*

   2.6.3 Using the mouse to save a file to, and retrieve a file from, a floppy disk *31*

Exercise 1 *33*

CHAPTER 3   DATA HANDLING IN SPSS *35*

3.1 INTRODUCTION *36*

3.2 SOME RESEARCH TERMS *36*

3.3 ENTERING AND EDITING DATA *41*

   3.3.1 Data from a between subjects experiment *41*

   3.3.2 Obtaining the Data Editor window *43*

   3.3.3 How many decimal places? *44*

   3.3.4 Variable names and value labels *45*

   3.3.5 Using the keyboard to enter data *49*

   3.3.6 Entering the data into the Data Editor window *50*

   3.3.7 Editing data *51*

   3.3.8 Data from a within subjects experiment *53*

   3.3.9 Entering string variables *55*

   3.3.10 Missing values *56*

3.4 SAVING AND RETRIEVING SPSS FILES *57*

   3.4.1 Saving a file *57*

   3.4.2 Reading in SPSS files *59*

   3.4.3 Importing and exporting data *60*

3.5 LISTING DATA *61*

   3.5.1 Listing cases *61*

   3.5.2 Displaying data file information *63*

3.6 PRINTING IN SPSS *64*

3.7 SOME SPECIAL OPERATIONS *65*

    3.7.1   Case selection *66*

    3.7.2   The weighting of cases by their frequencies of occurrence *68*

    3.7.3   Splitting files *70*

Exercises 2-3 *71*

CHAPTER 4   LISTING AND EXPLORING DATA *77*

4.1 INTRODUCTION *78*

    4.1.1   Exploratory data analysis (EDA) *78*

    4.1.2   The influence of outliers and asymmetry of distributions *80*

    4.1.3   Formal tests, statistical models and their assumptions *80*

4.2 FINDING MENUS *82*

4.3 DESCRIBING DATA *82*

    4.3.1   Describing categorial data *83*

    4.3.2   Describing interval data *87*

    4.3.3   Other graphical procedures *96*

4.4 MANIPULATION OF THE DATA SET *108*

    4.4.1   Reducing and transforming data *108*

    4.4.2   The COMPUTE procedure *108*

    4.4.3   The RECODE procedure *111*

Exercises 4-8 *114*

CHAPTER 5   CHOOSING A STATISTICAL TEST *127*

5.1 INTRODUCTION *128*

5.2 THE RESEARCH QUESTION *128*

    5.2.1   The nature of the data *129*

    5.2.2   The plan or design of the research *130*

5.3 TWO OR MORE SAMPLES *131*

    5.3.1   Choosing tests for comparing averages between (and among) samples of interval data *131*

    5.3.2   Interval data *133*

    5.3.3   Ordinal data *143*

    5.3.4   Nominal data *134*

5.4 ONE-SAMPLE TESTS *136*

5.5 THE ANALYSIS OF DATA FROM FACTORIAL EXPERIMENTS *138*

5.6   MEASURING STATISTICAL ASSOCIATION BETWEEN TWO VARIABLES *138*

5.7   REGRESSION *141*

5.8   MULTIVARIATE STATISTICS *141*

5.9   DATA ANALYSIS WITH SPSS *143*

5.10 GETTING HELP *145*

CHAPTER 6   COMPARING THE AVERAGES OF TWO SAMPLES *147*

6.1   INTRODUCTION *148*

6.2   PARAMETRIC METHODS: THE t-TESTS *150*

    6.2.1   Assumptions underlying the use of the t-test *150*

    6.2.2   Paired and independent samples *150*

    6.2.3   The paired samples t-test *152*

    6.2.4   The independent samples t-test *155*

6.3   NONPARAMETRIC METHODS *157*

    6.3.1   Related samples: Wilcoxon, Sign and McNemar tests *158*

    6.3.2   Independent samples: Mann-Whitney test *159*

Exercises 9-11 *161*

CHAPTER 7   THE ONE-FACTOR BETWEEN SUBJECTS EXPERIMENT *170*

7.1   INTRODUCTION *171*

7.2   THE ONE-WAY ANOVA *173*

    7.2.1   The mnemonics experiment revisited *173*

    7.2.2   Procedure for the one-way ANOVA *173*

    7.2.3   Output listing for the one-way ANOVA *176*

7.3   NONPARAMETRIC TESTS *180*

    7.3.1   The Kruskal-Wallis test *180*

    7.3.2   The chi-square test *182*

Exercise 12 *183*

CHAPTER 8   FACTORIAL EXPERIMENTS (BETWEEN SUBJECTS) *186*

8.1   INTRODUCTION *187*

8.2   FACTORIAL ANOVA *190*

    8.2.1   Preparing the data for the factorial ANOVA *191*

    8.2.2   Exploring the data: Obtaining cell means and standard deviations *192*

8.2.3 Choosing a factorial ANOVA *193*

8.2.4 Output listing for a factorial ANOVA *195*

8.3 EXPERIMENTS WITH MORE THAN TWO TREATMENT FACTORS *202*

Exercise 13 *206*

CHAPTER 9   WITHIN SUBJECTS EXPERIMENTS *208*

9.1 INTRODUCTION *209*

9.2 ADVANTAGES AND DISADVANTAGES OF WITHIN SUBJECTS EXPERIMENTS *210*

9.3 WITHIN SUBJECTS ANOVA WITH SPSS *211*

9.4 A ONE-FACTOR WITHIN SUBJECTS ANOVA *212*

9.4.1 Some experimental results *212*

9.4.2 Entering the data *213*

9.4.3 Exploring the data - boxplots for within subjects factors *213*

9.4.4 Running the within subjects ANOVA *216*

9.4.5 Output listing for a one-factor within subjects ANOVA *219*

9.4.6 Unplanned multiple comparisons: Bonferroni method *221*

9.5 NONPARAMETRIC TESTS FOR A ONE-FACTOR WITHIN SUBJECTS EXPERIMENT *222*

9.5.1 The Friedman test for ordinal data *222*

9.5.2 Cochran's Q test for nominal data *224*

9.6 THE TWO-FACTOR WITHIN SUBJECTS ANOVA *225*

9.6.1 Results of a two-factor within subjects experiment *225*

9.6.2 Preparing the data set *226*

9.6.3 Running the two-factor within subjects analysis *227*

9.6.4 Output listing for a two-factor within subjects ANOVA *229*

9.6.5 Unplanned comparisons following a factorial within subjects experiment *231*

Exercises 14-15 *232*

CHAPTER 10   EXPERIMENTS OF MIXED DESIGN *235*

10.1 INTRODUCTION *236*

10.2 THE TWO-FACTOR MIXED FACTORIAL ANOVA *237*

10.2.1 Results of a mixed A × (B) experiment *237*

10.2.2 Preparing the SPSS data set *238*

10.2.3 Exploring the results: Boxplots and tables of means and standard deviations *238*

Contents

    10.2.4 Procedure for a mixed A × (B) ANOVA *241*

    10.2.5 Output listing for the two-factor mixed ANOVA *243*

10.3 THE THREE-FACTOR MIXED ANOVA *245*

    10.3.1 The mixed A × (B × C) experiment *245*

    10.3.2 The mixed A × B ×(C) experiment *247*

10.4 FURTHER ANALYSIS: SIMPLE EFFECTS AND MULTIPLE COMPARISONS *248*

Exercises 16-17 *249*

CHAPTER 11   **MEASURING STATISTICAL ASSOCIATION** *253*

11.1 INTRODUCTION *254*

11.2 CORRELATIONAL ANALYSIS WITH SPSS *256*

    11.2.1 Procedure for the Pearson correlation *258*

    11.2.2 Output listing for the Pearson correlation *259*

    11.2.3 Point-biserial correlation *261*

11.3 OTHER MEASURES OF ASSOCIATION *261*

    11.3.1 Measures of association strength for ordinal data *261*

    11.3.2 Measures of association strength for categorial data *264*

Exercises 18-19 *271*

CHAPTER 12   **REGRESSION** *277*

12.1 INTRODUCTION *278*

    12.1.1 Simple, two-variable regression *278*

    12.1.2 Multiple regression *278*

    12.1.3 Residuals *279*

    12.1.4 The multiple correlation coefficient *279*

12.2 SIMPLE REGRESSION *279*

    12.2.1 Procedure for simple regression *280*

    12.2.2 Output listing for simple regression *283*

12.3 MULTIPLE REGRESSION *287*

    12.3.1 Procedure for simultaneous multiple regression *289*

    12.3.2 Procedure for stepwise multiple regression *291*

    12.3.3 The need for a substantive model of causation *294*

12.4 SCATTERPLOTS AND REGRESSION LINES *295*

Exercises 20-21 *298*

Contents

CHAPTER 13   LOGLINEAR ANALYSIS *302*

13.1 INTRODUCTION *303*

    13.1.1 Comparison with ANOVA *303*

    13.1.2 Why 'loglinear' analysis? *304*

    13.1.3 Constructing a loglinear model *305*

    13.1.4 Small expected frequencies *305*

13.2 AN EXAMPLE OF A LOGLINEAR ANALYSIS *306*

    13.2.1 A three-way contingency table *306*

    13.2.2 Procedure for a loglinear analysis *308*

    13.2.3 Output listing for a loglinear analysis *311*

    13.2.4 Comparison with the total independence model *315*

Exercise 22 *317*

CHAPTER 14   DISCRIMINANT ANALYSIS *319*

14.1 INTRODUCTION *320*

    14.1.1 Discriminant analysis *320*

    14.1.2 Types of discriminant analysis *322*

    14.1.3 Stepwise discriminant analysis *322*

14.2 DISCRIMINANT ANALYSIS WITH SPSS *323*

    14.2.1 Procedure for discriminant analysis *323*

    14.2.2 Output listing for discriminant analysis *325*

    14.2.3 Predicting group membership *331*

Exercise 23 *332*

CHAPTER 15   FACTOR ANALYSIS *335*

15.1 INTRODUCTION *336*

    15.1.1 The nature of factors *336*

    15.1.2 Stages in a factor analysis *337*

    15.1.3 The extraction of factors *338*

    15.1.4 The rationale of rotation *338*

    15.1.5 Confirmatory factor analysis and structural equation modelling *338*

15.2 A FACTOR ANALYSIS OF DATA ON SIX VARIABLES *339*

    15.2.1 Procedure for factor analysis with raw scores *340*

    15.2.2 Output listing for factor analysis *343*

15.3 USING SPSS COMMAND LANGUAGE *348*

    15.3.1 The power of SPSS syntax: an example *348*

    15.3.2 Using a correlation matrix as input for factor analysis *351*

    15.3.3 Progressing with SPSS syntax *354*

Exercise 24 *355*

REFERENCES *357*

INDEX *359*

READER'S NOTES *364*

PREFACE

SPSS for Macintosh Made Simple is similar in scope and intended readership to our three earlier books for the PC platform. We wrote those books because, although comprehensive texts on SPSS were available, there was an evident need for an introductory book, especially one specifically addressing the requirements of psychologists, social scientists, and educational researchers. The gratifyingly positive reception strongly confirmed the need for a text of this kind. There have been many enquiries from Macintosh users about the availability of such a book for the Macintosh platform. We hope that this one will meet their requirements.

Like its predecessors, *SPSS for Macintosh Made Simple* is the product of many years of experience in teaching the use of SPSS (and other packages) for the analysis of psychological data. There is an abundance of illustrative material and worked examples, which include selections of SPSS output and screen images of application windows and dialog boxes. These are accompanied by comments clarifying the points that, over the years, have arisen most frequently from students' queries during our SPSS practical classes at the University of Aberdeen. As the title indicates, the emphasis has been upon simplicity and clarity, rather than upon comprehensiveness. The range of problems and techniques covered is, however, much wider than the selections available in comparable introductions to SPSS.

This book is intended for the reader with access to a Macintosh computer who has never worked with SPSS and wants to get started. No previous experience with SPSS (nor indeed with any other computing package) is assumed; although we expect that many of our readers will already have had at least some experience of computing. More experienced users may wish to skip some of the material in the earlier chapters, which are concerned with computer basics.

In outline, the structure of the book is as follows. Chapter 1 introduces the reader to some general basic principles of computing. Chapter 2 introduces the Macintosh operating system and describes some elementary Macintosh operations. Chapter 3 describes the inputting and editing of data in some detail. Chapter 4 concerns the description and exploration of data sets with SPSS. Chapter 5 offers some advice on selecting an appropriate statistical test from the bewildering variety of options available in SPSS. This chapter is also a sort of sketch map of the remainder of the book: there are signposts indicating where, in the later chapters, the relevant commands can be found. The remaining chapters describe the access and use of a variety of statistical methods: t-tests and their nonparametric equivalents (Chapter 6); the analysis of variance for common experimental designs (Chapters 7 - 10); correlation (Chapter 11); regression (Chapter 12); loglinear analysis of complex contingency tables (Chapter 13); discriminant analysis (Chapter 14); and factor analysis (Chapter 15).

We have been most fortunate in having the advice, encouragement and expertise of John Lemon, Senior Computing Adviser at Aberdeen University's Directorate of Information Systems and Services, who has given us the benefit of his own extensive experience with SPSS. We are also fortunate having several Departmental colleagues who are expert Macintosh users, and we are especially grateful to Dr Annalena Venneri and Dr Alan Milne, who have been most generous with their time and expertise. Dr Leslie Ord, our Departmental Computing Officer, has been tireless in arranging and maintaining the necessary hardware and networking facilities. We are also grateful to Caroline Green, Teaching Fellow, for her many helpful suggestions.

Preface

Finally, we would like to express our gratitude to all those people who, though too numerous to mention individually, have contributed advice or comments, or have helped in some other way. In particular, we must make special mention of our students, whose comments have been a continual source of enlightenment and support.

Colin Gray and Paul Kinnear.

July 1998

CHAPTER 1

THE MACINTOSH PERSONAL COMPUTER

1.1 INTRODUCTION
1.2 THE MACINTOSH KEYBOARD
1.3 BEGINNING AND ENDING A SESSION ON THE MAC

1.1 INTRODUCTION

1.1.1 To The Reader

We anticipate that our readers will vary considerably in their computing background: some will certainly be experienced users of computing systems and packages; but others, just as certainly, will be newcomers to computing. Should you be in the former category, you may wish to skip the remainder of this chapter, which is about computer basics, and move directly to Chapter 2. Otherwise, we suggest you begin here and familiarise yourself with some basic computing terminology, with the nature and functions of an operating system, and with the organisation of information that you want to store into files and folders. Should any of these terms be unfamiliar to you, they will be explained in the following sections.

1.1.2 Computers in general

A computer is a device for processing information. This processing has three aspects, all of which can be monitored on the screen of the computer's **visual display unit (VDU)**:

(1) the **inputting** of information;

(2) the **central processing** of the input;

(3) the **output** of the results.

Inputting information to the computer

There are several ways of inputting information to a computer. The user can type it in from a keyboard resembling that on a typewriter; but information can also be retrieved electronically from a storage medium such as a **floppy disk**, or transferred from another computer in a **network** (see below).

Central processing of the input

The central processing of information is controlled by **commands** typed on the keyboard or selected from a **menu** by means of a **mouse**, a **trackball**, a **trackpad**, or a **light pen**. A **mouse** is a device which, when moved around on a flat surface (a special high-friction mat, or **mouse pad**, is recommended), controls the position of a **screen pointer**. There are now many mouse analogues, such as the **trackball** (which is stationary), the **trackpad**, which respond to the touch of a finger, and the **light pen**, which the user applies to the screen. But although the basic principle is always the same, many users prefer the original, 'mouse-like' form, and use that wherever possible. The mouse (we shall retain this as a generic term for all such devices) continues to be one of the mainstays of modern computing.

Outputting the results

The inputting of information, the giving of commands to the computer, and computer output can all be monitored on the screen. It is often necessary, however, to use a printer to obtain a permanent record, or **hard copy**, of the work the computer has done.

1.1.3 Memory

An important aspect of computing is **memory**, the retention of information both in the **short term** (for the duration of a computing session) and in the **long term** (indefinitely). Information is stored in units called **files**, which are patterns of electromagnetic disturbance on the surfaces of disks, the latter being driven by hardware called **disk drives**. By the operation of a disk drive, information is stored in (**saved to**) and **read from** files. Until quite recently, there have been two main types of disks:

(1) **floppy disks** (or '**floppies**'), which are physically accessible to the user, have limited storage capacity and are portable;

(2) **hard disks**, which are an integral part of the hardware, have a relatively large storage capacity, and cannot be withdrawn by the user.

Modern desktop computers, however, often have additional **compact disk (CD) drives** which can store more information than can floppy disks. For additional back-up storage, particularly in **mainframes** (large non-portable computers), electronic **recording tape** is used. The contents of the hard disks of desktop computers can also be backed up on tape, a useful recourse if one is about to change to a new computer.

In the early days of desktop computers, floppy disks (and hard disks too) could only too easily be damaged, or **corrupted**, so that the information they contained was lost. Since then, although disks have certainly become more robust, corruption can still occur, and it is still sound practice to duplicate (or **back up**) files by storing them on another disk or on another computer, such as the **file server** in a network.

Before a new floppy disk can be used, it must first be **formatted**: that is, it must be prepared for use with a specific **operating system** - see below. Until recently, it was standard practice for users to format their own disks, but now disks intended for a particular **platform** (computer plus operating system) often come ready-formatted from the manufacturer.

1.1.4 Programs, programming and packages

There are many programming languages, and expertise in programming takes some time to acquire. Fortunately, there are available prewritten sets, or **packages**, of programs, which can be used by those with little or no programming experience. The **Statistical Package for the Social Sciences (SPSS)** is a computing package which, over the years, has developed and changed with the latest advances in computing technology and statistics. Whether one's computer is a stand-alone machine or a unit in a network, the procedure for operating **SPSS for Macintosh** is basically the same, barring a few minor local details, such as the manner in which one enters and leaves the system, and how one prints the output.

1.1.5 Operating systems and interfaces

An **operating system (OS)** is the software that runs the computer. An important aspect of any computing system is the **user interface**, that is, the working environment within which the user gives commands, makes choices and monitors the results of the computer's response. It is through the interface that the user accesses and runs programs. As well as creating the interface, an OS has several other functions over which the user has direct control. These include disk formatting, file management and the running of programs.

In this book, we shall be concerned with the **Macintosh Operating System (MACOS)**. Other operating systems, however, are also in use. For example, the **Windows** operating system was designed by the Microsoft Company for **IBM Personal Computers (PCs)** and their compatibles, the latter being widely known as **PC clones**. Microsoft also devised the earlier **Microsoft Disk Operating System (MS-DOS, or DOS** for short).

The combination of computer and operating system is known as a **platform**. The Mac computer and MACOS are just one of several platforms in use at present: an IBM PC clone running Windows is another; and a computer running the UNIX operating system yet another. Although, in recent years, the environments created by the Macintosh and Windows operating systems have become rather similar, there remain some important differences which must be borne in mind should the need to change platforms arise.

Some environments, such as Microsoft DOS, require the user to type commands in from the keyboard. In a **graphical interface**, however, the user communicates with the computer by working with small pictures on the screen called **icons** and inputting information to larger arrays called **dialog boxes**. MACOS provides a graphical interface, known as the **Graphical User Interface (GUI)**, pronounced 'gooey' by Mac buffs.

1.1.6 Files and folders

The manner in which information is stored by a computing system may be clarified by analogy with an office filing system. In a computing system, information is also stored in units called **files**. Files can usefully be thought of as individual documents, like letters, or manuscripts. Files are stored in larger units called **folders**, which are analogous to the labelled folders that hang in a filing cabinet.

To be useful, a file or folder must have a name. A Mac file name can be as long as 31 characters, which can be letters, spaces, punctuation marks, arithmetical operators, diacritics (such as accents) and so on. Only the colon (:) is forbidden. The following, therefore, are legitimate file names: **accounts, accounts 1997-98, ?### accounts?;** but the name **##: accounts** is not allowed, because it contains a colon. Note that spaces are allowed in Mac names. This is a very useful feature indeed.

There can be folders within folders within folders, so that a file may be buried several layers beneath the surface of a complex hierarchical storage system. Fortunately, as we shall see in the next chapter, it is remarkably easy to retrieve a Mac file or folder, provided that file names are kept as distinctive as possible, and that a systematic and sensible storage strategy is followed.

1.1.7 Changing from MACOS: Windows conventions for file names

On occasion, perhaps in order to access a particular package or to add a file to an existing set on another platform, the user may want to transfer a file from a Macintosh platform to, say, a PC clone with Windows. Nowadays, there is much more compatibility than there used to be between MACOS and Windows. The user, however, is warned that care is needed when transferring a Mac file (say a document created with a word-processing application such as Word 6) to the equivalent package in Windows, because Windows has a much stricter set of rules governing the naming of files, and cannot open Mac files with names that do not conform to these rules.

1.2 THE MACINTOSH KEYBOARD

The information in this section is partly intended for later reference, once the user has learned some Mac basics. There is no substitute for hands-on experience with the keyboard, particularly for those who have had no previous experience of typing. One of the best ways of familiarising yourself with the workings of the Mac keyboard is to access a word processor such as Word for Macintosh and try to produce some text. Before doing that, however, the reader may find it helpful to study the following short account of the Mac keyboard, preferably with a keyboard at hand, on which the principal keys and other structures can be identified.

The two keyboards most commonly in use with Mac computers are the 81-key Apple keyboard and the Apple Extended Keyboard. There are, however, many variants of these two basic types. On portable laptop machines (or Powerbooks), the keyboards have fewer keys, and some non-essential functions may be missing.

1.2.1 Arrangement of the keys on a Mac keyboard

To the proficient typist, the Mac keyboard will look very familiar (see Figure 1). The letter keys are arranged exactly as they are on an ordinary typewriter. The difference is that when a key is pressed, the effects are seen on the monitor screen, rather than anything being actually typed. The location of control on the screen (i.e. the typist's 'place') is indicated by a blinking (but stationary) image called the **cursor**. (The term **insertion point** is also used.) There is a **space bar** running along the bottom of the keyboard, a single press of which moves the cursor one space to the right, without any character appearing.

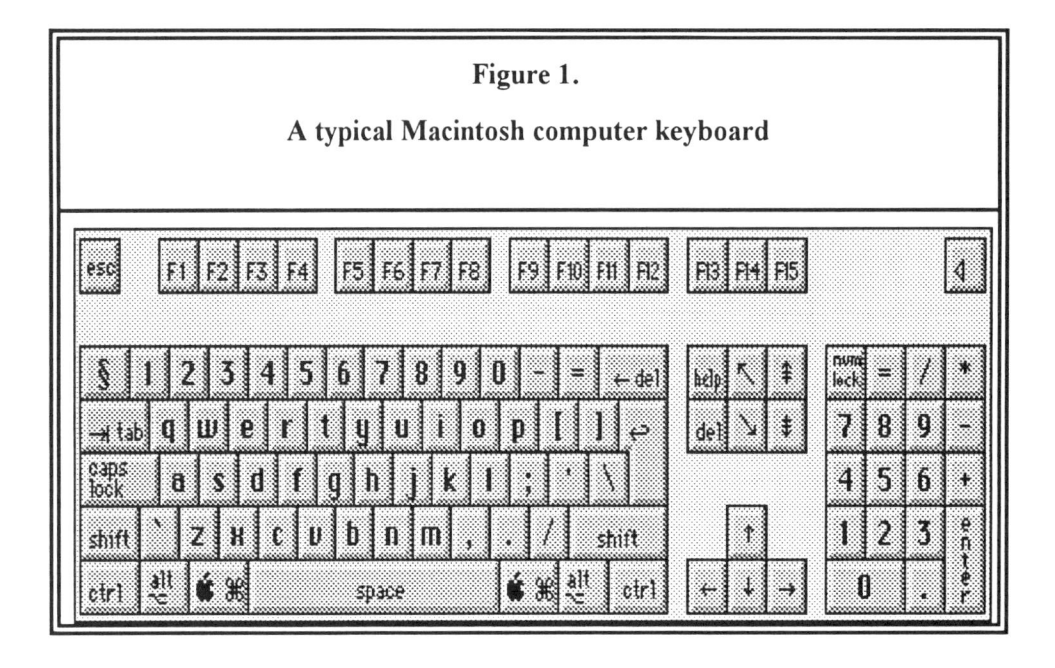

Figure 1.

A typical Macintosh computer keyboard

Like an ordinary typewriter, the Mac keyboard has two **shift keys** (Figure 1). Some keys have more than one character printed on them. When a shift key is pressed and held down, pressing a double-character key such as that bearing the characters 8 and *, will produce the asterisk, not the 8.

The shift keys also control whether letters are printed in **lower** or **UPPER** case. In the original, or **default**, set-up, pressing a letter key (say that marked **E**) will show that letter on the screen in lower case (**e**). But if, after a shift key has been pressed and held down, the same letter key is pressed, the letter on screen will appear in upper case (**E**). Should the user wish to type several letters in upper case, a single press of the **Capitals Lock (Caps Lock)** key will achieve this; lower case is restored by another press of Caps Lock. The Caps Lock key thus functions as a toggle switch: one press of which produces a change in the state of the system, which is reversed when the key is pressed again. Toggle keys often have an indicator light on the keyboard to show the state of the system.

In this book, to make it clear that a key is to be pressed, rather than a sequence of letters typed, the key will be referred to by its name (or a shortened form of this) or its symbol, as in the instruction **Shift**, meaning 'Press the shift key'.

Holding down one key (such as Shift) and then pressing another will be represented by using the slash character (/), thus **Shift/E**, means 'Hold down the Shift key, then press and release E'. In MACOS, the command key is often used in this way, as in the key combination **Command/?**, which summons the **Macintosh Guide**.

Sometimes, two or more keys are held down together. This will be indicated by separating the names of the keys by hyphens within a single set of square brackets: thus **Option-Command-Escape** means that the three keys so labelled are to be pressed and held down together. (We shall see that the decision to use this combination should not be taken lightly!)

Be sure to make a clear distinction between the digit **zero (0) key** (which is one of the number keys above the top row of letters) and the letter **O (O) key**, which is in the top row of letters. The computer treats these two characters quite differently.

On a full computer keyboard, there are several additional keys with functions specific to computing. For example, to the right of the main keyboard there may be an extra set of number keys, known as the **number pad**, which is useful when one is typing in a succession of numerical values.

1.2.2 A glossary of keys for future reference

The following, for your future reference as you work through this book, is a list of the keys on a typical Mac keyboard. At this point, they will be described briefly, and you should try to identify them on a real keyboard at the earliest opportunity. With experience, the user may find other ways of carrying out some of the operations accessed by these keys.

Alternative (Alt)

This the **Option** key (see below), which occasionally bears the label **Alt**. There are two of these keys on most Powermac keyboards; but there is only one on a Powerbook keyboard.

Arrow keys (←, ↑, →, ↓)

The four **arrow keys** move the cursor in the directions indicated.

Backspace/Delete (← Del)

The long horizontal key on the upper right with the left-pointing arrow is the **Backspace/Delete** key (the Del label may be missing.) If you press Backspace/Delete, the cursor will move one space to the left and delete any character that happens to be in that space. This key should not be confused with the **Delete key (Del)** which is often (but by no means always) present on the same keyboard (see **Delete**, below).

Capitals Lock (Caps Lock)

As explained earlier, the **Capitals Lock** or **Caps Lock** key is a toggle switch, determining whether letters are shown in upper or in lower case. The Caps Lock key affects only the letter keys.

Command (⌘ or)

The **Command** key, which is usually marked with a ⌘ character (and often also with the Apple motif , a silhouette of an apple with a piece bitten out of it) is arguably the most important on the Mac keyboard and has a variety of functions. (On a full-sized Mac keyboard there are two Command keys.) The Command key is a **modifier key**, that is, it works only in combination with other keys. There are three other modifier keys: **Option**, **Shift** and **Control**. For example, in combination with other keys, the Command key can be used to effect some commands more quickly than by accessing them on menus with the mouse.

Control (Ctrl)

Like the Command key, the **Control** key is a modifier key. This key, however, is used comparatively rarely, usually in combination with Command, to make more options available. On a full-sized Mac keyboard, there are two Control keys.

Delete (Del)

A single press of the **Delete** key on a full-sized Mac keyboard erases the character at the position of the cursor and replaces it with the next character on the right. The position of the cursor on the screen, however, is unchanged. The effect of continuing to press **Del** has the effect of 'sucking in' text from the right and deleting it, while the cursor remains stationary. The **Del** key, therefore, should not be confused with the Backspace/Delete key, which cannot perform this 'sucking-in' function. On small Powerbook keyboards, the Delete key is absent and unwanted space can be removed by using the **Backspace/Delete** key.

Enter

The **Enter** key, which is variously marked on different keyboards, is used to confirm a choice from a dialog box. In this respect, it has the same effect as the **Return** key (see below).

Escape (Esc)

The Escape key is often used to change (or 'escape') from one activity to another, but its precise function depends upon which program you are using.

Function keys F1, F2, ...

Along the top of the keyboard is a row of function keys, labelled F1 to F12. These are not normally used in SPSS for Macintosh.

Option

The **Option** key is an important modifier key, which (in combination with other keys) is used to extend the range of commands. The Option key sometimes bears the label **Alt**.

Power (◁)

In some models, this key turns the computer on and off.

Return (Rtn or ↵)

On the keyboard, to the right of the letter keys, there is a large, L-shaped key labelled **Return**, which may be marked with a crooked arrow. In word-processing, the purpose of the Return key is to move the cursor to the beginning of a new line, as when one is beginning a new paragraph. In other applications, however, such as SPSS, the Return key has another function: in a dialog box, pressing Return has the same effect as clicking on the OK button, which initiates the execution of the command. In this respect, Return has the same function as the Enter key (see above).

Shift (⇧)

On every keyboard, there are two identical keys, situated to the right and left of the letter keys, which are either labelled **Shift** or bear broad upward-pointing arrows. Their function was described at the beginning of Section 1.2.1 .

Tabulation (Tab or →/)

On the left of the keyboard, above Caps Lock, is the **Tabulation (Tab)** key. As with an ordinary typewriter, pressing **Tab** moves the cursor directly to a predetermined position a set number of columns ahead. This was obviously invaluable to the typist of yesteryear who was producing tables of data. In modern word processing, however, tables are constructed by selecting special tabulation commands, which do not involve the Tab key.

1.3 BEGINNING AND ENDING A SESSION ON THE MAC

At the outset, it is essential for the user to be aware of certain processes that are started up when one switches on a computer; and it is even more important to be aware of what a computer does when one has indicated that one wishes to finish a session and shut the computer down. Never simply switch off a computer; nor should Command-Option-Escape be used in anything but an emergency (as when the computer **hangs** - see below). The computer should be warned that a session is about to end, so that it can close down files properly and remind the user to save any that have been worked on since they were last saved.

1.3.1 Booting up

When a computer is switched on, the first thing it does is to **boot up** (short for 'bootstrap'), that is, an operation by which preliminary computer operating instructions are loaded into main memory in order to bring in further material from an external storage device. In this way, the computer makes itself, in a sense, more powerful, hence the 'bootstrap' metaphor. Nowadays, bootstrapping is carried out automatically when a computer is switched on.

Sometimes, during the course of a computing session, the system may freeze, **crash** or **hang up**: that is, it will no longer respond to the user's instructions. When this happens, there is nothing for it but to **reboot**, that is, start the computer again. A complete rebooting, which involves all the checking routines, is known as a **hard reboot**. One should have recourse to a hard reboot only in the direst emergency, when all else has failed. Do not, however, simply switch the machine off (with Powerbooks, in fact, that might not be possible): there will be a button somewhere on the computer (perhaps at the back) which, when pressed, shuts down the system, whether the computer is running on mains or battery. When the computer is next turned on, MACOS will inform you of its displeasure at being shut down so suddenly. Rather than shutting down the computer, however, one can try a **warm reboot**, by pressing **Command-Control-Power**. This move (which does not always work) will, if successful, bring about a limited rebooting process, which omits many of the routine checks in a hard reboot and earns no rebuke from MACOS. Even with a soft reboot, the user must accept the annoying fact that all information in current memory that has not been saved to a file on disk may be lost. With some applications, therefore, you are advised to save frequently, so that if the system crashes, only the processing that took place since the last save will be lost. (Note, however, that SPSS offers the option of frequent automatic saving of files.)

1.3.2 Using a machine in a network: Logging in and logging out

For security, and efficient resource management, access to a communal computing system usually requires a procedure by which the user, having already made arrangements to use the system beforehand, presents proof of identification, in the form of a user number and a password. This is known as **logging in**, and has the effect of making some of the computer's processing capacity and storage available to the user for the duration of the session. It is therefore essential, at the end of the session, to inform the system that these resources will no longer be needed, a procedure known as **logging out**. As in the use of a stand-alone computer, it is bad practice simply to switch off. Although such an action would not shut the system down, part of the system's capacity may continue to be monopolised for longer than necessary; moreover, there is also the danger that other users may be able to access your files!

CHAPTER 2

BASIC MACINTOSH OPERATIONS FOR SPSS

2.1	THE GRAPHICAL USER INTERFACE (GUI)
2.2	THE MENU BAR
2.3	THE MACINTOSH HARD DISK WINDOW
2.4	SOME USEFUL OPERATIONS WITH THE FILE MENU
2.5	THE APPLE MENU
2.6	BEGINNING SPSS FOR MACINTOSH

Chapter 2 - Basic Macintosh Operations for SPSS

2.1 THE GRAPHICAL USER INTERFACE (GUI)

This chapter is not intended to be a comprehensive guide for the Mac user. Many such manuals are already available, one of the best of which is *The Macintosh Bible*, by Darcy DiNucci and her colleagues (DiNucci *et al.*, 1994). In a lucid and friendly style, their book explains virtually every aspect of Macintosh use. The purpose of this chapter is to consider only those aspects that are relevant to the use of SPSS for Macintosh. Should the reader wish to explore a topic in more depth, DiNucci et al. are likely to have the answer to any question that might arise.

At the outset, it is important to be aware that the **Macintosh Operating System (MACOS)** is a powerful and complex system which can often perform a particular function (such as finding and opening a file, or accessing an application) in a variety of ways. Exploring the different approaches is an excellent way of familiarising oneself with the ins and outs of the system.

2.1.1 What happens when you turn on the Mac

In what follows, we shall assume that the user has available a stand-alone machine, such as a **Powermac** or a **Powerbook**. When you turn on the computer, the process of **booting up** is initiated. During this process, a **welcome sign** will appear, followed by a display in which an initially empty rectangle is gradually filled to make a solid bar. At the same time, along the bottom of the screen, a series of icons appears, each representing one of the applications that have been loaded. Finally a **wrist-watch icon** appears for a short time, indicating that the user must wait until the process of booting up is complete. In general, the appearance of the wrist-watch means that 'something is happening', and the user must wait for further developments.

2.1.2 The desktop

Figure 1 shows how the screen might typically appear when the booting up process is complete and the computer is ready to interact with the user.

The large grey area is known as the **desktop**. The desktop contains several **icons**. An icon, it will be recalled from Chapter 1, is a little picture representing a disk, a file, a folder, or something else that the user might wish to access. Some of the icons are located in a lighter strip across the top of the screen called the **Menu bar**. The Menu bar contains lists of **commands** that can be given to the computer to carry out specific operations; but there are other important items as well, such as the Apple menu (with the Apple motif) on the left, the **Guide menu** (with a question-mark) on the right, from which the user can obtain information about many aspects of Mac use, and the **Application menu** (an image of a VDU screen), which enables the user to control the running of several applications at the same time.

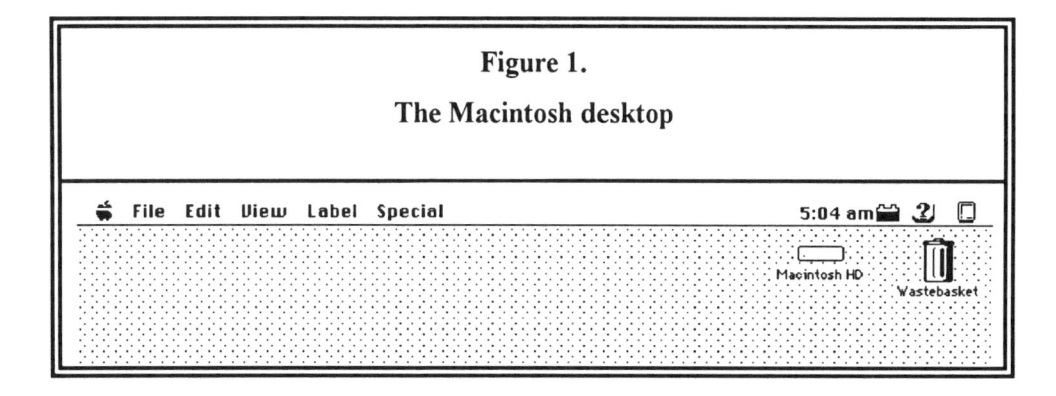

Figure 1.

The Macintosh desktop

Lower down on the desktop are the **Macintosh HD** (The Mac's Hard Disk) and the **Wastebasket**. There may well be other icons, depending upon the applications that have been loaded. In the Macintosh HD, are numerous files and folders, which may include the **system software** (which runs MACOS). If so, the Macintosh HD is the **startup disk**, because the system software controls the booting-up process. The Wastebasket is a temporary dump for files and folders that the user wishes to remove from the HD. Later, the user will encounter other kinds of icons, such as **documents** (like dog-eared pieces of paper) and **folders** (like the hanging folders in a filing cabinet). Document files do not initially appear on the desktop (though they can be stored there): they are usually to be seen only when the contents of a disk or folder are displayed.

2.1.3 The screen pointer: Handling the mouse

On the screen should be a **pointer**, in the form of an arrow pointing diagonally upward to the left. Initially, the pointer will retain the arrow shape wherever it is situated on the desktop, but in other circumstances it changes shape, depending on its location and the current activity of the computer. When the Mac is busy, for example, and does not wish to be interrupted, the arrow turns into the wrist-watch icon. Sometimes, as when one is working with text, the pointer takes the form of an I-beam (or girder). When one is working with an array of numbers (as in SPSS), the pointer often takes the form of a cross. In fact, the pointer can take many different shapes, which the user soon learns to recognise.

Positioning the pointer with the mouse

The position of the screen pointer is controlled by the mouse. Running the mouse around on the surface of the desk (or, preferably, a high-friction **mouse-mat**) will change its position on the screen.

Running out of mouse-mat space

Sometimes, the user may find that the mouse has been moved to the edge of the available space on the desk (or mouse-mat) before the pointer has reached the desired position. In that case, simply lift the mouse and reposition it on the surface. This trick also works with other mouse moves such as the **click-and-drag** operation (see below); though in that case, you need to keep the mouse button pressed down while the mouse is being lifted.

Clicking on an icon to activate it

Initially, the Macintosh HD icon has the form of an unfilled rectangle, with the title caption below it. Move the mouse so that the pointer lies on the icon. If you click the mouse button, the icon will turn black and its caption will appear in **inverse video** (white on black, rather than vice versa). The icon has been **activated** and certain operations can now be carried out.

The action just described is known as **clicking on** an icon. You will notice that when you click on the HD icon, the **Label** menu appears in bold font. This means that you can now access the commands on that menu (see below). Clicking on an icon affords the user the opportunity of **renaming** the item concerned, which is easily done simply by typing in the new name. If, having activated the icon, you now click on the desktop, the icon will appear in normal video and the Label menu will be dimmed once again. The icon has been **deactivated**.

Try clicking on the **time display** in the Menu bar. The **current date** will briefly appear, after which the display will revert to the time.

Relocating an icon: The click-and-drag operation

Position the pointer on **Macintosh HD** once again. Press the mouse button and keep it held down, while moving the mouse. The original icon remains in place, but a dotted outline of the icon, known as a **ghost**, moves with the arrow to whatever new location the user chooses. When the mouse button is released, the original icon jumps to the new position. This is known as a **click-and-drag** operation.

2.2 THE MENU BAR

The **Menu bar** (Figure 1) contains the headings **File**, **Edit**, **View**, **Label** and **Special**. Each of these is a **menu**, that is, a list of commands from which the user makes a selection, either by using the mouse, or by making a combination of key presses. Notice also that immediately after the system has booted up, two of the menus, **View** and **Label**, are **dimmed**, that is, the commands they contain are not yet accessible to the user. The other menus, however, are all available to the user at the outset.

In addition to the time display, there are one or two other items in the menu bar as well, such as a digital reading of the time and, if one is using a Powerbook, perhaps an image of a battery indicating how long the user can continue without a mains supply.

2.2.1 Getting help: the Guide menu

Position the mouse on the icon of the Guide menu (with the question mark). To obtain the menu, press the mouse button and hold it down. (If the button is not held down, the menu will disappear.) A **drop-down menu** appears, with the following headings: **About Apple Guide**; **Show Balloons**; **Macintosh Tutorial**; **Macintosh Guide**; and **Shortcuts**. Drag the screen pointer down to **Show Balloons** and release the button. The menu will disappear, but the user now has now engaged (or **enabled**) **Balloon Help**. Try moving the pointer around the desktop from icon to icon. At each port of call, a balloon will appear containing a caption explaining the meaning of the icon. This can be very useful in the early stages of Mac use, when the user is exploring the ins and outs of MACOS for the first time.

Balloon help, however, soon becomes tedious, and can be a positive hindrance in some situations. To **disable** Balloon help, enter the Guide menu once again. This time, instead of the choice **Show Balloons**, the user will find, in the same place, **Hide Balloons**. Disable Balloon help by dragging the screen pointer to **Hide Balloons** and releasing the mouse button.

The other commands on the Guide menu are all worth exploring fully, beginning with the **Macintosh Tutorial**. In the long term, the most useful command of all is **Macintosh Guide**, which prompts the user for a key word and (provided the word is recognised), provides an explanation.

2.2.2 The Application Menu

The rightmost menu in the menu bar is the **Application Menu**. Click-and-hold on the menu's icon to obtain the drop-down menu. The following selection will appear: **Hide Finder**; **Hide Others**; **Show All**; and **Finder**, the last having a screen icon to the left. That option is also likely to have a tick on the left, indicating that the Finder is active. The **Finder** is the program that produces the desktop display and keeps track of the files one has in store. There may be circumstances in which the Finder is inactive, in which case the Wastebasket and the startup disk will not appear. The Finder can always be reactivated by Clicking on the Application menu and choosing Finder in the usual way.

The Application menu is useful when has two or more applications running at the same time, such as SPSS and a word processor such as Word. In such cases, the applications in use will appear in the menu, and the user can switch back and forth between them by dragging the screen pointer from one to the other.

Chapter 2 - Basic Macintosh Operations for SPSS

2.2.3 How new folders and files are created

Click-and-hold on the **File** menu, to obtain a long list of choices, the uppermost of which is **New Folder**. Drag the screen pointer to New Folder and release. A new icon will appear in inverse video on the desktop, with the temporary caption **untitled folder**. Type the name **Rubbish**, and it will appear as the name of the folder. We have chosen this name because very soon, this item is going to be disposed of by using the **Wastebasket**.

Notice that there is no command in the File menu for creating a file: files are created by **applications**, such as word processors or SPSS.

2.2.4 The disk icons and the Wastebasket

Below the Menu bar, in the large grey area of the desktop, are other icons, notably the **Hard disk** (labelled **Macintosh HD**) and the **Wastebasket**. There may be others as well.

Inserting a floppy disk

When a floppy disk is inserted into the computer, a new icon will appear, with the form of a floppy disk, under which, in **inverse video** (white on black, rather than vice versa), is the caption **Untitled**. If the inserted disk is IBM PC-formatted, the letters PC will appear on the icon. If it has already been Macintosh-formatted, no letters will appear on the icon. Should the disk not have been formatted at all, a **dialog box** will appear offering the option of **initialising** (formatting) the disk (see Figure 2).

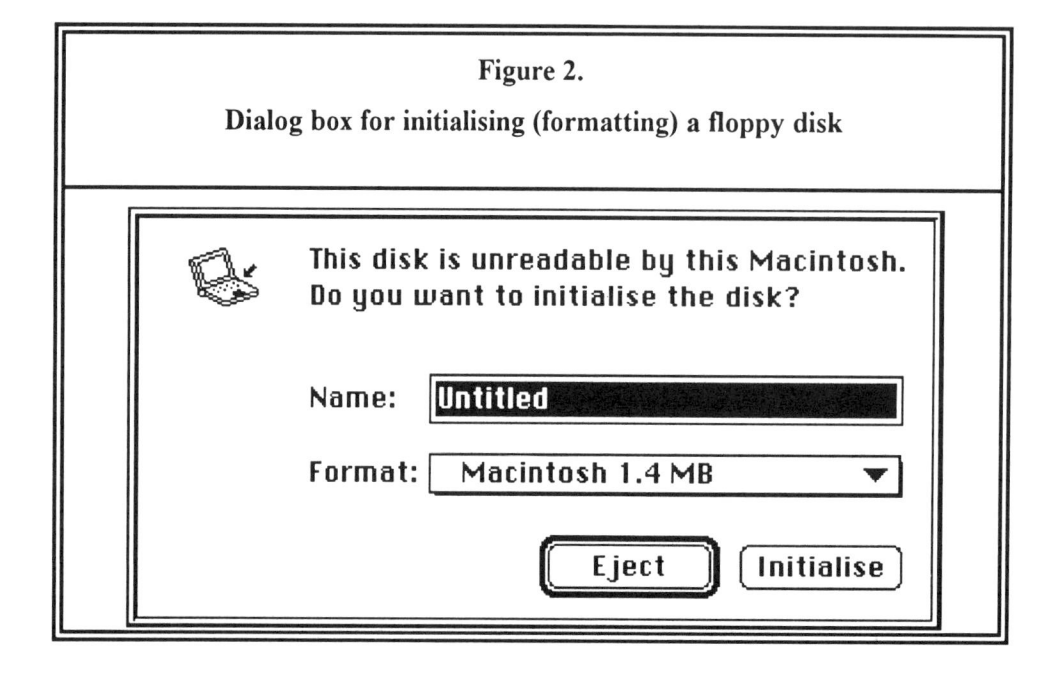

Figure 2.

Dialog box for initialising (formatting) a floppy disk

This disk is unreadable by this Macintosh. Do you want to initialise the disk?

Name: Untitled

Format: Macintosh 1.4 MB

Eject   Initialise

Ejecting a floppy disk

To eject a floppy disk, click-and-drag its icon over to the Wastebasket and release the mouse button. The floppy disk will now be expelled from the computer's floppy disk drive and the disk icon will disappear from the desktop. There is another way of ejecting a floppy disk by using the **Special** menu. We do not recommend that method, however, since the user is liable to get into a loop in which reinsertion of the disk is repeatedly requested. We suggest you always eject a floppy disk by dragging its icon over to the Wastebasket.

Using the Wastebasket to remove unwanted files or folders

The main purpose of the Wastebasket is the removal of unwanted files and folders from storage in the Mac computer. To eject an item, simply click-and-drag it to the Wastebasket icon and release the mouse button. Try this with the 'Rubbish' folder that has just been placed on the desktop. You will see that when the button is released, the folder disappears. Initially, the Wastebasket icon, a picture of a dustbin, has straight vertical sides. Now, its sides bulge outwards, indicating that it contains an object. Double-click the icon to confirm that the contained object is indeed the Rubbish folder.

The contents of the Wastebasket will be displayed. To eject the unwanted folder finally from MACOS, click-and-hold on the Special menu, in which one command is **Empty Wastebasket . . .** , where the ellipsis (...) indicates that when this command is selected, a dialog box will appear so that the user can confirm that the items are to be finally ejected. As in the present example, however, we have already checked the contents of the Wastebasket by double clicking on its icon, and decided that we want to eject its contents without further scrutiny. In that case, press and hold down the Option key before accessing the Special menu. When this is done, the command **Empty Wastebasket** appears without an ellipsis, and if it is chosen, the material will be removed permanently from the Wastebasket without further input from the user (no dialog box will appear). The command, then, is

Option
    Special
        Empty Wastebasket

2.3 THE MACINTOSH HARD DISK WINDOW

One of the most important aspects of the GUI interface is a rectangular display known as **a window**, through which the user can see displayed the contents of a disk, folder, or file. Unlike a superficially similar array called a **dialog box**, a window simply *displays* items: no input is requested from the user. (There are also hybrid displays known as **control panels** which, while having some of the features of windows, also prompt the user for information.)

2.3.1 Opening the window

To open an iconised item, the mouse button must be located on the icon and clicked twice in quick session, an operation known as **double-clicking**. Try double-clicking on the HD icon, to obtain the **Macintosh HD window** (see Figure 3).

Figure 3.

The Macintosh hard disk window

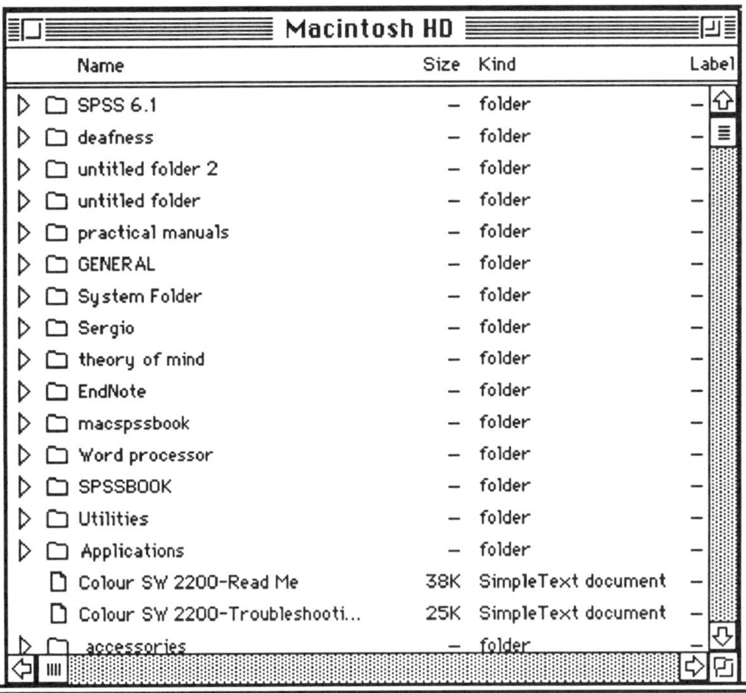

Name	Size	Kind	Label
▷ ☐ SPSS 6.1	—	folder	—
▷ ☐ deafness	—	folder	—
▷ ☐ untitled folder 2	—	folder	—
▷ ☐ untitled folder	—	folder	—
▷ ☐ practical manuals	—	folder	—
▷ ☐ GENERAL	—	folder	—
▷ ☐ System Folder	—	folder	—
▷ ☐ Sergio	—	folder	—
▷ ☐ theory of mind	—	folder	—
▷ ☐ EndNote	—	folder	—
▷ ☐ macspssbook	—	folder	—
▷ ☐ Word processor	—	folder	—
▷ ☐ SPSSBOOK	—	folder	—
▷ ☐ Utilities	—	folder	—
▷ ☐ Applications	—	folder	—
☐ Colour SW 2200-Read Me	38K	SimpleText document	—
☐ Colour SW 2200-Troubleshooti...	25K	SimpleText document	—
▷ ☐ accessories	—	folder	—

Through the window, can be seen a list of items. The appearance of the items in a window can be controlled by using the **View menu** (see below).

2.3.2 Controlling the window display: The View menu

You may have noticed that the **View** menu, which had been dimmed at startup, changed to bold when the **Macintosh HD** window was opened up. Click-and-hold on the **View** menu to inspect the commands that it offers.

Each command is an instruction to the Mac to sort and present the contents of the hard disk in a certain way:

- The **by Name** command lists the names of the various items in alphabetical order;
- The **by Date** command re-arranges the labels of the items according to the dates on which they were last worked on, the most recent item being at the top of the list;
- The **by Icon** command produces an array of icons, each representing a particular item.

The present setting is indicated by an arrow opposite one of the commands. For present purposes, the arrow should be opposite the **by Icon** command (although, in fact, icons of varying size are present in all the formats).

2.3.3 Viewing the contents of the Macintosh HD window

The icons in the window representing the folders and files on the hard disk are of two types.

- **Folder icons** resemble the folders in a filing cabinet, each with a protruding 'label' at the top left.
- A **file icon**, like a much-thumbed letter or document, has a 'dog-ear' at the top right.

The title bar

Across the top of the window is the **title bar**, with the title of the window, 'Macintosh', written on it. On the left side of the title bar is a small rectangle ☐ called the **close box**. Clicking on the close box will close the window. Try that, and reopen the window by double-clicking on the HD icon once again. On the right side of the title bar is another rectangle ⊡ called the **zoom box**. Clicking on the zoom box will enlarge the window and show details of at least some of the folders and files that the hard disk contains. Clicking on the zoom box again will restore the window to its original size. (The reader who is meeting these terms for the first time may find it helpful to establish the terminology by engaging **Guide/Balloon Help** at this point, and moving the screen pointer around the various parts of the window.)

Positioning the window

By positioning the pointer in the title bar and clicking-and-dragging, the window can be moved to any desired position on the screen. Try this, and position the window so that all four of its borders are visible.

The size box

There are other ways of changing the size or shape of a window. In the bottom right corner of the border of the window is a small picture of two overlapping rectangles ▣ . This is called the **size box**. Place the mouse pointer on the size box. By clicking-and-dragging the size box, the size and shape of the window can be changed at will. Experiment with this.

The scroll bar

Only some of the folders and files contained in the hard disk can be seen through the window. Notice, however, the grey borders on the right and base of the window. These are known as **scroll bars**. The vertical scroll bar can be used to change the position of the window vertically and bring other items into view. (The horizontal scroll bar changes the position of the window horizontally, and is useful for viewing items to the right or left of those items that are visible in the window at present.) Notice that each scroll bar has an arrow at either end, and contains a small darker rectangle within it known as the **scroll box**.

By clicking on an arrow ▲ or ▼ at either end of the vertical scroll bar, the window can be made to shift a little in the indicated direction, so that a few more folders or files come into view; and correspondingly, a few of those initially in view disappear. To scroll through the contents of the hard disk even faster, by complete windows, click once within the vertical scroll bar. Even greater scrolling speed can be achieved by clicking-and-dragging the scroll box within the scroll bar. The last move is especially valuable when one is working with a large document in a word processor.

2.3.4 Opening a file: The Memory Control Panel

In MACOS, there can be folders within folders within folders; and the file we are looking for may be many layers deep. In the present case, we shall locate a file known as the **Memory Control Panel**, which controls the amount of memory upon which an application such as SPSS can draw.

The System Folder

Among the contents of the HD viewable through the Macintosh window can be seen (provided the Macintosh HD is the startup disk) the **System Folder**, which contains the files that run the Macintosh operating system. If you double-click on the System Folder, other files and folders will be seen, the former dog-eared, the latter with the protruding label at top left. (The user may find, incidentally, that the contents of the System Folder are obscured by the HD window. If so, they can readily be brought into view by clicking on the title bar of the System Folder, which will activate that folder and bring it to the forefront of the windows on the screen.)

Chapter 2 - Basic Macintosh Operations for SPSS

The Control Panels

Within the System Folder window can be seen another folder, labelled **Control Panels**. A control panel is a special kind of window which allows the user to control an aspect of the system by entering specifications. For example, one of the control panels bearing the title Keyboard allows the user to control keyboard layout, the time that a key must be held down for before it begins to repeat, and so on.

The Memory Control Panel

If you double-click on Control Panels, you will obtain a file (note the dog-ear, which indicates that it is a file and not a folder) called **Memory**. Double-click on the Memory Control Panel file to view its contents (Figure 4). The following notation summarises the steps just taken to locate the Memory Control Panel:
Hard Disk
    System Folder
        Control Panels
            Memory

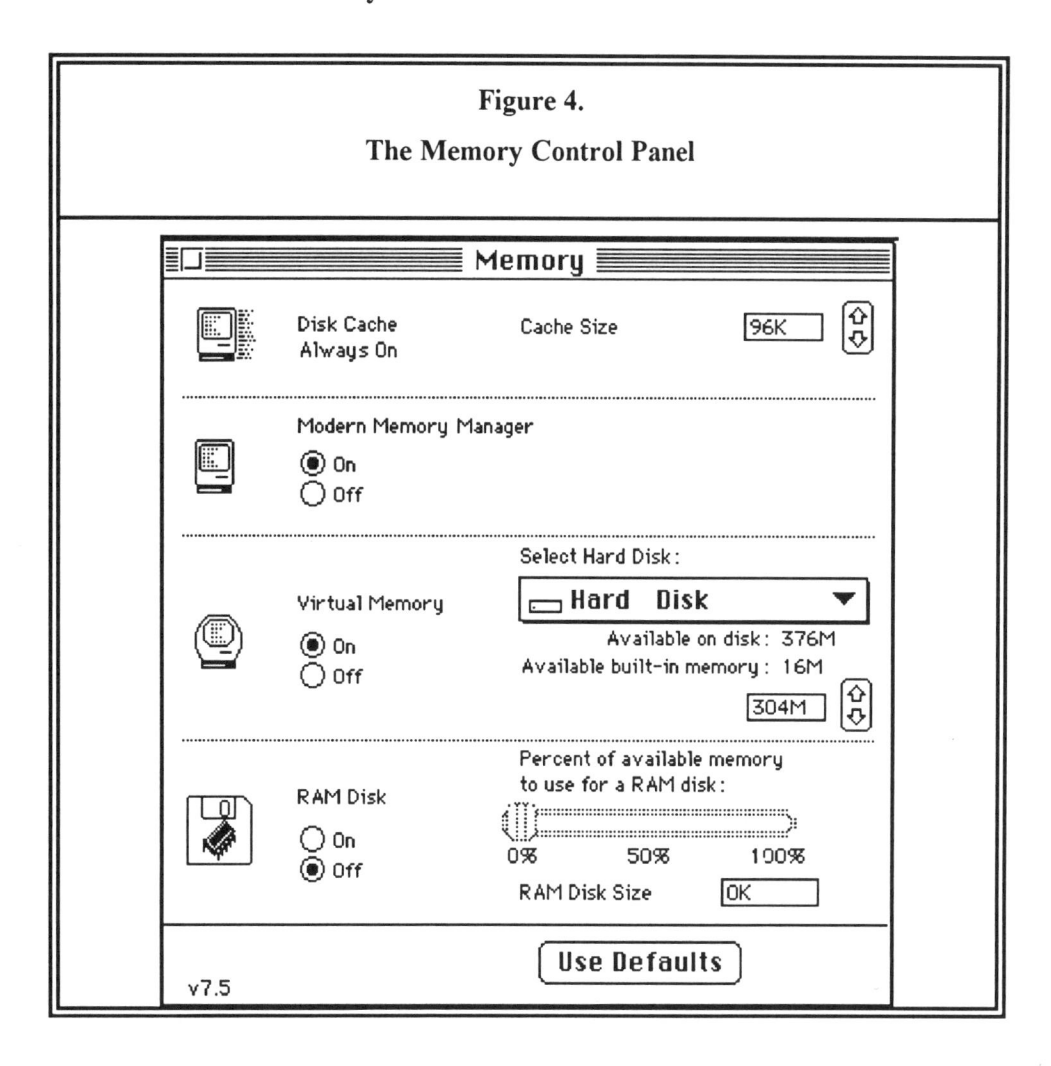

Figure 4.
The Memory Control Panel

	Memory	
Disk Cache Always On	Cache Size	96K
Modern Memory Manager ● On ○ Off		
Virtual Memory ● On ○ Off	Select Hard Disk: ⎯ Hard Disk ▼ Available on disk: 376M Available built-in memory: 16M	304M
RAM Disk ○ On ● Off	Percent of available memory to use for a RAM disk: 0% 50% 100% RAM Disk Size	0K
v7.5	Use Defaults	

21

Making sure that SPSS has sufficient memory

The **Memory Control Panel** is an important one for the SPSS user because, since SPSS constructs large temporary files during the course of a computing session, the package requires a considerable amount of memory. First make sure that the radio button ⦿ for **virtual memory** is **on**. For the moment, you need take note of only one feature of the Panel, the section labelled **Hard Disk** or **Macintosh HD** (it varies from computer to computer). This controls the **disk cache**, which is the amount of memory set aside for running programs. To run SPSS successfully, you may have to increase the size of the disk cache. You can do this by clicking on the upward-pointing arrow in the smaller box under the box containing the Macintosh HD label. Adjust the value shown to 100K - that should suffice. Note, however, that this new allocation to the disk cache will only take effect when the Mac is closed down and started up again.

2.4 SOME USEFUL OPERATIONS WITH THE FILE MENU

Place the pointer on the heading of the **File** menu and click (and hold down) the left-hand mouse button. The menu is shown in Figure 5.

Figure 5.

The File menu

You will see that there is a long list of items on the File menu, reflecting its importance in the operation of MACOS.

2.4.1 The Find ... command

Choose
File
    Find ...

to obtain the **Find File** dialog box (Figure 6). You will observe that the entries in the **Find File** dialog box take the form of an incomplete sentence:

    Find items on "Macintosh HD" whose name contains _____.

Complete the sentence by typing the word *memory* in the empty bar.

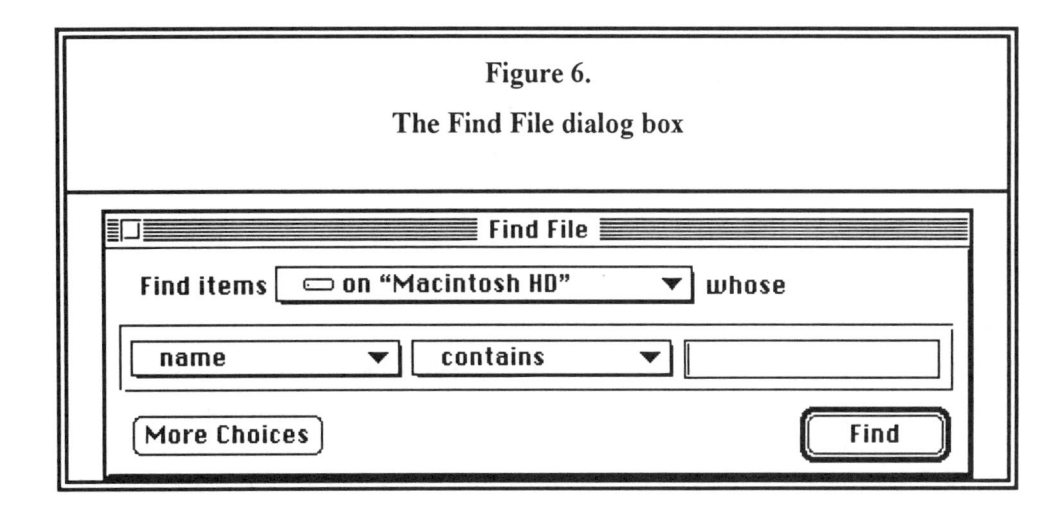

Figure 6.
The Find File dialog box

Next, click on the **Find** button. This will bring to the screen the **Items Found** window (Figure 7).

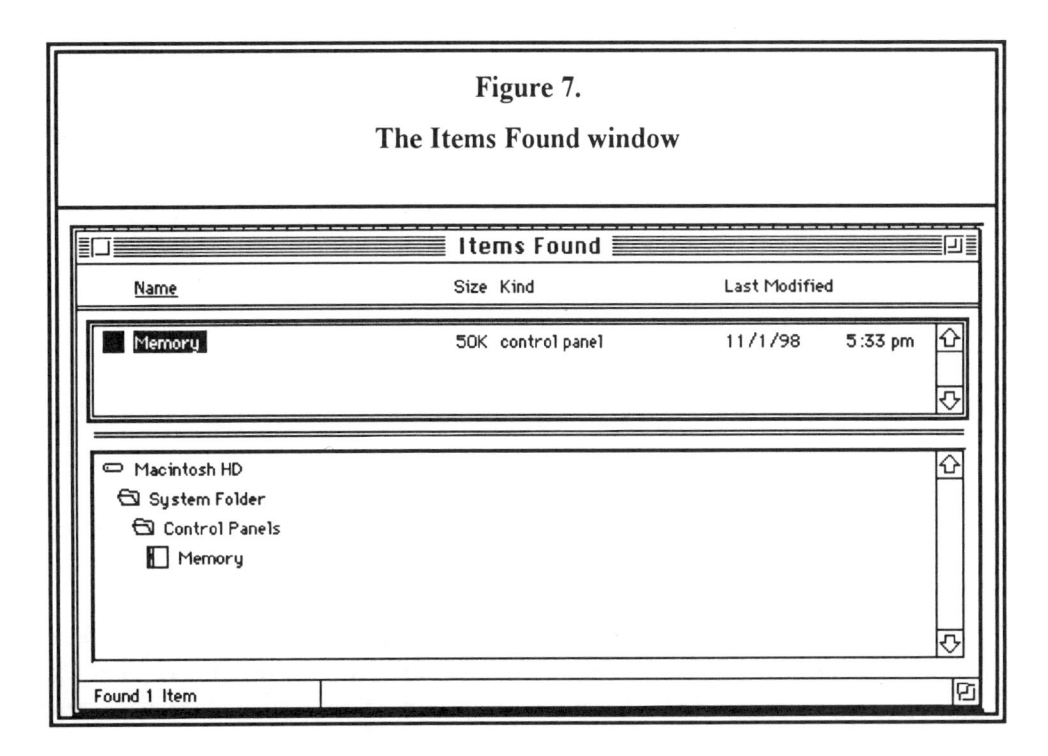

Figure 7.
The Items Found window

23

In the upper part of the **Items Found** window, can be seen the **Memory** control panel. In the lower part of the window can be seen the item's location in MACOS:

Macintosh HD
    System Folder
        Control Panels
            Memory

The **Find File** command, therefore, has given us speedy access to the file that we previously found by a laborious process of double-clicking on a series of icons.

Finding the SPSS program

Assuming that SPSS has already been loaded on to your computer, click on the **Close** box of the **Items Found** window and return to the **Find File** dialog box, where the word *memory* can still be seen, in inverse video. Now type in the name of the folder that contains SPSS (say *SPSS*) and click on the **Find** button. The **Items Found** window appears again, with the name of the specified folder (*SPSS*) in the upper half of the window, and its position in the MACOS storage hierarchy (**Macintosh HD/SPSS**) shown in the lower half.

Modifying the Find command

It will have been noticed that in the Find File dialog box there are downward-pointing black arrows to the right of each of the head-words **on "Macintosh HD"**, **name** and **contains**. Each black arrow indicates the availability of a **pop-up menu** giving a list of alternative specifications. For example, the pop-up menu with the caption **name** offers several specifications other than the file name, including **date created** and **date modified**; and the pop-up menu with the default caption **contain** offers **doesn't contain**, **starts with** and **ends with**, among other options. The power of the Find command is further enhanced by the provision of more search options if the user clicks on **More Choices**. These extra options include the head words **size** and **is less than**, each of which has its own pop-up menu: for example, with **is less than** is the choice **is greater than**. If, in the pop-up menu with the head-word **name** is chosen **date created**, the appropriate date will appear in the rectangle on the right of the display.

The MACOS **Find** command is clearly a very powerful tool indeed and with careful choice of specifications, it can be used to find any stored item, however thickly wrapped in folders it may be.

2.4.2 Short cuts: Using key combinations

To the right of each of the commands in the File menu is a combination of key presses which accesses the same command without going into the File menu first at all. For example, to the right of the first command on the menu **New Folder**, is written ⌘ N. This means that you can create a new folder directly by pressing **Command/N**. If one does this, an icon with the caption **Untitled folder** will appear on the desktop. The user need only type in the desired name.

The new folder can be stored anywhere in the MACOS hierarchy: for example, it can be placed in another folder at any depth by opening that folder and clicking-and-dragging the new folder from the desktop into the target folder's window. Alternatively, if the window of the target folder is opened first, and the command **File/New Folder** is selected, the icon of the new (unnamed) folder will appear in the window of the target folder directly, and no clicking-and-dragging is necessary.

2.4.3 Creating an alias

There will certainly be some files and programs (such as SPSS) which are so frequently used that especially rapid access to them is desirable. Such ready access is arranged by the operation known as **creating an alias**. An alias is a copy of the icon of a file which, although the latter may be stored deep in the hierarchy of folders, enables the user to access the file immediately. Create an alias of the SPSS program as follows:

- Choose **File/Find** to locate the SPSS folder, and double-click on the folder to open it. The SPSS application icon can now be seen in the SPSS window.

- Activate the icon by clicking on it. The caption underneath now appears in inverse video.

- Choose the command **File/Make Alias**. The effect of this is to produce a new icon with the caption **SPSS alias**.

- Click-and-drag this new icon to the desktop.

- Click on the desktop outside the icon to deactivate it.

On the desktop, there is now an icon which is an exact replica of the original in the SPSS folder. The only difference is that its caption reads **SPSS alias**, rather than simply **SPSS**.

The SPSS alias icon can be used to access the application: to run SPSS, simply double-click on the alias. We shall see, however, that the desktop is not necessarily the best place for an alias. Over the months, the user is likely to have created aliases for several applications and, were they all to be stored on the desktop, the latter would become rather cluttered. We shall now consider what is often a better location for aliases: the **Apple menu**.

Chapter 2 - Basic Macintosh Operations for SPSS

2.5 THE APPLE MENU

The Apple menu, indicated by the Apple motif , is on the extreme left of the Menu bar. Originally this menu was intended only to permit the user to use desktop accessories such as the Calculator while using an application such as a word processor. (At that time, it was not possible to run more than one application at the same time.) Now, it is possible to run several applications at the same time, and the Apple menu has become a useful means of holding in readiness any programs that the user wishes to access quickly. (See DiNucci *et al.*, 1994; p.16 and elsewhere, for more information about the Apple menu.)

The Apple menu has a unique feature: it is possible to add items to it, thus **customising** the menu. That is not possible with any of the other menus.

2.5.1 A look at the Apple menu

When the Apple menu is accessed (by clicking-and-holding on the icon), a list of items appears, among which are some familiar terms such as **Control Panels** and **Find File** (Figure 8).

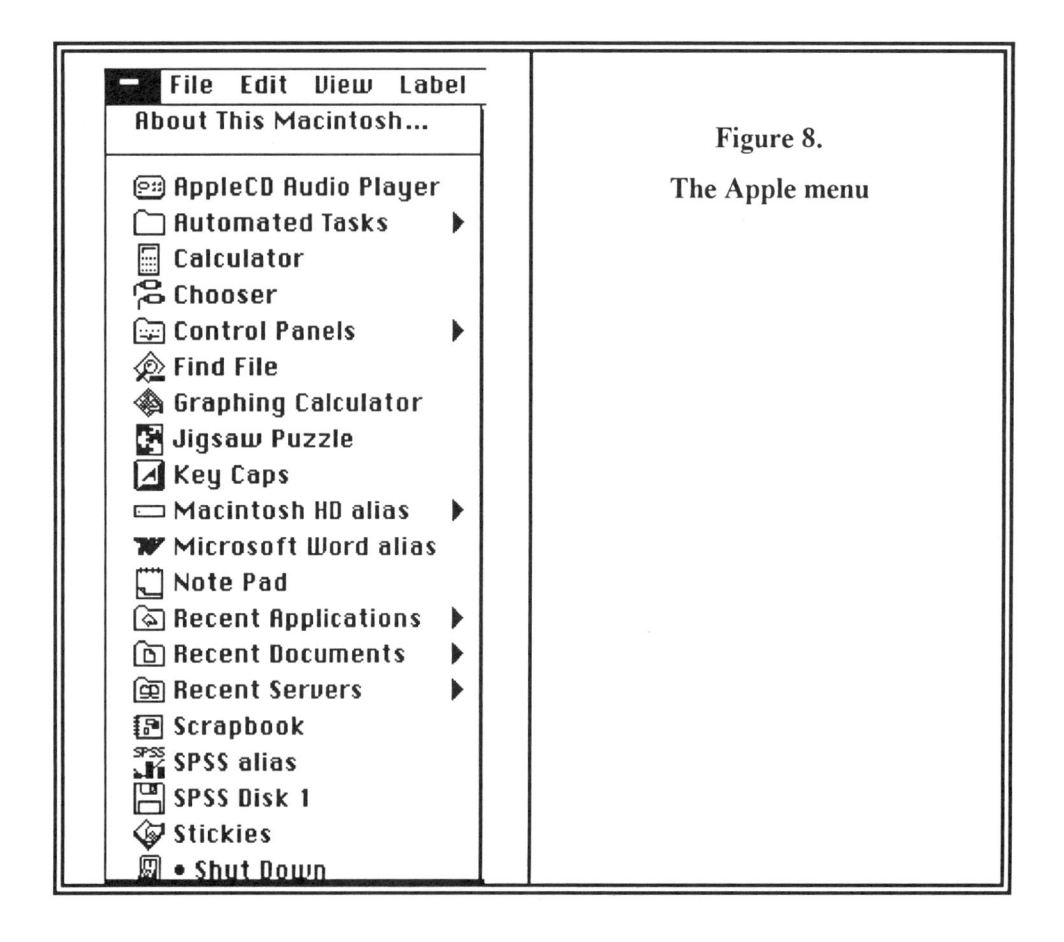

Figure 8.

The Apple menu

Here the advantage of the Apple menu becomes obvious, for the user need only click on **Find File** to obtain the dialog described 2.4.1. Similarly, on choosing **Control Panels**, the contents of the Control Panels Folder are listed immediately.

In addition to such short-cuts, however, there are some items that are unique to the Apple menu. For example, the item **About This Macintosh** gives the memory specifications of the user's computer, such as the capacity of its hard disk and the amount of **RAM** available (Random Access Memory, the sort you need when running an application such as SPSS).

You will also notice one or two desktop accessories, such as the **Calculator** and the **Chooser**, which specifies the printers to which the computer is to send its output.

Notice the **Shut Down** command. This is a quicker way of shutting the computer down than by going into the **Special menu** with **Special/Shut Down**.

By choosing **Control Panels**, the user obtains a list of the contents of the **Apple Menu Items** folder, including the **Memory**, **Keyboard**, and **Date and Time** Control Panels. There is an obvious saving of time in accessing these files by a single selection from the Apple menu.

2.5.2 Customising the Apple menu: The Apple Menu Items folder

To have an item included in the Apple menu, it is only necessary to drag its icon on to the icon of the **Apple Menu Items** folder. Thereafter, that item will appear in the Apple menu whenever that is accessed.

Transferring an alias to the Apple menu

Use
Macintosh HD
    Systems Folder
        Apple Menu Items

to access the **Apple Menu Items** folder. If the application alias (or the original item) is dragged on to that folder, that application will appear in the list of commands that appears when the Apple Menu is opened.

Find the **SPSS** folder once again, open it to show the SPSS icon and use the command **File/Make alias** to create another SPSS alias icon. Locate the **Apple Menu Items folder** as above, and drag the SPSS alias on to that icon. This action transfers the SPSS alias to the Apple menu; but the alias that was created earlier and located on the desktop will stay where it is. There can be several copies of the same alias in various locations, where each has its own special use.

Try making an alias of the Macintosh hard disk as well and transferring that to the Apple menu:

- Activate the hard disk.

- Use **File/Make alias** to create the Macintosh HD alias.
- Find the Apple Menu Items folder with
  Macintosh HD
      Systems Folder
          Apple Menu Items.
- Drag the Macintosh HD alias on to the Apple Menu Items icon.

This action will transfer the Macintosh HD alias to the Apple menu.

2.6 BEGINNING SPSS FOR MACINTOSH

Given that SPSS has been loaded into your machine, two conditions must be met before you can use the package:

(1) the **licence** must be current;

(2) there must be **sufficient memory** available to run SPSS (see 2.3.4).

Assuming that both these conditions have been met, there are several ways of accessing SPSS. If no aliases have been created, the user must enter the folder containing the SPSS icon and double-click on that to activate the package. Should an SPSS alias be available on the desktop, that icon must be double-clicked to start the package; unless the data set one wishes to work with has already been entered during a previous session, in which case a short-cut is available (see below). If an SPSS alias has been added to the Apple menu, it is only necessary to choose that item on the menu to run the application.

2.6.1 The Data Editor window

Data for SPSS is entered into a spreadsheet-like array called the **Data Editor window** (Figure 9). Notice the numbered rows and that the columns all have the label **var** at the top. The headings are dimmed, because, as yet, the cells of the **Data Editor** contain no data; nor have the columns been given names. Notice also that, at this point, the window bears the title **untitled data**.

In an SPSS data set, each row represents a single case, or subject. Each column represents some attribute or property (height, weight, gender) that has been recorded in the subjects under investigation. Each cell of the **Data Editor** grid, rather like a point on a graph, can be thought of as having a horizontal and a vertical co-ordinate, where the horizontal co-ordinate represents a particular subject and the vertical co-ordinate represents a particular variable: thus the cell at the interaction of the fourth row and the third column is the score of the *fourth subject* on the *third variable*. Within generous limits, there can be any number of subjects and variables.

Chapter 2 - Basic Macintosh Operations for SPSS

Figure 9.
The SPSS Data Editor window

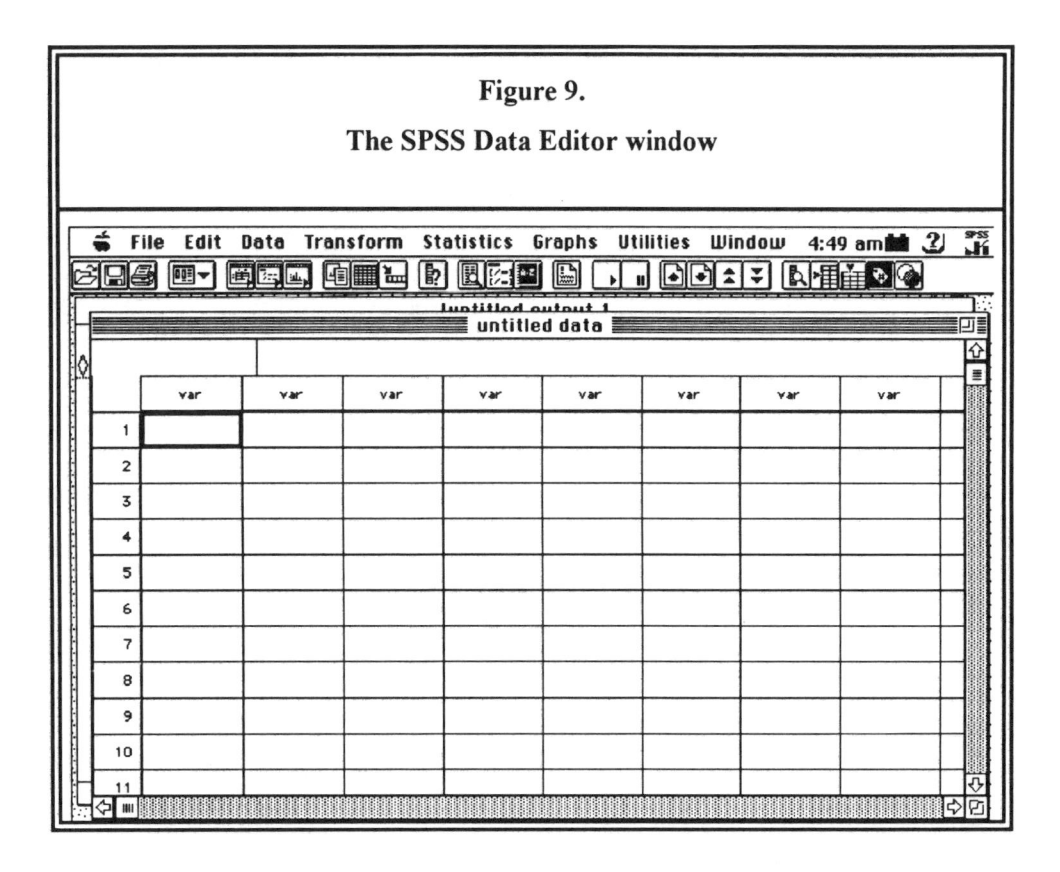

We suggest that the reader might double-click on the first column in the **Data Editor** grid to open up the **Define Variable** dialog box (Figure 10).

Figure 10.
The Define Variable dialog box

In the rectangle labelled **variable name**, type in a name such as *weight* and close the dialog box by clicking on the **OK** button. Instead of **var**, the word **weight** will now appear, in bold, at the head of the first column. (Note that in the SPSS **Data Editor** grid, variable names always appear in lower case, irrespective of whether the user typed them in lower case or not.) Now type in the weight (in pounds) of someone you know: *173* will do. The figure will appear, not in any of the cells of the grid below the columns headings, but in a space below the title bar known as the **cell editor**. When the **Data Editor** is first accessed, the cell at the head of the first column should have a thick black border. Notice that this border can be moved to other cells by using the arrow keys; but restore the border to its original position before entering the data. On pressing Return, the number *173* will be transferred to the thick-bordered cell in the grid and the border will move to the cell below. Type in another number, say *203*, and press Return again. Do this a few more times, so that you have a short column of numbers in the **Data Editor**.

Choose
File
    Save as ...

to bring the **Save as** dialog box to the screen (Figure. 11).

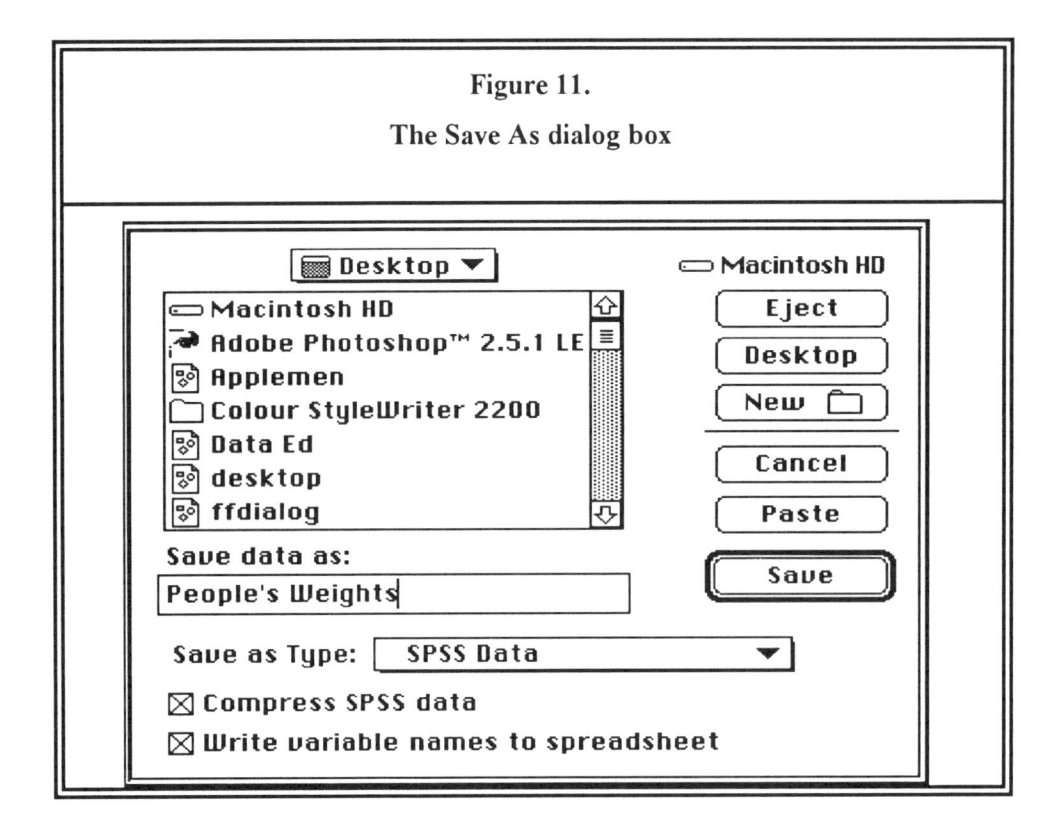

Figure 11.

The Save As dialog box

There are three pieces of information that this dialog is looking for:

- The file *name*;
- The *type* of file;
- The *location* at which the file is to be saved.

In the uppermost central rectangle is a specified target location for the saved file. Click on the **desktop** button on the right, to make sure that the file will be saved on the desktop. In the **Save as Type** rectangle at the bottom, choose **SPSS Data**. This choice will save the data in the form that preserves all the specifications of the data given to the **Data Editor** by the user. Name the file by typing, in the

Save data as rectangle, *People's Weights*. On pressing the **Save** button, the title of the **Data Editor** window will change from **untitled data** to **People's Weights**. Meantime the data in the **Data Editor** have been copied and saved to a file named **People's Weights**, located on the desktop.

Now, leave SPSS by choosing **Quit** within the **File** menu. (Alternatively, use **Command/Q** to quit SPSS.) Before the user is allowed to leave SPSS, a dialog box will appear with the question: **Save contents of SPSS output window !untitled output 1?** Click on the **Don't Save** button. On doing this, you will be allowed to leave SPSS. On the desktop can now be seen, along with the usual icons (Macintosh HD, Wastebasket, and so on) rather an ornate icon, People's Weights, clearly marked as an SPSS data file.

2.6.2 Resuming work on a saved data set: A short-cut

There are several ways of resuming work on a data set, either for the purpose of carrying out statistical analysis, or of adding further data. One can, of course, access SPSS and bring the saved data into the **Data Editor** by choosing **Open** within the **File** menu and then selecting *People's Weights* in **Desktop**. This choice, however, involves inputting these specifications into a dialog box, and there is a quicker method. When a data set has been entered into SPSS and saved to a named file before closing the application, the data can be quickly re-accessed in SPSS by dragging the data file to the icon of the SPSS alias. This takes considerably less time that simply entering the application and calling up the file on the application's own File menu. On the desktop, there should be, in addition to the data file *People's Weights*, an SPSS alias. Click-and-drag the *People's Weights* icon on to the SPSS alias. The application will start up immediately without any additional input from the user, and the **Data Editor** will appear with the data in place.

2.6.3 Using the mouse to save a file to, and retrieve a file from, a floppy disk

Saving a file to a floppy disk

Assuming that your Mac desktop contains the icon of the file *People's Weights*, it is a very simple matter to save a back-up copy on to a floppy disk: simply click and drag the icon on to the floppy disk icon, then release the mouse button. A message will appear telling you that the file is being copied. When the operation is complete, the icon of *People's Weights* will still appear on your desktop, but by double-clicking on the floppy disk icon, it can be seen that a copy of the file has been saved to the floppy disk.

Chapter 2 - Basic Macintosh Operations for SPSS

Retrieving a file from a floppy disk

To retrieve a file from a floppy disk and save it on the Mac's hard disk, insert the floppy disk in the floppy disk drive. An icon of an untitled floppy disk will then appear on the desktop, together with icons of any folders on the disk. If the file is not in a folder, click on the floppy disk icon to enable file icons to appear on the desktop.

The existence of these folder and file icons on the desktop, however, does not mean that they have been safely stored there. If the floppy disk were to be removed at this stage (by transferring its icon on to the **Wastebasket** icon), these folder and file icons would disappear. To save a file from a floppy disk permanently on the Mac, it is necessary to drag its icon on to the **Hard Disk** icon. After that, the file's icon can safely be transferred back from the hard disk to the desktop for convenient access, irrespective of whether the floppy disk is there or not.

EXERCISE 1
SOME BASIC MACINTOSH OPERATIONS

INTRODUCTION

If you are already familiar with the Mac computer, there is no need to carry out this exercise, and we suggest you proceed you begin with Exercise 2 at the end of the next chapter. If you are just starting on the Mac, however, the following exercises should prove helpful.

This exercise will work irrespective of whether you are an individual user with your own Mac computer or have access to a network. Before beginning this session, we suggest you have available a floppy disk. If you are an individual user, we assume that SPSS has been installed, and the licence is up to date.

GETTING STARTED

Familiarising yourself with the computer keyboard
Should you be unfamiliar with a typewriter keyboard, you may find it helpful to read Section 1.2.1 and identify the various keys on a real Mac computer. Unfamiliarity with the layout of keys can be a major obstacle to progress.

The value of practising with a word-processor
The best way of getting to know the computer keyboard is by accessing a word processor and trying to prepare text. Whether you are using a network or a stand-alone machine, there will almosst certainly be a word processor available to you. Some Powerbooks and Powermacs, for example, come with a word processor such as Simple Text already installed. If so, there will also be a tutorial available on your Mac, which we strongly recommend that you work your way through.
Word-processing skills are useful not only because they help you learn to find your way around the keyboard, but also because they include procedures (including certain editing operations) which are used with SPSS.

THE DESKTOP

Basic mouse operations
Assuming that your computer has booted up satisfactorily, you should have before you the screen array known as the desktop (Section 2.1). The important thing now is to get used to certain operations with the mouse, which controls the screen pointer. We suggest you work through the exercise described in Section 2.1.3.

The menu bar
Having gained control of the mouse, proceed with Section 2.2, and familiarise yourself with the menu bar. We suggest you try **Balloon Help** for a while, until the various icons become familiar (Section 2.2.1).

Creating a new folder
Create a new folder, as described in Section 2.2.3. Try the exercise by choosing **New Folder** from the **File** menu and by using the key combination **Command/N**.

Inserting and ejecting a floppy disk
Insert a floppy disk into the slit of the disk drive, as described in Section 2.2.4. If it is a Macintosh disk, you may need to format it by clicking on the **Initialise** button on the dialog box (Figure 2). Observe the appearance of the new floppy disk icon on the Desktop, with the name **untitled**. Eject the disk in the manner described.

THE MACINTOSH HARD DISK WINDOW

Explore the **Macintosh Hard Disk (HD) window**, as described in Section 2.3. You may find it helpful to engage **Balloon Help** (in the **Guide** menu), to remind you of the names of the various parts. Try double-clicking on some of the items shown in the window to open them.

USING SPSS

Finding the application folder
If yours is a stand-alone computer, with SPSS installed, follow the instructions in Section 2.4.1 to locate the folder containing the application. To find the application program itself, you will need to double-click on the containing folder to open it.

Making SPSS more accessible: creating an alias
Try making SPSS more accessible by creating an alias on the Desktop, as described in Section 2.4.3.

Putting SPSS on the Apple menu
Create another SPSS alias as described in Section 2.4.3. Get into the **Apple Menu Items** folder, as described in Section 2.5.2, and drag the new alias into that folder. Confirm that the SPSS alias now appears in the Apple menu.

Accessing SPSS
Double-click on the SPSS icon to obtain the **Data Editor**. Work through Section 2.6 to create a data set. Save the data to a file as described in Section 2.6.1.
Exit from SPSS, either by choosing
File
    Exit
from the SPSS **File** menu, or with the key combination **Command/Q**.

Retrieving the data set
Try restoring the Data Editor, complete with data, by dragging the data file (which should be stored on the Desktop) on to the **SPSS Alias** icon.

Saving files to and retrieving them from a floppy disk
Follow the procedure of Section 2.6.3 to save the data file to the floppy disk. Eject the floppy disk by dragging it to the Wastebasket and releasing the button. Drag the data file to the Wastebasket to dispose of it. Restore the floppy disk and double-click on the icon to view the stored file.
Store the data file in the Mac as described in Section 2.6.3.

CHAPTER 3

DATA HANDLING IN SPSS

3.1 INTRODUCTION

3.2 SOME RESEARCH TERMS

3.3 ENTERING AND EDITING DATA

3.4 SAVING AND RETRIEVING SPSS FILES

3.5 LISTING DATA

3.6 PRINTING IN SPSS

3.7 SOME SPECIAL OPERATIONS

3.1 INTRODUCTION

Before any exploration of data or statistical analyses can take place, it is necessary to input the data to *SPSS for Macintosh* (hereafter simply SPSS) in a suitable form and to check that the data have been correctly transcribed either by inspecting them on the screen or by printing them out. Any corrections or modifications can then be made by invoking one of the editing procedures. It may also be desirable to select (or exclude) cases, and to invoke the **Weight Cases** procedure if the data represent frequencies rather than scores. In this chapter, the operations of inputting, editing, saving, listing, printing, selecting and case-weighting will be fully explained and demonstrated with examples.

3.2 SOME RESEARCH TERMS

Variables

A **variable** is a characteristic or property of a person, an object or a situation, which comprises a set of different values or categories. **Quantitative variables**, such as height, weight or extraversion, are possessed in **degree** and can be measured; **qualitative** variables, such as sex, blood group or nationality, are possessed in **kind**.

Hypothesis

A **hypothesis** is a provisional supposition about nature, which is stated in such a way that it can be tested empirically, that is, by gathering data. Often, a hypothesis states that there is a causal relationship between two variables: it is an assertion that the value of one variable at least partially determines that of another.

Experimental and correlational research

In **correlational research** (a strategy often forced on the investigator), variables are measured as they occur in the individuals studied. As a consequence, it is often difficult to make an unequivocal decision about the research hypothesis, because the effects of the supposedly causal variables are entangled, or **confounded**, with the effects of other variables, such as the personal characteristics of the subjects studied. The difficulty with correlational research can be summed up in the aphorism:

Correlation does not imply causation

A correlation between two variables may indeed reflect the fact that one variable influences the other; but such a finding is equally compatible with the view that both the correlated variables are themselves caused by a third variable which has not been studied.

In **experimental** as opposed to **correlational** research, one variable, which is hypothesised to exert a causal influence upon another, is manipulated directly by the experimenter, the manipulated variable being known as the **independent variable (IV)**, the variable it supposedly influences being the **dependent variable (DV)**. (Should a mnemonic be necessary, one might think of the values of the DV as 'depending' upon - i.e. being partly determined by - those of the IV.) The IV is decided upon and controlled *before the experiment is carried out*; whereas the DV is *measured during the course of the investigation*. While this usage is common, there are several well-known authors (e.g. Tabachnick & Fidell, 1996; Howell, 1997) who use the term IV to refer to *any* supposedly causal variable, whether it is manipulated directly by the experimenter or not, and use the term *independent variable* in the context of correlational, as well as experimental, research. At times, for convenience, we shall also follow this practice.

The principle of control

The great advantage of the experimental strategy is that, since there is an independent variable, the experimenter is in a stronger position to draw causal inferences from the data, provided that there has been adequate **control** of the effects of potential confounding, or **extraneous variables**. In correlational research, on the other hand, the absence of an independent variable makes it impossible to draw causal inferences unequivocally.

Factors

In experimental design, a **factor** is a set of related conditions or categories. The conditions or categories making up a factor are known as **levels**, even though, as in the qualitative factors of gender or blood group, there is no sense in which one category can be said to be 'higher' or 'lower' than the other. Some factors are independent variables: that is, the experimenter manipulates them to ascertain their effects upon selected dependent variables. They are not inherent subject characteristics. Other factors, however, such as gender, or age, are **subject variables**, and are usually included in the experimental design for purposes of control. For the purposes of statistical analysis, subject variables are often treated as if they were true independent variables.

It should be noted that the term **factor** has more than one meaning in psychological data analysis. In this section, it has been presented as a term in experimental design. Experimental factors are decided upon at the planning stage of the research: they do not emerge from the data yielded by the investigation. Later, however, in the context of correlational research, the statistical technique known as **factor analysis** (Chapter 15) will be introduced. This technique is applicable when a battery of tests is given to a (large) sample of subjects, the purpose being to identify the comparatively few underlying variables supposedly underlying the observed correlations among the tests in the battery. In this second usage, a **factor** is a descriptive, classificatory variable, derived from the data gathered in the process of an essentially correlational investigation.

In summary, the terms **factor** and **level** are the equivalents, in the context of experimental design, of the more general terms **variable** and **value**, respectively. A **factor** is a special kind of variable, created by the design of an experiment. In the context of experimental design, a factor is either a true independent variable or a grouping variable such as gender, which we 'manipulate' *statistically*, rather than experimentally, by sampling so-many men and so-many women, or so-many people from each of some other set of categories.

Between subjects and within subjects factors

Some factors are **between subjects**: that is, the subject is tested under only one condition, or level, of the factor. (Subject variables such as Gender must always be between subjects factors.) Other factors are **within subjects**, that is, the subject is tested under all the different conditions (levels) making up the factor. A design with a within subjects factor is also said to have **repeated measures** on the factor.

In order to ascertain the effectiveness of a drug, an investigator tests the performance on a vigilance task of two groups of subjects:

(1) a group who have ingested a dosage of the drug;

(2) a comparison, or **control**, group, who have received a placebo.

In the terminology of experimental design, this experiment has **one treatment factor (Drug)**, comprising two conditions or **levels**: Drug Present and Drug Absent. Since different samples of subjects perform under the different conditions, this is a **between subjects experiment**. Should the investigator wish to study the effectiveness of more than one drug, the performance of two or more groups of subjects could be compared with that of the controls. In that case, there would still be one treatment factor, but with three or more levels.

Another investigator wishes to test the hypothesis that words presented in the right visual hemifield are recognised more quickly than those presented in the left hemifield. Fifty subjects are each presented with 40 words in the left and right hemifields and their median response times are recorded. In this experiment (as in the drug experiment), there is **one treatment factor** (Hemifield of Presentation) comprising two conditions: Left Field; Right Field. But this time, *the same subjects perform under both conditions*. This experiment is said to be of **within subjects** design, or to have **repeated measures on the hemifield factor.** In the general case of a one-factor, within subjects experiment, the factor would comprise three or more treatment conditions, or levels, and each subject would perform under all conditions.

For example, to test the hypothesis that the accuracy with which a subject shoots at a target depends upon the shape of the target's perimeter, each subject might be tested with circular, square and triangular targets, in which case the treatment factor (Shape of Target) would have three levels.

In Table 1, the designs of the between subjects and within subjects one-factor experiments are shown schematically.

Table 1.
Between subjects and within subjects experiments with one treatment factor

	(a) The one-factor between subjects experiment			
	Levels of the factor: Drug			
	Control	Drug A	Drug B	Drug C
Subjects	Group 1	Group 2	Group 3	Group 4
	(b) The one-factor within-subjects experiment			
	Levels of the factor: Shape of Target			
	Circle	Square	Triangle	Diamond
Subjects	The same group of subjects perform with all four shapes			

Factorial designs: Between subjects, within subjects and mixed designs

It is common for experiments to have two or more factors, in which case they are said to be of **factorial** design. For example, in addition to the effects of different drugs upon fresh subjects, our drugs researcher might wish to investigate the effects of the drugs upon those who have voluntarily gone without sleep for twenty-four hours. Accordingly, an experiment is planned, the design of which is shown in Table 2.

Table 2.		
A two-factor factorial between subjects experiment		

	Levels of the factor: Drug	
Levels of the factor: State	Drug A	Drug B
Fresh	Group 1	Group 2
Tired	Group 3	Group 4

Notice that a different sample of subjects performs at each of the four combinations of the two treatment factors, Subject's State (Fresh, Tired) and Drug (A, B). Since each subject is tested only once, this type of experiment is said to be of **between subjects factorial** design. It is also described as having **two factors with no repeated measures**.

Table 3 shows a **within subjects** experiment, in which there are two factors:

(1) Shape of Target (Triangle, Square);

(2) Colour of Target (Blue, Green).

Alternatively, the experiment can be said to have **repeated measures on both factors.**

Table 3. A two-factor factorial within subjects experiment				
Levels of the factor: Shape	Triangle		Square	
Levels of the factor: Colour	Blue	Green	Blue	Green
Subjects	The same subjects perform under all four combinations of shape and colour			

Suppose that, in addition to the effects of target colour, the experimenter wishes to test the hypothesis that men and women may not produce their best performances with targets of the same colour. Table 4 shows the experimental design with two factors, the first between subjects, the second within subjects:

(1) Sex (Male, Female);

(2) Colour of Target (Red, Blue).

Factorial experiments in which some (but not all) factors are within subjects are known as **mixed** (or **split-plot**) factorial experiments.

Table 4. A two-factor mixed factorial experiment with one between subjects factor (Sex) and one within subjects factor (Colour of Target)		
	Levels of the factor: Colour of Target	
Levels of the factor: Sex	Red	Blue
Male	Each is tested with red and blue targets	
Female	Each is tested with red and blue targets	

3.3 ENTERING AND EDITING DATA

3.3.1 Data from a between subjects experiment

A between subjects experiment

In an experiment on the relative efficacy of two mnemonic methods for the recall of verbal material, each individual in a pool of 30 participants is randomly assigned to one of three equal-sized groups:

(1) a **control** group, which receives no training;

(2) a group trained to use the **Galton's Walk** method (**Mnemonic A**);

(3) a group trained to use the **Peg** method (**Mnemonic B**).

Each participant is presented with verbal material and asked (at a later stage) to reproduce it in free written recall. The dependent variable is the number of words recalled. The results of the experiment are shown in Table 5.

Table 5. The numbers of words recalled by subjects with different mnemonic training methods									
Control Group	3	5	3	2	4	6	9	3	8	10
Mnemonic A	10	8	15	9	11	16	17	17	7	10
Mnemonic B	20	15	14	15	17	10	8	11	18	19

Laying out the data in a form suitable for entry into SPSS

In Chapter 2, we saw that data for processing by SPSS is entered into a spreadsheet format called the **Data Editor** window, in which each row represents a particular participant and each column represents a variable on which that person has been measured.

To make them suitable for analysis with SPSS, the results of an experiment or survey may have to be recast in a new format. In Table 5, for example, where each row represents the scores of ten participants, the data do not conform to the requirement that each row contains the data from only one person.

In this experimental design, there are two variables:

(1) Mnemonic Training Method, with three levels (Control, Mnemonic A, and Mnemonic B);

(2) the dependent variable, Number of Words Recalled (a person's score).

Chapter 3 - Data Handling

Since different subjects are used for each mnemonic training method, the experimental design is of the **between subjects** type.

In the SPSS data set, the scores of all the participants in the experiment can be entered into the first column, under the variable name *score*. (An SPSS variable name must not exceed 8 characters, and there must be no gaps.)

In the second column of the **Data Editor** window, we can place, opposite each person's score, a code number indicating the method (Control, Mnemonic A or Mnemonic B) under which she was tested: so the second column of the **Data Editor** window will contain so-many 1s (for the control subjects), so-many 2s (for the Mnemonic A group) and so-many 3s (for the Mnemonic B group). We shall have constructed what is known as a **grouping** or **coding** variable, which will carry, in a single column, information about the independent variable. This second column can be named *group*.

Note although the second column of the **Data Editor** window will contain numbers, those numbers are merely *category labels*: they are not *measurements* of the degree to which some property is possessed. Their values, therefore, are entirely arbitrary: any three numbers will do, as long as they are different.

Table 6.

The data of Table 5, recast in a form suitable for entry into SPSS

(Note that the shaded items have been included here for explanation only: they are not actually entered into SPSS. Only the unshaded variable names and values are entered in the Data Editor window.)

	Variable Names		
	group	score	
Subject 1	1	3	
Subject 2	1	5	
...	...	...	Group 1: The controls
Subject 9	1	8	
Subject 10	1	10	
Subject 11	2	10	
Subject 12	2	8	
...	...	...	Group 2: Mnemonic A
Subject 19	2	7	
Subject 20	2	10	
Subject 21	3	20	
Subject 22	3	15	
...	...	...	Group 3: Mnemonic B
Subject 29	3	18	
Subject 30	3	19	

In summary, each column in the **Data Editor** window will contain the values of one (and only one) variable: in the present case, one column will contain the independent (grouping) variable, that is, the code numbers (*1, 2* or *3*) identifying the condition under which each subject in each row performed; the other will contain all the scores.

In Table 6, the results in Table 5 have been recast, so that each row now contains two data per subject:

(1)   a code number showing the mnemonic training method *group* to which that person was assigned (the **IV**);

(2)   the *score* that person achieved under the coded condition(the **DV**).

Note that the requirement that each row contains data from only one subject has now been met.

Now that the data from the experiment have been re-organised into a format suitable for entry into the **Data Editor** window, we are ready to proceed to enter the data.

3.3.2   Obtaining the Data Editor window

Our first acquaintance with the **Data Editor** window was made at the end of Chapter 2. When SPSS is accessed, three important items appear:

(1)   the **SPSS application menu**;

(2)   the **Output** window (captioned **!untitled output1**);

(3)   the **Data Editor** window (captioned **untitled data**).

All three arrays are shown in Figure 1.

Running along the bottom of the screen is a horizontal band, in which various messages appear from time to time. When SPSS is accessed, the message reads: 'SPSS Processor is ready'. The horizontal band is known as the **status bar**, because it reports not only upon whether SPSS is ready to begin, but also on the stage that an analytic procedure has reached. If, for example, a large data set is being read from a file, progress is continually monitored, case by case, in the status bar. This **case counter** is one of several useful types of message that appear: there is also information about the weighting of cases (**weight status**), the selection of specified portions of the data set (**filter status**), and whether the data set has been split into separate groups for analysis (**split file status**).

Notice that initially, in both the **Data Editor** window and the **SPSS Application menu**, the title bars are coloured on the screen; whereas that in the **Output** window is grey. This indicates that, of the three arrays, only the first two (in order of mention) are presently **active**, that is, the items therein can be accessed directly by clicking within the appropriate areas.

Initially, as we saw in Chapter 2, every column in the **Data Editor** window has the heading *var*, and all the cells are empty.

Chapter 3 - Data Handling

Figure 1.
The SPSS Application menu

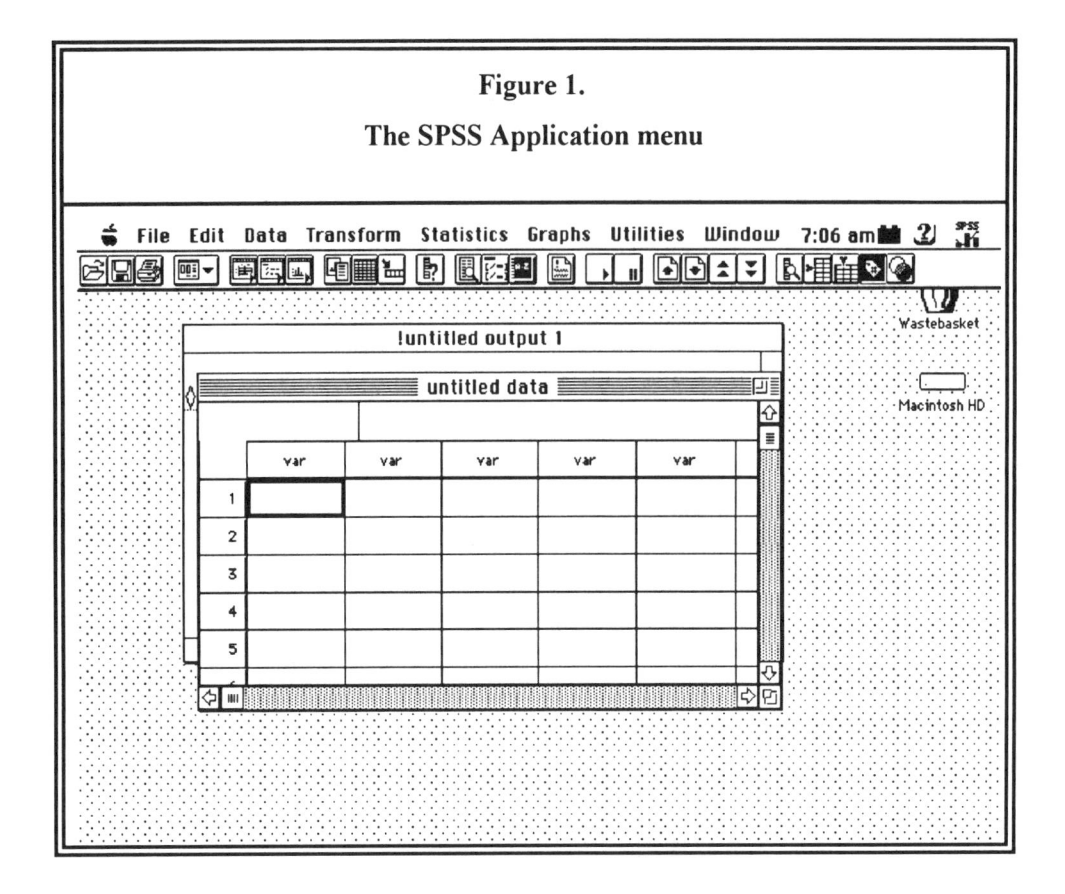

3.3.3 How many decimal places?

Since we are about to enter numbers into the **Data Editor** window, we need to consider the form (i.e. how many decimal places - if any) in which those values will be displayed. A convenient procedure is to specify a standard, or **default**, format for all values, which can then be over-ridden (if necessary) for specified variables only.

- From the **SPSS application menu**, choose
  Edit
     Preferences

  to obtain the **Preferences** dialog box (Figure 2).

- Within the **Display Format for New Variables** box are two **text boxes**, labelled **Width** and **Decimal Places**, in each of which a number is already entered. If those numbers are *8* and *2*, a total of eight spaces will be allocated to each value and all values will be displayed to two places of decimals, even if they are integers (i.e. *3* will appear as *3.00*). All the data in Table 5, however, are integers, so there is no need for values to be written as decimals at all. Click on the **Decimal Places** box, press ←**Del** to erase the number and type in a zero. The effect of this change will be to show all values as integers, and the data display will be much easier to read.

- Leave the **Preferences** dialog box by clicking on **OK**.

Incidentally, the user might take the opportunity to change the **Display Order for Variable Lists** to **File** instead of **Alphabetical** (the default setting): this has the effect of listing variable names within dialog boxes that contain lists of variables in the same order as they are displayed in the **Data Editor** window, rather than in alphabetical order.

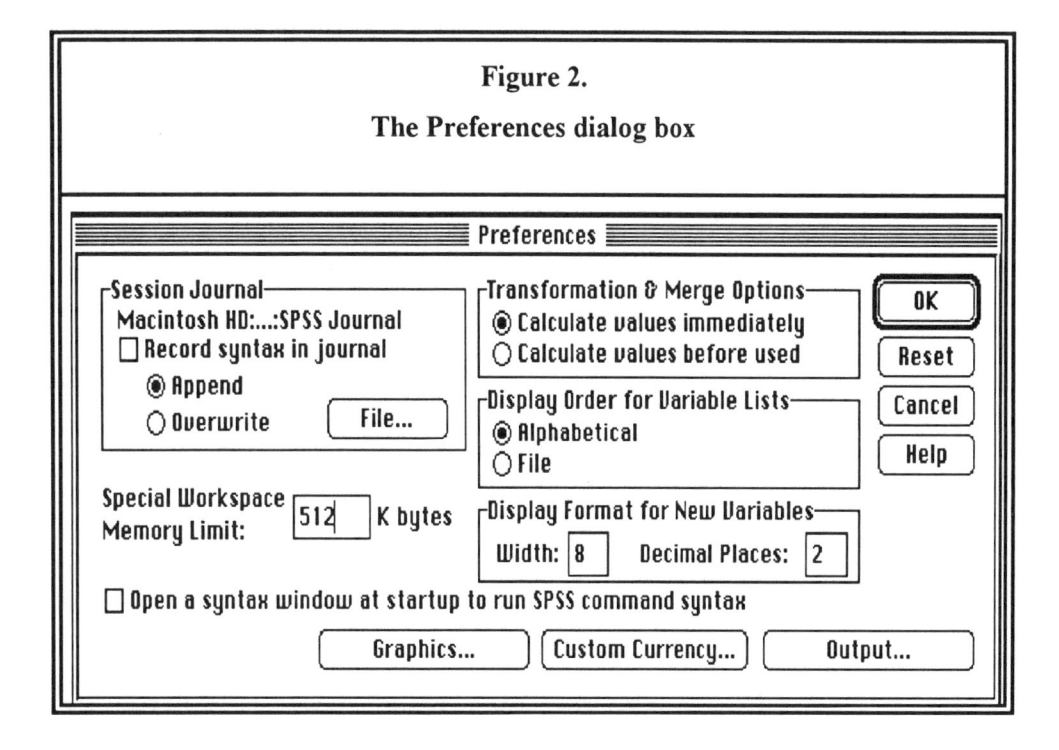

Figure 2.
The Preferences dialog box

3.3.4 Variable names and value labels

Having recast the results in Table 5 into the form shown in Table 6, we are now almost ready to begin entering the data into SPSS. Before doing that, however, we must first assign sensible names to our variables and (for the grouping variable) explanatory labels to the values. In Table 6, the first column contains the code numbers of the grouping variable, and the second contains the scores of the subjects tested under the conditions codified in the first column. We shall name the first and second columns *group* and *score,* respectively.

A notational convention

In this book, we shall use *italics* to indicate those variable names and values which are to be typed into the **Data Editor** window. Note that whether we type in lower or uppercase, the Editor will record (at the head of the appropriate column) a name in lower case only: for example, if we type *Field*, the name will be recorded as *field*. This is not true, however, of variable name labels and values (see below), which will appear in the SPSS output as they have been typed. We shall use a **bold** typeface for the names of menus, the names of dialog boxes and the items therein. Emboldening will also be used for emphasis and for technical terms.

Chapter 3 - Data Handling

Rules for naming variables

The choice of names for variables is governed by a set of six rules: A variable name:

- (1) must not exceed **eight characters**. (A **character** is a letter, a digit or a symbol.)

- (2) must **begin with a letter or @**.

- (3) must **not end with a full stop**.

- (4) **can** contain letters, digits or any of the characters @, #, _, or $.

- (5) must **not** contain either of the following:
  - (i) a blank;
  - (ii) special characters, such as !, ?, and *, other than those listed in (4).

- (6) must **not be** one of the keywords (such as AND, NOT, EQ, BY and ALL) that SPSS uses as special computing terms.

The names we have chosen, *group* and *score*, clearly meet the requirements of all the above rules. Note, however, that while the name *group1* would also have been satisfactory, *group 1* would not, because it contains a space, violating rule 5. The name *1group* would violate rule 2 since it does not start with a letter. Be careful about length, too (rule 1): *red_cube* is satisfactory; but *red_cubes* is not, because the total number of characters (including the underline symbol) exceeds the permitted limit of 8.

Assigning the chosen variable names

To assign the variable name *group* to the first column in the **Data Editor** window, proceed as follows:

- Double-click on the grey area at the top of the first column. This will obtain the **Define Variable** dialog box (Figure 3).

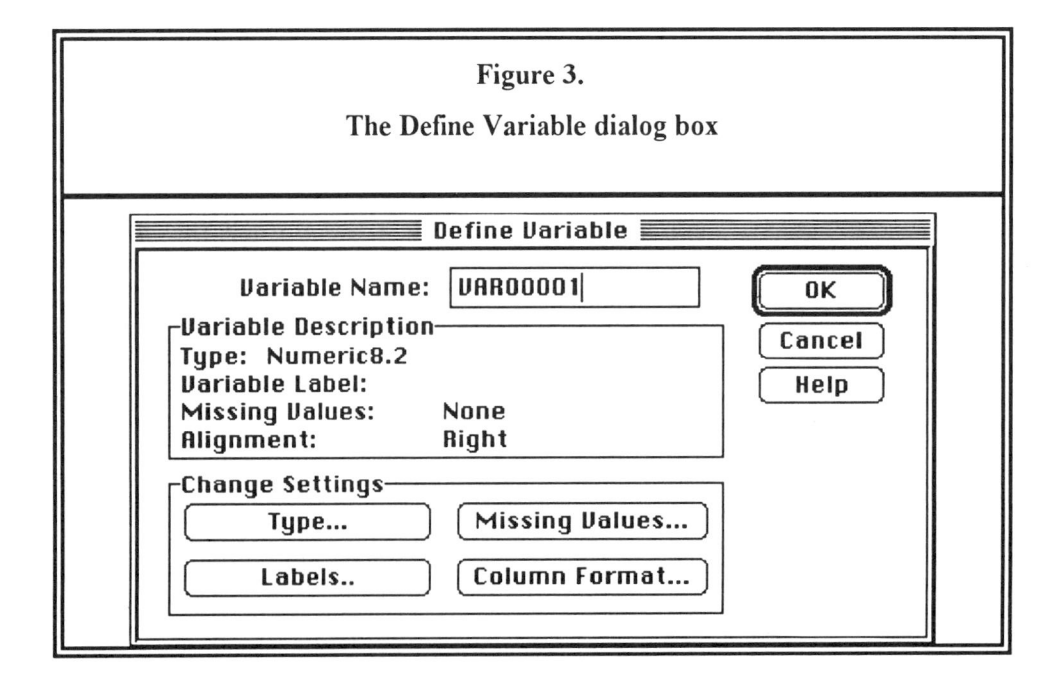

Figure 3.

The Define Variable dialog box

```
┌─ Define Variable ─────────────────┐
│                                   │
│  Variable Name: [VAR00001]   [ OK ]│
│  ┌Variable Description─────┐      │
│  │ Type:  Numeric8.2       │ [Cancel]│
│  │ Variable Label:         │      │
│  │ Missing Values:  None   │ [ Help ]│
│  │ Alignment:       Right  │      │
│  └─────────────────────────┘      │
│  ┌Change Settings──────────────┐  │
│  │  [ Type... ]  [Missing Values...]│
│  │  [ Labels.. ] [Column Format...]│
│  └─────────────────────────────┘  │
└───────────────────────────────────┘
```

46

Chapter 3 - Data Handling

- **The Variable Name** text box contains a default variable name, *var00001*. The **Variable Description** box contains the information that the **Type** (of variable) is **Numeric8.0**. These are the default specifications that were set in **Preferences** (see Section 3.3.3). Notice that the **Change Settings** box contains four subdialog command buttons: **Type, Labels, Missing Values** and **Column Format**. These permit the user to make specifications that apply only to one particular variable.

- In the **Variable Name** text box, click-and-drag to select the area in the rectangle and type *group*. There is no need to remove the default variable name (*var00001*) first: provided the area has been selected first, the default name will be overwritten when the chosen name is typed in. The name *group*, although reminding the reader that this is a grouping variable, conveys no further information. A longer, more meaningful, label is required. To assign one, click on the **Labels** subdialog button to obtain the **Define Labels** dialog box (Figure 4).

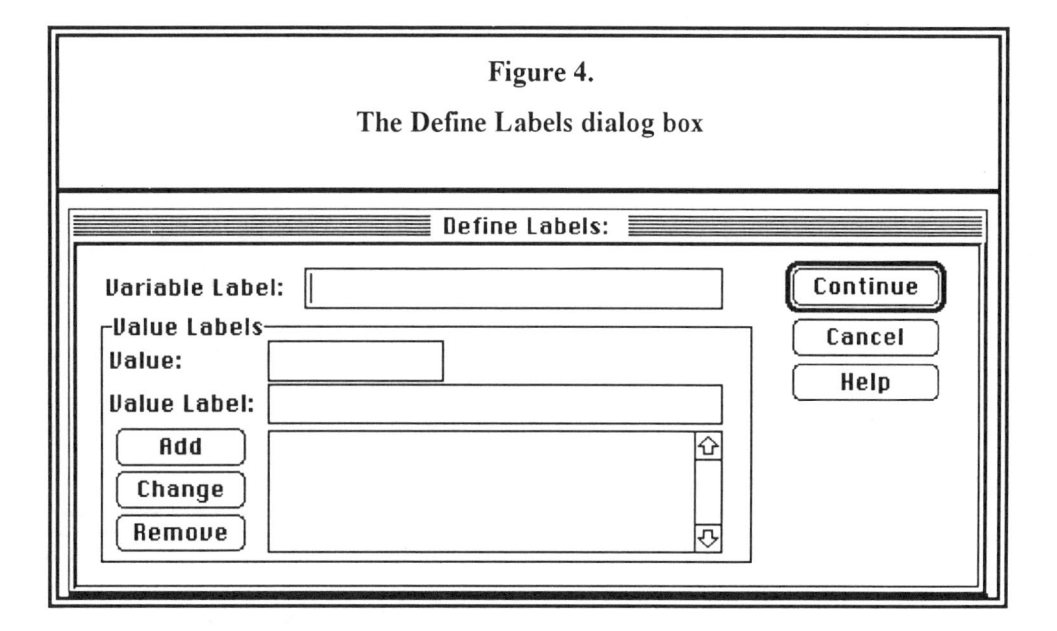

Figure 4.

The Define Labels dialog box

- The **Variable Label** text box gives the user the opportunity to supply a fuller label for the grouping variable. This will make the statistical output easier to interpret. Type in an informative name such as *Mnemonic Training Method*.

The rules governing the naming of variables do not apply to the assignment of labels in the **Define Labels** dialog box. Here, the name can be anything up to 120 characters in length and (as in *Mnemonic Training Method)* can include spaces. Expanded variable names often clarify the output when these fuller names appear in tables and diagrams. Moreover, unlike the naming of variables, assigned variable labels are case sensitive and displayed exactly as they are entered. It should be borne in mind, however, that should a name with the maximum of 120 characters be chosen, fewer characters (usually the first 40) will actually be displayed in the output though the precise number varies in different procedures.

Chapter 3 - Data Handling

Assigning value labels

Since a grouping variable comprises arbitrary code numbers, it is well to incorporate a decoding key into the **Data Editor** explaining what those numerical labels represent. This is done by assigning **value labels**.

- Type the lowest code number *1* into the **Value** text box.
- In the **Value Label** text box, type *Control*. This will embolden the **Add** button below.
- When **Add** is clicked, the following will appear in the lowest box:

    1 = "Control".

    In a similar manner, proceed to label the values *2* and *3,* so that in the lowest box can be seen:

    1 = "Control"

    2 = "Mnemonic A"

    3 = "Mnemonic B"

    Value labelling, like variable labelling, is governed by much looser constraints than is variable naming. A value label can be up to 60 characters in length, is case sensitive and can contain spaces. As with variable labels, however, fewer than the maximum of 60 characters (usually only about 20) will actually be displayed in the output.

    The completed **Define Labels** dialog box for *group* is shown in Figure 5.

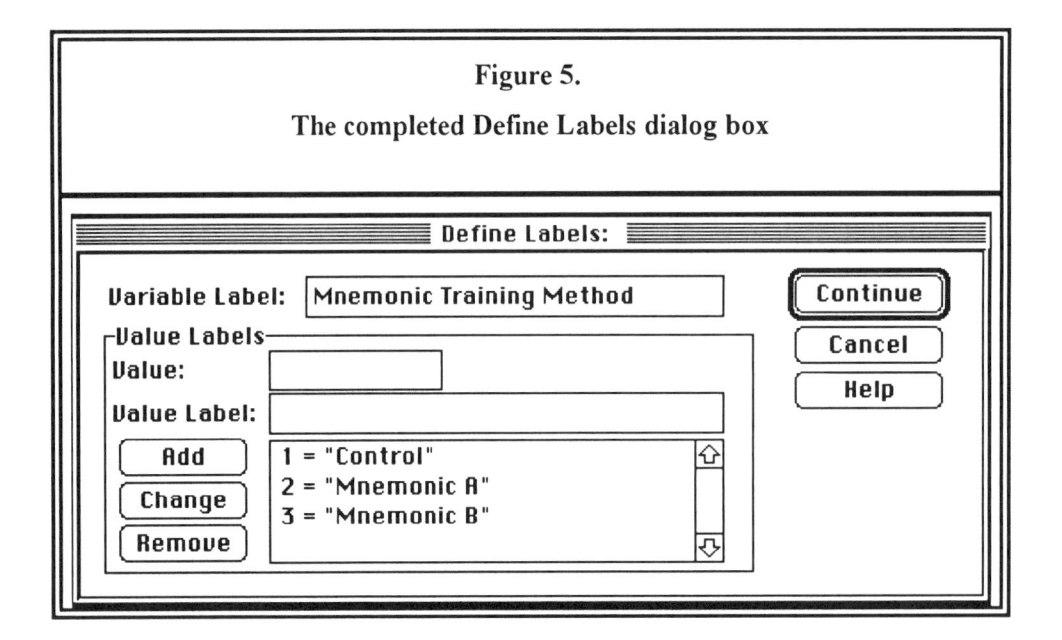

Figure 5.

The completed Define Labels dialog box

- Now that all three values of the grouping variable have been labelled, click on **Continue**. We are now back in the **Define Variable** dialog box again, but it now appears as in Figure 6. Notice that the **Variable Description** box now contains a fuller label for the grouping variable.
- Return to the **Data Editor** window by clicking on **OK**. Notice that the first column is now headed *group*.

- Double click on *var* at the top of the second column and name the variable *score*. As *score* is a quantitative variable, it does not have value labels, but an expanded variable label can be added if desired

This completes the naming of the two variables required for the data in Table 5.

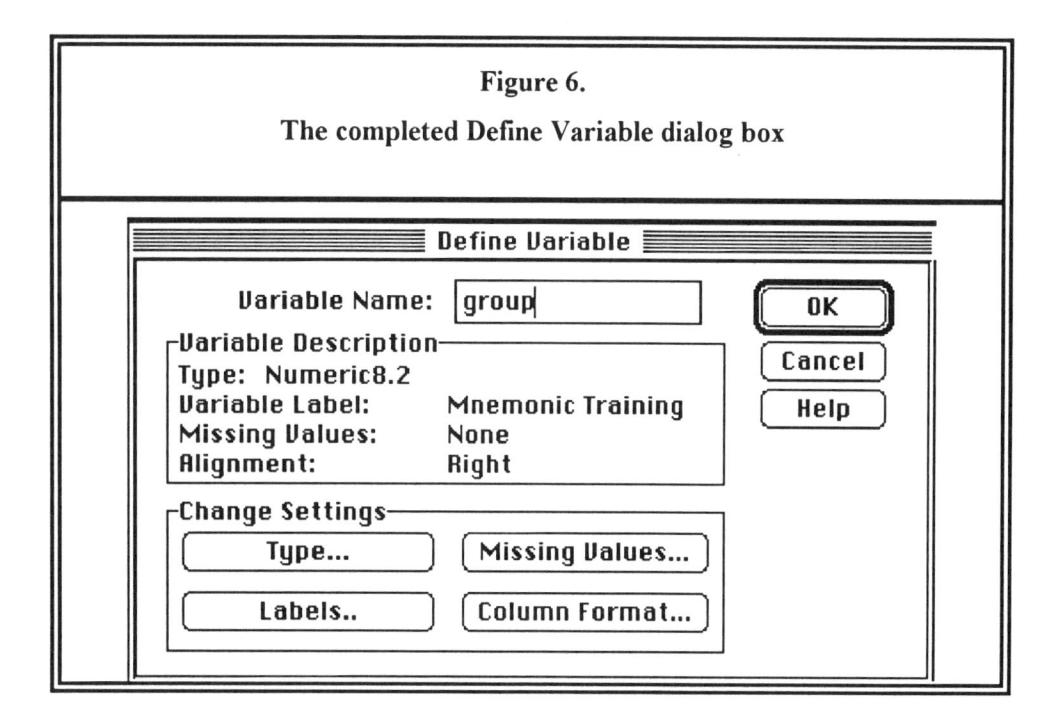

Figure 6.
The completed Define Variable dialog box

3.3.5 Using the keyboard to enter data

In the **Data Editor** window (Figure 1), just underneath the title bar, is a white bar. This is the **cell editor**. Beneath the cell editor, around the top left cell in the empty grid, can be seen a black rectangle, the **cell highlight**, formed by a thickening of the cell's borders. The cell highlight can readily be relocated by using the arrow keys.

A value typed in from the keyboard will appear in the cell editor. If a cursor key (or ↵) is pressed, this value (or its associated label as defined in the **Define Labels:** dialog box) is transferred to the highlighted cell. Whether the value or its label appears is determined by the state of the toggle item **Value Labels** in the **Utilities** drop-down menu: if it is ticked, then the label will appear; if not, the value will appear.

The subsequent location of the highlight depends upon which key is pressed: if the ↑ or ↓ arrow key is pressed, the new location is a cell above or below the original position; if the ← or → cursor key is pressed, the highlight moves to the left or the right, respectively. An alternative way of moving down is to use ↵. The position of the cell highlight can also be controlled by using the mouse. Clicking on any cell will highlight it and its row and column co-ordinates will appear in the cell editor.

The position of the highlight determines which cell of the grid will receive the next number typed into the cell editor. Try entering a few numbers into the empty

Chapter 3 - Data Handling

Data Editor window. Once numbers have been entered in the window, the location of the cell highlight will be shown in an entry on the left of the cell editor. For example, the entry **2:group** locates the highlight at the cell in the *second* row of the column headed *group*. Try moving the highlight around with the arrows keys (or ↵) and notice that the co-ordinates given in the cell editor change accordingly. Remove the numbers entered into the grid by clicking-and-dragging the cursor over the cells concerned to highlight them, and then pressing Delete.

3.3.6 Entering the data into the Data Editor window

It is easiest to enter the data by columns as shown in the completed **Data Editor** window in Figure 7.

Figure 7.

The completed Data Editor window for the 30 subjects taking part in the learning experiment

	group	score		group	score
1	Control	3	16	Mnemonic A	16
2	Control	5	17	Mnemonic A	17
3	Control	3	18	Mnemonic A	15
4	Control	2	19	Mnemonic A	7
5	Control	4	20	Mnemonic A	10
6	Control	6	21	Mnemonic B	20
7	Control	9	22	Mnemonic B	15
8	Control	3	23	Mnemonic B	14
9	Control	8	24	Mnemonic B	15
10	Control	10	25	Mnemonic B	17
11	Mnemonic A	10	26	Mnemonic B	10
12	Mnemonic A	8	27	Mnemonic B	8
13	Mnemonic A	15	28	Mnemonic B	11
14	Mnemonic A	9	29	Mnemonic B	18
15	Mnemonic A	11	30	Mnemonic B	19

(continued in next column)

In the first column labelled *group*, type in ten ones, ten twos and ten threes to identify the subjects in the three treatment groups. (In Section 3.3.7, a quicker way of entering repeated numbers will be described.) The values in the second column *score* of Table 6 are entered as described in Section 3.3.6, because each cell contains a different value. Whether the entries in the column headed *group* appear as code numbers or value labels, depends upon whether there is a tick opposite the command **Value Labels** in the **Utilities menu**. Notice that the numbers entered for the variable *group* have been replaced with the value labels previously defined in the **Value Labels:** dialog box.

In this example there is just one grouping variable (**between subjects factor**). The entry procedure is easily extended to deal with more than one grouping variable: a two-factor case will be considered in Section 3.7.2.

Notice particularly that data from an experiment having repeated measures (**within subjects factors**) are entered differently, because such data do not require any grouping variables at all (provided all the factors are within subjects). In this experimental design, the data from each of the levels of a within subjects factor are entered in a separate column as will be explained in Section 3.3.8.

3.3.7 Editing data

The **Data Editor** offers a range of functions, some of which are extremely useful, not only for amending data that are already in the **Data Editor** window, but also for inputting data values that are to be repeated many times.

Changing individual values

Enter a few numbers in the **Data Editor** window. Any of these can be changed at will by targeting the cell concerned with the black rectangle, typing a new value and pressing a cursor key or Return.

Blocking, copying and pasting

Initially, only one cell in the **Data Editor** window is highlighted. In Chapter 2, however, we saw that it is possible to highlight a whole block of cells. This **blocking** operation is achieved very simply, either by a click-and-drag with the mouse or by proceeding as follows:

Press and hold **Shift** and press the ↓ cursor a few (say four) times. It will be seen that five cells are now highlighted: the original cell and four new ones below, whose entries now appear in **inverse video** (that is, in white against a black background).

The blocking operation can be used to copy, say, the values in one column into another column or to lower down in the same column (see below).

- Highlight a column of values that you wish to copy. Now, choose
  Edit
    Copy.

Chapter 3 - Data Handling

- Next, highlight the cells of the target column, choose
  Edit
    Paste

and the values in the source column will now appear in the target column. (Make sure that the number of highlighted target cells is equal to the number of cells copied.)

As an example, the repeated values 1, 2, 3 used for identifying the Mnemonic Training Method group could have been entered using this copy-and-paste method.

- To enter the first (unbracketed) column of values of Table 6 into the window, place the value *1* in the first (topmost) cell of the first column *group*. Use the arrow key to return the highlight to the cell that now contains the value *1*.

- Choose
  Edit
    Copy

and highlight cells 1 to 10 in the first column using the **Shift** and downward cursor keys.

- It will be found that on choosing
  Edit
    Paste,

the value *1* will appear in each of the highlighted cells.

- Target the 11th cell in the first column and enter the value *2* in that cell.

- Proceed as above to enter the value *2* in all of the cells from 11 to 20, inclusive.

- In similar fashion, enter the value *3* in each of the cells from 21 to 30, inclusive.

Deletion of values

To delete the values in a cell (or block):

- Highlight the area concerned and press **Shift/ Delete**.

- To delete a whole row of values, click on the grey box containing the row number (see Figure 1). This will highlight every cell in the row. Pressing **Delete** will remove the whole row from the **Data Editor** window. (Press firmly and look for the wrist-watch screen pointer: this means that the **Delete** procedure has been successfully activated.)

- Similarly, clicking the grey box containing the name of a column will highlight all the cells in the column, and pressing **Delete** will remove the entire column of values from the **Data Editor** window.

Inserting additional variables and cases, and changing the order of variables

Additional variables (i.e. new named columns) and additional cases (i.e. new rows) can always be added on at the right and foot of the existing data respectively, but it is sometimes convenient to be able to insert a new variable beside an existing variable within a large data set or to insert a new case (e.g. an additional male) at the end of a block of cases rather than at the foot of the entire data set. Likewise it is sometimes useful to change the positions of variables so that certain variables are adjacent to one another.

All these operations are easily achieved as follows:

- Highlight the variable **to the right of the position desired for the new variable** or highlight **the case above which the desired new case is to be inserted**.

- Choose the **Data** drop-down menu and then select the appropriate item. A blank column or a blank row will then be created.

- If a variable is to be moved to this new column, highlight the existing variable, select
  Edit
     Cut

  and highlight the new column.

- Finally select
  Edit
     Paste.

  The variable will then be pasted into its new position.

3.3.8 Data from a within subjects experiment

A within subjects experiment

Suppose ten subjects participate in an experiment designed to investigate whether recognition of patterns is affected by the shapes of their perimeters. Perhaps, for instance, it is easier to recognise a pattern with a square perimeter than one with a circular perimeter. Each subject is tested on pattern recognition with three perimeter shapes: a triangle, a circle and a square. In this experiment, there is one treatment factor, Shape of Perimeter, comprising three levels, or conditions:

(1) Triangle;

(2) Circle;

(3) Square.

The dependent variable is Recognition Time.

Notice that, in contrast to the mnemonics experiment, each subject is tested under all the three conditions making up the treatment factor. The factor Shape of Perimeter, therefore, has **repeated measures**: it is a **within subjects factor**.

Entering the data into the Data Editor window

Table 7 shows how the data are entered in the **Data Editor** window. Observe that the heading Shape (the treatment factor in this experiment) is not entered in the **Data Editor** window: only the conditions *triangle, circle, square* are entered as variable names.

Chapter 3 - Data Handling

Table 7.

Recognition times for 3 shapes viewed by the same sample of subjects

(Only the unshaded items are entered in the Data Editor window)

Subject	Levels of the factor: Shape		
	triangle	circle	square
1	220	300	260
2	250	290	300
3	260	280	290
4	230	340	190
5	190	300	250
6	220	270	240
7	250	320	270
8	280	290	260
9	270	340	250
10	240	300	350

We have seen earlier that the **Data Editor** can accept only two kinds of variables:

(1) **grouping variables**, which identify (by codes) the condition under which each subject has been tested;

(2) **dependent variables**, comprising measurements.

At the moment, therefore, the **Data Editor** has no knowledge of the experimenter's interest in making comparisons among the three different shape columns. As far as the Data Editor is concerned, the data comprise **three dependent variables**. Later, we shall see that some statistical programs can be informed that the three columns in the **Data Editor** window are to be treated, not as separate dependent variables, but as comprising a single (repeated measures) treatment factor.

After defining the variable names as *triangle*, *circle*, *square* and entering the recognition times into the columns, the **Data Editor** window is as in Figure 8.

Entering data with between subjects and within subjects variables

Data from an experiment with **both between subjects variables and within subjects factors** is entered in the **Data Editor** window as a combination of the procedures illustrated in this Section and those in Section 3.3.6. For example, if the subjects for the recognition of patterns experiment had been coded for sex, then all that would be required is an extra column for the variable *sex* with a code such as *1* for Males and *2* for Females.

```
            untitled data
        triangle   circle   square
   1     220.00    300.00   260.00
   2     250.00    290.00   300.00
   3     260.00    280.00   290.00
   4     230.00    340.00   190.00
   5     190.00    300.00   250.00
   6     220.00    270.00   240.00
   7     250.00    320.00   270.00
   8     280.00    290.00   260.00
   9     270.00    340.00   250.00
  10     240.00    300.00   350.00
```

Figure 8.

The layout in the Data Editor window for a within subjects (repeated measures) design

3.3.9 Entering string variables

A **string** is a sequence of characters (letters, symbols, blanks, digits) which is treated as a label by the system. A **string variable** is a qualitative variable whose categories are entered into the window as strings, rather than numbers. Thus a string can be a simple letter M, a word such as French, or a person's name such as Abraham Lincoln.

A **short string variable** has string values of up to eight characters in length; a **long string variable** has values exceeding eight characters in length. The distinction is important, because some SPSS procedures only work with short string variables or truncate long string variables to the first eight characters.

Suppose we want to record the names of all the subjects taking part in the learning experiment and that the longest name does not exceed 20 characters in length.

- In the **Data Editor** window (Figure 1), double-click on the grey area at the top of the third column to obtain the **Define Variable** dialog box (Figure 9).

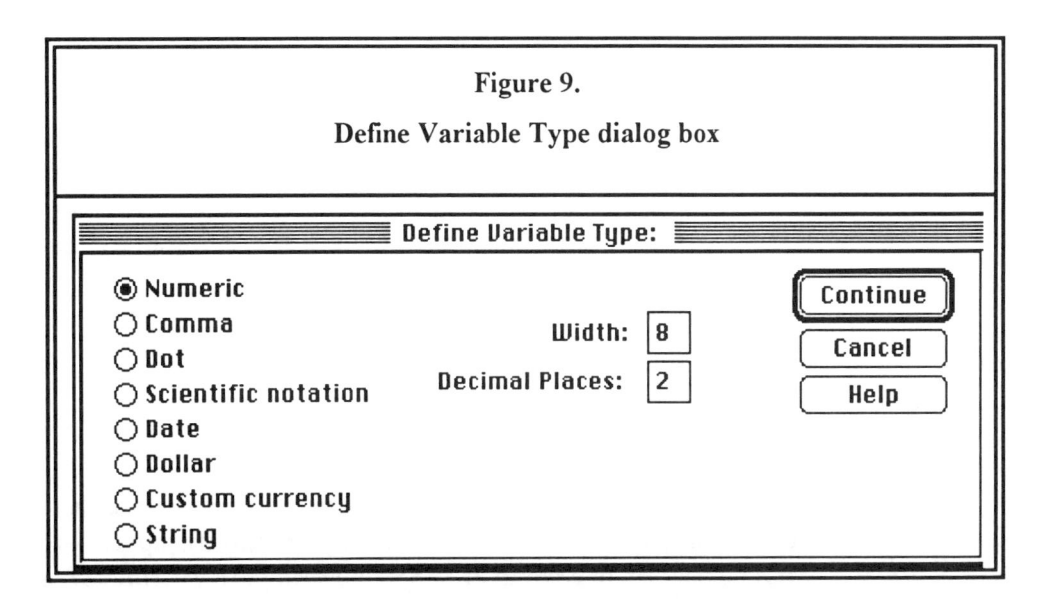

Figure 9.
Define Variable Type dialog box

```
============ Define Variable Type: ============
  ⦿ Numeric                                        ( Continue )
  ○ Comma                      Width:       [ 8 ]
  ○ Dot                                            ( Cancel   )
  ○ Scientific notation        Decimal Places: [ 2 ]
  ○ Date                                           ( Help     )
  ○ Dollar
  ○ Custom currency
  ○ String
```

- In the **Variable Name** text box, type the name of the string variable *name*. Notice, however, that in the **Variable Description** box is the entry **Type: Numeric8.0**. Until it receives information to the contrary, SPSS for Windows always assumes that variables will be of the numeric type.

- To specify a string variable, click on **Type**, to obtain the **Define Variable Type** dialog box (Figure 11).

- In the box is a list of eight variable types, each with a radio button. SPSS initially marks the **Numeric** button. Click on the **String** button at the foot of the list. The **Decimal Places** text box immediately disappears, leaving only the **Width** box, with the value *8* that was set in **Preferences**.

- Delete *8* in the **Width** box and type in *20*.

- Click on **Continue** and then on **OK**. The variable *name* will now appear at the head of the third column, which is now much wider than before. The names of the subjects can now be typed into each row of this column.

3.3.10 Missing values

In SPSS, there are no empty cells within the data file, which is assumed to be rectangular. If no value has been entered (as shown by a dot in a cell), the system supplies the **system-missing** value, which is indicated in the **Data Editor** window by a full stop. SPSS will exclude system-missing values from its calculations of means, standard deviations and other statistics.

It may be, however, that for some purposes the user wishes SPSS to treat certain responses actually present in the data set as missing. For example, suppose that, in a survey of political opinion, five categories are used (A, B, C, D & E), but category E was recorded when the person refused to answer and D was a category that indicated a failure to understand the question. The user wants SPSS to treat responses in both categories as missing, but to retain information about the relative frequencies of such responses in categories D and E in the output listings. In SPSS terminology, the user wants certain responses to be treated as **user-missing** values.

In analysing a set of exam results, for instance, the user might wish SPSS to treat as missing:

(1) any marks between, say, 0 and 20;

(2) cases where the candidate walked out without giving any written response. (A walk-out could be coded as an arbitrary, but salient, number, such as *-9*: the negative sign helps it to stand out and cannot be a valid exam mark.)

To define such user-missing values:

- Open the **Define Variable** dialog box and click on **Missing Values**. This will obtain the **Define Missing Values** dialog box (Figure 10).

- Initially, the **No missing values** radio button is marked. The three text boxes underneath give the user the opportunity to specify up to three **Discrete Missing Values**, referred to in SPSS as *missing (1)*, *missing (2)*, and *missing*

(3). These may either be numerical, as with a grouping variable, or short string variables, but must match the original variable type. The other options in the dialog box are for quantitative variables: the user may define a missing value as one falling within a specified range, or one that falls either within a specified range or within a specified category.

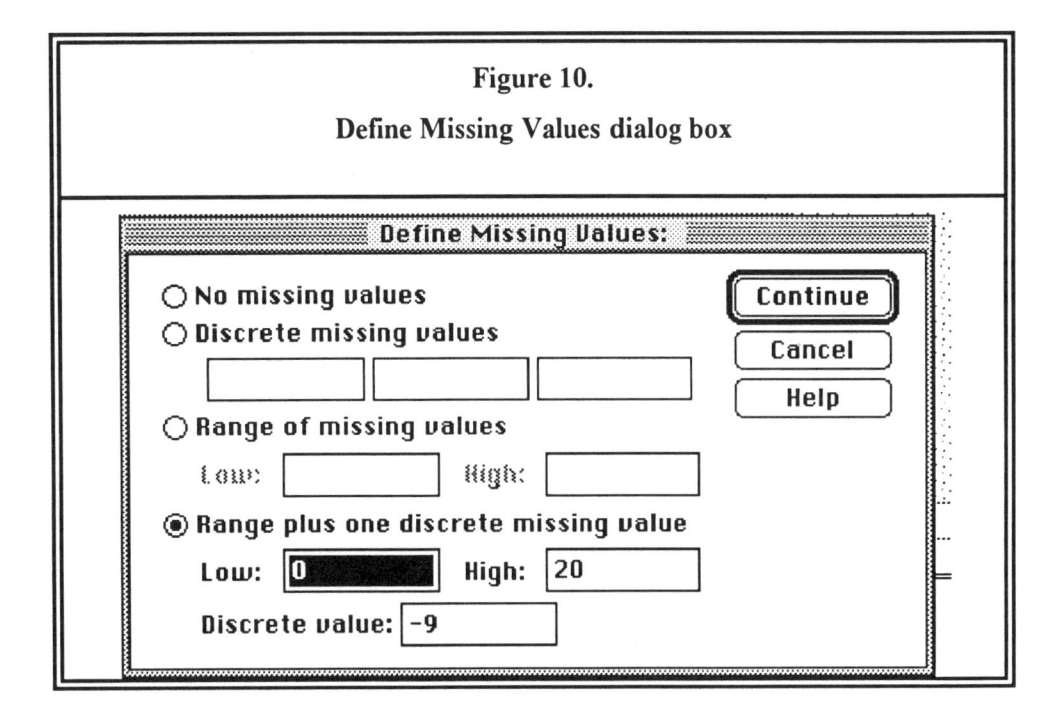

Figure 10.
Define Missing Values dialog box

- Click on the **Range plus one discrete missing value** button, entering the values *0* and *20* into the **Low** and **High** boxes, respectively, and *-9* into the **Discrete value** box.

- Click on **Continue** to return to the **Define Variable** dialog box.

3.4 SAVING AND RETRIEVING SPSS FILES

3.4.1 Saving a file

Suppose that we have entered a set of data such as the results of the learning experiment in Table 7 into the **Data Editor** window. We want to save this data set to a file named *learning*, and to store that file in a folder called **SPSS Data**. We want the folder to be located in the **Macintosh Hard Disk**. Neither the file nor the folder exists at the moment.

To ensure that the folder will be located in the Hard Disk, double-click on the **Hard Disk** icon to open the **Macintosh Hard Disk** window. The double-click will transfer control to the **Desktop**. To ensure that the folder will be created in the Hard Disk, activate the **Hard Disk** window by clicking on its title bar.

Choose
File
   New Folder

This will produce, in the **HD** window, a highlighted folder icon, with a title such as **untitled folder 2** in inverse video within a double-bordered frame. The desired name **SPSS Data** can be typed in directly. Click outside the frame to establish the folder's new name. Return to the **Data Editor** window by clicking on its title bar.

Now choose
File
   Save Data

to obtain the **Save Data As** dialog box (Figure 11).

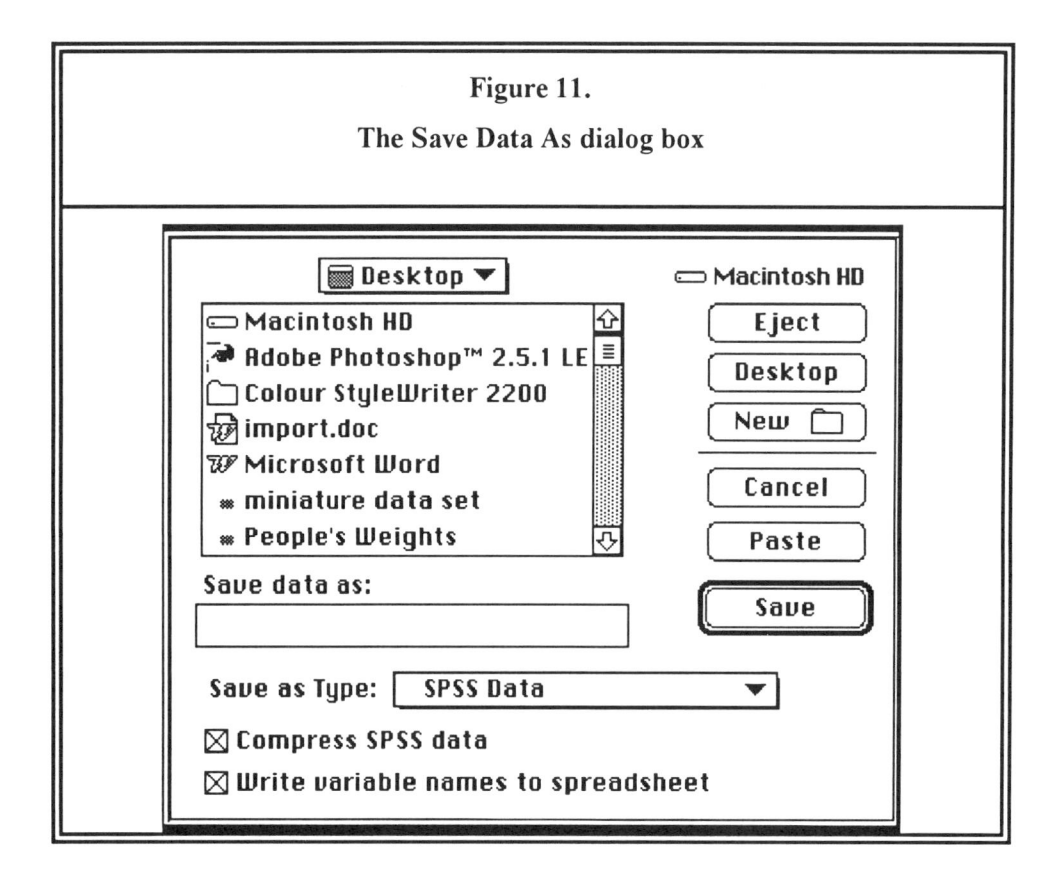

Figure 11.

The Save Data As dialog box

The **Save Data As** dialog box is an example of a **directory dialog box**. Similar boxes appear in all operations involving the saving or accessing of files or folders, and appear (in one form or another) whenever the user is working with any kind of SPSS output, whether data, output listings or graphics. Note the central **name box**, which contains a list of items known as a **directory**. (There is also a scroll bar at the side, for viewing items not immediately visible in the name box.)

The narrow box [Desktop ▼] at the top is a **pop-up menu**. The name presently showing is the present location of all the items listed in the name box, in this case, the **Desktop**. Moreover, if no further adjustment to the dialog box were to be made, any file named by typing a title (in our example, *learning*) into the **Save Data As** box underneath the name box would appear on the **Desktop**.

Double-click on the **Hard Disk** icon to bring the caption **Macintosh HD** into the pop-up menu box at the top. In the name box will appear (scroll down if necessary) the folder **SPSS Data**. Double-clicking on **SPSS Data** will bring this folder name into the pop-up menu at the top. This is the location at which the data set will be stored, under whatever name is typed into the **Save Data As** box. Clicking-and-holding on the pop-up menu will show the items, **SPSS Data**, **Macintosh HD** and **Desktop**. The pop-up menu always contains all levels from the present one to the highest, which is the **Desktop**. Complete the dialog box by typing the file name *learning* into the **Save Data as:** box and clicking on the **Save** button.

In the lowest box in the **Save As** dialog box is a second pop-up menu **Save as Type:** showing the data specification as **SPSS Data**. The file *learning* will be saved as SPSS Data, and will be recognised as such by SPSS in future. If you click on this pop-up menu, however, you will see other specifications, such as **SPSS Portable Data**, **Tab-delimited Data**, and so on. (The former choice would produce an SPSS file that could be read by SPSS for Windows, an EXCEL spreadsheet, and other applications.)

The procedure we have just described also applies whenever the user wishes to save other kinds of SPSS material, such as output and graphics. A basically similar dialog box will appear.

It is often advisable to back up important files on floppy disk, especially if the user's computer is in a network. There are two ways of doing this:

(1) Drag the file's icon over to the **floppy disk icon** and release the mouse button.

(2) In the **Save As** dialog box, place the screen pointer in the pop-up menu at the top of the **Save As** dialog box and choose the option **untitled** (assuming that an unnamed floppy disk has been placed in the computer's disk drive). Clicking on the **Save** button will direct the file to the floppy disk.

3.4.2 Reading in SPSS files

As we saw at the end of Chapter 2, reading an SPSS data file into the **Data Editor** window is simplicity itself. Simply drag the data file on to the SPSS icon. Alternatively, double-click on the data file to achieve the same result.

It is also possible, of course, to use the **Open** option within the **File** menu:

- Choose
  File
    Open

  from the Application menu. This will produce the **Open Data File** dialog box (Figure 12). In appearance, this box is very similar to the **Save Data As** box.

- In the name box, double-click on **Macintosh HD** to produce a directory of the items contained in the HD, among which will be the folder **SPSS Data**.

- Double-click on the icon of the folder **SPSS Data** to open it. The new name box will contain the file name *learning*. Highlight the *learning* item in the directory.

Chapter 3 - Data Handling

Figure 12.
The Open Data File dialog box

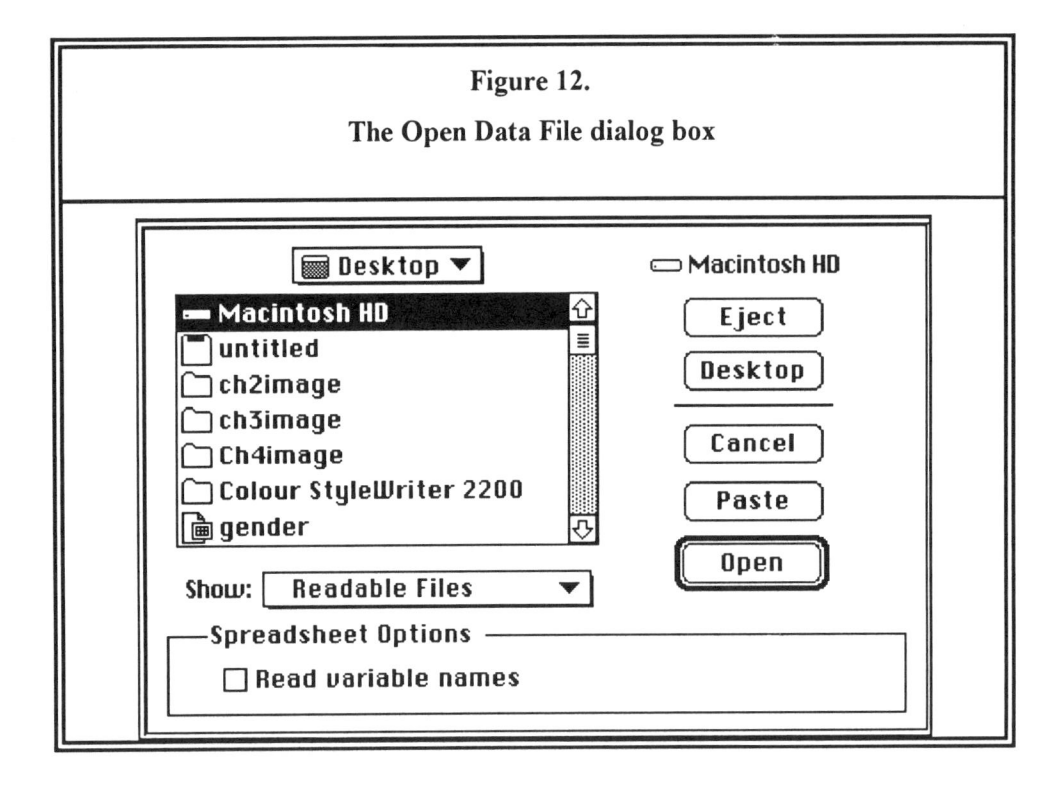

- Click on **Open** to return to the **Data Editor** window, which will now contain the desired data set, as before.

While data are being read into the **Data Editor** window from a file, the wristwatch will appear and messages will appear in the **Status Bar** at various stages in the operation. The message **SPSS Processor is ready** signals the end of the procedure.

3.4.3 Importing and exporting data

It is possible to import into SPSS for Macintosh data from applications on other platforms such as SPSS for Windows, Microsoft Excel, and as ASCII tab-delimited (i.e. values are separated by tabulation symbols) or fixed format (i.e. variables are recorded in the same column locations for each case) files. For example, to import an Excel file, choose
File
    Open

to obtain the **Open File** dialog box (Figure 12). Make sure, by making the correct selection from the pop-up menu at the top, that the location of the file is correct. Click on the pop-up menu **Show** and drag the screen pointer to select **Excel Spreadsheets**. On the same menu, there is a separate command for the importation of ASCII data. Click on **Open** to enter the data into the **Data Editor** window.

It is also possible to export an SPSS data file in a format compatible with another application. An existing SPSS data file can be saved in a wide range of formats, such as **SPSS Portable Data**. Full details of importing and exporting files are available in the **Help** facility.

3.5 LISTING DATA

3.5.1 Listing cases

It is sometimes convenient to be able to list the data for a particular variable (or perhaps a few variables) rather than having to scan a particular column (or columns) in the **Data Editor** window.

Table 8.
Blood group, sex, height & weight of 32 subjects

Blood	Sex	Height	Weight	Blood	Sex	Height	Weight
O	M	178	75	O	M	183	70
O	M	196	100	B	M	182	85
A	M	145	60	A	M	170	72
O	M	170	71	O	M	160	77
B	M	180	80	O	M	170	95
O	M	175	69	AB	M	172	68
AB	M	185	78	B	M	190	120
A	M	190	90	O	M	180	75
O	F	163	60	O	F	162	62
O	F	142	51	B	F	182	80
A	F	150	55	O	F	165	67
O	F	165	64	A	F	171	50
A	F	160	53	O	F	146	55
O	F	175	50	AB	F	151	48
O	F	182	72	O	F	164	59
B	F	169	65	B	F	176	71

For example, although two variables may be several columns apart in the **Data Editor** window, the user might wish to see them side-by-side. Let us assume that

Chapter 3 - Data Handling

a data set (Table 8) consisting of two quantitative variables *Weight* and *Height*, and two qualitative variables *Gender* and *Blood*, has already been set up in the **Data Editor** window.

- Choose
  Statistics
  Summarize
  List Cases

  and then complete the **List Cases** dialog box (Figure 13) indicate which variables are to be listed.

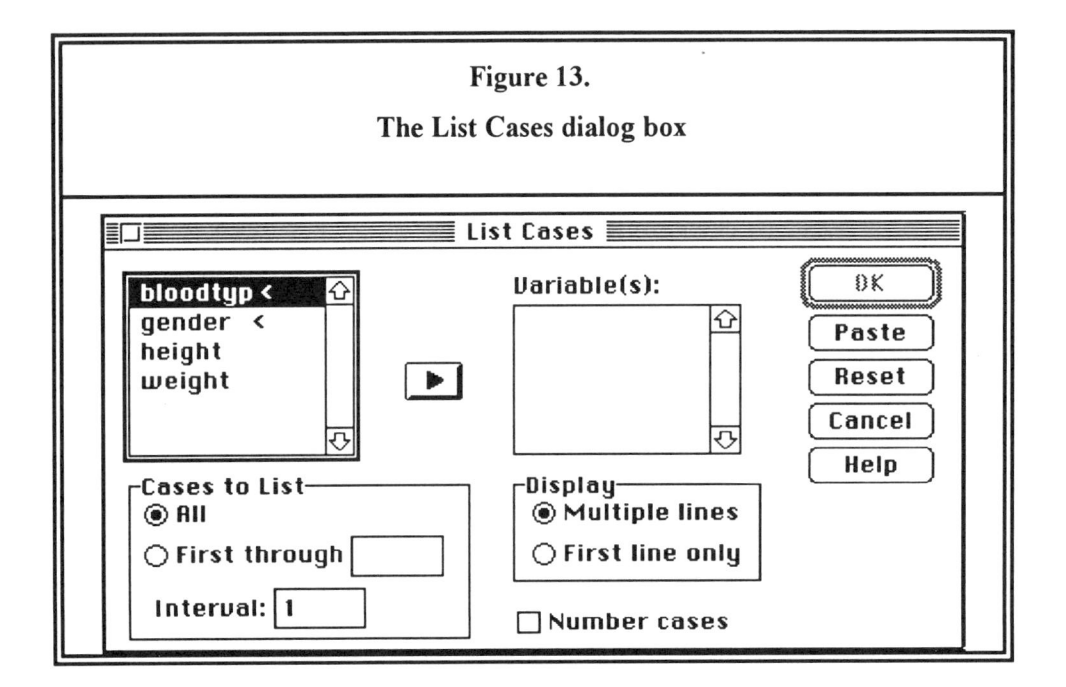

Figure 13.
The List Cases dialog box

- Select the variables of interest (for example, *gender* and *bloodtyp*) by clicking on the variable name and then on ▶ to enter it into the **Variable(s)** box.

- It is also useful to click on the **Number cases** box in order to have the data listed with case numbers. For illustrative purposes, we have chosen to list only the first ten cases by activating the **First through** radio button and inserting *10* in the box within the **Cases to List** box.

- Click on **OK**.

The output is shown in Output Listing 1

```
╔═══════════════════════════════╗
║ ▣☐▤  !untitled output 1  ▤▣▤ ║
║            BLOODTYP  GENDER   ║
║         1    O         M      ║
║         2    O         M      ║
║         3    A         M      ║
║         4    O         M      ║
║         5    B         M      ║
║         6    O         M      ║
║         7    AB        M      ║
║         8    A         M      ║
║         9    O         M      ║
║        10    B         M      ║
╚═══════════════════════════════╝
```

Output Listing 1.

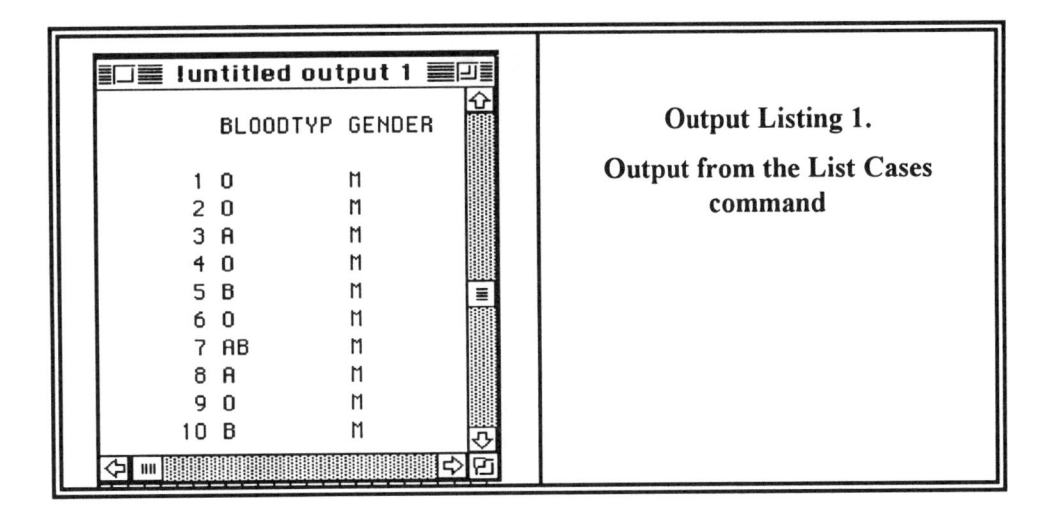

Output from the List Cases command

3.5.2 Displaying data file information

It is useful to be able to see details of variables such as their names, types, values and value labels (if any) in a data file, particularly if it is a large one and one has perhaps forgotten how many values were defined for several variables. This can be done for either the current file in the **Data Editor** window or for a stored file.

In the case of a stored file (but not currently displayed in the **Data Editor** window), choose

File
    Display Data Info...

and then select the appropriate file name from the **Display Data Info** dialog box. The listing of the details of the SPSS file for the data set we have just been discussing includes the information that

- There were 32 cases.

- None of the variables was weighted (weighting is explained in Section 3.7.2).

- The variable GENDER has two defined string levels M and F together with their value names with a format of just one character in width (A1).

- WEIGHT and HEIGHT are numeric variables with a format of 8 non-decimal digits (F8).

- BLOODTYP has four defined string values together with their value names with a format of two characters (A2).

In the case of the data file currently displayed in the **Data Editor** window, choose

Utilities
    File Info.

Details of the variables will immediately be listed in the Output window.

Chapter 3 - Data Handling

3.6 PRINTING IN SPSS

It is always reassuring to have a hard copy of important computer output. For example, after a series of complicated editing operations, the user may wish to print out the contents of the **Data Editor** window to have a permanent record of the finalised data set. It may be necessary to check that a suitable printer is connected to the computer (or to the network) by inspecting the information within the **Page Setup** item in the **File** drop-down menu where an option for changing the orientation of the printing from portrait to landscape may be invoked by clicking on one or other of the icons under **Orientation:** (see Figure 14). Click on **OK** to close the dialog box and run the listing.

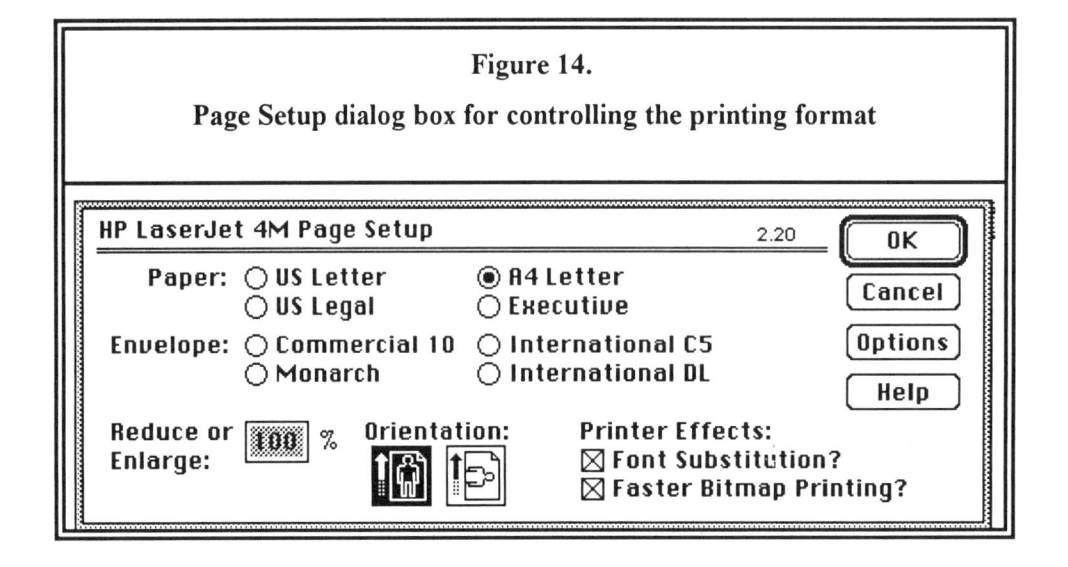

Figure 14.

Page Setup dialog box for controlling the printing format

When the **Print** item in the **File** drop-down menu is selected, the **Print** dialog box (Figure 15) will appear. Bear in mind that only the contents of the **active** window will be printed: thus if the data set is to be printed out, the **Data Editor** window must be active. Similarly, if it is the output listing that is to be printed, the **Output** window must be active. Charts and graphs are in the **Chart Carousel** window. A window can be activated by clicking anywhere on it, or by selecting the appropriate window title from the Windows drop-down menu.

Printing out the entire data set

To print out the entire contents of the **Data Editor** window, ensure that it is active as described above and choose
File
     Print...
This obtains the **Print** dialog box (see Figure 15).

If the **All** button is marked, the entire data set will be printed out. (If the **Selection** button is marked, only a selected part of the data set will be printed out - see below.) The user can also amend the entry in the **Copies** text box to obtain multiple hard copies. Click on **OK** to start the printing.

Chapter 3 - Data Handling

Printing out a selection from the data set

To print out only selected parts of the data set, use the click-and-drag method to define the target sections by blackening them. This requires a little practice: it will be found that when the mouse arrow touches the lower border of the window, the latter will scroll down to extend the blackened area to the desired extent. If it touches the right border, it will scroll rightwards across the **Data Editor** window.

When the **Print** dialog box (Figure 15) appears, the marker will now be on **Selection**. Click on **OK** to obtain a hard copy of the selected areas.

Figure 15.

The Print dialog box

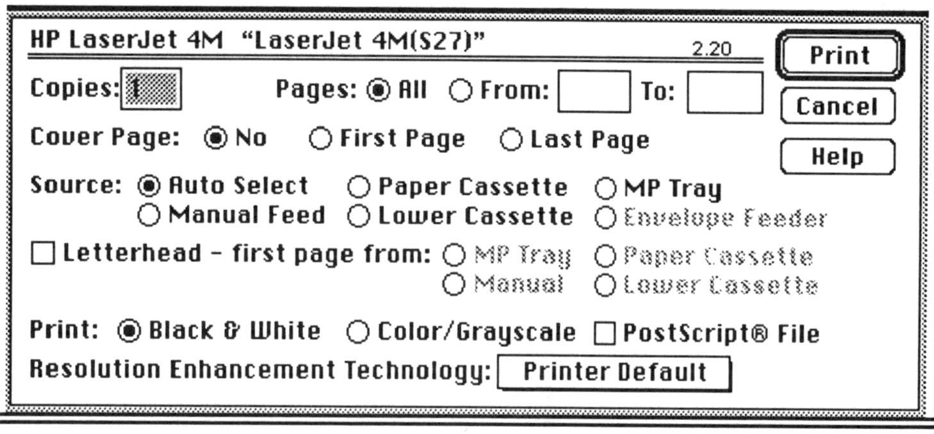

Printing other items

To print items such as listings of tables and results, graphs, scatterplots, and diagrams, ensure that the correct window is active before following the procedures that have just been described.

3.7 SOME SPECIAL OPERATIONS

So far, the emphasis has been upon the construction of a complete data set, the saving of that set to a file on disk, and its retrieval from storage. There has also been consideration of a number of widely applicable editing functions.

There are occasions, however, on which the user will want to operate selectively on the data. It may be, for instance, that only some of the rows comprising a data set are of interest (those contributed by the subjects in one category alone, perhaps); or the user may wish to exclude subjects with outlying values on specified variables. In this section, some of these more specialised manoeuvres will be described.

Transformations and recoding of data will be discussed in Chapter 4.

65

Chapter 3 - Data Handling

3.7.1 Case selection

Let us assume that we have the data of our Mnemonic Training Method example in the **Data Editor** window: there are two variables, *group* and *score*. Suppose, for example, that we want to analyse only the data from the two mnemonic groups (i.e. exclude the control group) of the experiment presented in Section 3.3.1:

- Choose
  Data
    Select Cases

  to produce the **Select Cases** dialog box (see Figure 16).

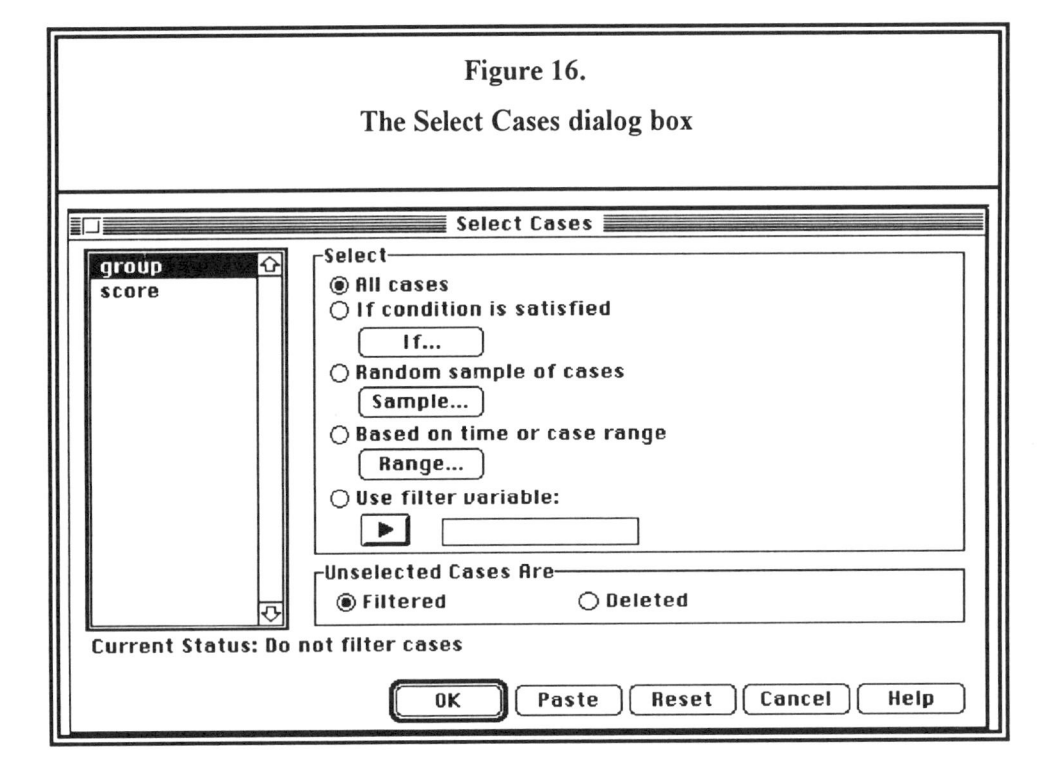

Figure 16.

The Select Cases dialog box

- Click on the **If condition is satisfied** radio button and then on **If...** to open the **Select Cases: If** dialog box (completed version is shown in Figure 17).

- On the left in Figure 17 is the same list of the variables. Highlight *group* and click on ▶ to transfer it to the upper box on the right. The simplest way (but not the only way) of selecting the cases with values *2* or *3* is to type *>1* directly into this box after *group*. Alternatively, the same expression can be assembled by clicking on buttons in the lower box. The completed dialog box is shown in Figure 17.

- When the conditional expression has been completed, click on **Continue** and then on **OK** to return to the **Data Editor** window, where it will be noticed that a new column labelled **filter_$**, and containing *1*s and *0*s, has appeared (Figure 18).

Chapter 3 - Data Handling

Figure 17.

The conditional expression for selecting groups 2 and 3

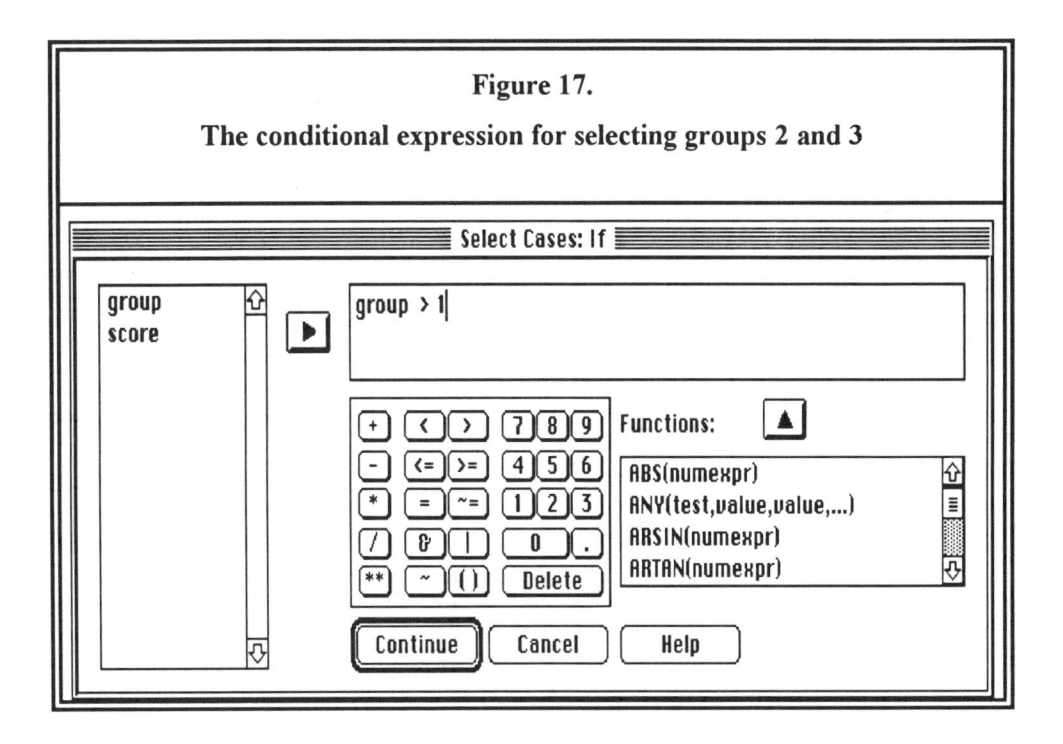

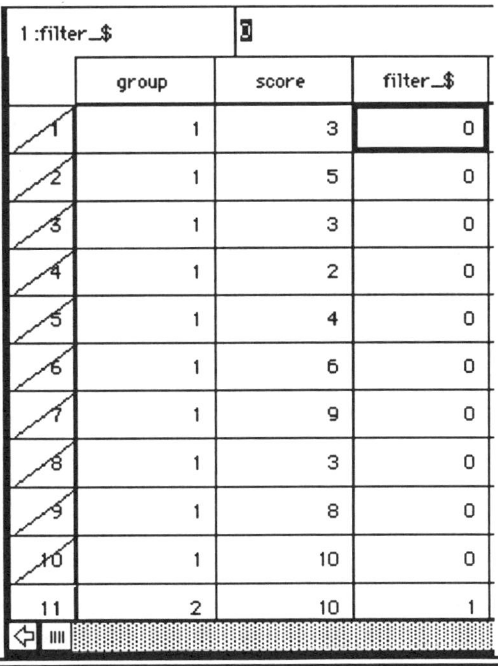

[Select Cases: If dialog box showing variables "group" and "score" on the left, expression "group > 1" in the expression area, with operator buttons and Functions list (ABS(numexpr), ANY(test,value,value,...), ARSIN(numexpr), ARTAN(numexpr)), and Continue, Cancel, Help buttons]

	group	score	filter_$
1	1	3	0
2	1	5	0
3	1	3	0
4	1	2	0
5	1	4	0
6	1	6	0
7	1	9	0
8	1	3	0
9	1	8	0
10	1	10	0
11	2	10	1

Figure 18.

Part of the Data Editor showing the deselected cases

The *1*s and *0*s represent the selected and unselected cases, respectively. The row numbers of the unselected cases have also been marked with an oblique bar. This is a useful indicator of **case selection status.** The status bar (if enabled at the foot of the **Data Editor** window) will carry the message **Filter On**.

Any further analyses of the data set will exclude the cases within group 1. The case selection can be cancelled as follows:

- Select the **Select Cases** dialog box and click on **All cases**.
- Click on **OK**.

67

3.7.2 The weighting of cases by their frequencies of occurrence

Suppose that fifty women and fifty men are asked whether they disapprove of a popular, but violent, television programme. Their responses can be summarised in what is known as a **contingency table** (Table 9).

Table 9. A contingency table		
	Disapprove	
Sex	Yes	No
Female	30	20
Male	10	40

The purpose of constructing a contingency table is to bring out whatever relationship there may be between two qualitative or nominal variables. In the present example, the qualitative variables are Sex (with levels Male and Female) and Disapprove (with levels Yes and No). It is clear from Table 9 that there is indeed a relationship between the two variables: a markedly higher proportion of the female respondents disapproved of the programme.

As with the data in Table 5, a contingency table must be recast to make it suitable for entry into SPSS. Earlier, it was said that SPSS expects a data set in the form of a matrix whose rows are subjects and whose columns are variables. Clearly, the arrangement of the data in Table 9 does not conform to this requirement: the two columns represent values of the same variable; and a row represents the responses of several subjects.

In part, the solution is to carry the variables in columns of codes, as we did with the data from the mnemonics experiment (see Table 6). This meets the requirement that each column in the **Data Editor** window relates to a single variable. In the present case, however, it must still be made clear to SPSS that each cell entry represents the response not of one, but of several people. This is achieved by entering the cell frequencies into the third column in the **Data Editor** window.

In Table 10, the code numbers of the variable *sex* (*1* and *2*) have been assigned the labels *M* and *F* for *female* and *male*, respectively (by using **Labels**); and the code numbers (*1* and *2*) of the variable *disapp* have been labelled *Y* and *N*, respectively, again by using the **Labels** procedure. SPSS can then be instructed to weight the category combinations by multiplying them by the corresponding frequencies in the third variable *freq* using the **Weight Cases** option with the **Data** drop-down menu.

Chapter 3 - Data Handling

Table 10. Recasting the data in Table 9 for entry into SPSS		
sex	disapp	freq
M	Y	30
M	N	20
F	Y	10
F	N	40

To enter the data set in Table 10:

- Name the variables taking care to change the **Type** for *sex* and for *disapp* to **String** and assign labels as described in Section 3.3.4.

- Enter the data into the **Data Editor** window.

- Choose
  Data
      Weight Cases

  to open the **Weight Cases** dialog box (the completed version is in Figure 19) in order to inform SPSS that each row of entries under *sex* and *disapp* is to be weighted by the corresponding entry in *freq*. Initially, the box on the left contains a list of the variables in the data set: *sex, disapp, freq*. We want to weight each row (case) by the corresponding frequency in the third column.

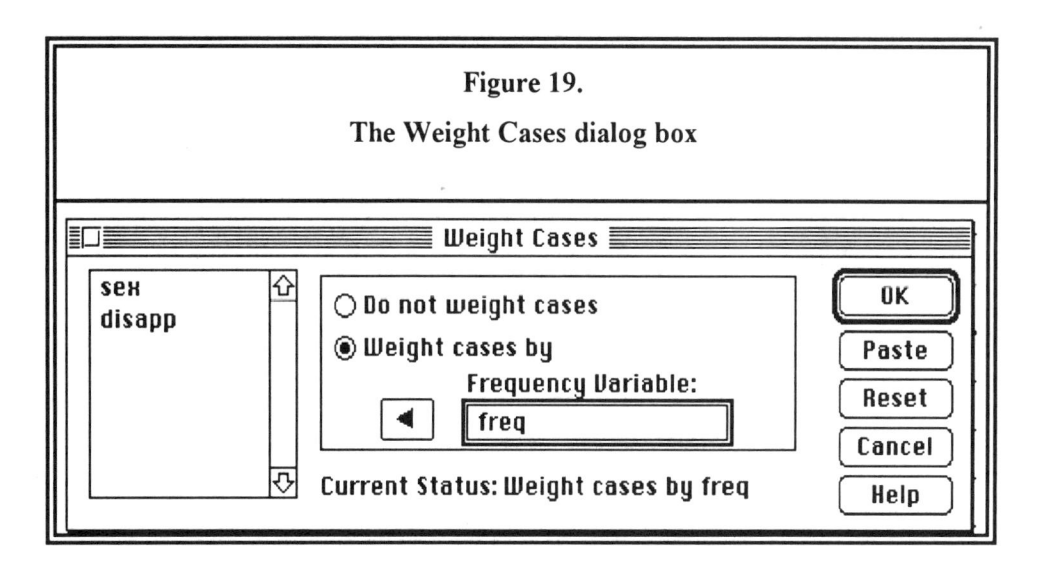

Figure 19.

The Weight Cases dialog box

- Click on the **Weight cases by** radio button. Highlight the variable *freq*. This will embolden the arrow button which, when clicked, will transfer the name *freq* to the **Frequency Variable** text box.

- Click on **OK** to run the procedure.

Chapter 3 - Data Handling

The weighting of cases is an essential preliminary to the analysis of nominal data in the form of contingency tables, as described in Chapter 11.

3.7.3 Splitting files

It is sometimes convenient to split a file by the levels of a grouping variable (or by combinations of more than one grouping variable) so that any subsequent exploratory data analysis or statistical analysis is conducted automatically on each level (or combinations of levels) separately. For example, the blood group data in Table 8 could be split by the levels of *bloodtyp*.

Choose
Data
    Split File

to obtain the **Split File** dialog box and complete it as shown in Figure 20.

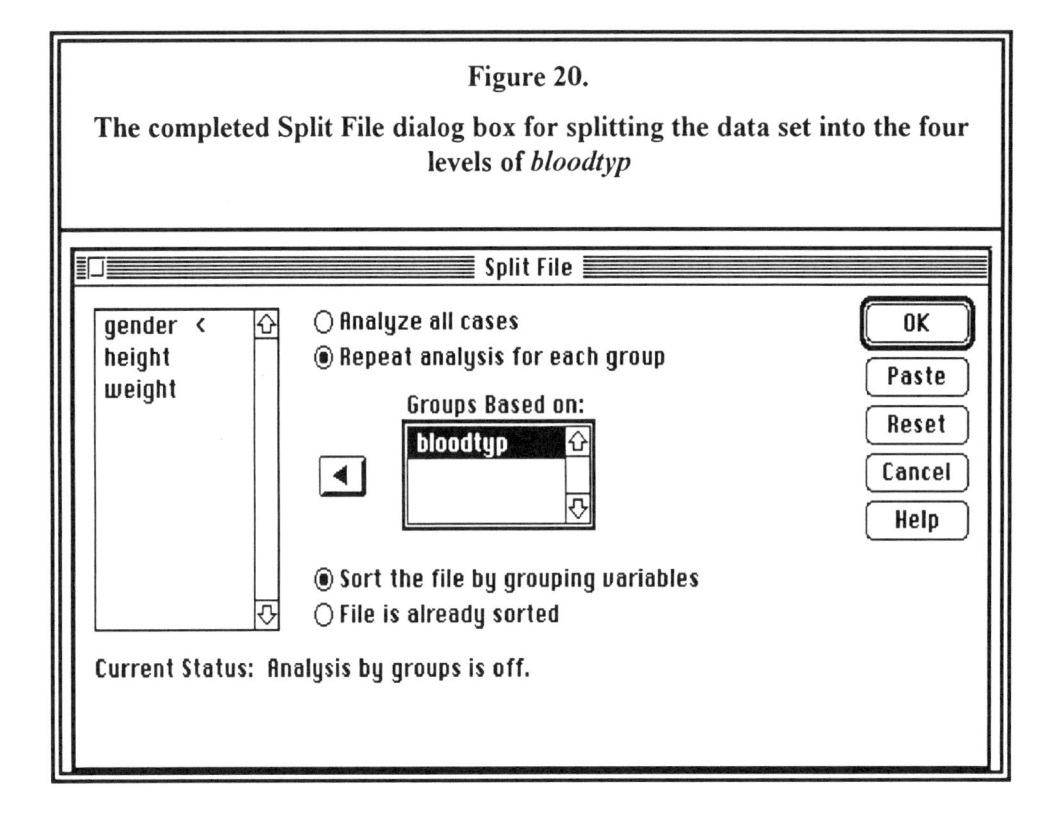

Figure 20.

The completed Split File dialog box for splitting the data set into the four levels of *bloodtyp*

When you return to the **Data Editor** window, you will notice that the cases have now been sorted into the different blood groups. More dramatically, you will discover later that when you command SPSS to carry out a statistical analysis of the data in this file, there will be a separate analysis for each blood group.

Chapter 3 - Data Handling

EXERCISE 2

QUESTIONNAIRE DATA

INTRODUCTION

Exercises 2 to 8 are concerned with the preparation and entry of data into SPSS, and with various **exploratory data analysis (EDA)** procedures such as calculating descriptive statistics, drawing graphs, transforming and selecting data and so on. In this Exercise, the reader is asked to complete a short questionnaire and the data from it into SPSS. In the next exercise, the reader's data will be merged with a larger data set, comprising the responses of 334 other people to the same questionnaire. Subsequently, the merged file will be used as the data set for the various EDA procedures described in later exercises.

THE QUESTIONNAIRE

Please complete the questionnaire below by entering the values or circling the appropriate options. Afterwards, you will enter your data in SPSS's **Data Editor** window. Later, you will access a data set comprising the responses of 334 others to the same questionnaire.

QUESTIONNAIRE			
What is your age in years?			
What is your sex?		M	F
What is your Faculty of study?	Arts		1
	Science		2
	Medicine		3
	Other		4
What is your status?	Undergraduate		1
	MSc postgraduate		2
	PhD postgraduate		3
	Other		4
What is your approximate weight?	Use British or metric measures		
British units	Stones		
	Pounds		
Metric units	Kilograms		
(Questionnaire continued on next page)			

71

+---+
| (Questionnaire continued from previous page) |
| What is your approximate height? Use British or metric measures |
| British units   Feet |
| Inches |
| Metric units   Metres (include two decimal places)|
| Do you smoke?   Y N |
| If so, how many a day? |
+---+

Entering the data

Successful file merging does not require that the variables necessarily appear in order in the two data sets. It is essential, however, that the variables common to both data sets have exactly the same names. Using the methods described in Section 3.3.4, assign the following names to the variables in the questionnaire. Note that, for those respondents giving their weights or heights in British units, two SPSS columns will be allocated to each variable: stones and pounds for weight, and feet and inches for height.

Name the variables as follows: age, sex, faculty, status, stones, pounds, kilos, feet, inches, metres, smoker, npday (i.e 'number smoked per day').

Assign the appropriate values labels to the variables faculty and status.

For the variables sex and smoker, specify the type as 'string' and respond with either Y or N according to whether you smoke or not, and with M or F to indicate your gender.

Saving the data

Once you have entered the data set and checked it for accuracy, select
File
    Save
to obtain the **Save As** dialog box. Having decided on a suitable target location for the file (perhaps by creating a folder called SPSS Data and opening it by double-clicking on the folder's name in the name box), type a file name such as **mydata** into the **Save Data As:** box. Click on **Save** to save your own questionnaire responses as the SPSS file **mydata**.

FINISHING THE SESSION

Close down SPSS and any other open windows before logging out of the computer.

Chapter 3 - Data Handling

EXERCISE 3

QUESTIONNAIRE DATA (continued)

AIMS OF THIS EXERCISE

This exercise shows you how to open a saved file, how to merge your data with those of others, how to obtain information about the structure of a data file, and how to print out a file. The relevant sections are 3.4.2 (opening a file), 3.5.2 (displaying data file information) and 3.6 (printing in SPSS).

OPENING YOUR SAVED FILE

First of all open the file that you saved (perhaps under the name **mydata**) from the previous exercise by selecting

File
    Open

and manipulating the **Open File** dialog box as described in Section 3.4.2 to obtain the Data Editor, complete with your own questionnaire data entered.

MERGING YOUR DATA WITH THE LARGER FILE

The larger data set with which you are going to merge your own data is to be found at the following WWW address:

        http://www.psyc.abdn.ac.uk/teaching/spss/spssbook.htm

It would be a good idea to download the data on to a floppy disk for easy access.

To carry out the merger, select

Data
    Merge Files
        Add Cases

to obtain a directory subdialog dialog box (Figure 1) allowing you to specify the file (the large data set) from which you want to extract further cases.

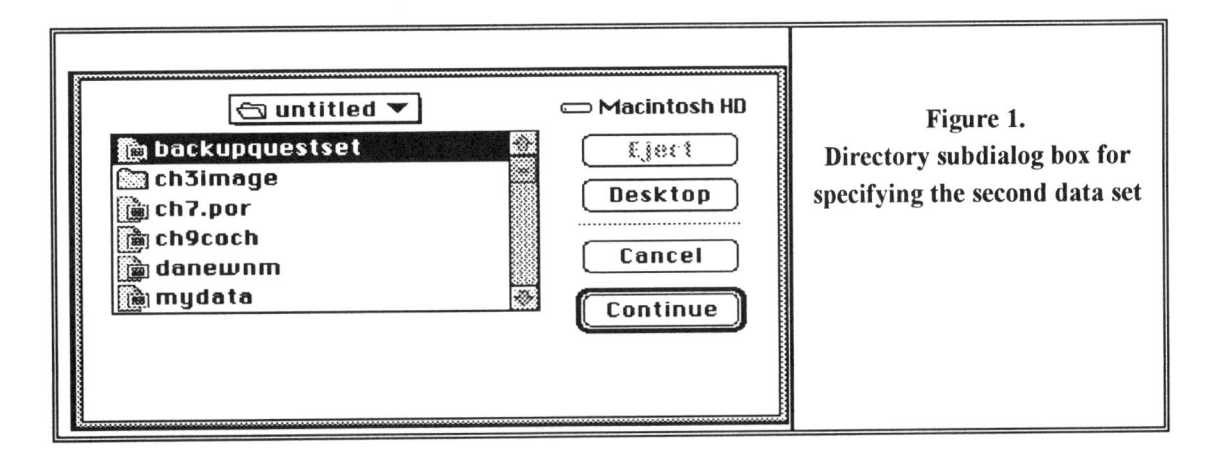

Figure 1.
Directory subdialog box for specifying the second data set

Click on Continue, to obtain the **Add Cases from ...** dialog box (Figure 2).

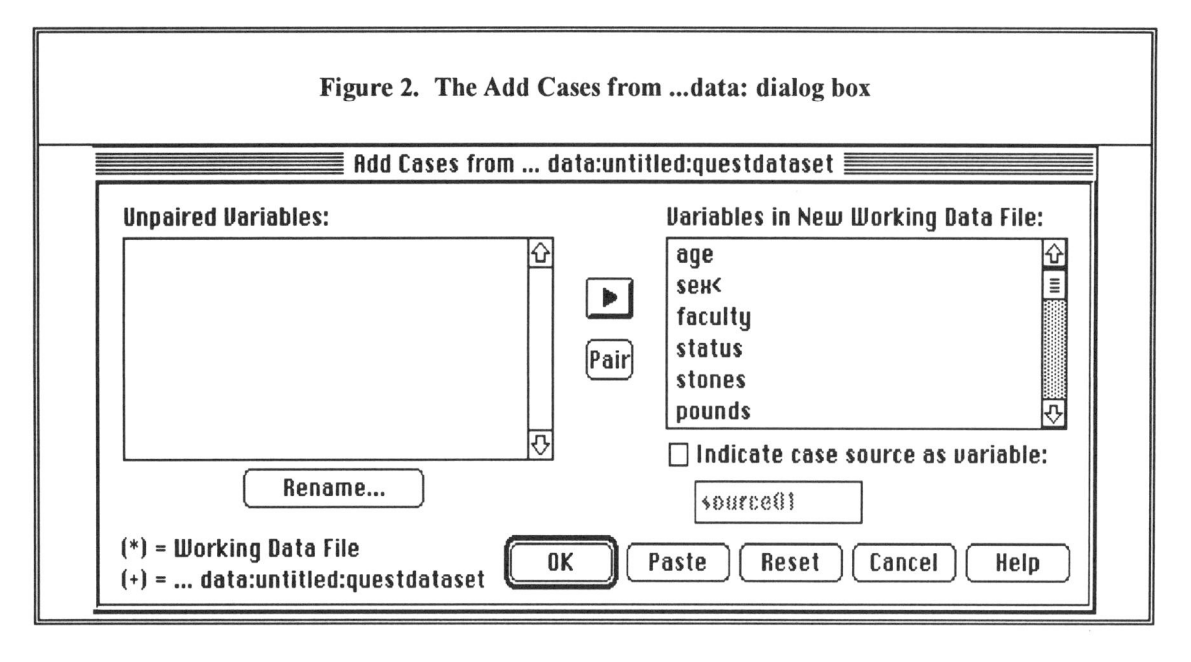

Figure 2. The Add Cases from ...data: dialog box

Notice that the name box on the right contains the names of all the variables; the box on the left is empty. That is very much as it should be. Suppose, however, there had been a mismatch between one of the variable names you had typed into the Data Editor and the name of the corresponding variable in the large data set: suppose that, instead of typing *age* as the variable name, you had typed *aged*. The pair of variables, **aged** and **age**, would have appeared in the left hand name box as **Unpaired Variables** (see Figure 2). You would then have had to select one of the variables (by highlighting it) and clicked on the **Rename** box to obtain another dialog box, allowing you to rename the selected variable with the name of the other file. When this has been done, the desired variable name can be transferred to the right hand box, which shows the **Variables in the New Working Data File**.
Click on **OK** to complete the merger. You will be returned to the Data Editor, which now contains your own data in the first row, and the data from the 334 cases in the other data set in the rows underneath.

A warning

In the large data set, the categorial variable was of the numeric type, with values assigned as follows: 1 = Arts, 2 = Science, 3 = Medicine, 4 = Other. Suppose that you had assigned the 1 to Science and the 2 to Arts, instead of the other way round, and that as a scientist, you had recorded a 1 in our own data set. SPSS will not warn you of the discrepancy. Instead, it will adopt your convention throughout the merged data set and all those people who recorded 1s in the larger original data set, will now be recorded as scientists, not arts students.
When two files are being merged, it is the value assignments of the first that determine those for the entire merged file, even when, as in the present example, the former contains only a single case.
Save the merged data file in the usual way.

Chapter 3 - Data Handling

DISPLAYING DATA FILE INFORMATION

It is often useful to be able to see a list of variable names, formats, values and value labels for a particular file. There are two ways of doing this: one uses the File menu; the other is on the Utilities menu. the choice between them depends upon whether the file of interest is in the SPSS Data Editor at present.

Procedure when the file is not in the Data Editor

Select
File
    Display Data Info ...
which brings a directory dialog box. Locate and select the target file by higlighting it. Then click on the **Get Info** button. All the desired information appears in the output listing: the names and order of the variables in the data set, the value labels of category variables, and so on.

Procedure when the file is in the Data Editor

The foregoing procedure will not work if the target file is in the Data Editor. The procedure then is to select
Utilities
    File Info
The absence of an ellipsis after **File Info** indicates that the desired information will appear directly, without the appearance of any dialog box. The information will be found in the output listing.

Editing the output listing for printing

SPSS adds extra information and page throws to the output listing which the user may not always want, especially if there is a charge for each printed page!

- **Deleting material: You may wish to delete some of the preliminary material about the file (but leave the file name) and also each page throw. A new page is created on the printer when there is a small solid black rectangle located at the left-hand edge of the text followed by a line of text including the date and a page number. To delete material, use the cursor and the mouse button to highlight the sections of the text to be deleted and then press the Delete key. After removing a page throw, you can remove some of the extra blank lines by placing the cursor at the left-hand end of a blank line and pressing Delete.**

- **Adding material: You can insert any extra material such as the date and details of the file simply by moving the cursor to the desired point of insertion and then typing in the material.**

Saving the output listing

The procedure for saving any kind of SPSS output - data files, graphics or output listings - is always basically the same. First, you must activate the window containing the material you wish to save. You can do this either by clicking on the window, or selecting the window from the **Windows** drop-down menu.

Select
File
> **Save SPSS Output ...**

This will bring a directory dialog box allowing you to choose a name for your storage file. Effect the save by clicking on the **Save** button.

Printing the output listing file

Finally, to print a copy of this listing file, select
File
> **Print**

You may need to change the printer set-up by clicking on **Setup...** and changing the printing arrangements according to local circumstances.

FINISHING THE SESSION

Close down SPSS and any other windows before logging out of the computer.

CHAPTER 4

EXPLORING AND GRAPHING DATA

4.1 INTRODUCTION
4.2 FINDING MENUS
4.3 DESCRIBING DATA
4.4 MANIPULATION OF THE DATA SET

Chapter 4 - Exploring and Graphing Data

4.1 INTRODUCTION

The SPSS package has been designed to carry out a wide range of statistical tests with ease and rapidity. Before the user can proceed with any data analysis, however, certain preparatory steps must first be taken.

First of all, it is essential to check whether the data have been correctly entered into the computer: a chain is no stronger than its weakest link and it is of paramount importance to ensure that all subsequent inferences rest upon a firm factual foundation. Having checked that the data have been correctly entered using the procedures described in Chapter 3, one might be tempted to proceed immediately to command SPSS to perform various formal statistical tests. The user, however, is strongly warned against this.

The process of data analysis should be thought of as taking place in two phases:

(1) exploration and description of the data;

(2) confirmatory statistical analysis.

This chapter is primarily concerned with the first phase: exploration and description of the data.

4.1.1 Exploratory data analysis (EDA)

The need to explore the data set

The availability of powerful computing packages such as SPSS has made it a simple matter to subject a data set to all manner of statistical analyses and tests of significance. To proceed immediately to such formal analysis, however, is a decidedly risky practice.

There are two main reasons for caution. Firstly, the user who proceeds immediately to carry out various tests may miss the most illuminating features of the data. Secondly, the performance of a statistical test always presupposes that certain assumptions about the data are correct. Should these assumptions be false, the results of statistical tests may be misleading.

In recent years, statisticians have devised a set of statistical methods specially designed for the purpose of examining a data set. Together, they are known as Exploratory Data Analysis (EDA). (For a readable account of EDA, see Howell, 1997). These useful methods have now found their way into all good computing packages, including SPSS.

The purpose of formal statistical tests

The researcher who explores a data set may find interesting patterns. There is always the possibility, however, that these were merely chance occurrences and that, were the research to be repeated with fresh subjects, they might not recur. The purpose of a statistical test is to **confirm** a characteristics of a data set, in the sense that the researcher wants to be able to say, with a high degree of confidence, that the same pattern would be obtained again were the study to be repeated. The purpose of a statistical test, then, is to establish that a result is **robust** to repetition (or **replication**) of the study.

Nominal, ordinal and interval data sets

The researcher works with several different kinds of data:

(a) **interval data** (measurements on an independent scale with units);

(b) **ordinal data** (ranks or assignments to ordered categories);

(c) **nominal data**, which are merely statements of qualitative category membership.

Of the three kinds of data, types (a) and (b) relate to **quantitative** variables; whereas (c) refers to **qualitative** variables. The term *categorial* is sometimes used to include qualitative data and quantitative data in the form of assignments to ordered categories. This term thus straddles the foregoing distinction between types (b) and (c).

Suppose we have a set of measurements, say the heights in centimetres of a group of children. There are usually three things we want to know about such a data set:

(1) the general **level**, or **average value**, of their heights;

(2) the **dispersion** of height, i.e. the degree to which the individual scores tend to **vary** around or **deviate** from the average, as opposed to clustering closely around it;

(3) the **distribution shape**, i.e. the relative frequencies with which heights are to be found within various regions of the total range of the variable.

In this book, we must assume that you already have some knowledge of the statistics that measure the level and dispersion of a set of scores. The most well-known measures of level are the **mean**, the **median** and the **mode**; and dispersion is measured by the **standard deviation** and **quantile range** statistics. We also assume that you understand some terms relating to the distribution of the data set, such as **skewness**, **bimodality** and so on. Different statistics are appropriate for data of different types: there is little point in finding the mean of a set of ranks, for example, because the resulting average would depend solely upon the number of people (or objects) in the sample. Should you be a little rusty on such matters, we strongly recommend that you read the relevant chapters of a good textbook on the topic, such as Gravetter & Wallnau (1997: chapters 1 to 4) or Howell (1997: chapters 1 and 2).

4.1.2 The influence of outliers and asymmetry of distribution

Statistics such as the mean and standard deviation are intended to express, in a single number, some characteristic of the data set as a whole: the former is intended to express the **average**, that is, the general level, typical value, or **central tendency**, of a set of scores; the latter is a measure of their **spread**, or **dispersion**. There are circumstances, however, in which the mean and standard deviation are very poor measures of central tendency and dispersion, respectively, as when the distribution of scores is markedly skewed, or when extreme values, or **outliers**, exert undue **leverage** upon the values of these statistics.

4.1.3 Formal tests, statistical models and their assumptions

The making of a formal statistical test of significance always presupposes the applicability of a statistical **model**, that is, an interpretation (usually in the form of an equation) of the data set as having been generated in a certain manner. The model underlying the one-sample t-test, for example, assumes that the data are from a normal population. To some extent, statistical tests have been shown to be robust to moderate violations of the assumptions of the models upon which they are based: that is, the nominal error rates are not markedly altered. But there are limits to this robustness, and there are circumstances in which a result, declared by an incautious user to be significant beyond, say, the 0.05 level, may actually have been much more probable under the null hypothesis than the given tail probability would indicate. There is no way of avoiding this pitfall other than by thoroughly exploring the data first to ascertain their suitability for specified formal tests.

4.2 FINDING MENUS

Before considering the various exploratory statistical measures available on SPSS, it might be useful to remind the reader how to find the various menus, how to complete the dialog boxes, and how to amend the information that they contain.

In the **SPSS Application menu bar** are eight captioned drop-down menus, plus the **Apple** menu icon on the left, and the **Guide** and **Application** menu icons on the right (Figure 1).

Chapter 4 - Exploring and Graphing Data

Figure 1.

The SPSS drop-down menus

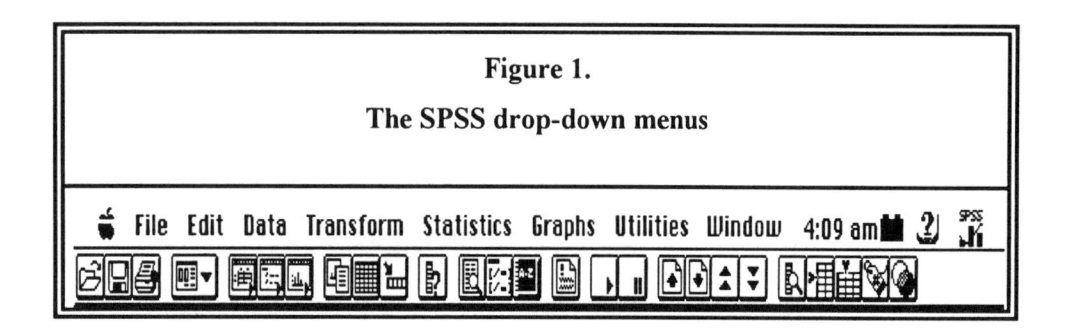

File Edit Data Transform Statistics Graphs Utilities Window 4:09 am

Some items in the **Data Menu (Define Variable, Select Cases, Weight Cases)** have already been considered in Chapter 3. (There are, as we have seen, other ways of accessing some of these commands.) For this chapter, the relevant menus are **Statistics, Graphs,** and **Transform.** Within the **Statistics** menu (Figure 2), are **Summarize** and **Compare Means.**

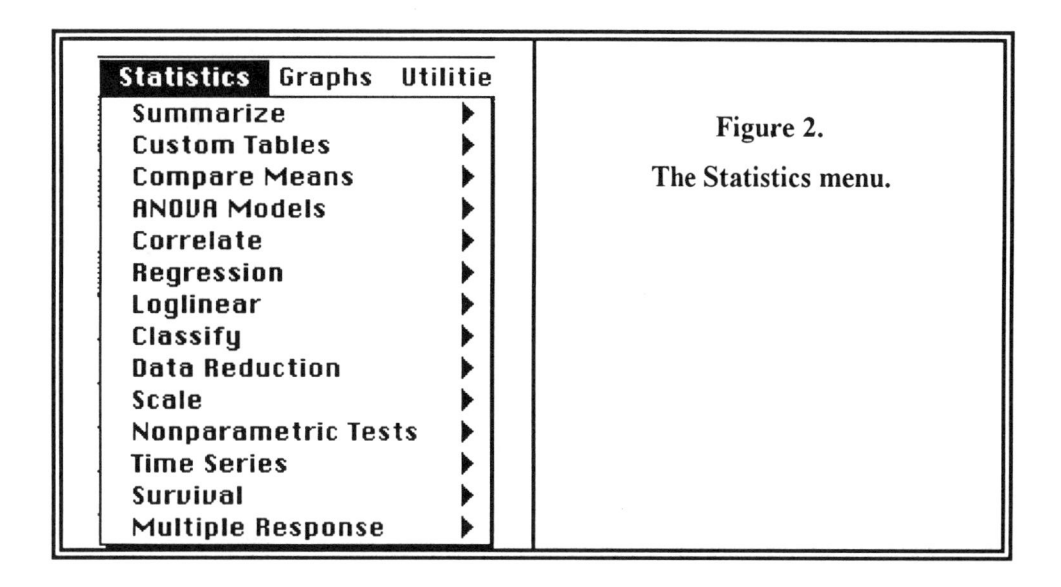

Statistics Graphs Utilitie
Summarize
Custom Tables
Compare Means
ANOVA Models
Correlate
Regression
Loglinear
Classify
Data Reduction
Scale
Nonparametric Tests
Time Series
Survival
Multiple Response

Figure 2.

The Statistics menu.

By highlighting **Summarize** or **Compare Means,** the submenus shown in Figure 3 appear. It can be seen that the submenu of **Summarize** includes **Frequencies, Descriptives, Explore,** and **Crosstabs,** and that for **Compare Means** includes **Means.**

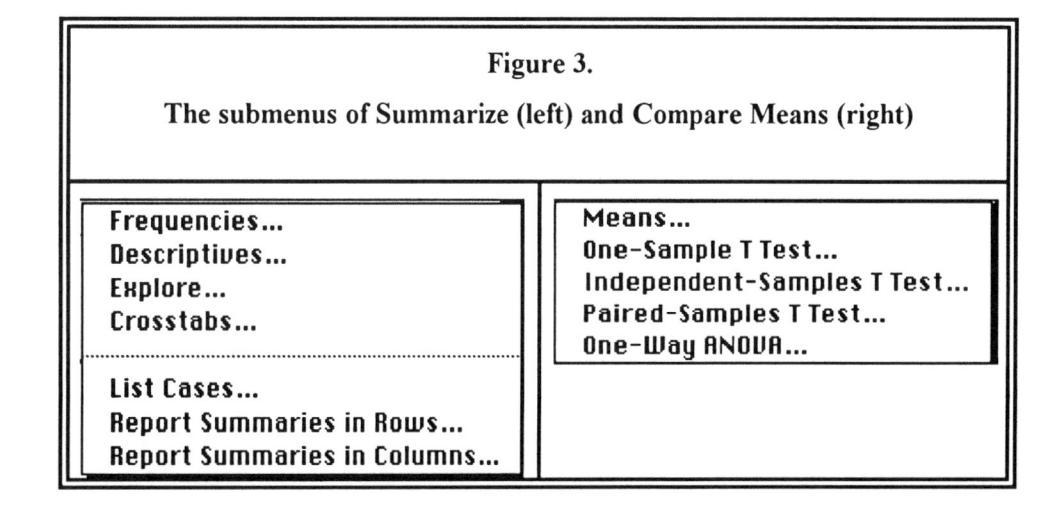

Figure 3.

The submenus of Summarize (left) and Compare Means (right)

Frequencies...
Descriptives...
Explore...
Crosstabs...

List Cases...
Report Summaries in Rows...
Report Summaries in Columns...

Means...
One-Sample T Test...
Independent-Samples T Test...
Paired-Samples T Test...
One-Way ANOVA...

81

The **Graphs** menu (Figure 4) offers a choice from a range of graphs, including **Bar**, **Line**, **Pie**, **Boxplot**, **Error Bar**, **Scatter** (for a scatterplot) and **Histogram**. Since, however, some of these graphs are also available in other procedures in the **Summarize** menu, we shall consider those later.

Finally, within the **Transform** menu (Figure 4) are **Compute** and **Recode**. The meanings of these commands will be explained later.

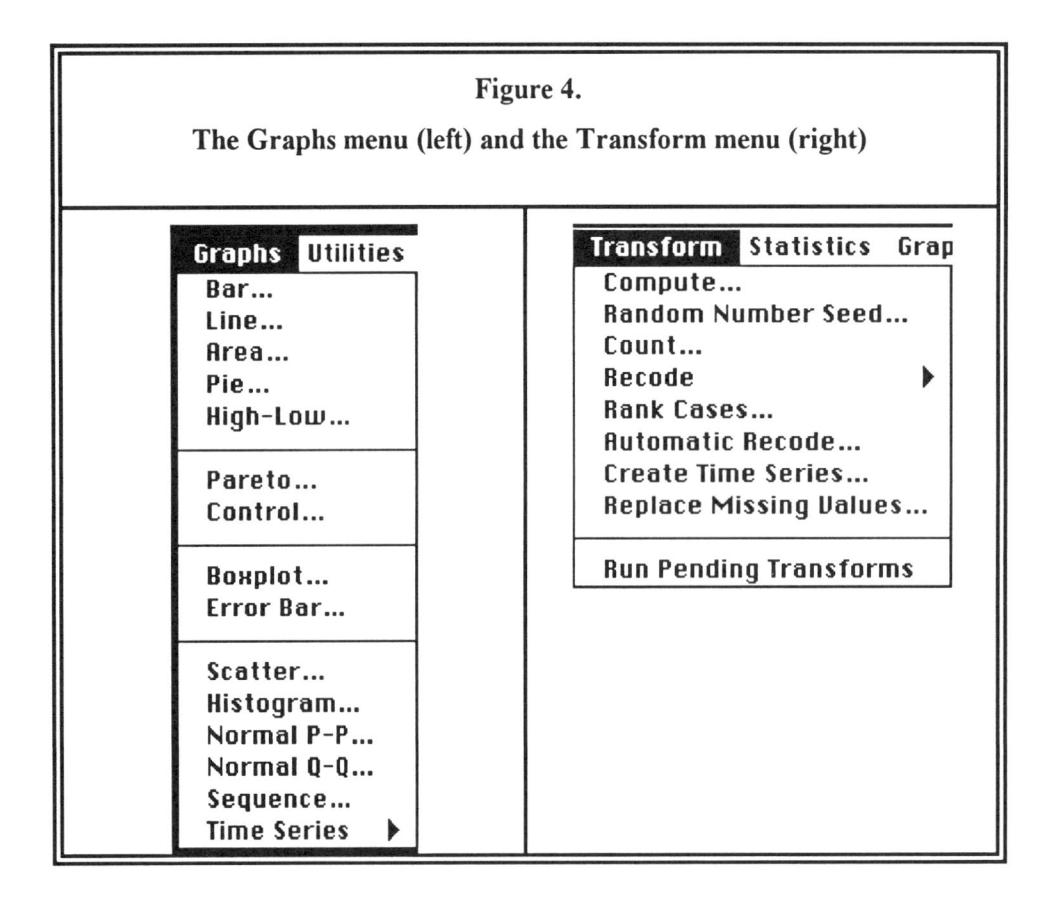

Figure 4.
The Graphs menu (left) and the Transform menu (right)

```
Graphs  Utilities              Transform  Statistics  Grap
  Bar...                         Compute...
  Line...                        Random Number Seed...
  Area...                        Count...
  Pie...                         Recode              ▶
  High-Low...                    Rank Cases...
                                 Automatic Recode...
  Pareto...                      Create Time Series...
  Control...                     Replace Missing Values...

  Boxplot...                     Run Pending Transforms
  Error Bar...

  Scatter...
  Histogram...
  Normal P-P...
  Normal Q-Q...
  Sequence...
  Time Series  ▶
```

4.3 DESCRIBING DATA

Before illustrating the use of various menu items, it is necessary to have a suitable data set such as the one already used in Chapter 3 (Table 8), which comprises two quantitative variables *weight* and *height*, and two qualitative variables *gender* and *bloodtyp*. Let us assume the data have already been set up in the **Data Editor** window (only the first seven of the thirty-two cases are shown in Figure 5).

Chapter 4 - Exploring and Graphing Data

	gender	weight	height	bloodtyp
1	M	75	178	O
2	M	100	196	O
3	M	60	145	A
4	M	71	170	O
5	M	80	180	B
6	M	69	175	O
7	M	78	185	AB

Figure 5.
The first 7 cases of the data set in the Data Editor window

4.3.1 Describing categorial data

The **summarize** item within the **statistics** drop-down menu contains procedures for describing qualitative and categorial data, namely **Frequencies** and **Crosstabs**. Items from the **Graphs** drop-down menu can also be used; but these will not be described in this section, since some of them are also available within **Frequencies**.

Frequencies gives frequency distributions for all types of data (nominal, ordinal, and interval). There are options for additional statistics, and for plots such as barcharts and histograms (see also **Explore** below for other ways of displaying barcharts and histograms).

Crosstabs generates **contingency tables**, which display cell frequencies for categorial data classified on at least two variables. The tables also show row and column frequencies and percentages. Various statistics computed from contingency tables, such as **chi-square**, the **phi coefficient**, the **contingency coefficient**, **lambda**, **Kendall's tau-b** and **tau-c**, **Pearson's correlation coefficient r**, and **gamma**, are available in the **Options** box in **Crosstabs**.

Frequencies

The following example demonstrates the use of the descriptive statistics procedures for the qualitative variables *bloodtyp* and *gender*.

- Choose
  Statistics
     Summarize
        Frequencies

to open the **Frequencies** dialog box (Figure 6).

Chapter 4 - Exploring and Graphing Data

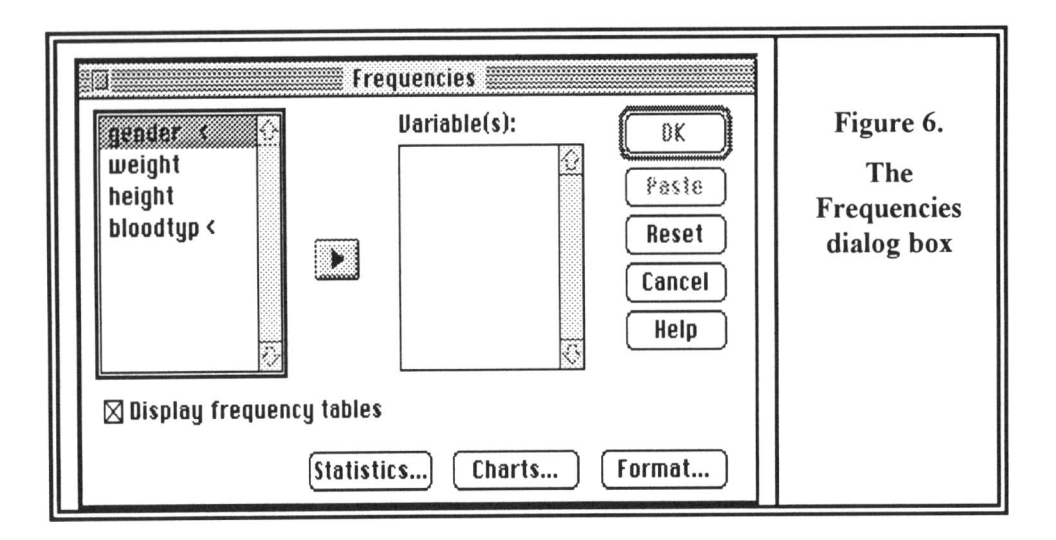

[Figure 6. The Frequencies dialog box]

- Highlight the variables *bloodtyp* and *gender*, and click on ▶ to transfer them to the **Variable(s)** box. The Frequencies dialog box should now appear as in Figure 7.

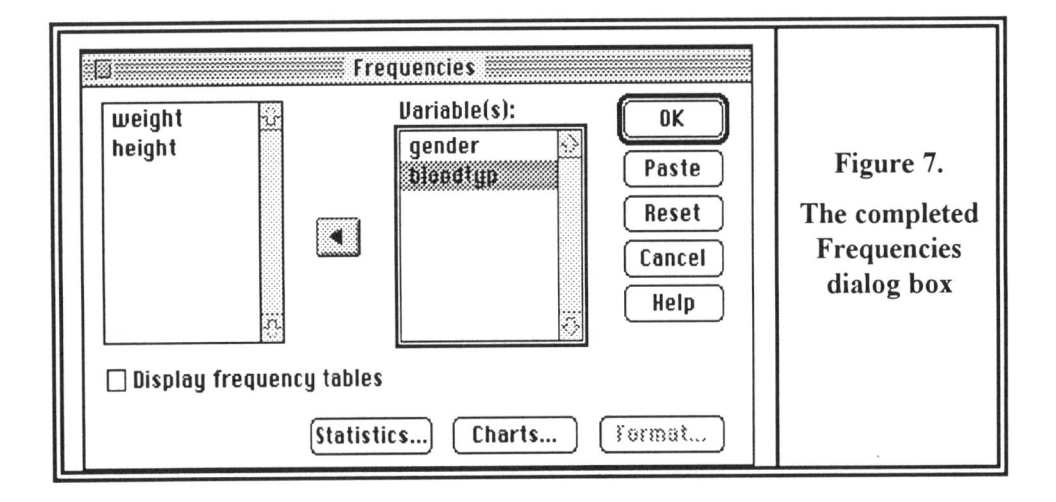

[Figure 7. The completed Frequencies dialog box]

- Click on **Charts** to obtain the **Frequencies: Charts** dialog box (Figure 8) and select the **Bar Chart(s)** radio button. There is also the choice of frequencies or percentages for the y axis in the **Axis Label Display** box.

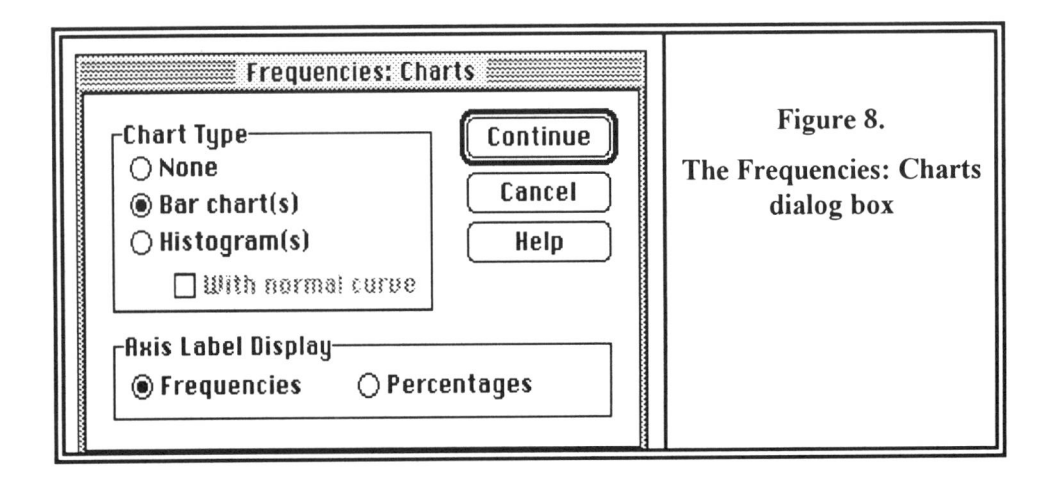

[Figure 8. The Frequencies: Charts dialog box]

Chapter 4 - Exploring and Graphing Data

- Click on **Continue** to get back to in the **Frequencies** dialog box and then on **OK**.

The output consists of a table and bar chart. All listings and tables appear in the **Output window**, whereas charts and graphs appear in the **Chart Carousel window**, where further editing can be carried out if necessary. The output table is shown in Output Listing 1 and the edited bar chart for *bloodtyp* is shown in Figure 9. Note that the bar chart can also be requested directly with **Graphs/Bar**.

Output Listing 1.

Frequency listing for *bloodtyp* and *gender*

```
GENDER
                                                  Valid     Cum
Value Label             Value  Frequency  Percent  Percent  Percent

Female                    F       16       50.0    50.0     50.0
Male                      M       16       50.0    50.0    100.0
                                -------  -------  -------
                        Total     32      100.0   100.0

BLOODTYP
                                                  Valid     Cum
Value Label             Value  Frequency  Percent  Percent  Percent

Group A                   A        6       18.8    18.8     18.8
Group AB                 AB        3        9.4     9.4     28.1
Group B                   B        6       18.8    18.8     46.9
Group O                   O       17       53.1    53.1    100.0
                                -------  -------  -------
                        Total     32      100.0   100.0
```

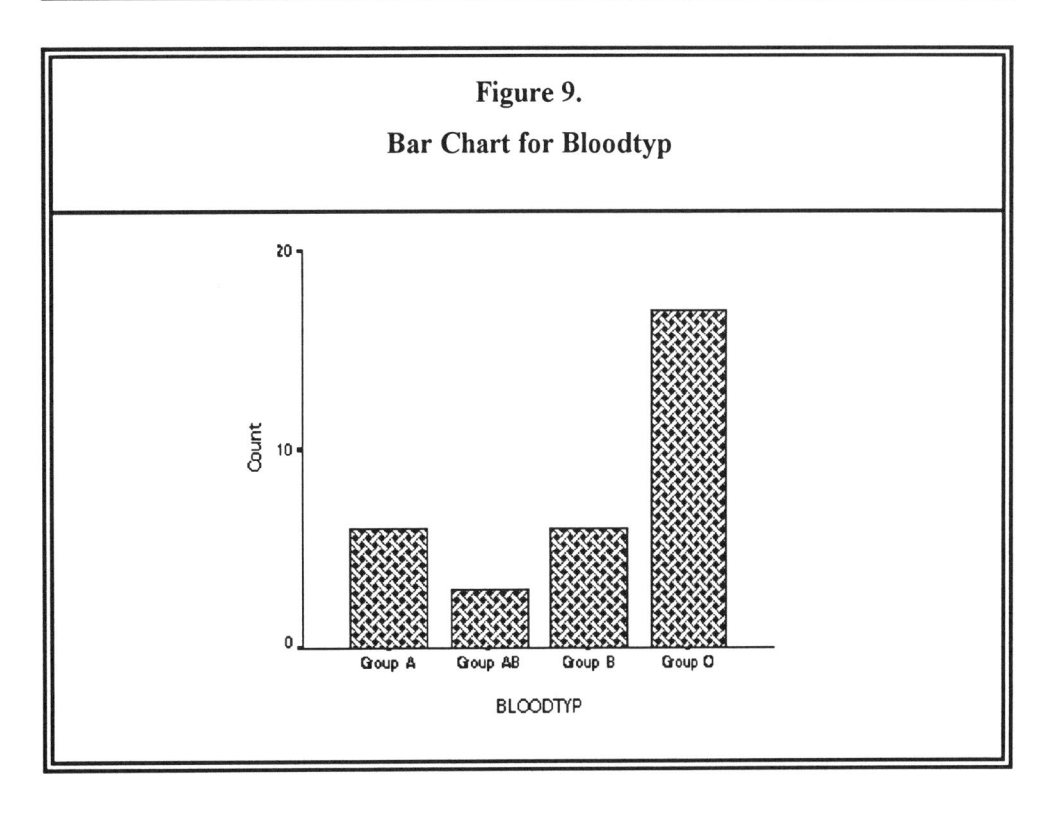

Figure 9.

Bar Chart for Bloodtyp

85

Chapter 4 - Exploring and Graphing Data

Crosstabs

Crosstabs generates contingency tables from nominal or ordinal categorial data. Here we illustrate the procedure with *bloodtyp* and *gender*.

- Choose
  Statistics
    Summarize
      Crosstabs

  to open the **Crosstabs** dialog box (Figure 10).

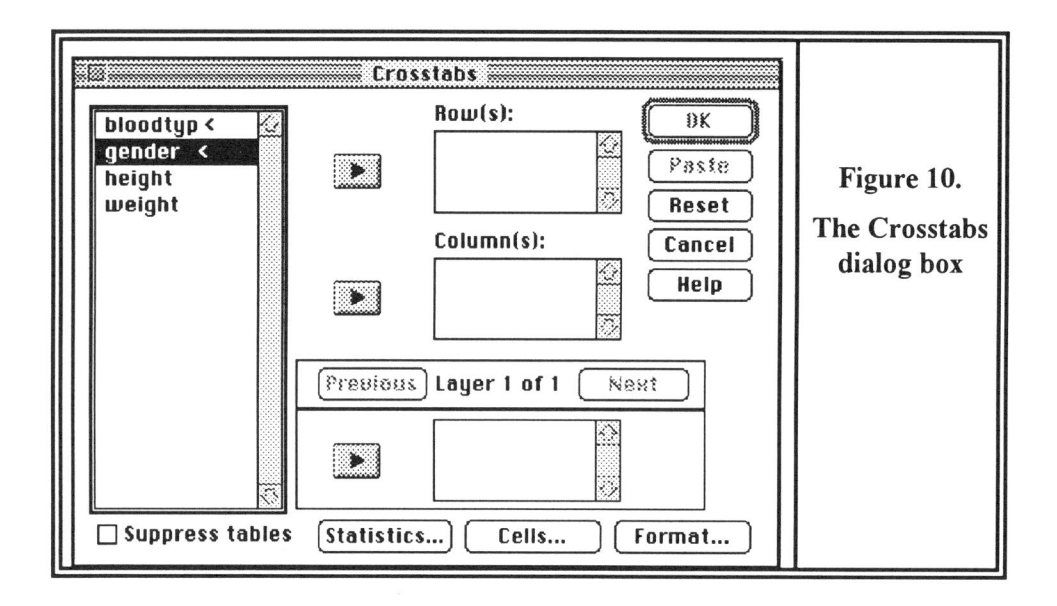

Figure 10. The Crosstabs dialog box

- Enter one of the variables into the **Row(s)** box by clicking on its name and then on ▶.
- Enter the other variable into the **Column(s)** box.
- Click on **OK**.

The output is shown in Output Listing 2.

Output Listing 2.

Contingency table from Crosstabs

```
GENDER   by  BLOODTYP

                   BLOODTYP                                Page 1 of 1
            Count
                   Group A  Group AB  Group B   Group O
                                                           Row
                      A       AB        B          O       Total
   GENDER
                F     3        1        3          9       16
     Female                                                50.0

                M     3        2        3          8       16
     Male                                                  50.0

            Column    6        3        6         17       32
            Total   18.8      9.4     18.8       53.1     100.0

Number of Missing Observations:  0
```

86

Chapter 4 - Exploring and Graphing Data

It is important to be clear that **Crosstabs** is only applicable to contingency tables as described in Section 3.7.2 of Chapter 3: it should be requested only for **categorial data** (i.e. nominal data or those that are assignments to ordered categories). Crosstabs should not be requested for interval data or ranks.

4.3.2 Describing interval data

The principal commands for describing and exploring interval data are
Statistics
    Summarize
        Descriptives,
Statistics
    Summarize
        Explore

and
Statistics
    Compare Means
        Means

The second and third procedures allow quantitative variables to be classified by categories of a qualitative variable (e.g. *gender* in the present data set). **Descriptives** provides a quick way of obtaining a range of common descriptive statistics, both of central tendency and of dispersion. **Means** calculates the means and standard deviations of sub-populations (as defined by values of a grouping or coding variable). There is also the option of a one-way analysis of variance. Note especially that **Means** cannot be used for variables that have not been grouped by another variable: for such variables, **Descriptives** must be used instead. **Explore** contains a large variety of graphs and displays (also available directly from the **Graphs** drop-down menu) as well as a variety of statistics.

The command **Summarize/Frequencies**, though primarily intended for nominal and ordinal data, can be used with interval data for computing specified percentile values, measures of central tendency and dispersion, and drawing histograms (with or without a superimposed normal curve).

Frequencies

The first example illustrates the use of **Frequencies** to draw a histogram, compute some descriptive statistics, and to display some percentile values with the variable *height*. Proceed as follows:

- Choose
  Statistics
      Summarize
          Frequencies.

- In the **Frequencies** dialog box (Figure 7), enter the variable name *height* into the **Variables** box.

- Click on **Charts** to open the **Frequencies: Charts** dialog box (Figure 8).

Chapter 4 - Exploring and Graphing Data

- In the **Chart Type** box, click on the **Histogram(s)** button, and mark the **With normal curve** box by clicking on that also. Click on **Continue**.

- Back in the **Frequencies** dialog box, click on the **Statistics** button to open the **Frequencies: Statistics** dialog box (Figure 11).

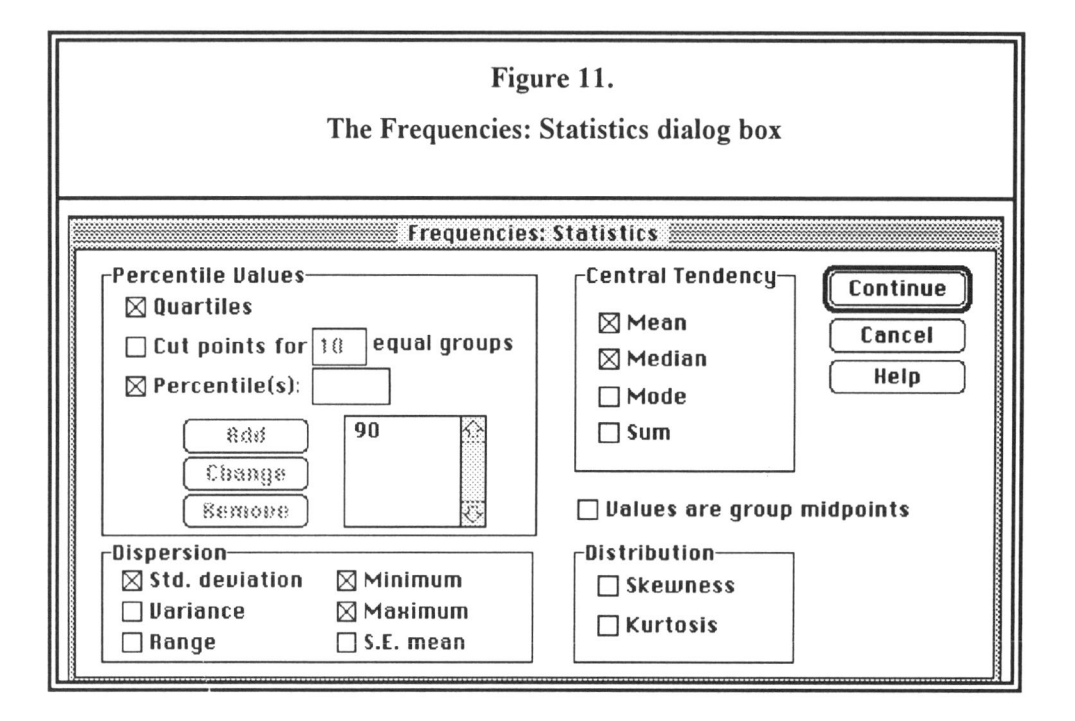

Figure 11.

The Frequencies: Statistics dialog box

[Frequencies: Statistics dialog box showing:
- Percentile Values: ☒ Quartiles, ☐ Cut points for 10 equal groups, ☒ Percentile(s): 90, with Add/Change/Remove buttons
- Central Tendency: ☒ Mean, ☒ Median, ☐ Mode, ☐ Sum
- Dispersion: ☒ Std. deviation, ☐ Variance, ☐ Range, ☒ Minimum, ☒ Maximum, ☐ S.E. mean
- Distribution: ☐ Skewness, ☐ Kurtosis
- ☐ Values are group midpoints
- Continue, Cancel, Help buttons]

- In the **Central Tendency** box, click on the **Mean** and **Median** check boxes.

- In the **Dispersion** box, click on the **Std. deviation** check box.

- In the **Percentile Values** box, click on the **Quartiles** check box: this will print the 25th, 50th and 75th percentile values. Other percentiles can be specified if desired by clicking on the **Percentile(s)** box and filling in whatever values are wanted (e.g. 90, 95).

- Click on **Continue** to get back into the **Frequencies** dialog box. Back in the **Frequencies** dialog box, make sure that the **Display frequency tables** check box is turned off. If the check box contains a cross, click on it to remove it.

- Click on **OK** to run the procedure.

The statistical output is shown in Output Listing 3 and the edited histogram in Figure 12.

Output Listing 3.
The mean, standard deviation, quartiles for height

```
HEIGHT    Height in Centimetres


Hi-Res Chart   # 1:Histogram of height in centimetres

Mean         170.281     Median      170.500     Std dev       13.679
Minimum      142.000     Maximum     196.000


Percentile     Value      Percentile    Value      Percentile     Value

   25.00      162.250        50.00     170.500        75.00      181.500
   90.00      188.500

Valid cases      32     Missing cases       0
```

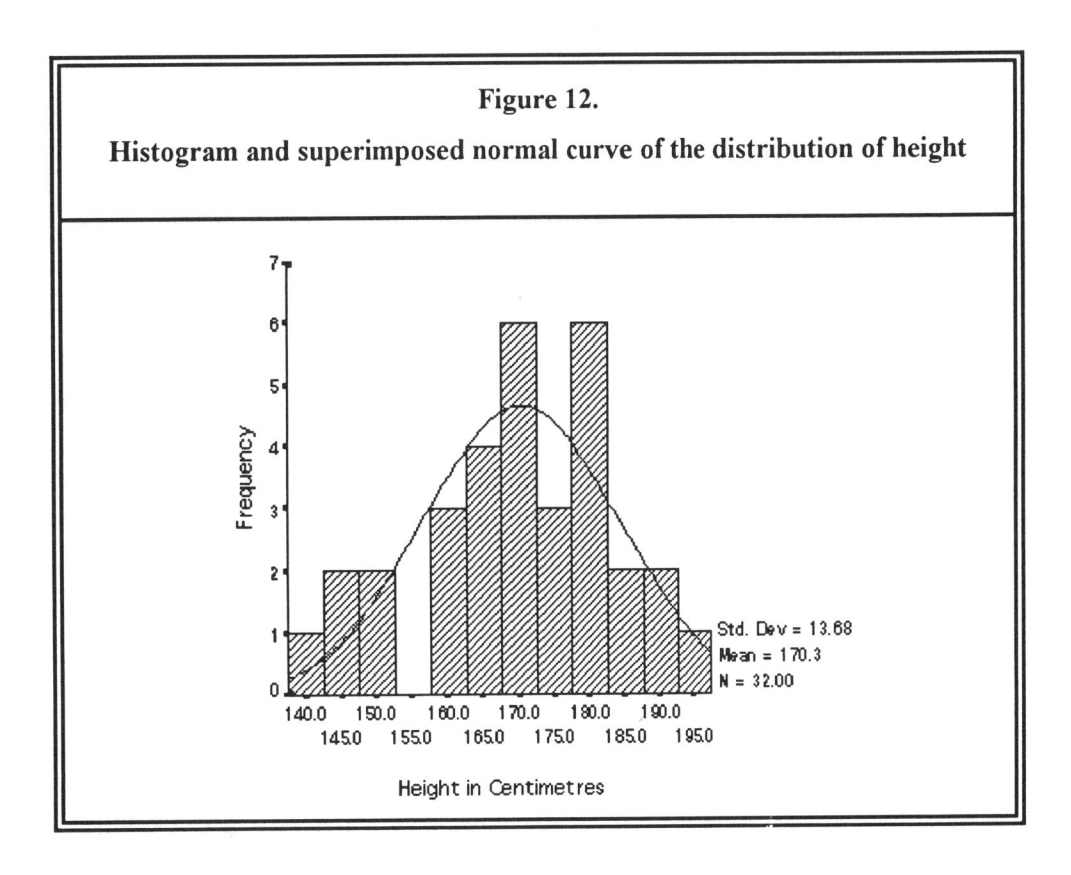

Figure 12.
Histogram and superimposed normal curve of the distribution of height

[Histogram of Height in Centimetres with superimposed normal curve; Std. Dev = 13.68, Mean = 170.3, N = 32.00]

A histogram can also be requested directly from the **Graphs** menu by selecting **Histogram**.

Chapter 4 - Exploring and Graphing Data

Descriptives

Descriptives provides a quick way of generating several common, one-number statistics such as the mean, standard deviation, variance, maximum and minimum values, range and sum.

- Choose
   Statistics
      Summarize
         Descriptives

   and open the **Descriptives** dialog box (not shown).

- Transfer the variables names *height* and *weight* into the **Variable(s)** box.

- Click on **Options** to open the **Descriptives: Options** dialog box (Figure 13).

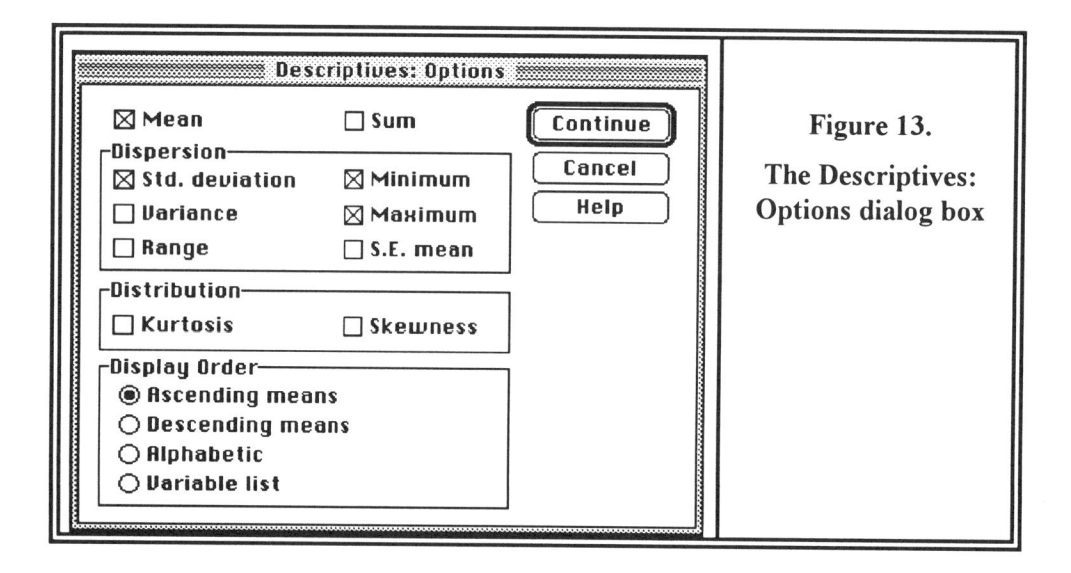

Figure 13.

The Descriptives: Options dialog box

- Select the statistics of interest by clicking on the check boxes (here we have selected just a few of them).

- Click on **Continue** (to get back into the **Descriptives** dialog box) and then on **OK** to run the procedure.

The output is shown in Output Listing 4.

					Valid	
Variable	Mean	Std Dev	Minimum	Maximum	N	Label
WEIGHT	70.22	15.93	48	120	32	Weight in Kilograms
HEIGHT	170.28	13.68	142	196	32	Height in Centimetres

Output Listing 4. The descriptive statistics for weight and height

Chapter 4 - Exploring and Graphing Data

Means

When statistics such as the mean and standard deviation are required for one variable that has been grouped by categories of another (e.g. height grouped by gender), the appropriate procedure is **Means**. Proceed as follows:

- Choose
  Statistics
     Compare Means
        Means

  to open the **Means** dialog box.

- Click on *height* and on ▶ to transfer the name *height* into the **Dependent List** box.

- Click on *gender* and on ▶ to transfer the name *gender* into the **Independent List** box. The completed dialog box is shown in Figure 14.

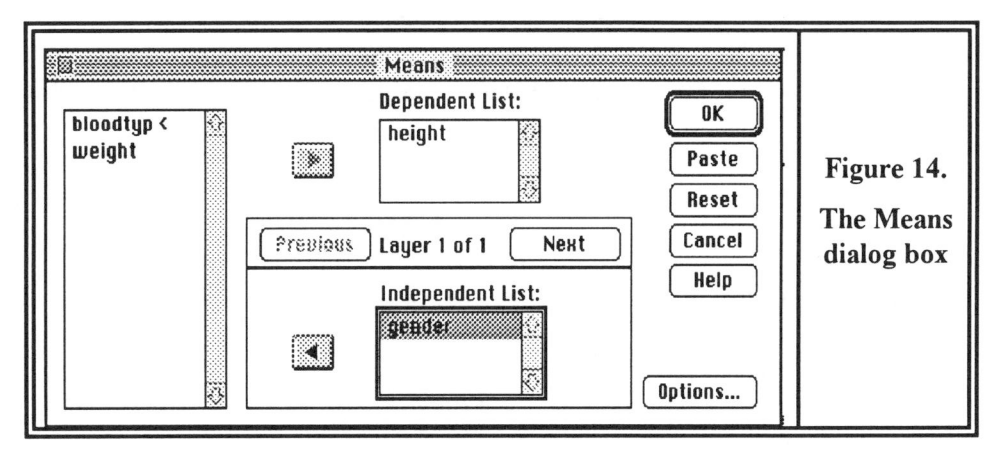

Figure 14. The Means dialog box

- Click on **OK** to run the procedure.

The output is listed in Output Listing 5. You can see that the **Means** command has obtained statistics such as the mean and standard deviation for the male and female participants separately.

Output Listing 5.

The mean height for each level of gender requested with Means

```
Summaries of      HEIGHT      Height in Centimetres
By levels of      GENDER


Variable      Value  Label                Mean      Std Dev      Cases

For Entire Population                  170.2813     13.6789        32

GENDER        F      Female           163.9375     12.0635        16
GENDER        M      Male             176.6250     12.4626        16

Total Cases = 32
```

91

Chapter 4 - Exploring and Graphing Data

Breaking down the data with two or more classificatory variables: Layering

In Figure 14, notice the centrally located box containing two sub-dialog buttons **Previous** and **Next,** as well as the caption **Layer 1 of 1**. Here a **layer** is an independent (grouping) variable, such as *gender*. If you click on **Next**, you can add another independent variable such as *bloodtyp*, so that the data are classified thus:

1st Layer *Gender* Male Female

2nd Layer *Bloodtype* A AB B O A AB B O

SPSS will give the mean and standard deviation of all the combinations of gender and bloodtype as shown in Output Listing 6. This **layering** is very useful when one is calculating the means and standard deviations of data from a factorial analysis of variance (see Chapters 8-10).

Output Listing 6.

The use of layering to compute means and standard deviations for all combinations of gender and blood type. (The dependent variable is height.)

```
Variable         Value   Label                Mean       Std Dev

For Entire Population                       170.2813    13.6789

GENDER           F       Female             163.9375    12.0635
  BLOODTYP       A       Group A            160.3333    10.5040
  BLOODTYP       AB      Group AB           151.0000        .
  BLOODTYP       B       Group B            175.6667     6.5064
  BLOODTYP       O       Group O            162.6667    12.4700

GENDER           M       Male               176.6250    12.4626
  BLOODTYP       A       Group A            168.3333    22.5462
  BLOODTYP       AB      Group AB           178.5000     9.1924
  BLOODTYP       B       Group B            184.0000     5.2915
  BLOODTYP       O       Group O            176.5000    10.6637

Total Cases = 32
```

It is perhaps worth noting that, had you not clicked on the **Next** button before adding the second classificatory variable, the output would have consisted of one-way classifications of *height* by *gender* and of *height* by *bloodtyp* separately: that is, only a single layer would have been used for each analysis.

Explore

The **Explore** command (which is in **Statistics/Summarize**) offers many of the facilities already illustrated with other commands, and (like **Means** and **Compare Means**) allows quantitative variables (such as height) to be subdivided by the categories of a qualitative variable, such as gender. If, for example, a data set contains the heights of 50 men and 50 women collected into a column headed *height* and (in another column) code numbers making up the grouping variable *gender*, the command **Explore** will produce statistical summaries, graphs and

Chapter 4 - Exploring and Graphing Data

displays either for the 100 height measurements considered as a single group, or the heights of males or females (or both) considered separately.

A useful first step in the analysis of data is to obtain a picture of the data set as a whole, that is, to construct a **graph** of the data. The **Explore** routine offers three kinds of graphs:

(1) **histograms**;

(2) **stem-and-leaf displays**;

(3) **boxplots**.

Readers unfamiliar with these can find, in Howell (1997), clear descriptions of histograms (and bar graphs) on pp17-20, of stem-and-leaf displays on pp21-23, and of boxplots on pp54-57.

The basis of all three types of graph is a table called a **frequency distribution**, which sets out either (in the case of qualitative or nominal data) the categories comprising a qualitative variable and gives the frequency of observations in each category or (with interval data) divides the total range of values into arbitrary **class intervals** and gives the frequency of measurements that fell within each interval, that is, had values within the upper and lower **bounds** of the interval concerned. With data on height recorded in centimetres, for example, the total range could be divided into the class intervals (140-149, 150-159, 160-169, and so on), and the frequency distribution would give the **frequencies** of heights within each of these ranges.

A **bar graph** (SPSS calls it a 'bar chart': see Figure 9) is suitable for qualitative (nominal) data, such as the numbers of people in a sample belonging to the various blood groups. In a bar graph, the bars are separated to clarify the fact that the horizontal axis contains no scale of measurement; in fact, the order of the bars in Figure 9 is arbitrary, since the Group B bar could as well have followed the Group A bar. A **histogram**, on the other hand, is appropriate for interval data such as a set of height measurements: the class intervals are stepped out on the horizontal axis; and on each interval a bar is erected, whose height represents the number of people whose heights fell within that interval. *In a histogram, in contradistinction to a bar graph, the bars touch one another - there are no spaces.*

To run **Explore**, proceed as follows:

- Choose
  Statistics
    Summarize
      Explore

  to open the **Explore** dialog box (the completed version is shown in Figure 15).

- To see how *height* varies with *gender*, click on the variable name *height* and on ▶ to transfer it to the **Dependent List** box.

- Click on *gender* and on ▶ to transfer it to the **Factor List** box.

- Click on **Plots** to open the **Explore: Plots** dialog box (Figure 16) and select the **Stem-and-leaf** check box in the **Descriptive** box. The default setting for the **boxplots** is a side-by-side plot for each level of the factor (i.e. Female and Male).

- Click on **Continue** and then on **OK** to run the procedure.

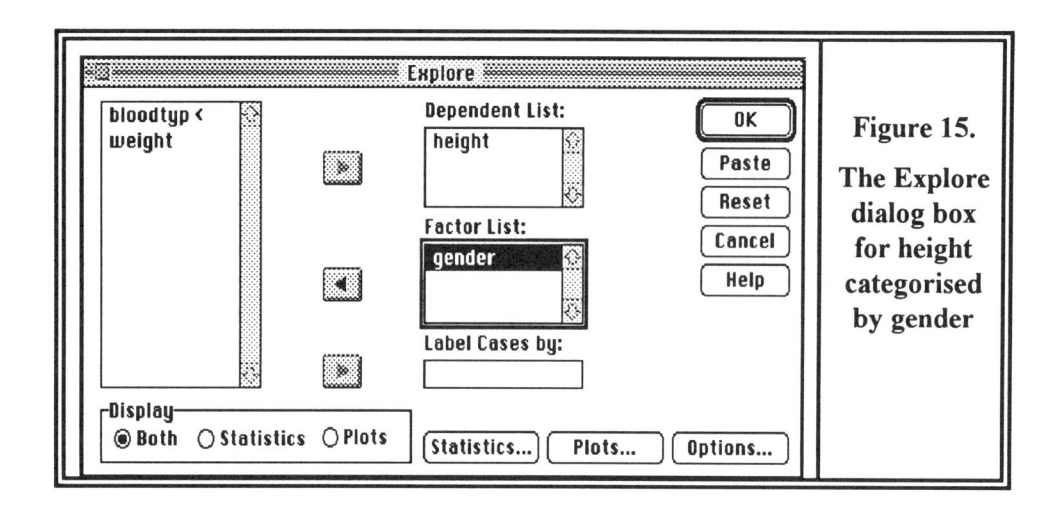

Chapter 4 - Exploring and Graphing Data

Figure 15. The Explore dialog box for height categorised by gender

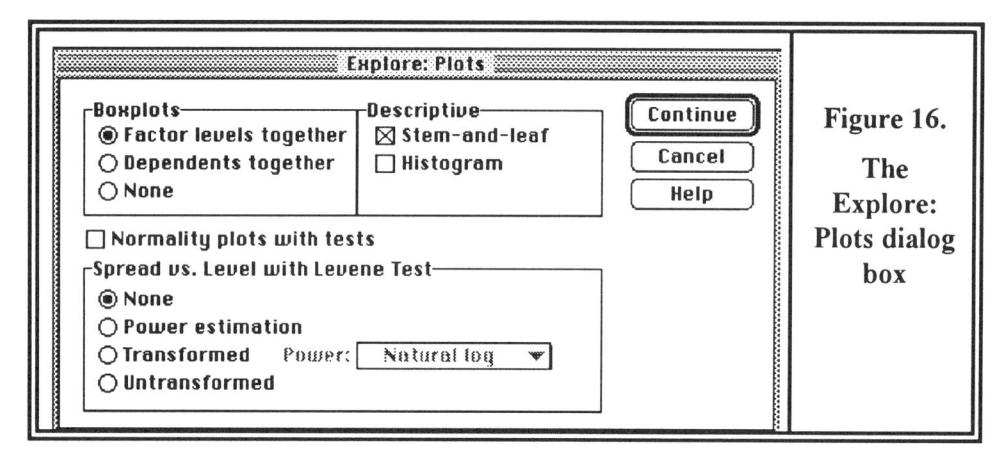

Figure 16. The Explore: Plots dialog box

Should one wish to have boxplots of two dependent variables side-by-side at each level of a classificatory variable (such as gender, or blood group), both dependent variables must be entered into the **Dependent List** box, and (in the **Boxplots** dialog box) the **Dependents together** radio button must be selected. In the present example, of course, it would have made no sense to plot boxplots of *height* and *weight* side-by-side at each level of gender, since height and weight measurements have quite different scales.

The descriptive statistics and the stem-and-leaf display of *height* for Males (one of the levels of *gender*) is shown in Output Listing 7; the output for Females is not reproduced here.

Look at the example of a **stem-and-leaf display** given in the lower half of Output Listing 7. The central column of numbers (16, 16, 17, 17, ..., 19) is the **stem** of the display representing the leading digit or digits (here they are the hundreds and tens of centimetres); the numbers in the column headed **Leaf** are the final digits (here they are centimetres). Each stem denotes the lower bound of the class interval: for example, the first number, 16, represents the lower bound of the class interval from 160 to 169, and 17 represents the lower bound of the interval from 170 to 179. If there are a large number of leaves for a single stem, SPSS may split the stem into two using an asterisk * for the leaves 0-4 and a dot for the leaves 5-9. (Sometimes SPSS may split the stem into five, using the stems * for leaves 0 and 1, t for leaves two and three, f for leaves four and five, s for leaves six and seven, and . for leaves 8 and 9.) The column headed **Frequency** lists the number of cases in each stem. As an example, look at stem 18 *: there are four cases with a height between 180 and 184 centimetres and they are 180, 180, 182 and 183 since the leaves are listed as 0, 0, 2, 3. The stem-and-leaf display is very useful for displaying small data sets, but for large sets, the histogram is generally preferred.

Output Listing 7.

Descriptive statistics, and stem-and-leaf display for height categorised by gender (only the output for Males shown here)

```
     HEIGHT    Height in Centimetres
By   GENDER    M        Male

Valid cases:        16.0   Missing cases:      .0   Percent missing:      .0

Mean       176.6250  Std Err    3.1157  Min      145.0000  Skewness     -.9470
Median     179.0000  Variance 155.3167  Max      196.0000  S E Skew      .5643
5% Trim    177.3056  Std Dev   12.4626  Range     51.0000  Kurtosis     1.6419
95% CI for Mean (169.9841, 183.2659)    IQR       14.5000  S E Kurt     1.0908

Frequency    Stem &  Leaf

    1.00 Extremes    (145)
    1.00        16 * 0
     .00        16 .
    4.00        17 * 0002
    2.00        17 . 58
    4.00        18 * 0023
    1.00        18 . 5
    2.00        19 * 00
    1.00        19 . 6

Stem width:        10
Each leaf:      1 case(s)
```

Figure 17 shows the **boxplots** of the heights of the male and female subjects considered separately, but plotted side-by-side, for comparison. In a boxplot, the box itself represents that portion of the distribution falling between the 25th and 75th percentiles, i.e. the **lower** and **upper quartiles** (in EDA terminology these are known as **hinges**). The xth percentile is the value below which x% of the distribution lies: so 50% of the heights lie between the 25th and 75th percentiles. The horizontal line across the interior of the box represents the median. The vertical lines outside the box, which are known as **whiskers**, connect the largest and smallest values that are not categorised as outliers or extreme values.

A boxplot **outlier** (o) is defined as a value more than 1.5 box-lengths away from the box, and an **extreme value** (*) as more than 3 box-lengths away from the box. The number(s) alongside o and * are the case number(s).

Skewness is indicated by an eccentric location of the median within the box. Notice that the distribution of heights for females is much more symmetric than that for males. The o^3 under the Male boxplot indicates the existence of an outlier and that it is the value for case 3. This value (145cm) is well below the average height for males and its presence is also noted in the stem-and-leaf display in Output Listing 7.

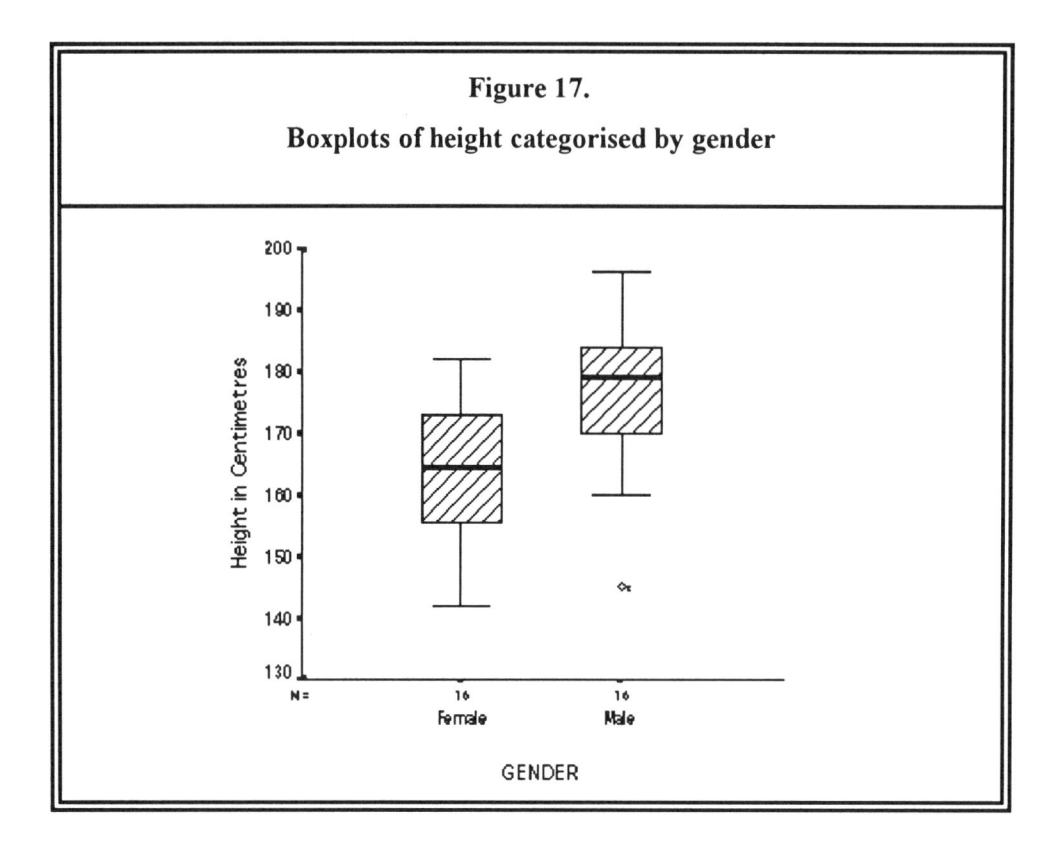

Figure 17.
Boxplots of height categorised by gender

Boxplots are especially useful for identifying outliers and extreme values in data sets, and can be requested directly by choosing the **Graphs/Boxplot**.

4.3.3 Other graphical procedures

A wide range of graphs and charts (some of which we have already considered) are available for exploring and representing data. Here, before we go on to discuss some more graphical methods, we shall first outline some general aspects of graph-drawing in SPSS.

Requesting graphs and charts

The dialog boxes for specifying graphs and charts are accessed from the **Graphs** drop-down menu or from options within various procedures - for example, the **Frequencies** dialog box (Figure 7) contains an option **Charts** (see Figure 8).

It is worth spending a few moments considering the variable names and labels that may be plotted in charts or graphs, in case the user might want to change some of them within the data file before going ahead with the chosen figure. If some data are missing from the data file, remember to specify whether (as in a bar chart, for example) missing data should be included in the plot. Missing data can be

Chapter 4 - Exploring and Graphing Data

excluded by turning off the **Display groups defined by missing values** box in the **Options** dialog box.

If extensive editing is not anticipated, it is quicker to add a title (if desired) at this stage rather than at the editing stage (though for boxplots, titles can be added only at the editing stage) by clicking on the **Titles** box and typing in the appropriate title.

It should be noted that not all boxes in a dialog box need necessarily be completed. For example, **Label Cases by** boxes can be left empty when that option is not required. The critical test of whether enough information has been specified in a dialog box is whether the **OK** button is operative or not: if that is still dimmed, more information must be supplied before the command can be executed.

Seeing the graph or chart on screen

After a graph or chart has been completed by SPSS, it will appear in the **Chart Carousel** window. If the pointer is clicked on another window or another window is requested from the **Window** drop-down menu, the Chart Carousel window will temporarily disappear. It can easily be retrieved, however, by reselecting it from the **Window** menu.

Editing a graph or chart

After a graph or chart has appeared on the screen, the following options are available:

1. Accept the image as it is and save it, print it or copy it for pasting into a document.

2. Reject the image by clicking on the **Discard** button on the right.

3. Edit the image as described below.

It is tempting to save all relevant charts, but the reader should be aware that charts take up a lot of computer space. If storage space is limited, save only the most important charts: it is easy to recreate them from saved data files later if necessary.

The **Chart Editor** allows a wide range of alterations and additions to be made to a graph or chart; though such editing is a slow process and proficiency takes some practice to acquire. The editor offers an array of important menus (Figure 18), some of which offer long lists of commands, and the user will need to experiment with these to learn how to apply them.

Figure 18.

The Chart Editor menu bar (with tool bar underneath).

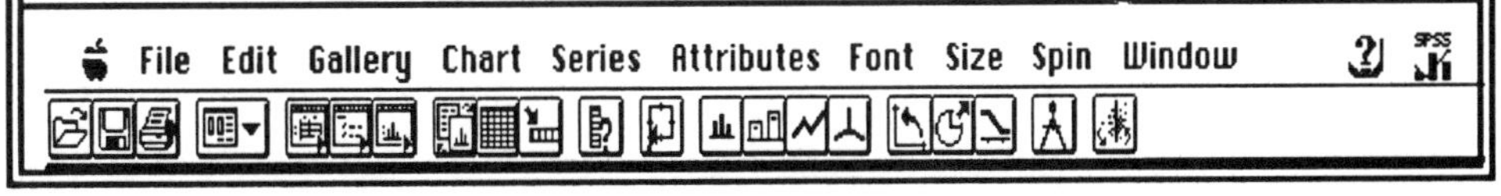

Chapter 4 - Exploring and Graphing Data

The most important menus are **Gallery**, **Chart**, **Series** and **Attributes**, details of which are shown in Figure 19.

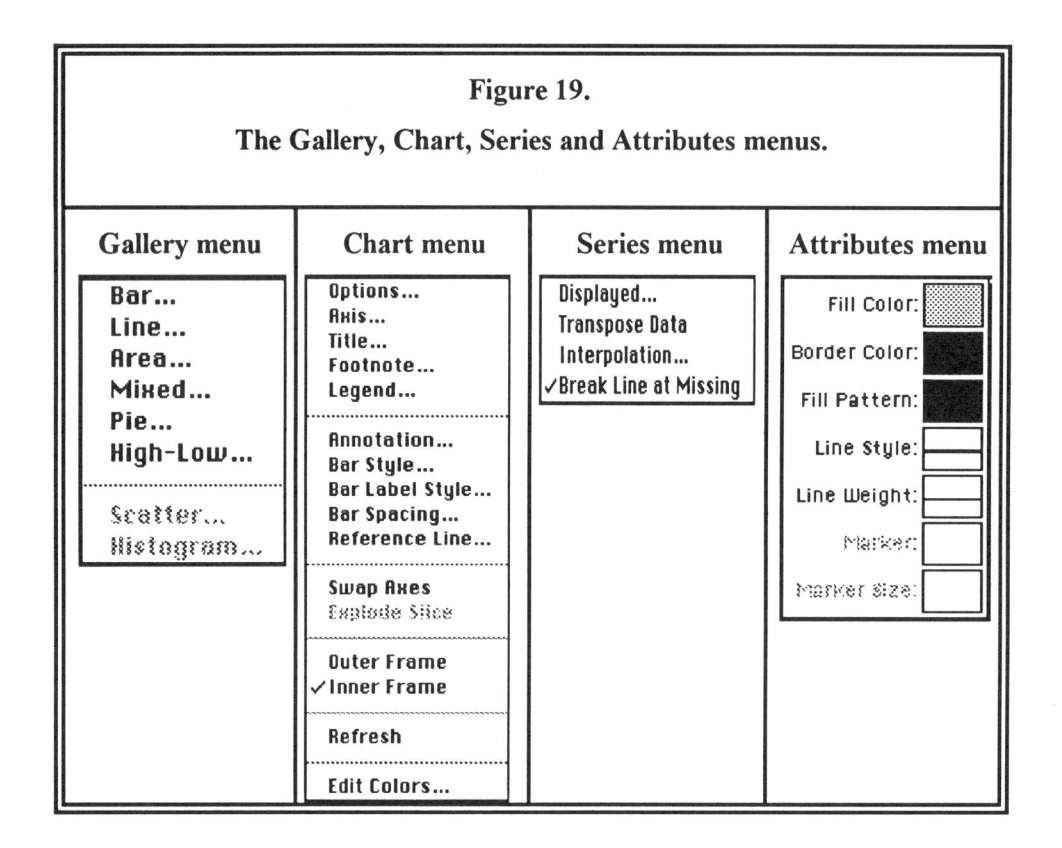

Figure 19.
The Gallery, Chart, Series and Attributes menus.

Gallery menu	Chart menu	Series menu	Attributes menu
Bar... **Line...** **Area...** **Mixed...** **Pie...** **High-Low...** Scatter... Histogram...	Options... Axis... Title... Footnote... Legend... Annotation... Bar Style... Bar Label Style... Bar Spacing... Reference Line... Swap Axes Explode Slice Outer Frame ✓Inner Frame Refresh Edit Colors...	Displayed... Transpose Data Interpolation... ✓Break Line at Missing	Fill Color: Border Color: Fill Pattern: Line Style: Line Weight: Marker: Marker Size:

---

* The **Gallery** menu offers pie charts, high-low graphs and a command **Mixed...** for producing hybrid graphs (see below).

* The **Chart** menu has commands for adding labels and legends, as well as changing the spacing between bars, putting frames around the graph, swapping axes, and so on.

* The **Series** menu has commands for interpolating lines between the markers in some types of graph and displaying only selected categories.

* The **Attributes** menu has commands for changing the colour of the bars in a bar chart, the colour of the border, the fill pattern, the line style and weight, and the marker and marker size. (Not all of these options will be applicable to any one kind of graph: with a bar graph, for example, there are no markers.)

If a series of similar graphs or charts are going to be requested, the reader should consider saving the edited first chart and then specifying the file when using the **Chart Template** option for the second and subsequent charts.

In summary, it is possible to customise a graph or a chart to a considerable extent and to maximise clarity for reproduction by a monochrome printer by replacing colours with uncoloured patterns.

Chapter 4 - Exploring and Graphing Data

Clustered bar charts

Several types of bar charts can be drawn. Returning to the data set shown in Table 8 of Chapter 3, consisting of the blood groups, heights and weights of 16 men and 16 women, we have already considered the production of bar graphs showing the frequency distributions of gender or blood group considered separately. Now suppose that having constructed a bar graph of the frequency distribution of blood group in the sample of 32 people, we would like to be able to compare that distribution in the males with the same distribution in the females. In other words, instead of having a simple bar graph with a bar for each of the four blood groups, we want two clusters of bars, each cluster showing the frequencies of the different blood groups within either the males or the females in the sample. Such a **clustered bar graph** (edited) is shown in Figure 20. In this graph, there are two parts, a male part and a female part, each consisting of its own blood group distribution.

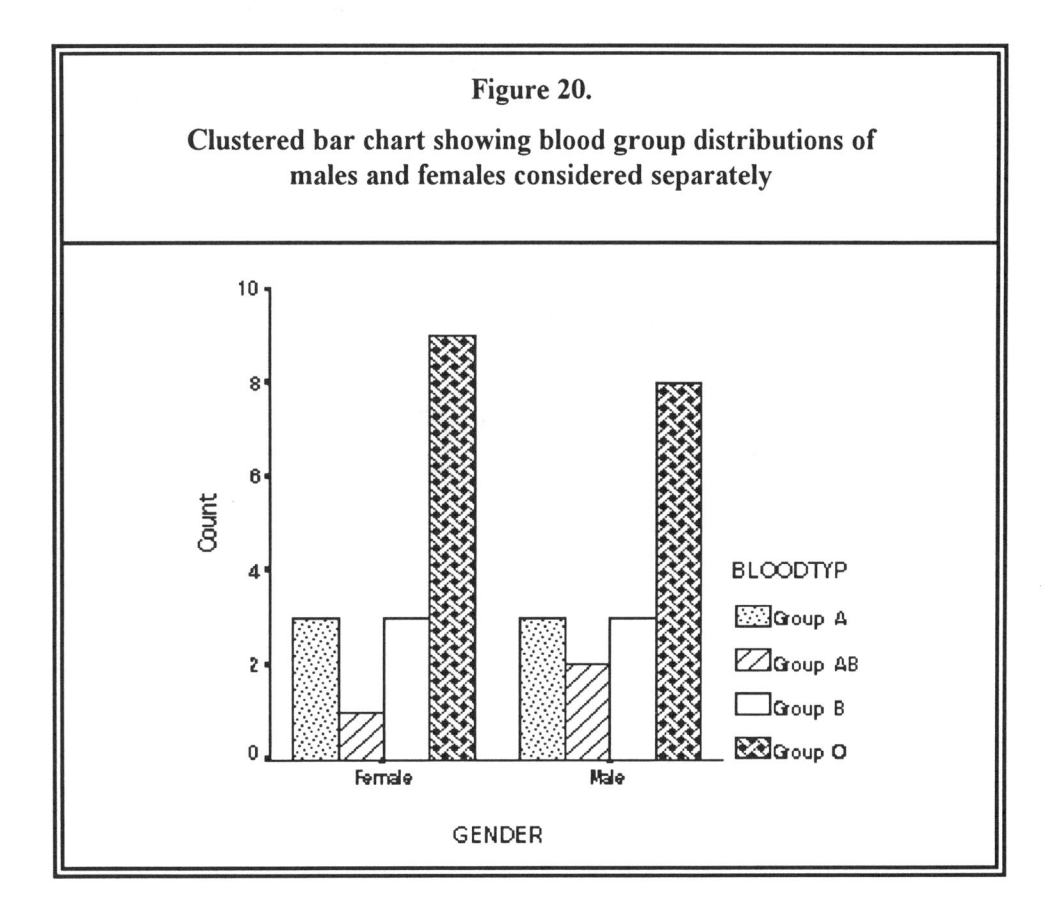

Figure 20.

Clustered bar chart showing blood group distributions of males and females considered separately

To obtain this clustered bar graph, proceed as follows.

- Choose
   Graphs
      Bar...

to obtain the **Bar Charts** dialog (Figure 21).

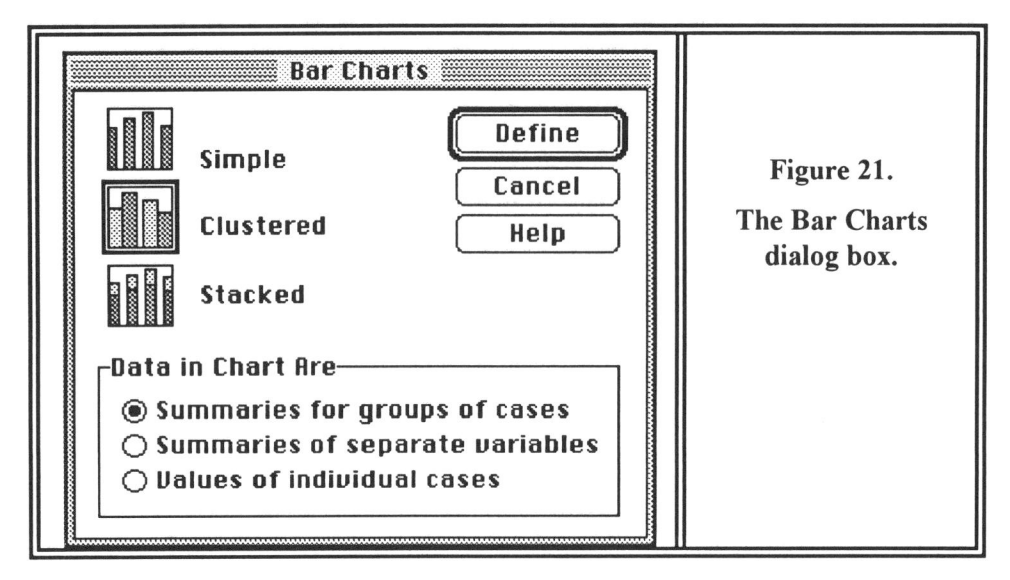

Chapter 4 - Exploring and Graphing Data

Figure 21. The Bar Charts dialog box.

- Choose **Clustered** by clicking on the middle diagram to get the black border (which, initially, will be round the **Simple** option) to move down to the **Clustered** diagram.

- Click on the **Define** button to obtain another dialog box with the rather ponderous caption: **Define Clustered Bar: Summaries for Groups of Cases** (the completed dialog box is shown in Figure 22).

Figure 22.

The Define Clustered Bar: Summaries for Groups of Cases dialog box.

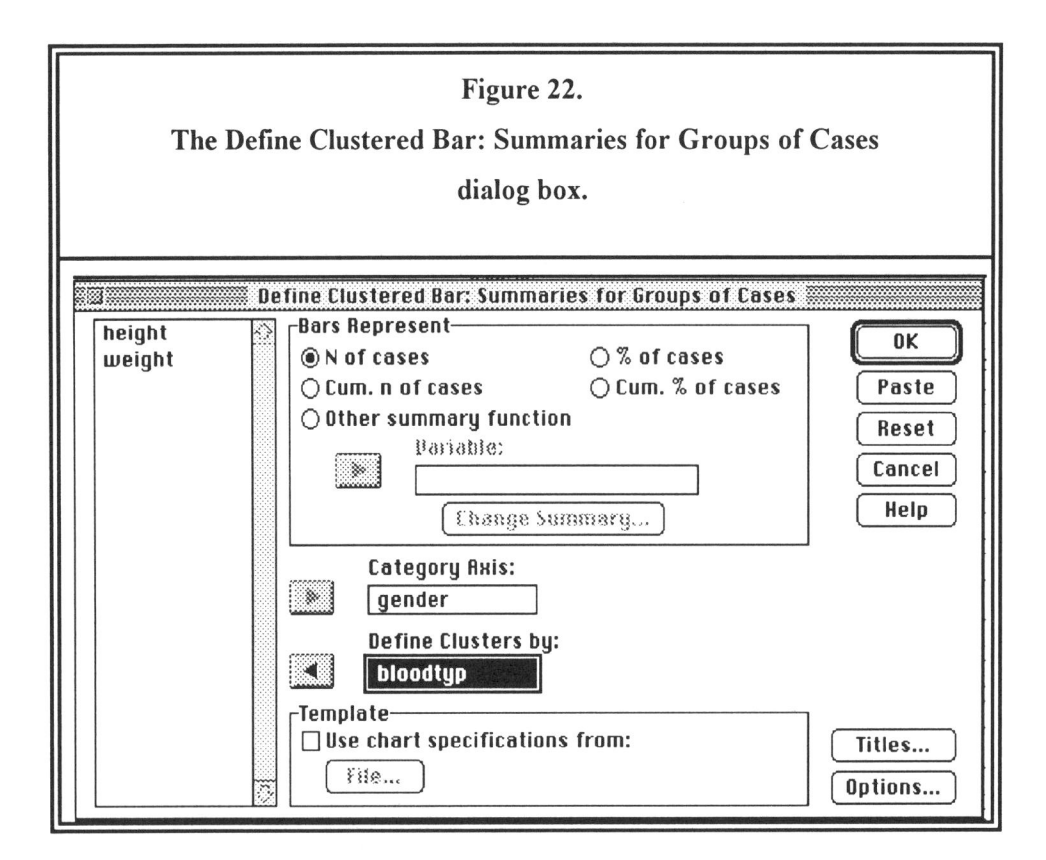

- We want a clustered bar graph showing the frequency distributions of blood group for the males and females separately, but presented side by side for comparison, in the one diagram. In the **variable window** on the left of the dialog box will appear the variable names *height*, *weight*, *gender* and

Chapter 4 - Exploring and Graphing Data

bloodtyp. When any of these is selected (by clicking on it), the arrows to the left of the two lower text boxes on the right, **Category Axis** and **Define Clusters by**, will come alive. (The uppermost box, **Variable**, will remain dim unless the lowest of the three radio buttons, **Other summary function**, is selected. For this exercise, however, the correct radio button is **N of cases**.) In our example, the category axis is *gender*, and the clusters are defined by *bloodtyp*. Transfer those two variables into the boxes accordingly, leaving *height* and *weight* behind in the variable box.

- (Note that had we wanted, instead of frequencies, the mean height of the subjects in each of the six gender by blood group categories, we should have chosen the lowest radio button, **Other Summary Function**, and transferred the variable *height* into the text box there.)

- Click on the **OK** button to obtain a clustered bar chart similar to that shown in Figure 20. (Note, however, that if you are going to be printing in black and white, it is best to use the graphics editor to change the colours of the graph to shades of grey. Figure 20 is such an edited version, produced by procedures which will be described in the next section.)

Editing a bar chart

A bar chart can be edited to improve reproduction clarity by replacing the default colour shadings of the boxes by grey and black. This is done by clicking on the **Edit** box to access the **Graph-editing menu** bar. By choosing **Window/Toolbar**, the **Chart Editor** menu bar can be obtained (Figure 18). (You might wish to engage **Balloon Help** to identify the various icons in the toolbar.)

Should you wish to change the colour of a bar graph, the fill pattern, or some other attribute, click on the bar to select it. (Selection will be indicated by the appearance of four black filled squares around the bar.) From the **Attributes** menu select the appropriate box and make the adjustment. This will not be possible unless part of the figure has been selected first.

Several modifications are available for changing the pattern of bars in the chart as shown in the **Bar Spacing** dialog box in Figure 22, which is obtained by choosing **Chart/Bar Spacing**. The settings can then be altered as desired.

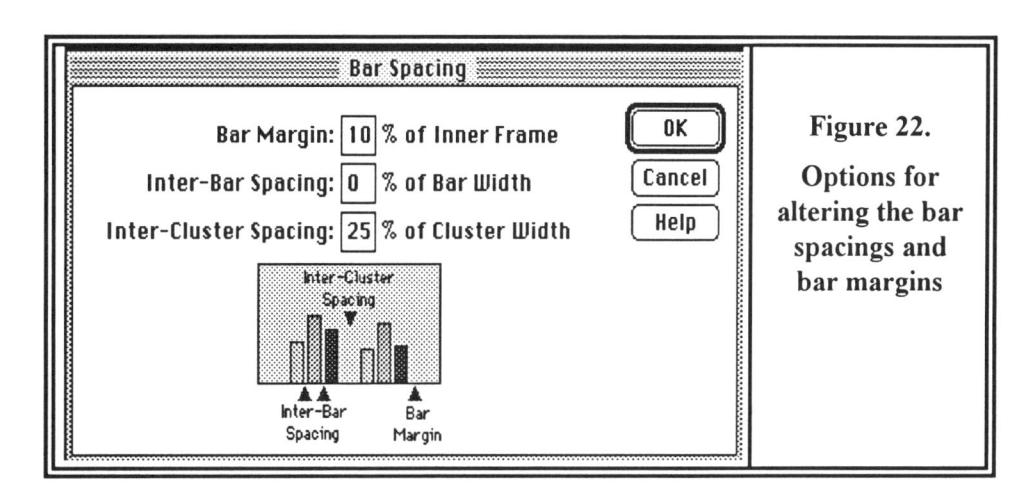

Figure 22.

Options for altering the bar spacings and bar margins

101

Chapter 4 - Exploring and Graphing Data

Error bar charts

An alternative to a bar graph is what SPSS terms an **error bar chart**, in which the mean of the scores in a particular category is represented by a single point and the spread (standard deviation, standard error of the mean or confidence interval for the mean - the user can choose one of these) is represented by a vertical line passing through the point. Figure 23 shows an error bar chart for the heights of the men and women in the sample we have been using for the other displays.

To obtain an error bar chart, proceed as follows.

- Choose
  Graphs
    Error Bar

  and make the appropriate selection of variables from the dialog box.

- In the **Bars Represent** box, specify whether you want the bars to be **Confidence interval for mean** or multiples (choose the multiplier with the appropriate entry in the **Multiplier** box) of the **standard deviation** or the **standard error of mean**. Here we have selected **Standard deviation** and set the **Multiplier** to 1. Click on the **OK** button to produce the **Error Bar Chart**.

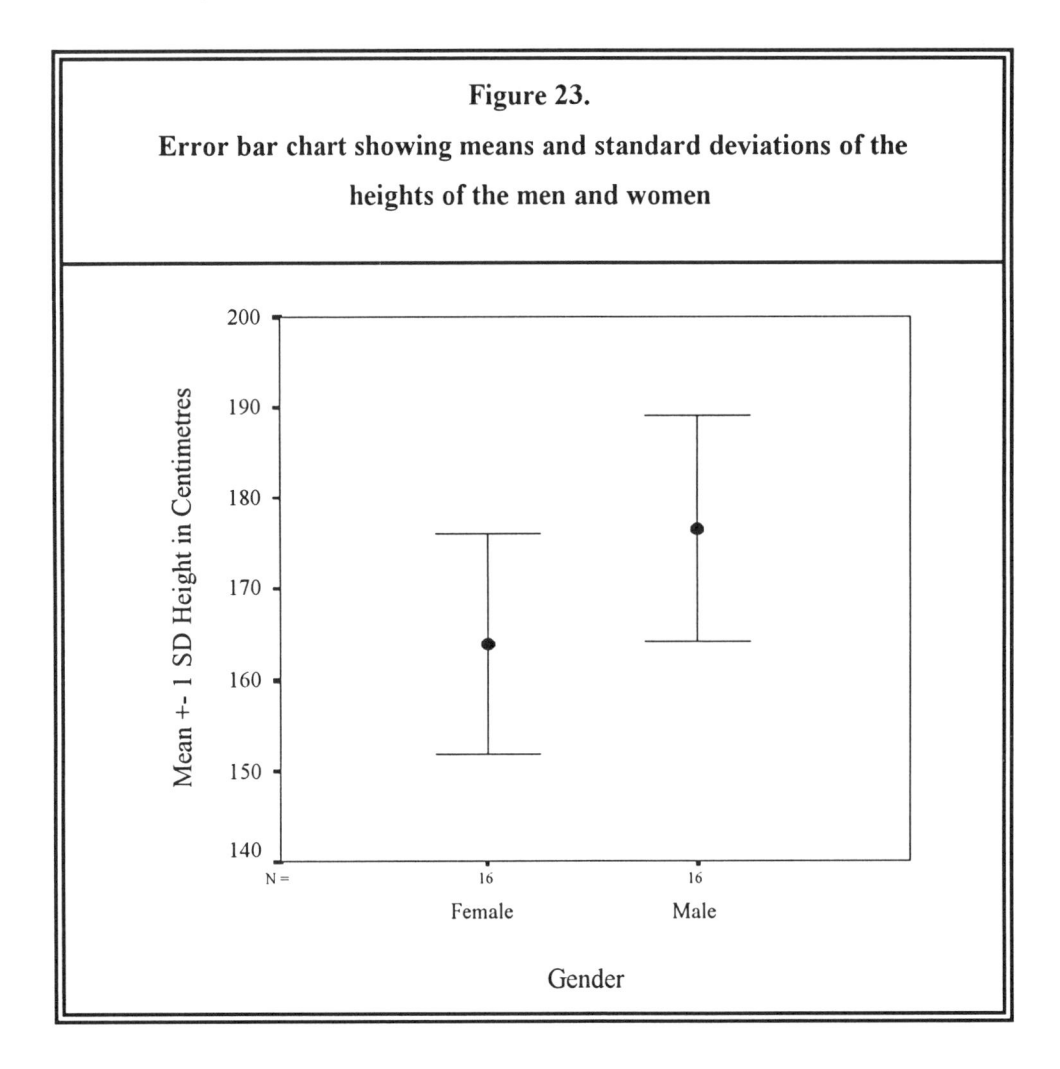

Figure 23.

Error bar chart showing means and standard deviations of the heights of the men and women

You will notice that in Figure 23, there are no lines joining the markers. This is entirely appropriate, since Female and Male are qualitatively distinct categories.

Chapter 4 - Exploring and Graphing Data

In other circumstances, however, as when the categories are ordered, it may be desirable to join up the markers with straight lines. This is easily achieved by choosing **Series/Interpolation** and selecting the appropriate command (the correct choice is obvious from the icons in the dialog box).

Producing hybrid graphical displays: Bar graphs with error bars

By appropriate choices from the menus, it is possible to produce graphs that combine features of different displays. For example, one may wish to produce a bar graph which also has error bars representing the spread of the scores around their mean for the various categories. An example of such a hybrid chart is shown in Figure 24.

The procedure is as follows:

- Obtain an error bar chart as described above.

- Click on **Edit** to obtain the **Chart Editor** menu bar. Select
  Gallery
    Mixed
      Replace

  to obtain the **Mixed Charts** dialog box, and click on **Replace**. In response to a warning that you will lose your error bar chart if you proceed, click on **Yes**. You are now in the **Bar/Line/Area Displayed Data** dialog box.

- In the **Display box**, you will see highlighted, **M + 1 SD Height in Centimetres** (in this example, we are using the variable *height*). In the **Series Displayed As** box below and to the left, click on the **Line** radio button. Move the highlight to **M - 1 SD Height in Centimetres** and click on the **Line** radio button again. Finally, highlight **Mean Height in Centimetres** and click on the **Bar** radio button. Click on **OK** to obtain a figure which looks like a combination of a bar graph and a line graph. This, however, is only an intermediate stage.

- Choose
  Series
    Interpolation

  to obtain the **Line Interpolation** dialog box. The thick black border should be around the icon labelled **None**. Click on **Apply All** and the window's close box to obtain the next intermediate figure, which is a bar graph with two points along the vertical axis of each bar.

- Choose
  Chart
    Options

  to obtain the **Bar/Line/Area Options** dialog box. In the **Line Options** box, select the **Connect markers within categories** check box and click on **OK** to produce the **bar chart with error bars**. At this stage, perhaps with a view to printing in black and white, you might wish to change the colouring of the bars to grey and the lines and markers to black.

Chapter 4 - Exploring and Graphing Data

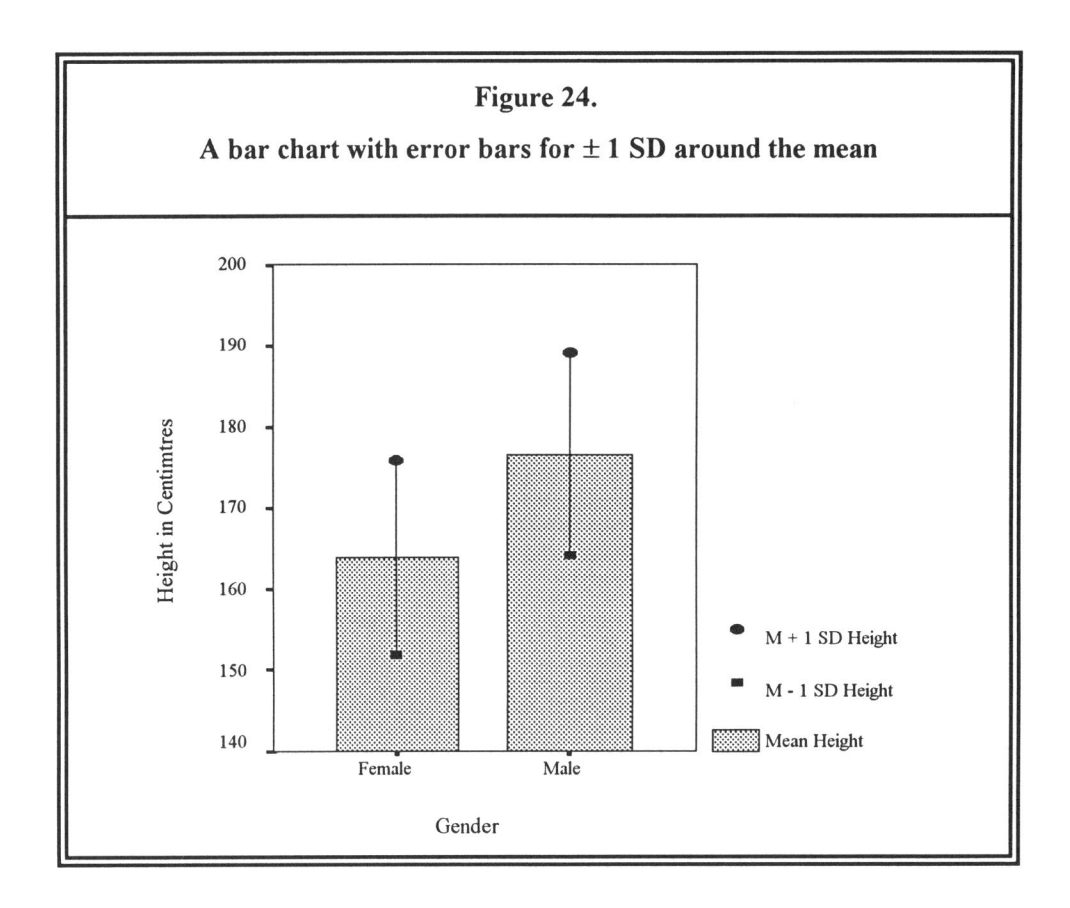

Figure 24.

A bar chart with error bars for ± 1 SD around the mean

Other graphs: Pie charts

The **pie-chart** provides a picturesque display of the frequency distribution of a qualitative variable.

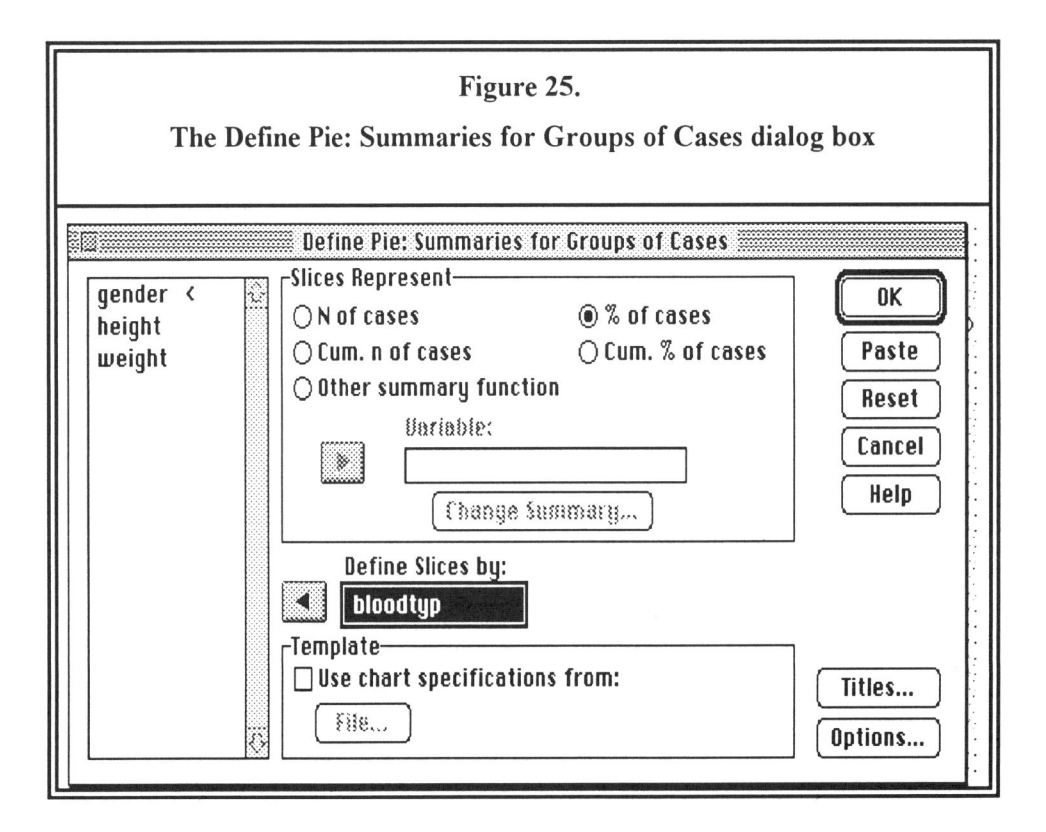

Figure 25.

The Define Pie: Summaries for Groups of Cases dialog box

Chapter 4 - Exploring and Graphing Data

To draw a pie chart of the categories within *bloodtyp*:

- Choose
  Graphs
  Pie

  to open the **Pie Charts** dialog box (not reproduced here).

- Click on **Define** to open the **Define Pie: Summaries for Groups of Cases** dialog box (the completed version is shown in Figure 25).

- Click on *bloodtyp* and on ▶ to paste the name into the **Define Slices by** box.

- Click on **% of cases** so that the slices represent percentages rather than the values of N.

- Finally, it is desirable to have a title: click on **Titles** and type the desired title into the box (e.g. *Blood Group Distribution*), click **Continue** and then **OK** to draw the pie-chart, which is reproduced in Figure 26.

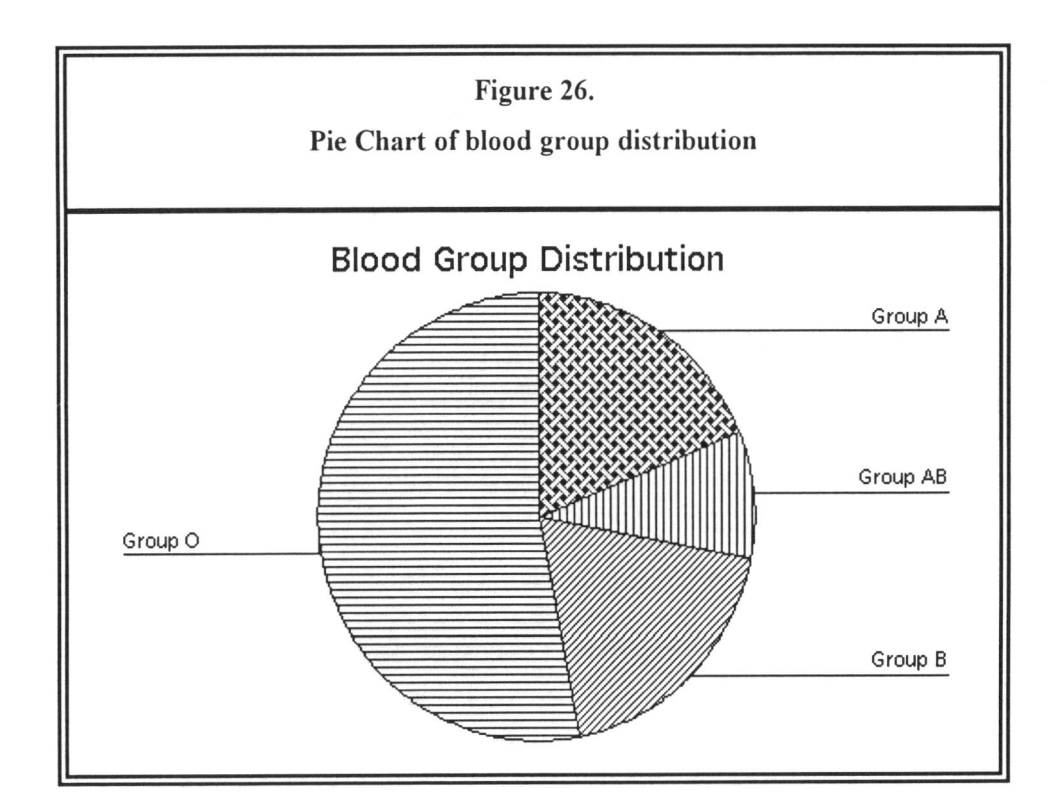

Figure 26.

Pie Chart of blood group distribution

Blood Group Distribution

(Pie chart showing Group A, Group AB, Group B, Group O)

Line graphs

Suppose that in the data set we have been studying, the total range of the heights of the participants were to be divided into the class intervals <155, 156-165, 166-175, 176-185, >185, and that these intervals were to be assigned the ordered category labels 1, 2, ..., 5, respectively. The ordering of these categories is not, of course, arbitrary, because height is a quantitative variable. The creation of a new variable *hghtcat*, containing the height categories of the participants is easily achieved by using the **Recode** command (see below). The key to the code can be supplied by using **Define Variable/Labels**.

Chapter 4 - Exploring and Graphing Data

The distribution of the quantitative variable height can be graphed by means of a histogram. An alternative, however, is the **line graph**, in which the frequency of observations falling within each class interval is plotted as a point above the mid-point of the interval, and the points are joined with straight lines.

A line graph is obtained by choosing
Graphs
    Line

and completing the **Line Charts** (Choose **Simple** and click on **Define**) and the **Define Simple Line: Summaries for Groups of Cases** dialog boxes. Figure 27 shows the completed dialog box for a line graph of mean *weight* against *hghtcat* (height category).

Figure 27.

Completed Define Simple Line: Summaries for Groups of Cases dialog box

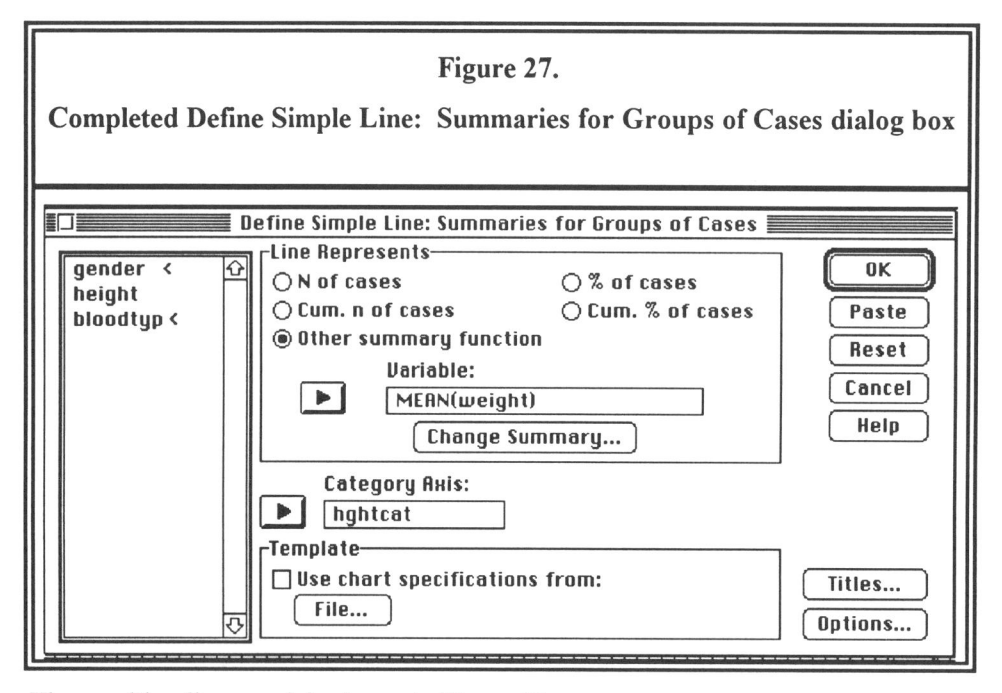

The resulting line graph is shown in Figure 28.

Figure 28.

Line graph showing the plot of mean weight against height category.

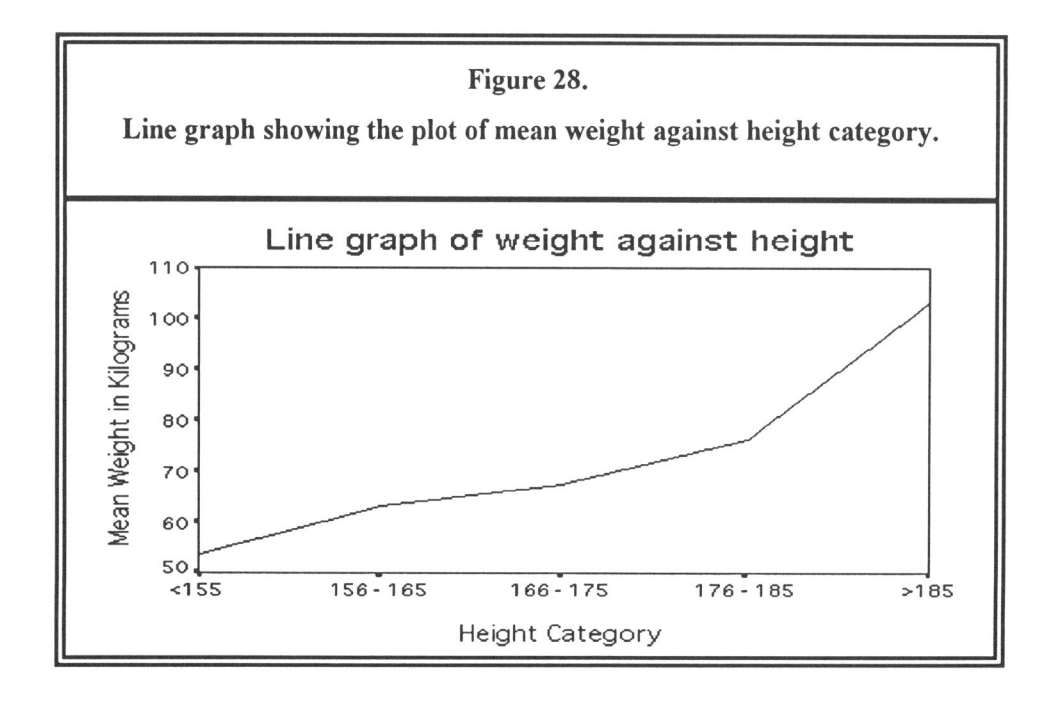

106

Chapter 4 - Exploring and Graphing Data

Scatterplot

The scatterplot depicts the bivariate distribution of two quantitative variables and should always be examined before calculating a correlation coefficient (Chapter 11) or conducting a regression analysis (Chapter 12). To obtain the scatterplot of *weight* against *height*, choose

Graphs
     Scatter

to open the **Scatterplot** dialog box (not reproduced here). Click on **Define** to open the **Simple Scatterplot** dialog box (the completed version is shown in Figure 29).

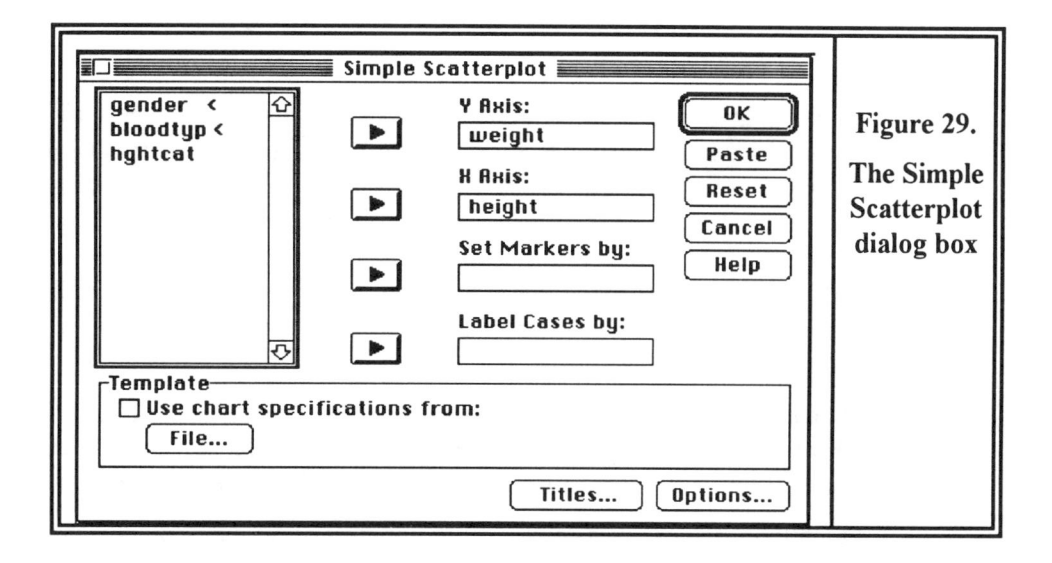

Figure 29. The Simple Scatterplot dialog box

Enter *height* into the **X Axis** box and *weight* into the **Y Axis** box by clicking on each variable name and then on the corresponding ▶ button. Click on **OK** to execute the plot, which is shown in Figure 30.

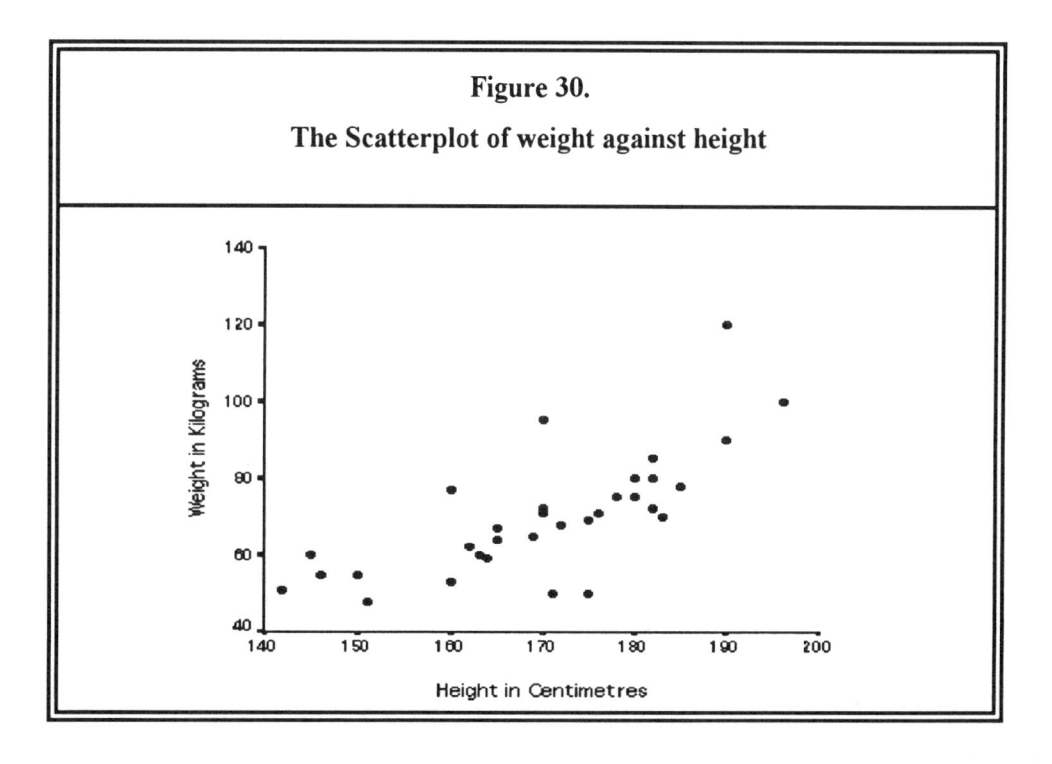

Figure 30.

The Scatterplot of weight against height

107

Chapter 4 - Exploring and Graphing Data

Further examples of scatterplots (e.g. plotting bivariate data subdivided by a grouping variable such as sex; adding regression lines to the plots) will be considered in Chapters 11 and 12.

4.4 MANIPULATION OF THE DATA SET

4.4.1 Reducing and transforming data

After a data set has been entered into SPSS, it may be necessary to modify it in certain ways. For example, an exploratory data analysis may have revealed that atypical scores, or **outliers**, have exerted undue influence, or **leverage**, upon the values of statistics such as the mean and standard deviation. One approach to this problem is to remove the outliers and repeat the analysis with the remaining scores, on the grounds that it is better to have statistics that describe 95% of the data well than 100% of them badly. Cases can be dropped from the analysis by using **Select Cases** (Chapter 3).

Sometimes it is necessary to **transform** the values of a variable in order to satisfy the distribution requirements for the use of a particular statistic. Transformations such as the square root or the logarithm, are easily made with **Compute**.

Finally, it is sometimes convenient to combine or alter the categories that make up a variable. This is achieved with the **Recode** procedure, which can construct a new variable with the new category assignments.

4.4.2 The COMPUTE procedure

The **Compute** procedure is used to transform the values of a variable to, say, their logarithms, or their square roots. The most commonly used transformation functions are:

    LG10   logarithm to the base 10

    SQRT   square root

    ABS   absolute value

The transformed values can either replace the existing values in a variable column (dangerous) or form a new variable in another column (much safer). Suppose, for example, that in the data set we have been using we want to look at the distribution not of height but of the square root of height.

- Choose
Transform
    Compute
to open the **Compute Variable** dialog box (Figure 31).

Chapter 4 - Exploring and Graphing Data

Figure 31.
The Compute Variable dialog box

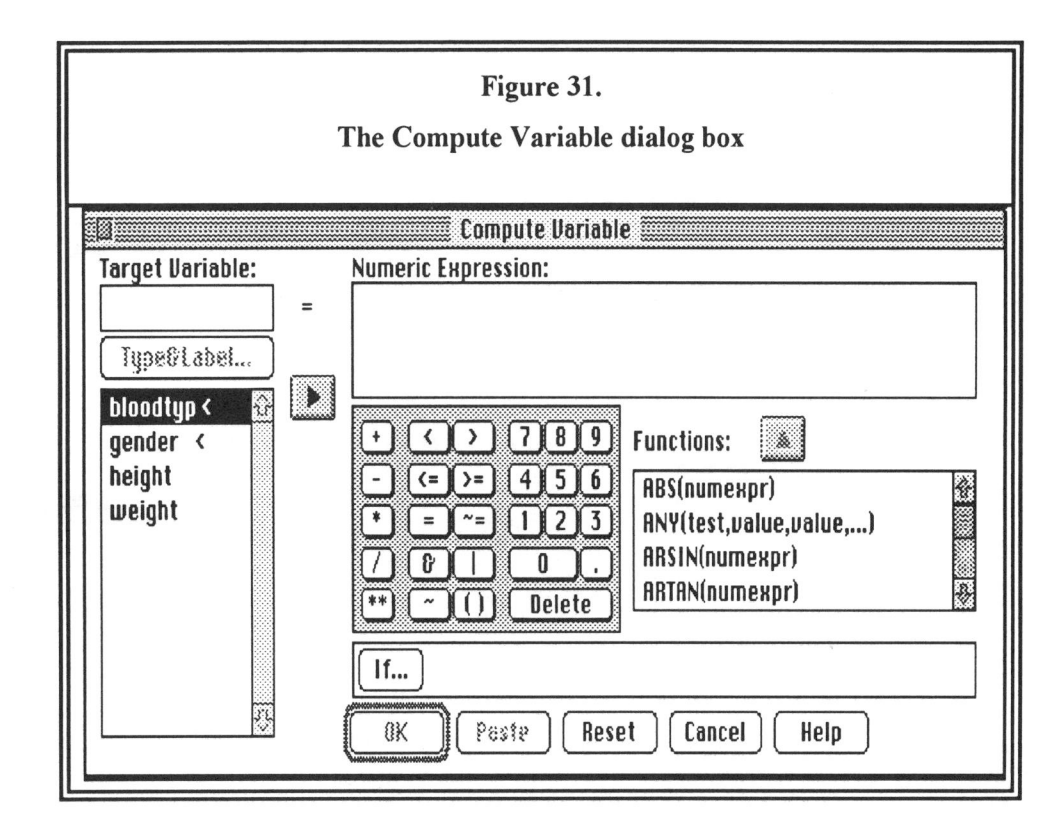

- In the lower left hand text box will appear the names of the four variables in the data set: *height*, *weight*, *gender* and *bloodtyp*. Click in the **Target Variable** box at top left to locate control there and type in the name of the new variable, *roothght*.

- Next, scroll down through the **Function** box on the right to find the square root function. Click on **SQRT[numexpr]** and then ▲ to paste it into the **Numeric Expression** box where it will appear as **SQRT[?]**.

- Click on *height* and ▶ to make this variable the argument of the square root function (i.e. replacing ?). The expression **SQRT[height]** will now appear in the **Numeric Expression** box. The final pattern of the dialog box is shown in Figure 32.

- Click on **OK** to run the procedure.

A new column *roothght*, containing the square roots of the values of *height*, will appear in the **Data Editor** window. (It may be necessary to change **Variable Type** to show decimals - see Chapter 3.)

Compute can also be used to combine values of variables. For example, the procedure can compute a new variable *meanval* from the equation *meanval = (french + german + spanish)/3*, which sums the three scores and divides by three; if any value is missing, a system-missing result is recorded. Alternatively, the function *mean* can be used (e.g. *meanval = mean (french, german, spanish)*). *Mean* computes the mean of the valid values; the result is recorded as missing only if all three scores are absent.

Finally, conditional computations can be commanded by clicking on the **If** button in the **Compute Variable** dialog box and then clicking on **Include if case satisfies the condition**. A conditional statement, such as the one in Figure 33, can then be compiled within the box.

Chapter 4 - Exploring and Graphing Data

Figure 32.

The completed Compute Variable dialog box

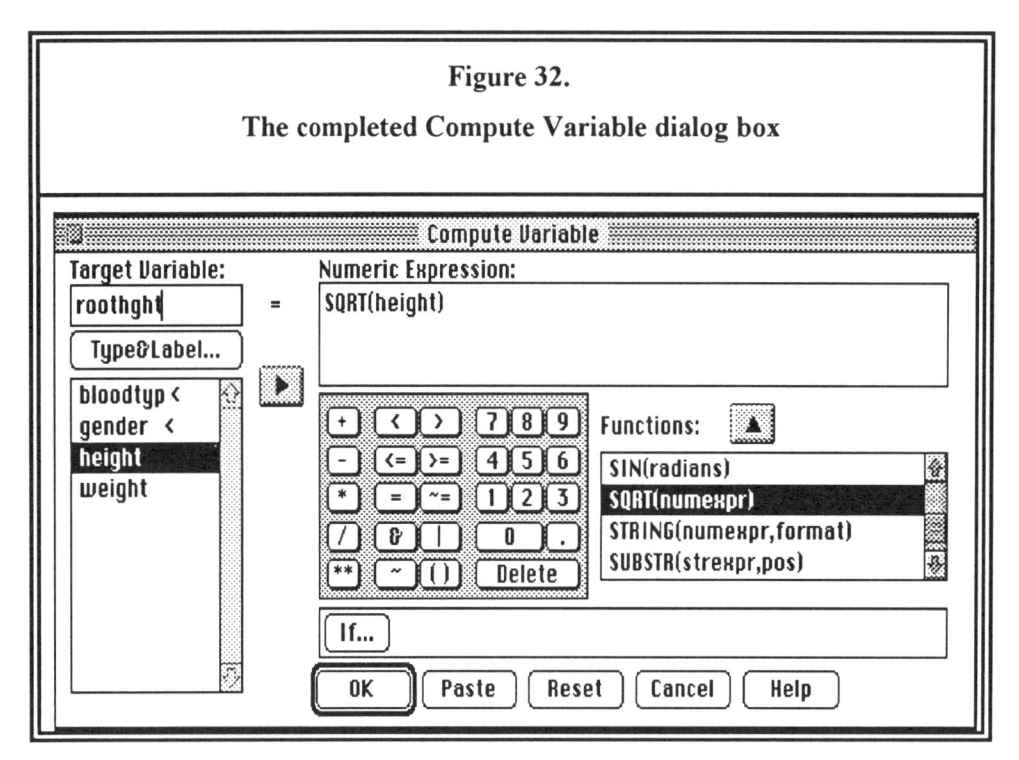

Click on **Continue** to return to the **Compute Variable** dialog box where, for example, the **Target Variable** might be nominated as *group* and the **Numeric Expression** as *1*. This would then have the effect of categorising all males with bloodgroup AB into value *1* of the variable *group*. Other values for *group* could be assigned by specifying other combinations of *gender* and *bloodtyp*.

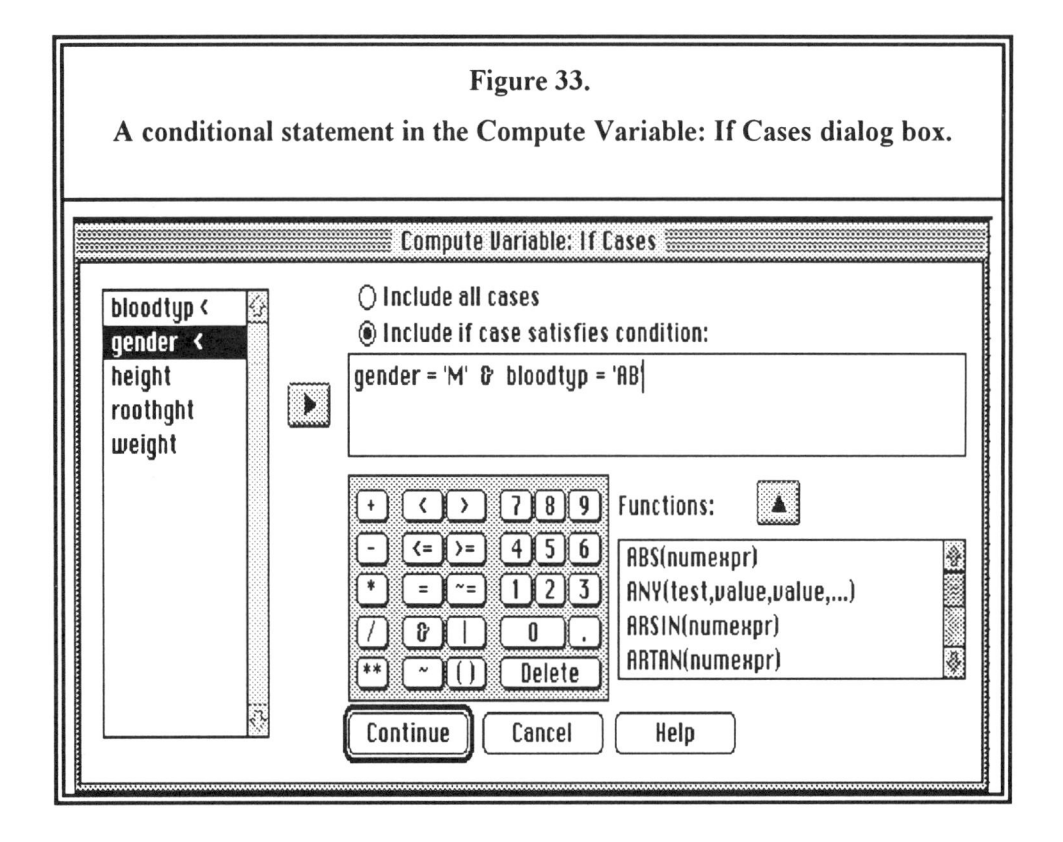

Figure 33.

A conditional statement in the Compute Variable: If Cases dialog box.

Chapter 4 - Exploring and Graphing Data

4.4.3 The RECODE procedure

We have seen that the **Compute** procedure operates upon one or more of the variables in the data set, so that there will be as many values in the transformed variable as there were in the original variable. Sometimes, however, the user, rather than wanting a transformation that will convert all the values of a variable systematically, may want to assign relatively few code numbers to values that fall within specified ranges of the variable.

For example, suppose we have a set of 20 children's examination marks on a scale from 0 to 100 (Table 1). If the pass mark is 50, it may be convenient to recode each child's mark into a Pass (P) or a Fail (F). This can easily be done by using the **Recode** command.

We suggest you enter these data into the SPSS Data Editor in a single variable named *marks* and try the recoding procedure as follows.

- Choose
  Transform
      Recode

  and click on **Into Different Variables** to open the **Recode into Different Variables** dialog box (Figure 35). Just as in the case of **Compute**, it is possible to change the values to the recoded values within the same variable; but we recommend storing the recoded values in a new variable, perhaps *passfail*.

Table 1.
Children's Examination Marks

Child	Mark	Child	Mark
s1	81	s11	62
s2	78	s12	51
s3	71	s13	50
s4	70	s14	50
s5	70	s15	42
s6	68	s16	40
s7	68	s17	40
s8	65	s18	40
s9	63	s19	38
s10	62	s20	30

Chapter 4 - Exploring and Graphing Data

Figure 35.
The Recode into Different Variables dialog box

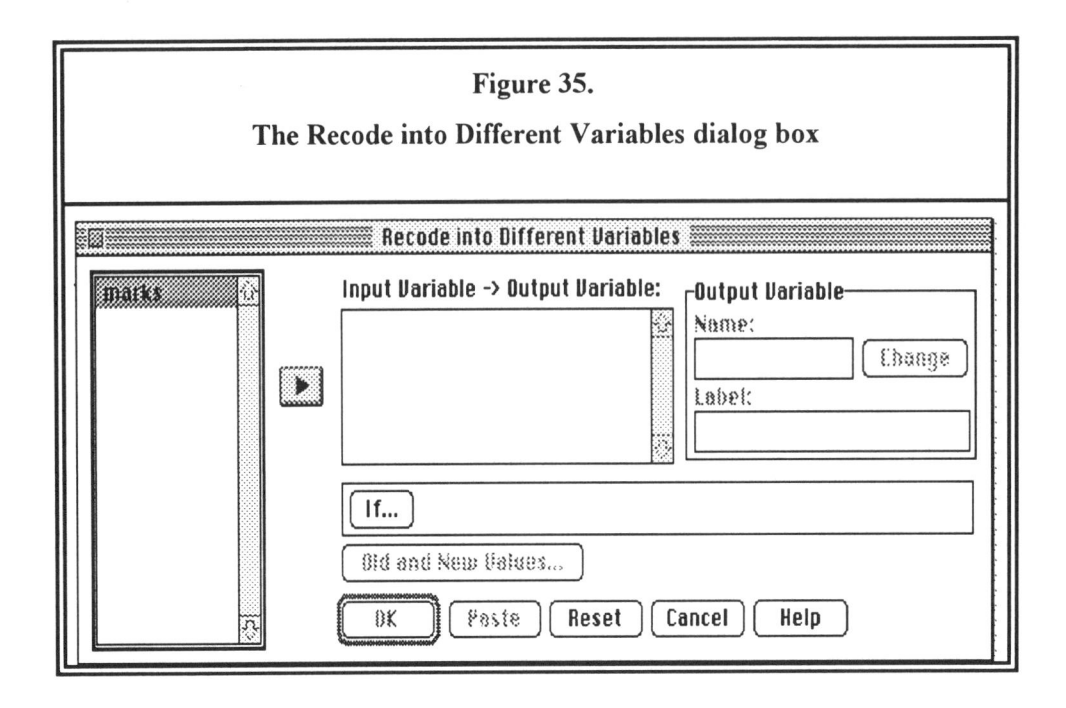

- Click on *marks* and on ▶ to paste the name into the **Numeric Variable -> Output Variable** box.

- Type the name of the output variable *passfail* into the **Name** box and click **Change** to insert the name into the **Numeric Variable -> Output Variable** box.

- Click on the **Old and New Values** box to open the **Recode into Different Variables: Old and New Values** dialog box (the partly completed dialog box is shown in Figure 36).

Figure 36.
The Recode into Different Variables: Old and New Values dialog box

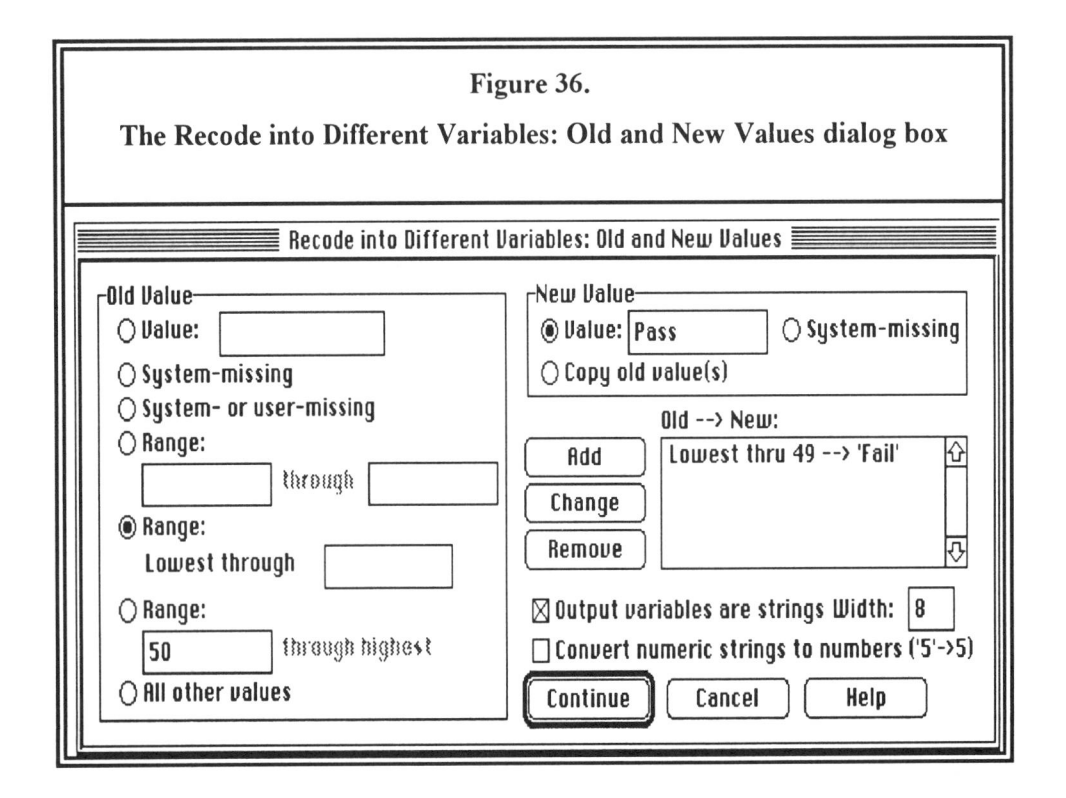

Chapter 4 - Exploring and Graphing Data

- Activate the radio button opposite the range: **Lowest through** ☐. Enter the number 49 in the box. Mark the checkbox captioned **Output Variables are Strings**. In the **Value** box, type *Fail* and click on **Add**. In the box will appear: **Lowest thru 49→ 'Fail'**.

- Activate the radio button opposite the range: ☐ **through highest**. Type *50* in the box (as shown in Figure 36). In the Value box type *Pass* and click on Add. In the box will appear: **50 thru Highest → 'Pass'**. Notice that the word **through** includes the specified value either before or after the word. Thus this procedure will categorise all exam marks less than 50 as *Fail* and all those of 50 and above as *Pass*.

- Click on **Continue** and then on **OK** to run the procedure.

A new column, headed *passfail* and containing the recoded values, will appear in the **Data Editor** window (Figure 37).

	marks	passfail
10	62	Pass
11	51	Pass
12	50	Pass
13	50	Pass
14	42	Fail
15	40	Fail
16	40	Fail
17	40	Fail
18	38	Fail
19	32	Fail
20	30	Fail

Figure 37.
Part of the Data Editor showing the new variable *passfail*.

If a variable has non-integer values (e.g. height in metres), great care has to be taken in recoding the values into ranges such as tall, medium and short. For example, if short is to be defined as less than 1.6 metres, medium as 1.6 to 1.8 metres, and tall as more than 1.8 metres, then the ranges should be set within the **Recode** dialog box as follows:

```
Lowest thru 1.5999 -> 'Short'
1.6 thru 1.8 -> 'Medium'
1.8001 thru Highest -> 'Tall'
```

Chapter 4 - Exploring and Graphing Data

EXERCISE 4

EXPLORATORY DATA ANALYSIS (EDA)

This exercise explores the data in your saved file of merged data, consisting of the responses of 345 people (including yourself) to a questionnaire. To begin this exercise, open this data file in the usual way. We shall refer to the file as *mergerdata*.

Describing categorial data: Obtaining a frequency distribution

Use the **Frequencies** procedure described in **4.3.1** to obtain a frequency listing for the variable *smoker* in the Output window, remembering to click on the **Charts...** box in order to be able to select **Bar Chart(s)** within the **Frequencies: Charts** dialog box.

Inspect the frequency table. Is it what you expected? Before taking any steps to remedy the situation, inspect the bar chart in the **Chart Carousel.**

The bar chart

Charts always appear in the **Chart Carousel** window. You will notice immediately that, although the variable *smoker* was supposed to consist only of Y and N responses, the horizontal axis of the bar chart implies that the entries included two extra categories: T and a dot. To investigate such a mishap, transfer to the output listing window by selecting

Window
>!untitled output 1

to obtain the output listing. There you will find a table informing you that, as far as the variable smoker is concerned, in the 335 cases that were processed, there was one T entry and one missing value (indicated by the full stop). Move back into the Data Editor by selecting

Window
>**mergerdata**

There, notice that the observation for the 11th case is missing, and that for the 15th case, a T has been entered. It is obvious that the T entry should have been Y, since he is recorded as smoking 5 cigarettes per day. Such mistakes are common when one is preparing large data sets. The T response is beside Y on the computer's keyboard; moreover, the response T is semantically similar to Y. It is also very easy to press Return without actually keying in a datum. Such transcription errors can be avoided by carefully checking the data set as we are doing in this exercise.

To remedy the false T entry, simply change the T to a Y in the Data Editor.

Handling missing values

It is more satisfactory to enter a specially defined code or value for a missing datum rather than leave the cell blank. In this way you can be sure that you have not simply overlooked the cell when entering the data. When a code for a missing value is declared, SPSS ignores it when drawing a bar chart. Follow the procedure described in Section 3.3 to define 999 as a missing value. Go to the cell containing the dot and replace that entry with 999.

You may prefer to indicate the presence of missing values in the data set by arranging to have the word 'missing' appear in the appropriate cells. In that case, select

Chapter 4 - Exploring and Graphing Data

Define Variable
   Labels ..
to define the value 999 as 'missing'. Then select
Utilities
   Value labels
This command will cause the word 'missing' to appear in the cells with missing values. (This will only work if there is a tick beside Value Labels indicating that this option has been activated.)
Save the corrected data file, using the **Save Data** item within the **File** drop-down menu.
Now re-run the **Frequencies** command, but cancel the **Bar Chart** option. Notice the difference in the listing table. The message is that EDA is useful for detecting any false data before more extensive statistical analyses are conducted.

Obtaining a bar chart from the Graphs drop-down menu

You can obtain a bar chart directly, without any additional statistics, by selecting
Graphs
   Bar ...
to obtain the **Bar Charts** dialog box. You will find that the default settings are **Simple** and **Summaries for Groups of Cases**. This is quite correct for present purposes.
Click on **Define** to open the **Define Simple Bar: Summaries for Groups of Cases** dialog box. Check that in the **Bars Represent** box the **N of cases** option is selected, and then enter the variable name *smoker* into the **Category Axis** box. To prevent the missing cases from appearing as an unwanted category on the horizontal axis of the graph, click on **Options** and deselect **Display groups defined by missing values**. Click on **Continue** to return to the main dialog box. Click on **OK** to obtain the bar chart, which will appear in the Carousel window.

Editing a bar chart

Initially boxplots (and other graphics) will appear in colour on the screen of your Mac. Such a screen image, however, does not print well in black-and-white. To make the image suitable for balck-and-white printing, some editing will be necessary. Proceed as follows.
Click on the Edit box. To edit any part of the figure, you must select that part of the screen figure. Highlight the bars by clicking on one of them so that each corner has little black squares.
Click on the **Attributes** menu. The boxes on the right will show the default settings for the colours, borders and fill patterns that were used for the screen image. Change the fill colour by clicking-and-dragging the screen pointer into the **Fill Color** box and selecting black. Do not be alarmed when the bars turn black!
Click on the **Attributes** menu once again and drag the screen pointer into the **Fill Pattern** box to select an attractive black-and-white fill pattern.
After completing the change of pattern, click anywhere in the Chart window to turn off the bar highlighting. It is possible to control many other features of charts and graphs by using the Chart Editor. For example, by double-clicking on an axis, a dialog box will appear enabling you to label the axis and position the label either centrally or to right or left. There are many other adjustments that can be made; but the way forward is to try it yourself.
It is also possible to alter other aspects of the screen figure, such as the aspect ratio, and the spacing of bars and boxes in graphs. All this can be done while you are in the Chart Editor. The **aspect ratio** (the height of a graph divided by its width) is controlled by the **Graphics ...** option within the **Preferences** dialog box:
Click on
Edit
   Preferences

to open the **Preferences** dialog box.

Click on the **Graphics ...** box to bring the **Preferences: Graphics** dialog box into view.

The default setting for the Chart Aspect Ratio is at **Best for Display (1.67).** Notice that the recommended setting for the printer is 1.25, as shown by the line **Best for printer (1.25).** To improve the appearance of bars and boxes in SPSS graphs, it is well worth experimenting with aspect ratios such as 1 by clicking on the radio button for **Custom**, inserting 1 in the box, and then clicking on **Continue** and **OK**.

The spacing of the bars is controlled by the Bar Spacing option within the Chart menu. There are two aspects of bar spacing:

(1) the Inter-Bar Spacing (expressed as a percentage of bar width, and which can vary from 0% to 100%);
(2) the Bar Margin, which is the distance of the outermost bars from the inner frame, an invisible rectangle with the horizontal and vertical axes of the graph as two of its sides.

Increasing the bar margin will make the bars narrower, since the inter-bar spacing has been fixed at a specified relative value. It is recommended that the reader experiment with varying combinations of aspect ratio, bar margin and inter-bar spacing.

To save your edited chart select

File
> **Save As ...**

to obtain a directory dialog box with **Save this chart as** written beside the text box at the bottom.

Use the pop-up menu at the top and the icons on the right to choose a suitable target storage location for the bar chart. Type a suitable name into the **Save this chart as** textbox. Note that there is a new folder icon on the right, clicking on which enables you to store the graph inside. You might wish to try that.

Try printing out your chart, following the instructions in Chapter 3, Section 3.6.

Describing categorial data: crosstabulation

Next we are going to produce some contingency tables, using the **Crosstabs** procedure (Section 4.3.1). A **Crosstabulation** is a table showing the frequency of observations in each combination of two categorial variables. Here we shall crosstabulate the *sex* and *faculty* of the cases in our merged data set.

Choose

Statistics
> **Summarize**
>> **Crosstabs**

to open the **Crosstabs** dialog box.

Enter one of the variables into the **Row(s)** box by clicking on its name and then on ▶. Enter the other variable into the **Column(s)** box. Click on **OK**.

To save the crosstabulation output, first edit out the unnecessary parts, retaining only the table itself. Then select **Save**, and complete the dialog box. (When you quit SPSS, you will be given this option anyway.) When you double-click on the saved document, the edited contents of the output window will reappear; but the original data set will not appear in the Data Editor. Further editing of the material in the output window can be carried out and the amended version saved in the usual way.

You can print out a selection from the output window by highlighting it and choosing

File
> **Print Selection**

Chapter 4 - Exploring and Graphing Data

FINISHING THE SESSION

Close down SPSS and any other windows before logging out of the computer.

EXERCISE 5

EDA (continued)

For this exercise, you should have available the merged data set that you corrected in the course of the previous exercise.

Describing interval data

Use the **Frequencies** procedure outlined in Section 4.3.2 to obtain a histogram with a superimposed normal curve and a table showing the mean, standard deviation and quartiles for *age*. Select the same options as in the **Frequencies: Statistics** dialog box in Section 4.3.2. Remember to ensure that the **Display frequency tables** box is turned off. Save both the histogram and the output listing.

- **Edit the histogram to make it suitable for black-and-white printing**
- **Print the histogram**.

Manipulation of the data set - transforming variables

It is sometimes useful to change the data set in some way. For instance, in the current data set, some people have entered their weight in stones and pounds, and others in kilograms. Likewise, height has been entered both in British units (feet and inches) and in metres. In order to be able to produce useful data on weight and height, we must use the same units of measurement.
In this exercise we shall adopt metric units (kilograms and metres). Thus we must convert any other measurements into metric measurements.
Use the **Compute** procedure (Section 4.4.2). Select
Transform
    Compute ...
to obtain the **Compute Variable** dialog box. In the **Target Variable** box, type the name of the variable (*kilos*) which contains the kilograms data In the **Numeric Expression** box, enter the conversion factor. Thus you will enter (**stones*14 + pounds) * 0.453** to convert pounds to kilograms using the conversion factor that 1 pound is 0.453 kilograms and remembering to convert stones to pounds by multiplying by 14. Note that in computing, the symbol * is used for multiplication. There remains one further problem: what about cases whose weight is already in *kilos* and do not have any values in the *stones* and *pounds* variables? If the formula above were to be immediately applied, these people would end up with no values in the *kilos* column. Therefore to convert only the cases with stones and pounds measurements, you must select the **If** box in the **Compute Variable** dialog box, then the **Include if case satisfies condition** box and enter the following expression **stones > 0** which tells the program to calculate the kilograms if the entry in *stones* is greater than 0 (we assume that no-

Chapter 4 - Exploring and Graphing Data

one has a weight of less than 1 stone!). Select **Continue** and then **OK.** You will see a message which asks **Change existing variable?**. Select the **OK** option. Now the program will calculate all the missing *kilos* data and enter them in the data set. Check that it has done this.

(It is often regarded as a safer procedure to recode data into a new variable since it allows one to check that the correct recoding procedure has been requested. We have not done that here, because we wanted to preserve the values already present for some cases in *kilos*.)

Save the file, but use the **Save As** option for this, giving the amended file a new name (e.g. *metric data*). This ensures that you still have a copy of the old file, in case you have made any mistakes in calculation and you wish to retrieve the old data at some future time.

Now do a similar conversion for the height data, converting feet and inches to metres. To do this you will need to know that 1 inch is 0.0254 metres. Work out a conversion factor with this in mind. Remember to change the condition to **feet >0**. When you have converted the height data, save the file again.

Describing interval data - means of cases categorised by a grouping variable

We can obtain a table of means for one variable at different categories (or combinations) of another variable (or variables).

Use the **Means** procedure described in Section 4.3.2 to obtain a two-way table of means for *metres* by *sex*. Then use the same procedure to obtain a three-way table of *kilos* by *sex* by *faculty*. (Look carefully at Section 4.3.2 to see how to layer the variables, using the **Next** facility, to produce the three-way table).

- **Print the listing output of this exercise.**

FINISHING THE SESSION

Close down SPSS and any other windows before logging out of the computer.

EXERCISE 6

MORE CHARTS AND GRAPHS

BEFORE YOU START

This exercise shows you how to request various charts and graphs. Restore the data file saved in the previous exercise to the Data Editor window.

Chapter 4 - Exploring and Graphing Data

CHARTS AND GRAPHS

Stem-and-leaf plot and boxplot

It is often useful to present data in a graphical form, which is easily read and conveys the information quickly and effectively. Use the **Explore** procedure (Section 4.3.2) to produce stem-and-leaf plots and boxplots of *metres* categorised by *sex*.

The **stem-and-leaf plot** provides more information about the original data than does a histogram. As in a histogram, the length of each row corresponds to the number of cases that fall into a particular interval. However, the stem-and-leaf plot represents each case with a numeric value that corresponds to the actual observed value. This is done by dividing observed values into two components - the leading digit or digits, called the **stem**, and a trailing digit, called the **leaf**. For example, the value 64 would have a stem of 6 and a leaf of 4. In the case of heights in metres, the stems are the metres expressed to the first decimal place, the leaves are the second decimal place. Thus the modal height (i.e. the most frequent height) for males is shown with a stem of 17 (1.7 metres), the leaves being the second decimal place. The * and . after the stem are used in some stem-and-leaf plots to split the leaves into two sections: the * row includes the leaves from 0 to 4; the . row includes the leaves from 5 to 9. In other plots, the leaves are broken down into * (noughts and ones), t (twos and threes), f (fours and fives), s (sixes and sevens), and . (eights and nines).

The **boxplot** is another type of display, which is more fully explained in Section 4.3.2. The main box spans 50% of the cases (those between the upper and lower quartiles) and the extensions (**whiskers**) cover the remaining cases, provided they are not deemed to be outliers (shown as o's) or extremes (shown as asterisks).

- **Prepare the boxplot for printing in black-and-white, and print the output listing.**

Within the female group, which stem contains the most leaves?
Examine the boxplot for males and note the case numbers of the outliers so that you can check their actual heights in the data set. There is a procedure for locating a specific case in the data set. Select
Data
    Go to case ...
to obtain the **Go to Case** dialog box. You then enter the required case number and click on **OK**.

- **Write down the actual heights of the males denoted by the outliers on the box plots.**

Bar charts

Draw a bar chart of *kilos* and *metres* by *sex* using the **Bar** option within the **Graphs** drop-down menu. Choose
Graphs
    Bar
        Clustered
and select the radio button for **Summaries of Separate Variables** in the **Data in Chart Are** box.
Click on **Define** and then enter *kilos* and *metres* into the **Bars Represent** box and *sex* into the **Category Axis** box.

- **Study the chart produced. Does this seem a sensible graphic representation of the two variables? If not, why not? You do not need to print the chart, but make a note of why the representation is not appropriate and what would be a better way of displaying the mean heights and weights of subjects split by sex.**

The moral behind this is that you must always consider what your output is likely to be. SPSS will produce the graph that you ask for, but the end result may not be a sensible representation of the data. It is best to draw by hand a rough representation of what you expect the graph to look like before requesting SPSS to do so.

Transposing data on a graph or chart

It is possible to transpose data on graphs and charts which have more than one variable or factor plotted so that the lines or bars are replotted in a transposed manner. This will become clearer with an example.

Plot a new bar chart of the mean number of cigarettes smoked (*npday*) categorised by *sex* and by *faculty*. Do this by choosing

Graphs
    Bar
        Clustered

and select the radio button for **Summaries for groups of cases** in the **Data in Chart Are** box.

Click on **Define** and then click on **Other summary function** within the **Bars Represent box**. Then enter *npday* into the **Variable** box (it will appear as **MEAN(npday)**), *sex* in the **Category Axis** box, and *faculty* in the **Define Clusters by** box. Deselect **Display groups defined by missing values**.

You should then see in the Chart Carousel window a bar chart arranged by sex, with each cluster consisting of bars representing the three Faculties (apparently no-one in the Other category smokes). Suppose, however, that you would rather see a chart with three clusters (Faculties) of two (sex) instead of two clusters (sex) of three (Faculties). This could be done by returning to the dialog box and changing *sex* and *faculty* around, but a quicker method is to use the **Transpose Data** option within the **Series** drop-down menu. This menu becomes accessible after clicking on **Edit**. Select (while you are in the Chart Carousel window)

Edit
    Series
        Transpose Data

You will now see that the data have been transposed on the chart.

Pie chart

Another way of presenting data is in the form of a **pie chart**. Draw a pie chart (see Section 4.3.3) for *status* and give the chart a title, including your **own** name in the title (e.g. Pie Chart of Status produced by Mary Smith).

Edit the chart to show actual percentages for each slice. You can do this by selecting in the **Chart Carousel** window

Edit
    Chart
        Options
            Percents
                OK

Save the chart in the usual way.

- **Edit the chart to make it suitable for black-and-white printing. Print the pie chart.**

FINISHING THE SESSION

Close down SPSS and any other windows before logging out of the computer.

Chapter 4 - Exploring and Graphing Data

EXERCISE 7

RECODING DATA; SELECTING CASES; LINE GRAPH

RECODING DATA

Sometimes you may wish to recode values or categories within a variable (e.g. you might want to combine more than one value or category into a single new value or category). Suppose that you are not particularly interested in whether people are doing a MSc degree or a PhD degree, but just want to know whether they are postgraduates. You can change the database to give you this information, either within the original variable, *status*, or by creating a new variable containing the recoded information. In this session we are going to use a new variable, since this retains the original variable *status* for checking that the recoding has been done correctly. It also maintains the original values in the data set.

Use the **Recode** (Section 4.4.3) procedure to recode the status codes MSc Postgrad and PhD Postgrad (i.e. categories 2 and 3) into a new category 1 and the codes Undergraduate and Other (i.e. categories 1 and 4) into a new category 2. You will need to follow the section carefully. The recode procedure creates a new variable which you are asked to name: we suggest *postgrad*. To do this, you will have to choose the **Recode into Different Variables** option within the **Recode** procedure.

Choose

Transform

    Recode

        Into Different Variables

to open the **Recode into Different Variables** dialog box. Highlight *status* and click on ▶ to transfer it into the **Input Variable → Output Variable** box. Type *postgrad* in the **Name** box within the **Output Variable** box and click on **Change**. The new variable name *postgrad* will now appear alongside *status*. Click on **Old and New Values** and then fill in the corresponding values in the Value box of Old Value and in the Value box of New Value, clicking on **Add** each time. The following should then appear in the right-hand box: 1 → 2, 2 → 1, 3 → 1, 4 → 2. Finally click on **Continue** and **OK**.

When you have followed this procedure, check that you have the new variable at the far right of your data set. Double-click on the variable name *postgrad* and then click on **Labels** within the **Change Settings** box to label the new categories 1 as Yes and 2 as No. Click on **Continue** and then **OK**. To see whether this has worked, click on the **Value Labels** item within the **Utilities** drop-down menu. This will allow you to relate the new values or categories in the new variable *postgrad* to any other variable. Save the file again.

We shall now use the **Recode** procedure to recode the heights of people as tall, medium or short. Give the new variable the name *new_ht* containing the underline, not the hyphen, symbol. This is allowed in a variable name but the hyphen or a space is not.

Use the following table for recoding the heights into values (we shall attach the labels later):

Chapter 4 - Exploring and Graphing Data

Range	Value	Label
Under 1.7 metres	1	Short
Between 1.7 and 1.8 metres	2	Medium
Over 1.8 metres	3	Tall

You will need to use the **Range Lowest through** facility for short people, the **Range** facility for medium people, and the **Range through highest** facility for tall people, taking particular care to ensure that there is no ambiguity about the group into which a height will be assigned. SPSS recodes values from the smallest upwards. Thus 1.7 will be included in Short unless it is defined as **Lowest thru 1.6999**. Re-read the end of Section 4.4.3 for extra help.

Check your data to make certain that they have all been classified in the manner that you planned. Note that although you may see only two decimal places in the Data Editor, so that a value such as 1.70 may in fact be 1.7068. If the value is highlighted, the true value will appear in the Cell Editor box above the variable names.

Once the new variable *new_ht* has been created, double-click on the variable name, click on **Labels** and enter the value labels *short*, *medium* and *tall* for values 1, 2 and 3 respectively. Click on **Continue** and then on **OK**. These labels should then appear in the Data Editor window.

Pie chart

Produce a pie chart with a title showing what percentages of the cases are tall, medium or short. Edit the pie chart to show the percentage for each slice using the **Pie Options** dialog box (see Exercise 6 if you need to refresh your memory).

- **Edit the pie chart to prepare it for black-and-white printing. Print the pie chart.**

SELECT CASES

It is also useful to be able to select the cases you want to analyse. Suppose, for example, that you wished to consider only the data relating to females.

Use **Select Cases** (Section 3.7.1) to specify that only the female cases will be analysed. Remember that since *sex* is a string variable, you will need to enter F in quotes (i.e. sex='F') when filling in the **Select Cases** dialog box.

Now suppose that, since smoking is said to suppress appetite, you wanted to see whether female smokers were lighter in weight than non-smokers. Use the **Compare Means** (Section 4.3.2) procedure to do this. Remember the Dependent variable will be *kilos* and the Independent variable *smoker*.

- **Print the table produced. Note that as a result of the Select Cases procedure you have just followed, this table will apply to the female respondents only.**

- **Are there any differences between the smokers and the non-smokers? Comment briefly on any differences you find. (When you think about this, bear in mind the difference in size between the smoking and non-smoking groups)**

LINE GRAPH

A **line graph** is suitable when there is an interval or ordinal scale for one of the variables with not more than about ten values. When the scale is nominal, a bar chart is preferable. Now that we have an ordinal scale of height with three values in the variable *new_ht*, we can draw a line graph of *sex* agains *new_ht*.

First, however, the selection of females in the previous section must be reversed by returning to the **Select Cases** dialog box and clicking on the **All cases** radio button. Then choose

Graphs
> **Line**
>> **Multiple**
>>> **Summaries for groups of cases**

to open the **Define Multiple Line: Summaries for Groups of Cases** dialog box. Then insert the variable *new_ht* into the **Category Axis** box and *sex* into the **Define Lines by** box. Click on **Options** and deselect **Display groups defined by missing values**. Click on **Continue** and then **OK** to plot the lines. A two-line graph should then appear, one line for M and one line for F, with the points on the abscissa labelled Short, Medium and Tall.

In order to differentiate the sexes clearly in the printed graph, change one of the lines to a discontinuous line using the editing facility (see Section 4.3.3). Click on the **Edit** box, then click on the selected line to highlight it. From the **Attributes** menu, change the line style from continuous to dotted. Prepare the graph for black-and-white printing by entering the **Attributes** menu and changing the fill colour to black. You may also wish to show the markers for the different categories, in which case, enter the **Series** menu, choose **Interpolation ...** and check the **Display Markers** box. Although there is an **Apply** button, it may be necessary simply to close the dialog box to get back to the line graph in the Carousel window. You will then need to enter the **Attributes** menu to change the colour of the markers to black.

Save the chart in the usual way.

- **Print out the line graph.**

FINISHING THE SESSION

Close down SPSS and any other windows before logging out of the computer.

EXERCISE 8

THE ANALYSIS OF NOMINAL DATA

BEFORE YOU START

Before proceeding with this practical, we strongly recommend you to read Sections 5.3.4 (Nominal data) and 5.4 (One-sample tests) in this Chapter, and Section 11.3.2 (Measures of association strength for categorial data) in Chapter 11.

GOODNESS-OF-FIT

Some nominal data on one qualitative variable

Suppose that a researcher, interested in children's preferences, suspects a spatial response bias towards the right hand side. Thirty children enter a room containing three identically-marked doors: one to the right; another to the left; and a third straight ahead. They are told they can go through any of the three doors. Their choices are shown in Table 1.

Table 1.
The choices of one of three exit doors by thirty children

Door		
Left	Middle	Right
5	8	17

It looks as if there is indeed a preference for the rightmost door, at least among the children sampled. Had the children been choosing at random, we should have expected about 10 in each category: that is, the theoretical, or expected distribution (E), of the tallies is a **uniform** one. The observed frequencies (O), on the other hand, have a distribution which is far from uniform.

Pearson's chi-square test can be used to test the goodness-of-fit of the expected to the observed distribution. Its rationale is lucidly discussed in any good statistics textbook (e.g. Howell, 1997). Here, we shall merely describe the SPSS procedure.

Procedure for the chi-square test of goodness-of-fit

Prepare the SPSS data set by proceeding as follows:

Define the variable *position* for the three positional categories and a second variable *freq* for the numbers of children in the different categories. Use the **Labels** procedure to assign the code numbers *1*, *2* and *3* to the *position* categories *Left*, *Centre* and *Right*, respectively.

Run the Weight Cases procedure

To ensure that SPSS treats the entries in *freq* as frequencies rather than scores, follow the procedure described in Section 3.12.2.
To obtain the correct dialog box, select

Statistics
> **Nonparametric Tests**
>> **Chi-Square**

to open the **Chi-Square Test** dialog box. Click on *position* (not on *freq*) and on ▶ to transfer *position* to the **Test Variable List** box. Click on **OK** to run the test.

- Write down the value of the chi-square statistic and its p-value. Does the test show significance, i.e. is the p-value sufficiently small to constitute evidence against the null hypothesis? Write down the implications for the experimenter's research hypothesis.

Running the goodness-of-fit test on a set of raw data

When the researcher carried out the experiment, the door that each child chose was noted at the time. In terms of the code numbers, their choices might have been:

1 1 3 2 1 1 3 3 3, ..., and so on.

If the user defines the variable *position*, and enters the 30 (coded) choices that the children made, the chi-square test is then run directly: there is no weighting of cases.

THE CHI-SQUARE TEST OF ASSOCIATION BETWEEN TWO QUALITATIVE VARIABLES

The reader should study Section 11.3.2 before doing this part of the exercise.

An experiment on children's choices

Suppose that a researcher, having watched a number of children enter a room and recorded each child's choice between two objects, wants to know whether there is a tendency for boys and girls to choose different objects. This question concerns two variables: *gender* and *choice*. In statistical terms, the researcher is asking whether they are associated: do more girls than boys choose one of the objects and more boys than girls choose the other object? Suppose that the children's choices are as in Table 2.

Table 2.
Choices by 50 children of one of two objects

Object	Boys	Girls
A	20	5
B	6	19

Procedure for the chi-square test of association between two variables

The use of the **Crosstabs** procedure is fully described in Section 11.3.2. We recommend the inclusion of the option for obtaining the expected frequencies (using the **Cells...** option) so that you can check for the presence of cells with unacceptably low expected frequencies (see Section 11.3.2 for details). Remember to select **Chi-square** and **Phi and Cramér's V** from the **Statistics** option.

Output listing for the chi-square test of association

The listing is discussed in Section 11.3.2. First, a crosstabulation table is listed showing the observed and expected frequencies in each cell, along with row and column totals. Second, a table of various chi-square statistics, together with their associated significance levels, is listed. Third, the values of Phi and Cramér's V are given, together with their associated significance levels.

- **Write down the value of the Pearson chi-square and its associated tail probability (p-value). Is it significant? In terms of the experimental hypothesis, what has this test shown?**

- **Write down the value of Phi.**

CHAPTER 5

CHOOSING A STATISTICAL TEST

5.1 INTRODUCTION
5.2 THE RESEARCH QUESTION
5.3 TWO OR MORE SAMPLES
5.4 ONE-SAMPLE TESTS
5.5 THE ANALYSIS OF DATA FROM FACTORIAL EXPERIMENTS
5.6 MEASURING STATISTICAL ASSOCIATION BETWEEN TWO VARIABLES
5.7 REGRESSION
5.8 MULTIVARIATE STATISTICS
5.9 DATA ANALYSIS WITH SPSS
5.10 GETTING HELP

5.1 INTRODUCTION

The need for formal statistical tests

Chapter 4 was concerned with the first stage of data analysis, the description and exploration of the data set. In the present chapter, we turn to the second stage, namely, the making of formal statistical tests. Neither stage can be omitted: to rush into formal testing without first examining the data is foolhardy; but to rest one's case purely on the characteristics of one's own data is to ignore the possibility that a fresh sample of data, even one gathered in exactly the same way, might not show those characteristics. We shall need to confirm that the patterns we have observed in our data were not merely chance occurrences and are 'robust', in the sense that they would be replicated were the research project to be repeated.

While this is not a statistics textbook, it was felt that in view of the great variety of statistical tests offered to the user by SPSS, there should be at least some guidance here on how to make a reasonable choice from among such a daunting array of possibilities.

Considerations in choosing a formal statistical test

It may be helpful to suggest that choosing a statistical test depends upon three general considerations:

(1) the **research question**;

(2) the **nature of the data**;

(3) the **plan**, or **design**, of the research.

5.2 THE RESEARCH QUESTION

Consider the following two situations:

a) Suppose that, in order to determine whether it is easier to shoot at a square target than at a circular one, you ask two groups of subjects to shoot, say fifty times, at either a square or a circular target. Each person will have a score in the range from 0 to 50, inclusive. You want to know whether the accuracy rate is typically higher in one group than in the other. Translating your question into statistical terms, you want to know whether the *average* hit rate is higher for one target than for the other: your research question is one of **comparing averages**. In terms of formal statistical testing, you want a statistical test that will tell you whether the difference, *in your own data set*, between people's hit rates when shooting at square and circular targets is sufficiently great for you to be able to claim that if someone else were to repeat your experiment, they would find a similar difference.

b) Now suppose that you want to know whether there is a tendency for tall and short fathers to have tall and short (first) sons, respectively. In statistical terms, you are asking whether there is an **association** between the measured variables of Father's Height and First Son's Height.

The answers to questions of comparison (situation a) and association (situation b) are provided by quite different statistical tests. There are, of course, many other questions you might ask about a set of data. For example, you might be interested in the spread of scores obtained under one condition in comparison with another. Or you might be interested the sequencing of a subject's choices. Such questions, however, often arise in the context of research that has basically been designed to compare averages, or establish the presence of an association.

5.2.1 The nature of the data

The choice of a specific test depends on other considerations apart from the research question that motivated the enquiry. Another crucial consideration when choosing a statistical test is the nature of the data set.

In Chapter 4 (Section 4.1.1), three kinds of data were described:

(1) **interval** data, which are measurements on an independent scale with units;

(2) **ordinal** data, consisting of ranks, of assignments to ordered categories, or of sequencing information;

(3) **nominal** or **categorial** data, which are records of qualitative category membership.

Strictly, only the first category contains 'measurements', in the familiar sense of the term; although the first and second categories both refer to quantitative variables. While *all* data are numerical, in the sense that even the categories making up a qualitative variable may be assigned arbitrary code numbers, a nominal datum is merely a *label*, not an expression of the degree to which the attribute is possessed.

Different statistics are appropriate for descriptions of the three types of data; and the corresponding formal tests are also different.

Another important aspect of a data set is the number of measured variables. If a data set comprises measurements on only **one** variable (e.g. reaction time), the **data are univariate data**. If, on the other hand, subjects are measured on **two** variables (e.g. height and weight), the data are **bivariate**. If there are **three or more** variables, the data are **multivariate**.

5.2.2 The plan or design of the research

The number of samples

A crucial consideration in the choice of a statistical test is the number of samples in the data set. The exercise of observing and noting the sex of people passing through a theatre door would yield one sample of nominal data. If, on the other hand, we were to note which of three theatre doors people pass through over a period of time, the operation would also yield one sample of nominal data; but since there are now three categories in the variable we are studying, the choice of a statistical test would be different in the second case.

If the skilled performance (measured on a scale from 0 to 100) of a group of people who have ingested a drug A is compared with that of a control (placebo) group, we shall obtain two samples of scores; but if, on the same skilled task, we test a third group, who have ingested drug B, there will be three samples. Again, the choice of formal statistical tests will be different in the two cases.

Independent versus related samples

If we select, say, 100 participants for an experiment and randomly assign half of them to an experimental condition and the rest to a control condition, we have a situation where the assignment of an individual to a particular group has no effect on the group to which another participant is assigned, or vice versa. This experiment will yield two **independent samples** of scores. With independent samples of data, there is no basis for pairing the scores in one sample with those in the other: there is no way in which, say, the first person selected for one group has anything more in common with the first person selected for the other group than with any of the other people in that group.

Now suppose that each of fifty people shoots fifty times at a triangular target and fifty times at a square target of the same area. This experiment will also yield two samples of scores. This time, however, every score in either sample can be paired with the score in the other sample that the same subject produced. This experiment will yield two **related samples** of scores.

The scores in two related samples are likely to be substantially correlated; whereas that is unlikely to be the case with scores in independent samples. Accordingly, different statistical tests are appropriate for use with independent and related samples of data.

Between subjects and within subjects factors

In Chapter 3, some basic terms in research design were introduced. A pivotal concept is that of a **factor**, a related set of conditions, treatments or categories known as **levels**. Another key notion, from the point of view of selecting a statistical test, is the distinction between **within subjects** (or **repeated measures**) **factors** and **between subjects** factors.

If an experimental design has only between subjects factors, the experiment will yield independent samples of scores. If, on the other hand, there are within subjects factors, that is, if there are repeated measures on some factors, the

Chapter 5 - Choosing a Statistical Test

experiment will yield related samples of scores. There are quite distinct statistical models for the two situations, requiring the use of different statistical tests.

5.3 TWO OR MORE SAMPLES

Suppose we have a set of data comprising two or more samples from a one-factor experiment. In the simplest case, there are two samples; but in principle, there can be any number of samples, provided each sample was obtained under one of a single set of related conditions or categories, that is, from an experiment (or study) with a *single treatment factor*.

Table 1 (see next page) outlines a scheme for classifying situations and research questions in the manner described in the Introduction to this chapter. In each cell of the table, a statistical test is specified.

To enter the table, one must consider:

(1) whether the samples of data are related or independent (i.e. whether the design is between subjects or within subjects);

(2) how many samples of data there are;

(3) the type of data (interval, ordinal or nominal) that will be used in the test.

5.3.1 Choosing tests for comparing averages between (or among) samples of interval data

To explore Table 1, we shall begin by assuming that we have a set of interval data, that is, independent measures on a scale with units.

Suppose we have two samples of data. Table 1 suggests that an **independent samples t-test** may be the appropriate test for comparing the means of the two samples. The decision about whether the design is between subjects (producing independent samples) or within subjects (producing related samples) is absolutely crucial for a correct choice of test. Consideration of the theory behind the independent and related t-tests is beyond the scope of this book: the reader is referred to statistical texts such as Howell (1997) or Winer, Brown & Michels (1991). In the present book, the computerisation of a t-test is described in Chapter 6.

Table 1.
Choosing a test for comparing the averages of two or more samples of scores from experiments with one treatment factor.

Type of data	Experimental Design	
	Between subjects (independent samples)	**Within subjects** (related samples)
	TWO SAMPLES	**TWO SAMPLES**
Interval	Independent samples t-test	Paired samples t-test
Ordinal	Wilcoxon-Mann-Whitney test	Wilcoxon signed ranks test. Sign test
Nominal	Chi-square test	McNemar test
	THREE OR MORE SAMPLES	**THREE OR MORE SAMPLES**
Interval	One-way ANOVA	Repeated measures ANOVA
Ordinal	Kruskal-Wallis k-sample test	Friedman test
Nominal	Chi-square test	Cochran's Q test (dichotomous nominal data only)

As another example, suppose we have three or more samples of scores, as when people's performance under two or more experimental conditions is compared with their performance under a control condition for comparison. To test the null hypothesis of a constant level of performance in the population at all levels, the **one-way analysis of variance (ANOVA)** can be used as described in Chapters 7 and 8. Note that 'one-way' means 'one factor'; although the term is used only for between subjects designs.

5.3.2 Interval data

Parametric and nonparametric tests

The t-test is an example of a **parametric test**, that is, it is assumed that the data are samples from a population with a normal distribution. Other tests, known as **nonparametric tests**, do not make specific assumptions about population distributions. For that reason, they are often referred to as **distribution-free tests**.

While some authors (e.g. Siegel & Castellan, 1988) strongly recommend the use of nonparametric tests, others (e.g. Howell, 1997) emphasise the robustness of the parametric t-tests to violations of their assumptions and the loss of power incurred by the use of equivalent nonparametric tests. We suggest that, provided the data show no obvious contra-indications such as the presence of outliers, marked skewness or great disparity of variances (especially if the last is coupled with greatly disparate sample sizes), a t-test can safely be used; otherwise a nonparametric equivalent should be considered. If, however, the data comprise measurements at the ordinal level in the first place, as with sets of ranks or nominal data, a nonparametric test is the only option. Ratings are a grey area: there has been much dispute as to whether they should be analysed with parametric or nonparametric tests.

Reducing interval data to ordinal data

Nonparametric tests can be used with samples of interval data by converting the original data into another, derived data set which preserves only some of the information present in the original. For example, suppose two samples of children have taken part in a between subjects experiment: one sample has performed a task under an experimental condition; the other has performed the same task under a control condition. Such an experiment will result in two independent samples of scores. The **Wilcoxon-Mann-Whitney statistic W** is obtained by ranking all the scores in order, noting which group each score came from. The value of W is calculated by counting the numbers of scores in, say, the experimental group that have ranks higher than each of the scores in the control group. The Wilcoxon-Mann-Whitney test, therefore, uses only the sequential or ordinal information present in the original data set. Of course, all the procedures just described are carried out automatically by SPSS (see Chapter 6).

Nonparametric tests are also available for comparing the averages of the related samples of data resulting from a within subjects experiment. If, say, thirty subjects identify material presented to the left and right visual hemifields, the experiment will result in a set of paired data. In the **Wilcoxon signed ranks test**, a single column of difference scores is obtained, the differences are ranked in order of their absolute size, and the test is made with the statistic T+, which is the sum of the ranks of the positive differences.

Another test available for paired data is the **sign test**, which uses only the nominal information present in the original paired samples of interval data. As in the Wilcoxon signed ranks test, the values in each column of data are subtracted from the corresponding data in the other column; but *only the sign* of each difference is noted. The result is a sequence of pluses and minuses. The null hypothesis

Chapter 5 - Choosing a Statistical Test

implies equal numbers of pluses and minuses, and the binomial test is used to ascertain whether the number of pluses (or, equivalently, the number of minuses) is such as to constitute evidence against the null hypothesis.

So far, we have been considering the use of nonparametric alternatives to t-tests. For data sets comprising more than two sets of interval data, however, there are also equivalent nonparametric tests. The **Kruskal-Wallis k-sample test** is equivalent to the one-way ANOVA (which is appropriate for independent samples of interval data). The **Friedman test** is a nonparametric equivalent of the one-factor within subjects ANOVA.

5.3.3 Ordinal data

Consider, however, an experiment in which subjects rank ten objects in order of preference. This would generate ten related samples of data, each sample comprising the ranks given by the subjects to one particular object. Here we have a set of inherently ordinal data, not independent measurements on a scale with units. In this case, the use of a nonparametric test is required by the nature of the data: a parametric ANOVA is not an option here.

5.3.4 Nominal data

With nominal data, the question of comparing *averages* does not really arise, because all we have are the frequencies of people in each category. Nevertheless, it is often of interest to know whether there is a robust tendency for people to produce a response more often in some conditions than in others.

Independent samples of dichotomous nominal data

Suppose that twenty-four subjects are divided into three groups: two experimental groups (Group A and Group B) and a Control group, eight subjects being randomly assigned to each group. Each subject is tested with a criterion problem, a 1 being recorded if they pass, and a 0 if they fail. Table 2 shows the results of the experiment.

With such a nominal data set, a **chi-square test** can be used to test the null hypothesis that, in the population, there is no tendency for the problem to be solved more often in some conditions than in others (see Chapter 11).

Three or more sets of correlated dichotomous nominal data: Cochran's Q test

A nominal data set resembling the data in Table 2 would also result from a within subjects experiment, that is, if each person had been tested under all three conditions. In that case, however, the data set would comprise three *related samples* of nominal data. Table 1 shows that an appropriate test of the null hypothesis of no difference in performance among the three conditions is the **Cochran's Q test**, which is described in Chapter 9.

Table 2.
A set of nominal data from a one-factor between subjects experiment

Control Subject	Score	Group A Subject	Score	Group B Subject	Score
s1	0	s9	0	s17	1
s2	0	s10	1	s18	1
s3	0	s11	0	s19	1
s4	0	s12	0	s20	1
s5	1	s13	0	s21	1
s6	0	s14	0	s22	1
s7	0	s15	0	s23	1
s8	0	s16	1	s24	1

Two correlated samples of dichotomous nominal data: McNemar test

Suppose that ten people are asked whether they are for or against a proposal before and after hearing a debate on the issue. On both occasions of testing, each person's response is coded either as 0 (against) or 1 (for). Table 3 shows the results.

Table 3.
A set of correlated nominal data from a one-factor within subjects experiment

Subject	Before	After	Subject	Before	After
s1	0	1	s6	0	1
s2	0	1	s7	0	1
s3	0	0	s8	0	1
s4	1	0	s9	0	1
s5	0	1	s10	0	1

Here an appropriate test of the null hypothesis that hearing the debate has no effect upon people's opinions on the issue is tested with **McNemar's change test** described in Chapter 6.

Chapter 5 - Choosing a Statistical Test

5.4 ONE-SAMPLE TESTS

Much psychological research involves the drawing of two or more samples of data. This is by no means always true, however: sometimes the researcher draws a *single* sample of observations in order to study just one population.

One-sample tests with nominal data
A question about a single population is often one of **goodness-of-fit**: has the sample been drawn from a population with certain specified characteristics? For example, suppose a researcher wants to know whether 5-year-old children of a certain age, when leaving a room, show a preference for one of two doors, A and B. One hundred 5-year-olds are observed leaving the room and their choices are noted. Here the population comprises the choices (A or B) of 5-year-olds in general. Of the hundred children in our study, 60 leave by door A and 40 by door B. The null hypothesis states that the probability of choosing A (or B) is 0.5 : more formally, it states that we have sampled 100 times from a Bernoulli population with $p = 0.5$. Does this theoretical distribution fit our data?

Table 4 is a scheme for choosing appropriate one-sample tests in various situations.

	Table 4. Scheme for choosing a one-sample test	
	Two categories	**More than two categories**
Nominal Data	Binomial test	Chi-square test
	Randomness	**Distribution**
Ordinal Data	Runs test	Kolmogorov-Smirnov test
	Mean	**Distribution**
Interval Data	t-test	Kolmogorov-Smirnov test

Selection of a test from the Table is on the basis of (1) the type of data, and (2) whether there are more than two categories or values. According to Table 4, with a sample of nominal data such as the children's choices in the present example, the **binomial test** is appropriate. Should the children have had more than two doors to choose from, a **chi-square** test could have been used to test the null hypothesis of no preferences among the three or more alternatives.

Chapter 5 - Choosing a Statistical Test

Using sequential information: Tests of randomness

Many of the most well-known statistical tests assume that the scores in the data set are a random sample from the population. There are circumstances, however, in which this fundamental assumption can be questioned. Suppose we learn that a child, when given a choice between two apparently identical objects on each of ten trials, chose the left on five trials and the right on the remainder. On the basis of this information alone, it would seem reasonable to suppose that the child has been choosing at random. But if we know that the sequence of choices was L, L, L, L, L, R, R, R, R, R, the supposition of randomness seems less tenable. To test the assumption of randomness in such sequences of events, the **Runs test** can be used. Notice that the use of the Runs test requires that we have the necessary **ordinal** information (see Table 4).

Testing for goodness-of-fit with ordinal and interval data: Kolmogorov-Smirnov test

The histogram of a sample of scores may suggest that it has been drawn from a normal population (or one which is nearly so). The **Kolmogorov-Smirnov** test can be used to test the assumption of normality of distribution. This test compares the centiles of the observed distribution of the data with the corresponding centiles of the normal distribution. The test statistic is the largest discrepancy between the observed and theoretical centiles. The Kolmogorov-Smirnov test is not confined to testing for normality: as long as the theoretical centiles can be specified, the test is also applicable to Poisson distributions, rectangular distributions, chi-square distributions, and so on.

Has the sample been drawn from a population with a specified mean value?

With interval data, as when we ask whether the performance of a group of schoolchildren on a standardised test is typical of those in their age group, a **one-sample t-test** can be used to test the null hypothesis that the population mean has the putative 'population' value (Table 4).

Note that the t-test used with two samples of correlated interval data is really a *one-sample* test. Essentially, a single column of differences is created by consistently subtracting the scores in one column from the corresponding scores in the other. If the null hypothesis is true, there is no difference in the population between people's average performance under the two conditions. In terms of the columns of differences (rather than the original scores), the mean difference in the population is zero. Here, rather than thinking of having correlated samples from two populations (or a single sample from a bivariate population) we have reinterpreted the situation as one in which a single sample (of differences) has been drawn from a population (of differences). Now, we need only carry out a one-sample t-test to test the null hypothesis of a population mean (μ) of zero (see Howell, 1997, pp. 175 - 188).

5.5 THE ANALYSIS OF DATA FROM FACTORIAL EXPERIMENTS

There may be two, three or more factors in an experimental design. Experiments with more than one factor are known as **factorial** experiments. In Chapter 3 (Section 3.2), three different types of factorial experiments were described:

(1) between subjects;

(2) within subjects;

(3) mixed.

The basis of this classification is whether the experiment has factors with repeated measures, and if so, whether *all* factors have repeated measures (within subjects designs), *some* (but not all) factors have repeated measures (mixed designs), or *none* has repeated measures (between subjects designs). Beware of an alternative use of the term *mixed* (usually in the term *mixed model*) in some textbooks such as Howell (1997, p.422) which refers to the mixed model as the combination of *fixed* and *random effects* factors, a fixed effects factor being one with fixed selected levels whereas a random effects factor is one with randomly selected levels. Random effects factors are rare in psychological experiments.

Corresponding to the three different types of factorial experiment described, between subject, within subjects and mixed, are three different analysis of variance models, the between subjects, within subjects and mixed models, respectively. A separate chapter will be devoted to the use of SPSS to analyse data from each of these three different types of experiments - see Chapters 8, 9 and 10.

5.6 MEASURING STATISTICAL ASSOCIATION BETWEEN TWO VARIABLES

Consider the following research question: do tall fathers tend to have tall sons? Your question is whether there is a **statistical association** between the two variables Father's Height and Son's Height. To answer the question, you would need the heights of a substantial sample of fathers and those of their first sons and (since you would have interval data), an appropriate statistic would be a **Pearson correlation coefficient**. Now suppose we have asked two judges to rank twenty paintings in order of preference. We should have a data set consisting of (20) pairs of ranks. Do the judges agree? Again, our question is one of statistical association, but a rank correlation would be an appropriate statistic. Other measures of association are appropriate for data in the form of contingency tables (nominal data).

Table 5 shows some of the correlation coefficients and other measures of strength of association that are available for the different kinds of psychological data. As before, the choice of a measure depends upon consideration of the type of data one has.

Table 5. Measures of association between two variables	
	Statistic
Interval Data	Pearson correlation (r)
Ordinal Data	Spearman's rho, Kendall's tau-a, tau-b, tau-c
Nominal Data	Phi; Cramér's V

Measuring association with interval data: The Pearson correlation

If we have the heights of 200 fathers, paired with those of their 200 eldest sons, we have a set of interval data. According to Table 5, we should consider the use of a correlation coefficient to measure the strength of association between the variables of father's height and son's height.

It may be well, however, even at this point, to warn the reader of the dangers lurking in the incautious use of the correlation coefficient. Some of the difficulties are discussed in Chapter 11. For the moment it should suffice to say that, taken by itself, the value of a correlation coefficient, whether calculated by SPSS or by any other means, may give quite a wrong impression of the real nature of the association (if any) between two variables. It is always necessary to examine the scatterplot of the two variables in a correlation. Fortunately, it is very easy to command SPSS to produce a scatterplot (see Chapters 4 and 11).

Measuring association with ordinal data: Spearman rank correlation and Kendall's tau statistics

If two judges rank ten paintings on order of their quality, we shall have a set of ordinal data in the form of ranks. Most statistical packages now offer two alternative measures of association for such data:

(1) Spearman's rank correlation;

(2) one of Kendall's tau statistics.

The manner in which one enters bivariate data in the form of ranks into the SPSS Data Editor window and obtains a rank correlation or a Kendall statistic are considered in detail in Chapter 11.

Chapter 5 - Choosing a Statistical Test

Measuring association in nominal data: Contingency tables

Suppose that Fred claims to possess telepathic powers. Accordingly, in an experiment designed to test this claim, an experimenter tosses a coin 100 times, and Fred, seated behind a screen, states, on each occasion, whether the coin turned up heads or tails. Table 6 presents the results of the experiment.

Table 6.
A contingency table

Fred's Guess	Experimenter's toss	
	Head (H)	Tail (T)
H	45	9
T	8	38

The presence of an association can be confirmed by using a **chi-square test** (see Chapter 11). Since the value of the chi-square statistic depends partly upon the sample size, it is unsuitable as a measure of the strength of association between two qualitative variables. Table 5 specifies two statistics, **Cramér's V** and the **phi coefficient**, which measure such association.

The point-biserial correlation

Table 5 is by no means comprehensive; in fact, many other measures of association are in use. One of the most important of these is the **point-biserial correlation**.

Suppose that in an experiment on skilled performance, the scores of 20 subjects under a special experimental condition are compared with the scores of 20 controls. The results of such an experiment can be entered into the SPSS Data Editor window in the manner described in Chapter 3: all the scores are entered into a single column of the grid, and the group membership of each subject is carried by another column containing code numbers, such as *0* for the control group and *1* for the experimental group. Such a variable is known as a **grouping variable**.

The **Data Editor** thus contains two columns of numbers:

(1) the scores;

(2) values of the grouping variable.

The Pearson correlation between the two columns of numbers, where one variable has been measured and the other is merely a grouping variable, is known as the **point-biserial correlation**.

It will be found that if a point-biserial correlation proves to be significant, then so also will be the pooled t-test of the difference between the means of the two groups, and *vice versa*. This is because the point-biserial correlation and the t-statistic are both completely determined by the difference between the group means and the spread of the scores within the groups. It will be found that the values used to label the groups are entirely arbitrary: *any* numbers will do, as long as they are different. This fact, though interesting, may not seem to be particularly useful. Nevertheless, the point-biserial correlation is a useful conceptual bridge between the making of comparisons and the measurement of association.

5.7 REGRESSION

Simple regression

If there exists an association between two variables, this can be exploited to estimate the values of one variable from knowledge of those of the other. For example, if there is an association between the heights of fathers and their sons (which there certainly is), can we make use of this association to estimate the height of a son whose father is, say, five feet ten inches in height? This is a problem in **simple regression**, and its solution is described in Chapter 12.

Estimating one variable from knowledge of two or more other variables: multiple regression

It may be that a young man's height is associated not only with that of his father but also the father's financial circumstances. In **multiple regression** (Chapter 12), knowledge of a person's scores on two or more variables (the **regressors**) is used to estimate that person's score on a target variable (the dependent variable, or **criterion**). We can expect that if height and father's income are indeed correlated, multiple regression will produce a more accurate prediction of a young man's height than will a simple regression upon either of the two regressors considered on its own.

5.8 MULTIVARIATE STATISTICS

In all the experimental examples so far considered, there was just one dependent variable. In factorial ANOVA, for example, there may be several *independent* variables (i.e. factors); but there is only one *dependent* variable. The ANOVA, therefore, is **a univariate statistical test**. There is, however, available a set of methods designed for situations in which there are two or more dependent variables. These methods are known as **multivariate statistics**.

Multivariate analysis of variance (MANOVA)

Suppose that in a one-way experiment on memory, the performance of two groups of subjects, each group trained in a different mnemonic technique, is compared with that of a control sample. Suppose also that performance is measured in two ways:

(1) number of items recalled;

(2) number of errors in recall.

In **multivariate analysis of variance (MANOVA),** these dependent variables are combined into a single variable in such a way that the mean scores of the different groups on this new variable are spread out, or dispersed, to the greatest possible extent. The differences among the group means on the single new dependent variable are then tested by methods similar in rationale to univariate analysis of variance. Although we shall not consider MANOVA in any detail in this book, references will be made to the technique from time to time, in the hope that the foregoing simplified characterisations of ANOVA and MANOVA may serve as useful co-ordinates in the exploration of what may be unfamiliar territory. For most purposes, however, researchers usually find it more informative to use a univariate ANOVA on each DV separately.

Discriminant analysis

In an experimental study where cases have been classified into two or more groups with two or more dependent variables, the dependent variables can be combined to produce a new dependent variable for maximising the correct classification of the cases into the groups. This new combination variable can then become a **regressor** for predicting group membership of other non-classified cases. Thus **discriminant analysis (DA)** is the obverse of MANOVA: the same composite variable is computed with a view to predicting group membership. In fact, in many ways, discriminant analysis is mathematically equivalent to MANOVA. Discriminant analysis is the subject of Chapter 14.

Factor analysis

In all the situations so far described, the variables, whether measured during the course of the study, or manipulated by the experimenter, have been *overt*, in the sense of being directly observable. Suppose, however, that people are tested on a number of psychological tests, and the correlations among them are calculated. Among the correlations, certain patterns may emerge suggesting that subgroups of the original set of variables are manifestations of underlying, or **latent**, psychological variables. **Factor analysis** (see Chapter 15) is a set of methods designed to identify the latent psychological variables thought to underlie the correlations among a set of tests. In **exploratory factor analysis**, the object is to find the minimum number of latent variables, or **factors**, necessary to account for the correlations among the psychological tests. In **confirmatory factor analysis**, specified models are compared to see which gives the best account of the data.

Complex contingency tables

In the past two decades, there have been dramatic developments in the analysis of nominal data in the form of multiway contingency tables. Before that time, the analysis of contingency tables with three or more attributes was often carried out by ignoring some of the factors in the classification, in order to produce two-way tables to which chi-square tests could be applied. That approach is fraught with risk, and such tests may give highly misleading results. The application of modern **loglinear models** of the cell frequencies in such tables, however, has made it possible to tease out the relationships among the attributes in the classification in a way that was not possible before (see Chapter 13). Such models permit the construction of models with interaction terms strongly reminiscent of those in ANOVA models.

5.9 DATA ANALYSIS WITH SPSS

The analysis of a set of data takes place in two phases:

(1) **data entry and exploration** at a general level;

(2) **formal statistical testing**.

Phase 1 - Data Entry and Exploration

The scheme below shows the steps taken in entering data into SPSS, their subsequent exploration, inspection, transcription corrections, data transformations, case selections and so on.

Prepare data file in **Data Editor** window

⬇

Within the **Statistics** menu, explore data with procedures from the **Summarize** submenu such as **Frequencies**, **Descriptives**, **Explore**, **Crosstabs**

⬇

Inspect listings on the screen, check for outliers, study the distributions

⬇

If necessary, deselect outliers or transform distributions with procedures from the **Data** or **Transform** menus

---

Chapter 5 - Choosing a Statistical Test

Phase 2 - Formal Statistical Analysis

After the data have been entered, corrected, and explored as described in Phase 1, the user is then ready to engage in further statistical analysis of the data. Table 7 tabulates the SPSS statistical procedures which will be discussed in subsequent chapters of this book. The names in **bold type** are items within the **Statistics** drop-down menu; the names in *italics* are sub-items from the main items.

After running a statistical test and inspecting the output, the user can re-run the analysis slightly differently by returning to the original dialog box(es) and changing the variables or selecting different options. The analysis may lead to the identification of more outliers and the need to repeat the analysis with a reduced data set. Further refinements may be added: additional statistics can be commanded; tables of residuals can be requested; and plots of the results obtained. Once an analysis has been carried out to the user's satisfaction, the various outputs (listings, charts, graphs) may be stored and/or printed.

Table 7.

SPSS statistical procedures (bold type) within the Statistics drop-down menu and their sub-items (italics)

Significance of differences in level between or among variables	Degree of relationship among variables	Prediction of group member-ship	Finding latent variables
Compare Means: *Various T-Tests* *One-way ANOVA* **ANOVA Models:** *Simple Factorial* *Repeated measures* **Nonparametric Tests:** *2 Independent Samples* *K Independent Samples* *2 Related Samples* *K Related Samples*	**Summarize:** *Crosstabs* **Correlate:** *Bivariate* **Regression:** *Linear* **Loglinear**	**Classify:** *Discriminant*	**Data reduction:** *Factor*

144

Chapter 5 - Choosing a Statistical Test

5.10 GETTING HELP

In a book of this sort, which is primarily concerned with the use of a computing package, it is not possible to offer more than a few signposts to the reader wishing to select and use a statistical test correctly. In the following sections we offer two suggestions.

Useful textbooks

Of the many textbooks that offer advice on the selection of statistical tests, we have found Howell (1997) to be among the most consistently helpful. Like several other authors (Siegel & Castellan, 1988; Tabachnick & Fidell, 1996), Howell offers a decision tree to help the reader make the correct selection. The trees offered by different authors vary considerably in appearance, a fact reflecting the different approaches advocated by their authors (Siegel was an advocate of nonparametric statistics; Howell emphasises parametric univariate ANOVA methods; Tabachnick & Fidell are more concerned with multivariate statistics). From the point of view of the modern experimental psychologist, Howell's decision tree is perhaps the most helpful.

While such decision trees are very helpful in the early stages of study, one inevitably meets situations to which none of the proposed schemes really applies convincingly. Some situations, in fact, require the construction of a special statistical model, rather than the application of any standard test, in which case it is best to consult a statistician.

Getting help in SPSS

SPSS offers a very useful Help facility. By selecting **Guide/SPSS Help**, the window **Help: SPSS for the Macintosh** is obtained (Figure 1).

The effective use of SPSS Help takes practice. The **Keyword** option presents no problems: that command obtains a useful glossary of the terms that SPSS will recognise. Beware of **Search**, however: SPSS Help will embark upon a lengthy search for all occurrences of the chosen phrase.

The underlined headings are very useful. For example, for a one-sample t-test, the user is directed to the dialog box for a **related-samples t-test** and is given clear instructions there on how to modify the data set for the one-sample test.

Chapter 5 - Choosing a Statistical Test

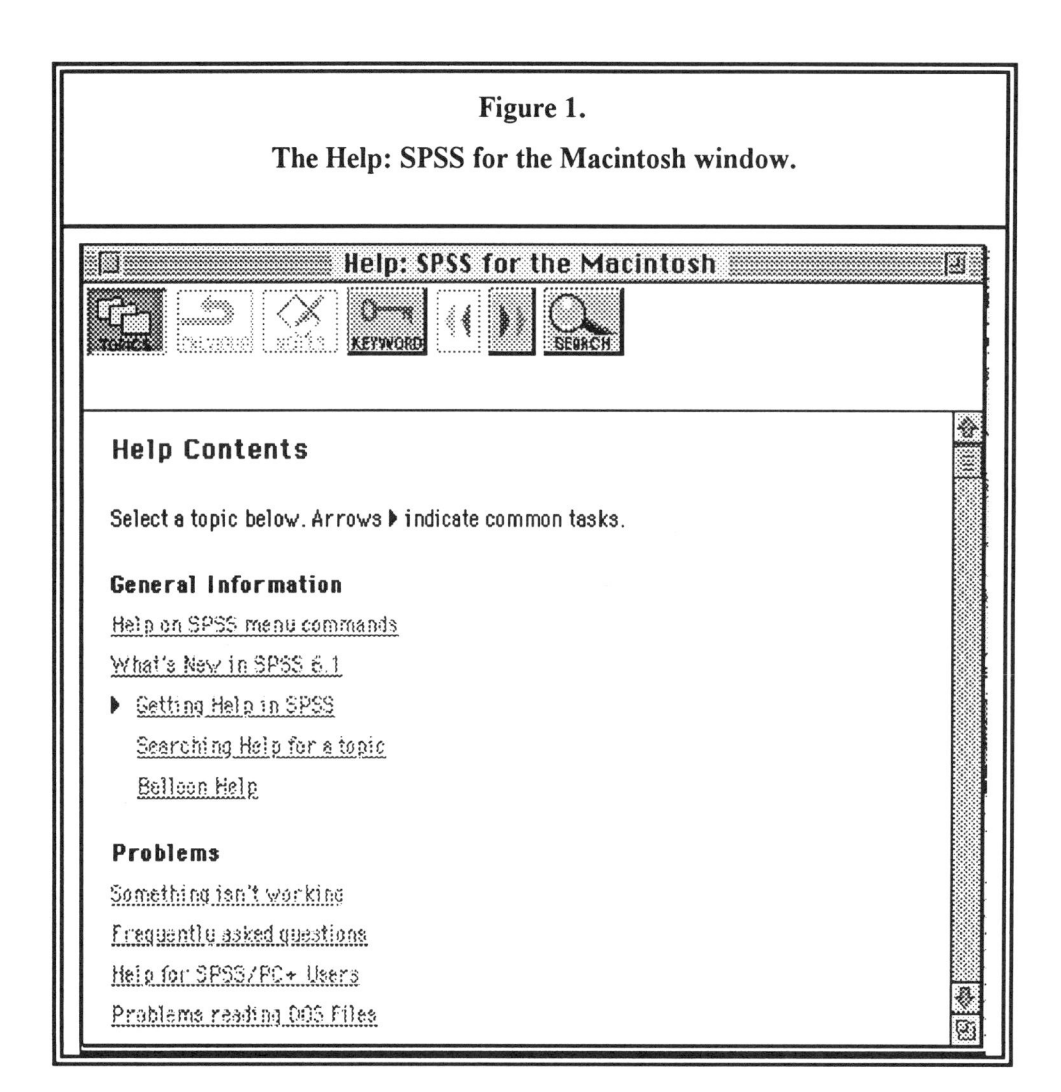

Figure 1.

The Help: SPSS for the Macintosh window.

CHAPTER 6

COMPARING THE AVERAGES OF TWO SAMPLES

6.1 INTRODUCTION
6.2 PARAMETRIC METHODS: THE T-TESTS
6.3 NONPARAMETRIC METHODS

Chapter 6 - Comparing the Averages of Two Samples

6.1 INTRODUCTION

Suppose that an experiment has been carried out, in which the performance of two groups of people has been measured under two conditions, an experimental condition and a control. For example, the task could be the memorisation of the content of a written passage, and the purpose of the experiment might be to compare the recall performance of a group of subjects who have been given special training in a mnemonic technique with that of an untrained control group. We may find that the mean performance of the experimental (trained) group is higher than that of the untrained (control) group, but we need to confirm this apparent treatment effect with a statistical test.

The t-test is commonly used to ascertain the significance of a difference between two means. Our hypothesis is that the mnemonic technique enhances recall. This is the **experimental hypothesis**. In traditional significance testing, however, it is not the experimental hypothesis that is directly tested but its **negation**, which is known as the **null hypothesis** (H_0). In this example, H_0 states that, in the population, there is *no difference* between performance under the mnemonic and control conditions. If H_0 fails the test, we shall conclude that our experimental hypothesis, which in statistical terms is known as the **alternative hypothesis**, is correct.

The performance of a statistical test requires a knowledge of the **sampling distribution** of the test statistic. The **p-value** of a statistic such as t or F (or some other test statistic) is the probability, assuming that H_0 is true, of obtaining a **value at least as extreme as the one actually obtained**. Should the p-value be small, this is taken as evidence against H_0, because a value that extreme is unlikely (though possible) under H_0. Traditionally, H_0 is rejected if the p-value is no more than 0.05; but in many areas, an even lower p-value, say 0.01, is now the conventional criterion for rejection. When the p-value of a statistic is at least as small as the conventional value, the value of the statistic is said to be **significant**.

Should the p-value be larger than the conventional small value, H_0 is **accepted**. This does not mean that it is actually true: it means only that the evidence is insufficient to justify rejection.

To sum up:

1) if the p-value is greater than 0.05, **H_0** is accepted and the result is **not significant**;

2) if the p-value is less than 0.05 but greater than 0.01, **H_0** is rejected and the result is **significant beyond the 5 per cent level**;

3) if the p-value is smaller than 0.01, **H_0** is rejected and the result is **significant beyond the 1 per cent level**.

In this book, we assume that you are familiar with the t-test, at least to some extent. If you are not, we strongly recommend that you read the relevant sections of a good statistical text: e.g. Gravetter & Wallnau (1997; chapters 9-11) give a lucid account. With independent samples, the t statistic is calculated by dividing the difference between the sample means by an estimate of the standard deviation of the distribution of differences, known as the **standard error of the difference**.

Should the sample variances have similar values, it is common practice to work with a pooled estimate of the supposedly constant population variance; but if they do not, the pooled estimate is not used and a **separate variance** test is made. The null hypothesis is rejected if the obtained value of *t* lies in either tail of the sampling distribution. The precise value of *t* needed for significance depends upon the **degrees of freedom** of the distribution, which in turn depends upon the sizes of the samples in the experiment; but an absolute value of *t* greater than or equal to *2* is usually significant, unless the samples are very small indeed. Very small samples should be avoided in any case, because the test would have insufficient power to reject H_0. (The **power** of a statistical test is the probability that H_0 will be rejected given that it is false.)

Table 1 shows the SPSS menus and sub-menus (in upper case letters) for the various two-sample situations.

Table 1.

SPSS menus and submenus (upper case words) within the Statistics drop-down menu for various two-sample situations

Data derived from populations assumed to have normal distributions and equal variances		No specific assumptions about the population distributions	
Independent samples	Paired samples	Independent samples	Related samples
COMPARE MEANS ↓ INDEPENDENT SAMPLES T-TEST	COMPARE MEANS ↓ PAIRED SAMPLES T-TEST	NON-PARAMETRIC TESTS ↓ 2 INDEPENDENT SAMPLES	NON-PARAMETRIC TESTS ↓ 2 RELATED SAMPLES

↓ indicates that the item below is part of the submenu of the item above

The left half of Table 1 deals with parametric tests (i.e. those making assumptions about population distributions), the right half with nonparametric tests (i.e. those making no assumptions about population distributions). Each half is subdivided according to whether the samples are independent or related (SPSS refers to related samples as **paired samples** in the case of the t-test, but as **related samples** for nonparametric tests).

6.2 PARAMETRIC METHODS: THE T-TESTS

6.2.1 Assumptions underlying the use of the t-test

The model underlying a t-test assumes that the data have been derived from normal distributions with equal variance. Computer simulations have shown that even with moderate violations of these assumptions, one may still safely proceed with a t-test, provided the samples are not too small, do not contain outliers (atypical scores), and are of equal (or nearly equal) size. Should a preliminary exploration of the data (as recommended in Chapter 4) indicate that the assumptions of a t-test model have been seriously violated, an alternative test should be chosen from the portfolio of **nonparametric** tests in the **Nonparametric Tests** menu. Nonparametric tests do not carry specific assumptions about population distributions and variance.

6.2.2 Paired and independent samples

In an experiment on lateralisation of cortical functioning, a subject looks at a central spot on a computer screen and is told to press a key on recognition of a word which may appear on either side of the spot. As a check on whether the word has been truly recognised, the subject is also asked to type the word just identified. The experimental hypothesis is that words presented in the right visual field will be more quickly recognised than those in the left visual field, because the former are processed by the left cerebral hemisphere, which is thought to be more proficient with verbal information. For each subject, the median response time to forty words in each of the right and left visual fields is recorded, as indicated in Table 2.

This experiment is of **repeated measures**, or **within subjects**, design, because the performance of the same subjects has been measured under both conditions (word in right field, word in left field). Now suppose that **different** subjects had been tested with words in the right and left visual fields. The data table might appear as in Table 3.

This variant of the experiment has **no repeated measures**, or is of **between subjects** design: each subject is tested under only one condition. Notice that there is no basis on which the subjects in the two conditions can meaningfully be paired; indeed, with no repeated measures, the samples can be of different sizes. It is recommended, however, that samples should always be the same size wherever possible.

Table 2.

Paired data: Median word recognition times in milliseconds for words in the left and right visual fields

Subject	Left Field	Right Field
s1	323	304
s2	512	493
s3	502	491
s4	385	365
s5	453	426
s6	343	320
s7	543	523
s8	440	442
s9	682	580
s10	590	564

Table 3.

Independent samples: Median word recognition times in milliseconds for words in the left and right visual fields

Subject	Left Field	Subject	Right Field
s1	500	s11	392
s2	513	s12	445
s3	300	s13	271
s4	561	s14	523
s5	483	s15	421
s6	502	s16	489
s7	539	s17	501
s8	467	s18	388
s9	420	s19	411
s10	480	s20	467

With suitable paired data, the **paired samples t-test** can be used to test the difference between the means of the two sets of scores for significance. With suitable independent data, the **independent samples t-test** is used. These tests are available in **Compare Means** within the **Statistics** menu. Note that the data are entered differently in the two cases, as explained below.

Chapter 6 - Comparing the Averages of Two Samples

6.2.3 The paired samples t-test

Prepare the data file from the data in Table 2 as follows:

Using the techniques described in Chapter 3 (Section 3.3), define the variables *leftfld* and *rightfld* (fuller names, such as *Left Visual Field* and *Right Visual Field* can be assigned by using the **Define Labels** procedure). Type the data into the two columns and save the data set to a file.

To check for anomalies in the data before conducting the t-test, it is recommended that a scatterplot of the data points be constructed. Use **Graphs/Scatter** (Section 4.3.3) to obtain the scatterplot (Figure 1) with *leftfld* in the **Y Axis** box and *rightfld* in the **X Axis** box.

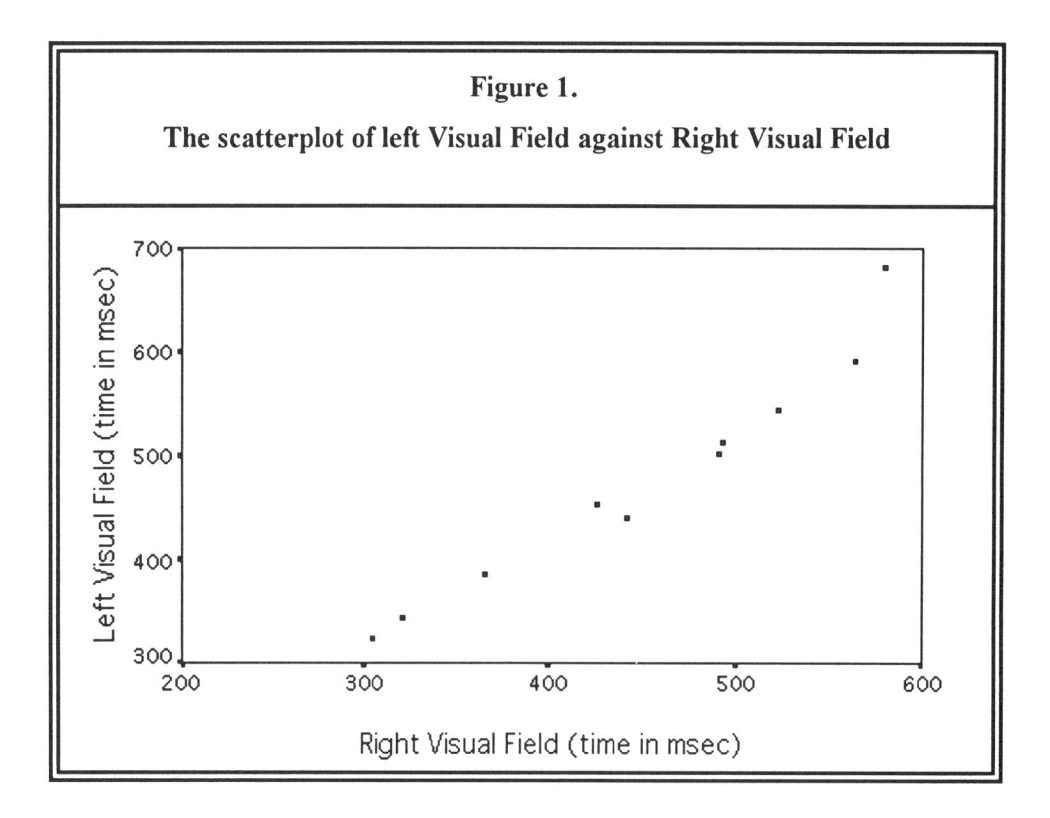

Figure 1.

The scatterplot of left Visual Field against Right Visual Field

No outlier appears in the scatterplot. It should be noted that the presence of an outlying pair of scores, even one showing a difference in the same direction as the others, can have the effect of increasing the denominator of the t statistic more than the numerator and so reduce the value of t to insignificance. This effect is illustrated in one of the Exercises. The vulnerability of the standard deviation to the leverage exerted by outliers derives from the fact that the elements of the variance are the **squares** of deviations from the mean, and large deviations thus continue to have a disproportionate influence, even after the square root operation by which the standard deviation is derived from the variance has been carried out.

When outliers are present, the user can either consider removing them or choose a nonparametric method such as the **Sign test** or the **Wilcoxon matched pairs test**. The former is completely immune to the influence of outliers; the latter is much more resistant than the t-test. Should there be no contra-indications against the use of the t-test however, the parametric t-test is preferable to a nonparametric

Chapter 6 - Comparing the Averages of Two Samples

test because the latter would incur the penalty of a loss of power.

The t-test is carried out by proceeding as follows:

- Choose
  Statistics (see Figure 2)
    Compare Means
      Paired-Samples T Test ...
  to open the **Paired-Samples T Test** dialog box (Figure 3).

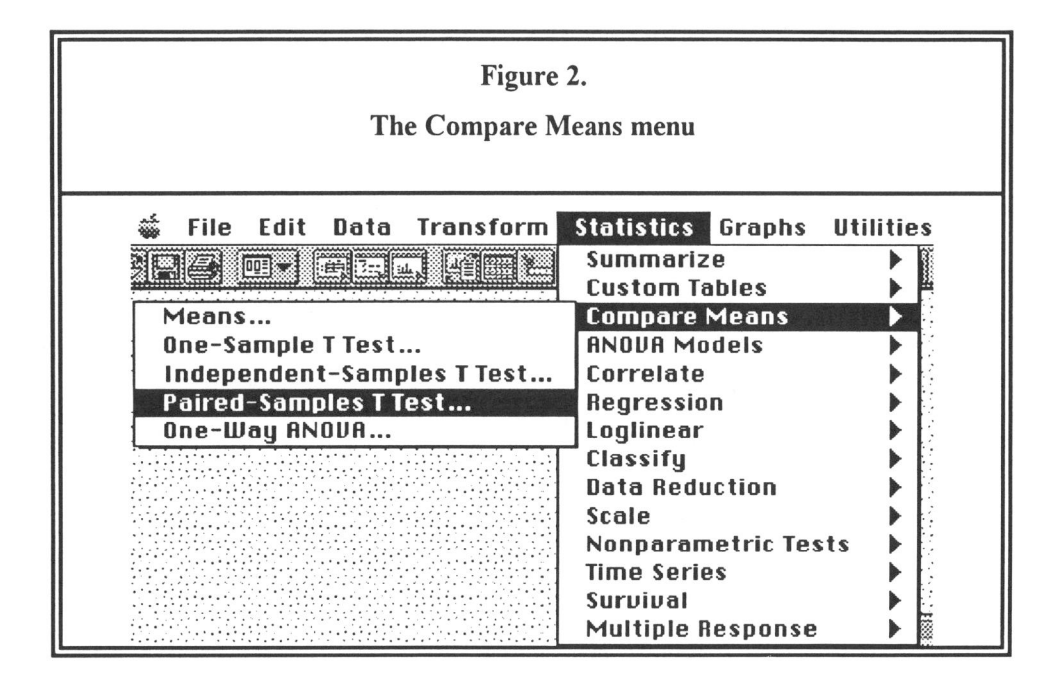

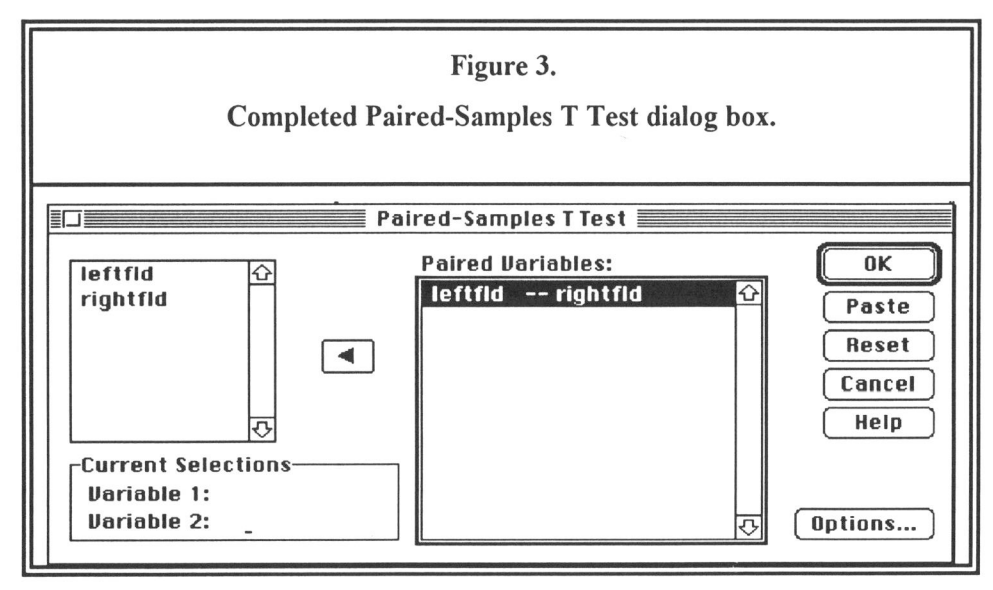

Figure 2.

The Compare Means menu

Figure 3.

Completed Paired-Samples T Test dialog box.

- Initially, the **Paired Variables:** box on the right will be empty, and the variable names *leftfld* and *rightfld* will appear in the left hand box. Highlight the upper variable label. Then, **keeping the Command key pressed down**, highlight the second variable name. Only then will the arrow box ▶ come alive. Click on that to transfer the two variable names to the **Paired Variables:** box, where they will appear joined by dashes as shown.

Chapter 6 - Comparing the Averages of Two Samples

- Click on **OK** to run the t-test command.

The output is shown in Output Listing 1. The listing begins with some statistics for each of the two variables considered separately, followed by statistics of the distribution of differences between the paired scores (Paired Differences).

Output Listing 1.

t-test output for paired samples

```
t-tests for Paired Samples


                      Number of              2-tail
Variable                 pairs      Corr      Sig          Mean          SD        SE of Mean

LEFTFLD     Left Visual Field                            477.3000     112.091         35.446
                           10       .975     .000
RIGHTFLD    Right Visual Field                           450.8000      97.085         30.701


            Paired Differences
    Mean          SD       SE of Mean         t-value         df         2-tail Sig

   26.5000      27.814        8.796             3.01          9             .015
   95% CI (6.603, 46.397)
```

The correlation coefficient for the two variables (0.975), the t-value (3.01) with its associated degrees of freedom (9), and the 2-tail p-value (0.015) are also given. The final item in the Output Listing 1 reads as follows:

95% CI (6.603, 46.397)

In words this is: 'The ninety-five per cent confidence interval is from 6.603 to 46.397'. The same values are listed in the Output Listing 1 under the heading: **95% Confidence Interval of the Difference**. In statistical inference there are two kinds of estimates:

(1) **point estimates**, which are single values (the sample mean and variance are point estimates of the corresponding population parameters);

(2) **interval estimates**, which are intervals within which the true values are stated, with specified levels of confidence, to lie.

The **ninety-five percent confidence interval (95% CI)** is an interval calculated from the data in such a way that it should include the true value of the parameter (in this case the mean difference in the population) in 95% of samples. This is what is meant by the term '95% confidence': the stated confidence interval does **not** mean: 'The probability that the true mean lies between 6.603 and 46.397 is 0.95'. Since this interval does not include the H_0 value of 0, the result is clearly significant.

The listing also shows that the null hypothesis can also be rejected on the basis of the t-test, since the t-test tail probability (labelled **2-tail Sig**) is .015 (or 1.5%) which is less than .05 (or 5%). Thus the difference between the means is significant. Write this as: $t = 3.01$; $df = 9$; $p < 0.05$.

Chapter 6 - Comparing the Averages of Two Samples

6.2.4 The independent samples t-test

Turning now to the independent samples t-test, we shall use the data set shown in Table 3. In Chapter 3 (Section 3.3.1), it was explained that data of this kind (from two or more samples of subjects) are entered into the **Data Editor** window in two columns: a single column of scores and a grouping variable consisting of code numbers indicating the group to which each participant belonged.

Using the techniques described in Chapter 3 (Section 3.3.4), define the grouping (independent) variable as *field* and the dependent variable as *rectime*. Fuller names (e.g. *Visual Field* and *Word Recognition Time*) and value labels (e.g. *Left Field* and *Right Field*) can be assigned by using the **Define Labels** procedure. Type in the data and save to a file.

- The t-test is selected by choosing
  Statistics
      Compare Means
          Independent-Samples T Test ...

to open the **Independent-Samples T Test** dialog box (Figure 4).

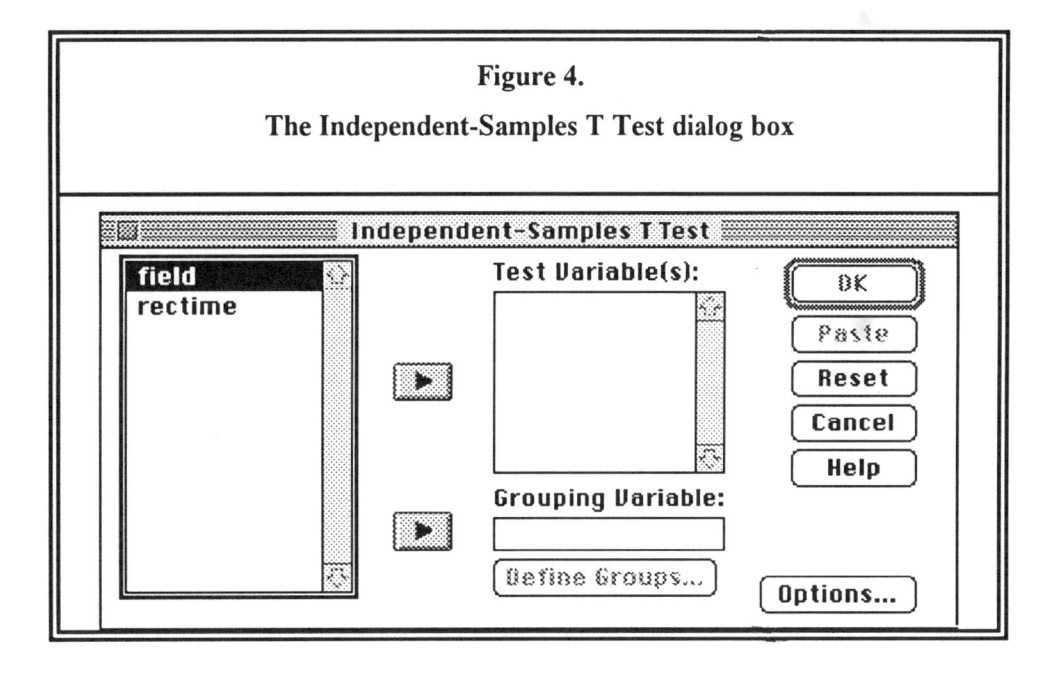

Figure 4.

The Independent-Samples T Test dialog box

- Highlight the dependent variable *rectime* in the left-hand box. Transfer *rectime* to the **Test Variable(s)** box by clicking on ▶. Similarly, highlight the grouping variable *field* and transfer it to the **Grouping Variable**. At this point the **Grouping Variable** box will appear with **? ?** as shown in Figure 5.

Figure 5.

The Grouping Variable part of the Independent-Samples t-test dialog box before defining the groups

Chapter 6 - Comparing the Averages of Two Samples

- Define the values of the groups by clicking on **Define Groups** (Figure 4) which will obtain the **Define Groups dialog box** (Figure 6).

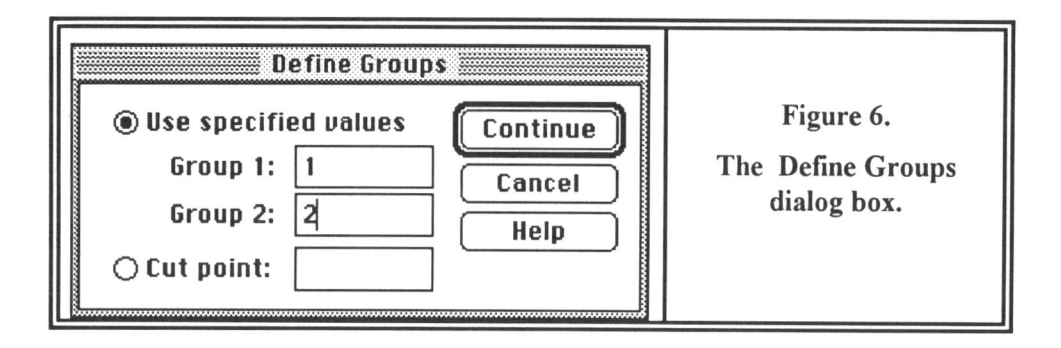

Figure 6.

The Define Groups dialog box.

- Type the value *1* into the **Group 1** box and the value *2* into the **Group 2** box, and click on **Continue**. The values 1, 2 will then appear in brackets after *field* in the **Grouping Variable** box as shown in the completed **Independent-Samples T Test** dialog box in Figure 7.
- Click on **OK** to run the t-test.

Figure 7.

The completed Independent-Samples T Test dialog box.

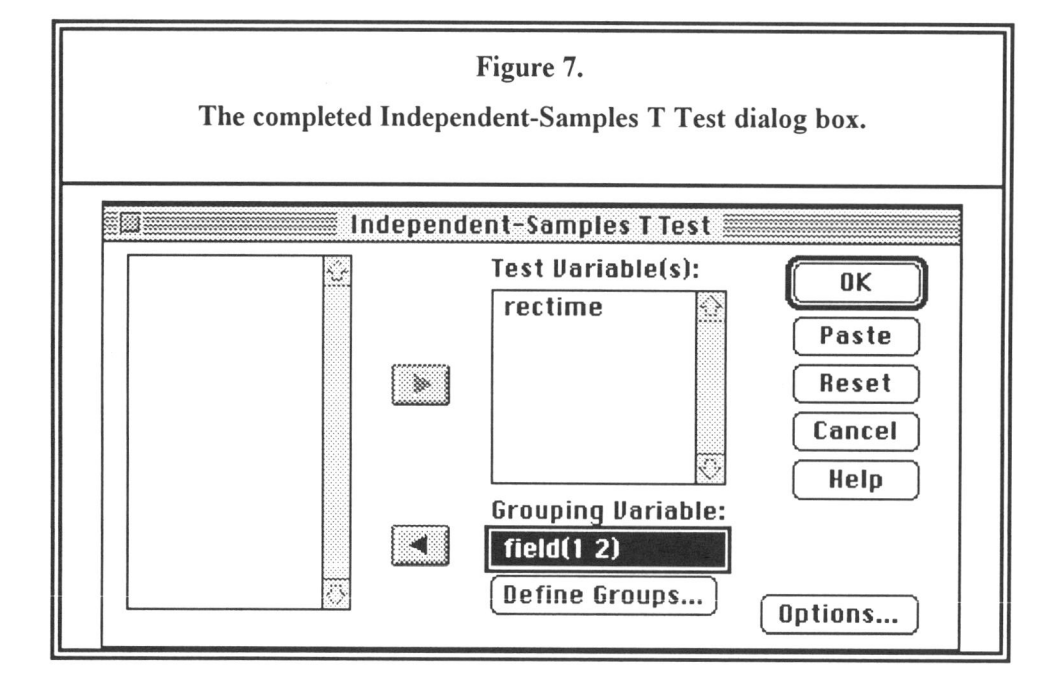

The output is shown in Output Listing 2.

The output starts with statistics of the two groups, followed by the value of the difference between means (Mean Difference). Since one of the assumptions for a valid t-test is homogeneity of variance, the **Levene Test** for homogeneity of variance is included. Provided the F value is **not significant** ($p > 0.05$), the variances can be assumed to be homogeneous and the **Equal Variances** line of values for the t-test can be used. If $p < 0.05$, then the homogeneity of variance assumption has been violated and the t-test based on separate variance estimates (**Unequal Variances** or **Equal variances not assumed**) should be used.

Output Listing 2.
t-test output for Independent Samples

```
t-tests for Independent Samples of FIELD    Visual Hemifield

                         Number
Variable                 of Cases      Mean       SD      SE of Mean

RECTIME

Left                        10       476.5000   73.083     23.111
Right                       10       430.8000   72.793     23.019

         Mean Difference = 45.7000

         Levene's Test for Equality of Variances: F= .068   P= .797

         t-test for Equality of Means                                95%
Variances   t-value    df     2-Tail Sig    SE of Diff         CI for Diff

Equal        1.40      18        .178         32.619       (-22.830, 114.230)
Unequal      1.40     18.00      .178         32.619       (-22.830, 114.230)
```

In this example, the Levene Test is not significant, so the t value calculated with the pooled variance estimate (Equal Variances) is appropriate. With a **2-Tail Sig** (i.e. p-value) of 0.178 (i.e. 17.8%), the difference between means is not significant. Write this as: t = 1.40; df = 18; NS.

This is confirmed by the **95% Confidence Interval** for the difference between means (-22.83 to 114.23) which includes the H_0 mean difference of 0. Had this interval been entirely positive, the result would have been significant.

6.3 NONPARAMETRIC METHODS

When there are serious violations of the assumptions of the t-test, nonparametric tests can be used instead. They should not be used as a matter of course, however, because should the data meet the requirements of the t-test, the comparable nonparametric test may lack the **power** to reject the null hypothesis, should that be false. It is best, therefore, to consider the parametric test first, resorting to the nonparametric alternative only if the data seriously violate the requirements.

SPSS has a wide selection of nonparametric tests in the **Nonparametric Tests** submenu of **Statistics**. The **Sign** and **Wilcoxon** tests are nonparametric counterparts of the paired samples t-test; the **Mann-Whitney** test is an alternative to the independent samples t-test.

Most nonparametric methods use measures, such as the median, that are resistant to outliers and skewness. In the tests described here, H_0 states that, in the population, the two **medians** are equal.

Chapter 6 - Comparing the Averages of Two Samples

6.3.1 Related samples: Wilcoxon, Sign and McNemar tests

- Choose
  Statistics
  　　Nonparametric Tests
  　　　　Related Samples ...

  to obtain the **Two-Related-Samples** dialog box (Figure 8).

- Highlight the variable names and transfer them to the **Test Pair(s) List** box. Click on **OK** to run the test.

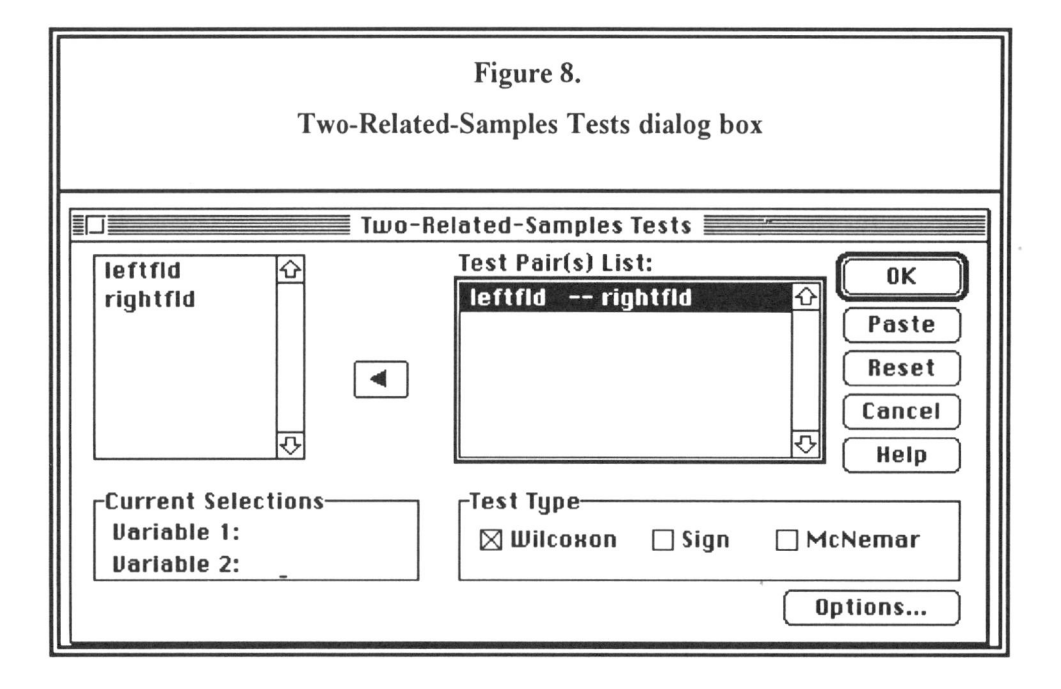

Figure 8.
Two-Related-Samples Tests dialog box

```
┌─────────────────── Two-Related-Samples Tests ───────────────────┐
│  leftfld              Test Pair(s) List:           ┌──OK──┐     │
│  rightfld             leftfld -- rightfld          ├─Paste┤     │
│                                                    ├─Reset┤     │
│                  ◀                                 ├─Cancel┤    │
│                                                    └─Help─┘     │
│  ┌Current Selections─┐  ┌Test Type─────────────────┐            │
│  │ Variable 1:       │  │ ☒ Wilcoxon  ☐ Sign  ☐ McNemar │        │
│  │ Variable 2:       │  │              ┌─Options...─┐  │        │
│  └───────────────────┘  └──────────────┴────────────┴──┘        │
└─────────────────────────────────────────────────────────────────┘
```

The results are shown in Output Listing 3.

The p-value for z (**2-tailed p**) is less than 0.01, confirming the t-test result that there is a significant difference between the visual fields. Write this as: z = 2.70; $p < 0.01$.

Although the Wilcoxon test assumes neither normality nor homogeneity of variance, it does assume that the two samples are from populations with the same distribution shape. It is also vulnerable to the influences of outliers - though not to nearly the same extent as the t-test. The **Sign test**, which is even more robust than the Wilcoxon, can be requested by clicking on its check box. The **McNemar test** is applicable to paired data relating to dichotomous qualitative variables.

Output Listing 3.

The output for the Wilcoxon test

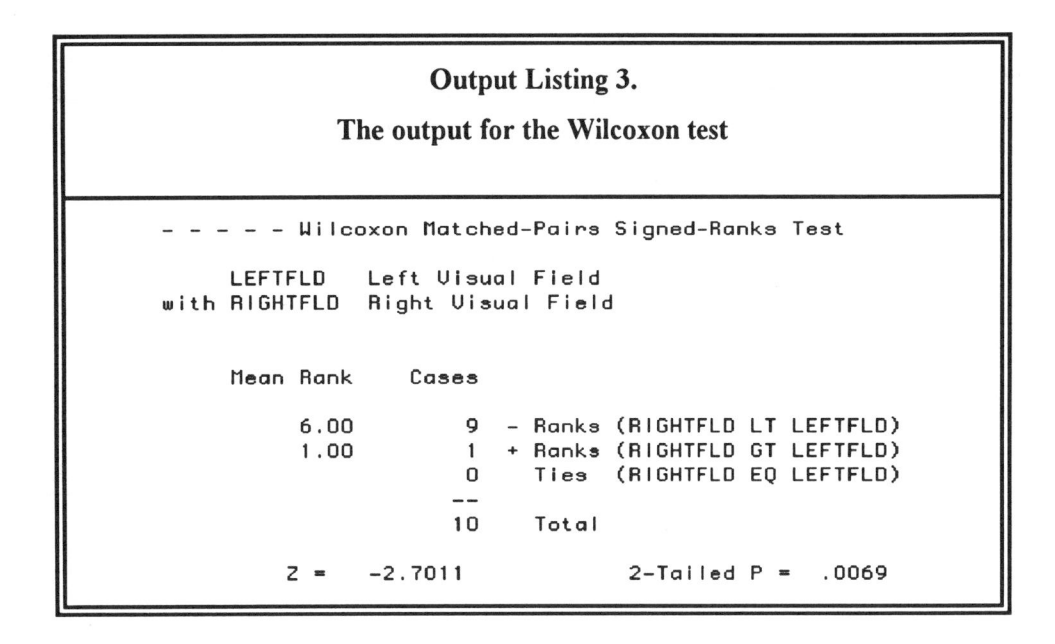

```
- - - - - Wilcoxon Matched-Pairs Signed-Ranks Test

    LEFTFLD    Left Visual Field
with RIGHTFLD  Right Visual Field

     Mean Rank    Cases

         6.00        9   - Ranks (RIGHTFLD LT LEFTFLD)
         1.00        1   + Ranks (RIGHTFLD GT LEFTFLD)
                     0     Ties  (RIGHTFLD EQ LEFTFLD)
                    --
                    10     Total

         Z =    -2.7011            2-Tailed P =   .0069
```

6.3.2 Independent Samples: Mann-Whitney test

- Choose
  Statistics
   Nonparametric Tests
    Independent Samples ...

to obtain the **Two-Independent-Samples** dialog box (Figure 9).

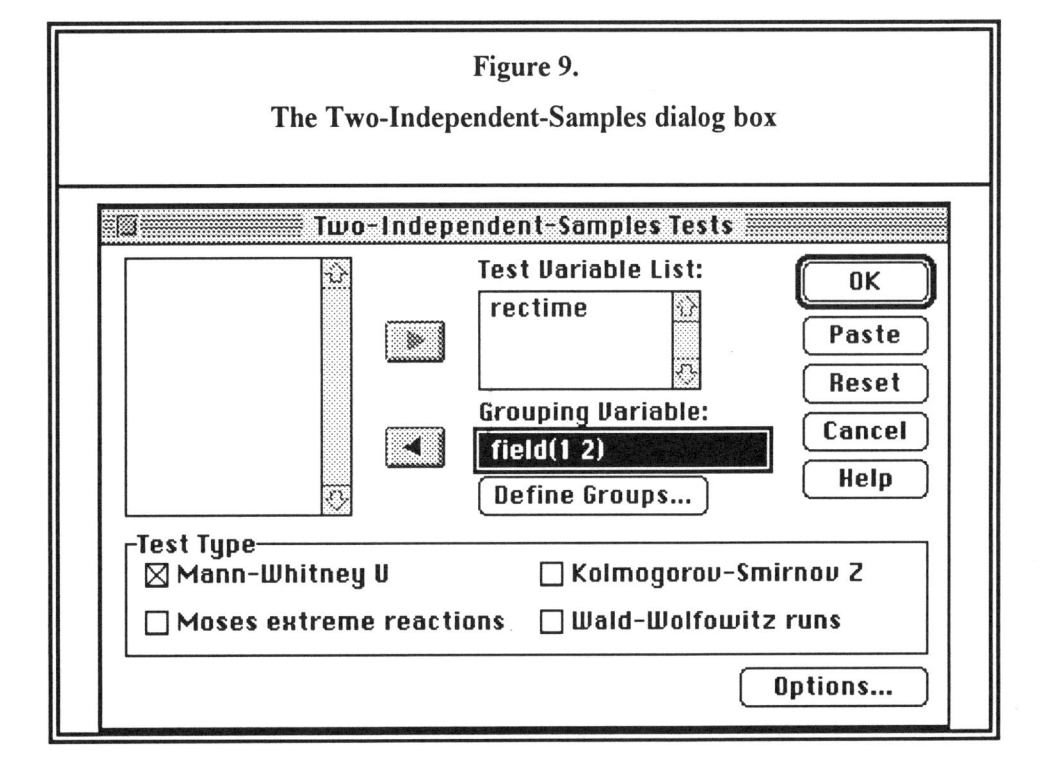

Figure 9.

The Two-Independent-Samples dialog box

Chapter 6 - Comparing the Averages of Two Samples

- Highlight the test variable name *rectime* and transfer it to the **Test Variable List** box. Highlight the grouping variable name *field* and transfer it to the **Grouping Variable** box; click on **Define Groups** and add the group numbers *1* and *2* in the usual way.

- Click on **Continue** and then on **OK** to run the test.

The results are shown in Output Listing 4.

```
                    Output Listing 4.
              The output for the Mann-Whitney test

 - - - - - Mann-Whitney U - Wilcoxon Rank Sum W Test
     RECTIME
  by FIELD       Visual Hemifield


     Mean Rank     Cases
        12.65      10    FIELD = 1  Left
         8.35      10    FIELD = 2  Right
                   --
                   20    Total
                              Exact             Corrected for ties
         U            W     2-Tailed P       Z         2-Tailed P
        28.5        126.5     .1051        -1.6259       .1040
```

The p-value for Z (**2-tailed p**) is greater than 0.05, confirming the t-test result that there is a no significant difference between the visual fields. Write this as: z = 1.63; NS.

160

EXERCISE 9

EXPLORING DATA FROM A SIMPLE TWO-GROUP EXPERIMENT

BEFORE YOU START

The previous exercises have used data from a questionnaire. The next few exercises will be based on data from experiments designed to test experimental hypotheses. In real experiments, of course, a larger number of subjects would have been used.

THE PROJECT

An investigation of the effects of a drug upon performance

The data we are going to explore in this exercise might have been produced by the following project. A team of investigators has good reason to believe that a small dosage of a certain drug increases the speed with which people can make decisions. They decide to try to confirm this by carrying out an experiment in which the decision times of 14 people who have ingested the drug are compared with those of a control group of 14 other people who have performed the task under a placebo condition. The experimenters expect that the decision times of the experimental group will tend to be shorter than those of the placebo group. The results are shown in Table 1.

Table 1.

Decision times of the experimental and placebo groups in the drug experiment

\multicolumn{4}{c	}{DRUG GROUP}	\multicolumn{4}{c}{PLACEBO GROUP}
Subject	Time	Subject	Time	Subject	Time	Subject	Time
1	471	8	425	15	446	22	440
2	494	9	421	16	749	23	471
3	386	10	407	17	599	24	501
4	323	11	386	18	460	25	492
5	660	12	550	19	390	26	392
6	406	13	470	20	477	27	578
7	345	14	393	21	556	28	398

Chapter 6 - Comparing the Averages of Two Samples

Constructing the SPSS data set

Construct the data set along the lines described in Section 3.3. The first column in the **Data Editor** window will represent the grouping variable (i.e. the type of treatment - drug or placebo) and we shall name it *group*. The second column will represent all the subjects' scores on the dependent variable and will be named *score*. Notice that this column will include the scores for **both** treatments; the first column, which represents the type of treatment, will be used by the computer to distinguish whether a score in the second column belongs to the drug group or to the placebo group.

Define the variables *group* and *score*, and enter the data of Table 1 into the **Data Editor** window in the manner described in Section 3.3. Use the labelling procedure to assign the value labels *drug* and *placebo* to the code numbers *1*, and *2*, respectively. Note that there is no need to enter the subject numbers, since each row of the Data Editor window is numbered automatically. When the data have been entered, save them to a file with a name such as **Drug Experiment**, from which they can be recalled at a later session.

Exploring the data

The first step is always to examine the data set to see whether there are any odd features.

Means and standard deviations

We shall want a table of means and standard deviations, together with indicators of distribution shape such as stem-and-leaf displays and boxplots. The statistics for the subgroups are most easily obtained with the **Means** procedure, and the plots from the **Explore** procedure. Follow the instructions in Section 4.3.2, remembering that the dependent variable name is *score* and the independent variable name is *group*.

- **Write down the values of the means and standard deviations**

Note that the **Means** procedure requires the presence of a grouping variable in the data set. To obtain the mean and standard deviation of a set of ungrouped data, use the **Descriptives** procedure.

Graphical displays of the data

To draw the plots, proceed as described in Section 4.3.2. The output listing begins with the stem-and-leaf displays for the two groups. The boxplots are then drawn in the **Chart Carousel**. When there is a marked discrepancy between the mean and median of a set of scores, it may be because the distribution is skewed or otherwise asymmetrical. Atypical scores, or **outliers** can also pull the value of the mean away from that of the median. Read Section 4.3.2 carefully for an explanation of SPSS's stem-and-leaf and boxplot displays.
- Identify any outliers by means of their row numbers.

Printing the listing

If you want to print out the listing, follow the procedure described in Section 3.6. The precise details will depend upon your local set-up.

Chapter 6 - Comparing the Averages of Two Samples

EXERCISE 10
COMPARING THE AVERAGES OF TWO INDEPENDENT SAMPLES

BEFORE YOU START

Before proceeding with this exercise, we suggest you read Chapter 6 carefully. This exercise concerns the **independent samples t-test** described in Section 6.2.4; the next will be concerned with the **paired samples t-test**, which is described in Section 6.2.3.

The data from Exercise 9 will be used again for the present exercise. In that experiment, the subjects were randomly assigned to either the Drug or the Placebo condition. Their scores, therefore, are two independent samples of interval data. Provided the distributions of the scores are appropriate, the independent samples t-test can be used to test the null hypothesis of no difference (in the population) between the means of the Drug and Placebo groups.

The **t-test** is an example of a **parametric** test: that is, it makes certain assumptions about the populations from which the samples have supposedly been drawn. It is assumed, for example, that the populations are normal, and that they have the same variance. When a data set is examined (by the methods of Chapter 4), it is often quite clear that neither the assumption of normality of distribution nor that of homogeneity of variance is tenable. This can mean that the **tail probability**, or **p-value**, given in the t-test output is misleading. One solution to this problem is to use a **nonparametric** test, a method which makes fewer assumptions about the population distributions. Later in this exercise, we shall use a nonparametric test, the **Mann-Whitney test** (sometimes called the Wilcoxon Mann-Whitney test), to compare the medians of the Drug and Placebo groups.

THE INDEPENDENT SAMPLES t-TEST

If you worked through Exercise 9 and stored the data to a file on floppy disk, they can easily be restored to SPSS by using the **Open** procedure. Otherwise, the data must be typed into the **Data Editor** window again and then saved.

Exploring the data

Before any formal statistical tests are carried out, it is essential to explore the data distributions. **Outliers** can also be detected at this stage. In this case, however, the data have already been thoroughly explored. In the previous exercise, it was found that both samples had practically identical variances (i.e. their standard deviations had very similar values) and the various plots (boxplots and stem-and-leaf displays) indicated that the distributions were such as to permit the use of a parametric test. The only untoward finding was that one of the subjects in the Placebo group had a score of *749*, which is highly atypical of the group as a whole.

Procedure for an independent samples t-test

Full details of the procedure for the independent samples t test are given in Section 6.2.4. Run the procedure as described in that section.

Output listing for the independent samples t-test

- **Guidance on how to interpret the listing is given in Section 6.2.4. We suggest you study that section and try to answer the following questions.**

Chapter 6 - Comparing the Averages of Two Samples

- **On the basis of the Levene test p-value, which row of the t-test results will you use?**
- **Write down the value of t and its tail probability. Is the p-value evidence against the null hypothesis? Remember that if the result is sufficiently unlikely (i.e. p < 0.05) under the null hypothesis, it is regarded as evidence against the null hypothesis and hence in favour of the experimental hypothesis.**
- **Write down your interpretation of the result of the test: has the t-test confirmed the pattern shown by the means of the two groups?**

A NONPARAMETRIC TEST: THE MANN-WHITNEY

When there are serious violations of the distribution assumptions of the t test, a nonparametric test should be considered. When there are two independent samples of scores, the **Mann-Whitney** test can be used to compare the averages of the two groups. It should be noted, however, that whereas in the parametric test the null hypothesis stated that the two population means are equal, the nonparametric test concerns **medians**, not means: in the **Mann-Whitney** test, the null hypothesis states that the population medians are equal.

Procedure for the Mann-Whitney test

The **Mann-Whitney** test procedure is fully described in Section 6.3.2. Run the procedure as described in that section.

Output listing for the Mann-Whitney test

The listing gives the values of the statistics U and W (the W statistic belongs to a test by Wilcoxon which is the exact equivalent of the Mann-Whitney), followed by an exact 2-tailed probability value, and then a standard normal deviate score Z and a 2-tailed probability value corrected for ties. If this p-value is less than 0.05, the null hypothesis can be rejected and the groups declared to differ significantly.

- **Write down the results of the Mann-Whitney test, including the value of U and its p-value. State whether the result is significant and whether the Mann-Whitney test confirms the result of the t-test. In what circumstances would you expect the p-values of U and t to differ?**

Chapter 6 - Comparing the Averages of Two Samples

EXERCISE 11

COMPARING THE AVERAGES OF TWO SAMPLES: PAIRED DATA

BEFORE YOU START

The methods described in the previous exercise, (the **independent samples t-test** and the **Mann-Whitney** test), are appropriate for data from a between subjects experiment, that is, one with independent samples of subjects in the two groups. Suppose, however, that the data had come from an experiment in which the same subjects had been tested under both the experimental and control conditions. Such a within subjects experiment would yield a set of paired (or related) data. In this exercise, we shall consider some methods for comparing the averages of the scores obtained under the experimental and control conditions when we have a set of paired data (SPSS calls this **paired samples**), rather than independent samples. Before proceeding with this exercise, the reader should review the material in Sections 6.2.2 and 6.2.3.

THE PAIRED SAMPLES T-TEST

An experiment on hemispherical specialisation

In an experiment investigating the relative ease with which words presented in the left and right visual fields were recognised, subjects were instructed to fixate a spot in the centre of the field. They were told that, after a short interval, a word would appear to the left or the right of the spot and they were to press a key as soon as they recognised it. In the trials that followed, each word was presented an equal number of times in each field, though the order of presentation of the words was, of course, randomised. From the results, a table of median decision times was constructed from the subjects' reactions to presentations of 40 words in each of the two visual fields (Table 1).
Do these data support the experimental hypothesis that there is a difference between the response times for words in the left and right visual fields?

Rationale of the paired samples t-test

In the **paired samples t-test**, the strategy is to subtract (consistently) either the first or the second member of each pair of scores from the other, producing a single column of difference scores. If there is, in the population, no difference between the mean scores for the right and left visual fields, the mean difference will be zero. The null hypothesis to be tested states that our 14 difference scores are a sample from a normal population with a mean of zero and a variance which can be estimated from the difference scores in the sample.
If we can assume that the population of differences is normally distributed, the null hypothesis can be tested with the statistic t, where

$$t = \frac{\text{mean difference}}{\text{standard error of the difference}}$$

If there are n pairs of data (i.e. n subjects), this t statistic has (n-1) degrees of freedom. In the present example, df = 13. The **one-sample t-test** presupposes that the difference scores are normally distributed. Should it turn out from preliminary inspection of the data that the differences are far from being normally distributed or that there are huge outliers, the user should beware of the t-test, especially with a small data set such as the present one, and should consider using a test that makes fewer assumptions about the data. For sets of paired data showing contraindications against the use of the related t-test, there are two nonparametric tests, neither of which assumes normality of the

Chapter 6 - Comparing the Averages of Two Samples

population distribution; both, moreover, are robust to the influence of outliers. These tests are:
(1) **Wilcoxon matched pairs test**;
(2) **Sign test**.
The latter is the more resistant to the leverage exerted by outliers; but, provided there are no outliers, the Wilcoxon is the more powerful test. (On the other hand, there are those who would say that if the data are good enough for the Wilcoxon, they are good enough for the paired samples t-test.)

Before proceeding with this exercise, we strongly urge you to read Section 6.2.3, which describes the procedure for a paired samples t-test.

Table 1.
Median decision times for words presented to the right and left visual fields

Subject	Right visual field	Left visual field	Subject	Right visual field	Left visual field
s1	323	324	s8	439	442
s2	493	512	s9	682	683
s3	502	503	s10	703	998
s4	376	385	s11	598	600
s5	428	453	s12	456	462
s6	343	345	s13	653	704
s7	523	543	s14	652	653

Preparing the SPSS data set

In the data set for the independent samples t-test, one of the variables must be a grouping variable, showing which subjects performed under which conditions. With the paired samples t-test, however, there was only one group and so no coding variable need be constructed. Define two variables: *rvf* with label *Right Visual Field*, and *lvf* with label *Left Visual Field*. Enter the data in the usual way, as described in Section 3.4. The two columns *rvf* and *lvf* are sufficient for SPSS to run a paired samples t-test. As always, however, it is wise to explore the data, rather than pressing ahead with the formal test automatically. Since the null hypothesis concerns only the population of differences (rather than the separate *rvf* and *lvf* populations), we first calculate the differences and see how those are distributed. It is a very simple matter to obtain the differences by using the **Compute** procedure (Section 4.4.2) to create a new variable, *diffs,* containing the (*rvf* - *lvf*) difference for each subject.

Exploring the data

To list the values within *diffs*, click on
Statistics
> **Summarize**
>> **List Cases ...**

to open the **List Cases** dialog box. Click on *diffs* and then on ► to paste the name into the **Variable(s)** box. Click on **OK**.
From inspection of the column of differences, it is quite clear that there is a glaring outlier. It is instructive to ascertain the effect of its presence upon the results of the t-test, in comparison with the nonparametric **Wilcoxon** and **Sign** tests. Although, in the paired samples t-test, the interest centres on the column of differences rather than the original scores, it is nevertheless of interest to see the scatterplot of *rvf* against *lvf,* which, ideally, should show an elliptical cloud of points indicating a bivariate normal distribution. Use the procedure in Section 6.2.3 to obtain a scatterplot of *lvf* against *rvf* and notice how the outlier shows up dramatically.

Running the paired samples t-test

Run the **paired samples t-test** by following the procedure described in Section 6.2.3.

Output listing for the paired samples t-test

From the details given in the t-test listing, it is clear that there are contraindications against the use of the paired samples t-test for the data in the present experiment. There is marked discrepancy between the standard deviations of the scores obtained under the *rvf* and *lvf* conditions. This arises from the presence of an outlier, which showed up dramatically in the scatterplot.

- **From the listing, write down the value of *t* and its p-value. Is *t* significant? Write down, in terms of the research hypothesis, the meaning of this result.**

What has happened here? You should find the t-test result paradoxical to say the least. Each of the fourteen pairs of data (one pair from each subject) shows a difference in the same direction: the *rvf* time is always lower than the *lvf* time. Moreover, in the case of the outlying pair of scores, the difference is even greater. Surely this should strengthen the evidence against the null hypothesis? Yet, in fact, the t-test does not show significance. This is because the outlier has exerted more leverage upon the denominator of the t statistic than it has upon the numerator, thus reducing the value of t (see Section 6.2.3).

NONPARAMETRIC ALTERNATIVES TO THE PAIRED SAMPLES T-TEST

The Wilcoxon matched pairs test

Now carry out the **Wilcoxon matched pairs** test, following the procedure described in Section 6.3.1.
- **Write down the value of the statistic and its p-value. Compare the p-value with that for the t-test. Relate the result of the Wilcoxon test to the experimental hypothesis.**

The Sign test

This test is based very simply on how many positive and negative differences there are between pairs of data, assuming that the value of one variable is consistently subtracted from the value of the other. It is a straightforward application of the binomial model to paired data, such as the results of the visual field experiment above. To merely record the signs (rather than the magnitudes) of the differences between the times for the left and right visual fields is certainly to lose a considerable amount of information. Indeed, when paired data show no contraindications, the related t-test is preferable to the Sign test, for to use the latter in such circumstances would be to make a needless sacrifice of power. The great advantage of the Sign test, however, is its robustness to the influence of outliers; moreover, there are no requirements about bivariate normality in the original paired data.

The procedure is very similar to that for the Wilcoxon test except that within the **Test Type** box, the **Wilcoxon** check box should be clicked off and the **Sign** check box clicked on. Click on **OK** to run the procedure.

- **Write down the results of the Sign test, including the p-value. Is the result significant? Compare this with the result of the paired samples t-test and explain any discrepancy.**

You may have noticed that the p-value for the **Sign** test is even smaller than that for the **Wilcoxon** test. This is because, although the Wilcoxon test is less sensitive to the presence of outliers than is the t-test, it is still affected by them to some extent.

ELIMINATING THE OUTLIERS

When there are contraindications for the **paired samples t-test**, the use of a nonparametric test is not the only alternative available. Another approach is to consider the possibility of eliminating some of the data. In the present set of paired data, there is one (*lvf-rvf*) difference which is much larger than all the others. This may have arisen because subject 10 has special difficulty in recognising words in the left visual field. At any rate, that subject's performance is quite atypical of this sample of participants and certainly calls into question the claim that he or she was drawn from the same population as the others. It is instructive to reanalyse the data after excluding the scores of Subject 10. This is done by using the **Select Cases** procedure (Section 3.7.1). Follow the procedure described in that section to eliminate the data from subject 10. (Hint: give the instruction to select cases if ABS(*diffs*) is less than 100; here, beware of negative scores.)

Now re-run the **paired samples t-test**, the **Wilcoxon** and the **Sign** test on the reduced data set. Examine the new listings.

- **Write down the value of t and its tail probability. Write down your interpretation of this new result. Similarly give the statistics and their p-values for the Sign and Wilcoxon tests, commenting on the relative sizes of the p-values.**

Appendix to Exercise 11

SOME NOTES ON ONE-SAMPLE TESTS

So far, we have been concerned with tests of the null hypothesis that, in the population, there is no difference between the averages of two correlated samples of data. There can arise, however, situations where one has a single sample of scores and wishes to test the null hypothesis that the sample has been drawn from a population with a specified mean, which may be other than zero.

The one-sample t-test

Suppose it is known that, over the years, the mean performance on a spelling test of children in a particular class at school is 51. One year, however, following the introduction of a new teaching method, it is hoped that a higher level of performance will be achieved. At the end of the year, it is found that the mean of the children's spelling scores is 60. Is this improvement significant? The null hypothesis that the population mean has value 51 could be tested by defining (in the **Data Editor** window) the variable *scores*, containing the children's marks. Then the **Compute** procedure could be used to define another variable *mean*, containing the constant value *51*. Finally the **paired samples t-test** could be used in the usual way to make the required one-sample test.

To demonstrate this procedure with the hemispherical specialisation data, use the **paired samples t-test** to test the hypothesis that the column *diffs* contains a sample of scores from a population whose mean is zero. Define by the **Compute** procedure the variable *hyp* (for hypothesis) by typing *hyp* in the **Target Variable** box and 0 in the **Numeric Expression** box. Click on **OK**. Then select *diffs* and *hyp* within the **paired samples t-test** dialog box and click on **OK**. You should finish with the same t value as previously.

The binomial test

Underlying the Sign test is the binomial model. There is also an explicit **binomial test** which can be used in situations such as the following. Suppose that a child is presented with a series of 20 pairs of objects, one member of each of which contains a reward. Sometimes the child makes the correct choice; but is this just good luck, or has the rule really been understood?

There are two ways of entering the data for the binomial test:

Method 1. You can decide upon a code for right and wrong guesses (e.g. 1 for a correct answer, 0 for a wrong one), and enter the person's performance as a series such as:

1 1 0 1 1 1 1 0 0 0 1 1 1 0 1 1 1 1 1 1

If we assume that there were only two choices for each question (i.e. the probability of a correct guess is ½ each time), the procedure for the first method is as follows:

Define the variable *guesses*, containing the above sequence of code numbers representing the subject's performance.
Next, choose
Statistics
    Nonparametric Tests
        Binomial
to open the **Binomial Test** dialog box. Click on *guesses* and on ▶ to transfer the name to the **Test Variable** box. Click on **OK** to run the procedure.

Method 2. Alternatively, the data can be entered as the numbers of correct and incorrect answers produced (in the current example, the child got 15 choices right and 5 wrong in a sequence of 20 trials). The **Weight Cases** procedure (see Section 3.7.2) instructs SPSS to treat the values *15* and *5* as frequencies rather than as scores.
As an exercise, try both methods to assess the child's performance.
So far, the binomial test has assumed the default value of 0.5 for the proportion of cases expected in the first category (i.e. the probability p of a case falling into the first category). In most experimental situations (and multiple-choice examinations), however, there are more than two choices at each trial. We need to be able to cope with situations where p is not 0.5. This is easily dealt with by changing the value of **Test Proportion** in the **Binomial Test** dialog box to whatever value is required. If there were four choices for each question, for example, the value would be 0.25.

CHAPTER 7

THE ONE-FACTOR BETWEEN SUBJECTS EXPERIMENT

7.1   INTRODUCTION
7.2   THE ONE-WAY ANOVA
7.3   NONPARAMETRIC TESTS

Chapter 7 - The One-Factor Between Subjects Experiment

7.1 INTRODUCTION

Suppose that an experiment has been carried out to compare the performance of two groups of subjects: an **experimental** group and a **control** group. Provided the data have certain characteristics (i.e. the samples have approximately normal distributions and comparable variances), an independent samples t-test can be used to test the null hypothesis (H_0) of equality of the two population means. If the test shows significance, we reject H_0: we conclude that there is a difference between the two population means, which is equivalent to the conclusion that the experimental manipulation does have an effect.

The same null hypothesis, however, can also be tested by using one of the set of techniques known as **analysis of variance (ANOVA** for short). Despite its name, the ANOVA, like the t-test, is concerned with the testing of hypotheses about **means**. In fact, if the ANOVA and the (pooled variance) t-test are applied to the data from a simple, two-group experiment, the tests will give the same result: if the t-test shows the difference between the means to be significant, then so will the ANOVA and vice versa.

The ANOVA, however, is more versatile than the t-test. Suppose that in an investigation of the effects of mnemonic training methods upon recall, three groups of subjects were tested:

(a) a group trained in Mnemonic Method A;

(b) a group trained in Mnemonic Method B;.

(c) a Control group, who had merely been asked to memorise the material as well as possible.

This type of experiment, in which each subject performs under only one of the conditions making up a single independent variable, is said to have **one treatment factor** with **no repeated measures**. It is also known as the **completely randomised experiment**. From such an experiment, we would obtain three samples of scores, one for each of the three groups. The 'one-way' ANOVA can test the null hypothesis that all three population means are equal, i.e. neither mnemonic technique improves recall (in comparison with the control group). Note that, unlike ANOVA, the t-test cannot be used to evaluate a hypothesis about three or more population means: it can substitute for ANOVA only if there are two groups in the experiment.

Why couldn't a series of t-tests be used to make comparisons among the three group means? Couldn't we simply use three t-tests to compare the Control group with the Mnemonic A and Mnemonic B groups, and Mnemonic A with Mnemonic B? The problem with that approach is that when multiple comparisons are made among a set of treatment means, the probability of at least one test showing significance **even when the null hypothesis is true** is higher than the conventional significance level (i.e. critical p-value) of 0.05 or 0.01; in fact, if there is a large array of treatment group means, the probability of at least one test showing significance is close to 1 (certainty)! This point is explained in greater detail in Gravetter & Wallnau (1997).

A lucid account of the rationale of the one-factor between subjects (one-way) ANOVA is given in Gravetter & Wallnau (1997), Chapter 13. Basically, the

ANOVA works like this. A group mean is taken to be an estimate of people's typical level of performance under that particular condition. But individual performance can vary widely and at times deviates markedly from the group mean. Think of this **within group** variability as background noise, or **error**. It may be, however, that mnemonic groups A and B achieved much higher average levels of performance than did the control group: in other words, there is high variability **between (i.e. among) groups**. The **ANOVA F statistic** is calculated by dividing an estimate of the variability **between groups** by the variability **within groups**:

$$F = \frac{\text{variance between}}{\text{variance within}}$$

If there are large differences among the treatment means, the numerator of F (and therefore F itself) will be inflated and the null hypothesis is likely to be rejected; but if there is no effect, the numerator and denominator of F should have similar values, giving an F close to unity. A high value of F, therefore, is evidence against the null hypothesis of equality of all three population means.

There remains a problem, however. If H_0 states that all the means are equal, the alternative hypothesis is that they are not. If the ANOVA F test gives significance, we know there is a difference **somewhere** among the means, but that does not justify us in saying that any **particular** comparison is significant. The ANOVA F test, in fact, is an **omnibus test**, and further analysis is necessary to localise whatever differences there may be among the individual treatment means.

The question of exactly how one should proceed to further analysis after making the omnibus F test in ANOVA is not a simple one, and an adequate treatment of it earns an extensive chapter in many statistical texts (e.g. Kirk, 1982, Chapter 3; Howell, 1997, Chapter 12). It is important to distinguish between those comparisons that were **planned** before the data were actually gathered, and those that are made as part of the inevitable process of unplanned **data-snooping** that takes place after the results have been obtained. Planned comparisons are often known as **a priori** comparisons. Unplanned comparisons should be termed **a posteriori** comparisons, but unfortunately the misnomer **post hoc** is more often used.

SPSS offers the user both planned comparisons and an assortment of unplanned data-snooping tests, such as **Tukey's Honestly Significant Difference (HSD) test, Scheffé's test**, and so on. If these are unfamiliar to you, we urge you to read the relevant chapters in the books we have cited.

7.2 THE ONE-WAY ANOVA

7.2.1 The mnemonics experiment revisited

In Chapter 3 (Section 3.3.1), an experiment was described in which the performance of two groups of subjects, each trained in a different mnemonic method (Mnemonic A or Mnemonic B), was compared with that of a group of untrained controls. The results are shown in Table 1, which is a reproduction of Table 5 in Chapter 3.

Table 1.

The numbers of words recalled by subjects with different mnemonic training methods

Control Group	3	5	3	2	4	6	9	3	8	10
Mnemonic A	10	8	15	9	11	16	17	17	7	10
Mnemonic B	20	15	14	15	17	10	8	11	18	19

Section 3.3.1 describes how this set of results is recast into a form suitable for entry into SPSS and Figure 7 in that Chapter is a reproduction of the **Data Editor** window comprising two variables *group* and *score*. The first variable *group* identifies the Control, Mnemonic A, and Mnemonic B groups, the second variable *score* contains each subject's score achieved under the condition coded by the *group* variable on the same row. The **Define Labels** dialog box (Chapter 3, Figure 5) was used to assign to the independent variable *group* the more informative variable label *Mnemonic Training Method*, and to assign the value labels *Control*, *Mnemonic A* and *Mnemonic B* to the values *1*, *2* and *3*, respectively.

We shall assume that the data set was saved and can therefore be recalled immediately to the **Data Editor** by using the procedure in Section 3.4.2.

7.2.2 Procedure for the one-way ANOVA

The following instructions assume that the data set shown in Chapter 3, Figure 7, has been restored to the **Data Editor** window.

Chapter 7 - The One-Factor Between Subjects Experiment

The one-way analysis of variance is selected by proceeding as follows.

- Choose
  Statistics
    Compare Means
      One-Way ANOVA

as shown in Figure 1. This will open the **One-Way ANOVA** dialog box (Figure 2).

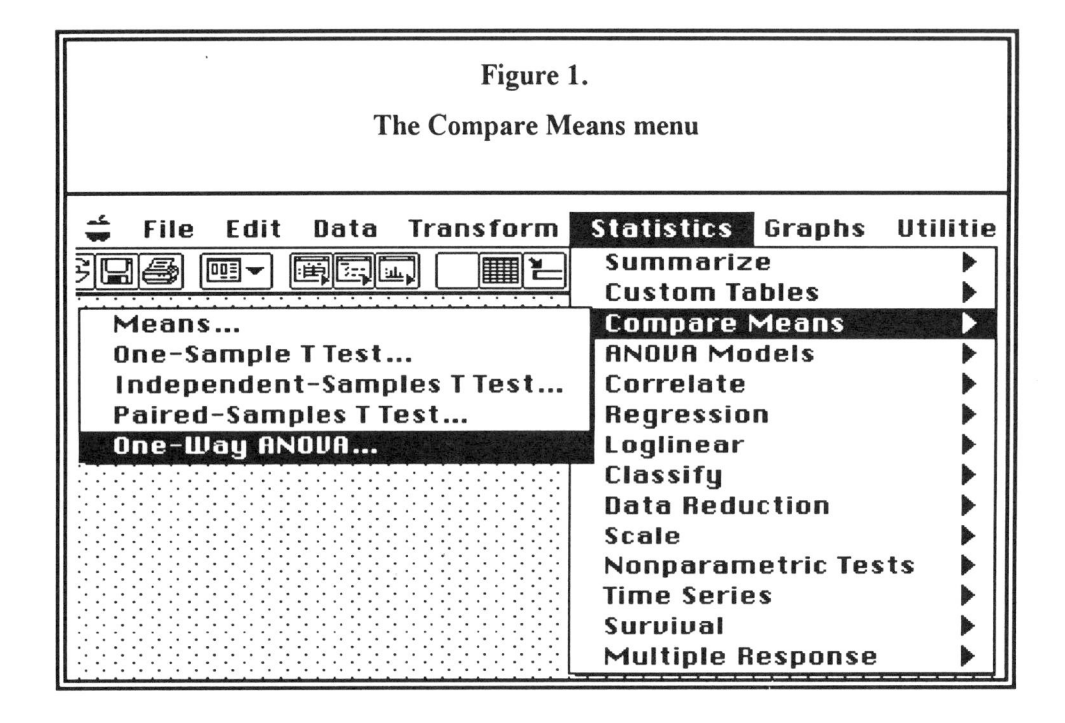

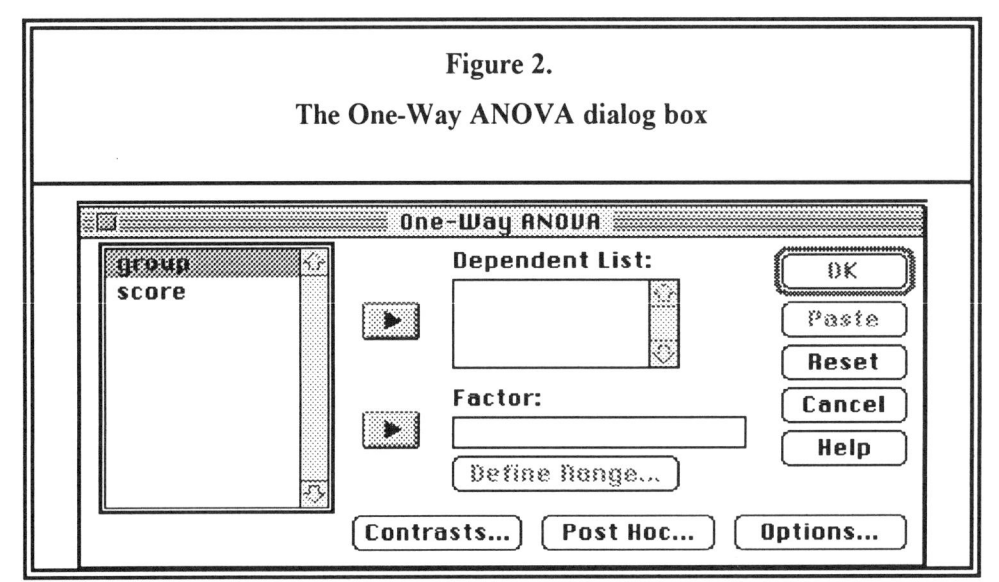

Figure 1.

The Compare Means menu

Figure 2.

The One-Way ANOVA dialog box

- Click on *group* and then on ▶ to transfer it to the **Factor** box. Click on the **Define Range** box to obtain the **Define Range Dialog box** (Figure 3).

174

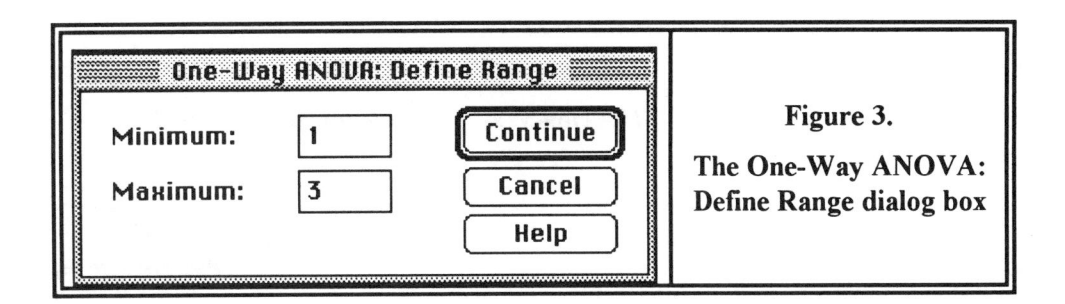

Chapter 7 - The One-Factor Between Subjects Experiment

Figure 3.

The One-Way ANOVA: Define Range dialog box

- Type the value *1* into **Minimum** box and *3* into the **Maximum** box. Click on **Continue**.

- Return to the variable names (Figure 2), click on *score* and then on ▶ to transfer it to the **Dependent List** box.

- Unplanned multiple pairwise comparisons among the means can be obtained by clicking on the **Post Hoc** button to obtain the **One-Way ANOVA: Post Hoc Multiple Comparisons** dialog box (Figure 4) and then clicking on the check box opposite **Tukey's honestly significant difference**.

Figure 4.

The One-Way ANOVA: Post Hoc Multiple Comparisons dialog box.

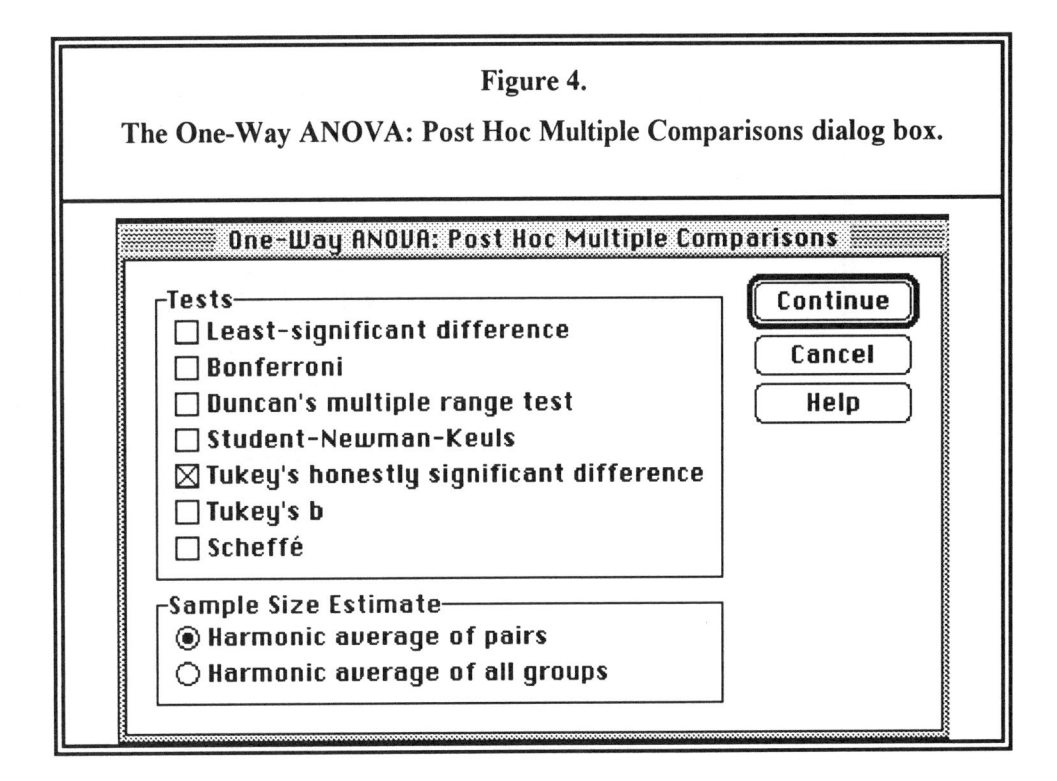

- Click on **Continue** to return to the **One-Way ANOVA** dialog box.

- If descriptive statistics are desired, they can be obtained by clicking on **Options** and then on the check box opposite **Descriptive** (see Figure 5).

175

Chapter 7 - The One-Factor Between Subjects Experiment

Figure 5.
The One-Way ANOVA: Options dialog box.

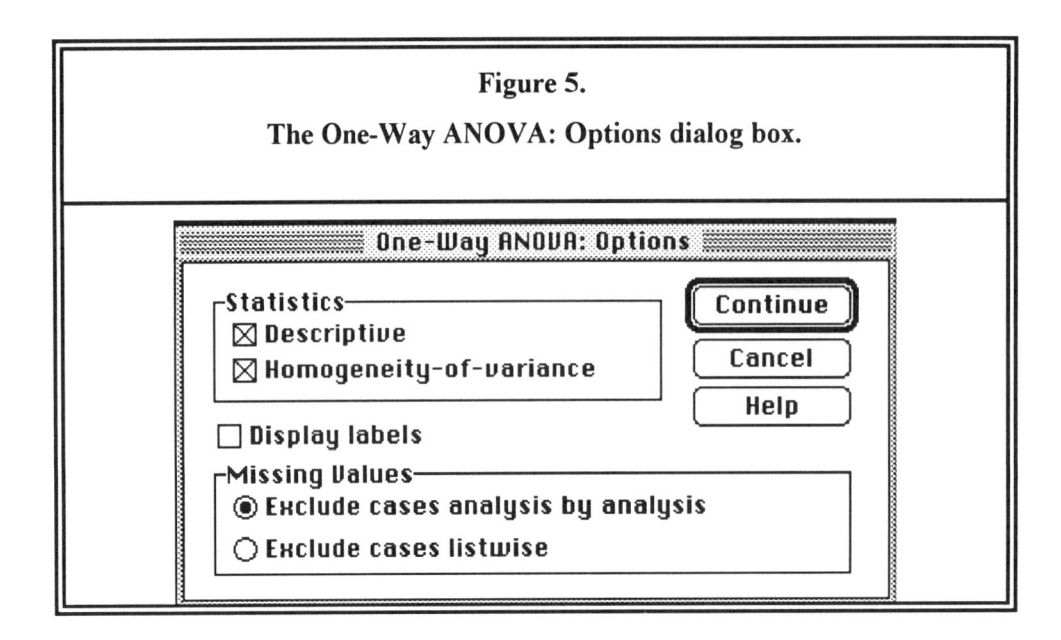

- The completed **One-Way ANOVA** dialog box is shown in Figure 6. Click on **OK** to run the ANOVA..

Figure 6.
The completed One-Way ANOVA dialog box

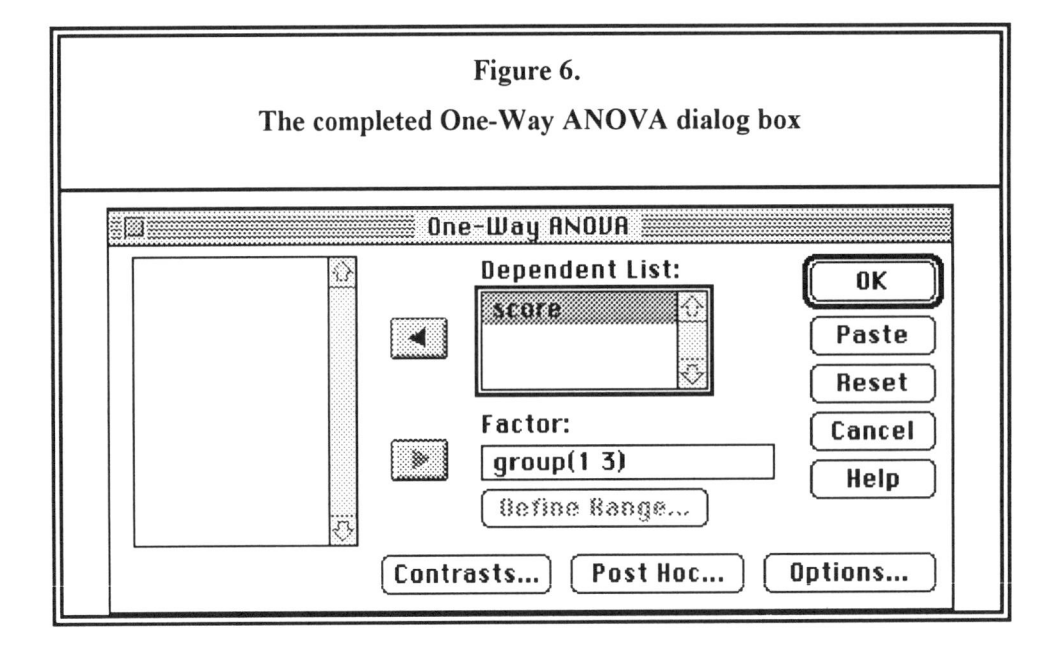

7.2.3 Output listing for the one-way ANOVA

The ANOVA summary table

The summary table for the one-way ANOVA is shown in Output Listing 1.

Note the **F Prob** value: this is the p-value of F (i.e. the probability under H_0 of a value at least as extreme as the one obtained). If the p-value is less than 0.05, F is statistically significant. The smaller the p-value, the stronger the evidence against the null hypothesis. In this example, H_0 can be rejected, since the p-value is very small indeed. (It is shown as .0000 in the listing, which means that it is less than 0.00005).

Output Listing 1.

The Summary Table for One-Way ANOVA

```
    Variable  SCORE
 By Variable  GROUP      Mnemonic Training Method

                         Analysis of Variance

                           Sum of       Mean          F       F
         Source    D.F.   Squares     Squares     Ratio   Prob.

Between Groups       2   463.4000    231.7000    18.7415   .0000
Within Groups       27   333.8000     12.3630
Total               29   797.2000
```

It is worth noting that in a scientific paper, it is not acceptable to write, 'p = .0000'. The results of the present ANOVA F test would be reported in a format like the following: $F(2, 27) = 13.74$; $p < 0.01$, where the bracketed numbers are the degrees of freedom of the numerator (here it is the Between Groups D.F.) and the denominator (here it is the Within Groups D.F.) of the F ratio.

Descriptive statistics for a one-way ANOVA

Output Listing 2 continues with the descriptive statistics.

Output Listing 2.

Descriptive statistics for One-Way ANOVA

```
                        Standard   Standard
Group     Count   Mean  Deviation    Error    95 Pct Conf Int for Mean

Grp 1       10   5.3000   2.8304    .8950      3.2753  TO    7.3247
Grp 2       10  11.8000   3.6148   1.1431      9.2141  TO   14.3859
Grp 3       10  14.7000   4.0014   1.2654     11.8376  TO   17.5624

Total       30  10.6000   5.2431    .9572      8.6422  TO   12.5578


GROUP      MINIMUM    MAXIMUM

Grp 1       2.0000    10.0000
Grp 2       7.0000    17.0000
Grp 3       8.0000    20.0000

TOTAL       2.0000    20.0000


Levene Test for Homogeneity of Variances
    Statistic    df1    df2    2-tail Sig.
       .7348      2      27        .489
```

Chapter 7 - The One-Factor Between Subjects Experiment

These include standard deviations, standard errors, 95% confidence intervals (confidence intervals are explained in Chapter 6, Section 6.2.3) and extreme values.

Levene's Test for Homogeneity of Variance was also requested (see the completed **One-Way ANOVA: Options** dialog box in Figure 5). The high p-value, or tail probability, indicates that there is no evidence for heterogeneity of variance.

Unplanned multiple comparisons with Tukey's HSD test

The results of **Tukey's HSD test** are tabulated in Output Listing 3.

Output Listing 3.

The Tukey-HSD test output

```
        Variable  SCORE
     By Variable  GROUP       Mnemonic Training Method

Multiple Range Tests:  Tukey-HSD test with significance level .05

The difference between two means is significant if
  MEAN(J)-MEAN(I)  >= 2.4863 * RANGE * SQRT(1/N(I) + 1/N(J))
  with the following value(s) for RANGE: 3.50

  (*) Indicates significant differences which are shown in the lower triangle

                              G G G
                              r r r
                              p p p

                              1 2 3
      Mean        GROUP

      5.3000      Grp 1
     11.8000      Grp 2      *
     14.7000      Grp 3      *

Homogeneous Subsets (highest and lowest means are not significantly different)

Subset 1

Group       Grp 1

Mean        5.3000
- - - - - - - - -

Subset 2

Group       Grp 2       Grp 3

Mean       11.8000     14.7000
- - - - - - - - - - - - - - -
```

In Output Listing 3, the means are ordered and displayed from smallest to largest in the first column (so the groups may not be in the same order as they were in the **Data Editor** window). To the right of this column is the following:

```
              G G G
              r r r
              p p p

              1 2 3
      GROUP

      Grp 1
      Grp 2   *
      Grp 3   *
```

This is a lower triangular matrix (i.e. where the items, if all present, would appear in the form of a triangle) of asterisks indicating which pairs of groups differ significantly at the 5% level. Here groups 2 and 3 each differ from group 1, but they do not differ from each other (in which case there would have been an additional asterisk at the intersection of the Group 2 column and the Group 3 row).

Finally, at the end of the listing, the groups are divided into homogeneous subsets, thus showing which means do *not* differ from one another (i.e. the members within each subset). Here Group 1 which differs from Groups 2 and 3 is in a separate subset from the other two groups which do not differ from one another.

The rationale of **Tukey's HSD** test is that if the treatment means are arranged in order of magnitude, and the smallest is subtracted from the largest, the probability of obtaining a large difference increases with the size of the array of means. To achieve significance, it requires that any pairwise difference must exceed a critical difference (CD) given by the formula

$$CD = q_{critical} \sqrt{\frac{MS_{error}}{n}}$$

where $q_{critical}$ is the critical value of a special statistic known as the **Studentized Range Statistic q**, MS_{error} is the mean square for the error term of the one-way ANOVA, and n is the number of scores in each treatment group (n).

The 0.05 or 0.01 critical value of **q** is obtained by looking up a table of critical values of the **Studentized Range Statistic** (see Howell, 1997; pp 680-681). To obtain the critical value, enter the table with the values of the following two parameters:

(1) the number of means in the array (i.e. the number of treatments);

(2) the degrees of freedom (df) of MS_{error} (MS_{error} is the quantity **Mean Square** for the row labelled **Within Groups** in Output Listing 1).

In this example, the number of means = 3 and the df for the **Within Groups** source of variance = 27. This value of 27 is k(n - 1) where k is the number of treatment means and n is the number of subjects in each treatment group (i.e. df = 3(10-1) = 27). For these values, $q_{critical}$ from the table for α = 0.05 is 3.50 (interpolating the values for 24 and 30 df because a value for 27 is not listed).

Hence inserting these values in the formula above,

$$CD = 3.50\sqrt{\frac{12.363}{10}} = 3.89$$

In Output Listing 3, SPSS specifies a variation of the formula for calculating the critical differences between means which allows for the possibility of the samples not being of the same size (i.e. N(I) and N(J) being the sizes of samples I and J respectively):

```
MEAN(J)-MEAN(I)  >= 2.4863 * RANGE * SQRT(1/N(I) + 1/N(J))
with the following value(s) for RANGE: 3.50
```

Here **RANGE** is the critical value ($q_{critical}$) as explained above. The value 2.4863 is computed from

$$\sqrt{\frac{MS_{error}}{2}} = \sqrt{\frac{12.363}{2}} = 2.4863$$

The **One-Way ANOVA: Post Hoc Multiple Comparisons** dialog box (Figure 4) listed several tests apart from **Tukey's HSD** test. The feature of **Tukey's HSD** test is that the critical value for the significance of any of the pairwise comparisons is determined partly by the size of the *entire array* of means. Other tests, such as **Student-Newman-Keuls**, adjust the critical value according to whether the two means are close together or far apart in the left-to-right order of magnitude. **Tukey's HSD** test, therefore, is more conservative than the **Student-Newman-Keuls** test: that is, it gives fewer significant differences. Details of several *post hoc* tests are given in Howell (1997) pp369-383.

7.3 NONPARAMETRIC TESTS

Should the data be unsuitable for ANOVA (as when there is marked heterogeneity of variance, or the data are highly skewed), one should consider using **nonparametric** tests, which assume neither homogeneity of variance nor a normal distribution. With inherently ordinal data, the parametric ANOVA cannot be used in any case (see Chapter 5).

7.3.1 The Kruskal-Wallis test

The nonparametric equivalent of the one-way (between subjects) ANOVA is the **Kruskal-Wallis Test**. To make this test, proceed as follows:

- Choose
  Statistics
    Nonparametric Tests
      K Independent Samples

  to open the **Tests for Several Independent Samples** dialog box (Figure 7).

Chapter 7 - The One-Factor Between Subjects Experiment

Figure 7.
The Tests for Several Independent Samples dialog box

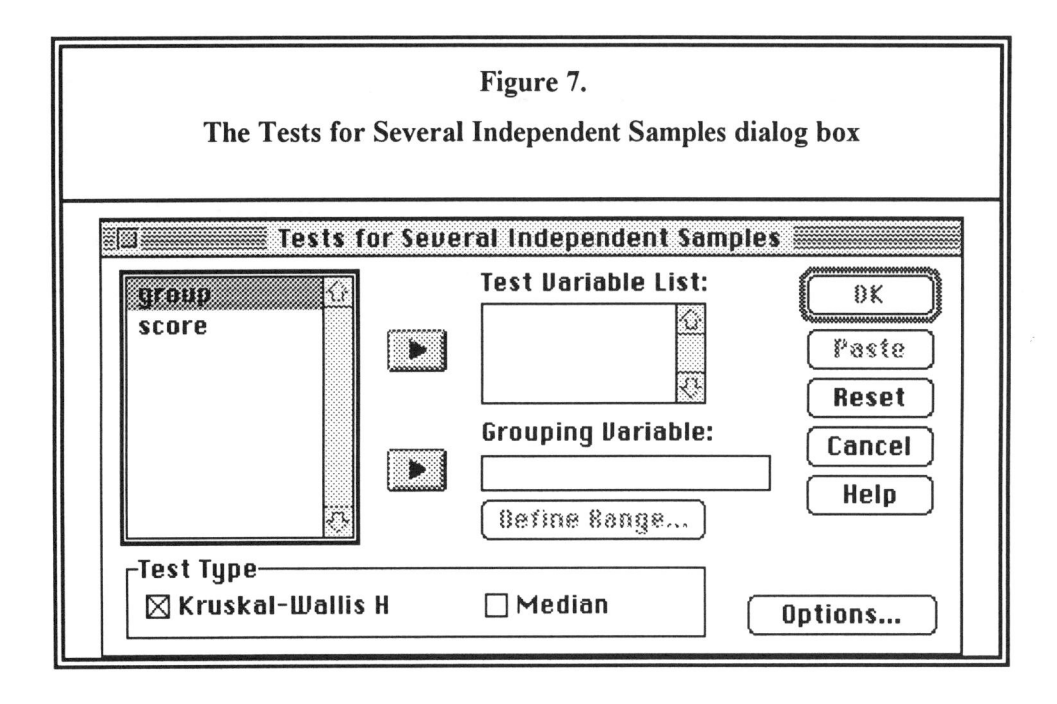

```
┌─────────── Tests for Several Independent Samples ───────────┐
│                                                              │
│  ┌─────────┐          Test Variable List:    ┌──────────┐   │
│  │ group   │         ┌──────────────┐        │    OK    │   │
│  │ score   │   ▶     │              │        └──────────┘   │
│  │         │         │              │        ┌──────────┐   │
│  │         │         └──────────────┘        │  Paste   │   │
│  │         │                                 └──────────┘   │
│  │         │          Grouping Variable:     ┌──────────┐   │
│  │         │         ┌──────────────┐        │  Reset   │   │
│  │         │   ▶     │              │        └──────────┘   │
│  │         │         └──────────────┘        ┌──────────┐   │
│  │         │          ┌──────────────┐       │  Cancel  │   │
│  │         │          │ Define Range │       └──────────┘   │
│  └─────────┘          └──────────────┘        ┌──────────┐  │
│                                                │   Help   │  │
│  ┌─Test Type────────────────────────────┐     └──────────┘  │
│  │  ⊠ Kruskal-Wallis H    ☐ Median      │     ┌──────────┐  │
│  └──────────────────────────────────────┘     │ Options… │  │
│                                                └──────────┘  │
└──────────────────────────────────────────────────────────────┘
```

- Complete the dialog box exactly as for one-way ANOVA and click on **OK**.

The result of the test is shown as a value of the **Chi-Square statistic** together with its p-value in Output Listing 4.

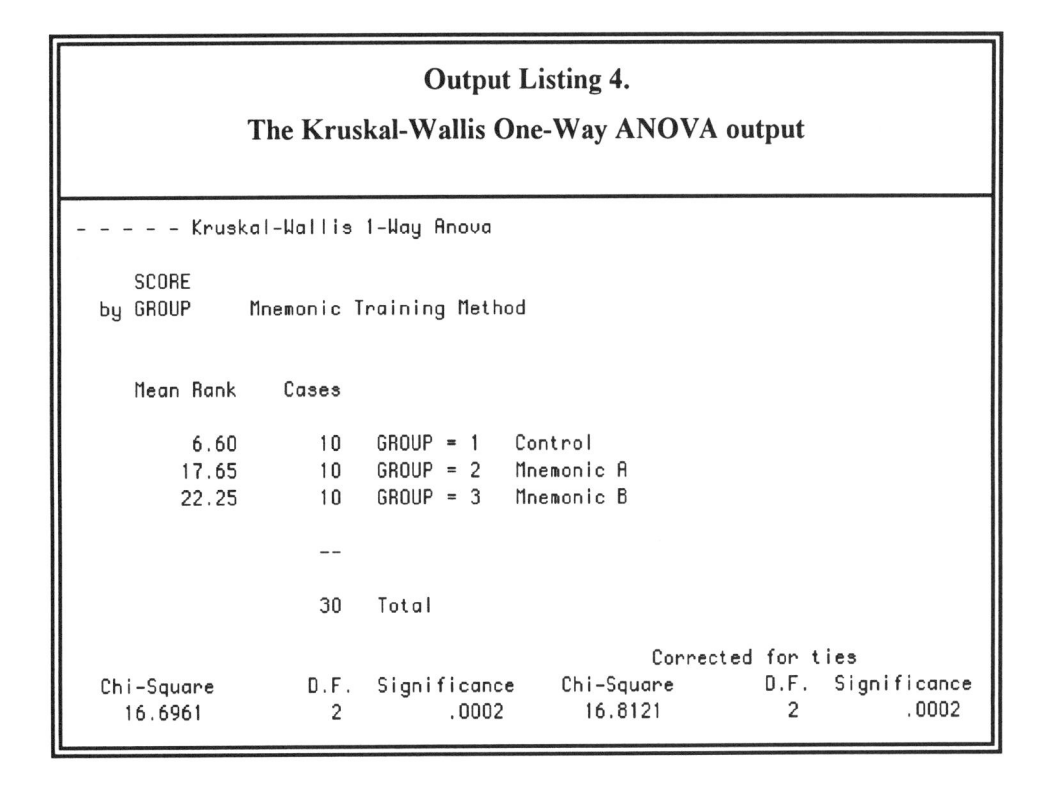

Output Listing 4.
The Kruskal-Wallis One-Way ANOVA output

```
- - - - - Kruskal-Wallis 1-Way Anova

    SCORE
 by GROUP     Mnemonic Training Method


   Mean Rank    Cases

        6.60      10    GROUP = 1    Control
       17.65      10    GROUP = 2    Mnemonic A
       22.25      10    GROUP = 3    Mnemonic B

                  --

                  30    Total

                                          Corrected for ties
 Chi-Square    D.F.   Significance    Chi-Square    D.F.   Significance
   16.6961       2        .0002         16.8121       2        .0002
```

The p-value (**Significance** or **Asymp. Sig.**) is much smaller than 0.01, confirming the parametric test that performance is not at the same level in all three groups. We can write this result as: Chi-square = 16.7; df = 2; p < 0.01.

Chapter 7 - The One-Factor Between Subjects Experiment

7.3.2 Dichotomous data: Chi-square test

When data are in the binary (dichotomous) form shown in Table 2 in Chapter 5, the **chi-square test** can be used to test the null hypothesis that, in the population, there is no tendency for the problem to be solved more often in some conditions than in others. The procedure is described in Chapter 11.

EXERCISE 12

ONE-FACTOR BETWEEN SUBJECTS ANOVA

BEFORE YOU START

We suggest that you review the material in Chapter 7 before working through this practical exercise.

THE EXERCISE

The purpose of this exercise

In one-factor between subjects ANOVA, the **F ratio** compares the spread among the treatment means with the (supposedly uniform) spread of the scores within groups about their group means. The purpose of this exercise is to help clarify the rationale of the F ratio by showing how its value is affected by various manipulations of some (or all) of the data. Before proceeding with this exercise, we ask you to suppose that a one-factor ANOVA has been carried out upon a set of data and yields an F value of, say, 7.23. Now suppose we were to multiply every score in the experimental results by a constant, say 10. What would happen to the value of F: would it still be 7.23? Or would it increase? Or decrease?

We also invite you to speculate upon the effect that adding a constant (say 10) to all the scores in just one of the groups would have upon F: suppose, for example, we were to add 10 to all the scores in the group with the largest mean. Would F stay the same, increase or decrease in value? Would the effect be the same if the constant were added to the scores of the group with the smallest mean?

As a first approach to answering these questions, we shall carry out a **one-factor ANOVA** on a set of data. Then we shall see what happens to the value of F when the data are transformed as described in the previous paragraphs.

Some data from a completely randomised experiment

Table 1. Results of a completely randomised experiment on the effects upon recall of logographic characters of different mnemonic systems										
No Mnemonic (10 control subjects)	4	6	4	3	5	7	10	4	9	11
Mnemonic 1 (10 subjects trained in Mnemonic 1)	11	9	16	10	12	17	18	16	8	11
Mnemonic 2 (10 subjects trained in Mnemonic 2)	21	16	15	16	18	11	9	12	19	20

Suppose a researcher is interested in how well non-Chinese-speaking students can learn Chinese characters using different kinds of mnemonic. Independent groups of participants are tested under three conditions: *No Mnemonic*, *Mnemonic 1* and *Mnemonic 2*. The dependent variable is the number of Chinese characters that are correctly recalled. The data are shown in Table 1.

Chapter 7 - The One-Factor Between Subjects Experiment

Construction of the SPSS data set

Recast the data of Table 1 into a form suitable for analysis by SPSS by following the procedure described in Chapter 3. Save the data set: we shall be using it again in the next exercise.

Exploring the data

As always, we recommend a preliminary exploration of the data set before any formal testing is carried out, in case there are contraindications for the use of the ANOVA. As in Exercise 8, use the **Means** procedure for descriptive statistics and **Explore** for checks on the distributions of the scores within the groups. (**Explore** inundates the user with a surfeit of statistics: the **Means** procedure is therefore preferred.)

- **Examine the output listing for the Means procedure. Do the means appear to differ? Are the standard deviations similar in value?**

The output listing for the **Explore** procedure begins with the stem-and-leaf displays for the three groups. It then plots the boxplots in the **Chart Carousel**: they can be seen on the screen by clicking on the **Carousel** icon or clicking on the **Window** drop-down menu and selecting **Chart**. Further details about the boxplots are given in Section 4.3.2.

- **Do the boxplots suggest any anomalies in the distributions of the data in any of the three groups? Write a statement assessing the suitability of the data for ANOVA.**

Procedure for the one-way ANOVA

The procedure for the one-way ANOVA is described in detail in Section 7.2.2.

Output listing for the one-way ANOVA

- **Write down the value of F and its associated p-value. Is F significant? What are the implications of this result for the experimental hypothesis?**

RE-ANALYSIS OF TRANSFORMED DATA SETS

In this section, we return to the question of the effects upon the ANOVA statistics of subjecting the data (or sections of the data) to such operations as multiplying every score by a constant.

1) Multiplying every score by a constant

We recommend that whenever you have occasion to transform the values of a variable in the SPSS data set, you should construct a new target variable, rather than change (perhaps irreversibly) the original data. Use the **Compute** procedure (Section 4.4.2) to multiply each value in the data set by a factor of 10. Follow the instructions in that section, choosing, for the target variable, a mnemonic name such as *allbyten*. Now change the **One-way ANOVA** dialog box so that the dependent variable is *allbyten* instead of *score* and click on **OK** to run the analysis.

Output listing for the one-way ANOVA

- **Write down the value of F and its associated p-value. Is F significant? What are the implications of this result for the experimental hypothesis?**

In the output listing, you will see that both the between groups and within groups variance estimates have increased by a factor of 100. This is not at all surprising, since it is easy to show algebraically that when each of a set of scores is multiplied by a constant, the new variance is the old variance times the square of the constant. Since, however, the factors of 100 in the numerator and denominator of the F ratio cancel out, the value of the F ratio remains unchanged.

2) Adding a constant to the scores in only one group

This time, we want a target variable which contains, for two of the three groups, the original scores; but to the values of the Mnemonic 2 group has been added a constant of +10. First, make a copy of the values in *score* to a new variable *g3plus10* in the **Data Editor** window using the technique described in Section 3.5.4. Second, use the **Compute** procedure to add the value *+10* to the values in this new variable when the grouping variable has the value *3*. In the **Compute** dialog box, type *g3plus10* into the **Target Variable** box, transfer it to the **Numeric Expression** box and add *+10* after the variable name. Click on **If** to open the **Compute Variable: If Cases** dialog box. Transfer the name *group* into the box and add the expression *=3*. Click on **Continue** and then on **OK** to run the procedure. In the **Data Editor** window, check that the values in *g3plus10* for the third group have changed but the rest have their original values. Now re-run the **one-way ANOVA**, using *g3plus10* as the dependent variable.

Output listing for the one-way ANOVA

- **Write down the value of F and its associated p-value. Is F significant? What are the implications of this result for the experimental hypothesis?**

You will see that the effect of adding a constant of *10* to all scores in the *Mnemonic 2* group has no effect at all upon the within groups variance estimate, which is not surprising, since adding the same constant to all the scores in a set has no effect upon the spread of the scores - it merely shifts the mean. The between groups mean square, however, computed from the values of the treatment means alone, has increased its value considerably. The within groups mean square, on the other hand, is the average of the variance estimates of the scores within groups and is quite independent of the spread among the group means. Consequently, it is quite possible to change the value of the former without affecting that of the latter and vice-versa. The effect of increasing the mean of the third group is to increase the spread of the three treatment means and hence the value of the numerator of the F ratio.

POST-HOC COMPARISONS: THE TUKEY TEST

If the ANOVA is significant, you will want to know which pairs of levels differ significantly. We recommend that you read Sections 7.1 and 7.2.3. With data from a completely randomised experiment, it is a simple matter to run various multiple comparisons procedures with SPSS, because these can be requested from the **One-way ANOVA** dialog box.

Specifying post-hoc comparisons with the one-way ANOVA

Proceed as for the **one-way ANOVA**, but this time click on the **Post-hoc** button to bring to the screen the **One-Way ANOVA: Post Hoc Multiple Comparisons** dialog box. Mark the check box for **Tukey's honestly significant difference**. Click on **Continue** and then on **OK** to run the ANOVA and the multiple comparisons procedure.

Output listing for post-hoc comparisons

Study the output listing for the multiple comparisons test, noting its presentation of the results.

- **Construct your own table showing clearly which pairs of levels are significantly different and which are not.**

CHAPTER 8

FACTORIAL EXPERIMENTS (BETWEEN SUBJECTS)

8.1 INTRODUCTION

8.2 FACTORIAL ANOVA

8.3 EXPERIMENTS WITH MORE THAN TWO TREATMENT FACTORS

Chapter 8 - Factorial Experiments (Between Subjects)

8.1 INTRODUCTION

Factors

The meaning of the term **factor** was explained in Section 3.2, where Table 1 showed a one-factor between subjects experiment. The analysis of variance of data from an experiment of this type was the subject of Chapter 7.

In Section 3.2, we also considered some experiments with two treatment factors. Designs with two or more factors are known as **factorial** designs. In the simplest case, there is a different sample of subjects for each possible combination of the levels of the factors. This arrangement is known as a **between subjects** (or **completely randomised**) factorial design.

In recent years, developments in computer graphics have given an enormous fillip to the study of human-machine interaction. In driving simulation, for example, the participant sits in the cabin of a car whose controls are linked to computer-generated images of a moving road to create, to the greatest possible extent, a realistic driving experience. In such a situation it is possible to test a person's performance in heavy traffic, icy conditions, or in emergencies requiring evasive action.

A researcher is commissioned to investigate the effects upon driving peformance of two new anti-hay fever drugs, A and B. It is suspected that at least one of the drugs may have different effects upon fresh and tired drivers, and the firm developing the drugs needs to ensure that neither has a deleterious effect upon driving performance.

The researcher decides to carry out a two-factor experiment, in which factors are:

(1) **Drug**, with levels **Placebo**, **A** and **B**;

(2) **Alertness**, with levels **Fresh** and **Tired**.

All participants are asked to take a flavoured drink which contains either (in the A and B conditions) a small dosage of a drug or (in the control, or **Placebo** condition) no drug. Half the participants are tested immediately on rising; the others are tested after twenty hours of sleep deprivation. A different sample of ten subjects is tested under each of the six treatment combinations: (Fresh, Placebo); (Fresh, Drug A); (Fresh, Drug B); (Tired, Placebo); (Tired, Drug A); (Tired, Drug B).

Notice that in this design, each level of either factor is to be found in combination with every level of the other: the two factors are said to **cross**. There are designs in which the factors do not cross: that is, not all combinations of conditions (or groups) are present; but those will not be considered in this book. The design can be represented as a table in which each row or column represents a particular level of one of the treatment factors, and a **cell** of the table (i.e. a single rectangle in the grid) represents one particular treatment **combination** (Table 1). In Table 1, the cell on the bottom right represents the combination (Tired, Drug B). The participants in Group 6 were tested under that treatment combination.

Chapter 8 - Factorial Experiments (Between Subjects)

Table 1.

A completely randomised, two-factor factorial experiment

Levels of factor: Alertness	Levels of factor: Drug		
	Placebo	Drug A	Drug B
Fresh	Group 1	Group 2	Group 3
Tired	Group 4	Group 5	Group 6

Suppose that the experiment is carried out, and the mean scores of the participants tested under the six different treatment combinations are as shown in Table 2. The row and column means, which are known as **marginal means**, are the mean scores at each level of either factor considered separately, ignoring the other factor in the classification.

Table 2.

Mean scores achieved by the participants in the drugs experiment

	Placebo	Drug A	Drug B	*Means*
Fresh	21.0	12.0	22.0	18.3
Tired	10.0	18.0	16.0	14.7
Means	15.5	15.0	19.0	16.5

Main effects and interactions

In a two-factor experiment, there are two kinds of possible treatment effects:

(1) **main effects**;

(2) an **interaction**.

Look at the column marginal means in Table 2. These represent the mean scores of the participants who were tested at the three levels of the Drug factor, *ignoring the other factor (Alertness) in the experiment*. Similarly, the row marginal means in Table 2 represent the mean scores of the fresh and tired participants, *ignoring the other factor (Drug) in the experiment.*

Should the differences among the means for the three levels of the drug factor be sufficiently great to indicate a difference in the population, The Drug factor is said to have a **main effect**. Similarly, should the difference between the two row means be sufficiently great, the Alertness factor is said to have a main effect also.

In general, if, in a factorial experiment, the mean scores are not the same at all levels of any of the factors, those factors are said to have main effects. Since there are marked differences among the marginal means in Table 2, it would appear that there may be main effects of both the Drug and Alertness factors.

Turning now to the cell means in Table 2, it is clear that the results of the experiment show another striking feature. If we look at the fresh subjects only, we see a sharp dip in performance with Drug A: that is, a dose of this drug actually has a deleterious effect upon the performance of fresh participants. Drug B, on the other hand, has no such effect: the mean performance of the participants under that condition is much the same as that of the placebo group. The corresponding means for the tired participants show a different pattern. Under Drug A, their performance is almost as good as that of the fresh placebo group. Drug B also appears to improve performance. It would appear, therefore, that the researcher's suspicions were well founded: Drug A may improve the performance of tired drivers; but it seems to have an adverse effect upon fresh drivers.

Definition of an interaction

The effect of one treatment factor (such as Drug) at one particular level of another factor (e.g. the Fresh participants only) is known as a **simple main effect** of the first factor at a specified level of the second.

The Alertness factor has different simple main effects at different levels of the Drug factor: it is diminished with Drug B and actually reversed with Drug A. When one treatment factor does not have the same simple main effects at all levels of another, the two factors are said to **interact**. The analysis of variance of data from a factorial experiment offers tests not only for the presence of main effects of each factor considered separately but also for interactions between (or among) the factors.

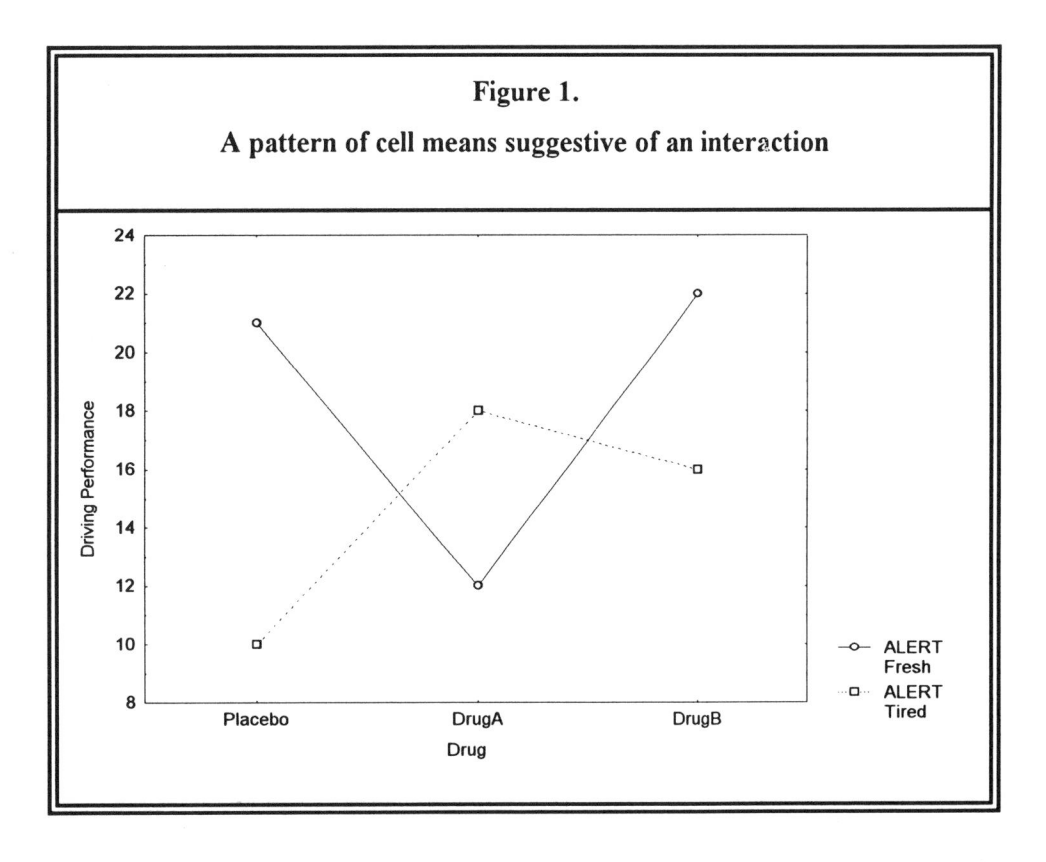

Figure 1.

A pattern of cell means suggestive of an interaction

Chapter 8 - Factorial Experiments (Between Subjects)

The interaction we have just described can be pictured graphically, as plots of the cell means against Drug group for the Fresh and Tired participants (see Figure 1). There is thus a **Fresh** subjects profile, which is V-shaped, and a **Tired** subjects profile below it, which rises to a plateau under the Drug A and Drug B conditions. **The presence of an interaction is indicated by profile heterogeneity across the levels of one of the factors.** An interaction between two factors A and B is often indicated by a multiplication sign: **A × B**; sometimes abbreviated to **AB**.

Algebraically, main effects and interactions are independent, so it is quite possible to obtain significant main effects without any significant interaction between the factors, and it is also possible to have significant interactions without any significant main effects.

The manner in which the ANOVA tests for the presence of main effects and an interaction is lucidly described in Gravetter & Wallnau (1997, Chapter 15). If you are unfamiliar with such ANOVA terms as **sum of squares**, **mean square** and **degrees of freedom**, we urge you to read their earlier ANOVA chapters also.

8.2 FACTORIAL ANOVA WITH SPSS

Table 3 shows the raw data from the two-factor factorial **Drug × Alertness** experiment.

Levels of the factor: Alertness	Levels of the factor: Drug		
	Placebo	A	B
Fresh	24 25 13 22 16	18 8 9 14 16	27 14 19 29 27
	23 18 19 24 26	15 6 9 8 17	23 19 17 20 25
Tired	13 12 14 16 17	21 24 22 23 20	21 11 14 22 19
	13 4 3 2 6	13 11 17 13 16	9 14 11 21 18

Table 3. Results of the Drug × Alertness factorial experiment

8.2.1 Preparing the data for the factorial ANOVA

It will be necessary to use *two* **coding (grouping) variables** to indicate the treatment combination under which each score was achieved. If the coding variables are *alert* and *drug*, and performance in the driving simulator is *drivperf*, the data file will consist of three columns: two for the coding variables, and a third for *drivperf*.

Proceed as follows:

- Define the three variables as described in Chapter 3, Section 3.3. Use the **Define Labels** dialog box to assign more meaningful names to the three variables: *Alertness*, *Drug Treatment*, and *Driving Performance* will be suitable.

- Use the **Value Labels** dialog box to provide keys to the code numbers that make up the grouping variables *alert* and *drug*: in the *alert* column, the values *1* and *2* can be assigned the value labels *Fresh* and *Tired*, respectively; in the *drug* column, the values *1*, *2*, and *3* can be assigned the value labels *Placebo*, *Drug A*, and *Drug B*, respectively.

- Use the cell editor to enter the data into the **Data Editor** window (Figure 2). The three values in row 1 indicate that subject 1 achieved a score of *24* while still fresh and without ingesting any drug; row 12 indicates that subject 12 achieved a score of *8* while still fresh, but having ingested a dose of Drug A.

- Save the file in the usual manner.

	alert	drug	drivperf
1	1	1	24
2	1	1	25
3	1	1	13
4	1	1	22
5	1	1	16
6	1	1	23
7	1	1	18
8	1	1	19
9	1	1	24
10	1	1	26
11	1	2	18
12	1	2	8

Figure 2.

Section of the Data Editor window showing some of the data from Table 3

(Each row represents one subject's score and the conditions under which it was achieved)

8.2.2 Exploring the data: Obtaining cell means and standard deviations

Before conducting the ANOVA, it is important to explore the data by computing the cell means and standard deviations to check for any wayward distributions. This information is also useful for interpreting any significant interactions which may appear in the ANOVA summary table.

To obtain the mean performance levels under each of the six treatment combinations, proceed as follows:

- Choose
  Statistics
   Compare Means
    Means

  to open the **Means** dialog box (see Figure 14, Chapter 4). In the box on the left are the variables *alert*, *drug* and *drivperf*.

- Highlight *drivperf* and click on ▶ to transfer it to the **Dependent List** box. Highlight *alert* and click on ▶ to transfer it to the **Independent List** box.

- Notice that the box above the **Independent List** box contains the caption **Layer 1 of 1**. So far, SPSS knows only of one layer of classification, created by classifying the dependent variable *drivperf* by the coding variable *alert*. Click the **Next** subdialog button and enter the next layer according to the grouping variable *drug*. The central caption will now read **Layer 2 of 2**, indicating that SPSS now knows of the two layers of classification.

- Click on **OK** to run the **Means** procedure, the output for which is shown in Output Listing 1.

Output Listing 1.

The means and standard deviations for each cell and for levels of Alert

```
                - - Description of Subpopulations - -
Summaries of     DRIVPERF    Driving Performance
By levels of     ALERT       Alertness
                 DRUG        Drug Treatment


Variable         Value  Label              Mean      Std Dev    Cases

For Entire Population                    16.5000     6.3846       60

  ALERT            1    Fresh            18.3333     6.3481       30
    DRUG           1    Placebo          21.0000     4.2947       10
    DRUG           2    Drug A           12.0000     4.4222       10
    DRUG           3    Drug B           22.0000     4.9441       10

  ALERT            2    Tired            14.6667     5.9731       30
    DRUG           1    Placebo          10.0000     5.6569       10
    DRUG           2    Drug A           18.0000     4.6428       10
    DRUG           3    Drug B           16.0000     4.7842       10

Total Cases = 60
```

Chapter 8 - Factorial Experiments (Between Subjects)

Unfortunately Output Listing 1 does not show the means for the levels of *drug* (i.e. for *Placebo, Drug A, Drug B*). To get those means, it is necessary to reset the dialog box and re-run it with *drivperf* as before in the **Dependent List** box but with just *drug* in the **Independent List** box. The means and standard deviations for the three drug conditions are given in Output Listing 2.

Output Listing 2.

The means and standard deviations for each drug condition.

```
              - - Description of Subpopulations - -
Summaries of      DRIVPERF    Driving Performance
By levels of      DRUG        Drug Treatment


Variable        Value  Label                 Mean      Std Dev    Cases

For Entire Population                       16.5000     6.3846      60

DRUG              1    Placebo              15.5000     7.4657      20
DRUG              2    Drug A               15.0000     5.3803      20
DRUG              3    Drug B               19.0000     5.6475      20

   Total Cases = 60
```

8.2.3 Choosing a factorial ANOVA

The factorial analysis of variance is run as follows:

- Choose
  Statistics
     ANOVA models
        Simple Factorial (Figure 3)

to open the **Simple Factorial ANOVA** dialog box (Figure 4).

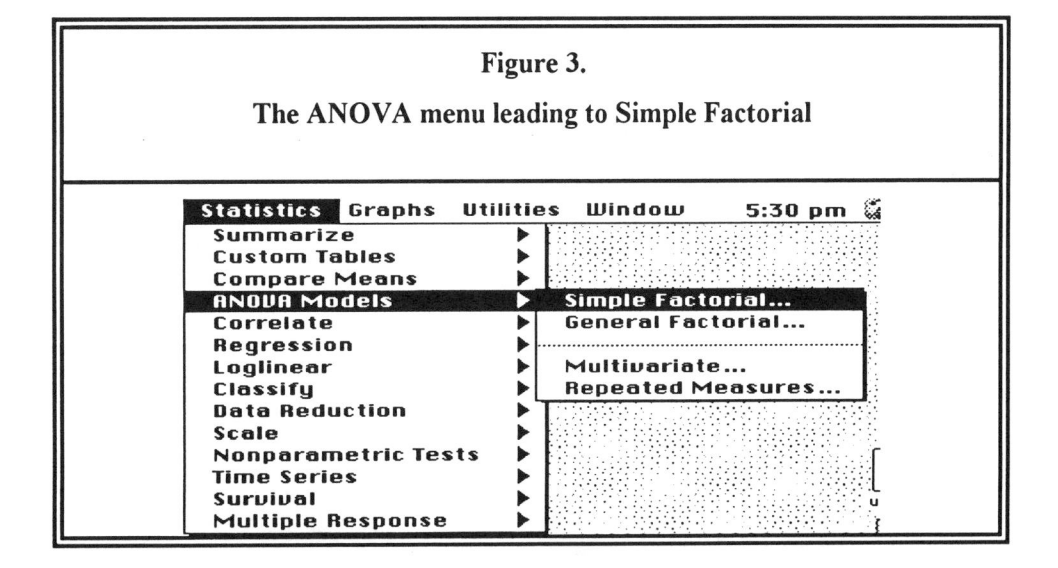

Figure 3.

The ANOVA menu leading to Simple Factorial

193

Chapter 8 - Factorial Experiments (Between Subjects)

Figure 4.
The completed Simple Factorial ANOVA dialog box

[Simple Factorial ANOVA dialog box showing:
Dependent: drivperf
Factor(s): alert(1 2), drug(1 3)
Define Range... button
Covariate(s): (empty)
Buttons: OK, Paste, Reset, Cancel, Help, Options...]

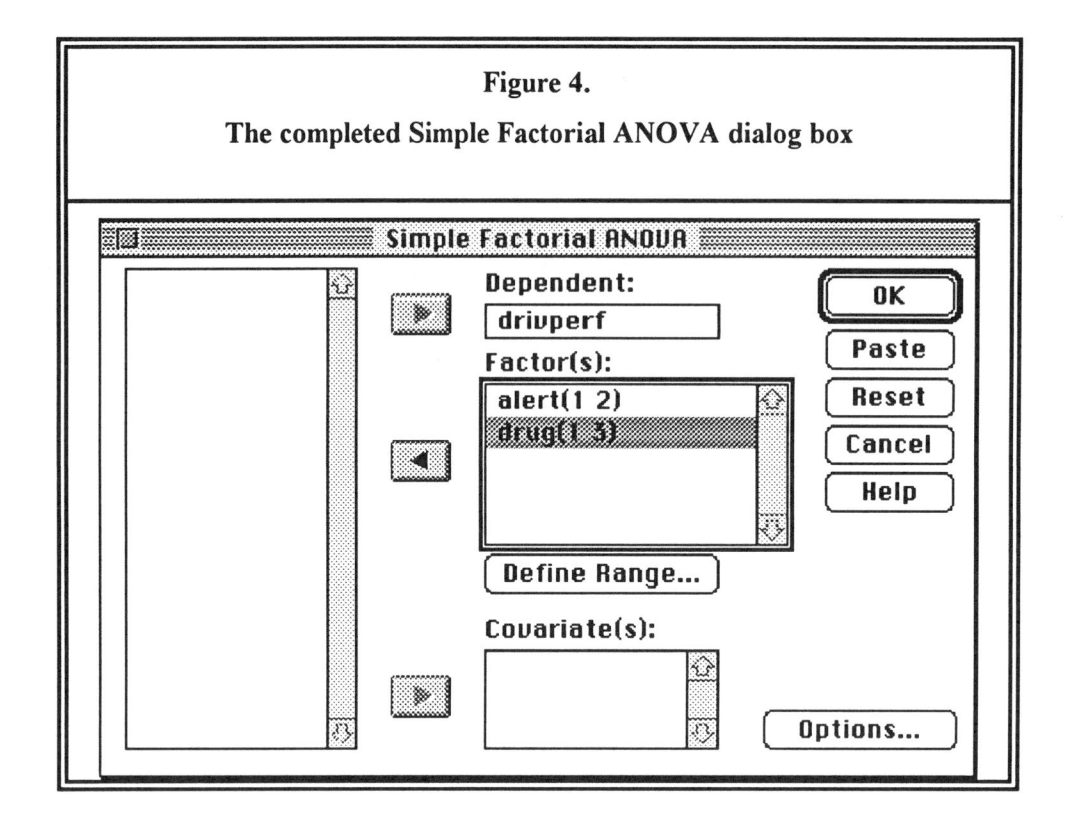

- Complete the box in the same manner as for the **Independent Samples T Test** (see Chapter 6) by clicking the grouping variables into the **Factors** box and adding the minimum and maximum values of their levels using the **Define Range** box. The dependent variable is *drivperf*.

- Click on the OK button to run the ANOVA.

Covariates

At the bottom of the **Simple Factorial ANOVA** dialog box, you will notice a box labelled **Covariate(s)**. A **covariate** is a variable which, although not of direct interest in the investigation, could be expected to correlate (covary) with the dependent variable. For example, suppose that our participants all belonged to an organisation which collected their IQ test scores. It would be interesting to know whether the mean IQs of the various experimental groups were similar in value; otherwise, genuine treatment effects could be confounded with differences in intelligence. There exist techniques known as **Analysis of Covariance (ANCOVA)** which essentially remove the effects of covariates from a data set and perform ANOVA on a 'purified' set. The advantage is often a reduction of 'data noise' and a resulting increase in the power of the ANOVA tests. To run an ANCOVA, transfer the variable name(s) of the covariate(s) into the covariate box.

8.2.4 Output listing for a factorial ANOVA

The factorial ANOVA summary table

The ANOVA table in Output Listing 3 tabulates the F ratios and their associated p-values for the main effects and the two-way interaction. The tables also include rows summing up all the **Main Effects**, all the **2-Way Interactions** (though here there is just one), and all the **Explained** variance (i.e. main effects plus interactions). Thus the remaining 'unexplained' variance is the row labelled **Residual** representing the error variance which (in this particular type of ANOVA) is used as the denominator for each of the F ratios.

Output Listing 3.

The factorial ANOVA summary table

```
       * * *   A N A L Y S I S   O F   V A R I A N C E   * * *

           DRIVPERF  Driving Performance
       by  ALERT     Alertness
           DRUG      Drug Treatment

           UNIQUE sums of squares
           All effects entered simultaneously


                          Sum of                Mean                  Sig
Source of Variation       Squares      DF       Square       F       of F

Main Effects              391.667       3      130.556      5.640    .002
   ALERT                  201.667       1      201.667      8.712    .005
   DRUG                   190.000       2       95.000      4.104    .022

2-Way Interactions        763.333       2      381.667     16.488    .000
   ALERT    DRUG          763.333       2      381.667     16.488    .000

Explained                1155.000       5      231.000      9.979    .000

Residual                 1250.000      54       23.148

Total                    2405.000      59       40.763


60 cases were processed.
0 cases ( .0 pct) were missing.
```

Note the **Signif of F** (i.e. p-value, or tail probability) for each F ratio. There are significant main effects for both the *alert* and *drug* factors: the former is significant beyond the 0.01 level; the latter beyond the 0.05 level, but not beyond the 0.01 level. In addition to main effects of both treatment factors, there is a significant interaction. The p-value is given as *0.000*, which means that it is less than *0.0005*. Clearly, the *drug* factor has different effects upon Fresh and Tired subjects; but to ascertain the nature of these effects, we shall need to examine the pattern of the treatment means more closely.

These results should be reported by specifying the name of the factor followed by the value of the F ratio (with the df of the numerator and the df of the denominator

Chapter 8 - Factorial Experiments (Between Subjects)

separated by a comma in brackets) and the p-value e.g. 'There was a significant main effect of the Alertness factor: $F(1,54) = 8.71; p < 0.01$'.

Exploring the interaction by graphing the cell means

The significant main effect and interaction in the ANOVA summary table can be explored by studying the patterns of the means in Output Listing 1. A graph, however, will clarify matters enormously. Proceed as follows:

- Select
  Graphs
    Line

    which will bring the **Line Charts** dialog box into view (Figure 5).

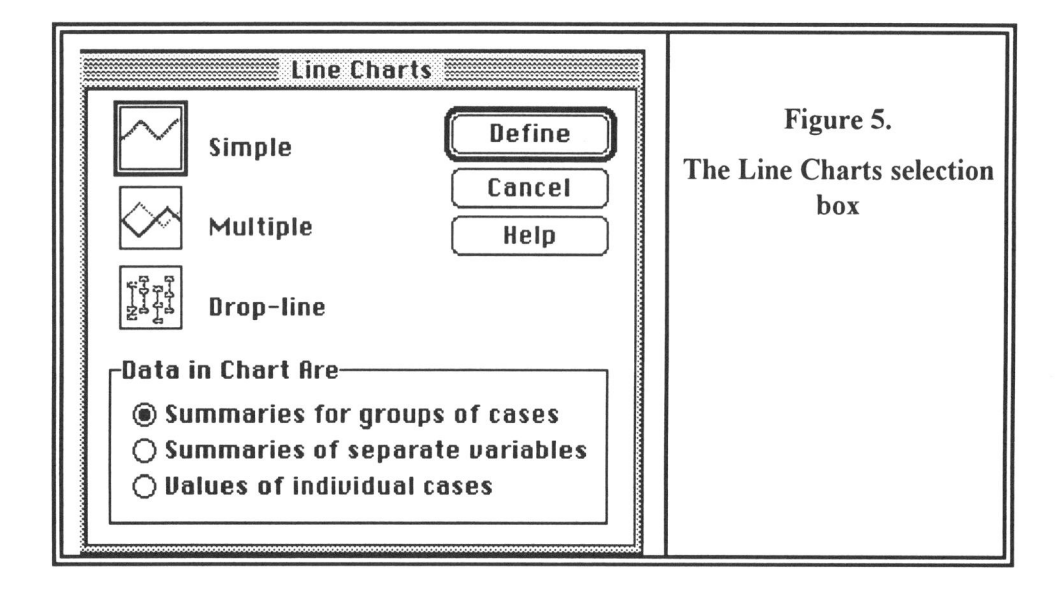

Figure 5.

The Line Charts selection box

- Highlight the **Multiple** box and click on **Define** to open the **Define Multiple Line: Summaries for Groups of Cases** dialog box (the completed version is shown in Figure 6).

- Within the **Lines Represent** box (Figure 6), mark the **Other Summary Function** radio button. By default, this choice selects the mean of whatever variable is entered into the **Variable** box (other functions, such as the median, can be selected by clicking on the **Change Summary** button.)

- When the dialog box is first opened, the variable names are listed alphabetically by default in the panel on the left (unless another specification has been made by selecting from **Preferences/ Display Order for Variable Lists/File**, as described in Section 3.4.2). Since we want to plot the cell means on the dependent variable, highlight *drivperf*, click on the radio button **Other summary function** and then ▶ to make it the subject (i.e. the *argument* - the mathematical term for variable, constant or expression on which a function will be calculated) of the function **MEAN[ ]** in the **Variable** box. The entry in the **Variable** box will then appear as **MEAN[drivperf]**.

Chapter 8 - Factorial Experiments (Between Subjects)

Figure 6.

The Define Multiple Line: Summaries for Groups of Cases dialog box

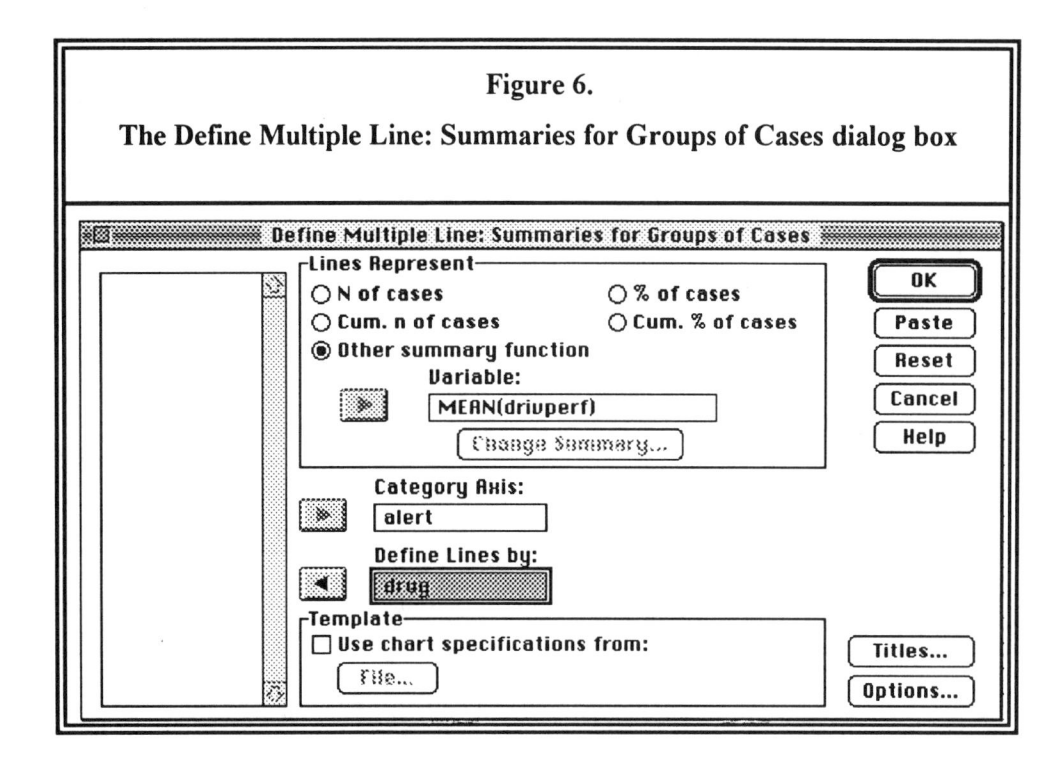

- Since we want to profile the two levels of the *alert* factor over the three conditions of the *drug* factor, we transfer the variable *drug* into the **Category Axis** box and the variable *alert* into the **Define Lines by** box.

- Click on **OK** to obtain the graph in Figure 7.

Figure 7.

The graph showing the profile of Drug treatments over the levels of Alertness

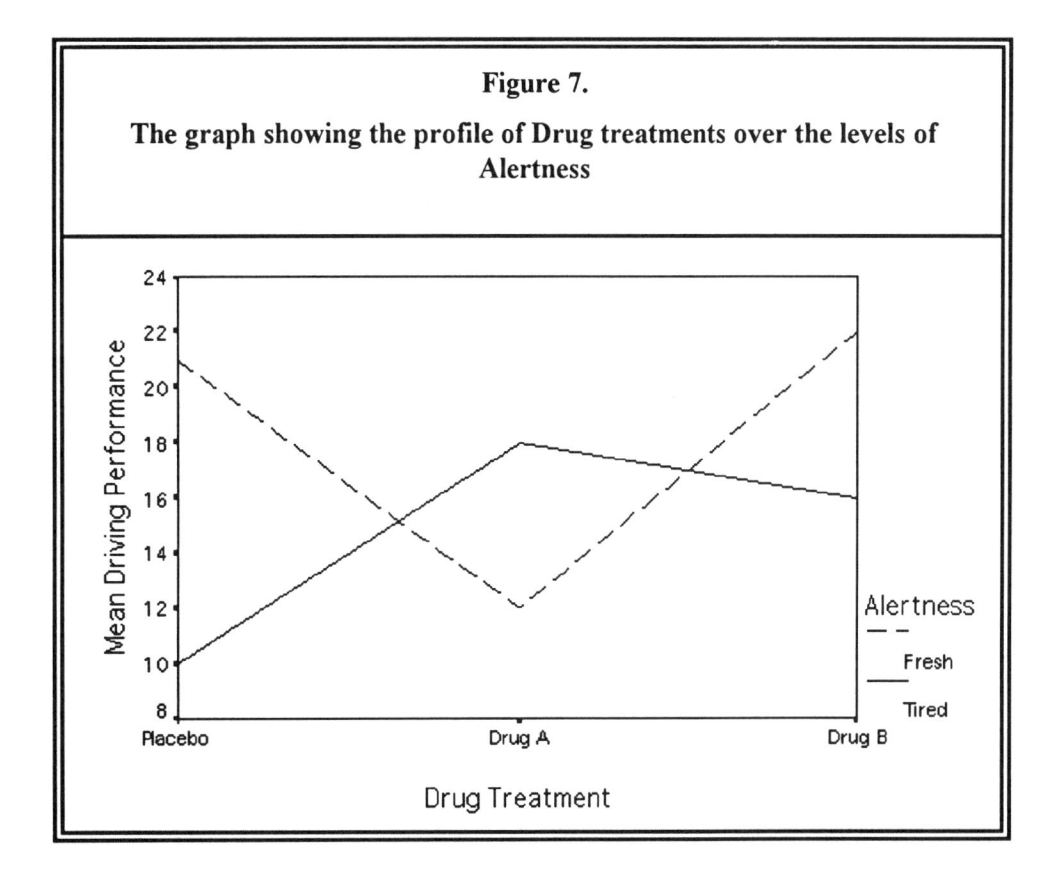

Figure 7 clearly shows several important experimental results.

(1) Alertness has a major effect on performance, as shown by the downward slope of the Placebo profile.

(2) Drug A does enhance the performance level of Tired subjects.

(3) But Drug A actually causes the performance of Fresh subjects to deteriorate.

(4) Drug B, while enhancing performance in both Fresh and Tired subjects, does not prevent performance from deteriorating as subjects become tired.

Notice that all the most interesting results from this experiment are to be found in the analysis of the cell means following the discovery of a significant interaction between the two factors Drug and Alertness. As is so often the case in factorial experiments, the presence of an interaction draws attention away from main effects (which, as we have seen, are apparent from considerations of the marginal means). In the present example, it is of relatively little interest to learn that the mean level of performance of drugged subjects is somewhat higher than that of undrugged subjects, because the three Drug profiles are so disparate. The finding that Fresh subjects outperform Tired subjects, while sensible, is hardly surprising.

Often, having made a preliminary graphical exploration of the cell means, the user will wish to make some unplanned pairwise comparisons among selected cell means to confirm the patterns evident in the graph. For example, Figure 7 suggests that the simple fact of tiredness led to a deterioration in performance. That would be confirmed should a comparison between the means for the combination (Placebo, Fresh) and (Placebo, Tired) prove significant. To confirm that Drug A actually has deleterious effect upon the performance of Fresh subjects, we should need to find a significant difference between the means for the (Placebo, Fresh) and (Drug A, Fresh) conditions. It is possible, too, that the improvement upon the performance of Fresh controls subjects achieved by Drug B may not be significant. That would be confirmed by a non-significant difference between the means for conditions (Placebo, Fresh) and (Drug B, Fresh).

Since the Alertness factor comprises only two conditions, the answer to the question of whether tiredness alone produces a significant decrement in performance is answered by a test for a **simple main effect** of Alertness at the Placebo level of the Drug factor. Tests for simple main effects are available on SPSS, but the user must know the syntax of the SPSS control language. Another approach is to perform an ANOVA only upon the data at the level of the qualifying factor concerned. If we go back to the **Data Editor**, select the data only from the Placebo condition and request a one-way ANOVA with Alertness as the single factor, we shall find that $F(1, 18) = 23.99$; $p = .0001$. This confirms the simple main effect of Alertness at the Placebo level of the Drug factor and hence that the difference between the means for the (Placebo, Fresh) and (Placebo, Tired) conditions is indeed significant.

Some of the other questions mentioned can only be answered by directly making pairwise comparisons between specified treatment means. Since many such comparisons are possible, it is necessary to protect against inflation of the *per family* type I error rate by using a conservative method such as the **Tukey test**, described in the following section.

Chapter 8 - Factorial Experiments (Between Subjects)

Unplanned multiple pairwise comparisons with Tukey's HSD test

Following a significant main effect or interaction, the user will often want to make unplanned comparisons either among the marginal means (to compare levels in a main effect) or among the cell means (to investigate the source of an interaction).

In the present case, the ANOVA showed a significant main effect of the Drug factor, and the user would naturally wish to know which of the pairwise differences among the three treatment means are significant. Here the trick is to pretend that the experiment had only one treatment factor *drug*, and run a one-way ANOVA with the **Tukey HSD** test. Simply choose the one-way ANOVA procedure and specify the Drug factor as the independent variable, ignoring the Alertness factor.

Should an interaction prove significant (as in the present example), it will often be illuminating to make comparisons among the **cell means** rather than the marginal means. The **Tukey HSD** test can be used for inter-cell comparisons; but this time we must pretend the data are from a one-factor experiment with as many levels in its single factor as there are cell means in the original two-way table of results. To achieve this, we must construct a new coding variable *cellcode*, containing a code number for each of the combinations *(1, 1)*, *(1, 2)*, *(2, 1)*, *(2, 2)*, *(3, 1)*, *(3, 2)* that coded the treatment combinations (Placebo, Fresh), (Placebo, Tired), (Drug A, Fresh), (Drug A, Tired), (Drug B, Fresh) and (Drug B, Tired).

To compute values 1 to 6 for each of these combinations in the variable *cellcode*, one method to use is the **Compute** procedure followed by the **Recode** procedure as follows:

- Click on **Transform** and **Compute** to obtain the **Compute Variable** dialog box (Figure 8). In the **Target Variable** box, type the name of the new variable *cellcode*.

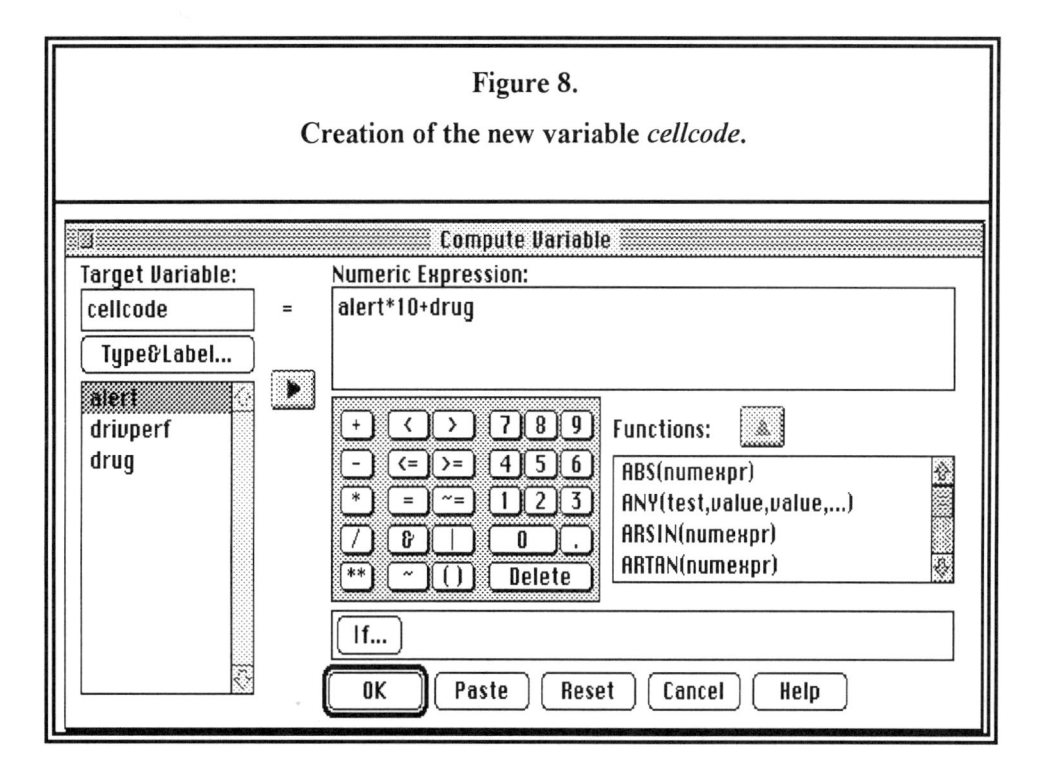

Figure 8.

Creation of the new variable *cellcode*.

Chapter 8 - Factorial Experiments (Between Subjects)

- Transfer *alert* with ▶ into the **Numeric Expression** box and type in *10 and +. Then transfer *drug* with ▶ into the box so that the whole expression is *alert*10 + drug*. Click **OK** to create (in the **Data Editor** window) the new variable *cellcode* with values of 11, 12, 13, 21, 22 and 23.

- Click on **Transform, Recode** and **Into Same Variables** to obtain the **Recode into Same Variables** dialog box. Transfer cellcode with ▶ into the **Variables** box.

- Click on **Old and New Values** box to open the **Recode into Same Variables: Old and New Values** dialog box (the completed version is shown in Figure 9) and then build up a list of 11→1, 12→2, 13→3, 21→4, 22→5, 23→6 in the **Old→New** box using the procedure described in Section 4.4.3. Click **Continue** and then **OK** to effect these changes in the variable *cellcode*. You can check that this has been done by inspecting the **Data Editor** window.

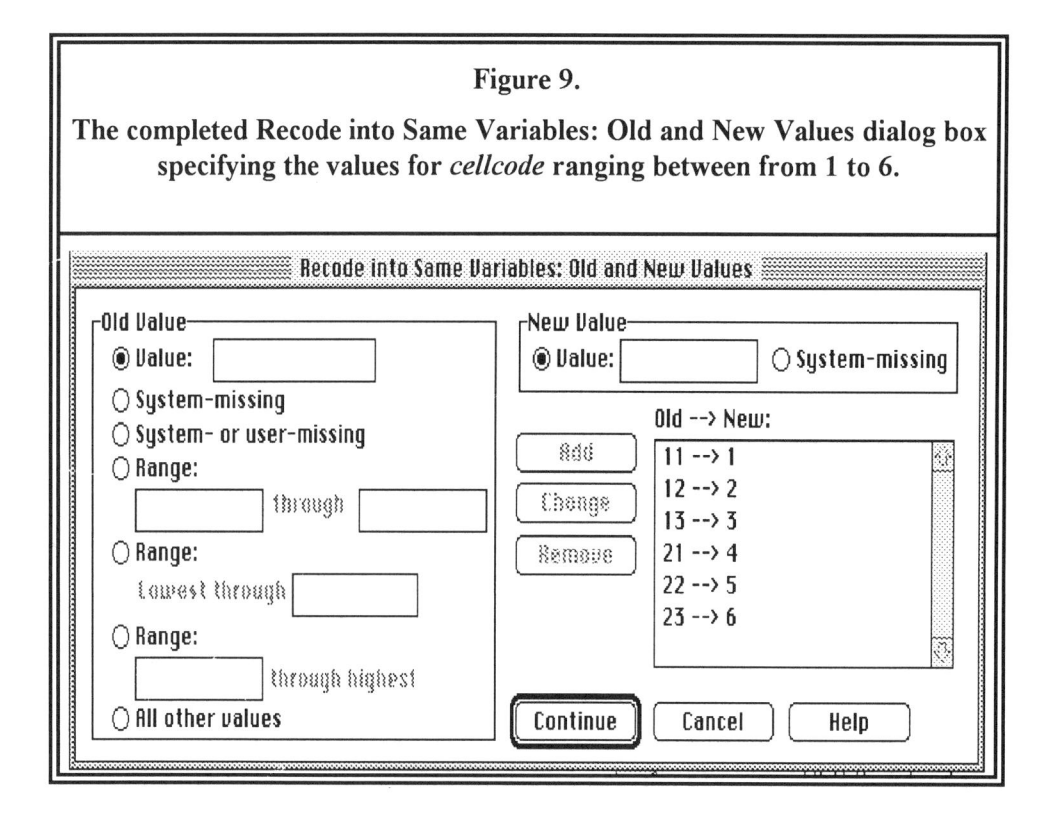

Figure 9.

The completed Recode into Same Variables: Old and New Values dialog box specifying the values for *cellcode* ranging between from 1 to 6.

- Now simply run the **one-way ANOVA** procedure, with *drivperf* as the dependent variable and *cellcode* as the independent variable with levels 1 to 6, opting for the **Tukey HSD** test.

Part of the output relating to the **Tukey HSD** test is shown in Output Listing 4. It is clear that Group 4 (Tired, Placebo) differs significantly from Groups 1 (Fresh, Placebo), 3 (Fresh, Drug B) and 5 (Tired, Drug A), and that Group 2 (Fresh, Drug A) differs from Group 1 (Fresh, Placebo) and Group 3 (Fresh, Drug B).

Chapter 8 - Factorial Experiments (Between Subjects)

Output Listing 4.

Part of Tukey HSD listing for the interaction of *drug* and *alert*

```
- - - - - O N E W A Y - - - - -

     Variable  DRIVPERF   Driving Performance
  By Variable  CELLCODE

Multiple Range Tests:  Tukey-HSD test with significance level .05

The difference between two means is significant if
  MEAN(J)-MEAN(I)  >= 3.4021 * RANGE * SQRT(1/N(I) + 1/N(J))
  with the following value(s) for RANGE: 4.18

   (*) Indicates significant differences which are shown in the lower triangle

                         G G G G G G
                         r r r r r r
                         p p p p p p

                         4 2 6 5 1 3
    Mean       CELLCODE

   10.0000    Grp 4
   12.0000    Grp 2
   16.0000    Grp 6
   18.0000    Grp 5    *
   21.0000    Grp 1    * *
   22.0000    Grp 3    * *
```

Unplanned multiple comparisons following the ANOVA of complex factorial experiments: Some cautions and caveats

In considering the making of unplanned multiple comparisons to explore a significant interaction, we have touched upon a difficult area, abounding in disagreement. The reader will look in vain, in the writings of the most respected statistical authorities, for a set of rules and procedures on which there is complete consensus. Few, however, would dispute the following statements.

(1) The making of unplanned multiple comparisons (and other *a posteriori* analyses following the initial ANOVA) carries a heightened risk of type I error, that is, obtaining a significant difference (or pattern) which has merely arisen through sampling variability. In factorial experiments, that is, there is a heightened risk of **capitalising upon chance**. Accordingly, the user must take precautions to prevent the *per family* (or experiment-wise) error rate from rising to unacceptable levels.

(2) The more complex the experiment (that is, the more factors there are and the more levels each factor has), the greater the risk of capitalising upon chance and so producing type I errors.

(3) The risks of capitalising upon chance are greatly increased if the researcher follows an indiscriminate dredging strategy, whereby every possible statistical test is automatically carried out: simple main effects of A at the various levels of B, simple effects of B at the different levels of A, comparisons between very possible pair of cell means, and so on. We have seen that only some comparisons are informative. In the present example, for instance, we should learn

little from a comparison of (Placebo, Tired) with (Drug A, Fresh), because it would be impossible to say whether the Drug or the Alertness factor was responsible for the difference.

(4) Whatever strategy one adopts, formal testing should be driven by considerations of theory and the meaningfulness, rather than a desire to milk every data set to the maximum possible extent in the hope of finding significance somewhere.

The **Tukey test** assumes that every possible paired comparison will be made. Since, however, the discriminating user will only wish to make selected comparisons, it may be felt that the Tukey test is unduly conservative. Certainly, with more complex factorial designs, with many treatment combinations, the Tukey criterion for a significant difference is a very exacting one. For this reason, some authors (e.g. Keppel, 1973; p244) suggest that a preliminary test for a simple main effect can justify defining the comparison family more narrowly, and carrying out a Tukey test only on the means relating to the simple main effect concerned. For example, returning to our current example of the effects of drugs upon fresh and tired subjects, the significant ANOVA interaction could be followed by tests of the simple main effects of the Drug factor at the Fresh and Tired levels of the Alertness factor. Since there is a significant simple main effect of Drug at the Placebo level of Alertness, we can enter the table of critical values of the **Studentized Range Statistic** with (number of means) = 3, instead of 6.

8.3 EXPERIMENTS WITH MORE THAN TWO TREATMENT FACTORS

SPSS can readily be used to analyse data from more complex factorial experiments, with three or more treatment factors. We should warn the reader, however, that experiments with more than three factors should be avoided, because interpretation of complex interactions involving four or more factors is often extremely difficult.

Here we illustrate how easily an analysis of a three factor ANOVA can be done in SPSS. Suppose the driving simulation data had included *sex* as an additional factor as shown in Table 4.

The data set in the **Data Editor** window would now have to include **three** coding variables (i.e. three columns) for *alertness*, *sex*, and *drug*, as well as a fourth column for the dependent variable *drivperf*. Figure 9 shows a section of the **Data Editor** window with the new coding variable *sex* added.

Chapter 8 - Factorial Experiments (Between Subjects)

Table 4.
Results of a three-way factorial experiment

Levels of the factor: Alertness	Levels of the factor: Sex	Levels of the factor: Drug		
		Placebo	A	B
Fresh	Male	24 25 13 22 16	18 8 9 14 16	27 14 19 29 27
Fresh	Female	23 18 19 24 26	15 6 9 8 17	23 19 17 20 25
Tired	Male	13 12 14 16 17	21 24 22 23 20	21 11 14 22 19
Tired	Female	13 4 3 2 6	13 11 17 13 16	9 14 11 21 18

Figure 10.
A section of the Data Editor window prepared for the analysis of the data in Table 4.

	alert	drug	drivperf	sex
1	1	1	24	1
2	1	1	25	1
3	1	1	13	1
4	1	1	22	1
5	1	1	16	1
6	1	1	23	2
7	1	1	18	2
8	1	1	19	2
9	1	1	24	2
10	1	1	26	2

To run the three-factor ANOVA, proceed as follows:

- Open the **Simple Factorial ANOVA** dialog box and complete it as shown in Figure 11 which is basically as in Figure 4, with the addition of the extra factor *sex*, together with its range of values, in the **Factor(s)** box.
- Click on **OK** to run the analysis.

Figure 11.
The completed three-way Simple Factorial ANOVA dialog box

Simple Factorial ANOVA

Dependent: drivperf

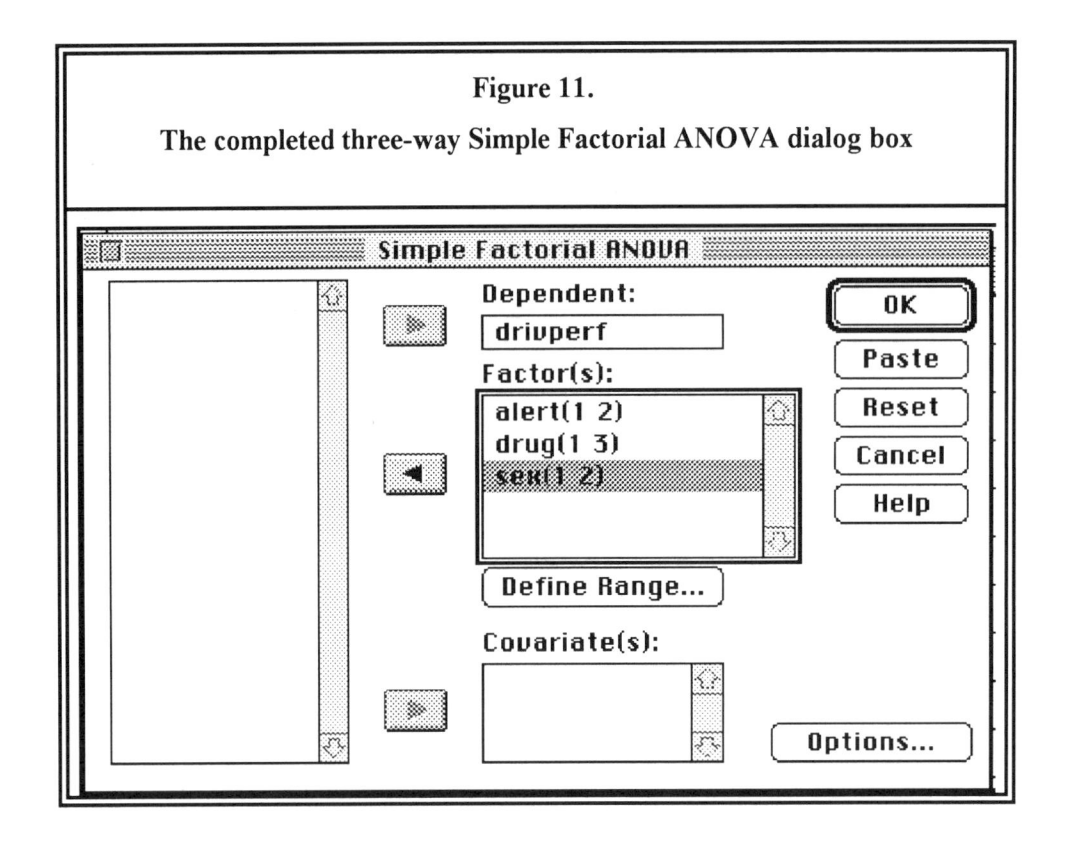

Factor(s):
- alert(1 2)
- drug(1 3)
- sex(1 2)

Covariate(s):

The output for the three-factor ANOVA is shown in Output Listing 5.

Output Listing 5.
The three-way factorial ANOVA summary table

Source of Variation	Sum of Squares	DF	Mean Square	F	Sig of F
Main Effects	593.333	4	148.333	8.452	.000
ALERT	201.667	1	201.667	11.491	.001
DRUG	190.000	2	95.000	5.413	.008
SEX	201.667	1	201.667	11.491	.001
2-Way Interactions	901.533	5	180.307	10.274	.000
ALERT DRUG	763.333	2	381.667	21.747	.000
ALERT SEX	123.267	1	123.267	7.024	.011
DRUG SEX	14.933	2	7.467	.425	.656
3-Way Interactions	67.733	2	33.867	1.930	.156
ALERT DRUG SEX	67.733	2	33.867	1.930	.156
Explained	1562.600	11	142.055	8.094	.000
Residual	842.400	48	17.550		
Total	2405.000	59	40.763		

60 cases were processed.
0 cases (.0 pct) were missing.

The first thing to notice in Output Listing 5 is that 60 cases were processed and there were no missing data. While that is reassuring, it is still a good idea to check that each entry in the **Data Editor** matches the score in Table 4.

With three factors, the ANOVA summary table becomes considerably longer than in the two-factor case. As before, there are main effects; but this time there are three, one for each of the three factors in the experiment. In the two-factor experiment, there can be only one two-way interaction; but in the three-factor experiment, there are three. Moreover, in the three-factor table a new interaction appears, *alert* × *drug* × *sex*. This is known as a **three-way**, or **three-factor interaction**.

A three-factor interaction is said to occur when there is heterogeneity of the interaction between two factors across the levels of a third. There is, however, no evidence of a three-factor interaction in the present data set: $F(2, 48) = 1.93$; NS. In addition to the significant main effects and interaction noted in Output Listing 3, there are now also a significant main effect *sex* and a significant interaction of *sex* and *alert*.

Chapter 8 - Factorial Experiments (Between Subjects)

EXERCISE 13

FACTORIAL BETWEEN SUBJECTS ANOVA (TWO-WAY ANOVA)

BEFORE YOU START

Before proceeding with this practical, please read Chapter 8. The following exercise assumes a knowledge of the standard **factorial ANOVA** terminology.

TWO-WAY ANOVA

An experiment on the memories of chess players

'Must have a marvellous memory!'. This is something often said of a good chess player; but do good chess players necessarily have better short-term memories than those who are mediocre? To find out, a psychologist tested chess players at three levels of proficiency on their ability to reconstruct board positions they had just been shown. Some of the positions used were from real games selected from tournaments; but others were merely random placings of the same pieces. The psychologist predicted that whereas the better players would show superior reconstructions of real board positions, this superiority would disappear when they tried to reproduce random placements. The dependent variable in this experiment was a subject's *score* on reconstruction. There were two independent variables (factors):

       (1)   Competence (Novice, Average, Good).
       (2)   Position   (Real, Random).

An important feature of the design of this experiment was that a different sample of subjects performed under each of the six treatment combinations: that is, each group of players at a given level was subdivided into those reconstructing Real positions and those reconstructing Random positions.

Table 1.
Results of the experiment on the reconstruction of positions by chess players

Position	Competence														
	Novice					Average					Good				
Real	38	39	42	40	40	65	58	70	61	62	88	97	79	89	89
Random	50	53	40	41	36	50	40	43	37	38	41	40	50	42	41

What the psychologist is predicting is that, when performance is averaged over Random and Real positions, the better players will achieve higher performance means; but this will turn out to be because of their superior recall of Real board positions only, and the beginners will be just as good at reconstructing Random positions. The **two-factor ANOVA**, therefore, should show a significant interaction between the factors of Competence and Position, as well as (possibly) a main effect of Competence. The latter might be expected to arise because the better players' much superior performance in reconstructing real board positions pulls up the mean value of their performance over both Real and Random positions, even though they may not excel beginners on the Random task. The results of the experiment are shown in Table 1.

Procedure for the two-factor between subjects experiment

Before proceeding further, we strongly recommend you to study Section 8.2.

Constructing the SPSS data set

Recast the data of Table 1 into a form suitable for entry into SPSS along the lines of the description in Section 8.2.1. You will need two coding variables, *compet* and *position*, and one dependent variable *score*. As always, save the data set.

Exploring the data

Before proceeding with the ANOVA, it is important to explore the data. Construct a table of means to include the cell means and the marginal means (i.e. row means and column means) by using the **Means** procedure twice, the first time including both *compet* and *position* in the **Independent List** box, the second time **layering** both the independent variables (see Section 8.2.2). The first operation obtains the marginal means, the second obtains the cell means. You should now have a table of cell means, and also the row and column means.

- **From inspection of the marginal means, are there any indications of main effects? Do the cell means give any indication of an interaction?**

Procedure for the two-way ANOVA

Follow the description in Section 8.2.3.

Output listing for the two-way ANOVA

The ANOVA summary table gives F ratios for the main effects of *compet* and *position* and also for the interaction between the two factors.

- **Write down the values of *F* (and the associated p-values) for the main effect and interaction terms. Do these results confirm your predictions from inspection of the output from the Means procedure? Relate these results to the experimental hypothesis about the short-term memory of chess players.**

Obtaining a graph of the cell means

Follow the procedure in Section 8.2.4. Inspect the graph and interpret the results of the ANOVA tests accordingly.

Post-hoc comparisons among the marginal and cell means

Follow up the main ANOVA with post-hoc comparisons among the marginal and cell means, as described in Section 8.2.4.

- **Construct your own table showing clearly which pairs of levels or cells are significantly different and which are not.**

CHAPTER 9

WITHIN SUBJECTS EXPERIMENTS

9.1 INTRODUCTION

9.2 ADVANTAGES AND DISADVANTAGES OF WITHIN SUBJECTS EXPERIMENTS

9.3 WITHIN SUBJECTS ANOVA WITH SPSS

9.4 A ONE-FACTOR WITHIN SUBJECTS ANOVA

9.5 NONPARAMETRIC TESTS FOR A ONE-FACTOR WITHIN SUBJECTS EXPERIMENT

9.6 THE TWO-FACTOR WITHIN SUBJECTS ANOVA

Chapter 9 - Within Subjects Experiments

9.1 INTRODUCTION

In Chapter 7, a one-factor between subjects experiment was described, in which the recall of a text by three groups of participants was compared, each group being tested at a different level of the treatment factor (Mnemonic Training Method). In other circumstances, however, it might be feasible to have just one sample of participants, and to test each person under all the conditions making up the treatment factor. In that case, the experiment would be described as a **one-factor within subjects experiment** or as a **one-factor experiment with repeated measures**.

For example, suppose that in a study of performance, the independent variable is Task Complexity, with three levels: Simple, Medium and High. The experimental design is shown in Table 1.

Table 1.
A one-factor within subjects experiment

	Levels of factor: Task Complexity		
	Simple	Medium	High
Subjects	Same group of subjects		

In Table 2, the subjects are represented individually, each row containing all the data from one subject.

Table 2.
Another representation of the design shown in Table 1

	Levels of factor: Task Complexity		
	Simple	Medium	High
Subject 1			
Subject 2			
...	...	...	....
Subject 30			

It can be seen from Table 2 that, although there is just one treatment factor (Task Complexity), the design could be thought of as having two factors:

(1)   the **Treatment** factor (Task Complexity) with 3 levels;

(2)   **Subjects**, with 30 levels (if there are 30 subjects in the experiment).

Moreover, the two factors **cross**: each level of either factor is to be found in combination with every level of the other. The one-factor within subjects design, in fact, resembles a two-factor between subjects experiment (Chapter 8) *with just one observation in each cell*. For this reason, the one-factor within subjects experiment is sometimes termed a **subjects by treatments** experiment. In this chapter, we shall consider only the analysis of experiments that have repeated measures on **all** treatment factors. In principle, as with between subjects experiments, there can be any number of treatment factors.

9.2   ADVANTAGES AND DISADVANTAGES OF WITHIN SUBJECTS EXPERIMENTS

A potential problem with between subjects experiments (Chapters 7 & 8) is that if there are large individual differences in performance, searching for a meaningful pattern in the data can be like trying to listen to a radio programme against a background crackle of interference. For example, in the Mnemonic Training Method experiment described in Chapter 7, some of the scores obtained by subjects in the control condition may well be higher than those of subjects who were trained to use a mnemonic: there are some people who, when asked to read through a long list, can, **without any training at all**, reproduce most of the items accurately; whereas others, even after training, would recall very few items. Individual differences, therefore, can introduce considerable **noise** into the data from between subjects experiments.

Essentially, the within subjects experiment uses each subject as his/her own control; and the crossed nature of the design makes it possible to separate the variance that has resulted from the manipulation of the treatment factor from that arising from individual differences.

Another drawback with the between subjects experiment is that it is wasteful of subjects: if the experimental procedure is a short one, a subject may spend more time travelling to and from the place of testing than actually performing the experiment. The great appeal of the within subjects experiment is that much more extensive use can be made of the subject who has taken the trouble to attend.

In summary, therefore, the within subjects experiment has two advantages over the between subjects experiment:

(1)   It cuts down data noise.

(2)   It makes more efficient use of time and resources.

Nevertheless, the within subjects experiment also has disadvantages, which in some circumstances can outweigh considerations of convenience and the maximisation of the signal-to-noise ratio. In designing an experiment, it is essential to try to ensure that the independent variable does not co-vary with an unwanted, or **extraneous** variable, so that the effects of the two are entangled, or **confounded**.

Suppose the mnemonics experiment had been of a within subjects design, and that each subject had first performed under the control condition, then under Mnemonic A and finally under Mnemonic B. Perhaps the improvement under mnemonic A was simply a **practice effect**: the more lists one learns, the better one becomes at learning lists. A practice effect is one kind of **carry-over effect**.

Carry-over effects do not always have a positive effect upon performance: recall of the items in a list is vulnerable to interference from items in previous lists (proactive interference). Carry-over effects may depend upon the sequence of conditions. For example, while performance under Mnemonic A may be unaffected by previous performance under the control condition, the converse may not be true: it may be difficult for subjects who have been trained in the use of a mnemonic to stop using it on demand. This is an example of an **order effect**. Carry-over and order effects can act as extraneous, confounding variables, making it difficult to interpret the results of a within subjects experiment.

One approach to the problem of carry-over effects and order effects is the procedure known as **counterbalancing**, whereby the order of presentation of the conditions making up a within subjects factor is varied from subject to subject, in the hope that carry-over and order effects will balance out across conditions. Counterbalancing is not always sensible, however, as in the mnemonics experiment, where (as we have seen) it would make little sense to have the control condition coming last. These matters must be carefully considered before deciding to perform an experiment with repeated measures on its treatment factors.

An additional problem with a within subjects design is that if there is **heterogeneity of covariance** (see next section), there is a heightened risk of statistical error. Covariance is a measure of statistical association between two variables: the Pearson correlation discussed in Chapter 11 is the covariance between two variables that have been standardised (i.e. they have means of zero and standard deviations of unity).

9.3 WITHIN SUBJECTS ANOVA WITH SPSS

To perform a within subjects ANOVA on SPSS, the user must select
Statistics
    ANOVA Models
        Repeated Measures....

Analysis of variance is a set of *univariate* statistical methods: that is, ANOVA was designed for data with *only one dependent variable (DV)*. In SPSS, however, all within subjects ANOVA procedures are run within SPSS's

MANOVA (Multivariate ANOVA) program. (MANOVA is a set of techniques designed for use with data sets with two or more DVs.) Initially, the MANOVA program treats the responses to the levels of the within subjects independent variable (IV) as separate DVs. Provided the factor levels are all linked with the name of a within subjects factor, the output will include (among other things) a univariate within subjects ANOVA.

Every statistical test implies that the data have been generated in a certain way, as specified by a statistical **model**. For example, the ANOVA for between groups experiments (Chapters 7 and 8) requires that there must be homogeneity of variance from group to group. The model for the within subjects ANOVA makes additional specifications, over and above those made by the between groups models. The most important of these is that the correlations among the scores at the various levels of the within subjects factor are homogeneous (i.e. the off-diagonal elements of the variance-covariance matrix are constant). This requirement is known as the assumption of **homogeneity of covariance** (or **sphericity**). If this assumption is violated, the true type I error rate (i.e. the probability of rejecting H_0 when it is true) may be inflated.

SPSS tests for homogeneity of covariance with the **Mauchly sphericity test**. Should the data fail the sphericity test (i.e. p-value < 0.05), the ANOVA F test can be modified to make it more *conservative* (less likely to reject the null hypothesis). The **Greenhouse-Geisser** test, available as an option (referred to as the **Epsilon corrected averaged F**) within one of the dialog boxes, reduces the degrees of freedom of the numerator and denominator of the F test by multiplying the original degrees of freedom values by a factor **e**, the value of which is given in the SPSS output under **Greenhouse-Geisser epsilon**. (The value of F remains the same as before: only the degrees of freedom are reduced.) For a helpful discussion of the rationale of the conservative test, see Howell (1997: Chapter 14).

9.4 A ONE-FACTOR WITHIN SUBJECTS ANOVA

9.4.1 Some experimental results

In an experiment on aesthetics, each subject was asked to produce three pictures using just one of three different materials for any one picture: Crayons, Paints or Felt-tip pens. The data are shown in Table 3.

The dependent variable was the rating a picture received from a panel of judges. The independent variable was the type of implement used to produce the picture. Since the subjects would certainly vary in artistic ability, it was decided to ask each to produce three pictures, one with each type of implement. In an attempt to neutralise carry-over effects, the order of implements was counterbalanced across subjects. This is a one-factor within subjects experiment. Alternatively, it could be described as a **one-factor experiment with repeated measures**, or as a **subjects by treatments** experiment.

Table 3. Results of a one-factor within subjects experiment			
	Levels of factor: Implement		
	Crayon	Paint	Felt-tip
s1	10	12	14
s2	18	10	16
s3	20	15	16
s4	12	10	12
s5	19	20	21
s6	25	22	20
s7	18	16	17
s8	22	18	18
s9	17	14	12
s10	23	20	18

9.4.2 Entering the data

When entering the data of Table 3 into the SPSS Data Editor, no grouping (code) variable is required, since the subjects have not been subdivided into groups. Using the procedures described in Section 3.4, define the variables *crayon*, *paint*, and *felttip*, and enter the data of Table 3 into the three columns.

9.4.3 Exploring the data: Boxplots for within subjects factors

To draw boxplots of the data at the various levels of a within subjects factor, follow the following steps:

- Select
  Graphs
    Boxplot...

Chapter 9 - Within Subjects Experiments

to open the **Boxplot** dialog box (Figure 1).

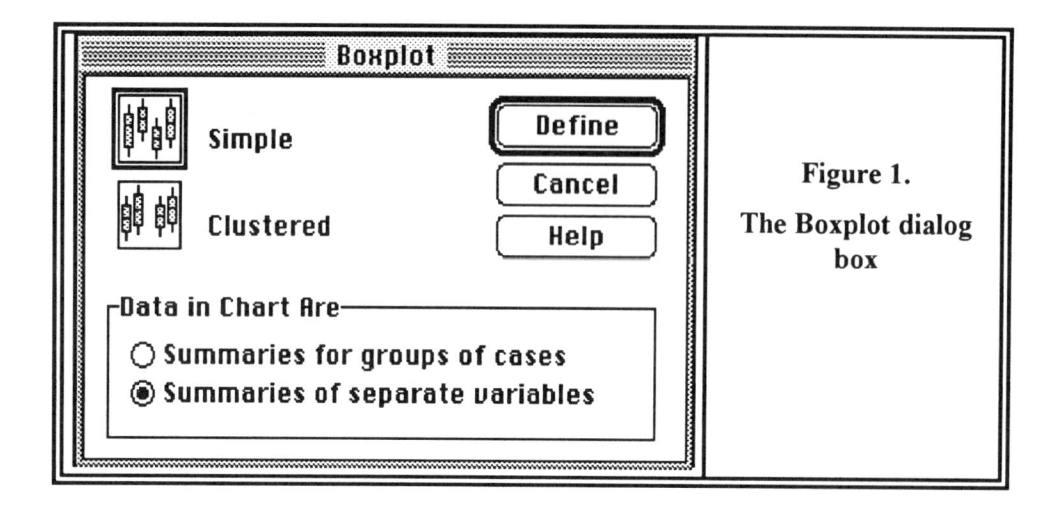

```
========== Boxplot ==========
  [icon] Simple           [ Define ]
                          [ Cancel ]
  [icon] Clustered        [  Help  ]
  ┌─Data in Chart Are─────────────┐
  │ ○ Summaries for groups of cases│
  │ ● Summaries of separate variables│
  └────────────────────────────────┘
```

Figure 1.
The Boxplot dialog box

- In the **Data in Chart Are** box, activate the **Summaries of separate variables** radio button. Click on **Define** (Figure 1) to open the **Define Simple Boxplot: Summaries of Separate Variables** dialog box (Figure 2).

Figure 2.
The Define Simple Boxplot: Summaries of Separate Variables dialog box

```
Define Simple Boxplot: Summaries of Separate Variables

  ┌─────────┐              Boxes Represent:      [   OK    ]
  │ crayon  │             ┌─────────┐
  │ felttip │             │         │            [         ]
  │ paint   │    [ ▶ ]    │         │            [  Reset  ]
  │         │             │         │            [ Cancel  ]
  │         │             └─────────┘            [  Help   ]
  │         │              Label Cases by:
  │         │             ┌─────────┐
  │         │    [ ▶ ]    │         │            [Options...]
  └─────────┘             └─────────┘
```

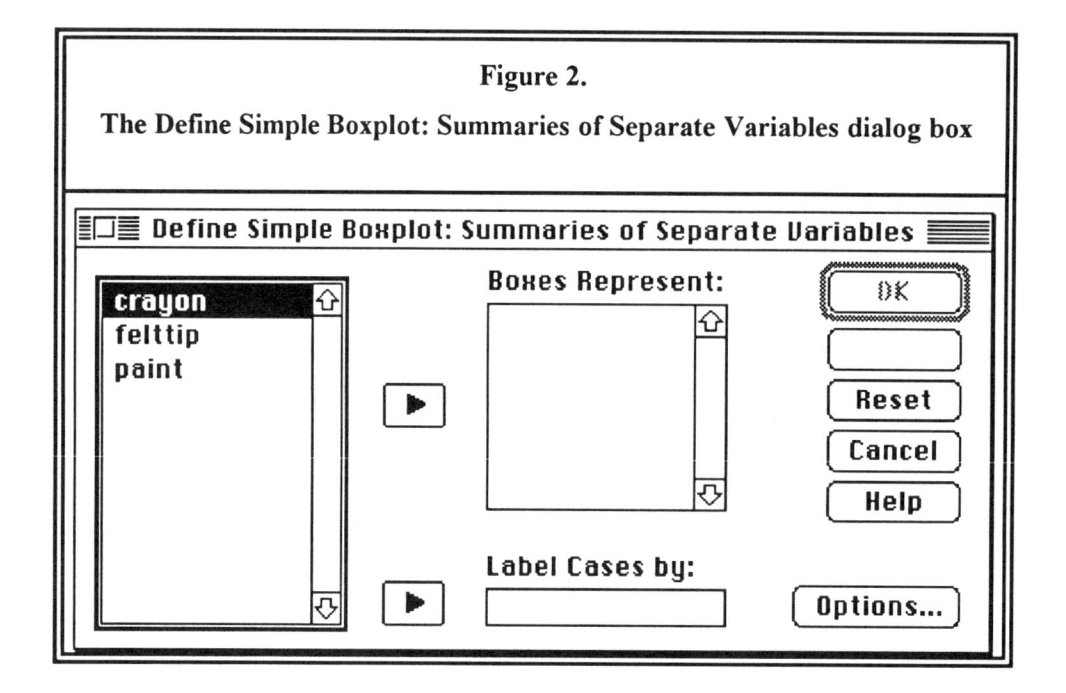

- In the box on the left (Figure 2), the variable names are normally listed in alphabetical order in the left-hand box. Transfer them one at a time in the sequence desired for the boxplot diagram. (If you would prefer to have the variables listed in the same left-to-right order of the columns in the **Data Editor**, it is possible to arrange this by changing the general **Preferences**. To do this, select **Preferences** at the foot of the **Edit** menu to open the **Preferences** dialog box and then change the default setting from **Alphabetical** to **File** in the **Display Order for Variables Lists**.)

- Click on **OK** to obtain the unedited boxplots (not shown). The edited boxplots are shown in Figure 3.

Figure 3.

Boxplots of within subjects data

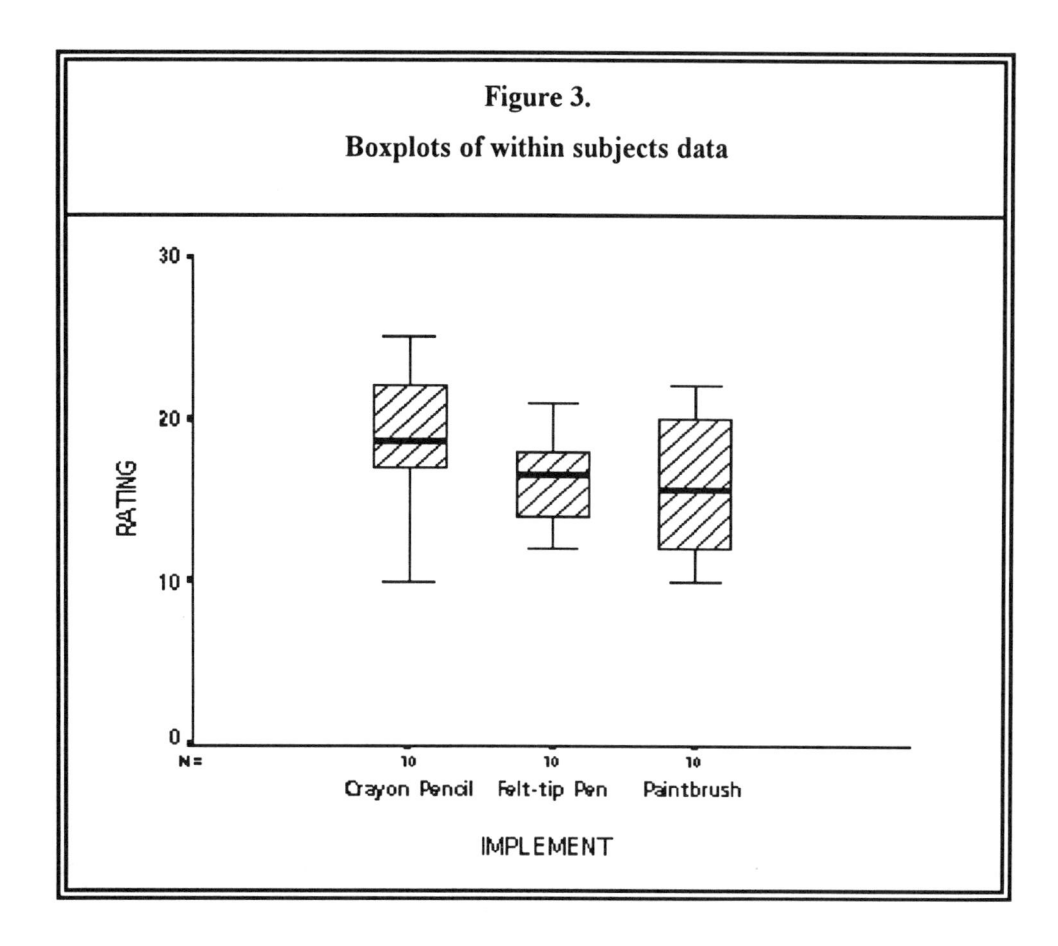

[Boxplot figure showing RATING (y-axis, 0 to 30) vs IMPLEMENT (x-axis): Crayon Pencil, Felt-tip Pen, Paintbrush, each with N = 10.]

Initially, the boxplots will appear in colour on the screen of your Mac. Such a screen image, however, does not print well in black-and-white. To make the image suitable for black-and-white printing, some editing will be necessary. Proceed as follows:

- Click on the **Edit** box.

- To edit any part of the figure, you must select that part of the screen figure. Highlight the boxes by clicking on one of them so that each corner has little black squares.

- Click on the **Attributes** menu. The boxes on the right will show the default settings for the colours, borders and fill patterns that were used for the screen image. Change the fill colour by clicking-and-dragging the screen pointer into the **Fill Color box** and selecting black. Do not be alarmed when the boxes turn black.

- Click on the **Attributes menu** once again and click-and-drag the screen pointer into the **Fill Pattern box** to select an attractive black-and-white fill pattern.

- After completing the change of pattern, click anywhere in the **Chart** window to turn off the box highlighting.

It is quite possible to alter other aspects of the screen figure, such as the aspect ratio, and the spacing of the boxplots. The aspect ratio (the height of a graph divided by its width) is controlled by the **Graphics...** option within the general **Preferences** dialog box:

Chapter 9 - Within Subjects Experiments

- Click on
  Edit
   Preferences ...
   to open the **Preferences** dialog box.

- Click on the **Graphics...** box to bring the **Preferences: Graphics** dialog box into view.

- The default setting for the **Chart Aspect Ratio** is at **Best for Display (1.67)**. Notice that the recommended setting for the printer is 1.25 as shown by the line **Best for printer (1.25)**. To improve the appearance of bars and boxes in SPSS graphs, it is well worth experimenting with aspect ratios such as 1 by clicking on the radio button for **Custom**, inserting 1 in the box, and then clicking on **Continue** and **OK**.

The spacing of the boxes is controlled by the **Bar Spacing** option within the **Chart** menu.

There are two aspects of spacing:

(1) the **Inter-Bar Spacing** (expressed as a percentage of bar width, and which can vary from 0% to 100%);

(2) the **Bar Margin**, which is the distance of the outermost bars from the **inner frame**, an invisible rectangle with the horizontal and vertical axes as two of its sides.

Increasing the bar margin will make the boxes narrower, since the inter-bar spacing has been fixed at a specified relative value. It is recommended that the reader experiments with varying combinations of aspect ratio, bar margin and inter-bar spacing.

9.4.4 Running the within subjects ANOVA

Since there seem to be no major problems with the data distributions such as outliers or extreme values (if there had been, it would be advisable to consider deselecting such cases from the analysis by the use of the **Select Cases** option in the **Data** drop-down menu), the within subjects ANOVA is run as follows:

- Select the **Repeated Measures** item from the **ANOVA Models** menu (Figure 4) by choosing
  Statistics
   ANOVA Models
    Repeated Measures
  to open the **Repeated Measures Define Factor(s)** dialog box (Figure 5).

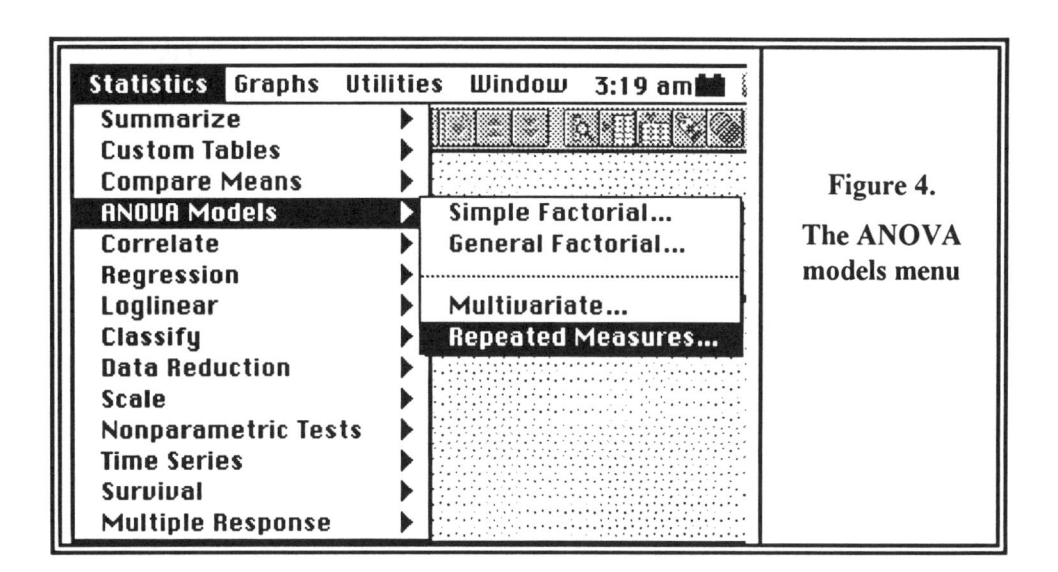

Chapter 9 - Within Subjects Experiments

Figure 4.
The ANOVA models menu

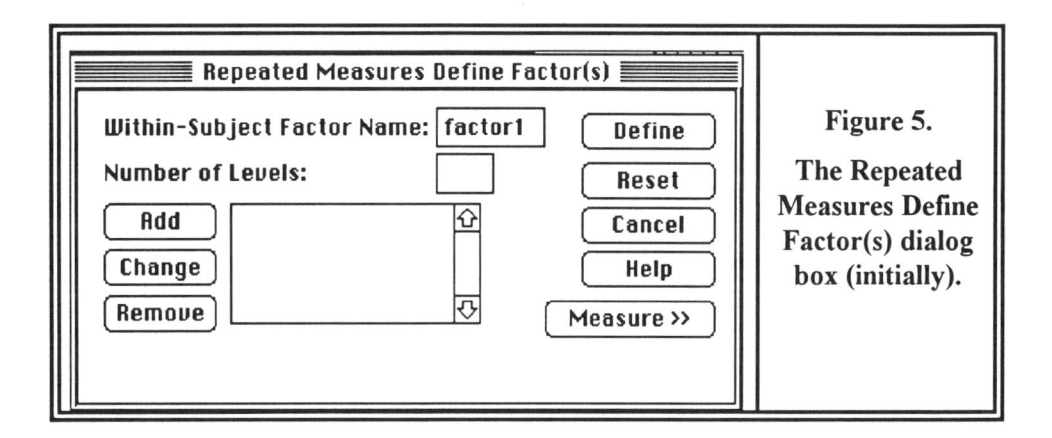

Figure 5.
The Repeated Measures Define Factor(s) dialog box (initially).

- In the **Within-Subject Factor Name** box, delete *factor1* and type in a generic name (such as *implem*), bearing in mind that the new name must not be that of any of the variables in the data set; moreover, it must not exceed 8 characters in length. In the **Number of Levels** box, type the number of conditions (*3*) making up the Implement factor. Click on **Add** to paste the factor name and number of levels into the lowest box (Figure 6).

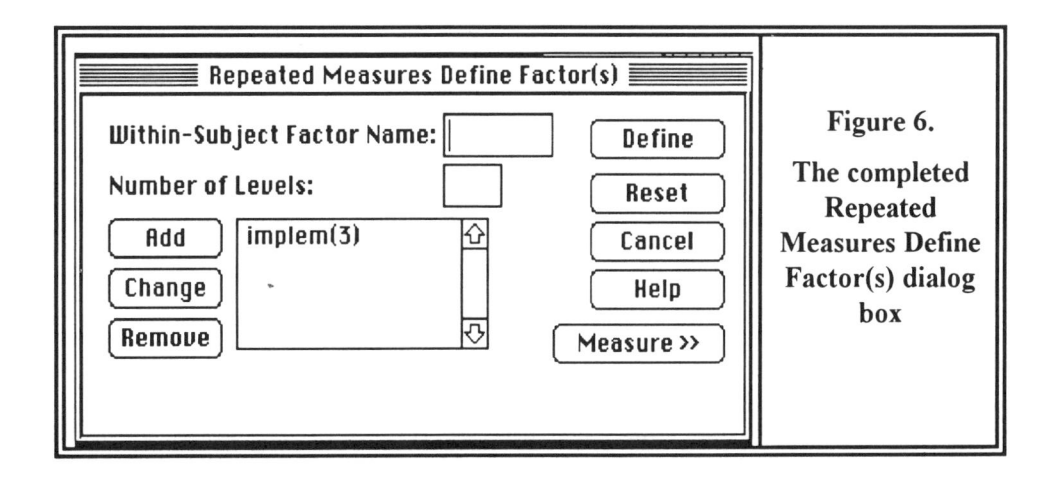

Figure 6.
The completed Repeated Measures Define Factor(s) dialog box

Chapter 9 - Within Subjects Experiments

- Click on **Define** to open the **Repeated Measures ANOVA** dialog box (Figure 7).

Figure 7.
The Repeated Measures ANOVA dialog box

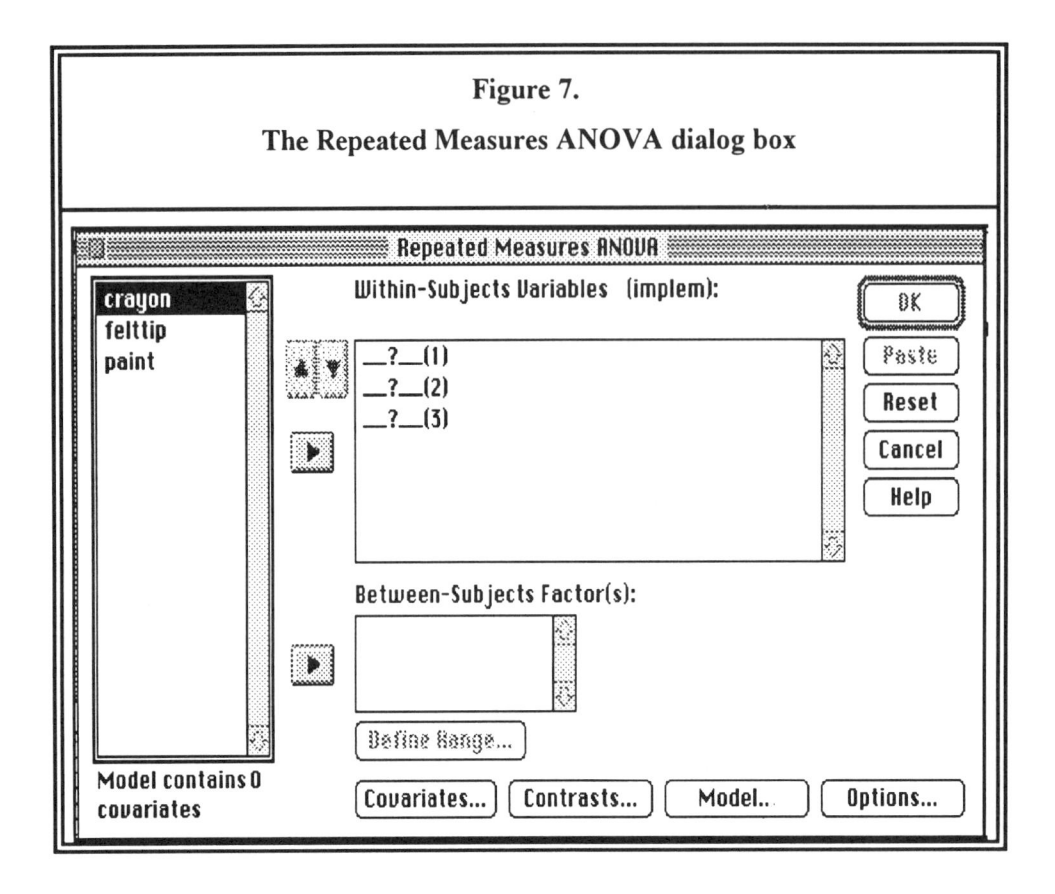

- You will see that the uppermost variable name has been highlighted. Press and hold down the Command key while clicking on the other two variable names successively. This will highlight all three variable names. Click on ▶ to transfer them into the double-bordered box on the right labelled **Within-Subjects Variables [implem]**. The question marks will be replaced by the variable names as shown in Figure 8.

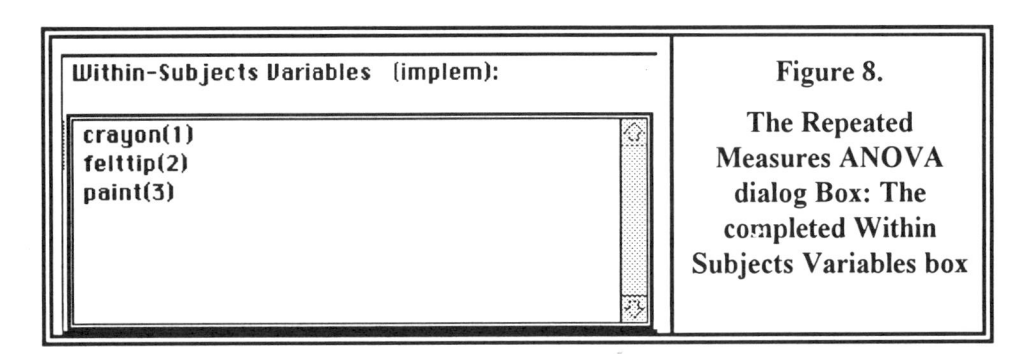

Figure 8.
The Repeated Measures ANOVA dialog Box: The completed Within Subjects Variables box

- Before leaving the **Repeated Measures ANOVA** dialog box, suppress the multivariate listing by clicking on **Model** to open the **Repeated Measures ANOVA: Model** dialog box (Figure 9). In the bottom left-hand corner, is a box labelled **Within-Subjects Tests** containing three check boxes. Click on the check box beside **Multivariate tests** to remove the ×.

218

Figure 9.
The Repeated Measures ANOVA: Model dialog box

[Dialog box: Repeated Measures ANOVA: Model, showing Specify Model options (Full factorial selected, Custom), Within-Subjects list containing "implem", Build Terms with Interaction dropdown, Within-Subjects Model, Between-Subjects, Between-Subjects Model, Model Options (Sum of squares: Unique, Error term: Within+Residual), Within-Subjects Tests (Multivariate tests, Averaged F checked, Epsilon corrected averaged F), Display (Transformation matrix, Hypothesis SSCP matrix), with Continue, Cancel, Help buttons.]

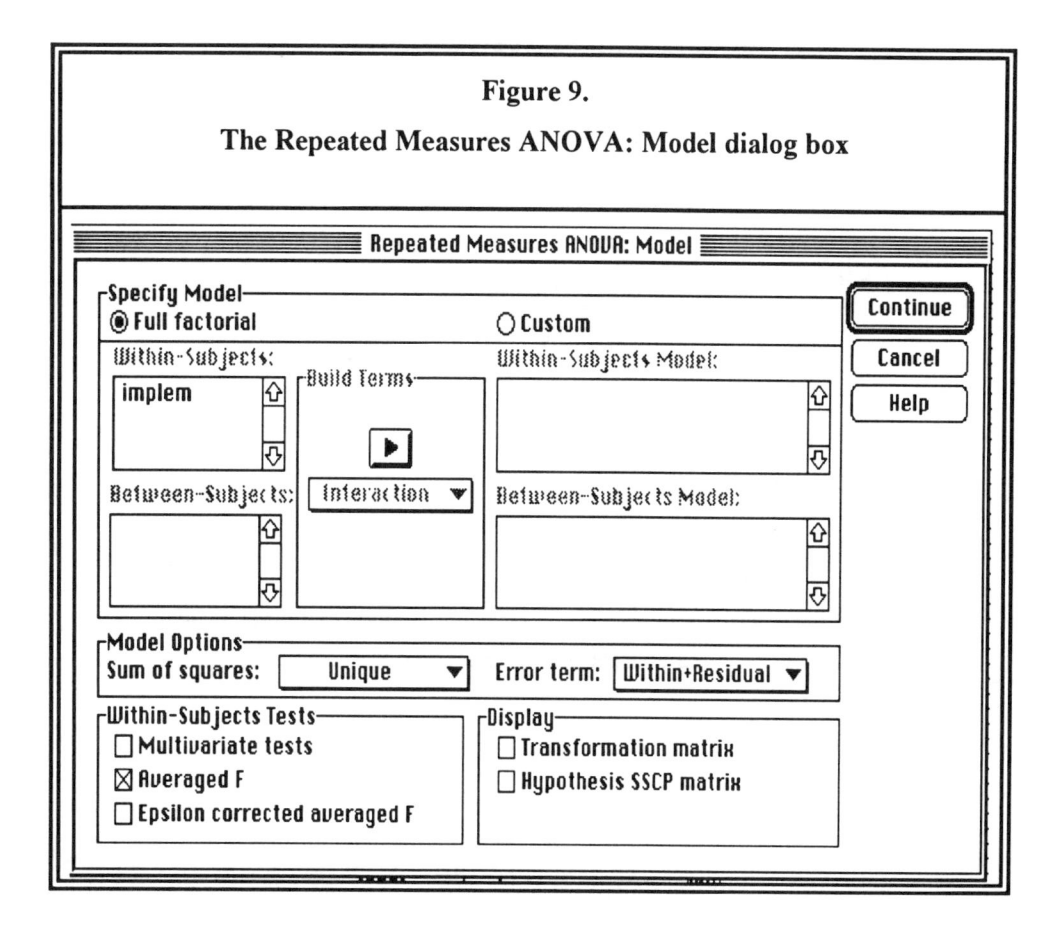

- Click on **Continue** to return to the **Repeated Measures ANOVA dialog box**, and then on **OK** to run the analysis.

9.4.5 Output listing for a one-factor within subjects ANOVA

The first part of the output listing (not reproduced here) is subtitled **Tests of Between Subjects Effects** and can be ignored, since this example has no between subjects variable.

The next section (shown in Output Listing 1) reports the result of the **Mauchly Sphericity Test** for homogeneity of covariance, which is important for the univariate approach. If the test is not significant (i.e. **Significance**, the p-value, has a value greater than 0.05), then the p-value given in the ANOVA summary table, which appears under the title **Averaged Tests of Significance**, can be accepted. If the test is significant (i.e. **Significance**, the p-value, has a value less than or equal to 0.05), then one can make a more conservative test, such as the **Greenhouse-Geisser test** by returning to the **Within-Subjects Tests** check boxes (Figure 9), clicking on the **Epsilon corrected averaged F** check box and re-executing the analysis. It is worth noting, however, that should the ordinary F-test have shown significance with a small p-value such as 0.03 or smaller, the conservative test will not reverse that decision: F will still be significant.

Chapter 9 - Within Subjects Experiments

Output Listing 1.

The Mauchly sphericity test and epsilon

Tests involving 'IMPLEM' Within-Subject Effect.

```
Mauchly sphericity test, W =      .90942
Chi-square approx. =              .75963 with 2 D. F.
Significance =                    .684

Greenhouse-Geisser Epsilon =      .91694
Huynh-Feldt Epsilon =            1.00000
Lower-bound Epsilon =             .50000
```

AVERAGED Tests of Significance that follow multivariate tests are equivalent to univariate or split-plot or mixed-model approach to repeated measures. Epsilons may be used to adjust d.f. for the AVERAGED results.

The conservative F-test only makes a difference when:

(1) there is heterogeneity of covariance (i.e. Mauchly test is significant);

(2) the F with unadjusted degrees of freedom is barely significant beyond the 0.05 level.

Should F have a lower tail probability, the null hypothesis can safely be rejected without making a conservative test.

In the present case, the Mauchly test gives a p-value of 0.684, so there is no evidence of heterogeneity of covariance. The usual ANOVA F test should therefore be used.

The ANOVA summary table is shown in Output Listing 2.

Output Listing 2.

The ANOVA summary table

```
* * * * * * A n a l y s i s   o f   V a r i a n c e -- design  1 * * * * * *

Tests involving 'IMPLEM' Within-Subject Effect.

AVERAGED Tests of Significance for MEAS.1 using UNIQUE sums of squares
Source of Variation         SS         DF        MS          F    Sig of F

WITHIN+RESIDUAL           72.73         18       4.04
IMPLEM                   39.27          2      19.63       4.86     .021
```

Note the **Signif of F** value for the *implem* within-subject factor is *0.021* (i.e. the obtained value of F is significant beyond the 5 per cent level, but not beyond the

0.01 level). Thus the type of implement used does affect the ratings that a painting receives. We can write this result as: $F(2,18) = 4.86$; $p < 0.05$.

In the present case, there was no need to make a conservative F-test because the Mauchly test was insignficant. It is instructive, however, to return to the **Repeated Measures ANOVA:Model dialog**, click the **Epsilon corrected averaged F** check box, and obtain the result shown in Output Listing 3. It is apparent from the **Sig of F** column that *in this particular example* these more conservative statistics in this case make no difference to the result of the ANOVA F-test.

Output Listing 3.
More conservative statistics when Mauchly is significant

```
Tests involving 'IMPLEM' Within-Subject Effect.

AVERAGED Tests of Significance for MEAS.1 using UNIQUE sums of squares
Source of Variation          SS         DF         MS         F      Sig of F

WITHIN+RESIDUAL            72.73        18        4.04
   (Greenhouse-Geisser)               16.50
   (Huynh-Feldt)                      18.00
   (Lower bound)                       9.00
IMPLEM                     39.27         2       19.63       4.86      .021
   (Greenhouse-Geisser)                1.83                  4.86      .024
   (Huynh-Feldt)                       2.00                  4.86      .021
   (Lower bound)                       1.00                  4.86      .055
```

9.4.6 Unplanned multiple comparisons: Bonferroni method

There is some dubiety as to whether, following significant main effects of within subjects factors, the Tukey HSD test affords sufficient protection against inflation of the *per family* type I error rate. Other methods, therefore, have been recommended. In Section 7.1, we distinguished between planned and unplanned tests. Suppose it is planned to make exactly *c* pairwise comparisons among a set of treatment means resulting from a one-factor experiment. It is desired to keep the *per family* error rate at 0.05. In the **Bonferroni method**, ordinary t-tests are used for the pairwise comparisons, but the *per family* error rate is divided by the number of planned comparisons. To achieve significance, therefore, each t-test must show significance beyond (sometimes well beyond) the 0.05 level.

The Bonferroni method, although primarily intended for the making of planned comparisons, can also be used to make *unplanned* pairwise multiple comparisons among a set of *k* treatment means following a one-factor ANOVA.

In this case, however, the *per family* type I error rate must be divided by the number of possible pairs (*c*) that can be drawn from an array of *k* means, which is given by

$$c = \frac{k!}{2!(k-2)!}$$

where the symbol ! means **factorial** (e.g. 4! is $4 \times 3 \times 2 \times 1 = 24$). For example, if there are five treatment means, $c = 5!/(2! \times 3!) = (5 \times 4 \times 3 \times 2)/(2 \times 3 \times 2) = 10$, and the test statistic will have to be significant beyond the $0.05/10 = 0.005$ level for a comparison to be deemed significant.

In the present example, the ANOVA has shown a significant main effect of the Implement factor. Here the number of treatment means (*k*) = 3, so *c* = 3. The Bonferroni t-tests, therefore, will have to show significance beyond the $0.05/3 = 0.02$ level, approximately.

To make the t-tests, we simply leave ANOVA and request **Paired-Sample T-Tests** for comparisons among the means of the *crayon*, *felttip* and *paint* columns in the **Data Editor**. When these are done with the present data, only the p-value for the difference between the means for the Paint and Crayon conditions is smaller than 0.02: thus only this difference is significant (p = 0.0146).

9.5 NONPARAMETRIC TESTS FOR A ONE-FACTOR WITHIN SUBJECTS EXPERIMENT

As with the one-factor completely randomised experiment, nonparametric methods are available for the analysis of ordinal and nominal data.

9.5.1 The Friedman test for ordinal data

Suppose that six people rank five objects in order of pleasingness. Their decisions might appear as in Table 4.

If we assume that the highest rank is given to the most pleasing object, it would appear, from inspection of Table 4, that Object 3 seems to be more pleasing to most of the raters than is Object 1. Since, however, each of the entries in Table 4 is not an independent measurement but a rank, the one-factor within subjects ANOVA cannot be used here. The Friedman test is suitable for ordinal data of the type shown in Table 4. Enter the data in the usual way in the **Data Editor** window, naming the variables *O1, O2, ... O5*.

Chapter 9 - Within Subjects Experiments

Table 4.

Six people's ranks of five objects in order of pleasingness

	Object 1	Object 2	Object 3	Object 4	Object 5
Person 1	2	1	5	4	3
Person 2	1	2	5	4	3
Person 3	1	3	4	2	5
Person 4	2	1	3	5	4
Person 5	2	1	5	4	3
Person 6	1	2	5	3	4

To run the Friedman test:

- Choose
  Statistics
  Nonparametric Tests
  K Related Samples

  to obtain the **Tests for Several Related Samples** dialog box (not shown).

- On the left, will appear a list of the variables in the **Data Editor** grid. This list should include the items *O1, O2, ..., O5*, which will contain the numbers shown in Table 4. Simply transfer these names to the **Test Variables** box in the usual way. Make sure the **Friedman** check box has been marked.

- Click on **OK**.

The Friedman results are shown in Output Listing 4. Clearly the rankings differ significantly across the objects since the p-value (**Significance** or **Asymp. Sig.**) is less than 0.01. We can write this result as: Chi-square = 17.2; df = 4; p < 0.01.

Output Listing 4.

Friedman test results

```
- - - - Friedman Two-Way Anova

Mean Rank    Variable

    1.50     OBJECT1
    1.67     OBJECT2
    4.50     OBJECT3
    3.67     OBJECT4
    3.67     OBJECT5

    Cases        Chi-Square        D.F.      Significance
      6           17.2000            4            .0018
```

9.5.2 Cochran's Q test for nominal data

Suppose that six children are asked to imagine they were in five different situations and had to choose between Course of Action *A* (coded *0*) and *B* (coded *1*). The results might appear as in Table 5. From inspection of Table 5, it would seem that Course of Action B (i.e. cells containing *1*) is chosen more often in some scenarios than in others. A suitable confirmatory test is **Cochran's Q** test, which was designed for use with related samples of dichotomous nominal data.

Table 5.
Courses of action chosen by six children in five scenarios

	Scene 1	Scene 2	Scene 3	Scene 4	Scene 5
Child 1	0	0	1	1	1
Child 2	0	1	0	1	1
Child 3	1	1	1	1	1
Child 4	0	0	0	1	0
Child 5	0	0	0	0	0
Child 6	0	0	0	1	1

To run Cochran's Q test:

- Bring the **Test for Several Related Samples** dialog box to the screen (see previous section).
- Click off the **Friedman** check box and click on the **Cochran** check box.
- Click on **OK** to run the **Cochran Q** test.

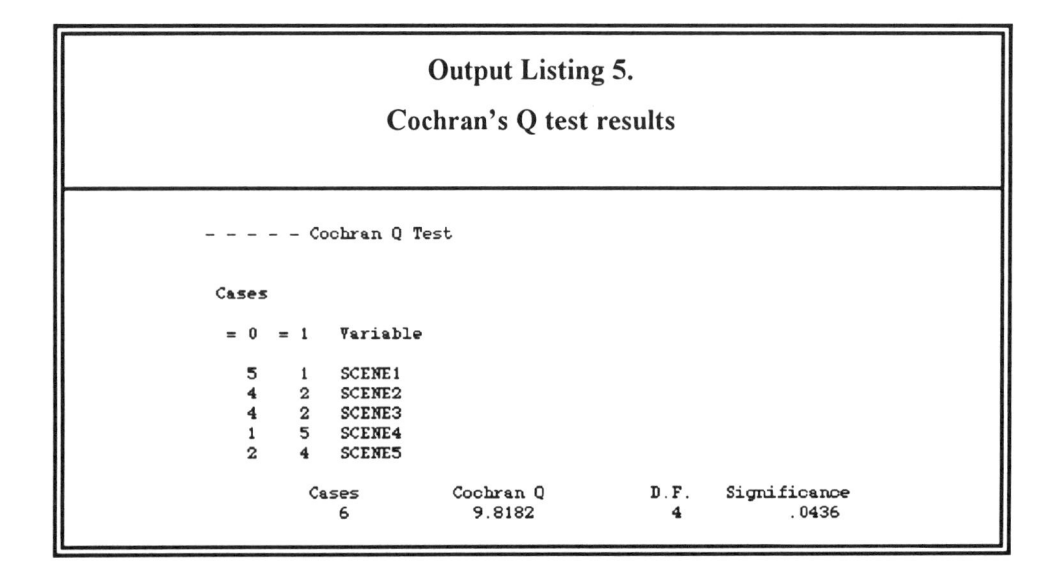

Output Listing 5.
Cochran's Q test results

```
- - - - - Cochran Q Test

Cases

  = 0   = 1   Variable
    5     1   SCENE1
    4     2   SCENE2
    4     2   SCENE3
    1     5   SCENE4
    2     4   SCENE5

        Cases       Cochran Q       D.F.    Significance
          6          9.8182           4         .0436
```

The results are shown in Output Listing 5. The output listings show that the differences in the courses of action taken by the children are just significant since the p-value (**Significance** or **Asymp. Sig.**) is marginally smaller than 0.05. We can write this result as: Cochran Q = 9.82; df = 4; p < 0.05.

9.6 THE TWO-FACTOR WITHIN SUBJECTS ANOVA

9.6.1 Results of a two-factor within subjects experiment

An experiment is designed to investigate the detection of certain theoretically-important patterns on a screen. The patterns vary in shape and solidity. The dependent variable (DV) is the Number of Errors made in responding to the pattern, and the two factors (IVs) are Shape (Circle, Square, or Triangle) and Solidity (Outline or Solid). The experimenter suspects that a shape's solidity affects whether it is perceived more readily than another shape. The same sample of subjects is used for all the possible treatment combinations, that is, there are repeated measures on both factors in the experiment. As with the one-factor within subjects experiment, the univariate ANOVA is performed by using SPSS's **Repeated Measures** option within the **ANOVA Models** menu. In this case, although each treatment combination will be treated as a separate dependent variable, the listing will contain a univariate ANOVA summary table with F tests of main effects and the interaction. The results are shown in Table 6.

Extra care is needed when analysing data from experiments with two or more within subjects factors. It is essential to ensure that SPSS understands which data were obtained under which combination of factors. In the present example, there are six data for each subject, each datum being a score achieved under a different combination of the two factors. We can label the data variables as *circsol*, *circlin*, *squarsol*, *squarlin*, *triansol* and *trianlin*, representing all possible combinations of the shape and solidity factors. Should there be many treatment combinations in the experiment, however, it would be very tedious to name the variables individually. In such cases, it is much more convenient to use the default variable names provided by the computer (e.g. *var00001*, *var00002*, *var00003* etc.), but a careful note must be kept about which combinations of levels of the within subjects factors are represented by which of these default variable names. This information must be borne in mind later when the user has accessed the **Repeated-Measures Define Variable(s)** dialog box (see below) and is naming the within subjects factors.

In the present example, remembering that the program initially treats each combination of levels of within subjects factors as a separate dependent variable, it can be seen that the sequence of names *circsol*, *circlin*, *squarsol*, *squarlin*, *triansol* and *trianlin*, represents successive columns of data in Table 6.

Table 6.
Results of a two-factor within subjects experiment

SHAPE:-	Circle		Square		Triangle	
SOLIDITY:-	Solid	Outline	Solid	Outline	Solid	Outline
S1	4	2	2	8	7	5
S2	3	6	2	6	8	9
S3	2	10	2	5	5	3
S4	1	8	5	5	2	9
S5	4	6	4	5	5	10
S6	3	6	4	6	9	12
S7	7	12	2	6	4	8
S8	6	10	9	5	0	10
S9	4	5	7	6	8	12
S10	2	12	12	8	10	12

9.6.2 Preparing the data set

The data file (part of which is shown in Figure 10) is prepared as before, except that there are now six columns rather than three. Care must be taken with the ordering of the columns - see the previous section.

Figure 10.
Part of the SPSS data file for the two-factor within subjects ANOVA

	circsol	circlin	squarsol	squarlin	triansol	trianlin
1	4	2	2	8	7	5
2	3	6	2	6	8	9
3	2	10	2	5	5	3
4	1	8	5	5	2	9

Chapter 9 - Within Subjects Experiments

9.6.3 Running the two-factor within subjects analysis

- Select
  Statistics
   ANOVA Models
    Repeated Measures

  and then complete the various dialog boxes as in the previous example, except that there is an extra repeated-measures factor to be defined. The completed **Repeated Measures Define Factor(s)** dialog box, with two generic names *shape* and *solidity* (together with their respective numbers of levels) is shown in Figure 11.

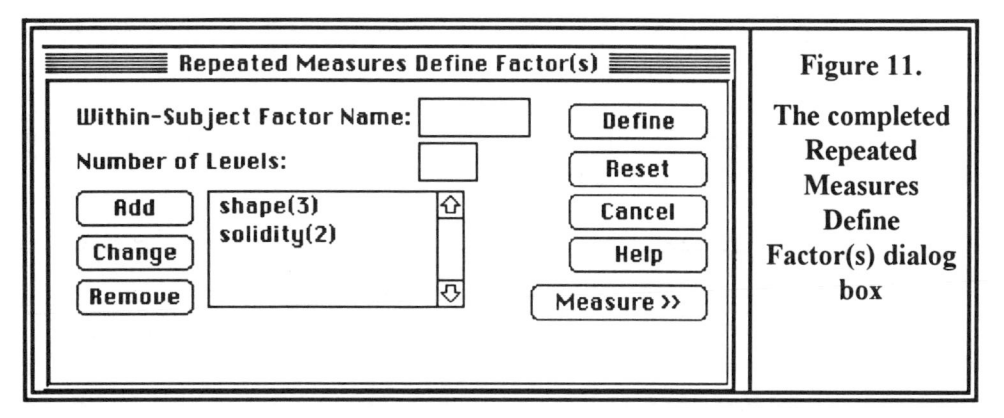

Figure 11. The completed Repeated Measures Define Factor(s) dialog box

- After the **Define** button has been clicked on, the **Repeated Measures ANOVA** dialog box appears (see Figure 12).

Figure 12. The Repeated Measures ANOVA dialog box

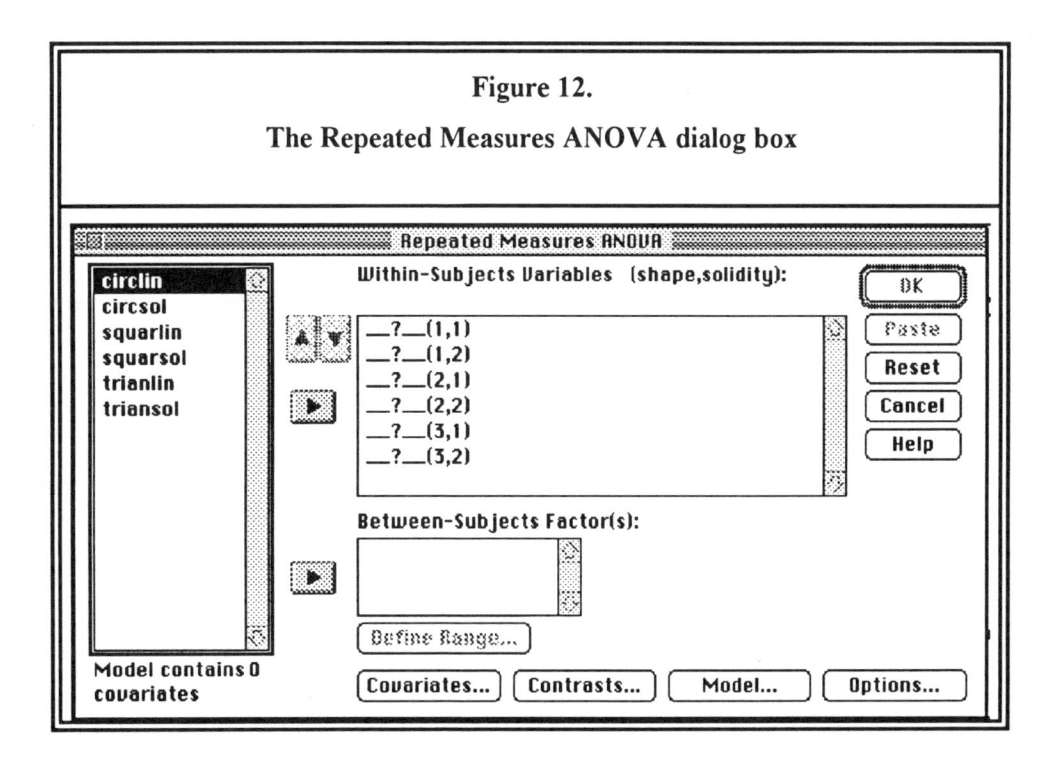

Chapter 9 - Within Subjects Experiments

On the left, the six variables are listed in alphabetical order. On the right, in the box labelled **Within-Subjects Variables [shape,solidity]**, appears a list of the various combinations of the code numbers representing the levels of each of the two treatment factors. It will be noticed that, as one reads down the list, the first number in each pair changes more slowly than the second.

When there is more than one within subjects factor, it is inadvisable to transfer the variable names in a block from the left-hand box to the **Within-Subjects Variables** box by a click-and-drag operation, as was done in the case of one within subjects factor. Care must be taken to ensure that the correct variable name is transferred to the correct slot. It is recommended that the variables are transferred one at a time, noting the numbers in the square brackets and referring to the names of the defined within subjects factors inside the square brackets in the caption at the head of the box (in Figure 12, the caption is **Within-Subjects Variables [shape, solidity]**).

Remember that unless the default setting has been changed in **Preferences** (within the **Edit** drop-down menu), the variables listed in the left-hand box will be in alphabetical order, which may not be the order of the variables in the **Data Editor**. Fort this reason, transfer the variables one at a time to the right hand box to make sure that the labelling is correct. A table such as Table 7 clarifies the numbering of the levels of within subjects variables. Thus the variable *circsol* is [shape 1, solidity 1] i.e. [1,1], *circlinl* is [1,2] and so on.

	Table 7. Numbering of levels in within subjects variables						
Shape Factor	\multicolumn{2}{c}{Shape 1 (Circle)}		\multicolumn{2}{c}{Shape 2 (Square)}		\multicolumn{2}{c}{Shape 3 (Triangle)}	
Solidity Factor	Solidity 1 (Solid)	Solidity 2 (Outline)	Solidity 1 (Solid)	Solidity 2 (Outline)	Solidity 1 (Solid)	Solidity 2 (Outline)
Variable name	*circsol*	*circlin*	*squarsol*	*squarlin*	*triansol*	*trianlin*

- The upper section of the completed **Repeated Measures ANOVA** dialog box is shown in Figure 13.
- Suppress the multivariate listing by clicking on **Model** (Figure 12) and removing the × beside **Multivariate tests** (Figure 9).

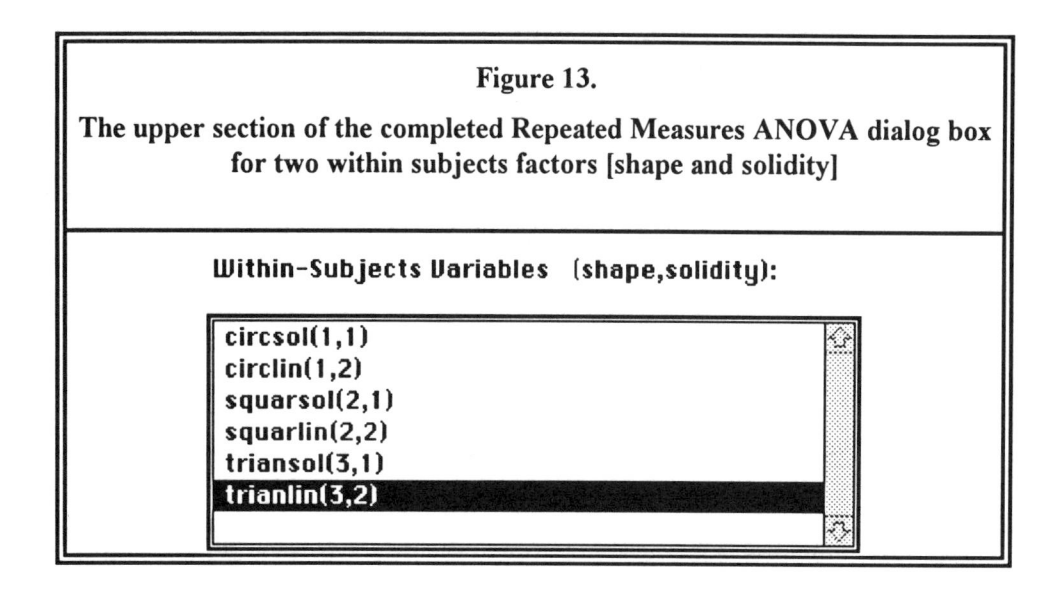

> **Figure 13.**
>
> **The upper section of the completed Repeated Measures ANOVA dialog box for two within subjects factors [shape and solidity]**
>
> **Within-Subjects Variables (shape, solidity):**
>
> ```
> circsol(1,1)
> circlin(1,2)
> squarsol(2,1)
> squarlin(2,2)
> triansol(3,1)
> trianlin(3,2)
> ```

9.6.4 Output listing for a two-factor within subjects ANOVA

The section subtitled **Tests of Between-Subjects Effects** (not reproduced here) can be ignored: here we are interested only in within subjects effects.

Tests for main effects

Output Listing 6 contains the **Mauchly sphericity test**, which is used to check the homogeneity of covariance assumption for the SHAPE within subject effect.

> **Output Listing 6.**
>
> **Some statistics of the SHAPE factor**
>
> ```
> * * * * * * A n a l y s i s   o f   V a r i a n c e -- design  1 * * * * * *
>
> Tests involving 'SHAPE' Within-Subject Effect.
>
> Mauchly sphericity test, W =      .66634
> Chi-square approx. =              3.24763 with 2 D. F.
> Significance =                    .197
>
> Greenhouse-Geisser Epsilon =      .74982
> Huynh-Feldt Epsilon =             .86638
> Lower-bound Epsilon =             .50000
>
> AVERAGED Tests of Significance that follow multivariate tests are equivalent to
> univariate or split-plot or mixed-model approach to repeated measures.
> Epsilons may be used to adjust d.f. for the AVERAGED results.
> ```

Output Listing 7.

The ANOVA summary table for SHAPE

```
Tests involving 'SHAPE' Within-Subject Effect.

AVERAGED Tests of Significance for MEAS.1 using UNIQUE sums of squares
Source of Variation        SS       DF       MS        F      Sig of F

WITHIN+RESIDUAL         138.97      18      7.72
SHAPE                    46.03       2     23.02      2.98      .076
```

In this case it is not significant, because the p-value (0.197) is greater than 0.05. Accordingly, the **Averaged Tests of Significance** (the univariate ANOVA shown in Output Listing 7) for SHAPE can be accepted. We can write this result as: $F(2,18) = 2.98$; NS.

Output Listing 8 examines the within subject factor SOLIDITY. With only two levels in this factor, the multivariate and univariate approaches are identical, and no sphericity test is necessary. This factor is significant beyond the 1 per cent level, since the **Significance of F** is listed as 0.000 (meaning that the p-value is less than .0005). We can write this result as: $F(1,9) = 54.56$; $p < 0.01$.

Output Listing 8.

The ANOVA summary table for SOLIDITY

```
Tests involving 'SOLIDITY' Within-Subject Effect.

Tests of Significance for T4 using UNIQUE sums of squares
Source of Variation        SS       DF       MS        F      Sig of F

WITHIN+RESIDUAL          19.40       9      2.16
SOLIDITY                117.60       1    117.60     54.56      .000
```

Test for an interaction

The next sections of the listing examine the interaction of the two within subject factors (SHAPE BY SOLIDITY). Since the **Mauchly sphericity test** is not significant (Significance = 0.663), the univariate test can be used as in Output Listing 9. The ANOVA summary table, however, shows that this interaction is not significant (**Significance of F** = 0.270). We can write this result as: $F(2,18) = 1.41$; NS.

In conclusion, the listing shows that only *solidity* is significant: the other systematic sources, namely, *shape* and its interaction with *solidity*, are not significant.

Chapter 9 - Within Subjects Experiments

> **Output Listing 9.**
> **The ANOVA summary table for the interaction**
>
> ```
> Tests involving 'SHAPE BY SOLIDITY' Within-Subject Effect.
>
> AVERAGED Tests of Significance for MEAS.1 using UNIQUE sums of squares
> Source of Variation        SS      DF      MS         F    Sig of F
>
> WITHIN+RESIDUAL         151.30     18     8.41
> SHAPE BY SOLIDITY        23.70      2    11.85      1.41     .270
> ```

Had the interaction proved significant, the next step would then have been to draw a graph of the cell means to display the heterogeneity of profiles, as described in Chapter 8. Because of the manner in which repeated measures data are entered into the Data Editor, however, the procedure for doing this is somewhat different from that described for between subjects data (Section 8.2.4). An example is given in Exercise 15.

9.6.5 Unplanned comparisons following a factorial within subjects experiment

In the example we have just considered, the question of unplanned multiple comparisons does not arise, because

(1) there is no interaction and

(2) the sole significant main effect involves a factor with only two levels, implying that the two means must be significantly different.

Had there been a significant interaction, however, the approach already described in the context of the one-factor within subjects experiment would also have been applicable here.

The problem with the **Bonferroni test** is that even with only six cells, it is very difficult to get a difference sufficiently large to be significant. With six cells, $c = 15$ and each t-test has to have a p-value of 0.003 or less to be deemed significant. There is, therefore, a case to be made for testing initially for **simple main effects** of the principal experimental factor of interest at various levels of the other factor.

A significant simple main effect may justify defining the comparison family more narrowly and improves the chances of finding significant differences. As in a between subjects factorial experiment, a simple main effect of a factor can be computed by carrying out a one-way ANOVA upon the data at only one level of the other factor. In the case of a within subjects factorial experiment, however, the data at different levels of either factor are not independent. It is wise, therefore, to adopt a stricter criterion for significance of a simple main effect in such cases, by applying the Bonferroni criterion and setting the significance level for each simple effect test at 0.05 divided by the number of tests that will be made.

EXERCISE 14

ONE-FACTOR WITHIN SUBJECTS (REPEATED MEASURES) ANOVA

BEFORE YOU START

Before proceeding with this exercise, we suggest you study Chapter 9.

ONE-FACTOR WITHIN SUBJECTS ANOVA

A comparison of the efficacy of statistical packages

Imagine an experiment which measures the time taken for ten subjects to perform an analysis using three statistical computer packages Pack1, Pack2 and Pack3. During the course of the experiment, each subject uses every package and the order of use is systematically varied across subjects. The results are shown in Table 1.

	Table 1. Times taken by participants to carry out an analysis with different computing packages
Subject	Pack1	Pack2	Pack3	Subject	Pack1	Pack2	Pack3
s1	12	15	18	s6	10	12	14
s2	18	21	19	s7	18	17	21
s3	15	16	15	s8	18	17	21
s4	21	26	32	s9	23	27	30
s5	19	23	22	s10	17	25	21

Preparing the SPSS data set

Prepare the SPSS data set as described in Section 9.4.2. Since there is just one group of subjects, there is no grouping variable.

Exploring the data

Use the methods described in Section 9.4.3 to check for any distribution problems.

Procedure for the within subjects (repeated measures) ANOVA

Follow the procedure described in Section 9.4.4.

Output listing for the within subjects (repeated measures) ANOVA

Section 9.4.5 offers some guidelines for the interpretation of the output listing. The most important item is the univariate ANOVA summary table for the Package factor.

- **What is the value of the F ratio and its associated p-value (tail probability) for** *package*? **Is** *F* **significant? What are the implications for the experimental hypothesis?**

At this point, however, we must issue a word of warning. In Chapter 9, attention was drawn to the fact that the model for repeated measures ANOVA makes an important assumption, over and above the usual requirements of homogeneity of variance and normality of distribution. This is the assumption of **homogeneity of covariance**. Often (indeed, usually) the data sets yielded by psychological repeated measures experiments show marked heterogeneity of covariance. If there is heterogeneity of covariance, the true p-value may be somewhat higher than that given in the ANOVA summary table. If, therefore, the p-value is very small, say, less than 0.01, it is safe enough to say that we have evidence against the null hypothesis. If, however, the p-value is just under 0.05, we need to look at the result more carefully, and consider the possibility of a **conservative F test** (see Howell, 1997; Chapter 14).

EXERCISE 15

TWO-FACTOR WITHIN SUBJECTS ANOVA

BEFORE YOU START

We suggest that you read Section 9.6 before proceeding. In this exercise, we consider the ANOVA of within subjects factorial experiments, that is, factorial experiments with crossed treatment factors and repeated measures on all factors.

THE TWO-FACTOR WITHIN SUBJECTS ANOVA

A two-factor within subjects experiment

An experiment is carried out to investigate the effects of two factors (independent variables) upon the recognition of symbols briefly presented on a screen, as measured by the number of correct identifications over a fixed number of trials. The factors are Symbol (with levels Digit, Lower Case, Upper Case) and Font (with levels Gothic, Roman). Each of the six subjects in the experiment is tested under all six combinations of the two treatment factors. The results are shown in Table 1.

Preparing the SPSS data set

Enter the data into the **Data Editor** window in the manner described in Section 9.6.2.

Exploring the data

Use the methods described in Section 9.4.3 to check for any distribution problems.

	Digit		Lower Case		Upper case	
	Gothic	Roman	Gothic	Roman	Gothic	Roman
s1	2	6	18	3	20	5
s2	4	9	20	6	18	2
s3	3	10	15	2	21	3
s4	1	12	10	9	30	10
s5	5	8	13	8	20	8
s6	6	10	14	10	16	6

Table 1. Results of a two-factor within subjects experiment

Running the two-factor within subjects ANOVA

To run the ANOVA, follow the procedure described in Section 9.6.3.

Output listing for the two-factor within subjects experiment

The output listing for the two-factor repeated measures ANOVA is explained in Section 9.6.4.

- **Examine the present listing and interpret the implications of the results of the tests for main effects and the interaction in terms of the aims of the study.**

Because of the way in which data from repeated measures experiments are entered into the Data Editor, the obtaining of graphs displaying interactions is just a little less straightforward than it is with data from a two-factor between subjects experiment. Proceed as follows:

Copy the data in the Data Editor to a file with a new name.

Construct a single column of data by successively copying and pasting the data from the second column onwards on to the end of the data in the first column.

Construct two coding variables to specify the conditions under which each of the scores in the first column was obtained. The first coding variable could be *style* (1 = Digit, 2 = Upper, 3 = Upper) and the second could be *font* (1 = Gothic, 2 = Roman).

Proceed exactly as described in Chapter 8, Section 8.2.4 to obtain a graph of the cell means.

CHAPTER 10

EXPERIMENTS OF MIXED DESIGN

10.1 INTRODUCTION

10.2 THE TWO-FACTOR MIXED FACTORIAL ANOVA

10.3 THE THREE-FACTOR MIXED ANOVA

10.4 FURTHER ANALYSIS: SIMPLE EFFECTS AND MULTIPLE COMPARISONS

Chapter 10 - Experiments of Mixed Design

10.1 INTRODUCTION

Mixed (or split-plot) factorial experiments

It is very common for factorial designs to have within subjects (repeated measures) factors on *some* (but not *all*) of their treatment factors. Since such experiments have a mixture of between subjects and within subjects factors, they are often said to be of **mixed** design. The term **split-plot** is also used, reflecting the agronomic context in which this type of experiment was first employed.

In psychological and educational research, the researcher often selects two samples of subjects (e.g. male and female groups) and performs the same repeated measures experiment upon each group. Suppose, for example, that samples of male and female subjects are tested for recall of a written passage with three different line spacings, the order of presentation of the three levels of the spacing factor being counterbalanced across subjects to neutralise order effects. In this experiment, there are two factors:

(1) Gender (Male, Female);

(2) Spacing (Narrow, Medium, Wide).

The levels of Gender vary **between** subjects; whereas those of Spacing vary **within** subjects. The experiment has thus one between subjects and one within subjects factor.

A notational scheme for mixed factorial experiments

In the foregoing experiment on the effects of Gender and Spacing upon Recall of written passages, the Gender factor was between subjects and the Spacing factor was within subjects. We shall adopt the convention whereby within subjects factors are bracketed, so that if A is Gender and B is Spacing, the reading experiment is of the type **A×(B)**, signifying a mixed design with repeated measures on factor B.

With three treatment factors, two mixed designs are possible: there may be one or two repeated measures factors, the former design being denoted by **A×B×(C)**, the latter by **A×(B×C)**.

Mixed factorial ANOVA with SPSS

The SPSS **Repeated Measures** program from the **ANOVA Models** menu is used for the analysis of data from experiments that have within subjects treatment factors. The procedure for defining the within subjects factors was explained in Chapter 9. In experiments of mixed design, however, there are also between subjects factors, with factor levels identified by means of a numerical code in the data file, as in between subjects experiments.

Chapter 10 - Experiments of Mixed Design

10.2 THE TWO-FACTOR MIXED FACTORIAL ANOVA

10.2.1 Results of a mixed A×(B) experiment

A researcher designs an experiment to explore the hypothesis that engineering students, because of their training in two-dimensional representation of three-dimensional structures, have a more strongly developed sense of shape and symmetry than do psychology students.

Three theoretically important types of shapes are presented to samples of Psychology and Engineering students under sub-optimal conditions on a monitor screen. All three types of shape are presented to each subject: hence Shape is a within subjects factor. The category of Student (Psychology or Engineering), on the other hand, is a between subjects factor. The dependent variable is the Number of Shapes correctly identified.

The results of the experiment are shown in Table 1.

Table 1.

Results of a two-factor mixed factorial experiment of type A×(B)

Levels of the factor: Category of Student	Subject	Levels of the factor: Shape		
		Triangle	Square	Rectangle
Psychology	s1	2	12	7
	s2	8	10	9
	s3	4	15	3
	s4	6	9	7
	s5	9	13	8
	s6	7	14	8
Engineering	s7	13	3	35
	s8	21	4	30
	s9	26	10	35
	s10	22	8	30
	s11	20	9	28
	s12	19	8	27

Chapter 10 - Experiments of Mixed Design

10.2.2 Preparing the SPSS data set

In Table 1, we chose to represent the experimental design with the levels of the within subjects factor arrayed horizontally and those of the between subjects factor stacked vertically, with the level Engineering under Psychology. We did so because this arrangement corresponds to the arrangement of the results in the SPSS data set.

The first column of the **Data Editor** grid will contain a single grouping variable Category representing the Psychologists (*1*) and the Engineers (*2*). The second, third and fourth columns will contain the results at the three levels of the Shape factor (i.e. Triangle, Square, and Rectangle).

Using the techniques described in Section 3.3, define four variables: *category* (the grouping variable), *triangle*, *square*, and *rectangl* (remember the variable names must not exceed 8 characters in length). Using the **Define Labels** procedure (Section 3.5.3), assign to the values of the *category* variable the value labels *Psychology Student* and *Engineering Student*. When the data of Table 1 have been entered into the **Data Editor** grid, the first five cases appear as shown in Figure 1.

	category	triangle	square	rectangl
1	1	2	12	7
2	1	8	10	9
3	1	4	15	3
4	1	6	9	7
5	1	9	13	8

Figure 1. The first five cases of the SPSS data set from the results in Table 1

10.2.3 Exploring the results: Boxplots and tables of means and standard deviations

As always, the first step is to explore the data set. The boxplot was described in Section 4.3.2; here the clustered boxplot (for different levels of the between subjects variable) is appropriate.

It can be obtained by proceeding as follows:

- Click on
  Graphs
    Boxplot

    to open the **Boxplot** dialog box.

Chapter 10 - Experiments of Mixed Design

- Select the **Clustered** option and (within the **Data in Chart Are** section) the **Summaries of separate variables** radio button. Press **OK** to enter the **Define Clustered Boxplot: Summaries of Separate Variables** dialog box.

- Transfer the variable names *triangle square rectangl* to the **Boxes Represent:** box and the variable name *category* to the **Category Axis** box.

- Click on **OK**.

The resulting boxplot will have the three boxes for Engineering on the left and the three boxes for Psychology on the right.

A table of cell means and standard deviations, together with the marginal means for the three different shapes, is desirable. Inspection of this table will indicate whether there has been a main effect of the within subjects factor *shape* or a *shape by category* interaction. The table can be obtained directly by using the **Means** procedure (see below).

We shall also want the marginal means for the between subjects factor to ascertain whether it had a main effect, too. These too can be obtained by running **Means**; but first it is necessary to use **Compute** to calculate the mean score achieved by each subject over the three different shapes.

Obtaining the cell means and the marginal means for the within subjects factor

- Choose
  Statistics
    Compare Means
      Means

  to open the **Means** dialog box. Detailed instructions are given in Section 4.3.2.

- Transfer the names of the three *shape* variables into the **Dependent List** box. Transfer *category* into the **Independent List** box.

- Click on **OK** to obtain a table showing the cell means and the marginal means for the *shape* factor. This table, however, does not include the marginal means for the between subjects factor, *category*. The next section describes a way of computing these remaining means.

Obtaining the marginal means for the between subjects factor

In order to use **Means** to calculate the marginal means for *category*, one must first define a new variable (e.g. *meancat*), which is the mean score that a subject achieves over the three different shapes.

- Choose
  Transform
    Compute

  to open the **Compute Variable** dialog box. Detailed instructions are given in Section 4.4.2.

- Type *meancat* into the **Target Variable** box. In the **Functions** box, scroll down to, and highlight, the function MEAN[numexpr, numexpr ....] and click on ▲ to transfer the function to the **Numeric Expression** box, where question marks will replace **numexpr**, inviting specific variable names. Delete the question marks and then successively highlight and transfer the variable names *triangle*, *square*, and *rectangl*, taking care to ensure that there is a comma between each name. The final entry is now **MEAN[triangle, square, rectangl]**.

- Click on **OK** to run the procedure.

Note that in order to display the values of the *meancat* variable in the **Data Editor** window to, say, two places of decimals, it may be necessary to override the general format instruction specified in **Edit/Preferences**, which may have specified that all variables will be displayed as integers. Within the **Define Variable** dialog box (accessed by double-clicking on the heading *meancat* column), click on **Type** and make the necessary adjustment to the value in the **Decimal Places** box. Now it is possible to compute the marginal means and standard deviations for *category* by returning to **Means** and transferring *meancat* to the **Dependent List** box, and *category* to the **Independent List** box. Click on **OK**.

The complete table of marginal and cell means and standard deviations

Table 2 combines the information from the computations described in the previous subsections.

Table 2.

Means of performance by two categories of students with three different shapes (standard deviations are given in brackets)

Levels of the factor: Category	Levels of the factor: Shape			*Means*
	Triangle	Square	Rectangle	
Psychology	6.00	12.17	7.00	8.39
	(2.61)	(2.32)	(2.10)	
Engineering	20.20	7.00	30.83	19.33
	(4.26)	(2.83)	(3.83)	
Means	13.08	9.58	18.92	13.86

The values of the marginal means in Table 2 strongly suggest main effects of both the Shape and Category factors. Moreover, the markedly superior performance of the engineers on triangles and rectangles is reversed with squares, suggesting the presence of an interaction.

10.2.4 Procedure for a mixed A×(B) ANOVA

- Select the **Repeated Measures** item from the **ANOVA Models** menu by choosing
  Statistics
     ANOVA Models
        Repeated Measures

  to open the **Repeated Measures Define Factor(s)** dialog box (the completed version is shown in Figure 2).

- In the **Within-Subject Factor Name** box, delete *factor1* and type a generic name (such as *shape*) for the repeated factor. This name must not be that of any of the three levels making up the factor and must also conform to the rules governing the assignment of variable names. In the **Number of Levels** box, type the number of levels (*3*) making up the repeated measures factor. Clicking on **Add** will result in the appearance of the entry *shape(3)* in the lowest box (Figure 2).

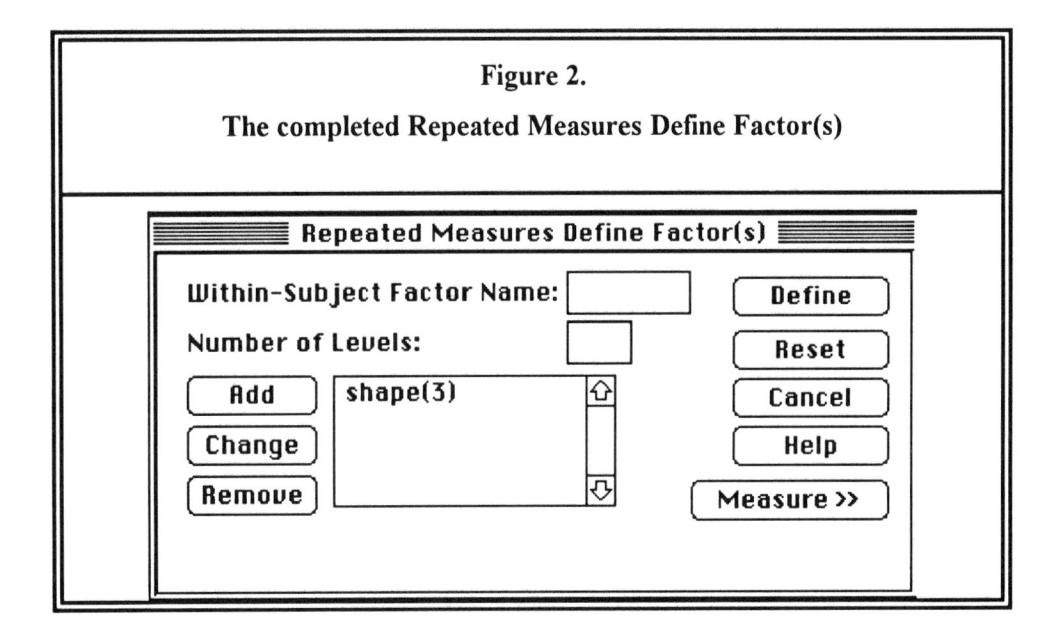

Figure 2.

The completed Repeated Measures Define Factor(s)

```
╔════════ Repeated Measures Define Factor(s) ════════╗
  Within-Subject Factor Name: [        ]    ( Define )
  Number of Levels:           [        ]    ( Reset  )
  ( Add    )  shape(3)                      ( Cancel )
  ( Change )                                ( Help   )
  ( Remove )                                ( Measure >> )
```

- Click on **Define** to open the **Repeated Measures ANOVA** dialog box (part of which is shown in Figure 3).

Chapter 10 - Experiments of Mixed Design

Figure 3.

Part of the Repeated Measures ANOVA dialog box before entering the names of the levels

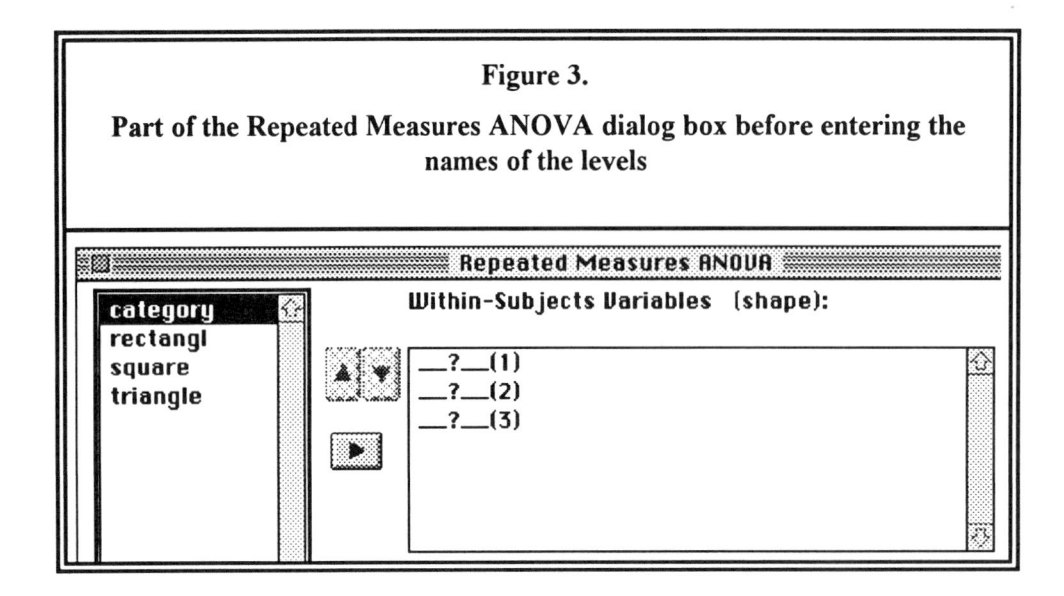

```
┌─────────────────── Repeated Measures ANOVA ───────────────────┐
│                         Within-Subjects Variables  (shape):    │
│  category                                                      │
│  rectangl       ▲▼    ─?─(1)                                   │
│  square               ─?─(2)                                   │
│  triangle             ─?─(3)                                   │
│                 ▶                                              │
└────────────────────────────────────────────────────────────────┘
```

- Click-and-drag the arrowhead down the variable names *rectangl, square, triangle* to highlight them, and click on ▶ to transfer them into the **Within-Subjects Variable(s) [shape]** box (Figure 4). So far, the procedure has been as described in Chapter 9.

Figure 4.

The completed Repeated Measures ANOVA dialog box with one within subjects variable (shape) and one between subjects variable (category)

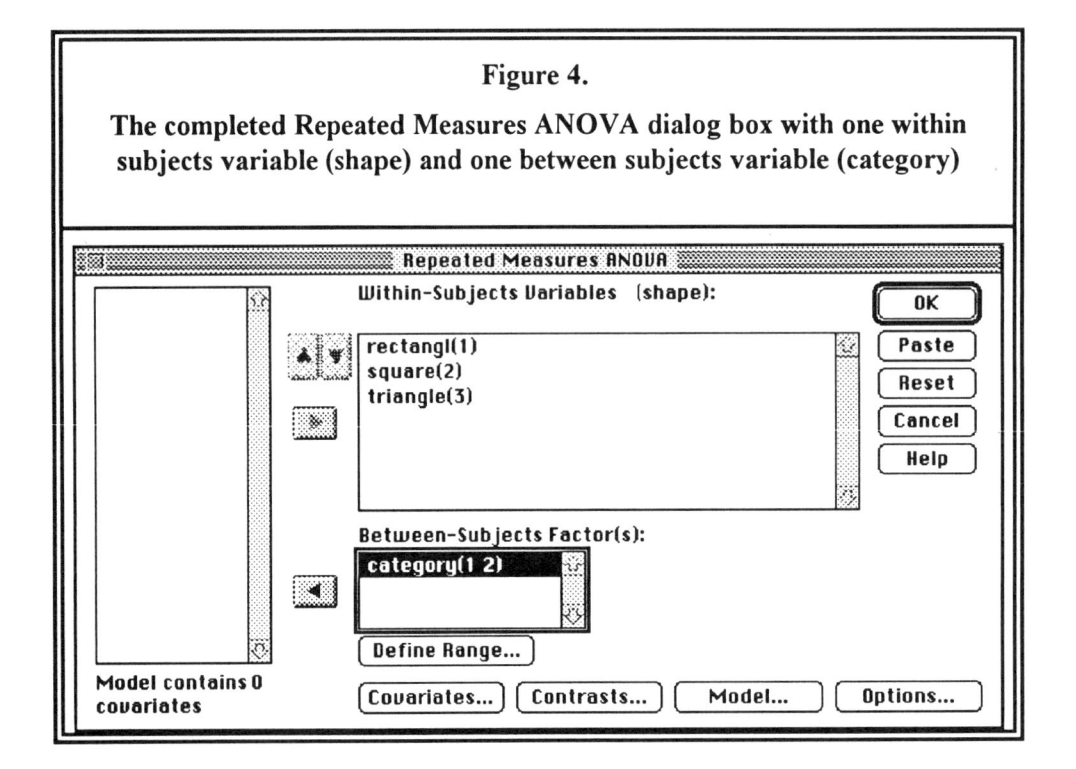

```
┌─────────────────── Repeated Measures ANOVA ───────────────────┐
│                   Within-Subjects Variables  (shape):   ┌──OK──┐│
│                   ▲▼   rectangl(1)                       │Paste ││
│                        square(2)                         │Reset ││
│                        triangle(3)                       │Cancel││
│                   ▶                                       │ Help ││
│                                                                │
│                   Between-Subjects Factor(s):                  │
│                   ◀    category(1 2)                           │
│                                                                │
│                        Define Range...                         │
│  Model contains 0                                              │
│  covariates       Covariates... Contrasts... Model... Options...│
└────────────────────────────────────────────────────────────────┘
```

- The new element is the presence of the between subjects factor *category*. Click on that variable name and transfer it to the **Between-Subjects Factor(s)** box by clicking on ▶ to the left of that box. On transferral, click on **Define Range** and type the value *1* into the **Minimum** box and *2* into the **Maximum** box.

- Click on **Continue** to return to the **Repeated Measures ANOVA** dialog box which now appears as shown in Figure 4.

- Finally, before running the ANOVA, we suggest that **Multivariate tests** should be turned off. Click on **Model** to open the **Within-Subjects Tests** dialog box, within which are the check boxes of the **Within-Subjects Tests** menu. Cancel the × beside **Multivariate tests** to disable that function (Figure 5).

┌Within-Subjects Tests─────────┐ □ Multivariate tests ☒ Averaged F □ Epsilon corrected averaged F	**Figure 5.** The Within-Subjects Tests check boxes

- Click on **Continue** to return to the **Repeated Measures ANOVA** dialog box, and then on **OK** to run the ANOVA.

10.2.5 Output listing for the two-factor mixed ANOVA

Between subjects effects

The tests for between subjects effects are shown in Output Listing 1.

Note that the factor *category* is significant beyond the 1 per cent level: the **Sig of F** (0.000) is less than 0.0005. This result would be reported as: $F(1,10) = 98.95$; $p < 0.01$. There is thus a significant difference in performance between the two groups of students.

Output Listing 1.

Tests for Between Subjects Effects

```
Tests of Between-Subjects Effects.

Tests of Significance for T1 using UNIQUE sums of squares
Source of Variation        SS       DF       MS          F  Sig of F

WITHIN+RESIDUAL         108.94      10    10.89
CATEGORY               1078.03       1  1078.03      98.95     .000
```

Tests for within subjects and interaction effects

Output Listing 2 shows the **Mauchly sphericity test** test for homogeneity of covariance in the within subjects *shape* factor. Since the statistic is not significant

(**Significance** is greater than 0.05), it can be assumed that the covariance matrix is homogeneous. Had the Mauchly test shown significance, it would have been necessary to make a conservative Greenhouse-Geisser test with fewer degrees of freedom by clicking on the **Epsilon corrected averaged F** test in the **Within-Subjects Tests** box (Figure 5).

Output Listing 2.

Statistics of the Within Subjects shape factor

```
Tests involving 'SHAPE' Within-Subject Effect.

Mauchly sphericity test, W =        .90277
Chi-square approx. =                .92059 with 2 D. F.
Significance =                      .631

Greenhouse-Geisser Epsilon =        .91139
Huynh-Feldt Epsilon =              1.00000
Lower-bound Epsilon =               .50000

AVERAGED Tests of Significance that follow multivariate tests are equivalent to
univariate or split-plot or mixed-model approach to repeated measures.
Epsilons may be used to adjust d.f. for the AVERAGED results.
```

Output Listing 3 shows the ANOVA summary table for the within subjects factor *shape* and the *category by shape* interaction.

Output Listing 3.

ANOVA summary table for shape main effect and for category by shape interaction

```
Tests involving 'SHAPE' Within-Subject Effect.

AVERAGED Tests of Significance for MEAS.1 using UNIQUE sums of squares
Source of Variation          SS       DF       MS         F     Sig of F

WITHIN+RESIDUAL           163.56      20      8.18
SHAPE                    533.56       2    266.78      32.62      .000
CATEGORY BY SHAPE       1308.22       2    654.11      79.99      .000
```

The ANOVA strongly confirms the patterns that were discernible in Table 2: the Shape and Category factors both have significant main effects and the interaction between the factors is also significant. For Shape, $F(2, 20) = 32.62$; $p < 0.01$ and for Category × Shape, $F(2, 20) = 79.99$; $p < 0.01$.

Unplanned comparisons following a significant interaction

The procedures described in the previous chapter can readily be applied to the analysis of data from experiments with a mixture of between and within subjects factors. In mixed experiments, it is the within subjects factors that are generally of principal interest. Following a significant interaction, therefore, one could proceed to test for **simple main effects of the within subjects factor** at the various levels of the between subjects factor. Following a significant simple main effect in the data from one group of subjects, **Bonferroni t-tests** could then be applied to make pairwise comparisons among the different levels of the within subjects factor.

Simple effects of between factors can readily be tested by performing **one-way ANOVAs** on the data at selected levels of within-subjects factors. (Since each test for a main effect uses a fresh set of data, there may be no need to use the Bonferroni method to make the tests specially conservative. Should a simple effect prove significant, the **Tukey HSD test** can be used to make unplanned pairwise multiple comparisons among a set of means comprising only those relevant to the main effect concerned.

10.3 THE THREE-FACTOR MIXED ANOVA

The procedures described in Section 10.2 can readily be extended to the analysis of data from mixed factorial experiments with three treatment factors. In Section 10.1.2, we introduced a notation for specifying a particular mixed design, whereby a within subjects factor is written in brackets, so that the designation **A×(B)** denotes a mixed, two-factor factorial experiment, where factor A is between subjects and factor B is within subjects. Here we consider the two possible mixed three-factor factorial designs:

(1) the **A×(B×C)** experiment, with two within subjects factors;

(2) the **A×B×(C)** experiment, with one within subjects factor.

10.3.1 The mixed A×(B×C) experiment

Suppose that to the A×(B) experiment described in Section 10.2.2 we were to add an additional within subjects factor C, such as the Solidity of the shape with two levels, either Solid or Outline. Thus the subjects (either Psychology or Engineering students) have to try to recognise either Solid or Outline Triangles, Squares, or Rectangles. We now have an A×(B×C) experiment, with 3×2 = 6 within subjects variables in the **Data Editor** window, each variable containing the data for a combination of Shape and Solidity. It is convenient (though not essential) to prepare these columns in the **Data Editor** window systematically by taking the first level of one variable and combining it in turn with each of the levels of the second variable, followed by the second level of the first variable

Chapter 10 - Experiments of Mixed Design

combined with each level of the second variable, and so on. Thus for this experiment the **Data Editor** window might appear as in Figure 6.

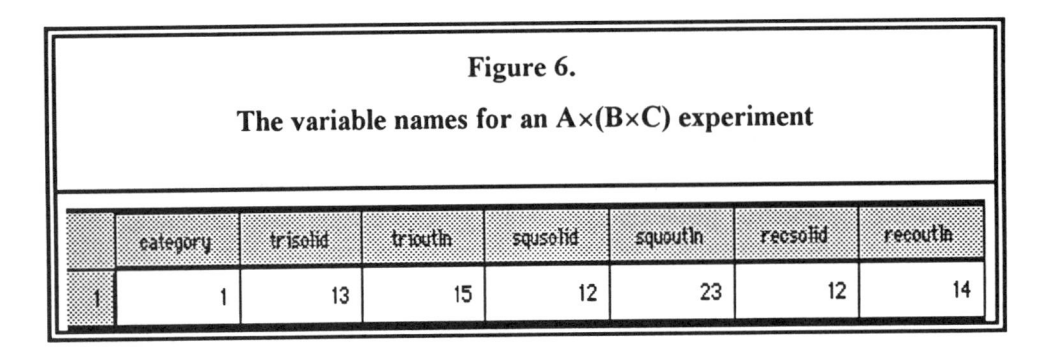

Figure 6.

The variable names for an A×(B×C) experiment

category	trisolid	trioutln	squsolid	squoutln	recsolid	recoutln
1	13	15	12	23	12	14

Care must be taken in transferring variable names within the **Repeated Measures ANOVA** dialog box. Remember that the order of variables listed in the left-hand box is alphabetic unless the default setting of **Alphabetical** has been changed to **File** in the **Display Order for Variable Lists** within the **Preferences** dialog box (see Section 3.4.2), in which case they will appear in the order of the columns in the Data Editor. It may, therefore, be necessary to transfer the variable names one at a time to the **Within-Subjects Variables** box to ensure that the correct names are fitted into the various slots. (The order of the defined factors is shown in square brackets above the box.) The completed dialog box is shown in Figure 7.

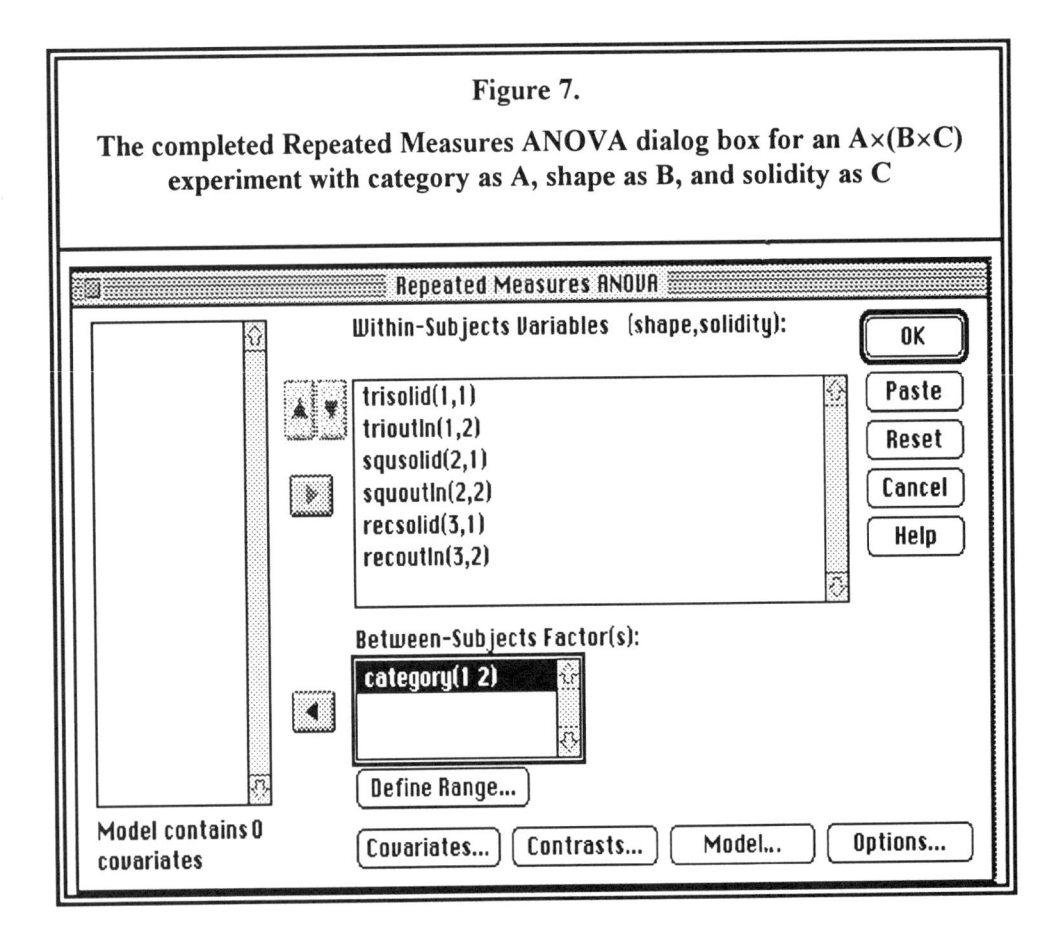

Figure 7.

The completed Repeated Measures ANOVA dialog box for an A×(B×C) experiment with category as A, shape as B, and solidity as C

Repeated Measures ANOVA

Within-Subjects Variables (shape,solidity):

trisolid(1,1)
trioutln(1,2)
squsolid(2,1)
squoutln(2,2)
recsolid(3,1)
recoutln(3,2)

Between-Subjects Factor(s):

category(1 2)

Define Range...

Model contains 0 covariates

[OK] [Paste] [Reset] [Cancel] [Help]

[Covariates...] [Contrasts...] [Model...] [Options...]

246

10.3.2 The mixed A×B×(C) experiment

This experimental design has two between subjects factors (A and B) and one within subjects factor (C). Suppose the A×(B) experiment described in Section 10.2.2 were to have an additional between subjects factor added, such as the Sex of the subjects. This variable has two levels Male and Female. Thus the subjects (either Psychology or Engineering students, and either Male or Female) have to try to recognise shapes (either Triangles, Squares, or Rectangles). The experiment is now of the A×B×(C) type.

There will now be two coding variables *category* and *sex*, and the three levels of the within subjects variable *rectangl*, *square*, and *triangle*. Thus for this experiment the **Data Editor** window might appear as in Figure 8.

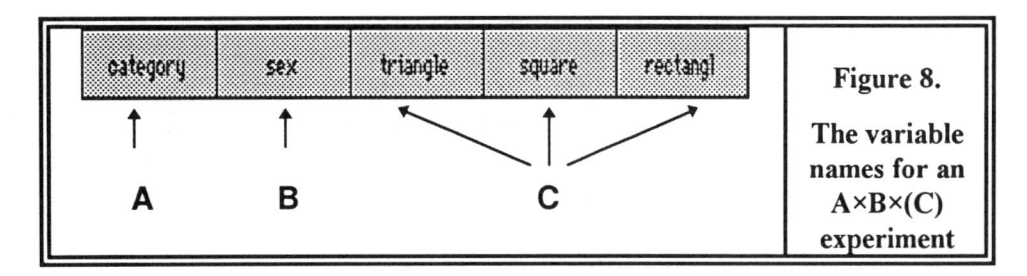

Figure 8. The variable names for an A×B×(C) experiment

The completed **Repeated Measures ANOVA** dialog box would then be as shown in Figure 9.

Figure 9.

The completed Repeated Measures ANOVA dialog box for an A×B×(C) experiment with category as A, sex as B, and shape as C

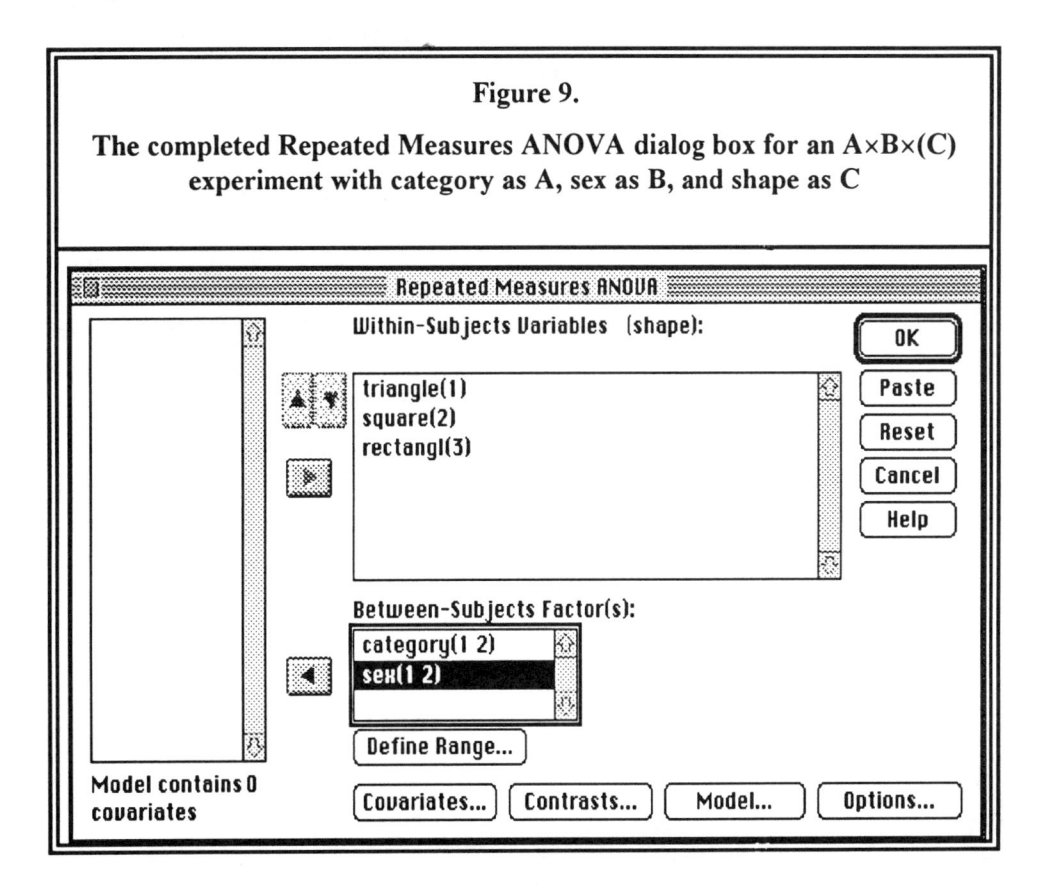

10.4 FURTHER ANALYSIS: SIMPLE EFFECTS AND MULTIPLE COMPARISONS

The analysis of variance is a large topic in statistics, and there are available many more techniques than we can mention in this book, which is primarily concerned with computing, rather than statistics as such. For example, following the confirmation that an interaction is significant, it is often useful to follow up the initial ANOVA with additional tests of the effects of one factor at specific levels of another. Such analyses of **simple effects** can be combined with both planned and unplanned multiple comparisons. We urge the reader who is unfamiliar with such methods to read the relevant chapters in a lucid textbook such as Howell (1997).

At this point, it may be worth reminding the reader that the dangers of committing a type I error in unplanned multiple comparisons increase enormously with the complexity of the experiment. Accordingly, the user must take precautions to attempt to control the *per family* type I error rate. The use of simple effects tests may give one justification for specifying a smaller subgroup of treatment means and so increasing the power of each test.

In an experiment of design A×(B×C), for example, the obtaining of a significant ABC interaction would lead one to suspect that the B×C interactions may not be homogeneous across the different levels of factor A (the between subjects factor).

By analogy with simple main effects, a **simple two-way interaction** is one considered only *at a particular level* of a third factor: thus there are simple BC interactions at $A_1, A_2, ..., A_a$, simple AB interactions at $C_1, C_2, ..., C_c$, and so on. A **three-factor interaction** is said to occur when the simple two-factor interactions are not homogeneous across all levels of a third factor.

One can test for the presence of simple BC interactions at particular levels of factor A by running two-factor (BC) within subjects ANOVAs on the data from those groups only. Then, having established that there is a simple interaction, one could proceed to use the methods of Chapter 9 to make pairwise multiple comparisons among the means for the combinations of factors B and C at the particular level of factor A concerned. As before, tests of simple effects (in this case, actually **simple simple main effects**) could be made in order to justify working with a particular subgroup of means.

We should warn the reader, however, that with complex factorial experiments, there is a heightened risk that some interaction or other will be found significant by chance alone. Should a particular interaction be thought crucial, it would be highly advisable to design another experiment to focus upon performance under those particular conditions, to see whether the pattern really is robust. Otherwise, the user is in great danger of capitalizing upon chance.

Chapter 10 - Experiments of Mixed Design

EXERCISE 16

MIXED ANOVA (BETWEEN AND WITHIN SUBJECTS FACTORS)

BEFORE YOU BEGIN

Readers should study Chapter 10 carefully before proceeding with this exercise.

THE TWO-FACTOR MIXED ANOVA

Effects of ambient hue and sound on vigilance

Table 1.
The results of a two-factor mixed design experiment

Colour	Subject	Signal Horn	Whistle	Bell
Red	s1	25	18	22
Red	s2	22	16	21
Red	s3	26	19	26
Red	s4	23	21	20
Red	s5	19	18	19
Red	s6	27	23	27
Blue	s7	19	12	23
Blue	s8	21	15	19
Blue	s9	23	14	24
Blue	s10	20	16	21
Blue	s11	17	16	20
Blue	s12	21	17	19

In an experiment investigating the effect of the colour of the ambient light upon performance of a vigilance task, subjects were asked to press a button when they thought they could discern a signal against a background of random noise.

The experimenter expected that the ambient colour would have varying effects upon the detection of different kinds of sound. Three types of signal were used: a horn, a whistle and a bell. Each signal was presented 30 times in the course of a one-hour monitoring session, during which the subject sat in a cubicle lit by either red or blue light. The dependent variable was the number of correct presses of the button. For theoretical purposes, it was necessary to use different subjects for the different colour

Chapter 10 - Experiments of Mixed Design

conditions; on the other hand, it was considered that there would be advantages in testing each individual with all three kinds of signal. In this experiment, therefore, the factor of Colour was between subjects; whereas the other factor, Signal, was within subjects.
The results are shown in Table 1.

Preparing the SPSS data set

Recast the data of Table 1 into a form suitable for entry into the **Data Editor**. You will need to define a grouping variable *colour* and three variables for the scores: *horn*, *whistle*, and *bell*. The last three variables will be the three levels of the within-subjects factor *signal*, which is not defined until the ANOVA procedure is actually being run. Follow the procedure described in Section 10.2.2.

Exploring the data set

Since there is a grouping variable, use the **Means** procedure as described in Section 10.2.3 to obtain means and standard deviations.

Obtain a graph of the cell means, to see whether there is likely to be an interaction. Copy the data in the Data Editor into a new file. Using the copy-and-paste procedure, transfer all the scores in the experiment into the first column of the Data Editor. Name the second column *colour*, and enter *1* or *2* for Red and Blue, respectively. Name the third column *signal*, enter 1, 2 or 3 for Horn, Whistle and Bell, respectively. Proceed as described in Chapter 8, Section 8.2.4 to construct the interaction graph.

- **Are there signs of main effects or an interaction?**

Procedure for the two-factor mixed ANOVA

Run the procedure as described in Section 10.2.4.

Output listing for the two-factor mixed ANOVA

The main features of the output are explained in Section 10.2.5.

- **Write down the values of *F* and their associated p-values. Relate these findings to the experimental hypothesis**

Chapter 10 - Experiments of Mixed Design

EXERCISE 17

MIXED ANOVA: THREE-FACTOR EXPERIMENT

BEFORE YOU START

Before proceeding with this exercise, you should study Section 10.3. From the procedural point of view, the analysis of mixed experiments with three factors is a fairly simple extension of the procedure for two-factor mixed experiments. In general, however, the interpretation of data from factorial experiments becomes increasingly problematic as more factors are added. In particular, where there is a complex design with repeated measures on some factors but not on others, the naming of the factors must be carried out with special care.

A MIXED FACTORIAL A x (B x C) EXPERIMENT

Imagine an experiment investigating the recognition of shapes under sub-optimal conditions on a monitor screen. There are three shapes (shape1, shape2, shape3), each of which can be either Open (outline) or Filled. Each subject in the experiment is tested under all six combinations of these two treatment factors, which can be labelled Shape and Shade. The between subjects factor group is the type of observer used: one group consists of Psychology students, the other of Engineering students. The dependent variable is the number of correct identifications over a fixed series of trials. The results are shown in Table 1.

Table 1.
Three-factor mixed factorial experiment with two within subjects treatment factors

	Shape:	Shape 1		Shape 2		Shape 3	
	Shade:	Open	Filled	Open	Filled	Open	Filled
Group	Subject						
Psychology	s1	2	12	3	1	4	5
	s2	13	22	5	9	6	8
	s3	14	20	8	7	5	7
Engineering	s4	12	1	3	9	6	10
	s5	11	2	8	10	5	9
	s6	12	7	2	4	4	10

Preparing the SPSS data set

Recast the results in Table 1 as described in Section 10.3.1. The data will comprise seven variables: a grouping variable and a variable for each combination of the two treatment factors. Define the variables appropriately, remembering to label the values of the grouping variable. Enter and save the data.

Chapter 10 - Experiments of Mixed Design

Exploring the data

Use the **Means** procedure to obtain tables of cell and marginal means. In a three-factor experiment, there is the possibility of a three-way interaction among all three factors. A three-way interaction is said to occur when the interaction between two factors is heterogeneous across the levels of a third factor. This definition might suggest that the presence of a three-way interaction might be rather easy to discern in a three-way table of cell means by simply comparing graphs of two-way interactions at the different levels of a third factor. In fact, the interpretation of graphs drawn from the cell means of three-way tables requires considerable practice. This is because, just as two-way tables of means (and their graphs) reflect the presence of main effects as well as the interaction, three-way tables (and their graphs) reflect the presence of two-way interactions as well as any three-way interaction that might be present. To the untrained eye, two-way graphs may look heterogeneous; but this may arise entirely from the presence of two-way interactions.

Using the procedure described in Exercise 16, graph the two-way interactions between Shape and Shade for the psychologists and the engineers separately.

- **Do the patterns of lines seem similar? If not, a three-way interaction may be present.**

Running the ANOVA procedure

The procedure is merely outlined in Section 10.3.1, but is a straightforward extension of the routine for the two-factor mixed experiment.

Output listing for the A x (B x C) mixed factorial experiment

Look for the table of 'Tests of Between-Subjects Effects' for the factor *group*. For the various 'Tests involving ..... Within-Subject Effect', **Mauchly** tests will appear for factors with more than two levels (i.e. the Shape factor and for the Shape x Shade interaction); check that the p-values are greater than 0.05.

- **Write down the F ratios (and p-values) for the three factors, their two-way interactions and the three-way interaction. Do the values of F confirm the patterns among the treatment means you saw earlier in your graphs?**

As always where there are repeated measures factors, special care is needed when interpreting an F ratio that is significant with a p-value just below 0.05.

CHAPTER 11

MEASURING STATISTICAL ASSOCIATION

11.1 INTRODUCTION

11.2 CORRELATIONAL ANALYSIS WITH SPSS

11.3 OTHER MEASURES OF ASSOCIATION

Chapter 11 - Measuring Statistical Association

11.1 INTRODUCTION

Statistical association in interval data

So far, this book has been concerned with statistical methods devised for the purpose of comparing averages between or among samples of data that might be expected to differ in general level: for example, right-handed people might be compared with left-handed people; the trained might be compared with the untrained; males might be compared with females.

Consider, however, a set of paired data of the sort that might be produced if one were to weigh each of a sample of one hundred men before and after they had taken a fitness course. Previously, our concern would have been with the **comparison** of the men's average weight before the course with their average weight afterwards. One would expect these data to show another feature, however: the person who was heaviest before the course is likely to be among the heaviest in the group afterwards; the lightest person before the course should be among the lightest afterwards; and one with an intermediate score before the course is likely to be in the middle of the group afterwards. In other words, there should be a statistical **association** or **correlation** between people's weights before and after the course.

Depicting an association: Scatterplot

The existence of a statistical association between two variables is most apparent in the appearance of a diagram called a **scatterplot** (see Section 4.3.3) which, in the foregoing example, would be constructed by representing each person as a point in space, using as co-ordinates that person's weights before and after taking the course. The cloud of points would take the shape of an ellipse (see bottom right scatterplot in Figure 1 on the next page), whose longer axis slopes upwards from left to right across the page. An elliptical scatterplot indicates the existence of **a linear relationship** between two variables. If the slope of the major axis is positive, the variables are said to be **positively correlated**; if it is negative, they are **negatively correlated**. The thinner the ellipse, the stronger the degree of linear relationship; the fatter the ellipse, the weaker the relationship. A circular scatterplot indicates the absence of any relationship between the two variables.

Linear association

The term **linear** means 'of the nature of a straight line'. In our current example, a straight line (known as a **regression line**) can be drawn through the points in the elliptical scatterplot so that it is as close to as many of the points as possible (though there may be one or two atypical scores, or **outliers** as they are termed). We can use the regression line to make quite a good **estimate** of a particular man's weight after the course from a knowledge of his weight before the course: if we have Weight Before on the horizontal axis and Weight After on the vertical axis, we need only move up to the point on the regression line vertically above his first weight, and then move across to the vertical scale to estimate his second weight. If we do that, we shall probably be in error, the difference between his true weight after the course and his estimated weight from the regression line being known as a **residual**. The value of the residual, however, is likely to be small in comparison with the man's true weight after the course.

Measuring the strength of a linear association: Pearson correlation

A **correlation coefficient** is a statistic devised for the purpose of measuring the strength, or degree, of a supposed linear association between two variables, each of which has been measured on a scale with units. The most familiar correlation coefficient is the **Pearson correlation (r)**. The Pearson correlation is so defined that it can take values only within the range from −1 to +1, inclusive. The larger the absolute value (i.e. ignoring the sign), the narrower the ellipse, and the closer to the regression line the points in the scatterplot will fall. A perfect correlation arises when the values of one variable are exactly predictable from those of the other and the Pearson correlation takes a value of ± 1, in which case all the points in the scatterplot lie on the regression line. In other cases, the narrower the elliptical cloud of points, the stronger the association, and the greater the absolute value of the Pearson correlation. When there is no association whatever between two variables, their scatterplot should be a roughly circular cloud, in which case the Pearson correlation will be about zero (top right in Figure 1).

Figure 1.

The scatterplots of sets of data showing varying degrees of linear association

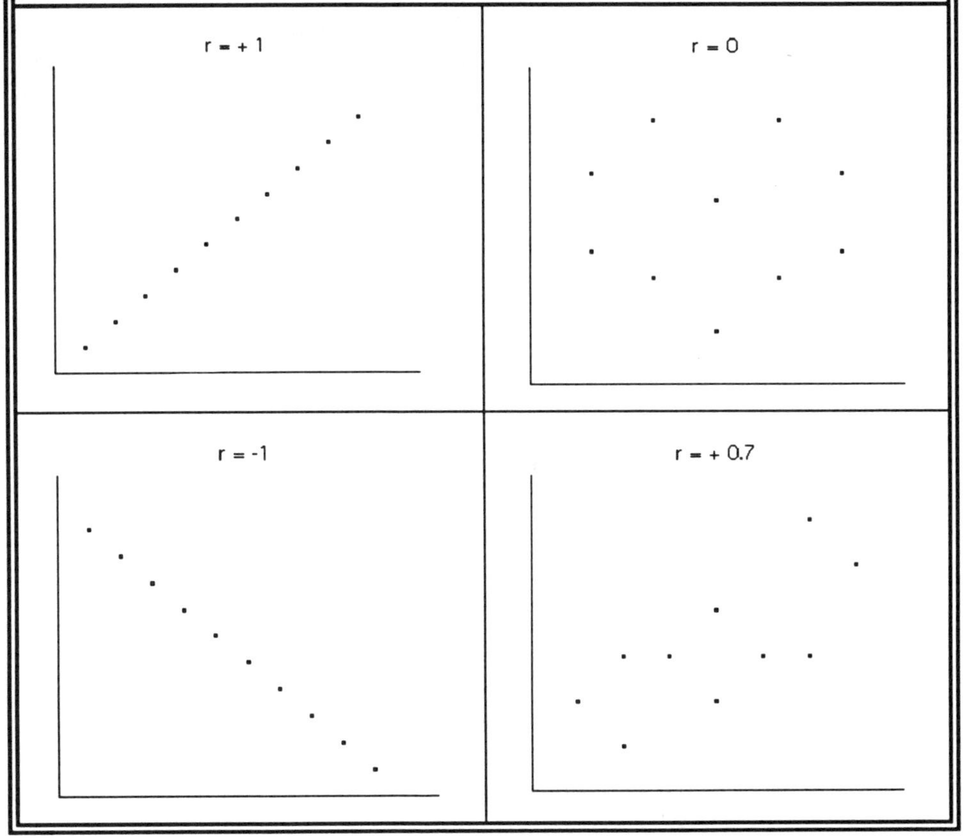

Chapter 11 - Measuring Statistical Association

A word of warning

It is quite possible, from inspection of a scatterplot, to do two things:

(1) see whether there is indeed a linear relationship between the variables, in which case the Pearson correlation would be a meaningful statistic to use;

(2) guess fairly accurately what the value of the Pearson correlation would be if calculated.

In other words, from inspection of their scatterplot alone, one can discern all the essential features of the true relationship (if any) between two variables. So if we reason from the scatterplot to the statistics, we shall not go seriously wrong.

The converse, however, is not true: **given only the value of a Pearson correlation, one can say nothing whatsoever about the relationship between two variables**. In a famous paper, the statistician Anscombe (1973) presents data which illustrate how misleading the value of the Pearson correlation can be. Basically, he shows that, wherever the scatterplot is neither elliptical nor circular (i.e. the variables are neither in a linear relationship nor independent), the value of the Pearson correlation is misleading. (Exercise 18 uses Anscombe's data to show this.) For example, data giving a zero Pearson correlation may show a very strong **non-linear** association in their scatterplot. Two variables may be unrelated (and most of the data may show a circular scatterplot), but the presence of one or two outliers can exert considerable **leverage** and yield a high Pearson correlation, suggesting a strong linear relationship.

The moral of this cautionary tale is clear: when studying the association between two variables, always construct a scatterplot, and interpret (or disregard) the Pearson correlation accordingly. In the same paper, Anscombe gives a useful rule for deciding whether there really is a robust linear relationship between two variables: should the shape of the scatterplot be unaltered by the removal of a few observations at random, there is probably a real relationship between the two variables.

To sum up, the **Pearson correlation** is a measure of a **supposed** linear relationship between two variables; and the supposition of linearity must be confirmed by inspection of the scatterplot.

11.2 CORRELATIONAL ANALYSIS WITH SPSS

The principal of a tennis coaching school thinks that tennis proficiency depends upon the possession of a degree of general hand-eye co-ordination. To confirm this hunch, she measures the hand-eye co-ordination (Initial Co-ordination) of some pupils who are beginning the course and their proficiency in tennis at the end of the course (Final Proficiency). The data are shown in Table 1.

Chapter 11 - Measuring Statistical Association

<table>
<tr><td colspan="6" align="center">Table 1.
A set of paired data</td></tr>
<tr><th>Pupil</th><th>Initial Co-ordination</th><th>Final Proficiency</th><th>Pupil</th><th>Initial Co-ordination</th><th>Final Proficiency</th></tr>
<tr><td>s1</td><td>4</td><td>4</td><td>s6</td><td>4</td><td>2</td></tr>
<tr><td>s2</td><td>4</td><td>5</td><td>s7</td><td>7</td><td>5</td></tr>
<tr><td>s3</td><td>5</td><td>6</td><td>s8</td><td>8</td><td>6</td></tr>
<tr><td>s4</td><td>2</td><td>2</td><td>s9</td><td>9</td><td>9</td></tr>
<tr><td>s5</td><td>10</td><td>6</td><td>s10</td><td>5</td><td>3</td></tr>
</table>

Preparing the SPSS data set

Using the techniques described in Section 3.3.4, define the variables *coordin* and *proficy* (fuller names, such as *Initial Co-ordination* and *Final Tennis Proficiency*, can be assigned by using the **Define Labels** procedure).

Obtaining a scatterplot

- Choose
  Graphs
    Scatter

  When the **Scatterplot** selection box (Figure 2) appears, click on **Define** (with a **Simple** scatterplot selected by default).

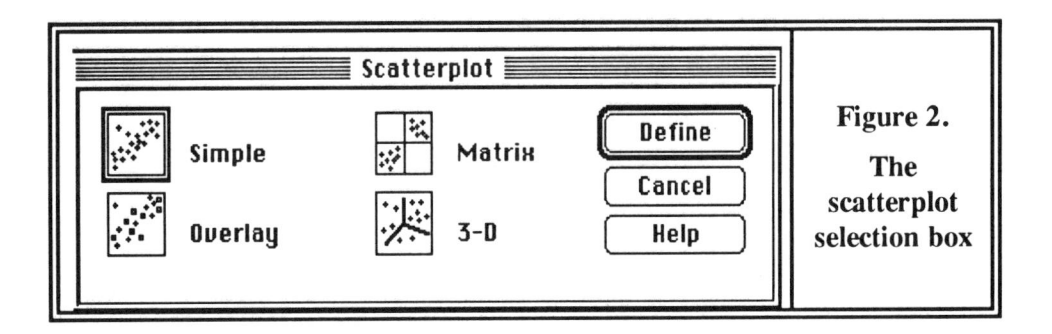

Figure 2. The scatterplot selection box

- Enter the variable names *proficy* and *coordin* into the **y-axis** and the **x-axis** box, respectively.
- Click on **OK**.

The scatterplot is shown in Figure 3. The plot shows a consistent trend, with no outliers.

It is possible to categorise points on a scatterplot by the levels of a grouping variable (e.g. sex) by inserting the grouping variable name in the **Set Markers by:** box. The points for males and females will be plotted in different colours.

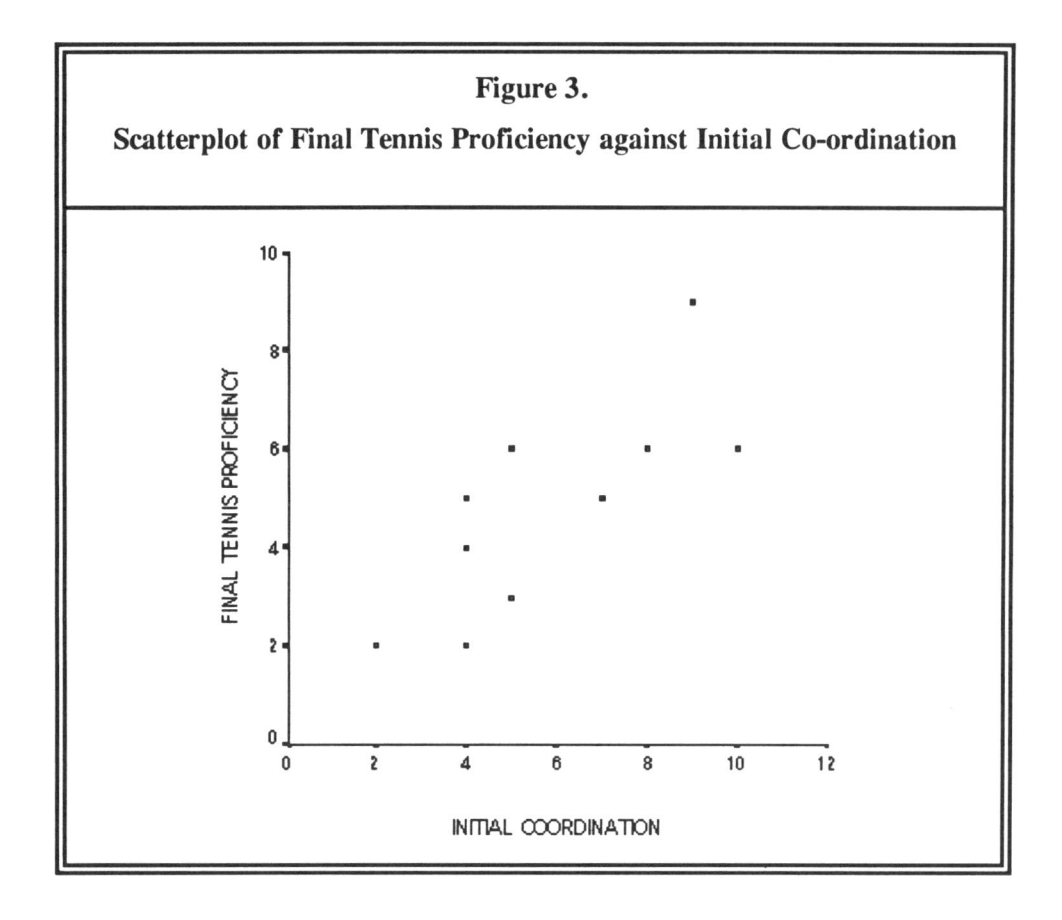

Figure 3.
Scatterplot of Final Tennis Proficiency against Initial Co-ordination

11.2.1 Procedure for the Pearson correlation

- Choose (Figure 4)
  Statistics
     Correlate
        Bivariate

  to open the **Bivariate Correlations** dialog box (the completed version is shown in Figure 5).

- Highlight both variables and click on ▶ to transfer the names to the **Variables** box. Click on **Options** and then click on the **Means and Standard Deviations** check box.

- Click on **Continue** and then on **OK** to run the correlation coefficient and the optional additional statistics.

Figure 4.
The Correlate menu

Figure 5.
The completed Bivariate Correlations dialog box

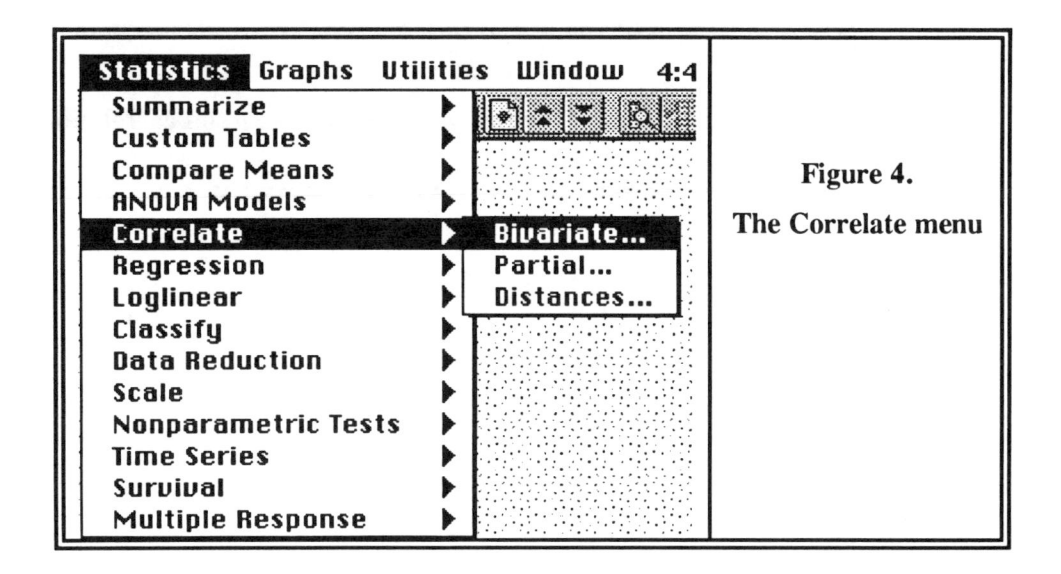

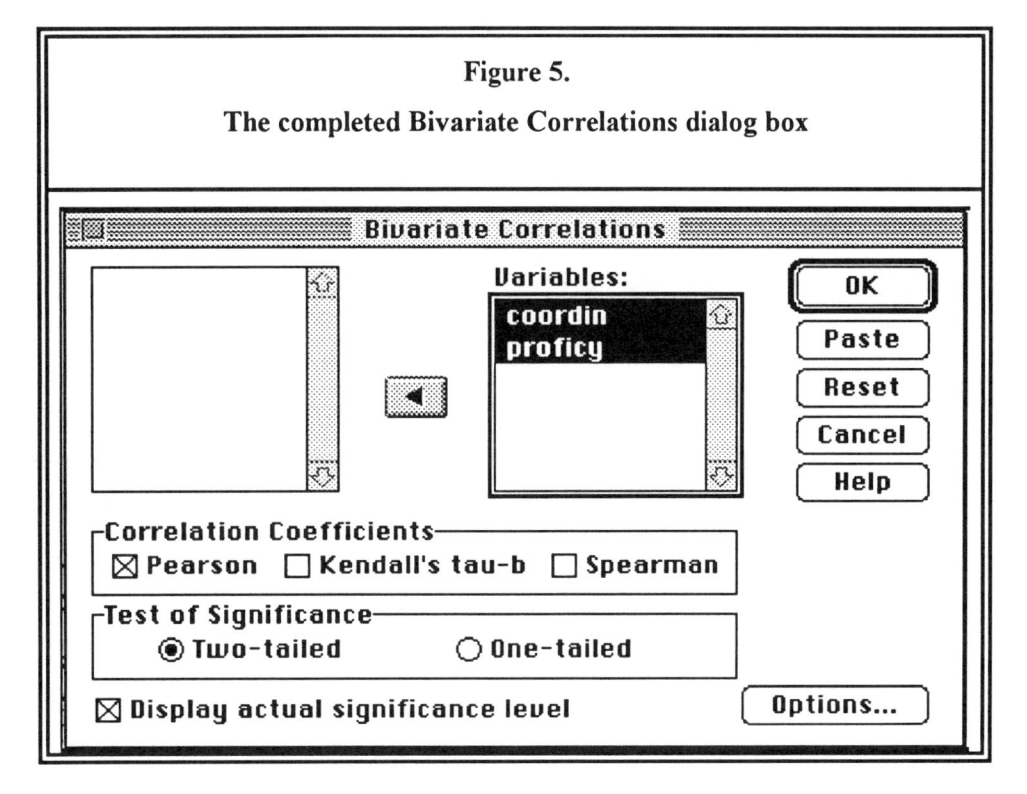

11.2.2 Output listing for the Pearson correlation

Output Listing 1 begins with a tabulation of the means and standard deviations of the two variables, as requested with **Options**. Then the correlation coefficient, together with its exact p-value, is listed. With a value for r of 0.7752 and a two-tailed p-value of 0.008, it can be concluded that the correlation coefficient is significant beyond the 1 per cent level. This is written as: $r = 0.77$; $n = 10$; $p < 0.01$.

Output Listing 1.
Statistics of the two variables and Pearson correlation

```
   Variable     Cases        Mean         Std Dev

   COORDIN       10         5.8000        2.5734
   PROFICY       10         4.8000        2.1499

                        - - Correlation Coefficients - -

                COORDIN     PROFICY

   COORDIN      1.0000       .7752
               (    10)    (    10)
               P= .         P= .008

   PROFICY       .7752      1.0000
               (    10)    (    10)
               P= .008      P= .
   (Coefficient / (Cases) / 2-tailed Significance)

   " . " is printed if a coefficient cannot be computed
```

If the **Display actual significance level** check box at the bottom left of the **Bivariate Correlations** dialog box is turned off (see Figure 5), the correlation is displayed as in Output Listing 2.

	- - Correlation Coefficients - -		**Output Listing 2.**
	COORDIN PROFICY		**Brief display of the significance of r**
COORDIN	1.0000 .7752**		
PROFICY	.7752** 1.0000		
* - Signif. LE .05	** - Signif. LE .01	(2-tailed)	

Obtaining a correlation matrix

When there are more than two variables, SPSS can be commanded to construct a **correlation matrix**, a rectangular array whose entries are the correlations between each variable and every other variable. This is done by entering as many variable names as required into the **Variables** box within the **Bivariate Correlations** dialog box (Figure 5).

11.2.3 Point-biserial correlation

When one of the variables is a dichotomy such as male/female or pass/fail, and the other is measured on a continuous scale and assumed to be distributed normally in the population, then the Pearson correlation can still be used though in this situation it is usually referred to as **point-biserial correlation** (r_{pb}). Thus in our example, a Pearson correlation (alias point-biserial) could have been calculated for Final Tennis Proficiency and Gender (assuming the genders of the players were known).

11.3 OTHER MEASURES OF ASSOCIATION

The Pearson correlation is suitable only for interval data. With categorial or ordinal data, other measures must be used. (**Ordinal** data are either ranks or records of **ordered** category membership; **categorial** data are records of **qualitative** category membership.)

11.3.1 Measures of association strength for ordinal data

The term ordinal data embraces all data relating to quantitative variables that are not measures on an independent scale with units. For example, if we rank a group of 10 people with respect to height, giving 10 to the tallest and 1 to the shortest, the resulting set of ranks is an ordinal data set, because an individual rank does not signify so many inches, centimetres (or some other unit of height): a rank merely expresses an individual's height in relation to the heights of the other people in that particular group.

If two judges are asked to rank, say, ten paintings in order of preference, they may well disagree in their orderings, especially if each judge is required to assign a different rank to each object and avoid 'ties'. (This stricture, however, is not always enforced and one or two ties may be tolerated.) The result of such an exercise would be a set of paired ordinal data.

In a rather different procedural paradigm, however, ties, rather than being, at best, tolerable may actually be built into the judgmental process. Judges may be asked to assign objects to a pre-specified set of ordered categories. If, as is usual, there are more objects than categories, tied observations are inevitable. Rating scales yield data in the form of assignments to ordered categories.

Chapter 11 - Measuring Statistical Association

The term **ordinal data** includes both ranks and assignments to ordered categories. When, as in the case of the two judges, ordinal data are paired, the question arises as to the extent to which the two sets of ranks of category assignments agree. This is a question about the strength of association between two variables which, although quantitative, are measured at the ordinal, rather than the interval level.

The Spearman rank correlation (r_S or ρ)

Suppose that the ranks assigned to the ten paintings by the two judges are as in Table 2.

It is obvious from Table 2 that the judges generally agree closely in their rankings: at most, the ranks they assign to a painting differ by a single rank. One way of measuring the level of agreement between the two judges is by calculating the Pearson correlation between the two sets of ranks. This correlation is known as the **Spearman rank correlation** r_S (or as **Spearman's rho** ρ). The Spearman rank correlation is usually presented in terms of a formula which, although it looks very different from that of the Pearson correlation, is actually equivalent, provided that no ties are allowed.

Table 2.
Ranks assigned by two judges to each of ten paintings

Painting	A	B	C	D	E	F	G	H	I	J
First Judge	1	2	3	4	5	6	7	8	9	10
Second Judge	1	3	2	4	6	5	8	7	10	9

The use of the Spearman rank correlation is not confined to ordinal data. Should a scatterplot show that the Pearson correlation is unsuitable as a measure of the strength of association between two quantitative variables which have been measured at the interval level, the scores on both variables can be converted to ranks and the Spearman rank correlation calculated instead.

With small samples, it is difficult to obtain an accurate p-value for a Spearman correlation, especially when there are tied ranks. When there are no tied ranks, one can obtain critical values for the Spearman rank correlation from tables in textbooks such as Neave & Worthington (1988). When ties are present, they must reduce one's confidence in the critical values given in the tables. The user can but hope that when there is only a tie or two here and there, the tables will still give serviceable p-values.

Kendall's tau (τ) statistics

Kendall's tau statistics represented by the Greek letter τ provide an alternative to the Spearman rank correlation as measures of agreement between rankings, or assignments to ordered categories. The basic idea is that one set of ranks can be converted into another by a succession of reversals of pairs of ranks in one set: the fewer the reversals needed (in relation to the total number of possible reversals), the larger the value of tau. The numerator of Kendall's tau is the difference between the number of pairs of objects whose ranks are concordant (i.e. they go in the same direction) and the number of discordant pairs. If the former predominate, the sign of tau is positive; if the latter predominate, tau is negative.

There are three different versions of Kendall's tau: **tau-a**, **tau-b** and **tau-c**. All three measures have the same numerator, the difference between the numbers of concordant and discordant pairs. It is in their denominators that they differ, the difference lying in the way they handle tied observations. The denominator of tau-a is simply the total number of pairs. The problem with tau-a is that when there are ties, its range quickly becomes restricted, to the point where it becomes difficult to interpret. The correlation tau-b has terms in the denominator that consider, in either variable, pairs that are tied on one variable but not on the other. (When there are no ties, the values of tau-a and tau-b are identical.) The correlation tau-c was designed for situations where one wishes to measure agreement between assignments to unequal-sized sets of ordered categories. Provided the data meet certain requirements, the appropriate tau correlation can vary throughout the complete range from -1 to $+1$.

Kendall's tau correlations have advantages over the Spearman correlation, especially with small data sets, in which there are tied assignments, where serviceable p-values can still be obtained.

Procedures for obtaining the Spearman and Kendall rank correlations

In the **Data Editor** window, define two variables, *judge1* and *judge2*. From Table 2, enter the ranks assigned by the first judge into the *judge1* column and those assigned by the second judge into the *judge2* column.

- Choose
  Statistics
     Correlate
        Bivariate

  to obtain the **Bivariate Correlations** dialog box (Figure 5).

- By default, the **Pearson** check box will be marked. Mark also the **Kendall's tau-b** and the **Spearman** check boxes.

- Click on **OK** to obtain all three statistics, shown in Output Listing 3.

Note that the calculation of Kendall's statistics with **categorial** data, in the form of assignments of target objects to ordered categories, is best handled by the **Crosstabs** procedure (see next section); indeed, tau-c can only be obtained in **Crosstabs**.

Output Listing 3 show the Pearson correlation between the two sets of ranks as *0.9515*, and the Kendall correlation as *0.8222*. This value is different from that of the Pearson correlation, but there is nothing untoward in this: the two statistics are based on quite different theoretical foundations and often take noticeably different values. Finally the Spearman rank correlation is *0.9515*, which is exactly the value given for the Pearson correlation. These would be written thus: $r_S = 0.9515$; $n = 10$; $p < 0.01$; $\tau = 0.8222$; $n = 10$; $p < 0.01$.

> **Output Listing 3.**
> **Correlations between two sets of ranks**
>
> ```
> - - - K E N D A L L   C O R R E L A T I O N   C O E F F I C I E N T S - - -
> JUDGE2      .8222
>            N(   10)
>            Sig .001
>            JUDGE1
>
> (Coefficient / (Cases) / 2-tailed Significance)
> " . " is printed if a coefficient cannot be computed
>
> - - - S P E A R M A N   C O R R E L A T I O N   C O E F F I C I E N T S - - -
> JUDGE2      .9515
>            N(   10)
>            Sig .000
>            JUDGE1
> (Coefficient / (Cases) / 2-tailed Significance)
> " . " is printed if a coefficient cannot be computed
> ```

11.3.2 Measures of association strength for categorial data

When people's membership of two sets of mutually exclusive and exhaustive categories (such as sex or blood group) is recorded, it is possible to construct a **crosstabulation**, or **contingency table** (see Section 3.7.2). In the analysis of categorial data, the crosstabulation is the analogue of the scatterplot. Note that the categories of each variable must be mutually exclusive, that is no individual or case can fall into more than one combination of categories.

In SPSS, crosstabulations are handled by **Crosstabs**, which is found in the **Summarize** menu. Within the **Crosstabs** dialog box, there is a **Statistics** subdialog box (this chapter, Figure 11) containing check boxes for several measures of association. Many of these are based on the familiar **chi-square** statistic χ^2, which is used for determining the presence of an association between two qualitative variables. The rejection of H_0 by means of chi-square, however, only establishes the **existence** of a statistical association: it does not measure its **strength**. In fact, the chi-square statistic is unsuitable as a **measure** of association, because it is affected by the total frequency.

A word of warning about the misuse of chi-square should be given here. It is important to realise that the calculated statistic is only **approximately** distributed as the theoretical chi-square distribution: the greater the expected frequencies, the better the approximation, hence the rule about minimum expected frequencies, which is stated later in this Section. It is also important to note that the use of the chi-square statistic requires that **each individual studied contributes to the count in only one cell in the crosstabulation**. There are several other potential problems the user should be aware of. A lucid account of the rationale and assumptions of the chi-square test is given by Howell (1997), and a survey of the errors and misconceptions about chi-square that abound in the research literature is given by Delucchi (1983).

Several measures of strength of association for categorial data have been proposed (see Reynolds, 1984). An ideal measure should mimic the correlation coefficient by having a maximum absolute value of 1 for perfect association, and a value of 0 for no association. The choice of the appropriate statistic depends on whether the variables are ordinal or categorial, and whether the contingency (crosstabulation) table is 2×2 (each variable has two categories) or larger. Guidance can be found by clicking on the **Help** box and choosing the various statistics in turn to find the most appropriate one. One such statistic, for example, is the **phi coefficient** ϕ, obtained by dividing the value of chi-square by the total frequency and taking the square root. For two-way contingency tables involving variables with more than two categories, however, another statistic, known as **Cramér's V**, is preferred because with more complex tables, Cramér's measure can still, as in the 2×2 case, achieve its maximum value of unity. Other measures of association, such as **Goodman & Kruskal's lambda**, measure the proportional reduction in error achieved when membership of a category on one attribute is used to predict category membership on the other. If the categories in the cross-tabulation are **ordered**, we have ordinal, not categorial, data and Kendall's statistics **tau-b** and **tau-c** are appropriate.

A 2 × 2 contingency table

Suppose that 50 boys and 50 girls are individually asked to select toys from a cupboard. The available toys have previously been categorised as mechanical or non-mechanical. The hypothesis is that the boys should prefer mechanical toys, and the girls non-mechanical toys. There are two categorial variables here: Group (Boys or Girls); and Children's Choice (Mechanical or Non-Mechanical). The null hypothesis (H_0) is that there is no association between the variables. Table 3 shows the children's choices.

From inspection of this 2×2 contingency table, it would appear that there is an association between the Group and Choice variables: the majority of the Boys did, in fact, choose Mechanical toys; whereas the majority of the Girls chose Non-Mechanical toys.

Table 3. A contingency table			
	Children's Choice		
Group	Mechanical	Non-Mechanical	Total
Boys	30	20	50
Girls	15	35	50
Total	45	55	100

Chapter 11 - Measuring Statistical Association

Procedure for crosstabulation and associated statistics (chi-square, phi and Cramér's V)

The SPSS data set for a contingency table must include two coding variables to identify the various cell counts, one representing the rows (*group*), the other the columns (*choice*).

- Using the techniques described in Section 3.3.4, define the variables *group*, *choice*, and *count*.

- In the *group* variable, the code numbers *1* and *2* can represent Boys and Girls, respectively.

- In the *choice* variable, the values *1* and *2* can represent Mechanical and Non-Mechanical, respectively.

- Type the data into the three columns, as shown in Figure 6.

	group	choice	count
1	1	1	30
2	1	2	20
3	2	1	15
4	2	2	35

Figure 6.

Part of the Data Editor window showing the coding of the children's choices

The next step is essential. Since the data in the *count* column represent cell frequencies of a variable (not values), SPSS must be apprised of this by means of the **Weight Cases** item within the **Data** menu (Figure 7).

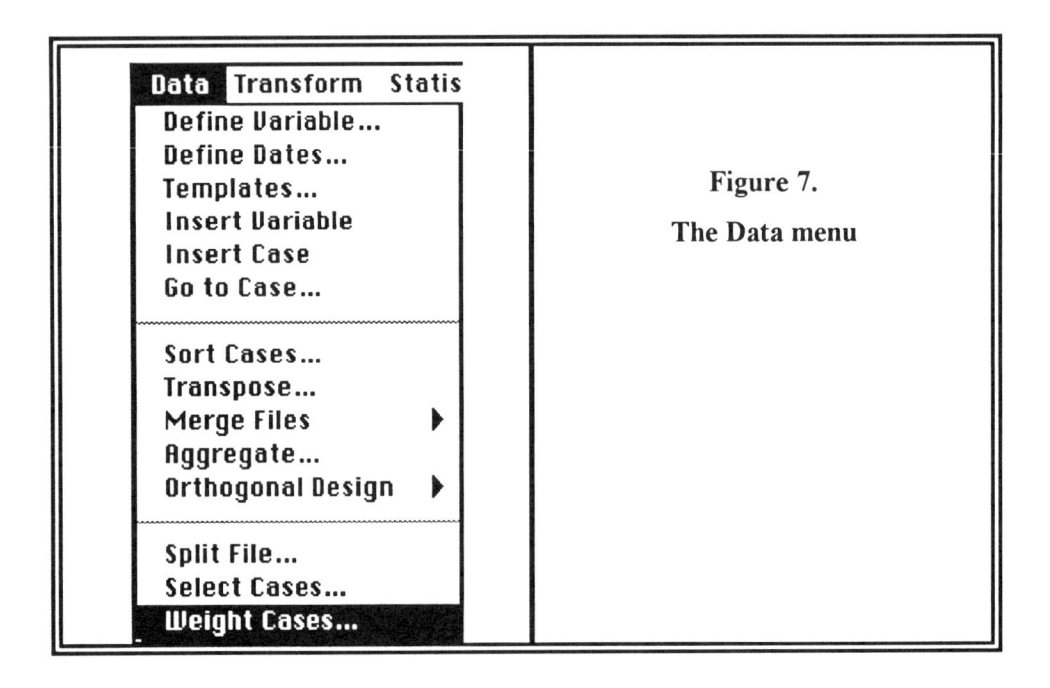

Figure 7.

The Data menu

266

Chapter 11 - Measuring Statistical Association

- Choose
  Data
  Weight Cases

  to open the **Weight Cases** dialog box (the completed one is shown in Figure 8).

- Click on the name of the variable that is to be weighted (*count*), then on the item **Weight cases by** (which cancels the default item **Do not weight cases**), and finally on ▶ to enter *count* into the **Frequency Variable** box.

- Click on **OK**.

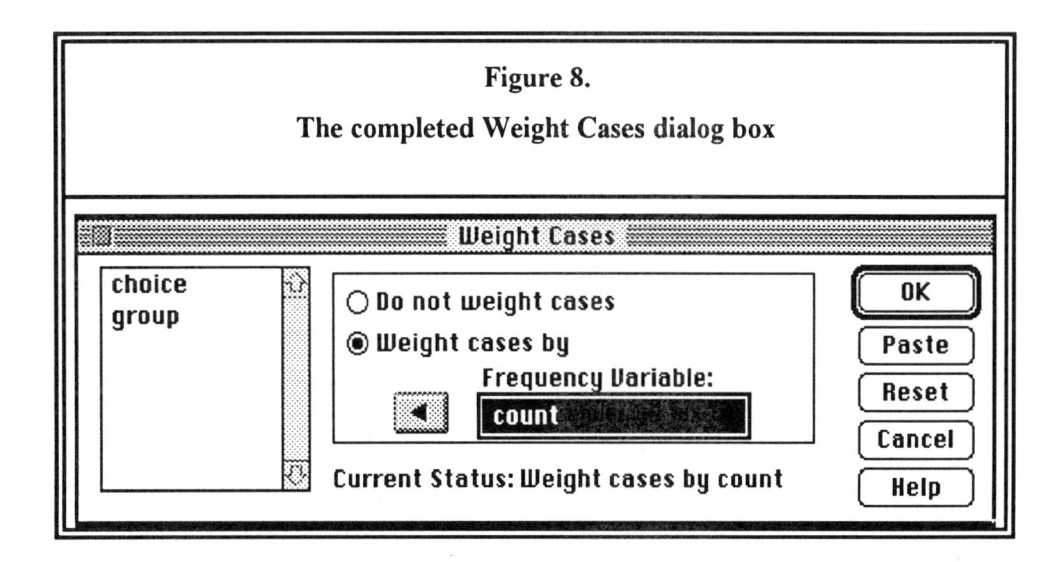

Figure 8.
The completed Weight Cases dialog box

To analyse the contingency table data, proceed as follows:

- Choose
  Statistics
  Summarize

  and then click on **Crosstabs** (Figure 9). This will open the **Crosstabs** dialog box (the completed version is shown in Figure 10).

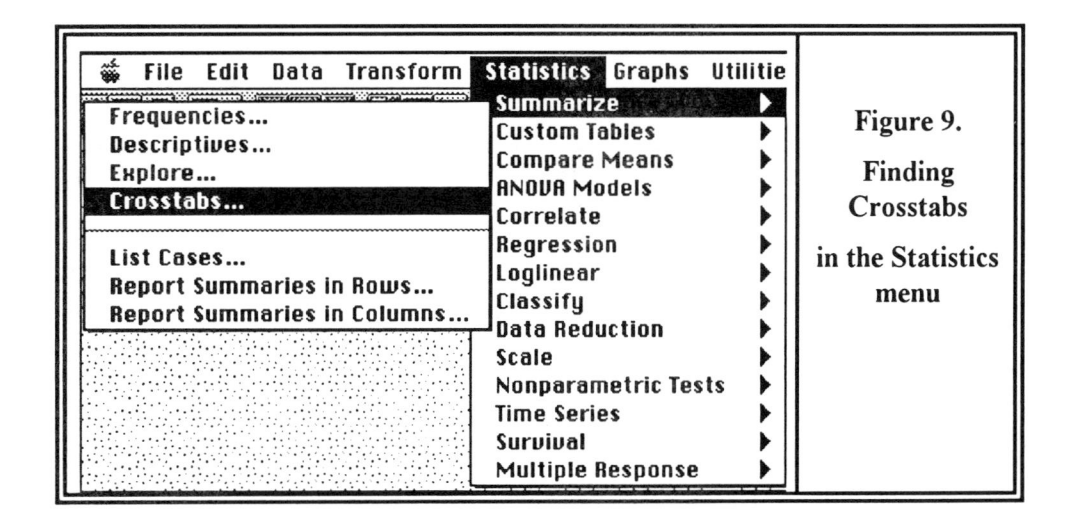

Figure 9. Finding Crosstabs in the Statistics menu

Chapter 11 - Measuring Statistical Association

- Within the **Crosstabs** dialog box, click on *group* and then on ▶ to transfer the name into the **Row(s)** box. Click on *choice* and then on ▶ to transfer the name into the **Column(s)** box (Figure 10).

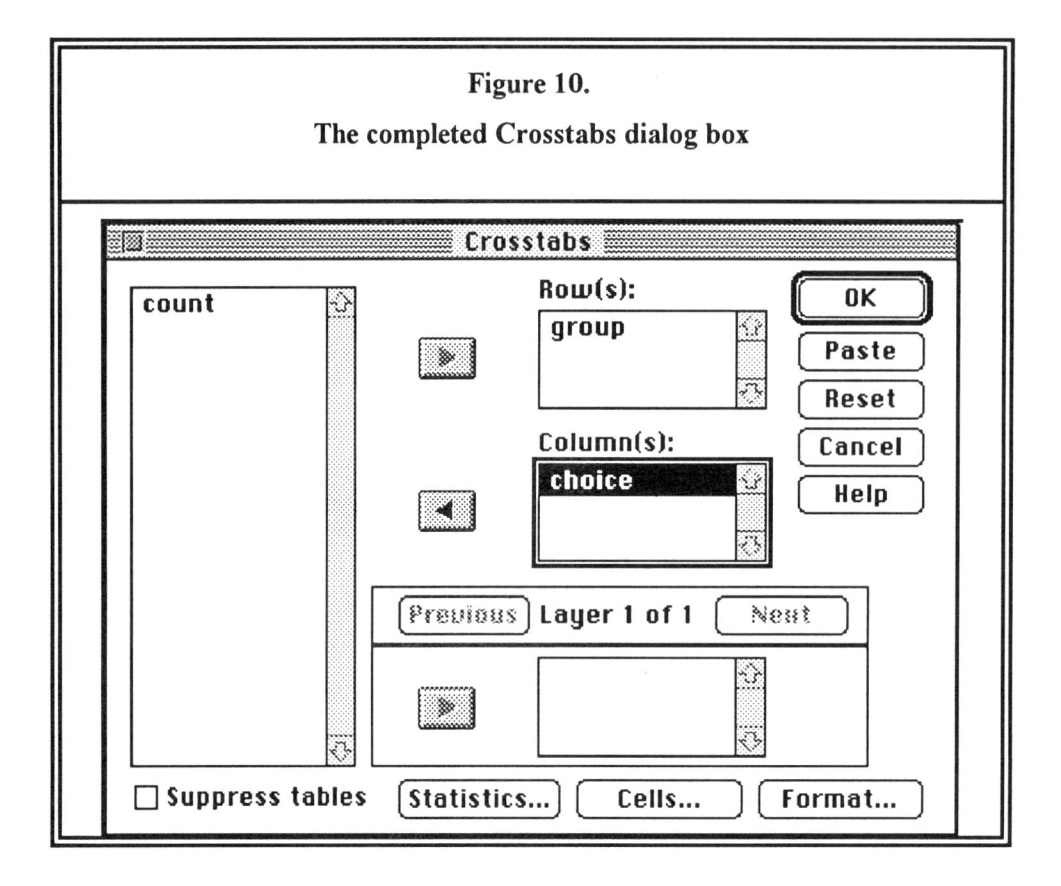

Figure 10.
The completed Crosstabs dialog box

- Click on **Statistics** to open the **Crosstabs: Statistics** dialog box (Figure 11).
- Within the **Nominal Data** list of check boxes, select **Chi-square** and **Phi and Cramér's V**.

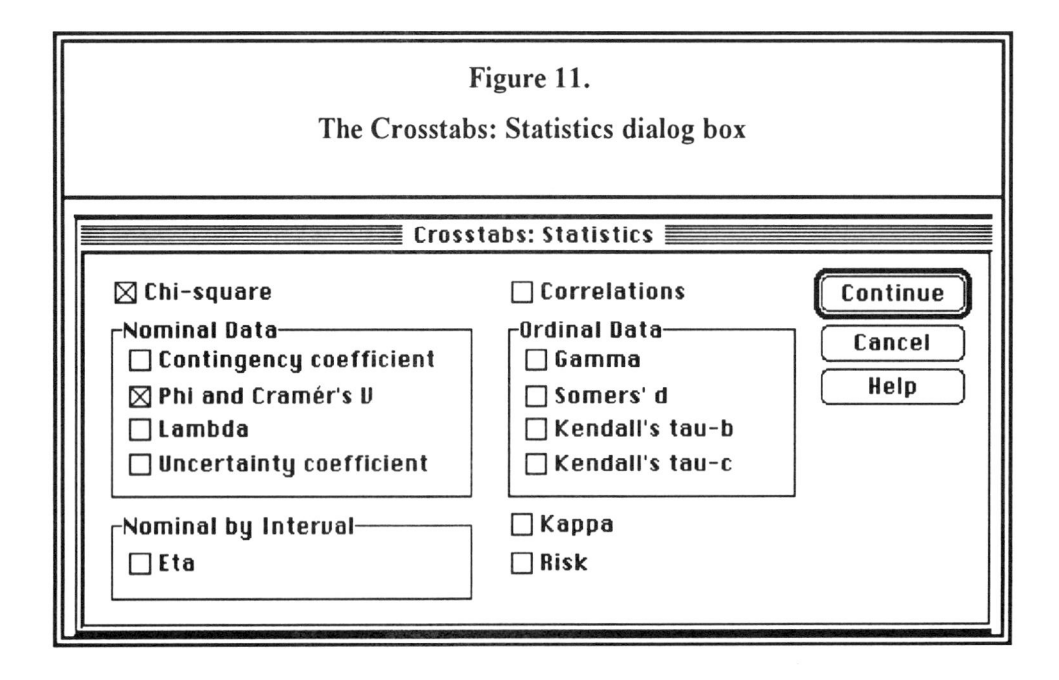

Figure 11.
The Crosstabs: Statistics dialog box

268

Chapter 11 - Measuring Statistical Association

- Click on **Continue** to return to the **Crosstabs** dialog box and then **OK**.

We recommend an additional option for computing the expected cell frequencies. This enables the user to check that the prescribed minimum requirements for the valid use of chi-square have been fulfilled. Although there has been much debate about these, the practice of leading authorities has been to proscribe the use of chi-square when:

(a) in 2 × 2 tables, any of the expected frequencies is less than 5;

(b) in larger tables, any of the expected frequencies is less than 1 or more than 20% are less than 5.

- Click on **Cells** at the foot of the **Crosstabs** dialog box (Figure 10) to open the **Crosstabs: Cell Display** selection box.

- Click on **Expected** in **Counts** box to display the expected frequencies in the output (the completed dialog box is shown in Figure 12).

- Click on **Continue** and then **OK**.

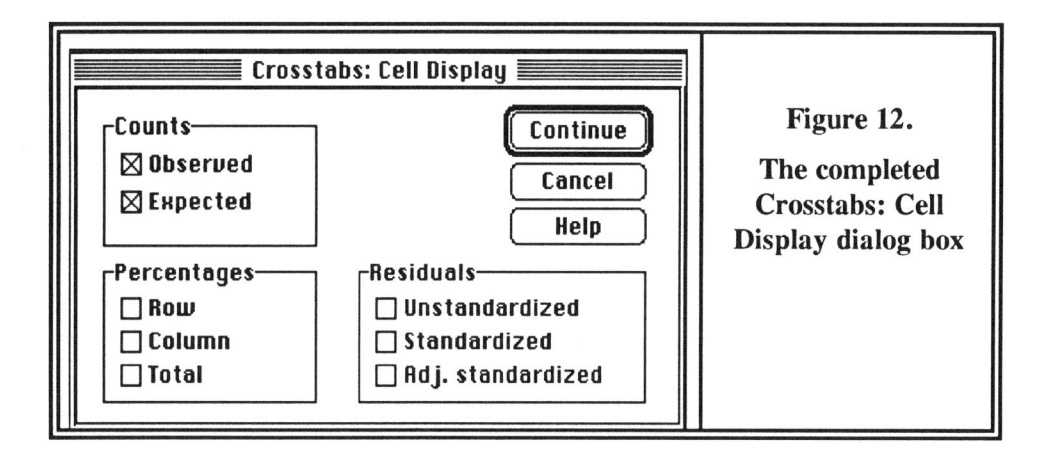

Figure 12.

The completed Crosstabs: Cell Display dialog box

Output listing for crosstabulation and associated statistics (chi-square, phi and Cramér's V)

```
GROUP  by  CHOICE  Children's Choice

                    CHOICE         Page 1 of 1
          Count
          Exp Val  Mechanic Non-mech
                   al       anical        Row
                          1        2|    Total
GROUP
             1       30       20       50
  Boys             22.5     27.5     50.0%

             2       15       35       50
  Girls             22.5     27.5     50.0%

          Column     45       55      100
          Total    45.0%    55.0%   100.0%
```

Output Listing 4.

A contingency table including the optional expected values

Output Listing 4 displays the cross-tabulation (contingency) table, with the observed and expected frequencies, as requested in the **Crosstabs: Cell Display** dialog box. None of the expected frequencies is less than 5.

Output Listing 5 shows the requested statistics.

Output Listing 5.

Statistics of a contingency table

```
        Chi-Square              Value         DF              Significance
        ----------              -----         --              ------------

Pearson                         9.09091        1                .00257
Continuity Correction           7.91919        1                .00489
Likelihood Ratio                9.24017        1                .00237
Mantel-Haenszel test for        9.00000        1                .00270
    linear association

Minimum Expected Frequency -   22.50
                                                                Approximate
        Statistic              Value         ASE1    Val/ASE0   Significance
        ---------              -----         ----    --------   ------------

Phi                             .30151                           .00257 *1
Cramer's V                      .30151                           .00257 *1


*1 Pearson chi-square probability

Number of Missing Observations:  0
```

The row labelled **Pearson** in Output Listing 5 lists the conventional chi-square statistic, along with its tail probability under H_0 (labelled **Significance** or **Asymp. Sig.**). Ignore the other rows in the Chi-Square section. It can be concluded that there is a significant association between the variables *group* and *choice*, as shown by the p-value (less than 0.01) for chi-square. This is written as: $\chi^2 = 9.09$; df = 1; p < 0.01.

Beneath the Chi-Square section in Output Listing 5 are the values of the extra requested statistics, the **phi coefficient** and **Cramér's V**. These provide a measure of the strength of the association rather like that of the Pearson correlation coefficient. This is written as: $\phi = 0.30$; p < 0.01.

EXERCISE 18

THE PEARSON CORRELATION

BEFORE YOU START

Before starting to work through this practical exercise we recommend that you read Chapter 11. The Pearson correlation *r* is one of the most widely used (and abused) of statistics. Despite its apparent simplicity and versatility, however, it is only too easy to misinterpret a correlation. The purpose of the present exercise is not only to show you how to use SPSS to obtain correlations, but also to illustrate how misleading a given value for *r* can sometimes be.

THE PROJECT

A famous data set

This exercise involves the analysis of four sets of paired data, which were contrived by Anscombe (1973). Each set yields exactly the same value for the **Pearson correlation**. The scatterplots, however, will show that in only one case are the data suitable for a Pearson correlation: in the others, the Pearson correlation gives a highly misleading impression of the relationship between the two variables. Ideally a scatterplot should indicate a **linear relationship** between the variables i.e. that all the points on the scatterplot lie along or near to a diagonal straight line as shown in the two left-hand plots in Chapter 11, Figure 1. Vertical or horizontal lines are not examples of linear relationships.

Table 1.
Anscombe's four data sets

Subject	X1	Y1	Y2	Y3	X2	Y4
s1	10.0	8.04	9.14	7.46	8.0	6.58
s2	8.0	6.95	8.14	6.77	8.0	5.76
s3	13.0	7.58	8.74	12.74	8.0	7.71
s4	9.0	8.81	8.77	7.11	8.0	8.84
s5	11.0	8.33	9.26	7.81	8.0	8.47
s6	14.0	9.96	8.10	8.84	8.0	7.04
s7	6.0	7.24	6.13	6.08	8.0	5.25
s8	4.0	4.26	3.10	5.39	19.0	12.50
s9	12.0	10.84	9.13	8.15	8.0	5.56
s10	7.0	4.82	7.26	6.42	8.0	7.91
s11	5.0	5.68	4.74	5.73	8.0	6.89

The data are presented in Table 1. The four sets we shall examine are *X1* with each of *Y1*, *Y2*, and *Y3*, and finally *X2* with *Y4*.

Preparation of the SPSS data set

Name the variables as shown in the data table above (omit subject numbers), enter the data and then save them in the file **anscombe** (this file will be used again in Exercise 19). If the numeric format does not include decimals, click on the **Type** button and enter *2* into the **Decimal Places** box.

Exploring the data

Obtain scatterplots of the four data sets, as described in Section 11.2. The plots can be produced either one at a time by choosing **simple scatterplot** or, more dramatically, by opting for a **matrix scatterplot**, which is a grid of scatterplots normally used when one is plotting all pairwise combinations of several variables. In the present exercise, however, we only want the plots of *Y1*, *Y2* and *Y3* against *X*, and of *Y4* against *X2*. It is best to obtain the plot of *Y4* against *X2* separately.
If the matrix scatterplot is selected and variables *X1*, *Y1*, *Y2* and *Y3* are transferred to the **Matrix Variables** box, only the first column of plots, those with *X1* on the horizontal axis, will be of interest.

- **What do you notice about the scatterplots in the first column? Which one is immediately suitable for a subsequent calculation of a Pearson correlation? What is wrong with each of the others?**

Return to the **Graphs** menu (it might be necessary to click on **Window**, and select the **anscombe** window), and set up a simple scatterplot with *X2* and *Y4* (see Section 4.3.3 or 11.2).

- **Is the plot suitable for a Pearson correlation?**

The plot of *Y1* against *X1* shows a substantial linear relationship between the variables. The thinness of the ellipse indicates that the **Pearson correlation** is likely to be high. This is the kind of data set for which the Pearson correlation gives an informative and accurate statement of the strength of linear relationship between two variables. The other plots, however, are very different: that of *Y2* against *X1* shows a perfect, but clearly non-linear, relationship; *Y3* against *X1* shows a basically linear relationship, which is marred by a glaring outlier; *Y4* against *X2* shows a column of points with a single outlier up in the top right corner.

Obtaining the Pearson correlations corresponding to the four scatterplots

Using the procedure described in Section 11.2.1, obtain the correlations between *X* and *Y* for the four sets of paired data.
The listing will include, in addition to the correlations of *X1* with the various *Y*s, the correlations among the four *Y* variables. The latter can be ignored.

- **What do you notice about the value of *r* for each of the correlations with *X1*?**

Return to the dialog box, click on the **Reset** box, and select *X2* and *Y4* for the remaining calculation.

- **What do you notice about the value of *r* in comparison with the values of *r* involving *X1*?**

The big surprise is that in all cases, the **Pearson correlation** has the same value (*0.817 or thereabouts*), even in the case where there appears to be no systematic relationship between *X* and *Y* at all! Anscombe's data strikingly illustrate the need to inspect the data carefully to ascertain the suitability of statistics such as the Pearson correlation.

REMOVING THE OUTLIERS

It will be instructive to recalculate the **Pearson correlation** for the data set (*X1*, *Y3*) when the values for Subject 3 have been removed. The outlier is the value *12.74* on the variable *Y3*. Use the **Select Cases** procedure to select cases which do not have a value of *12.74* on *Y3*. Since none of the other values exceed 10, it is simplest to eliminate any cases with a value greater than 10.

Return to the **Scatterplot** and **Bivariate Correlations** dialog boxes for *X1* and *Y3* (ignore the other variables) to re-run these procedures using the selected cases. Check that in the listing, only 10 rather than 11 cases have been used. You should find that the Pearson correlation for *X1* and *Y3* is now +1, which is what we would expect from the appearance of the scatterplot.

CONCLUSION

This exercise has demonstrated the value of exploring the data first before calculating statistics such as the **Pearson correlation**. While it is true that Anscombe's data were contrived to give his message greater force, there have been many misuses of the Pearson correlation with real data sets, where the problems created by the presence of outliers and by basically non-linear relationships are quite common.

EXERCISE 19

OTHER MEASURES OF ASSOCIATION

BEFORE YOU START

Please read Section 11.3 before proceeding with this practical exercise. The **Pearson correlation** was devised to measure a supposed linear association between quantitative variables. There are other kinds of data (ordinal and categorial), to which the Pearson correlation is inapplicable. Moreover, even with interval data, there may be considerations that debar the use of the Pearson correlation. Fortunately, other statistical measures of strength of association have been devised and in this exercise, we shall consider statistics that are applicable to ordinal and to categorial data.

ORDINAL DATA

The Spearman rank correlation

Suppose that two judges each rank ten paintings, A, B, ..., J. Their decisions are shown in Table 1.

Chapter 11 - Measuring Statistical Association

Table 1.
The ranks assigned to the same ten objects by two judges

	Best									Worst
First Judge	C	E	F	G	H	J	I	B	D	A
Second Judge	C	E	G	F	J	H	I	A	D	B

It is obvious from this table that the judges generally agree closely in their rankings: at most, the ranks they assign to a painting differ by two ranks. But how can their level of agreement be measured? The information in this table can be expressed in terms of numerical ranks by assigning the counting numbers from 1 to 10 to the paintings in their order of ranking by the first judge, and pairing each of these ranks with the rank that the same painting received from the other judge, as shown in Table 2.

Table 2.
A numerical representation of the orderings by the two judges in Table 1

Painting	C	E	F	G	H	J	I	B	D	A
First Judge	1	2	3	4	5	6	7	8	9	10
Second Judge	1	2	4	3	6	5	7	10	9	8

This is not the only way of representing the judgements numerically. It is also possible to list the objects (in any order) and pair the ranks assigned by the two judges to each object, entering two sets of ranks as before. Where the measurement of agreement is concerned, however, the two methods give exactly the same result.

Define two variables, *judge1* and *judge2*, and enter the ranks assigned by the judges into the two columns. Obtain the **Pearson correlation** between the two sets of ranks. This is the value of the **Spearman rank correlation**.

Use of the Spearman rank correlation where there is a monotonic, but non-linear, relationship

Consider a common problem. Table 3 shows a set of paired interval data. On inspecting the scatterplot, we see that there is a **monotonic relationship** between the two variables: that is, as X increases, so does Y. On the other hand, the relationship between X and Y is clearly non-linear, and the use of the **Pearson correlation** is therefore inadvisable.

Table 3.
A set of paired interval data showing a monotonic, but non-linear, relationship

Y	1.00	1.58	2.00	2.32	2.58	2.81	3.00
X	2.0	3.0	4.0	5.0	6.0	7.0	8.0

Enter these values into the **Data Editor**, calculate the **Pearson correlation** and obtain the scatterplot.

- **Describe the shape of the scatterplot and write down the value of the Pearson correlation.**

Since there is a perfect (but non-linear) relationship between X and Y ($Y = \log_2 X$), the degree of association is understated by the Pearson correlation coefficient.

Another approach (and arguably a better one) is to convert X and Y to ranks using the **Rank Cases** procedure within the **Transform** menu (the ranks will appear in new variables called *ran001* and *ran 002* respectively). Then calculate the Pearson correlation again using these new variables. Now compare this with your previous value of r.

- **Which value of r is the truer expression of the strength of the relationship between X and Y?**

Kendall's correlation coefficients

The association between variables in paired ordinal (and interval) data sets can also be measured by using one of **Kendall's correlation** coefficients, **tau-a**, **tau-b** or **tau-c** (see Section 11.3.1). (When there are no tied observations, **tau-a** and **tau-b** have the same value.)

With large data sets, **Kendall's** and **Pearson's correlations** give rather similar values and tail probabilities. When the data are scarcer, however, Kendall's statistics are better behaved, especially when there is a substantial proportion of tied observations, and more reliance can be placed upon the Kendall tail probability. Kendall's correlations really come into their own when the data are assignments to predetermined ordered categories (rating scales and so on).

There are two ways of obtaining **Kendall's correlations** in SPSS:
(1) In the **Bivariate Correlations** procedure, mark the **Kendall's tau-b** checkbox.
(2) Use the **Crosstabs** procedure (See Section 11.3.2).

Use the **Bivariate Correlations** procedure to obtain **Kendall's tau-a** (there are no ties) for the data in Tables 2 and 3.

- **Write down the values of tau-a and compare them with your previously obtained coefficient values.**

MEASURES OF ASSOCIATION STRENGTH FOR CATEGORIAL DATA

In an earlier exercise, we considered the use of the **chi-square statistic** to test for the presence of an association between two qualitative variables. Recall that, provided that the data are suitable, the **Pearson correlation** measures the strength of a linear association between two interval variables. In that case, therefore, the same statistic serves both as a test for the presence of an association and as a

Chapter 11 - Measuring Statistical Association

measure of associative strength. It might be thought that, with categorial data, the chi-square statistic would serve the same dual function. The chi-square statistic, however, cannot serve as a satisfactory measure of associative strength, because its value depends partly upon the total frequency.

To illustrate the calculation of measures of association for two-way contingency tables, we can recall an earlier example, concerning the possibility of a gender difference in the choice of objects by children. The data were as shown in Table 4.

Table 4.
The choices by boys and girls of two objects

Object	Boys	Girls
A	20	6
B	5	19

Prepare the data set for the **Crosstabs** procedure and run **Crosstabs** (Section 11.3.2). This time, however, select **Phi** and **Cramer's V** within the **Nominal Data** box of the **Crosstabs: Statistics** dialog box.

- **Write down the values of the chosen measures of association between the qualitative variables of Gender and Choice.**

CHAPTER 12

REGRESSION

12.1 INTRODUCTION

12.2 SIMPLE REGRESSION

12.3 MULTIPLE REGRESSION

12.4 SCATTERPLOTS AND REGRESSION LINES

Chapter 12 - Regression

12.1 INTRODUCTION

Much of Chapter 11 was devoted to the use of the **Pearson correlation** to measure the strength of the association between two quantitative variables, each of which has been measured on an interval scale.

But the associative coin has two sides. On the one hand, a single number can be calculated (a correlation coefficient) which expresses the **strength** of the association. On the other, however, there is a set of techniques, known as **regression methods**, which utilise the presence of an association between two variables to predict the values of one (the dependent variable) from those of another (the independent variable). It is with this predictive aspect that the present chapter is concerned.

To sum up, in **correlation**, the **degree of statistical association** between variables is expressed as a single number known as a **correlation coefficient**. In **regression**, the purpose is to **estimate** or **predict** some characteristic from a knowledge of others by constructing a **regression equation**.

12.1.1 Simple, two-variable regression

In **simple, two-variable regression**, the values of one variable (the dependent variable, y) are estimated from those of another (the independent variable, x) by a linear (straight line) equation of the general form

$$y' = b_0 + b_1(x)$$

where y' is the estimated value of y, b_1 is the slope (known as the **regression coefficient**), and b_0 is the intercept (known as the **regression constant**).

12.1.2 Multiple regression

In **multiple regression**, the values of one variable (the dependent variable y) are estimated from those of two or more other variables (the independent variables x_1, x_2, ... , x_p).

This is achieved by the construction of a linear equation of the general form

$$y' = b_0 + b_1(x_1) + b_2(x_2) + \ldots + b_p(x_p)$$

where the parameters b_1, b_2, ..., b_p are the partial **regression coefficients** and the intercept b_0 is the **regression constant**. This equation is known as the **multiple linear regression equation of y upon x_1, ... , x_p**.

12.1.3 Residuals

When a regression equation is used to estimate the values of a variable y from those of one or more independent variables x, the estimates y' will usually fall short of complete accuracy. Geometrically speaking, the data points will not fall precisely upon the straight line, plane or hyperplane specified by the regression equation. The discrepancies $(y - y')$ on the predicted variable are known as **residuals**. When using regression methods, the study of the residuals is of great importance, because they form the basis for measures of the accuracy of the estimates and of the extent to which the **regression model** gives a good account of the data in question. (See Lovie, 1991, for an account of the analysis of residuals, a topic known as **regression diagnostics**.)

12.1.4 The multiple correlation coefficient

One simple (though rather limited) measure of the efficacy of regression for the prediction of y is the Pearson correlation between the true values of the target variable y and the estimates y' obtained by substituting the corresponding values of x into the regression equation. The correlation between y and y' is known as the **multiple correlation coefficient R**. Notice that the upper case is used for the multiple correlation coefficient, to distinguish it from the correlation between the target variable and any one independent variable considered separately. In simple, two-variable regression, the multiple correlation coefficient takes the **absolute** value of the Pearson correlation between the target variable and the independent variable: so if $r = -0.90$, $R = 0.90$. It can be shown algebraically that the multiple correlation coefficient cannot have a negative value.

12.2 SIMPLE REGRESSION

Among university authorities, there is much concern about the efficacy of the methods used to select students for entry. How closely are performance on the selection tests and examination performance associated? How accurately can one predict university performance from students' marks on the selection tests?

Given data on students' final exam marks y and their performance x on the selection exam, a Pearson correlation can be used to measure the degree of statistical association between the former and the latter. It is also possible to use simple regression to predict exam performance at university from marks in the selection exam. It can be shown by mathematical proof, however, that when two or more independent variables are used to predict the target variable y, the predictions will, on average, be **at least as accurate** as when any one of the same independent variables is used: in other words, the multiple correlation coefficient *R* must be at least as great as any single Pearson correlation *r*. For the moment, however, we shall be considering the simple regression of university exam performance upon the marks in one selection exam.

12.2.1 Procedure for simple regression

Some data

In Table 1, the score *x* in each (*x, y*) pair is a student's mark in the final university exam, and the score *y* is the same student's mark in the selection exam. Table 1 contains the marks of 34 students: Student Number 1 (whose data are in the first row of the first two columns from the left) got 44 in the selection test and 38 in the university exam; Student 34 (whose data are in the sixth row of the last two columns on the right) got 49 in the selection test and 195 in the university exam.

Table 1.

Table of the final university exam (y) and the selection exam (x) scores

y	x	y	x	y	x	y	x	y	x
38	44	76	37	98	40	112	49	145	60
49	40	78	41	100	37	114	46	150	55
61	43	81	53	100	48	114	41	152	54
65	42	86	47	103	48	117	49	164	58
69	44	91	45	105	43	125	63	169	62
73	46	94	41	106	55	140	52	195	49
74	34	95	39	107	48	142	56		

Preparing the SPSS data set

Using the techniques described in Section 3.3, define the variables *finalex* and *selectex*, using the labelling procedure to assign the more informative names *University Exam* and *Selection Exam*. Type the data into the labelled columns.

Accessing the simple regression procedure

- Choose (Figure 1)
  Statistics
    Regression

  and click on **Linear** to open the **Linear Regression** dialog box (Figure 2).

Chapter 12 - Regression

Figure 1.
Finding the Linear Regression procedure

Figure 2.
Linear Regression dialog box

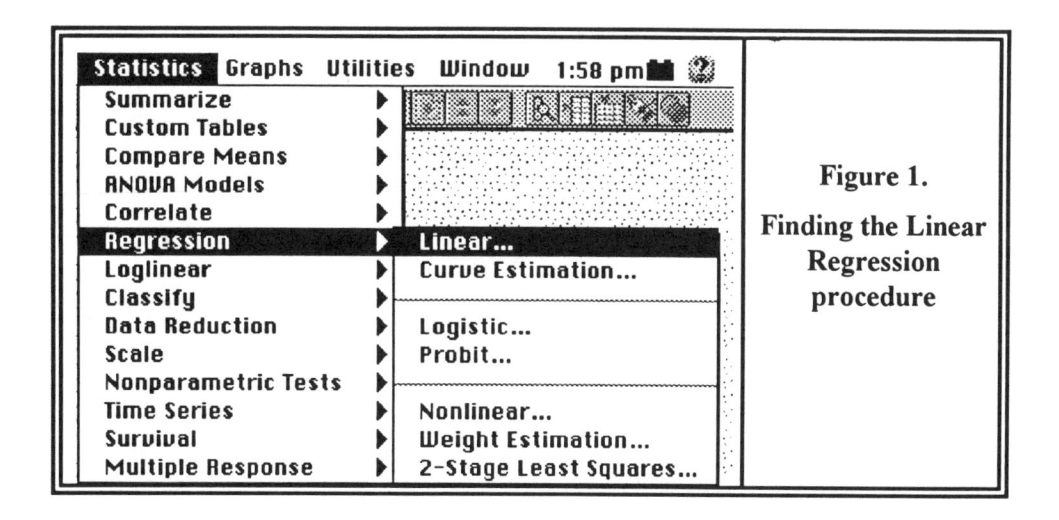

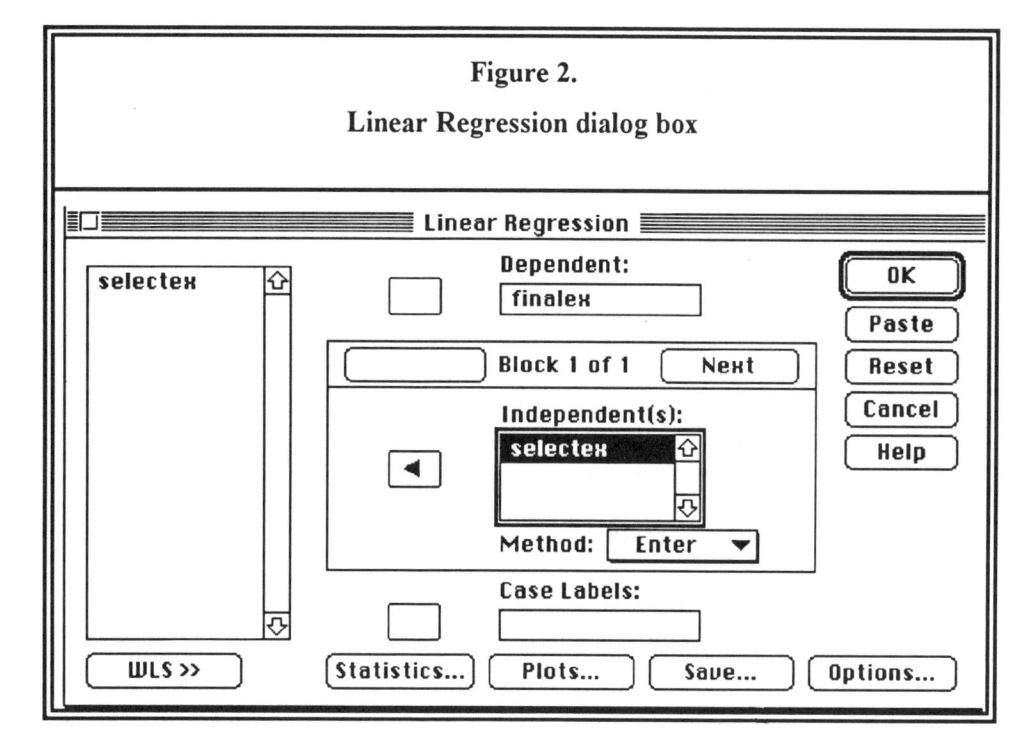

- The two variable names *finalex* and *selectex* will appear in the left-hand box. It is important to be clear about which variable is the dependent variable and which is the independent variable - in this example the dependent variable is the final university exam *finalex* and the independent variable is the selection exam *selectex*. Transfer these variable names into the appropriate boxes in the dialog box by clicking on the variable name and then on ▶ (Figure 2).

- It is advisable to request additional descriptive statistics and a residuals analysis. To obtain descriptive statistics, click on the **Statistics** button (Figure 2) to open the **Linear Regression: Statistics** dialog box (Figure 3). Click on the **Descriptives** check box and then on **Continue** to return to the **Linear Regression** dialog box.

Figure 3.
Linear Regression: Statistics dialog box

```
================ Linear Regression: Statistics ================
┌─Regression Coefficients─┐   ☒ Descriptives         ┌──Continue──┐
│ ☒ Estimates             │   ☒ Model fit            │   Cancel   │
│ ☐ Confidence intervals  │   ☐ Block summary        │    Help    │
│ ☐ Covariance matrix     │   ☐ Durbin-Watson        └────────────┘
└─────────────────────────┘   ☐ Collinearity diagnostics
```

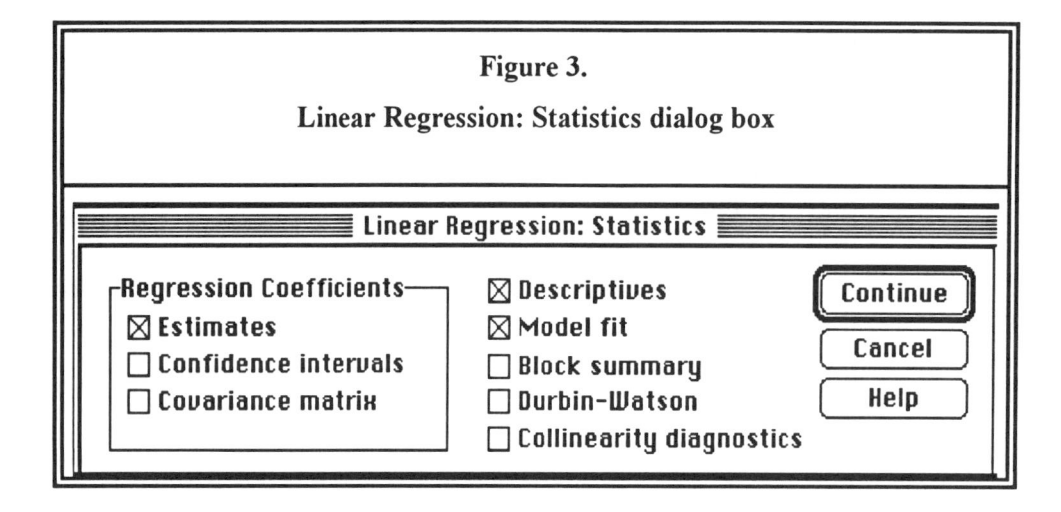

- Information about residuals is obtained by clicking on the **Plots** button (Figure 2) to open the **Linear Regression: Plots** dialog box (Figure 4). A **residual** (Section 12.1.3) is the difference between the actual value of the dependent variable and its predicted value using the regression equation. Analysis of the residuals gives a measure of how good the prediction is and whether there are any cases which are so discrepant that they might be considered as outliers and so dropped from the analysis. Click on the **Casewise plot** check box in the **Linear Regression: Plots** dialog box to obtain a listing of any exceptionally large residuals. Since systematic patterns between the predicted values and the residuals can indicate possible violations of the assumption of linearity, we recommend that a plot of the standardised residuals (*ZRESID*) against the standardised predicted values (*ZPRED*) is also requested by transferring *ZRESID* into the **Y:** box and *ZPRED* into the **X:** box as shown in Figure 4.

- Click on **Continue** and then on **OK** to run the regression for the first time.

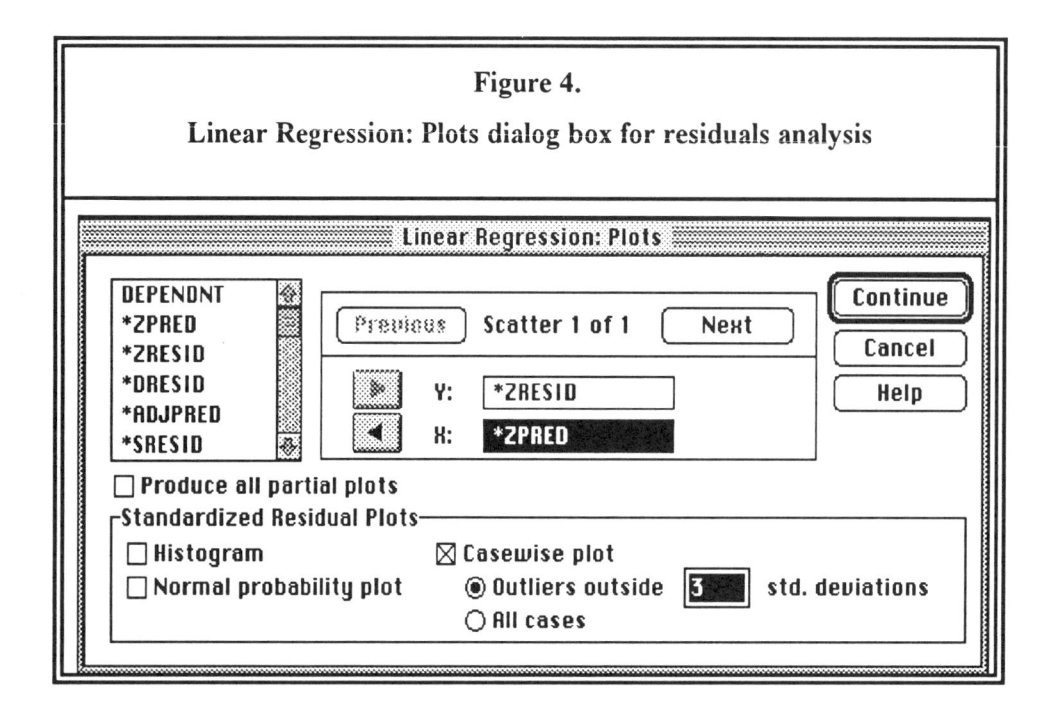

Figure 4.
Linear Regression: Plots dialog box for residuals analysis

```
================= Linear Regression: Plots =================
  DEPENDNT                                          ┌──Continue──┐
  *ZPRED       [Previous]  Scatter 1 of 1  [ Next ] │   Cancel   │
  *ZRESID                                           │    Help    │
  *DRESID         [▶]   Y:  *ZRESID                 └────────────┘
  *ADJPRED
  *SRESID         [◀]   X:  *ZPRED

  ☐ Produce all partial plots
  ┌─Standardized Residual Plots─────────────────────────────┐
  │ ☐ Histogram              ☒ Casewise plot                │
  │ ☐ Normal probability plot   ⦿ Outliers outside [3] std. deviations │
  │                             ○ All cases                 │
  └─────────────────────────────────────────────────────────┘
```

12.2.2 Output listing for simple regression

Indication of residual outliers

The **Casewise plot of standardized Residual** output in Output Listing 1 occurs after the following four items (these will be reproduced in a later section):

(1) means and standard deviations;

(2) the correlation coefficient;

(3) multiple R and regression ANOVA;

(4) the regression equation.

Output Listing 1 shows that Case 1 with a score of *195* for *finalex* (University Exam) is the only outlier. The next section describes how to eliminate this outlier and run the subsequent regression analysis.

Output Listing 1.

The casewise plot of standardized residual showing which outliers are greater than ± 3 standard deviations

```
Casewise Plot of Standardized Residual

Outliers = 3.    *: Selected    M: Missing

         -6.    -3.  3.    6.
  Case #  0:.......: :.......:0    FINALEX    *PRED      *RESID
    34   .          ..*       .       195     110.9517    84.0483


        1 Outliers found.
```

Elimination of outliers

- A more reliable regression analysis can be obtained by eliminating any outliers using the **Select Cases** procedure described in Section 3.7.1. Click on the **If condition is satisfied** radio button within the **Select Cases** dialog box and define the condition as *finalex ~=195*. (The symbol ~= means 'not equal to'.)

- Click on **Continue** and then on **OK** to deselect this case.

If there is more than one outlier, they can be deselected by defining the condition with an inequality operator (e.g. *finalex* < 150). Sometimes, in order to see what value to use in the inequality, it is convenient to arrange variables in order of value by choosing **Sort Cases** within the **Data** menu.

Chapter 12 - Regression

Output listing for simple regression after eliminating the outlier

When the regression analysis is run again, the descriptive statistics and the correlation coefficient for the remaining 33 cases are as shown in Output Listing 2.

Output Listing 2.

The descriptive statistics and correlation coefficient

```
                Mean    Std Dev   Label

  FINALEX      102.818   32.633   University Examination
  SELECTEX      47.273    7.539   Selection Exam

  N of Cases =    33

  Correlation, 1-tailed Sig:

             FINALEX    SELECTEX

  FINALEX     1.000       .729
                .         .000

  SELECTEX     .729      1.000
                .000        .
```

Output Listing 3 contains a value for **Multiple R** which in the case of just one independent variable has the same absolute value as the correlation coefficient *r* listed in Output Listing 2. There is also an ANOVA, which is intended to test whether there really is a linear relationship between the variables by forming an F ratio of the mean square for regression to the residual mean square.

In this example, the value of F in the ANOVA Table is highly significant. **It should be noted, however, that only an examination of the scatterplot of the variables can confirm that the relationship between two variables is genuinely linear.**

The other statistics listed are **R Square**, which is a positively biased estimate of the proportion of the variance of the dependent variable accounted for by regression, **Adjusted R Square** which corrects this bias and therefore has a lower value, and **Standard Error**, which is the standard deviation of the residuals.

Chapter 12 - Regression

Output Listing 3.

Multiple R and the regression ANOVA

```
         * * * *   M U L T I P L E   R E G R E S S I O N   * * * *

Equation Number 1    Dependent Variable..   FINALEX   University Examination

Block Number  1.  Method:  Enter      SELECTEX

Variable(s) Entered on Step Number
   1..    SELECTEX  Selection Exam

Multiple R           .72873
R Square             .53104
Adjusted R Square    .51592
Standard Error     22.70468

Analysis of Variance
                  DF      Sum of Squares       Mean Square
Regression         1         18096.32896       18096.32896
Residual          31         15980.58013         515.50258

F =     35.10424     Signif F =  .0000
```

Output Listing 4 is the kernel of the regression analysis, because it contains the regression equation. The values of the **regression coefficient** and **constant** are given in column **B** of the table. The equation is, therefore,

Predicted Final Exam Mark = **3.15** × (*Selection Exam Mark*) - **46.30**

Thus a person with a Selection Exam Mark of 60 would be predicted to score

$$3.15 \times 60 - 46.30 = 142.7 \qquad \text{(i.e. 143)}.$$

Notice from the data that the person who did score 60 on the selection exam actually scored 145 on the final exam. The residual is, therefore, 145-143 = +2.

Output Listing 4.

The regression equation and associated statistics

```
----------------- Variables in the Equation ------------------

Variable              B           SE B         Beta         T      Sig T

SELECTEX          3.154519      .532419      .728727     5.925    .0000
(Constant)      -46.304539    25.477326                 -1.817    .0788
```

Other statistics listed are **SE B** which is the standard error of the regression coefficient **B**, **Beta** which is the beta weight showing the change in the dependent variable (expressed in standard deviation units) that would be produced by a positive increment of one standard deviation in the independent variable, **T** which is a t-test for testing the regression coefficient for significance, and **Sig T** which is the p-value of **t** (here .000 means <0.00005, i.e. T is significant well beyond the 0.01 level).

Output Listing 5 is a table of statistics relating to the residuals. The variable *PRED* comprises the unstandardised predicted values, the variable *RESID* is the set of unstandardised residuals, the variable *ZPRED* contains the standardised predicted values (i.e. *PRED* has been transformed to a scale with mean 0 and SD 1), and the variable *ZRESID* comprises the standardised residuals (i.e. *RESID* standardised to a scale with mean 0 and SD 1).

Output Listing 5.

Table of statistics relating to the residuals

```
Residuals Statistics:

              Min       Max      Mean    Std Dev    N

*PRED       60.9491  152.4302  102.8182   23.7805   33
*RESID     -54.4943   30.9693     .0000   22.3471   33
*ZPRED      -1.7607    2.0862     .0000    1.0000   33
*ZRESID     -2.4001    1.3640     .0000     .9843   33

Total Cases =      33
```

Figure 5 is the scatterplot of the standardised residuals (*ZRESID*) against the standardised predicted values (*ZPRED*).

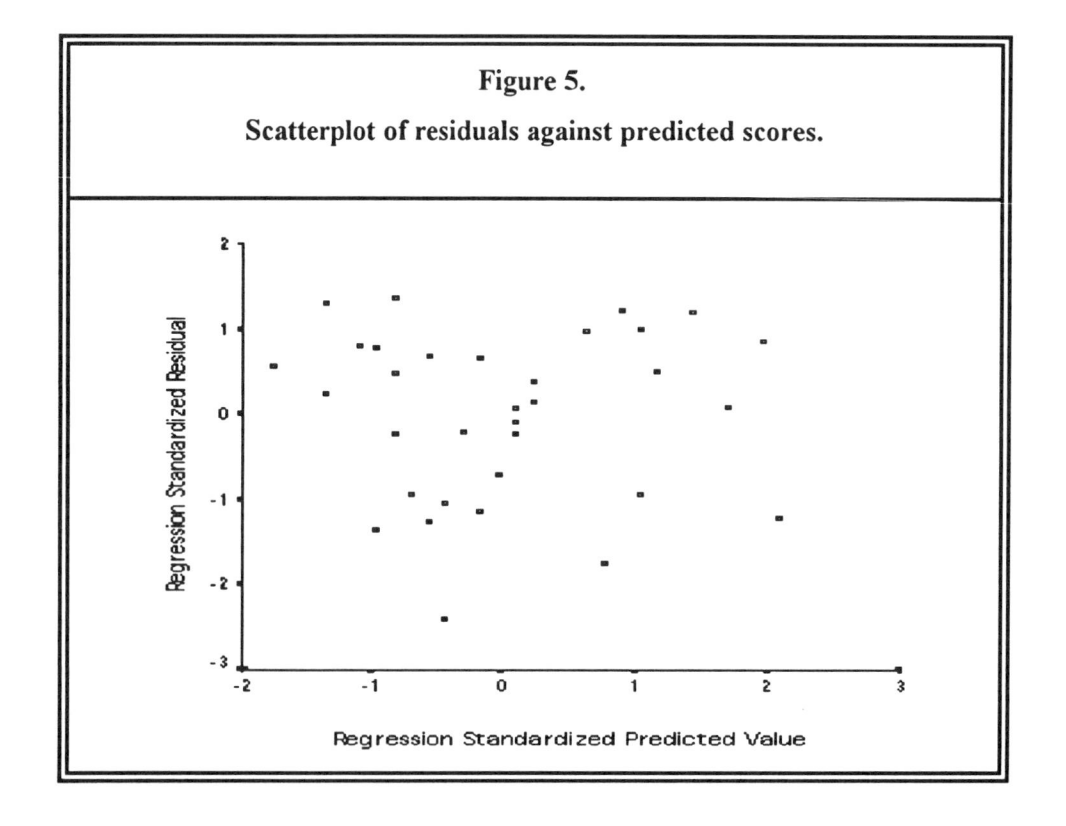

Figure 5.

Scatterplot of residuals against predicted scores.

286

The plot shows no obvious pattern, thereby confirming that the assumptions of linearity and homogeneity of variance have been met. If the cloud of points were crescent- or funnel-shaped, further screening of the data (or abandonment of the analysis) would be necessary.

Other diagnostic plots such as a histogram of the standardised residuals (ideally they should be distributed normally) and a cumulative normal probability plot (ideally the points should lie along or adjacent to the diagonal) could have been selected from within the **Standardized Residual Plots** box in Figure 4.

12.3 MULTIPLE REGRESSION

The process of constructing a linear equation that will predict the values of a target (dependent) variable from knowledge of specified values of a regressor (independent variable) can readily be extended to situations where we have data on two or more independent variables. The construction of a linear regression equation with two or more independent variables (or regressors) on the right hand side is known as **multiple regression**.

Some more data

In Table 2, two extra variables, the subjects' ages and the scores they obtained on a relevant academic project, have been added to the original variables *finalex* and *selectex* 1 in Table 1. The outlier that was detected in the preliminary regression analysis, however, has been removed.

In the following discussion, we shall be concerned with two main questions:

(1) does the addition of more independent variables improve the accuracy of predictions of *finalex*?

(2) of these new variables, are some more useful than others for prediction of the dependent variable?

We shall see that the answer to the first question is 'Yes'. The second question, however, is deeply problematic, and none of the available approaches to it is entirely satisfactory.

Many years ago, Darlington (1968) drew attention to some widespread misunderstandings among users of multiple regression; in fact, he was trying to do for regression what Lewis & Burke (1949) had done some years earlier for chi-square analysis. Darlington placed special emphasis upon the thorny problem of how to say which of the independent variables in a multiple regression equation is the most 'important', or 'useful' in accounting for variability in the dependent variable. (Of more recent non-technical treatments, the most lucid we have been able to find is by Cohen & Cohen, 1983.)

There are many problems; but most of them may be summed up in a well-known aphorism: **Correlation does not imply causation**. In a situation where everything correlates with everything else, **it is quite impossible to attribute variance in the dependent variable unequivocally to any one independent variable**.

Table 2.
An extension of Table 1, with data on two additional independent variables (outlier omitted)

Finalex	Selectex	Age	Project	Finalex	Selectex	Age	Project
38	44	21.9	50	103	48	22.3	53
49	40	22.6	75	105	43	21.8	72
61	43	21.8	54	106	55	21.4	69
65	42	22.5	60	107	48	21.6	50
69	44	21.9	82	112	49	22.8	68
73	46	21.8	65	114	46	22.1	72
74	34	22.2	61	114	41	21.9	60
76	37	22.5	68	117	49	22.5	74
78	41	21.5	60	125	63	21.9	70
81	53	22.4	69	140	52	22.2	77
86	47	21.9	64	142	56	21.4	79
91	45	22.0	78	145	60	21.6	84
94	41	22.2	68	150	55	22.1	60
95	39	21.7	70	152	54	21.9	76
98	40	22.2	65	164	58	23.0	84
100	37	39.3	75	169	62	21.2	65
100	48	21.0	65				

This fundamental dubiety is belied by considerations of some of the terms in the multiple regression equation, and by the availability of methods that have been specifically designed to evaluate the relative importance of the independent variables in the equation.

In a multiple regression equation, the coefficients of the independent variables are known as **partial regression coefficients**, meaning that they express the increase in the dependent variable that would be produced by a positive increase of one unit in the independent variable concerned, the effects of the other independent variables, both on the independent variable and the dependent variable, being supposedly held constant. Such **statistical control**, however, is no substitute for true **experimental** control, where the independent variable, having been manipulated by the experimenter, really is independent of the dependent variable.

If scores on all the variables in a multiple regression equation are standardised, the intercept of the regression equation disappears and each regression coefficient, referred to as a **beta weight**, expresses the change in the dependent variable, expressed in standard deviation units, that would be produced by a positive increment of one standard deviation in the independent variable concerned.

In this section, we shall consider two approaches to multiple regression, neither of which is entirely satisfactory. In **simultaneous** multiple regression, all the available independent variables are entered in the equation directly. In **stepwise** multiple regression, the independent variables are added to (or taken away from) the equation one at a time, the order of entry (or removal) being determined by statistical considerations. Despite the appeal of the second approach, however, there is the disconcerting fact that the addition of another 'independent' variable can completely change the apparent contributions of the other regressors to the variance of scores on the dependent variable.

Constructing the SPSS data set

Using the techniques described in Section 3.5, restore the original data set to the **Data Editor** window (removing the outlier), define the two new variables and type in the new data.

12.3.1 Procedure for simultaneous multiple regression

- In the **Linear Regression** dialog box, transfer the variable names *selectex*, *age* and *project* into the **Independent Variables** box by highlighting them and clicking on the appropriate button. The **Dependent Variable** box must contain the variable name *finalex*. For the **Method**, select **Enter** (for the simultaneous regression procedure).
- Click on **OK** to run the regression.

Output listing for simultaneous multiple regression

Output Listing 7 shows that the multiple correlation coefficient (**R**) is 0.77.

Recall that when one independent variable *selectex* was used to predict *finalex*, the value of R was 0.73. With R = 0.77, we see that the answer to the question of whether adding more independent variables improves the predictive power of the regression equation is certainly 'Yes', although the improvement is not very great.

But what about the second question? Do both new variables contribute substantially to the predictive power of the regression equation, or is one a passenger in the equation? From column **B** in the section headed **Variables in the Equation** in Output Listing 7, we learn that the multiple regression equation of *finalex* upon *selectex*, *age* and *project* is:

finalex' = 3.09 × (*selectex*) + 0.63 × (*project*) + 1.42 × (*age*) - 117.91

This, however, tells us nothing about the relative importance of the independent variables, because the **values of the partial regression coefficients reflect the original units in which the variables were measured**. From the fact that the coefficient for age is larger than that for project, therefore, one cannot conclude that age is the more important regressor.

Output Listing 7.

The simultaneous regression of finalex upon three regressors: selectex, age and project (ANOVA omitted)

```
Equation Number 1    Dependent Variable..   FINALEX    University Exam

Block Number  1.  Method:  Enter       PROJECT   AGE       SELECTEX

Variable(s) Entered on Step Number
    1..   SELECTEX   Entrance Exam
    2..   AGE
    3..   PROJECT    Project Mark

Multiple R          .76609

|----------------- Variables in the Equation -----------------

Variable            B          SE B        Beta        T       Sig T

PROJECT         .628040       .460888    .175991     1.363    .1835
AGE            1.423078      1.375600    .132812     1.035    .3094
SELECTEX       3.088891       .573397    .713567     5.387    .0000
(Constant)  -117.915892     46.421126               -2.540    .0167
```

The **beta** weights (in the column headed **Beta**) tell us rather more, because each gives the number of standard deviations change on the dependent variable that will be produced by a change of one standard deviation on the independent variable concerned. On this count, *selectex* still makes by far the greatest contribution, because a change of one standard deviation on that variable produces a change of 0.71 standard deviations on *finalex*, whereas a change of one standard deviation in *project* produces an increase of only 0.18 of a standard deviation in *finalex*. A change of one standard deviation in age produces a change of only 0.13 of a standard deviation in *finalex*. This ordering of the standardised beta weights is supported by consideration of the correlations between the dependent variable and each of the three regressors: the correlations between *finalex* and *project*, *selectex* and *age* are 0.40, 0.73 and −0.03, respectively. (These values are easily obtained by running the **bivariate correlations** procedure.) It is not surprising that the regressor with the largest beta weight also has the largest correlation with the dependent variable.

12.3.2 Procedure for stepwise multiple regression

If, in the **Linear Regression** dialog box, the choice of **Method** is **Stepwise**, rather than **Enter**, a *forward* stepwise regression will be run, whereby regressors are added to the equation one at a time. (In the **backward elimination** method, which is also available in SPSS, they are subtracted one at a time.)

Selected portions of the results are shown in Output Listing 9.

```
                        Output Listing 9.
                  Forward stepwise multiple regression


Block Number  1.  Method: Stepwise    Criteria   PIN  .0500   POUT  .1000
    PROJECT   AGE       SELECTEX

Variable(s) Entered on Step Number
    1..   SELECTEX   Entrance Exam

Multiple R         .72873

----------------- Variables in the Equation -----------------

Variable              B         SE B       Beta        T    Sig T

SELECTEX        3.154519     .532419     .728727    5.925  .0000
(Constant)    -46.304539   25.477326               -1.817  .0788

------------- Variables not in the Equation -------------

Variable       Beta In   Partial   Min Toler       T    Sig T

PROJECT        .210591   .294227    .915421     1.686   .1021
AGE            .178115   .250347    .926438     1.416   .1670
```

The most obvious feature of the output is the multiple correlation coefficient which is given as 0.729. This is smaller than the value given for simultaneous regression of *finalex* upon *selectex*, *project* and *age* (0.77). Nevertheless, the decision of the stepwise program is that the increment in R with the inclusion of the variables *project* and *age* is not robust, and so those variables are dropped from the final equation. Only *selectex* (the Selection Exam) is a reliable predictor of *finalex* (the University Exam).

Adding another variable

Why should *selectex* be a better predictor of *finalex* than is *project*? The researcher suspects that both the university exam and the selection exam tap the candidate's verbal ability, as well as motivation for the material of the curriculum. Adding the candidates' verbal IQs to the regression equation, therefore, should improve the accuracy of predictions from the multiple regression equation. To test this hypothesis, the researcher obtains the verbal IQs of the same students who provided the data on the other variables. These scores are given in Table 3.

Table 3.
The data from Table 2 plus IQs

F	S	Age	Proj	IQ	F	S	Age	Proj	IQ
38	44	21.9	50	110	103	48	22.3	53	134
49	40	22.6	75	120	105	43	21.8	72	140
61	43	21.8	54	119	106	55	21.4	69	127
65	42	22.5	60	125	107	48	21.6	50	135
69	44	21.9	82	121	112	49	22.8	68	132
73	46	21.8	65	140	114	46	22.1	72	135
74	34	22.2	61	122	114	41	21.9	60	135
76	37	22.5	68	123	117	49	22.5	74	129
78	41	21.5	60	133	125	63	21.9	70	140
81	53	22.4	69	100	140	52	22.2	77	134
86	47	21.9	64	120	142	56	21.4	79	134
91	45	22.0	78	115	145	60	21.6	84	132
94	41	22.2	68	124	150	55	22.1	60	135
95	39	21.7	70	135	152	54	21.9	76	135
98	40	22.2	65	132	164	58	23.0	84	149
100	37	39.3	75	128	169	62	21.2	65	135
100	48	21.0	65	130					

As an exercise, the reader may wish to add the variable *iq* to the data set and rerun both the simultaneous and the stepwise regressions. Selected parts of the results of the simultaneous regression of *finalex* upon *iq*, *age*, *projectex* and *selectex* are shown in Output Listing 10.

It can be seen from these Listings that the addition of *iq* improves the predictive power of the regression equation: the value of multiple R is now 0.87, which is noticeably larger than it was when there were only three regressors (0.77).

Looking at the standardised **beta** weights (column labelled **Beta**), we see that a change of one standard deviation in *selectex* produces a change of 0.58 of a standard deviation in *finalex* and the same change in *iq* increases *finalex* by 0.45 of a standard deviation. These appear to be substantial contributions, in comparison with those of *project* (0.14) and *age* (0.11).

Chapter 12 - Regression

Output Listing 10.

The simultaneous regression of finalex upon selectex, age, IQ and project

---

```
Equation Number 1    Dependent Variable..   FINALEX    University Exam
Block Number  1.  Method: Enter     PROJECT  AGE      SELECTEX  IQ

Variable(s) Entered on Step Number
   1..   IQ
   2..   AGE
   3..   PROJECT   Project Mark
   4..   SELECTEX  Entrance Exam

Multiple R          .87449

----------------- Variables in the Equation ------------------

Variable              B            SE B        Beta         T      Sig T

PROJECT         .503658        .354999      .141136      1.419    .1670
AGE            1.244163       1.057195      .116114      1.177    .2492
SELECTEX       2.494034        .458966      .576148      5.434    .0000
IQ             1.509827        .328181      .447155      4.601    .0001
(Constant)  -272.129581      48.935525                   -5.561    .0000
```

Output Listings 11 and 12 show selected parts of the output for the **forward stepwise** regression of *finalex* upon all four regressors.

Output Listing 11.

The first step in the forward stepwise regression of finalex upon IQ, age, project and selectex

---

```
Equation Number 1     Dependent Variable..   FINALEX    University Exam

Block Number  1.  Method: Stepwise    Criteria   PIN  .0500   POUT  .1000
    PROJECT  AGE       SELECTEX  IQ
Variable(s) Entered on Step Number
   1..   SELECTEX  Entrance Exam

Multiple R          .72873

----------------- Variables in the Equation ------------------

Variable              B            SE B        Beta         T      Sig T

SELECTEX       3.154519        .532419      .728727      5.925    .0000
(Constant)   -46.304539      25.477326                   -1.817    .0788
------------- Variables not in the Equation -------------

Variable      Beta In   Partial   Min Toler        T      Sig T

PROJECT       .210591   .294227   .915421       1.686    .1021
AGE           .178115   .250347   .926438       1.416    .1670
IQ            .466653   .645641   .897691       4.631    .0001
```

293

Chapter 12 - Regression

The first step in Output Listing 11 enters *selectex* into the equation. Notice that at this stage the model is identical with the forward stepwise regression of *finalex* upon *selectex*, *age* and *project*.

Output Listing 12 shows the second (and final) step in the analysis, which adds the new variable *iq* into the equation. The stepwise regression stops after it has added these variables to the equation. Notice that the final value of R is 0.85, which is close to the value of R when all four regressors are included in the regression equation (0.87). The decision of the regression procedure, therefore, is that the variables *project* and *age* do not contribute reliably to the regression equation.

Output Listing 12.

The second (and final) step in the forward stepwise regression of finalex upon IQ, age, project and selectex

---

```
Variable(s) Entered on Step Number
   2..    IQ

Multiple R              .85237

------------------ Variables in the Equation ------------------

Variable              B           SE B         Beta         T    Sig T

SELECTEX         2.508390       .436214       .579465     5.750   .0000
IQ               1.575662       .340252       .466653     4.631   .0001
(Constant)    -219.068451     42.224992                  -5.188   .0000


------------ Variables not in the Equation ------------

Variable        Beta In   Partial   Min Toler      T    Sig T

PROJECT         .171017   .311663    .840563     1.766   .0879
AGE             .151842   .279001    .829761     1.565   .1285
```

12.3.3 The need for a substantive model of causation

These results highlight an important consideration for the use of multiple regression as a research tool. The addition of new regressors can radically affect the relative contributions of those variables already in the equation. When planning a multiple regression and selecting regressors, the researcher must be guided by a substantive theoretical rationale. A *statistical* model, therefore, cannot by itself yield an unequivocal interpretation of regression results: the user must also be guided by a *substantive* model of causation.

12.4 SCATTERPLOTS AND REGRESSION LINES

A regression line can easily be added to a scatterplot such as Figure 3 in Chapter 11. Proceed as follows.

- After plotting the scatterplot in the usual way, click on the **Edit** box, and then select **Chart/Options** to open the **Scatterplot Options** dialog box (Figure 8).

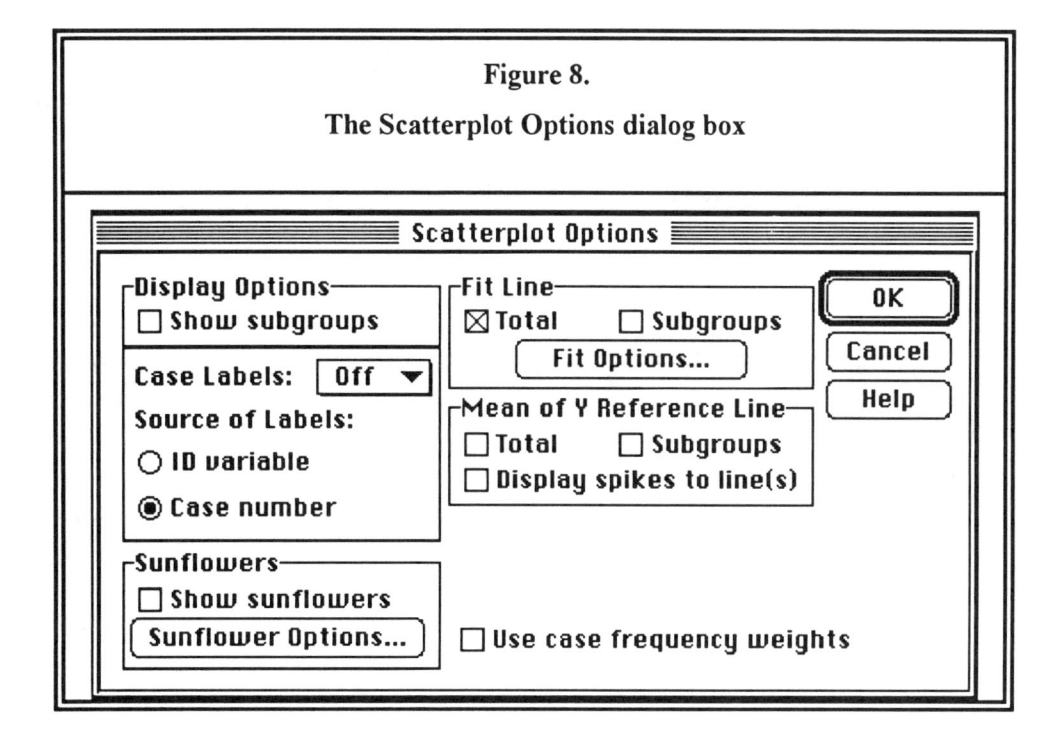

Figure 8.
The Scatterplot Options dialog box

- Within the **Fit Line** box, click on **Total**, and then on **OK** to obtain the (default) linear regression line. Should other regression lines (e.g. quadratic, cubic) be desired, click on the **Fit Options** box to open the **Scatterplot Options: Fit Line** dialog box (Figure 9).

- Here it is possible to select higher powered regression lines within the **Fit Method** box and also the confidence limits (95% is the default level) within the **Regression Prediction Line(s)** box. The value of R^2 can be displayed beside the scatterplot by clicking on the **Display R-squared in legend** box.

Chapter 12 - Regression

Figure 9.

The Scatterplot Options: Fit Line dialog box for selecting a regression line

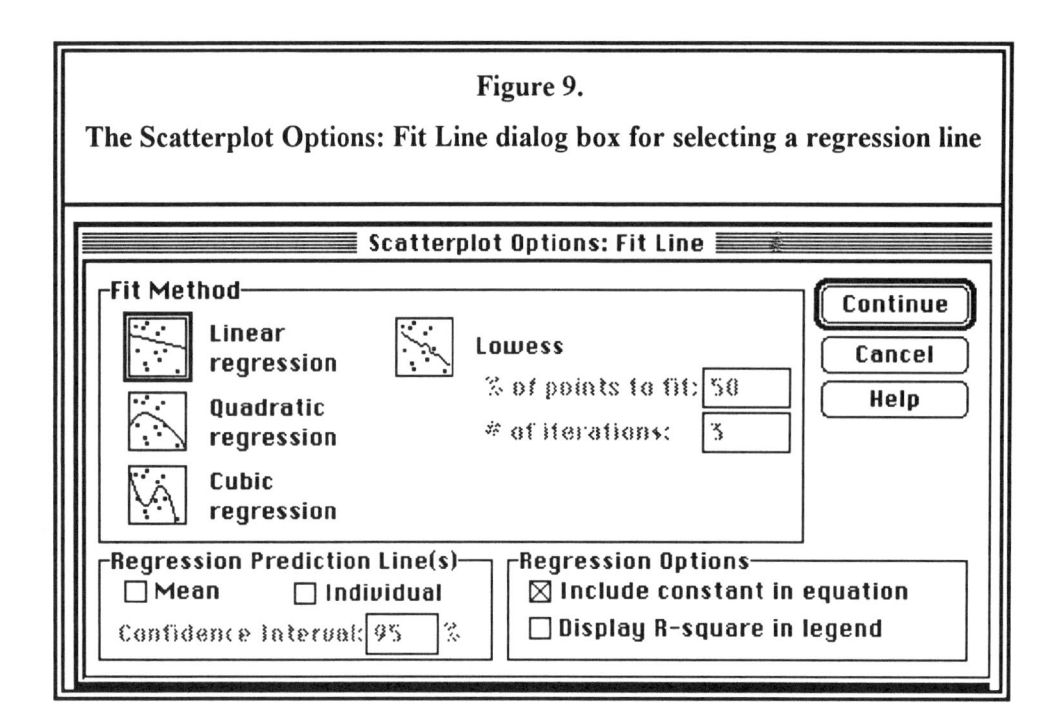

The resulting plot is shown in Figure 10.

Figure 10.

Scatterplot with regression line

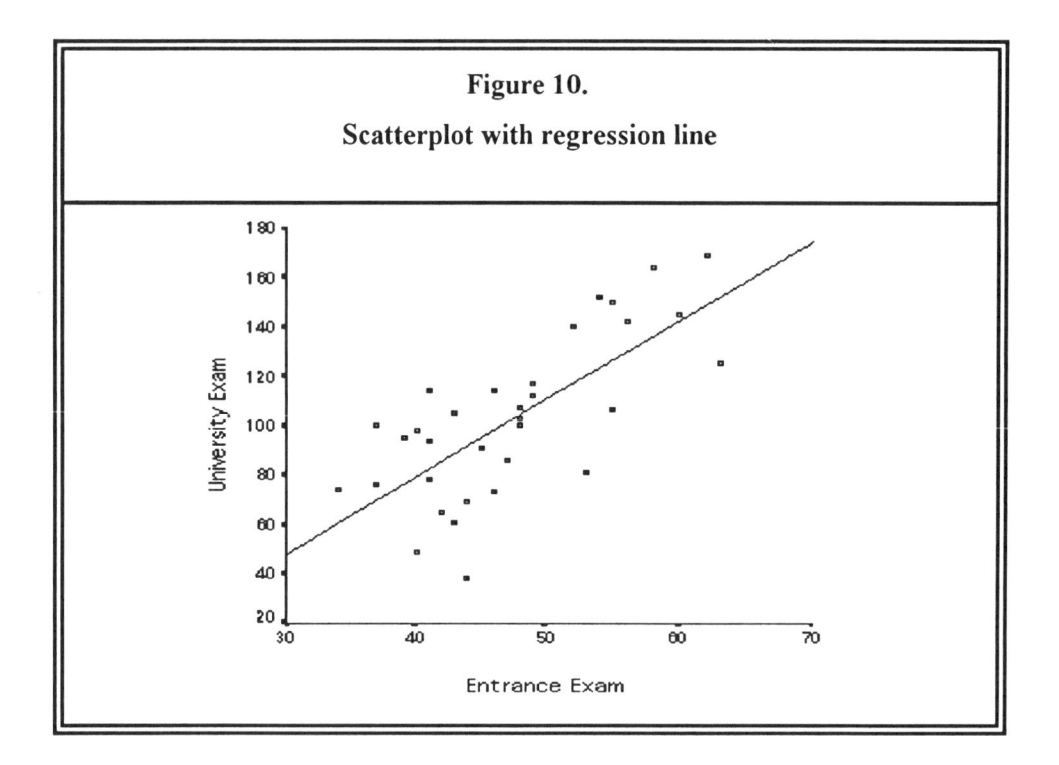

A **grouped scatterplot** is drawn by accessing the **Simple Scatterplot** dialog box and including a category variable in the **Set Markers by** box (here the category variable is *sex*). The result will be a scatterplot in which some of the points represent subjects in one category, and the remaining points represent the other subjects. In Chapter 4, for example, a data set was introduced which consisted of observations on four variables: height, weight, sex and blood group. A scatterplot of weight against height can be refined by entering sex as a category variable, when some of the points will represent males and others represent females.

Chapter 12 - Regression

In such a grouped scatterplot, it is possible to plot a regression line for the points in each category. With the height/weight/gender/blood group data in the Data Editor, proceed as follows.

- Choose **Graphs** and select **Scatter...**, to obtain the **Scatterplot** dialog box. Click on **Define**, to obtain the **Simple Scatterplot** dialog box.

- Transfer *weight*, *height* and *gender* to the **Y Axis**, **X Axis** and **Set Markers by** boxes, respectively. Press **OK** to obtain a scatterplot in which the males and females are represented by points of different colours.

- Click on the **Edit** button, change the colours to black, and change in turn the male and female symbols to small triangles and diamonds (or whatever symbols are preferred) using the **Colour** and **Marker** options within the **Attributes** menu.

- Select **Options** within the **Chart** menu to open the **Scatterplot Options** dialog box. In the area labelled **Fit Line**, mark the **Subgroups** checkbox. Click on **OK** to produce a scatterplot with a regression line drawn through each group of points.

- Finally change the colours of the regression lines to black and select appropriate line styles from the **Line Style** menu within the **Attributes** menu.

The completed scatterplot is shown in Figure 11.

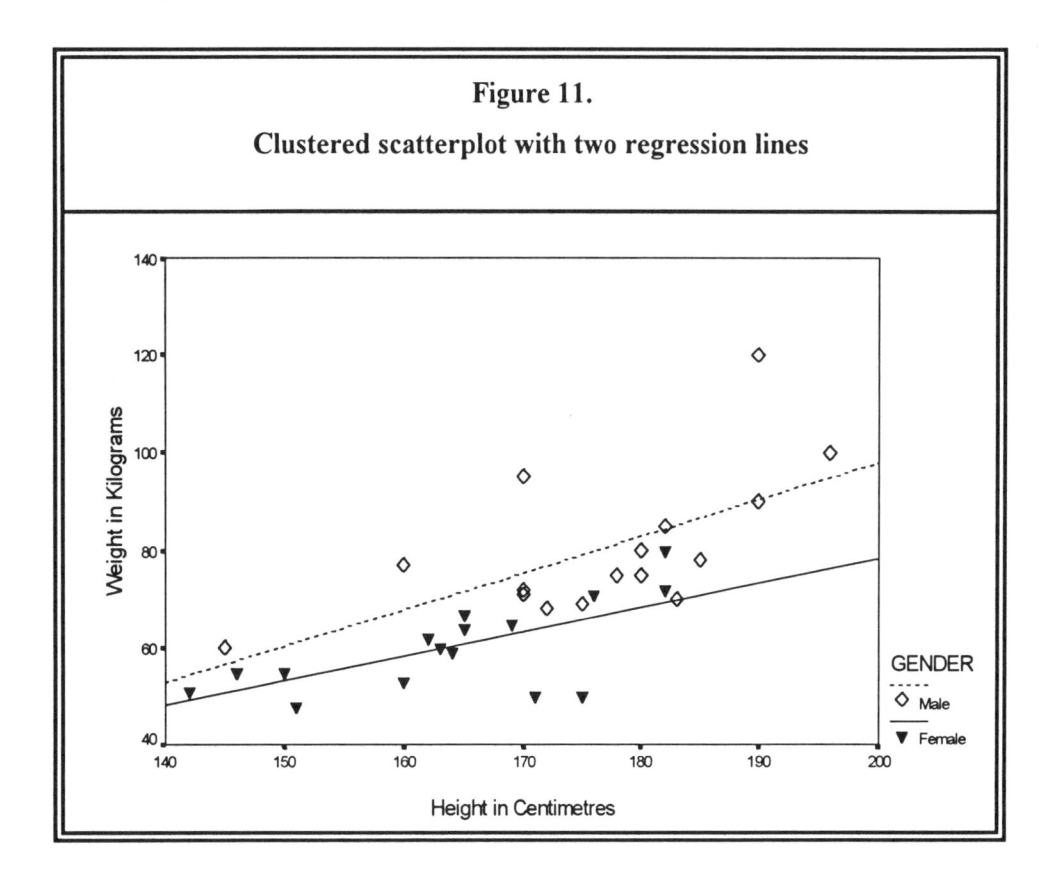

Figure 11.

Clustered scatterplot with two regression lines

Chapter 12 - Regression

EXERCISE 20

SIMPLE, TWO-VARIABLE REGRESSION

BEFORE YOU START

Before proceeding with this exercise, please read Chapter 12.

THE REGRESSION PROJECT

Purpose of the project

In this exercise, we shall look at some of the pitfalls that await the unwary user of regression techniques; in fact, as we shall see, all the cautions and caveats about the **Pearson correlation** apply with equal force to regression.

In Exercise 18, Anscombe's specially contrived data set (whose columns were named $X1$, $X2$, $Y1$, $Y2$, $Y3$, $Y4$) was saved in a file named **anscombe**. Scatterplots and correlation coefficients were obtained for the pairings $(X1, Y1)$, $(X1, Y2)$, $(X1, Y3)$ and $(X2, Y4)$. All sets yielded exactly the same value for the Pearson correlation. When the scatterplots were inspected, however, it was seen that the Pearson correlation was appropriate for only one data set: in the other sets, it would give the unwary user a highly misleading impression. One problem with the Pearson correlation is that it is very vulnerable to the leverage exerted by atypical data points, or **outliers** as they are termed. It can also show large values with monotonic but non-linear relationships. All this is equally true of the parameters of the regression equation. In this exercise, we return to Anscombe's data to investigate the statistics of the regression lines for the four sets of paired data.

Preparation of the data set

No preparation should be necessary: simply recall Anscombe's data set in file **anscombe** to the **Data Editor** window.

Running the simple regression procedure

Following the procedure described in Section 12.2, obtain the regression statistics of $Y1$, $Y2$ and $Y3$ upon $X1$ and of $Y4$ upon $X2$. Remember that the dependent variable is Y, and the independent variable is X. For present purposes, the plotting of the scatterplot of *ZRESID (**y-axis** box) against *ZPRED (**x-axis** box) should provide illuminating tests of the credibility of the assumption that the data are linear. Full details of preparing the **Linear Regression** dialog box are given in Section 12.2.1.

Since we want to carry out regression upon all four (X,Y) data sets, it will be necessary to prepare the **Regression** dialog box for the first pair to include a scatterplot of *ZRESID against *ZPRED, and then change the variable names on subsequent runs for the remaining three pairs. To return to the **Regression** dialog box after inspecting the scatterplot, click on the **Window** drop-down menu, select *anscombe*, click on the **Statistics** drop-down menu and select **Regression** again. After each run, you should record the value of **R Squared** and the regression equation, and note the appearance of the scatterplot.

Output listing for the simple regression analyses

The main features of the output listing of a simple regression analysis are fully explained in Chapter 12.

- **Compare the regression statistics and scatterplots for all four bivariate data sets. What do you notice about the values of R Squared and the appearances of the scatterplots?**

EXERCISE 21

MULTIPLE REGRESSION

BEFORE YOU START

The reader should study Section 12.3 before proceeding with this exercise.

THE PROJECT

A problem in reading research

Reading comprises many different component skills. A reading researcher hypothesises that certain specific kinds of pre-reading abilities and behaviour can predict later progress in reading, as measured by performance on reading tests taken some years after the child's first formal lessons. Let us, therefore, label the dependent variable (DV) in this study *progress*. While they are still very young indeed, many children evince a considerable grasp of English syntax in their speech. Our researcher devises a measure of their syntactic knowledge, *syntax*, based upon the average length of their uttered sentences. Some researchers, however, argue that an infant's prelinguistic babbling (which we shall label *vocal*) also plays a key role in their later reading performance. At the pre-reading stage, some very young children can acquire a sight vocabulary of several hundreds of words. The ability to pronounce these words on seeing them written down is known as logographic reading; but many authorities do not accept logographic reading. Our researcher, who views the logographic strategy as important, includes a measure of this skill, *logo*, in the study.

Preparing the data set

Fifty children are studied over a period beginning in infancy and extending through their school years. Their scores on the four measures, the DV *progress* (P), and the three IVs *logo* (L), *vocal* (V) and *syntax* (S), are listed in the appendix to this exercise. Since it would be very laborious for you to type in all the data during the exercise, we must hope that your instructor has already stored them in an accessible file. Let us suppose it is called **reading**. The data are also available in WWW (http://www.psyc.abdn.ac.uk/teaching/spss/spssbook.htm).

Exploring the data

The distributions of the variables are most easily explored by using the **Boxplot** option from the **Graphs** drop-down menu. Select **Boxplot**, click on the **Summaries of separate variables** button, and then click on **Define**. Transfer the variable names into the **Boxes Represent** box and click on **OK**. This will plot four boxes side-by-side for easy comparison.

Regression is most effective when each IV is strongly correlated with the DV but uncorrelated with the other IVs. Although the correlation matrix can be listed from within the regression procedure, it is often more useful to scrutinise the matrix before proceeding with a regression analysis in order to make judgements about which variables might be retained and which dropped from the analysis. For example, it might be advisable to make a choice between two variables which are highly correlated with one another.

Use the **Bivariate Correlations** procedure to compute the correlation matrix. The same procedure can conveniently be used for tabulating the means and standard deviations which are available as an option. After transferring the variable names to the **Variables** box, click on **Options** and select **Means and standard deviations** within the **Statistics** choice box. Click on **Continue** and then on **OK**. Notice that the DV *progress* shows substantial correlations with both *logo* and *syntax*. On the other hand, there is no appreciable correlation between *logo* and *syntax*. The remaining variable (*vocal*) shows little association with any of the other variables; although there is a hint of a negative correlation with *logo*.

Running the multiple regression analysis

Run the multiple regression of *progress* upon the three regressors, by following the procedure in Section 12.3. Remember that the **Dependent** variable is what you are predicting (*progress*) and the **Independent** variables are the predictors (*logo, vocal, syntax*). Use both the simultaneous (**Enter**) and stepwise (**Stepwise**) procedures.

Output listing for the multiple regression

The main features of a multiple regression output listing, both for the simultaneous and forward stepwise methods, are explained in Section 12.3 .

- **Do the decisions of the multiple regression procedure about which variables are important agree with your informal observations during the exploratory phase of the data analysis?**

- **Write out the regression equation which you would use to predict progress given a subject's values for logo, vocal and syntax.**

Appendix to Exercise 21 - The data

P	L	V	S	P	L	V	S	P	L	V	S	P	L	V	S
65	75	34	48	46	55	75	32	65	50	75	68	34	32	42	27
58	29	18	67	51	31	50	66	71	65	23	64	54	64	55	32
42	40	43	38	61	69	59	46	60	56	52	44	81	82	60	69
55	55	9	48	45	19	71	59	17	10	64	20	77	66	50	79
68	81	41	54	53	48	44	45	55	41	41	55	57	30	20	54
59	28	72	68	46	45	29	45	69	51	14	62	80	82	65	58
50	39	31	42	25	28	58	28	47	49	46	59	89	51	52	48
50	26	78	56	71	70	51	54	53	14	53	77	50	34	45	60
71	84	46	50	30	55	42	25	50	40	51	31	69	49	72	72
65	71	30	52	62	53	52	57	80	45	59	90	71	69	57	60
34	30	30	20	47	20	78	69	51	18	22	61	39	25	81	49
44	71	79	22	60	46	80	67	79	58	13	82				
47	62	26	30	70	66	40	61	51	43	31	50				

CHAPTER 13

LOGLINEAR ANALYSIS

13.1 INTRODUCTION

13.2 AN EXAMPLE OF A LOGLINEAR ANALYSIS

13.1 INTRODUCTION

The starting point for the analysis of nominal data on two or more attributes is a **contingency table**, each cell of which is the frequency of occurrence of individuals in various combinations of categories. In an earlier chapter (Chapter 11), we described the use of the chi-square test to test for the presence of an association between qualitative variables in a two-way contingency table.

In a two-way contingency table, the presence (or absence) of an association between the attributes is often very apparent from inspection alone: the formal statistical analysis merely confirms (or fails to confirm) a readily discernible pattern. It is quite possible, however, to have more complex contingency tables, in which individuals are classified with respect to three or more qualitative variables. In such multi-way contingency tables, it is often very difficult to discern associations; and indeed, it is only too easy to misinterpret what one does see. Recent years have seen great advances in the analysis of multi-way contingency tables (Everitt, 1977; Upton, 1978, 1986), and these new methods, collectively known as **loglinear analysis**, are now available in computing packages such as SPSS.

13.1.1 Comparison with ANOVA

To understand how loglinear analysis works, it may be helpful to recall some aspects of the completely randomised factorial analysis of variance, because there are some striking parallels between the two sets of techniques. In the ANOVA, it is possible to test for **main effects** and for **interactions**. Suppose that, following a three-factor experiment, all systematic sources are found to be significant. That would imply that the correct model for the experimental data must contain a term for each and every possible effect thus:

score = systematic effects* + error effects

(* 3 main effect terms + 3 two-way interaction terms + 1 three-way interaction term)

If, on the other hand, only one main effect and one of the possible two-way interactions were to prove significant, a much simpler model would account for a subject's score. This simplified model would contain, in addition to the error term, only one main effect term and one two-way interaction term thus:

score = systematic effects* + error effects

(* 1 main effect term + 1 two-way interaction term)

In the analysis of variance, the presence of an interaction often necessitates the re-interpretation of a significant main effect. Examination of the interaction may show that an experimental treatment has a strong effect at some levels (or combinations of levels) of other factors in the experiment, but no effect at other levels; in fact, the simple main effects of a factor may be in opposite directions at different levels of another factor.

Graphs of two-way tables of means are often very illuminating: if the factor profiles are non-parallel, a two-way interaction is indicated. Graphs of three-way tables, however, are more difficult to interpret visually, because, just as graphs of two-way tables reflect the presence of main effects as well as the two-way interaction, graphs of three-way tables reflect two-way interactions as well as the three-way interaction.

There are many parallels between the foregoing considerations and the loglinear analysis of multi-way contingency tables. Just as in the context of ANOVA, it is meaningful to speak of 'main effects' and of 'interactions' in loglinear analysis. Moreover, in interpreting multi-way tables by inspection alone, it is only too easy to confuse one effect for another. Loglinear analysis offers methods of testing the various effects separately. As in ANOVA, the presence of an interaction often necessitates the re-interpretation of a main effect; indeed, main effects, when considered on their own, can be highly deceptive. That is why the common procedure of 'collapsing' (i.e. combining the frequencies at all levels of some factors to exclude those factors from the classification) can produce misleading patterns in the data. The aim of a loglinear analysis is to find the model that best accounts for the data available. It contains both main effect terms and interaction terms, so that the values in the contingency table are expressed as the sum of main effects and interaction components.

There are, however, also important *differences* between loglinear and ANOVA models. In ANOVA, the target of the model is the **individual score** of a subject in the experiment. In loglinear analysis, the target is the **total frequency of observations in a cell.** The ANOVA model cannot predict the individual scores with perfect accuracy, because of the inevitable presence of errors of measurement, individual differences and experimental error. In contrast, as we shall see, it is **always** possible, by including all the possible terms in the loglinear model, to predict perfectly the cell frequencies in a contingency table. A model that contains all the possible effect terms is known as a **saturated model**. The purpose of a loglinear analysis is to see whether the cell frequencies may be adequately approximated by a model that contains **fewer** than the full set of possible treatment effects.

13.1.2 Why 'loglinear' analysis?

In the simple chi-square test of association in a two-by-two contingency table, the **expected frequencies** are obtained by **multiplying** marginal total frequencies and dividing the product by the total frequency. This is because the null hypothesis of independence of the variables implies that the probability of an individual occupying a cell of the classification is the **product** of the relevant main effect probabilities, the latter being estimated from the marginal totals. (Recall that the probability of the joint occurrence of independent events is the **product** of their separate probabilities.) Loglinear analysis exploits the fact that the logarithm (log) of a product is the **sum** of the logs of the terms in the product. Thus the **log** of the cell frequencies may be expressed as a **linear** (i.e. additive) function of the **logs** of the components. If one were to work directly with the cell frequencies, rather than their logs, one would require a **multiplicative** model for the data.

While that is feasible, the simplicity of a summative, ANOVA-type model would be lost.

13.1.3 Constructing a loglinear model

The purpose of a loglinear analysis is to construct a model such that the cell frequencies in a contingency table are accounted for in terms of a minimum number of terms. Several strategies can be followed in the construction of such a model, but the **backward hierarchical method** is perhaps the easiest to understand. The first step is to construct a **saturated model** for the cell frequencies, in which all the component effects are present. This model, as we have seen, will predict the cell frequencies perfectly. The next step is to remove the highest-order interaction, to determine the effect this would have upon the closeness with which the model predicts the cell frequencies. It may be that this interaction can be removed without affecting appreciably the accuracy of estimation of the target frequencies. The process of progressive elimination is continued, and each time a term is removed, a statistical test is carried out to determine whether the accuracy of prediction falls to a sufficient extent to show that the component most recently excluded should indeed be one of the components in the final model. The assessment of the goodness-of-fit at each stage of the procedure is made by means of a statistic known as the **likelihood ratio** (called **L.R. Chisq** by SPSS), which has a known distribution.

The evaluation of the final model is made by comparing the observed and expected frequencies for each cell using the likelihood ratio as described above; but it is also advisable to examine the distribution of **residuals** (the differences between the observed and expected frequencies), or more conveniently, the **standardised residuals** (the residuals expressed in standardised form) in a manner similar to that described for regression in the previous chapter.

13.1.4 Small expected frequencies

Just as in the case of the chi-square test, the size of the **expected frequency** (not the observed frequency) in each cell must be adequate for the analysis to be worth while. Small expected frequencies can lead to a drastic loss of power.

Problems with low expected cell frequencies should not arise provided:

(i) there are not too many variables in comparison with the size of the sample;

(ii) there are no categories with very few cases.

Tabachnick and Fidell (1996) recommend examining the expected cell frequencies for all **two-way associations** to ensure that all **expected frequencies** are greater than 1 and that no more than 20% are less than 5. If there is any doubt about the assumption of adequate expected cell frequencies, they can be checked out by using the **Crosstabs** procedure.

13.2 AN EXAMPLE OF A LOGLINEAR ANALYSIS

13.2.1 A three-way contingency table

In an investigation of the relationships between success on a second year university psychology statistics course and a number of possibly relevant background variables, researchers collected a body of information on a number of students, including whether or not they had taken an advanced school mathematics course and whether they had passed a data-processing examination in their first year at university. On each student's record, it was also noted whether he or she had passed the second year psychology statistics examination. (It will be noted that these yes/no variables are not true dichotomies, but artificial ones created from interval data. For present purposes, however, we shall assume that they are true qualitative variables.)

The data are presented in Table 1.

Table 1.
A three-way contingency table

Advanced Maths	Yes				No			
Data Processing	Pass		Fail		Pass		Fail	
Psychology Statistics	Pass	Fail	Pass	Fail	Pass	Fail	Pass	Fail
CELL FREQUENCIES	47	10	4	10	58	17	10	20

It is useful to summarise the cell frequencies for the categories of the variables considered separately, as shown in Table 2.

Table 2.
Summary of cell frequencies for the categories in each variable.

Advanced Maths	Yes	71	No	105	Total	176
Data Processing	Pass	132	Fail	44	Total	176
Psych Statistics	Pass	119	Fail	57	Total	176

It can be seen from Table 2 that of the 176 students in the study, 71 had taken advanced mathematics, and 105 had not. From Table 1, it can be seen that of those who had taken advanced mathematics, 57 passed first year data-processing and 14 did not, compared with 75 passes and 30 failures in the non-mathematical group. Relatively speaking, therefore, more of the mathematical group passed first year data-processing. Turning now to the statistics examination, it can be seen that of the mathematical group, the pass ratio was 51:20, compared with 68:37 in the non-mathematical group; and among those who had passed data-processing, the success ratio was 105:27, compared with 14:30 in the group that had failed data processing.

First, let us consider the (very unlikely) null hypothesis that there are **no links whatsoever** among the three variables studied. Suppose there is no tendency for those who have taken school mathematics to pass first year data-processing, no tendency for those who have passed data-processing to pass second year statistics and so on. It is a relatively simple matter, using a pocket calculator, to use the appropriate marginal totals to obtain the expected cell frequencies in a calculation similar to that appropriate for a two-way contingency table. Since there are three dichotomous (or pseudo-dichotomous) variables, there are 8 expected cell frequencies, the values of which are shown in Table 3. A way of computing these expected frequencies with SPSS will be described in Section 13.2.4.

Table 3.

Observed (O) and expected (E) cell frequencies for Table 1

Advanced Maths	Yes				No			
Data Processing	Pass		Fail		Pass		Fail	
Psychology Statistics	Pass	Fail	Pass	Fail	Pass	Fail	Pass	Fail
Cell Freq O	47	10	4	10	58	17	10	20
Cell Freq E	36.00	17.25	12.00	5.75	53.25	25.50	17.75	8.50

In several cells, the observed frequencies differ markedly from the expected values, suggesting that the complete independence model gives a poor account of the data. Clearly at least some associations are present among the three variables; but where exactly are they?

A loglinear analysis on SPSS can answer that question very easily. SPSS offers a hierarchical loglinear procedure within the **loglinear** menu. This procedure begins by constructing a fully saturated model for the cell frequencies, and works backwards in the manner described above, in order to arrive at a model with a minimum number of terms. Some of these are of little interest: for example, there are fewer subjects in the advanced mathematics group than there are in the non-mathematical group, so we can expect a main effect term for this variable in the final model. Main effects are usually unimportant in loglinear analysis. In the terms of ANOVA, we are seeking **interactions**, rather than **main effects**: the presence of associations among the three variables will necessitate the inclusion of interaction terms in the model.

13.2.2 Procedure for a loglinear analysis

- Using the procedures described in Section 3.5, define three coding variables: *maths*, *dataproc* and *psystats*. A fourth variable, *count* will contain the cell frequencies. Type in the data and save the set in the usual way. The complete SPSS data set is shown in Figure 1.

Figure 1.

The data grid showing the SPSS data set

	maths	dataproc	psystats	count
1	1	1	1	47
2	1	1	2	10
3	1	2	1	4
4	1	2	2	10
5	2	1	1	58
6	2	1	2	17
7	2	2	1	10
8	2	2	2	20

- It is now necessary to inform SPSS that the variable *count* contains frequencies and not simply scores. The procedure is described in Section 3.9.2. Choose
Data
    Weight Cases

to open the **Weight Cases** dialog box (Chapter 3, Figure 19), and transfer the variable *count* to the **Frequency Variable** box. Click on **OK**.

- The next stage is to confirm (by using the **Crosstabs** procedure in Section 11.3.2) that the expected frequencies are sufficiently large. Choose
Statistics
    Summarize
        Crosstabs

and then complete the **Crosstabs** dialog box (Figure 2) by transferring *dataproc* to the **Row(s)** box, *psystats* to the **Column(s)** box, and *maths* to the lowest box. Click on the **Cells** button to bring to the screen the **Crosstabs: Cell Display** dialog box (See Chapter 11, Figure 12). Within the **Counts** box, mark the **Expected** check box, click on **Continue** and then **OK**.

Chapter 13 - Loglinear Analysis

Figure 2.

The completed Crosstabs dialog box.

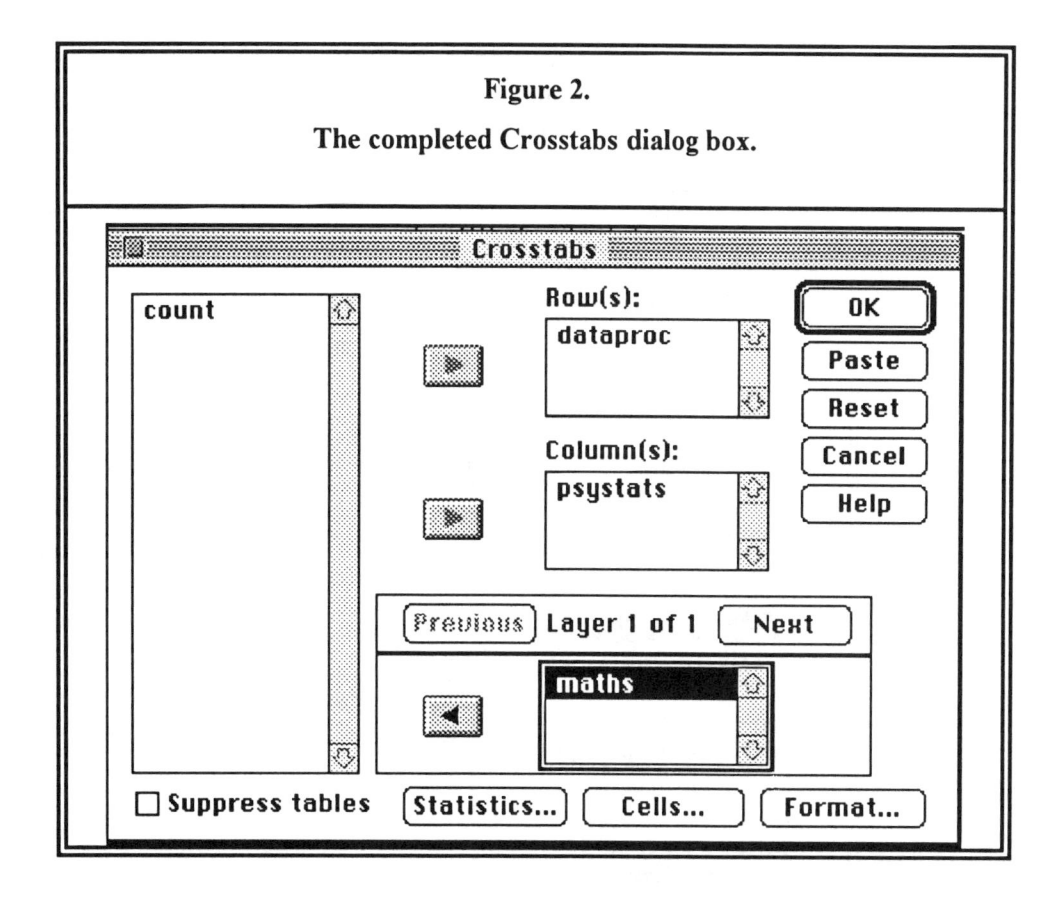

[Crosstabs dialog box showing count variable list, Row(s): dataproc, Column(s): psystats, Layer 1 of 1: maths, with OK, Paste, Reset, Cancel, Help buttons, and Suppress tables checkbox with Statistics..., Cells..., Format... buttons]

The **Crosstabs** procedure presents two-way contingency tables for each layer of *maths*, because that was chosen as the layering variable. The table for the first level of *maths* is shown in Output Listing 1.

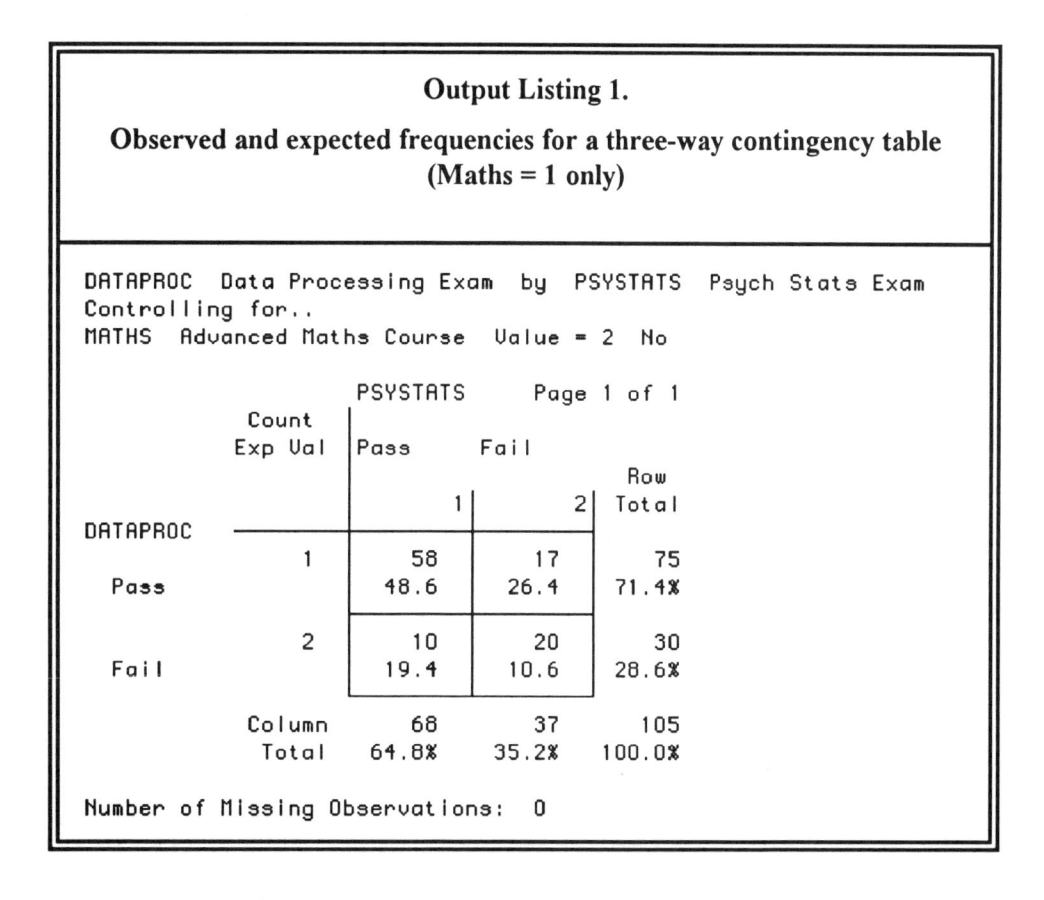

Output Listing 1.

Observed and expected frequencies for a three-way contingency table (Maths = 1 only)

```
DATAPROC  Data Processing Exam  by  PSYSTATS  Psych Stats Exam
Controlling for..
MATHS  Advanced Maths Course  Value = 2  No

                  PSYSTATS        Page 1 of 1
         Count
         Exp Val  Pass      Fail
                                      Row
                       1         2|  Total
DATAPROC
              1      58        17      75
         Pass      48.6      26.4    71.4%

              2      10        20      30
         Fail      19.4      10.6    28.6%

         Column     68        37     105
         Total    64.8%     35.2%   100.0%

Number of Missing Observations:  0
```

309

Chapter 13 - Loglinear Analysis

Provided the expected frequencies meet the criteria described in Section 13.1.4, the loglinear analysis can proceed, and in this case they clearly do (the expected frequencies for Maths = 2 are also adequate).

The hierarchical loglinear procedure is run as follows:

- Select
  Statistics
    Loglinear (Figure 3)

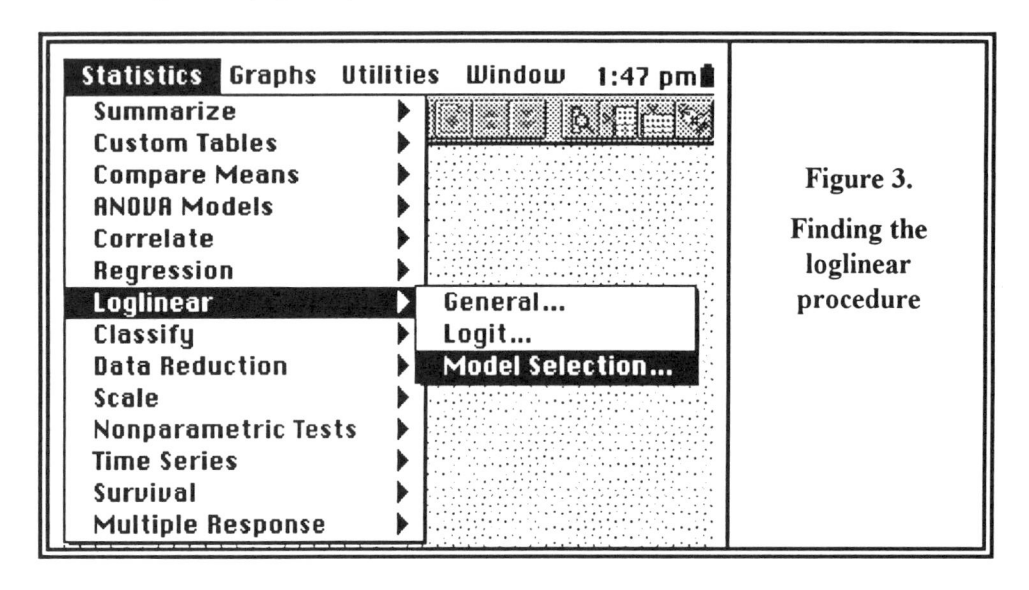

Figure 3. Finding the loglinear procedure

- Click on **Model Selection** to open the **Model Selection Loglinear Analysis** dialog box (the completed version is shown in Figure 4).

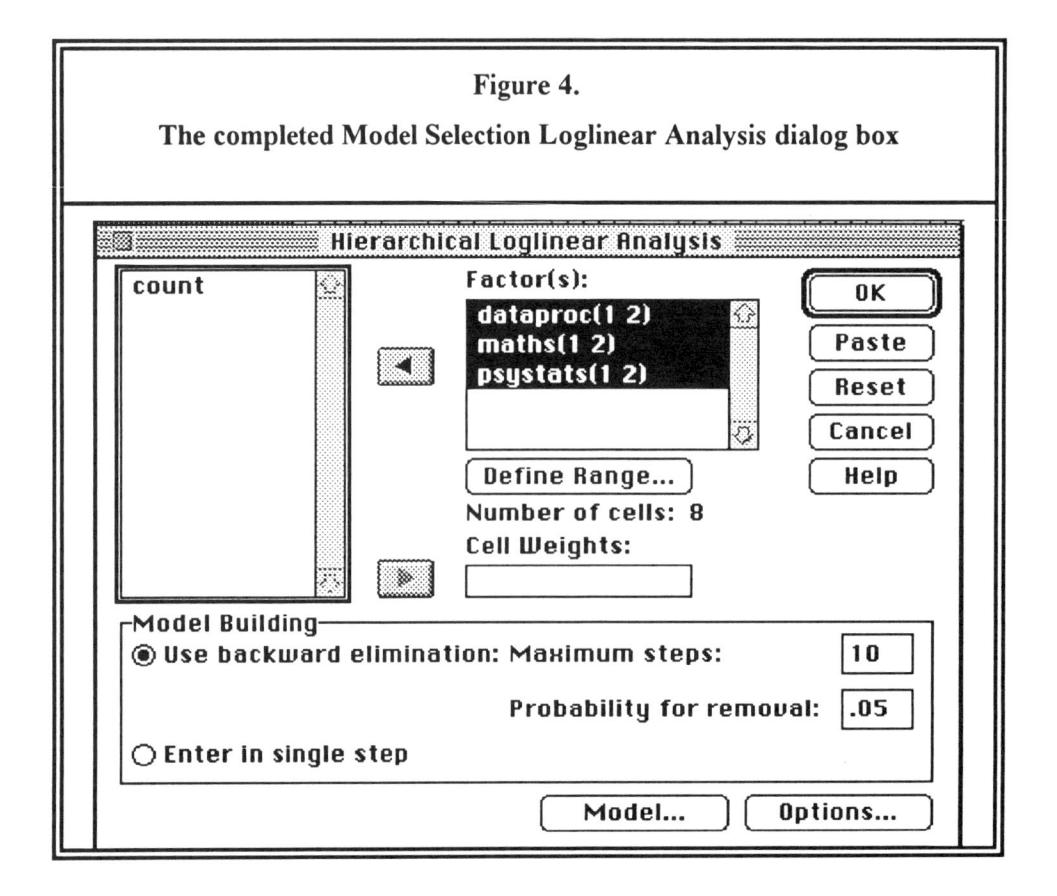

Figure 4. The completed Model Selection Loglinear Analysis dialog box

- Drag the cursor down the variable names *dataproc maths psystats* to highlight them, and click on ▶ to the left of the **Factor(s)** box to transfer these names into it. Click on **Define Range** and enter *1* into the **Minimum** box and *2* into the **Maximum** box. Click on **Continue**. The names will then appear with [1,2] after each of them (see Figure 4).

- Check that the radio button for the default model **Use backward elimination** is on and then click on **OK**.

13.2.3 Output listing for a loglinear analysis

Output Listing 2 contains information about the data and the factors.

This is followed by a table (not reproduced here) listing the counts (OBS count) for the combinations of the three factors. At this stage, SPSS is fitting a **saturated model**, MATHS*DATAPROC*PSYSTATS, to the cell frequencies. The table is useful for checking the accuracy of the data transcription.

```
Output Listing 2.
Basic design information

* * * * * * * *  H I E R A R C H I C A L    L O G    L I N E A R  * *

DATA    Information

        8 unweighted cases accepted.
        0 cases rejected because of out-of-range factor values.
        0 cases rejected because of missing data.
      176 weighted cases will be used in the analysis.


FACTOR Information

    Factor   Level  Label
    DATAPROC   2    Data Processing Exam
    MATHS      2    Advanced Maths Course
    PSYSTATS   2    Psych Stats Exam
```

Output Listing 3 shows tests of the various possible effects. It shows that K-way and higher order effects are zero, and that the K-way effects themselves are zero. These items give the tail probabilities for the effects of specified order and (where appropriate) a statement that an effect is significant. In this example, all effects are significant up to and including the two-way level of complexity. The three-way effect, however, is not significant.

Output Listing 3.
Tests of effects

```
******** HIERARCHICAL   LOG   LINEAR ********

Tests that K-way and higher order effects are zero.

    K    DF   L.R. Chisq   Prob   Pearson Chisq   Prob   Iteration

    3     1        .431   .5115           .426   .5141       3
    2     4      35.310   .0000         37.077   .0000       2
    1     7     110.282   .0000        123.000   .0000       0

- - - - - - - - - - - - - - - - - - - - - - - - - - - - - - - - -


Tests that K-way effects are zero.

    K    DF   L.R. Chisq   Prob   Pearson Chisq   Prob   Iteration

    1     3      74.972   .0000         85.923   .0000       0
    2     3      34.879   .0000         36.651   .0000       0
    3     1        .431   .5115           .426   .5141       0
```

Output Listings 4-7 show the most interesting part of the listing headed:

'Backward Elimination (p = .050) for Design 1 with generating class . . .'

The purpose of the analysis is to find the unsaturated model that gives the best fit to the observed data. This is achieved by checking that the model currently being tested does not give a significantly worse fit than its predecessor in the hierarchy.

Recall that in the hierarchical backward elimination method, the procedure starts with the most complex model (which in the present case contains all three factors, together with all their possible interactions), and progresses down the hierarchy of complexity, eliminating each effect from the model in turn and determining which decrement in accuracy is less than the **least-significant change in the chi-square value.** At each step, such an effect would be eliminated, leaving the remaining effects for inclusion:

'The best model has generating class . . . '

The procedure continues until no elimination produces a decrement with a probability greater than 0.05. The model containing the remaining effects is then adopted as 'The final model'. In this example, the final model is reached after four steps.

Output Listing 4.
Step 1 of the loglinear analysis

```
******* HIERARCHICAL  LOG  LINEAR *******

Backward Elimination (p = .050) for DESIGN 1 with generating class

  DATAPROC*MATHS*PSYSTATS

 Likelihood ratio chi square =      .00000    DF = 0  P = 1.000


If Deleted Simple Effect is           DF   L.R. Chisq Change   Prob   Iter

  DATAPROC*MATHS*PSYSTATS              1              .431    .5115    3

Step 1

  The best model has generating class

      DATAPROC*MATHS
      DATAPROC*PSYSTATS
      MATHS*PSYSTATS

  Likelihood ratio chi square =     .43090    DF = 1  P =  .512
```

At Step 2, MATHS*PSYSTATS is eliminated, because it has the largest probability (.6564).

Output Listing 5.
Step 2 of the loglinear analysis

```
If Deleted Simple Effect is           DF   L.R. Chisq Change   Prob   Iter

  DATAPROC*MATHS                       1            1.029    .3104    2
  DATAPROC*PSYSTATS                    1           32.098    .0000    2
  MATHS*PSYSTATS                       1             .198    .6564    2

Step 2

  The best model has generating class

      DATAPROC*MATHS
      DATAPROC*PSYSTATS

  Likelihood ratio chi square =     .62884    DF = 2  P =  .730
```

At Step 3, DATAPROC*MATHS is eliminated, because it has the larger probability (and it is greater than the criterion level of 0.05). Having processed all the interactions, it remains for any main effect which is not part of the remaining 2-way interaction to be included. In this case, MATHS is such a variable.

Chapter 13 - Loglinear Analysis

Output Listing 6.

Step 3 of the loglinear analysis

```
If Deleted Simple Effect is        DF    L.R. Chisq Change    Prob    Iter

DATAPROC*MATHS                      1           1.806        .1790    2
DATAPROC*PSYSTATS                   1          32.875        .0000    2

Step 3

  The best model has generating class

      DATAPROC*PSYSTATS
      MATHS

  Likelihood ratio chi square =    2.43511    DF = 3    P =  .487
```

At Step 4, neither of these effects can be eliminated, because both probabilities are less than 0.05. This, therefore, is adopted as the final model.

Output Listing 7.

The final step of the loglinear analysis

```
If Deleted Simple Effect is        DF    L.R. Chisq Change    Prob    Iter

DATAPROC*PSYSTATS                   1          32.875        .0000    2
MATHS                               1           6.610        .0101    2

Step 4

  The best model has generating class

      DATAPROC*PSYSTATS
      MATHS

  Likelihood ratio chi square =    2.43511    DF = 3    P =  .487
```

The final model includes the interaction between the variables representing the data processing exam and the psychology statistics exam, plus a main effect of maths. Note that there are no interactions involving the maths variable. Thus the most interesting finding is the interaction between the two examinations.

Finally, the computer lists the table of observed frequencies and the expected frequencies **as estimated by the final model** (Output Listing 8). The final chi-square test shows that these expected frequencies do **not** differ significantly from the observed frequencies (chi-square is not significant). This Table also lists the residuals and standardised residuals.

Output Listing 8.

Observed frequencies, expected frequencies and residuals estimated by the final model.

```
Observed, Expected Frequencies and Residuals.

      Factor         Code      OBS count  EXP count  Residual  Std Resid
   DATAPROC        Pass
    MATHS           Yes
     PSYSTATS       Pass         47.0       42.4       4.64       .71
     PSYSTATS       Fail         10.0       10.9       -.89      -.27
    MATHS           No
     PSYSTATS       Pass         58.0       62.6      -4.64      -.59
     PSYSTATS       Fail         17.0       16.1        .89       .22

   DATAPROC        Fail
    MATHS           Yes
     PSYSTATS       Pass          4.0        5.6      -1.65      -.69
     PSYSTATS       Fail         10.0       12.1      -2.10      -.60
    MATHS           No
     PSYSTATS       Pass         10.0        8.4       1.65       .57
     PSYSTATS       Fail         20.0       17.9       2.10       .50

Goodness-of-fit test statistics
   Likelihood ratio chi square =  2.43511    DF = 3   P = .487
            Pearson chi square =  2.39308    DF = 3   P = .495
```

13.2.4 Comparison with the total independence model

Notice that the expected frequencies estimated by the final model are much closer to the observed counts than those for the total independence model, whose values were listed in Table 3, and are reproduced in Table 4 for the purposes of comparison.

The reader might wish to use the loglinear procedure to check these values.

- After inserting the factor names and values in the **Factor(s)** box as before, click on the **Model** box. Within the **Specify model** box, select **Custom**. Enter the three factor names into the **Generating Class** box by clicking on each of *dataproc*, *maths* and *psystats*, following each variable name with ▶. Within the **Build Term(s)** box, click on **Interaction** and select **all 3-way**. Within the **Model Building** box, click on the **Enter in single step** option. The completed dialog box is shown in Figure 5.

- Click on **Continue** and then on **OK**.

Chapter 13 - Loglinear Analysis

Figure 5.

The completed dialog box for determining the expected frequencies assuming the total independence model

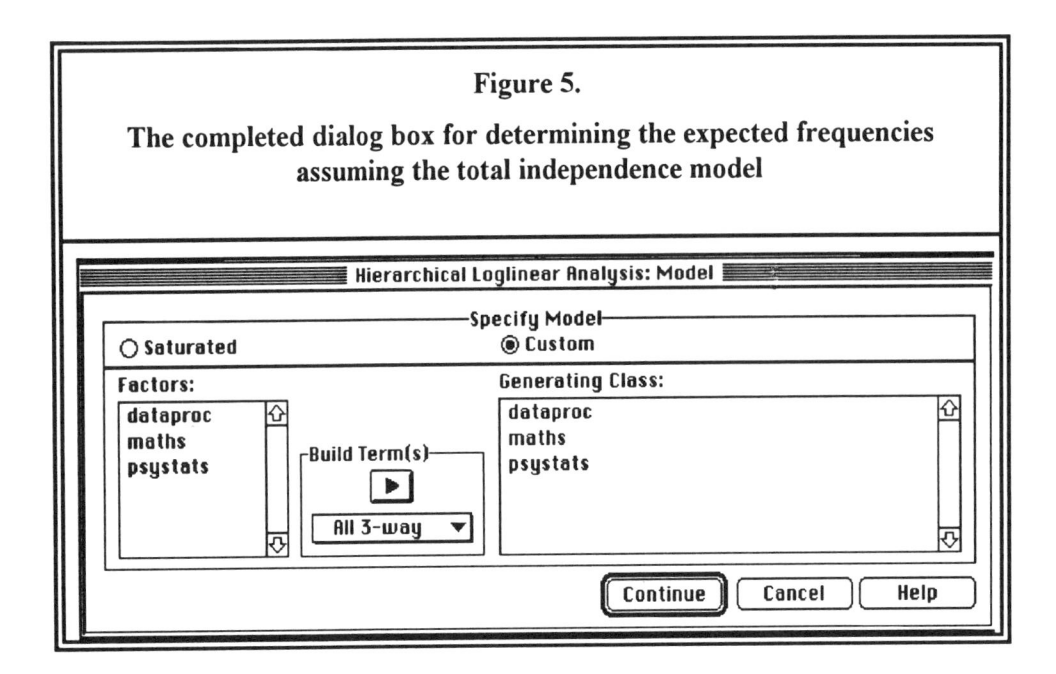

[Dialog box: Hierarchical Loglinear Analysis: Model — Specify Model: ○ Saturated ● Custom; Factors: dataproc, maths, psystats; Build Term(s): All 3-way; Generating Class: dataproc, maths, psystats; Continue, Cancel, Help]

Table 4 contrasts the observed and expected cell frequencies under the assumptions of the 'best model' generated by the loglinear procedure with the corresponding discrepancies under the total independence model.

Table 4.

Expected frequencies under the final loglinear model E(loglinear) and the total independence model E(independent)

Advanced Maths	Yes				No			
Data Processing	Pass		Fail		Pass		Fail	
Psychology Statistics	Pass	Fail	Pass	Fail	Pass	Fail	Pass	Fail
Cell Freq:								
Observed	47	10	4	10	58	17	10	20
E (loglinear)	42.4	10.9	5.6	12.1	62.6	16.1	8.4	17.9
E (independent)	36.0	17.3	12.0	5.8	53.3	25.5	17.8	8.5

EXERCISE 22

LOGLINEAR ANALYSIS

BEFORE YOU START

Before you proceed with this practical, please read Chapter 13.

THE PROJECT

Helping behaviour: The opposite-sex dyadic hypothesis

In the literature on helping behaviour by (and towards) men and women, there is much interest in three questions:

(1) Are women more likely to receive help?
(2) Are women more likely to give help?
(3) Are people more likely to help members of the opposite sex? (This is known as the **opposite-sex dyadic hypothesis**.)

A male or female confederate of the experimenter approached male and female students who were entering a university library and asked them to participate in a survey. Table 1 shows the incidence of helping in relation to the sex of the confederate and that of the subject.

Table 1.
Results of an experiment to test the opposite-sex dyadic hypothesis

Sex of Confederate	Sex of Subject	Help yes	Help no
Male	Male	52	35
	Female	21	43
Female	Male	39	40
	Female	23	75

Exploring the data

Before carrying out any formal analysis, however, a brief inspection of the contingency table may prove informative. First of all, we notice that, on the whole, help was more likely to be refused than given; moreover, the females helped less than did the males. In view of the generally lower rate of helping in the female subjects, therefore, there seems to be little support for the hypothesis that females help more. Finally, turning to the third question, although the male subjects did help the male confederate more often, the female subjects tended to be more helpful towards the male confederate. This provides some support for the opposite-sex dyadic hypothesis.

Procedure for a loglinear analysis

In order to answer the three research questions, these results will be subjected to a **hierarchical loglinear analysis** (following the **backward elimination** strategy), with a view to fitting the most parsimonious **unsaturated model**. Prepare the data set exactly as described in Section 13.2.2. There are three variables in the contingency table:

(1) Confederate's Sex (*confsx*).
(2) Subject's Sex (*subjsx*).
(3) Subject's Response (*help*).

Since there must be a coding variable for each of these, plus another variable of cell counts (*count*), the data set will comprise four variables in all. Prepare four columns in the Data Editor window, adding appropriate extended variable names and the value labels of the coding variables. Run the loglinear procedure (ignoring the preliminary Crosstabs operation) as described in Section 13.2.2.

Output listing for the loglinear analysis

The main features of the output listing for a hierarchical loglinear analysis are described in Section 13.2.3. The listing reports tests of models in which one of the two-way interaction terms has been left out. It can be seen that only the interaction between *confsx* and *subjsx* can be removed so that the increment in the **L-R chi-square** has a p-value not less than 0.05. That term, therefore, is dropped from the model. The final model has two interaction terms: *confsx*help* and *subjsx* help*.

- **Note down the p-value of the L-R chi-square along with its p-value associated with the best-fitting model. This is a measure of the success of the model to predict the cell frequencies: the greater the size of the p-value, the better the fit.**

Finally the listing shows a table of 'Observed, Expected Frequencies and Residuals'. Notice how small the residuals are.

Test the hypothesis of total independence of all three variables, using the procedure described in Section 13.2.4.

- **Write down the new value of the L-R chi-square along with its p-value. What do you conclude about the total independence model?**

CONCLUSION

It should be quite clear from the foregoing comparisons that the final loglinear model is a very considerable improvement upon the model of total independence. Loglinear models provide a powerful tool for teasing out the relationships among the variables in multi-way contingency tables.

CHAPTER 14

DISCRIMINANT ANALYSIS

14.1	**INTRODUCTION**
14.2	**DISCRIMINANT ANALYSIS WITH SPSS**

14.1 INTRODUCTION

14.1.1 Discriminant analysis

In Section 5.8, the rationale of multivariate analysis of variance (MANOVA) was outlined. Essentially, the multivariate technique known as **discriminant analysis** is the obverse of MANOVA. In the MANOVA situation, you know which categories the subjects belong to and you want to explore the possibility of identifying a composite variable which shows up differences among the groups. In other circumstances, however, one might wish to ascertain **category membership** on the basis of subjects' performance on the DVs. It would be of considerable value, for example, on the basis of records of children on a number of variables recorded during the earlier school years, to predict which children will go on to further education, which will secure immediate employment on leaving school, and which will join the ranks of the unemployed. Discriminant analysis offers answers to such questions.

The composite variable obtained in MANOVA is known as a **discriminant function**, because it is a weighted sum of the DVs, with the weightings chosen such that the distributions for the various groups are separated to the greatest possible extent. In discriminant analysis, the very same composite variable is constructed, so that category membership can be predicted to the greatest possible extent. Mathematically, therefore, the techniques of MANOVA and discriminant analysis have much in common. In the latter, however, the attempt is made to predict category membership using the discriminant function. There are other important differences between MANOVA and discriminant analysis (see Tabachnick & Fidell, 1996). For present purposes, however, their similarities are more notable than their differences, and it is worth noting that MANOVA computing programs can be used to perform discriminant analysis.

The reader will have noted that in the present book, having defined the terms **dependent variable** and **independent variable** in the context of experimental, as opposed to correlational, research, - see Section 3.2, we are now following the convention favoured by several other authors, such as Tabachnick & Fidell (1996) and Kerlinger (1986), whereby an independent variable is any variable that is supposed to have a causal effect upon another, irrespective of whether one is manipulating it directly, or merely measuring it as it occurs with other variables in the subjects studied. As a consequence of this, it is important to observe that in performing a discriminant analysis on data from an experiment with two or more DVs, the former DVs now become the **independent variables**, and the group variable is now the **dependent variable**.

The purpose of discriminant analysis is, given the independent variables IV_1, IV_2, ..., IV_p, to find a linear function (D) of the IVs such that when a **one-way ANOVA** is carried out to compare the categories of the qualitative dependent variable with respect to D, the ratio $SS_{between}/SS_{total}$ is as large as possible. The function D will be of the general form:

$$D = b_0 + b_1(IV_1) + b_2(IV_2) + \ldots + b_p(IV_p)$$

Chapter 14 - Discriminant Analysis

As in multiple regression, it is possible to identify those variables that make significant contributions to the predictive process and drop the others from the final function. There are many other parallels between the two statistical techniques.

Recall that in one-way ANOVA, the total sum of squares (SS_{total}), which is a measure of the total dispersion of the scores around the grand mean, can be partitioned into two components:

(1) $SS_{between}$

(2) SS_{within}

The first of these components is the dispersion of the group means around the grand mean; the second is the dispersion of the scores around their group means. The three sums of squares are related according to the identity:

$$SS_{total} = SS_{between} + SS_{within}$$

ANOVA will show a smaller p-value as the ratio of $SS_{between}$ to SS_{within} becomes greater, or equally, as the ratio of $SS_{between}$ to SS_{total} approaches unity (i.e. the group means show large dispersion, whereas the individual scores lie close to their group means). This second ratio (i.e. $SS_{between}/SS_{total}$) is sometimes known as **eta squared (η^2)** or the **correlation ratio**, and is one of the oldest measures of the strength of an experimental effect.

Ratios of variances are formed to test main effects and interactions using the familiar statistic *F*. This can be expressed in another way. In the univariate case (i.e. where there is just one dependent variable), the ratio SS_{within}/SS_{total} is the value of a statistic known as **Wilks' lambda (Λ)**. Hence

$$\eta^2 + \Lambda = \frac{SS_{between}}{SS_{total}} + \frac{SS_{within}}{SS_{total}} = \frac{SS_{between} + SS_{within}}{SS_{total}} = 1$$

Thus in the univariate case, Λ is $1 - \eta^2$. Because the relatively small dispersion of the individual scores around their group means implies a relatively large dispersion among the group means, *smaller* values of Λ are more likely to be significant.

In the multivariate case (i.e. where there is more than one dependent variable) as in discriminant analysis, Λ becomes a ratio of determinants of matrices of sums of squares and cross-products. It is used to assess whether a function of the independent variables (the discriminating variables) reliably discriminates among the categories of the dependent variable. Since the sampling distribution of Λ is very complex, its significance is more conveniently found from a chi-square approximation.

For each of the categories of the dependent variable, there will be a (supposedly normal) distribution of *D* for the members of that category. The distributions will usually overlap, of course; but the goal of discriminant analysis is to find values for the constants (b_0, b_1, . . ., b_p) in the discriminant function such that the overlap among the distributions of *D* is minimised. In other words, the idea is to spread out the distributions of *D* to the greatest possible extent. If there are only two categories in the dependent variable, only one discriminant function can be constructed.

14.1.2 Types of discriminant analysis

There are three types of discriminant analysis (DA): **direct**, **hierarchical**, and **stepwise**. In **direct** DA, all the variables enter the equations at once; in **hierarchical** DA, they enter according to a schedule set by the researcher; and in **stepwise** DA, statistical criteria alone determine the order of entry. In most analyses, the researcher has no reason for giving some predictors higher priority than others. The third (stepwise) method, therefore, is the most generally applicable and is the only one discussed in this chapter.

14.1.3 Stepwise discriminant analysis

The statistical procedure for stepwise discriminant analysis is similar to that for multiple regression, in that the effect of the addition or removal of an IV is monitored by a statistical test and the result used as a basis for the inclusion of that IV in the final analysis. When there are only two groups, there is just one discriminant function. With more than two groups, however, there can be several functions; though it is unusual for more than the first three to be useful.

Various statistics are available for weighing up the addition or removal of variables from the analysis, but the most commonly used is **Wilks' Lambda (Λ)**. The significance of the change in Λ when a variable is entered or removed is obtained from an **F test**. At each step of adding a variable to the analysis, the variable with the largest F (**F TO ENTER**) is included. This process is repeated until there are no further variables with an F value greater than the critical minimum threshold value. At the same time, any variable which had been added earlier, but which no longer contributes to maximising the assignment of cases to the correct groups because other variables in concert have taken over its role, is removed when its F value (**F TO REMOVE**) drops below the critical maximum threshold value. These critical values are listed in Output Listing 3.

Eventually, the process of adding and subtracting variables is completed, and a summary table is listed showing which variables were added or subtracted at each step. The variables remaining in the analysis are those used in the discriminant function(s). The first table thereafter shows which functions are statistically reliable. The first function provides the best means of predicting membership of the groups: later functions may or may not contribute reliably to the prediction process. Additional tables for listing the functions and their success rate for correct prediction can be requested. Plots can also be specified.

14.2 DISCRIMINANT ANALYSIS WITH SPSS

A problem in vocational guidance

A school's vocational guidance officer would like to be able to help senior pupils to choose which subjects to study at university. Fortunately, some data are available from a project on the background interests and school-leaving examination results of samples of architectural, engineering and psychology students. The students also filled in a questionnaire about their extra-curricular interests, including outdoor pursuits, drawing, painting, computing, and kit construction. The problem is this: can knowledge of the pupils' scores on a number of variables be used to predict their subject category at university? In this study, then, subject category at university (psychologists, architects or engineers) is the dependent variable, and all the other variables are the independent variables.

14.2.1 Procedure for discriminant analysis

Preparing the SPSS data set

Since the data for this example consists of the results of 118 persons over ten variables, it would be extremely tedious for readers to enter the data themselves into the **Data Editor** window but the data are available for anyone interested on WWW (http://www.psyc.abdn.ac.uk/teaching/spss/spssbook.htm).

Similar data would be entered in the following manner. Using the techniques described in Section 3.3, define the coding variable *studsubj* (full variable label: *Study Subject*), comprising three values: *1 = Architects, 2 = Psychologists, 3 = Engineers*. This is the dependent variable. Define the independent variables *sex* (which, like *studsubj*, is also a grouping variable), *conkit*, *model*, *draw*, *paint*, *outdoor*, *comput*, *vismod*, and *quals* (see Figure 2). Type in the data in the usual way. To specify the user-missing values, follow the procedure described in Section 3.3.10. For example, since the value of the independent variable *qual* does not exceed 30, an appropriate user-missing value would be a large number, such as 99 (see Figure 1).

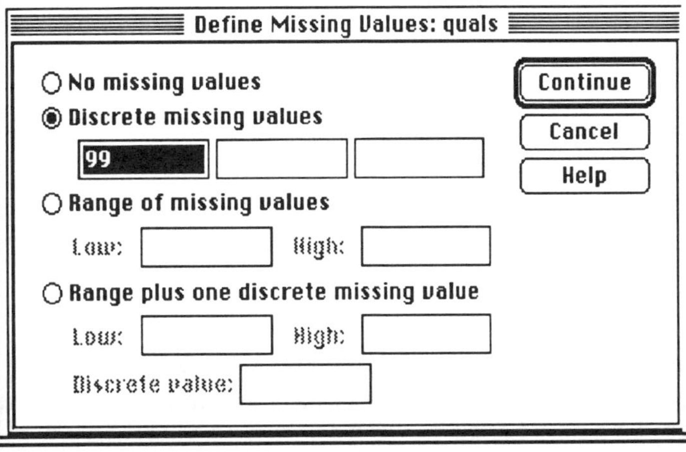

Figure 1.

Part of the Define Missing Value: quals dialog box specifying the user-missing value

Chapter 14 - Discriminant Analysis

Figure 2 shows the first four cases in the completed SPSS data set.

Figure 2.
The first four cases in the SPSS data set

	studs	sex	conkit	model	draw	paint	outdoor	comput	vismod	quals
1	1	1	2	3	2	0	1	0	5	99
2	1	1	3	2	6	2	2	0	6	10
3	1	2	5	5	6	7	0	3	4	8
4	1	1	5	6	7	1	4	3	6	99

Running discriminant analysis

Discriminant analysis is run as follows:

- Choose
  Statistics
     Classify (see Figure 3)
        Discriminant...

  to open the **Discriminant Analysis** dialog box (the completed version is shown in Figure 4).

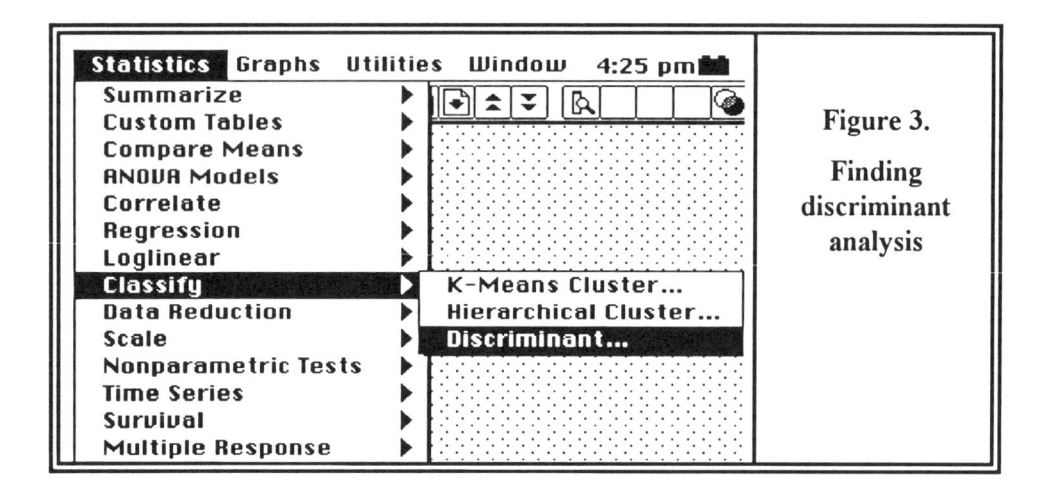

Figure 3. Finding discriminant analysis

- Select the dependent variable (here it is *studsubj*, the subject of study) and click on ▶ to the left of the **Grouping Variable** box to transfer the name. Click on **Define Range** and type *1* into the **Minimum** box and *3* into the **Maximum** box. Drag the cursor down the rest of the variable names to highlight them, and click on ▶ to the left of the **Independents** box to transfer them all. Since a hierarchical analysis is going to be used, click on **Use stepwise method**.

- Recommended options include one-way ANOVAs for each of the variables across the three levels of the independent variable and a final summary table showing the success or failure of the analysis. To obtain the ANOVAs, click on **Statistics** and within the **Descriptives** box, select **Univariate ANOVAs**. Click on **Continue**. To obtain the success/failure table, click on **Classify** and within the **Display** box, select **Summary table**.

- Click on **Continue** and then on **OK**.

Figure 4.
The completed Discriminant Analysis dialog box

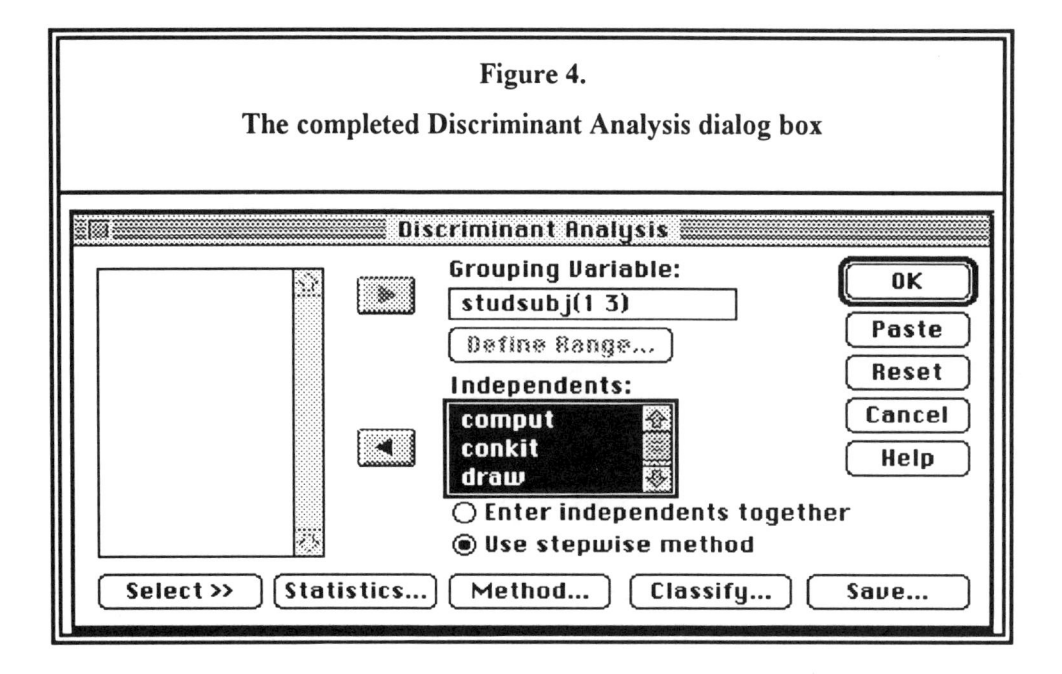

14.2.2 Output listing for discriminant analysis

Information about the data and the number of cases in each category of the grouping variable

The information about the data is shown in Output Listing 1.

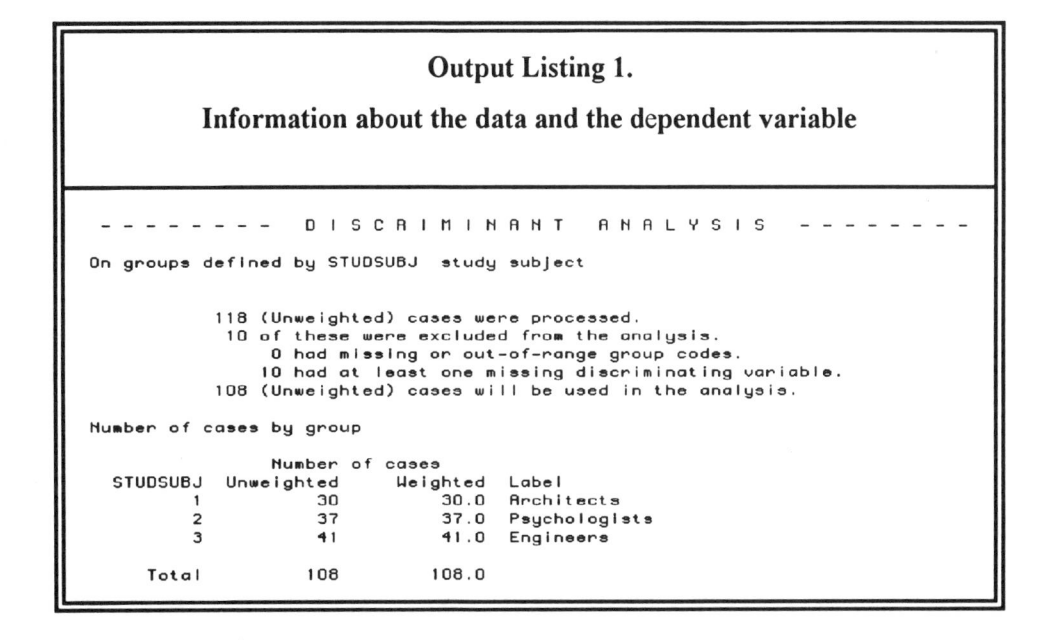

Output Listing 1.
Information about the data and the dependent variable

```
- - - - - - - -   D I S C R I M I N A N T   A N A L Y S I S   - - - - - - - -
On groups defined by STUDSUBJ   study subject

        118 (Unweighted) cases were processed.
         10 of these were excluded from the analysis.
            0 had missing or out-of-range group codes.
           10 had at least one missing discriminating variable.
        108 (Unweighted) cases will be used in the analysis.

Number of cases by group

             Number of cases
STUDSUBJ  Unweighted    Weighted  Label
       1          30        30.0  Architects
       2          37        37.0  Psychologists
       3          41        41.0  Engineers

   Total        108       108.0
```

Chapter 14 - Discriminant Analysis

Statistics

The optional **Univariate ANOVAs** selection is shown in Output Listing 2.

Output Listing 2.

Univariate ANOVAs

Wilks' Lambda (U-statistic) and univariate F-ratio
with 2 and 105 degrees of freedom

Variable	Wilks' Lambda	F	Significance
COMPUT	.99997	.0013	.9987
CONKIT	.84396	9.7064	.0001
DRAW	.89612	6.0862	.0032
MODEL	.96136	2.1099	.1264
OUTDOOR	.94183	3.2427	.0430
PAINT	.83454	10.4086	.0001
QUALS	.87670	7.3838	.0010
SEX	.76652	15.9914	.0000
VISMOD	.84351	9.7397	.0001

This indicates whether there is a statistically significant difference among the dependent variable means (*studsubj*) for each independent variable. All these differences are significant except *comput* and *model*.

Selection of variables

Details of Stepwise variable selection (Output Listing 3) and Canonical Discriminant Functions (not reproduced here) are listed. Notice the value of **Minimum F to enter** is 3.84 - this critical value is the minimum value for entering variables in a stepwise analysis.

Output Listing 3.

Rules for stepwise variable selection

```
Stepwise variable selection
    Selection rule:  minimize Wilks' Lambda
    Maximum number of steps................    18
    Minimum tolerance level................  .00100
    Minimum F to enter..................... 3.84000
    Maximum F to remove.................... 2.71000
```

Chapter 14 - Discriminant Analysis

Entering and removing variables step-by-step

The output listing starts with a table of variables and their **F to Enter** values (not reproduced) showing that *sex* has the highest **F to Enter** value. It is, therefore, selected as the first variable to enter at Step 1 (Output Listing 4).

At Step 2, the next variable with the highest **F-to-enter** value (*paint*) is entered.

Output Listing 4.

Entering and removing variables step-by-step

```
At step 1, SEX       was included in the analysis.

                               Degrees of Freedom    Signif.
Wilks' Lambda        .76652       1    2    105.0
Equivalent F       15.99140            2    105.0    .0000


---------------- Variables in the Analysis after Step 1 ------


Variable   Tolerance   F to Remove   Wilks' Lambda

SEX        1.0000000     15.9914

---------------- Variables not in the Analysis after Step 1 -

                       Minimum
Variable   Tolerance   Tolerance   F to Enter   Wilks' Lambda

COMPUT     .7450074    .7450074     4.2028382    .7091994
CONKIT     .9287215    .9287215     3.4285574    .7191062
DRAW       .9950388    .9950388     6.0381945    .6867722
MODEL      .9414225    .9414225     2.1991574    .7354177
OUTDOOR    .9826969    .9826969     1.4938129    .7451145
PAINT      .8832568    .8832568    10.1872805    .6409513
QUALS      .9834662    .9834662     7.6903191    .6677635
VISMOD     .9977884    .9977884     8.8257836    .6552981
```

This process of entering (and possibly removing) variables one at a time continues for a further five steps until Step 7 when the criteria shown in Output Listing 3 preclude any further steps.

Finally at Step 7:

Output Listing 4 (continued).
Entering and removing variables step-by-step

```
At step 7, COMPUT    was included in the analysis.

                                Degrees of Freedom    Signif.
Wilks' Lambda        .37391       7      2      105.0
Equivalent F        8.98587             14      198.0     .0000


---------------- Variables in the Analysis after Step 7 ------

Variable   Tolerance   F to Remove   Wilks' Lambda

COMPUT     .6995932       3.8543        .4030275
CONKIT     .8006370       4.3322        .4066375
OUTDOOR    .8426921       3.9592        .4038200
PRINT      .7344426      10.9168        .4563764
QUALS      .9145207      10.8321        .4557366
SEX        .5923199       7.4714        .4303510
VISMOD     .8998970       7.9591        .4340345


---------------- Variables not in the Analysis after Step 7 ------

                       Minimum
Variable   Tolerance   Tolerance   F to Enter    Wilks' Lambda

DRAW       .6280746    .5205052      .9114370      .3670851
MODEL      .7160546    .5718517      .3562813      .3712141


F level or tolerance or VIN insufficient for further computation.
```

The analysis stops at this point because neither of the **F to enter** values exceeds the critical value of 3.84. Thus two variables *draw* and *model* are excluded from the analysis.

The summary table

The stepwise variable selection section concludes with a **Summary Table** (Output Listing 5) showing the order in which the variables were entered or removed (though in this analysis none was removed), along with values of Wilks' Lambda and the associated probability levels.

Chapter 14 - Discriminant Analysis

Output Listing 5.

The summary table

```
                              Summary Table

         Action        Vars  Wilks'
Step Entered Removed    in   Lambda   Sig.   Label

  1  SEX                1    .76652  .0000   sex of student
  2  PAINT              2    .64095  .0000   Previous interest in painting
  3  QUALS              3    .53865  .0000   Total point count for highers
  4  VISMOD             4    .48073  .0000   Ability to visualise model
  5  OUTDOOR            5    .43903  .0000   Previous interest in outdoor pursuits
  6  CONKIT             6    .40303  .0000   Previous interest in construction kit
  7  COMPUT             7    .37391  .0000   Previous interest in computing
```

Statistics of the discriminant functions

Output Listing 6 shows the percentage (**Pct**) of the variance accounted for by each discriminant function and how many of them (if any) are significant. It also shows that both functions (**Fcn**) are highly significant (see the **Sig** column on the right).

Output Listing 6.

Statistics of the discriminant functions

```
                    Canonical Discriminant Functions

            Pct of  Cum  Canonical   After  Wilks'
Fcn Eigenvalue Variance Pct  Corr      Fcn  Lambda  Chi-square  df  Sig

                                    :  0  .373913   100.341    14  .0000
 1*   .6980    54.83   54.83  .6412  :  1  .634921    46.334     6  .0000
 2*   .5750    45.17  100.00  .6042  :

* Marks the 2 canonical discriminant functions remaining in the analysis.
```

Standardised coefficients and within groups correlations with discriminants

Two tables follow in the listing, the first (not reproduced here) being the standardised function coefficients, and the second (Output Listing 7) the pooled within groups correlations between the discriminating variables and the functions. It is clear from the output in Output Listing 7 that the first function is based on subjects' interests in painting, drawing, and visualising models, while the second is based on the sex of the subjects and their interest in kit construction. The asterisks mark the correlation with the higher value for each variable.

Chapter 14 - Discriminant Analysis

Output Listing 7.

The structure matrix

```
Structure matrix:

Pooled within-groups correlations between discriminating variables
                                    and canonical discriminant functions
(Variables ordered by size of correlation within function)

            Func  1     Func  2

VISMOD      -.50787*   -.09751
QUALS        .42584*   -.15639
PAINT       -.41858*    .36345
DRAW        -.21738*    .11537
MODEL       -.11505*    .07006
COMPUT       .00603*    .00007

SEX          .19409     .69570*
CONKIT      -.14833    -.54298*
OUTDOOR      .19267     .24970*

* denotes largest absolute correlation between each variable and any
discriminant function.
```

Success of predictions of group membership

The optional selection of **Summary table** from the **Classify** options in the **Discriminant Analysis** dialog box provides an indication of the success rate for predictions of membership of the grouping variable's categories using the discriminant functions developed in the analysis (see Output Listing 8). The table indicates that the overall success rate is 72.2%.

Output Listing 8 also shows that Engineers are the most accurately classified, with 75.6% of the cases correct. Architects are next with 73.3%, and Psychologists are last, with 67.6%. Notice that incorrectly classified Architects are more likely to be classified as Engineers than as Psychologists, and that incorrectly classified Psychologists are more likely to be classified as Engineers than as Architects!

> **Output Listing 8.**
> **Classification results**
>
> ```
> Classification results -
>
>                     No. of    Predicted Group Membership
>     Actual Group    Cases         1          2          3
>     -----------------------  --------  ---------  ---------
>
>     Group      1      30          22          2          6
>     Architects                  73.3%       6.7%      20.0%
>
>     Group      2      37           4         25          8
>     Psychologists               10.8%      67.6%      21.6%
>
>     Group      3      41           5          5         31
>     Engineers                   12.2%      12.2%      75.6%
>
>     Percent of "grouped" cases correctly classified:  72.22%
> ```

14.2.3 Predicting group membership

Sectional 14.2.1 posed the problem whether a knowledge of pupils' scores on a number of variables could be used to predict their subjects of study at university. The analysis has demonstrated that two discriminant functions can be generated using all the variables except *draw and model* and that these can predict 72% of the cases correctly. Furthermore, it is clear from Output Listing 7 that *sex*, *vismod* and *conkit* are the major contributors to the functions. However what about future students for whom only the data for predicting variables are known? Can the program be used to predict which subject they should study? The answer is yes.

Proceed as follows:

- Enter the data for the new students at the end of the data in the **Data Editor** window. Leave the grouping variable blank or enter an out-of-range number so that the analysis does not include these cases when it is computing the discriminant functions;

- Complete the **Discriminant Analysis** dialog box as before but, in addition, click the **Save** option and then click the radio button for **Predicted group membership**. Click **Continue** and then **OK** to run the analysis;

- The predicted group membership will appear in a new column labelled **Dis_1**.

EXERCISE 23

PREDICTING CATEGORY MEMBERSHIP: DISCRIMINANT ANALYSIS

BEFORE YOU START

Before proceeding with this practical, please read Chapter 14.

THE PROJECT

Prediction of reading success at the school-leaving stage

Just before they leave school, students in the most senior class of a school are regularly tested on their comprehension of a difficult reading passage. Typically, only 50% of students can perform the task. We shall also suppose that, for a substantial number of past pupils, we have available data not only on their performance on the comprehension passage but also on the very same variables that were investigated in the exercise on multiple regression, namely, the reading-related measures that we have referred to as *logo*, *syntax* and *vocal*, all of which were taken in the very earliest stages of the children's education.

The full data set is given in the appendix of this exercise. As with the multiple regression example, we can only hope that the data have already been stored in a file with a name such as **discrim**, the contents of which you can access by using the **Open** procedure. Table 1 shows the first and the last few lines of the data set.

The data are also available on WWW (http://www.psyc.abdn.ac.uk/teaching/spss/spssbook.htm).

\multicolumn{4}{c}{Table 1. Part of the data set}			
Logo	Syntax	Vocal	Comprehension
10	20	64	1
28	28	58	1
...	...	...	...
82	69	60	2
51	48	52	2

The rightmost variable is a coding variable whose values, *1* and *2*, denote, respectively, *failure* and *success* on the comprehension task.

Exploring the data set

Before moving on to the main analysis, a preliminary exploration of the data will bring out at least some of the important features. For example, if a particular variable is going to be useful in assigning individuals to categories, one might expect that, if its scores are subdivided according to category membership, there should be a substantial difference between the group means; if, on the other hand, there is no such difference, that would suggest that the variable will play a minimal role in the final discriminant function. To investigate these differences, **one-way ANOVAs** can be used to compare the group means on the various independent variables. These tests, however, are requested by options within the **Discriminant** procedure. We shall therefore return to the descriptive statistics when we come to prepare the dialog box.

Since discriminant analysis assumes that the distribution of the independent variables is multivariate normal, we shall also need to look at their empirical distributions to ascertain the credibility of that assumption.

Use the **Graphs** procedure to plot boxplots for the predictor variables as in Exercise 21 by choosing the **Summaries of Separate Variables** option and then defining the variables as *logo syntax vocal*.

- **Study the output and note whether the boxplots reveal any outliers. Do the side-by-side boxplots show anything of interest?**

Procedure for discriminant analysis

Run the discriminant analysis as described in Section 14.2.1. There, however, we recommended the **Stepwise** method of minimisation of **Wilks' lambda**. In the present example, because of its simplicity, it is better to use the default method known as **Enter**, in which all the variables are entered simultaneously. Since **Enter** is the default method, there is no need to specify it. Click on **Statistics** in the Discriminant Analysis dialog box to open the Discriminant Analysis: Statistics dialog box. Select **Univariate ANOVAs** and click on **Continue**. Click on **Classify** in the Discriminant Analysis dialog box to open the Discriminant Analysis: Classification dialog box. Select **Combined-groups** button in Plots and **Summary table** in Display. Click on **Continue** and then **OK**.

Output listing for discriminant analysis

The main features of the output for a discriminant analysis are explained in Section 14.2.2, which you should review.

In the present example, the first table shows the number of cases in each of the categories of the variable *comp*. The next table, headed 'Wilks' lambda (U-statistic) and univariate F-ratio', shows the F-ratios (and their associated p-values) for the comparisons between the groups on each of the three independent variables. The value of **Wilks' lambda** given in each of the ANOVAs is equal to one minus the **correlation ratio** (see Section 14.1.1).

- **Which variables have significant F ratios and which do not?**

There now follows the first of the tables showing the output of the discriminant analysis proper. Its title is 'Canonical Discriminant Functions'. Because there are only two groups, there is only one function.

The most important entries in the table are the statistic **lambda**, its **chi-square value** and the associated **p-value**. You will notice immediately that the value of lambda is smaller than the value for any of the three IVs considered separately. That is well and good: the discriminant function *D*, which uses the information in all the IVs should do a better job than any one IV alone. Here there is an

Chapter 14 - Discriminant Analysis

obvious parallel with multiple regression, in which the predictive ability of the multiple regression equation cannot be less than the simple regressions of the target variable on any one regressor alone. Just as, in multiple regression, predictions can only improve when more regressors are added, the addition of another variable to the discriminant function can only improve its efficacy (although, in the case of the variable *vocal*, the improvement is negligible). Since, however, two of the IVs can each discriminate reliably between the groups, the result of the chi-square test of lambda in the discriminant analysis table is a foregone conclusion. As expected, the p-value is very small. The discriminant function *D* can indeed discriminate reliably between the two groups on the basis of performance on the independent variables.

Ignore the table of standardized Canonical Discriminant Function Coefficients.

A more useful table is the next one, labelled 'Structure Matrix: Pooled-within-groups correlations between discriminating variables and canonical discriminant functions'.

- **Are the correlations as you expected?**

Examine the 'All-groups stacked histogram' to ascertain the success of the discriminant function in minimising the overlap between the distributions of D in the two groups. Notice that, although the groups are generally well separated, some 2s intrude into the area dominated by the 1s and vice versa. This means that, if category membership is unknown, SPSS will misassign some of the cases to the wrong group.

We have shown that the discriminant function D discriminates between the two groups; but how effectively does it do this? This is shown under the heading: 'Classification Results'.

- **Note down the percentage of grouped cases correctly classified, the percentage of correct group 1 predictions and the percentage of correct group 2 predictions.**

Now try out the discriminant function on some fresh data by adding them at the end of the data file (e.g. enter in the columns for *logo*, *syntax*, *vocal*, the values 50, 50, 50; 10, 10, 10; 80, 80, 80 and any others you wish). Leave the column blank for *compreh*. Then re-run the analysis after selecting **Save** in the **Discriminant Analysis** dialog box, clicking the radio button for **Predicted group membership**, and then clicking **Continue** and **OK**. The predicted memberships will appear in the variable called **dis_1**.

- **Will someone with logo, syntax and vocal scores of 50, 50, 50 respectively be expected to pass or fail the comprehension test?**

CONCLUSION

This exercise is intended to be merely an introduction to the use of a complex and sophisticated statistical technique. Accordingly, we chose an example of the simplest possible application, in which the dependent variable comprises only two categories. The simplicity of our interpretation of a number of statistics such as **Wilks' lambda** breaks down when there are more than two categories in the dependent variable. For a treatment of such cases, see Tabachnick & Fidell (1996).

CHAPTER 15

FACTOR ANALYSIS

15.1 INTRODUCTION
15.2 A FACTOR ANALYSIS OF DATA ON SIX VARIABLES
15.3 USING SPSS COMMAND LANGUAGE

15.1 INTRODUCTION

15.1.1 The nature of factors

Suppose that the subjects in a sample are each tested on several variables, perhaps an assortment of tests of intellectual ability, such as vocabulary, short term memory, reaction speed and so on. The correlations of performance on each test with every other test in the battery can be arranged in a rectangular array known as a **correlation matrix**, or **R-matrix**. Each row (or column) of R would contain all the correlations involving one particular test in the battery. The cells along the **principal diagonal** (running from the top left to the bottom right of the matrix) would remain empty (or contain the entry *1*), since each cell on that diagonal represents the combination of a particular test with itself; but each off-diagonal cell would be occupied by the correlation between the tests whose row and column intersect at that particular cell. The R-matrix can be the starting point for several statistical procedures, but in this chapter we shall consider just one: **factor analysis.**

The presence in the R-matrix of clusters of sizeable correlations among subsets of the tests in the battery would suggest that the tests in a subset may be measuring the same underlying psychological dimension, or ability. If the traditional British theories in the psychology of intelligence are correct, there should be fewer (far fewer) dimensions than there are tests in the battery. The purpose of factor analysis is to discern and to quantify the dimensions supposed to underlie performance on a variety of tasks. The **factors** produced by factor analysis are mathematical entities, which can be thought of as classificatory axes, with respect to which the tests in a battery can be 'plotted'. The greater the value of a test's co-ordinate, or **loading**, on a factor, the more important is that factor in accounting for the correlations between that test and others in the battery.

A factor, then, has the geometric interpretation as a classificatory axis in an axial reference system with respect to which the tests in the battery are represented as points in space.

But the term **factor** also has an equivalent algebraic, or arithmetical interpretation as a linear function of the observed scores that people achieve on the tests in a battery. For example, if a battery comprises 8 tests, and each testee were also to be assigned a ninth score consisting of the sum of the 8 test scores, that ninth, artificial, score would be a **factor score**, and it would make sense to speak of correlations between the factor and the real test scores. We have seen that the loading of a test on a factor is, geometrically speaking, the co-ordinate of the test point on the factor axis. But that axis represents a 'factor' in the second, algebraic sense, and the loading is the correlation between the test scores and those on the factor.

In factor analysis, a major assumption is that the mathematical factors represent **latent variables** (i.e. psychological dimensions), the nature of which can only be guessed at by examining the nature of tests that have sizeable co-ordinates on any particular axis. It should perhaps be said at the outset that this claim is controversial, and there are notable psychologists who hold that the factors of factor analysis are statistical realities, but psychological fictions.

The topic of factor analysis is not elementary, and the SPSS output bristles with highly technical terms. If you are unfamiliar with factor analysis, we suggest you read the lucid texts by Kim and Mueller (1978a, 1978b) and by Tabachnick and Fidell (1996), which contain relatively painless introductions to the technical jargon.

15.1.2 Stages in a factor analysis

A factor analysis usually takes place in three stages:

(1) a **matrix of correlation coefficients** is generated for all the variable combinations;

(2) from the correlation matrix, **factors** are extracted. The most common method is called **principal factors** (often wrongly referred to as **principal components** extraction, hence the abbreviation **PC**);

(3) the factors (axes) are **rotated** to maximise the relationships between the variables and some of the factors. The most common method is **varimax**, a rotation method which maintains independence among the mathematical factors. Geometrically, this means that during rotation, the axes remain **orthogonal** (i.e. they are kept at right angles).

A fourth stage can be added at which the scores of each subject on each of the factors emerging from the analysis are calculated. It should be stressed that these **factor scores** are not the results of any actual test taken by the subjects: they are estimates of the subjects' standing on the **supposed** latent variables that have emerged as mathematical axes from the factor analysis of the data set. Factor scores can be very useful, however, because they can subsequently be used as input for further statistical analysis.

It is advisable to carry out only Stage 1 initially, in order to be able to inspect the correlation coefficients in the correlation matrix R. Since the purpose of the analysis is to link variables together into factors, those variables must be related to one another and therefore have correlation coefficients larger than about 0.3. Should any variables show no substantial correlation with any of the others, they would be removed from R in subsequent analysis. It is also advisable to check that the correlation matrix does not possess the highly undesirable properties of **multicollinearity** and **singularity**. The former is the condition where the variables are very highly (though imperfectly) correlated; the latter arises when some of the variables are exact linear functions of others in the battery, as when the variable C is constructed by adding together the subjects' scores on variables A and B. Should either multicollinearity or singularity be present, it would be necessary to drop some of the variables from the analysis.

15.1.3 The extraction of factors

The factors (or axes) in a factor analysis are **extracted** (or, pursuing the geometric analogy, **constructed**) one at a time, the process being repeated until it is possible, from the loadings of the tests on the factors so far extracted, to generate good approximations to the correlations in the original **R matrix**. Factor analysis tells us how many factors (or axes) are necessary to achieve a reconstruction of R that is sufficiently good to account satisfactorily for the correlations it contains.

15.1.4 The rationale of rotation

If we think of the tests in the battery and the origin of the axis (factor) set as stationary points and rotate the axes around the origin, the values of all the loadings will change. Nevertheless, the new set of loadings on the axes, *whatever their new position*, can still be used to produce exactly the same estimates of the correlations in the R-matrix. In this sense, the position of the axes is quite arbitrary: the factor matrix (or **F-matrix**) only tells us *how many* axes are necessary to classify the data adequately; but it does not thereby establish that the initial position of the axes is the appropriate one.

In **rotation**, the factor axes are rotated around the fixed origin until the loadings meet a certain criterion. The set of loadings that satisfies the criterion is known as the **rotated factor matrix**. The purpose of any rotation is to achieve a configuration of loadings having the qualities collectively known as **simple structure** which, loosely conceived, is the set of loadings that shows the maximum number of tests loading on the minimum number of factors. The idea is that the fewer the factors that are involved in accounting for the correlations among a group of tests, the easier it is to invest those factors with psychological meaning. In fact, simple structure is an ideal never achieved in practice, partly because the concept, in its original form, is actually rather vague and embodies contradictory properties. Modern computing packages such as SPSS offer a selection of rotation methods, each based upon a different (but reasonable) interpretation of simple structure. The most commonly used method of rotation is known as **varimax**.

15.1.5 Confirmatory factor analysis and structural equation modelling

So far, we have considered the use of factor analysis to ascertain the minimum number of classificatory variables (or axes) we need to account for the shared variance among a set of tests. While the researcher will almost certainly have expectations about how many factors are likely to emerge, the process of factor extraction proceeds automatically until the criterion is reached, after which the process terminates. Even when the same battery of tests is used, the precise number of factors extracted will vary from study to study, although 'factor invariance' has been found with those factors accounting for the greatest amounts of variance (such as the general intelligence g factor and major group factors in tests of ability). Moreover, the pattern shown by the loadings in the final rotated factor matrix depends on the method of rotation used: some methods (such as varimax) keep the factor axes at right angles; but others (such as quartimax) allow **oblique** (correlated) factors. There has been much argument about which method of rotation is best, and the preferred method tends to reflect the theoretical views of the user. In the circumstances, traditional factor analytic methods seem ill-suited to the testing of specific hypotheses, and many hold the view that they are appropriate only in the early stages of investigation in a research area.

In view of this dubiety, the methods we have been describing have been termed **exploratory factor analysis** (Maxwell, 1977, p.60), and over the past three decades, there has been much interest in developing techniques for testing specific hypotheses about the factorial composition of specific test batteries (or other variables). In **confirmatory factor analysis**, the user decides in advance that there will be a specific number of factors; indeed, assumptions may also be made about the pattern of zero and non-zero loadings of the tests on the factors.

Recent years have seen dramatic developments in what is known as **structural equation modelling**, of which confirmatory factor analysis is just one aspect. There are also, for example, **causal modelling** (or **path analysis**), **regression models** with constrained weightings of the regressors, and **covariance structure models**, which test assumptions about a variance-covariance matrix, such as equality of the variances of all the tests in the battery. Several computing packages have been designed to test such models (see Bentler, 1993, on EQS; Joreskog & Sorbom, 1989, on LISREL). At present SPSS for Macintosh does not include a module for confirmatory factor analysis.

15.2 A FACTOR ANALYSIS OF DATA ON SIX VARIABLES

Suppose a researcher has available the marks of 10 children in six tests: **French, German, Latin, Music, Mathematics** and **Mapwork** as shown in Table 1.

Chapter 15 - Factor Analysis

Table 1
Scores of 10 children on six variables

Subject	French	German	Latin	Music	Maths	Mapwork
1	72	69	81	45	53	51
2	41	32	40	78	91	81
3	47	54	46	50	47	49
4	33	34	40	56	65	63
5	75	76	91	46	54	47
6	41	46	48	92	88	90
7	67	72	68	56	45	47
8	32	41	35	32	36	37
9	84	76	92	44	51	43
10	45	36	45	72	67	79

In order to identify the psychological dimensions tapped by these six variables, it is decided to carry out a factor analysis. There are two ways of doing this in SPSS:

1. The simpler way is to begin with a set of raw scores in the **Data Editor** and to run a factor analysis using dialog boxes in the usual manner.

2. The other way is to write commands in **command language** (referred to in SPSS as **syntax**) which will be described in Section 15.3. At first sight, SPSS syntax is highly opaque and it takes considerable effort to acquire a working knowledge of it. However we shall see that the use of syntax can save the experienced user considerable time and labour; moreover, there are some operations that be carried out only by using syntax.

15.2.1 Procedure for factor analysis with raw scores

Enter the data in Table 1 into the **Data Editor** in the usual way, using the procedures described in Section 3.5. Note that there are no grouping variables in this data set: this is a purely correlational (as opposed to experimental) study. Inasmuch as there can be said to be an 'independent' variable, it is one whose existence must be inferred from whatever patterns may exist in the correlation

Chapter 15 - Factor Analysis

matrix. It is the *raison d'être* of factor analysis to make such an inference credible. The first five subjects in the **Data Editor** are shown in Figure 1.

	french	german	latin	music	maths	mapwork
1	72	69	81	45	53	51
2	41	32	40	78	91	81
3	47	54	46	50	47	49
4	33	34	40	56	65	63
5	75	76	91	46	54	47

Figure 1. The data of the first five children on six variables

Running the factor analysis

- Choose
  Statistics
     Data Reduction
        Factor (Figure 2)

to open the **Factor Analysis** dialog box (Figure 3).

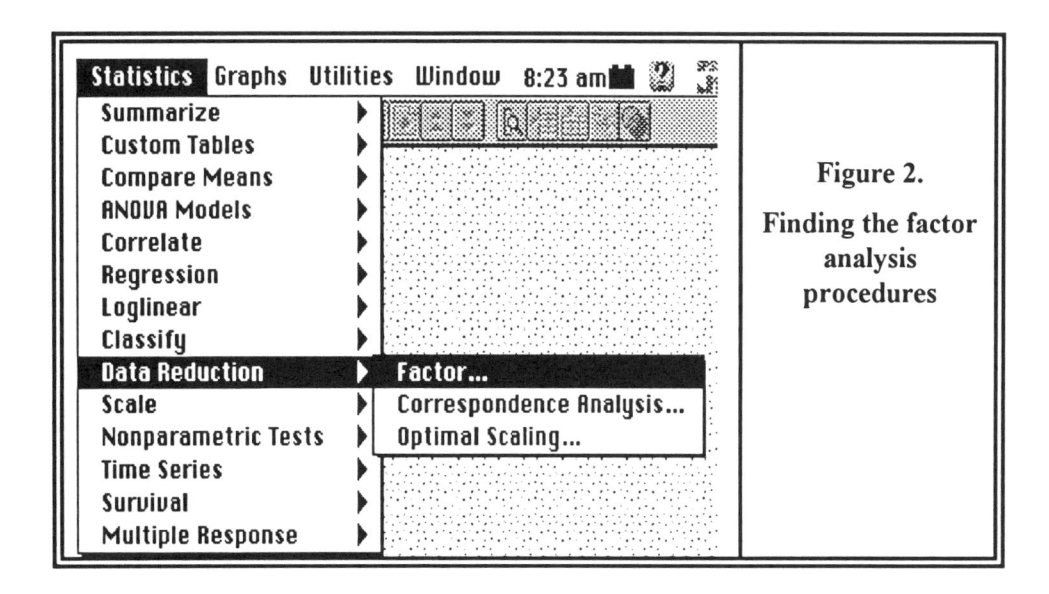

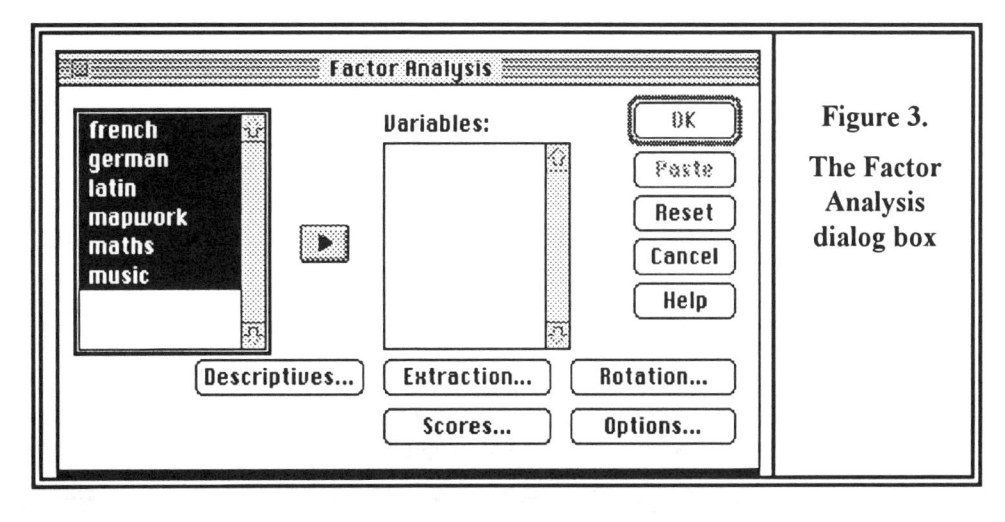

Figure 2. Finding the factor analysis procedures

Figure 3. The Factor Analysis dialog box

341

Chapter 15 - Factor Analysis

- Highlight all the variable names in the **Factor** dialog box and click on ▶ to transfer them to the **Variables** box.

Before running the analysis, it is necessary to select some options that regulate the manner in which the analysis takes place and produce some extra items of output. This is done by clicking on some of the buttons at the bottom of the main **Factor Analysis** dialog box.

- Click on the **Descriptives** button to open the **Factor Analysis: Descriptives** dialog box (Figure 4).

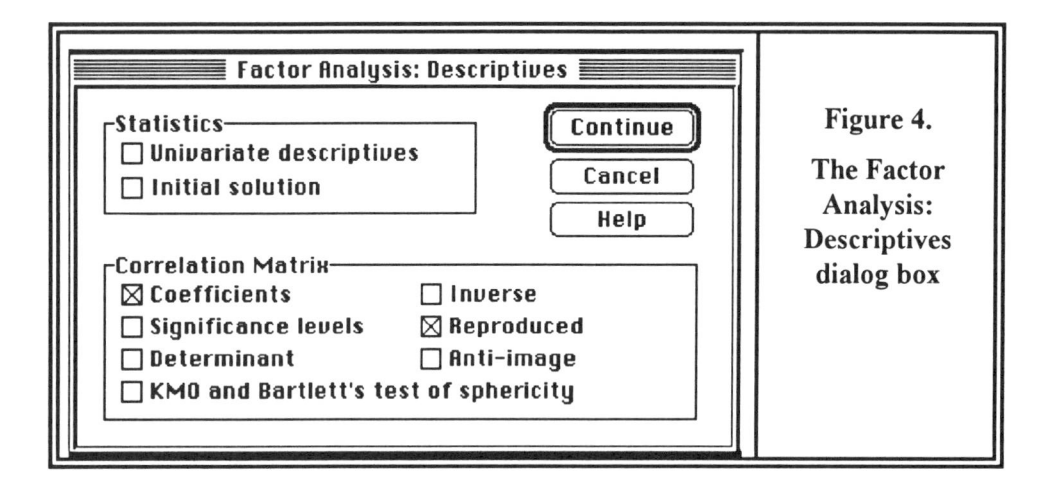

Figure 4.

The Factor Analysis: Descriptives dialog box

- Click on the following check boxes: **Coefficients** (which will tabulate the R-matrix) and **Reproduced** (which will produce an estimate of the R-matrix from the loadings of the factors extracted by the analysis along with the communalities and residuals between the observed and reproduced correlations).

- Click on **Continue** to return to the **Factor Analysis** dialog box.

- Now click on the **Extraction** button to open the **Factor Analysis: Extraction** dialog box (Figure 5). Click on the **Scree plot** check box which will draw the scree plot: this is a useful display which shows the relative importance of the factors extracted.

Figure 5.

The Factor Analysis: Extraction dialog box

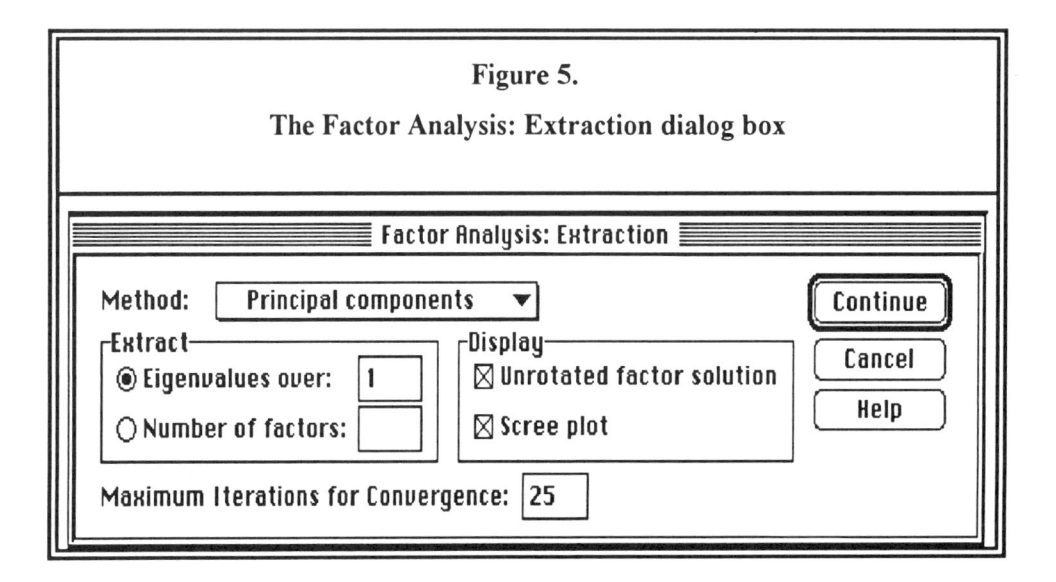

- Click on **Continue** to return to the **Factor Analysis** dialog box.
- To obtain the rotated F-matrix, click on the **Rotation** button to obtain the **Factor Analysis: Rotation** dialog box (Figure 6). In the **Method** box, activate the **Varimax** radio button.

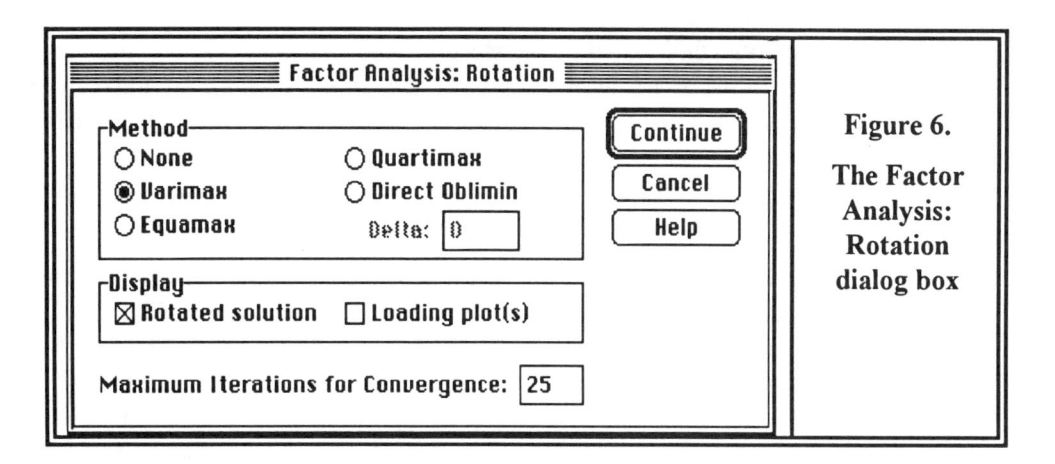

Figure 6. The Factor Analysis: Rotation dialog box

- Click on **Continue** and then on **OK** to execute the factor analysis.

15.2.2 Output listing for factor analysis

The correlation matrix

Output Listing 1 shows the correlation matrix, which may require some explanation.

Output Listing 1.

The correlation matrix

Correlation Matrix:

	FRENCH	GERMAN	LATIN	MAPWORK	MATHS	MUSIC
FRENCH	1.00000					
GERMAN	.93346	1.00000				
LATIN	.97744	.92814	1.00000			
MAPWORK	-.45633	-.61228	-.44833	1.00000		
MATHS	-.33491	-.51644	-.30970	.93885	1.00000	
MUSIC	-.35119	-.46754	-.36561	.96197	.90827	1.00000

In its basic form, a correlation matrix is *square*, that is, there are as many rows as there are columns. The diagonal of cells running from top left to bottom right is known as the **principal diagonal** of the matrix. Since the variables are labelled in the same order in the rows and columns of **R**, each of the cells along the principal diagonal contains the correlation of one of the variables with itself (i.e. *1*). The correlations in the off-diagonal cells are the same above and below the principal diagonal (the correlation of FRENCH with GERMAN is the same as that of GERMAN with FRENCH). A **triangular matrix** is that part of a square matrix comprising the entries along the principal diagonal and the off-diagonal entries either above or below the diagonal: the **upper triangular matrix** comprises the principal diagonal plus the entries above; the **lower triangular matrix** comprises the principal diagonal plus the entries below. Either of the triangular versions of **R** contains all the information in the square matrix. The matrix shown in Output Listing 1 is a **lower triangular correlation matrix**.

Inspection of the correlation matrix in Output Listing 1 reveals that there are two clusters of high correlations among the tests: one among FRENCH, GERMAN and LATIN; the other among MUSIC, MATHEMATICS and MAPWORK. Another interesting feature is that in either cluster, each test, while correlating highly with the others in the same cluster, does not correlate substantially with the tests in the other cluster. The abilities tapped by the two groups of tests, therefore, are independent. It is reasonable to interpret the pattern of the correlations in R as arising because each group of tests, while tapping a single psychological dimension, does not tap the principal abilities required by the other tests.

From inspection of the correlation matrix, therefore, it would appear that we can account for the pattern of correlations in R in terms of two independent, underlying psychological dimensions. Presently, we shall see whether such an interpretation is confirmed by the results of a formal factor analysis: are two factors (or axes) sufficient to account for the correlations among the tests?

A table of final statistics

Output Listing 2 presents the **final statistics** In the first column are listed the six variables used in the study. The **communality** of a test is the proportion of the variance of the test that is accounted for by the common factors extracted in the factor analysis (i.e. it is the proportion of the test variance that is **common factor variance**). For example, in the second column, we see that 98% of the variance of the scores on FRENCH is common factor variance.

To the right of the column of asterisks, there is a column (**Factor**) of those factors extracted that have an eigenvalue greater than 1, together with a corresponding column of **eigenvalues**, the percentage of variance (**Pct of Var**) attributable to each factor, and the cumulative variance (**Cum Pct**) for the factor and the previous factors. In the present context, an **eigenvalue** is the amount of the total test variance that is accounted for by a particular factor, the total variance for each test being unity (100%). For example, the eigenvalue of the first factor is 4.18, to two places of decimals. Since the total test variance that could possibly be accounted for by a factor is 6 [i.e. 100% × (number of tests)], the proportion of the total test variance accounted for by the first factor is 4.18/6 = 69.7%, the figure given in **Pct of Var**. The final column (**Cum Pct**) shows that the two factors extracted account for 96.7% of the variance.

Output Listing 2.
Some final statistics from the analysis

```
Final Statistics:

Variable    Communality  *  Factor   Eigenvalue   Pct of Var   Cum Pct
                         *
FRENCH         .98110    *    1       4.17894       69.6        69.6
GERMAN         .95707    *    2       1.62044       27.0        96.7
LATIN          .97860    *
MAPWORK        .98369    *
MATHS          .94664    *
MUSIC          .95228    *
```

Scree plot

Figure 7 shows the **scree plot** which was selected in the **Factor Analysis: Extraction** dialog box.

It shows that the amount of variance accounted for (the eigenvalue) by successive factors plunges sharply as successive factors are extracted. The point of interest is where the curve connecting the points starts to flatten out. This region of the curve has been fancifully likened to the rubble or scree on a mountain side. It can be seen that the curve begins to flatten out between the second and third factors. Notice also that Factor 3 has an eigenvalue of less than 1, so only the first two factors have been retained as shown in Output Listing 2.

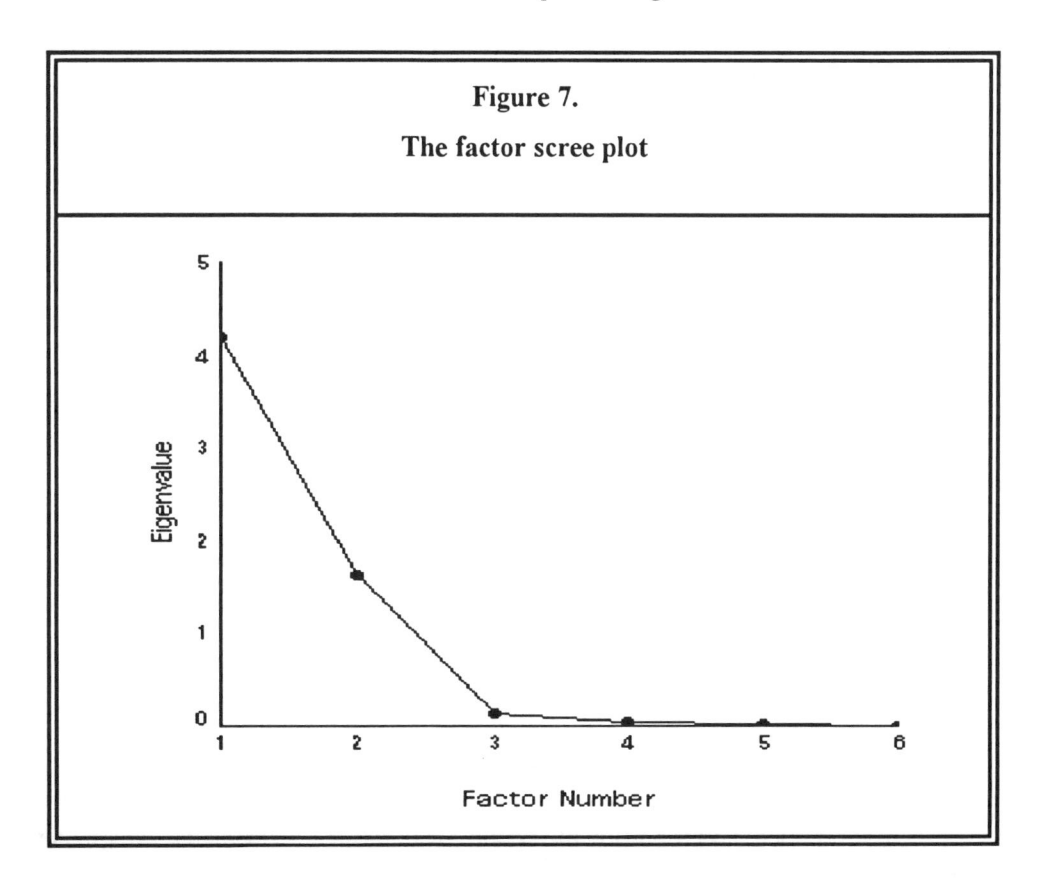

Figure 7.
The factor scree plot

Chapter 15 - Factor Analysis

The unrotated factor matrix

Output Listing 4 shows the unrotated factor matrix, containing the loadings of the six tests on the two factors extracted.

Output Listing 4.

The unrotated factor matrix

```
PC    extracted   2 factors.


Factor Matrix:


              Factor  1      Factor  2

FRENCH         .81031         .56965
GERMAN         .89241         .40084
LATIN          .80542         .57437
MAPWORK       -.88333         .45102
MATHS         -.80099         .55231
MUSIC         -.80956         .54489
```

When the factors are **orthogonal** (i.e. uncorrelated with each other), these factor loadings are the correlation coefficients between the variables and the factors. Thus the higher the absolute value of the loading (which can never exceed a maximum of 1), the more the factor accounts for the total variance of scores on the variable concerned.

It can be seen that the factor analysis has extracted two factors, in agreement with the impression given by the correlation matrix. On the other hand, it is not particularly easy to interpret the unrotated F-matrix. Both groups of tests show substantial loadings on both factors, which is not in accord with the obvious psychological interpretation of the original R-matrix.

Reproduced correlation matrix and residuals

Output Listing 5 shows the **reproduced correlation matrix** of coefficients, computed from the extracted factors. Each reproduced correlation coefficient is the sum of the products of the loadings of each of the two tests concerned on each successive factor extracted. For example, the sum of the products of the loadings of FRENCH and GERMAN on the two factors extracted is, from the loadings in the unrotated F-matrix in Output Listing 4, [(0.81 × 0.89) + (0.57 × (0.40)] = 0.95, which is the value given for the reproduced correlation between FRENCH and GERMAN in Output Listing 5. The correlation between FRENCH and GERMAN in the original correlation matrix is 0.93, only a 2% difference. The other correlations in the reproduced correlation matrix are similarly close to the reproduced correlations. The sentence at the foot of Output Listing 5 states the number and proportion of residuals (i.e. the differences) that are greater than 0.05.

Chapter 15 - Factor Analysis

There are none: in the present case, all the residuals are very small indeed, showing that the two-factor model accounts for the covariance among the six tests very well indeed. Had the residuals been large, there would have been reason to doubt the two-factor interpretation of the correlation matrix. The asterisked values in Output Listing 5 are the communalities, previously shown in Ouput Listing 2. Notice that they are all large - at least 90%.

Output Listing 5.

The reproduced correlation matrix, with residuals

```
Reproduced Correlation Matrix:

             FRENCH    GERMAN    LATIN    MAPWORK    MATHS    MUSIC

FRENCH      .98110*   -.01801   -.00239    .00252   -.00048  -.00559
GERMAN      .95147    .95707*   -.02086   -.00477   -.02301   .03651
LATIN       .97983    .94900    .97860*    .00407    .01820  -.02654
MAPWORK    -.45885   -.60751   -.45240    .98369*   -.01779   .00111
MATHS      -.33443   -.49343   -.32791    .95664    .94664*  -.04112
MUSIC      -.34560   -.50405   -.33907    .96086    .94940   .95228*

The lower left triangle contains the reproduced correlation matrix; the
diagonal, reproduced communalities; and the upper right triangle residuals
between the observed correlations and the reproduced correlations.

There are    0 (  .0%) residuals (above diagonal) with absolute values > 0.05.
```

The rotated factor matrix

Output Listing 6 shows the **rotated factor matrix**.

Output Listing 6.

The rotated factor matrix

```
          Rotated Factor Matrix:

                      Factor  1    Factor  2

          FRENCH      -.17192       .97547
          GERMAN      -.34924       .91384
          LATIN       -.16513       .97536
          MAPWORK      .94407      -.30400
          MATHS        .95725      -.17413
          MUSIC        .95807      -.18543
```

The purpose of rotation is not to change the number of factors extracted, but to try to arrive at a new position for the axes (factors) which is easier to interpret in psychological terms. In fact, the rotated factor matrix is much easier to interpret than the unrotated matrix. The three language tests now have high loadings on one factor alone (Factor 2); whereas *Mapwork*, *Mathematics* and *Music* have high loadings on the other factor (Factor 1). These factors are uncorrelated. This is quite consistent with what we gleaned from our inspection of the original R-matrix, namely, that the correlations among the six tests in our battery could be accounted for in terms of two independent psychological dimensions of ability.

15.3 USING SPSS COMMAND LANGUAGE

Throughout this book, the statistics provided by SPSS have been accessed by exploiting the advantages of the graphics environment that the Macintosh Operating System provides. Although this is by far the most painless way of familiarising oneself with SPSS, it is now time to consider an alternative approach.

It is also possible to run SPSS procedures and analyses by writing instructions in SPSS **command language**. This is done in a special **syntax window**, either by typing them in from the keyboard or pasting them in. Commands are then run by selecting (emboldening) them and pressing the **Run** button (see below).

For many users, SPSS syntax is pretty daunting. It is possible to appeal to **SPSS Help** and obtain what is known as a **syntax map**, but at first sight a syntax map seems even more opaque than the written commands themselves. There are, nevertheless, great advantages in learning how to use SPSS syntax because there are often more options available for some analyses than those accessible via dialog boxes. In addition, the syntax for a particular analysis run by the user (even one set up initially from dialog boxes) can be saved as a syntax file and re-used on a later occasion (perhaps with different data for the same variables, or for different variables, in which case the syntax variable names can be easily changed). If an analysis has been set up from dialog boxes, pressing **Paste** in the final dialog box will paste the hitherto hidden syntax into the **syntax window** from which it can be saved to a file in the usual way.

We believe that the most efficient way of learning SPSS syntax is by working from the dialog boxes in this way, rather than ploughing through the available texts on SPSS syntax, which are better left until one has already acquired a working knowledge of the language.

15.3.1 The power of SPSS syntax: An example

With the children's scores in the **Data Editor**, access the **Factor Analysis** dialog box in the usual way. Make the selections as before, remembering to press the

Chapter 15 - Factor Analysis

buttons at the bottom of the dialog box to specify the rotation, order a scree test, request a correlation matrix and so on. Now click on the **Paste** button (underneath **OK**). When this is done, a window with the title **!untitled syntax 1** will appear on the screen. This is the **syntax window**, which will contain the commands that have just been specified by our choices from the dialog boxes, written in SPSS command language (see Figure 8).

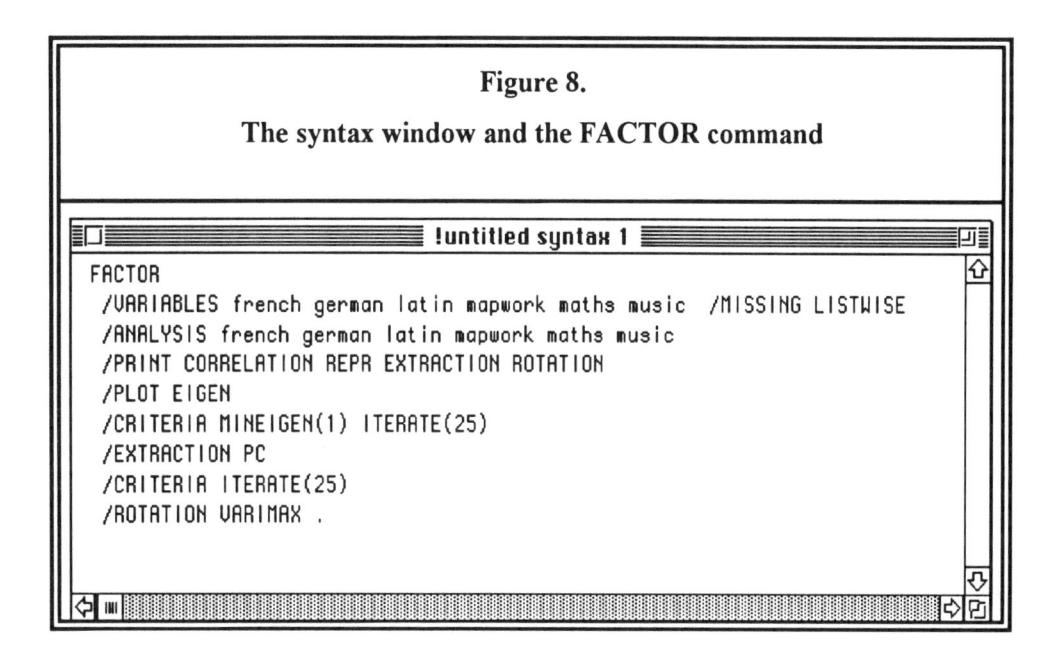

Figure 8.

The syntax window and the FACTOR command

```
!untitled syntax 1
FACTOR
  /VARIABLES french german latin mapwork maths music  /MISSING LISTWISE
  /ANALYSIS french german latin mapwork maths music
  /PRINT CORRELATION REPR EXTRACTION ROTATION
  /PLOT EIGEN
  /CRITERIA MINEIGEN(1) ITERATE(25)
  /EXTRACTION PC
  /CRITERIA ITERATE(25)
  /ROTATION VARIMAX .
```

The general appearance of SPSS syntax will be familiar to readers who have used SPSS/PC+ (see *SPSS/PC+ Made Simple, Kinnear & Gray, 1992*). Some **commands** (the **data commands**) control the entry of data into SPSS; others select and direct the statistical analysis. *In SPSS syntax, a command always ends in a full stop.* Notice that in the statement in the syntax window, there is only one full stop at the very end. In fact, there is only a single command: the FACTOR command. The statement, nevertheless, is not a short one. Notice the terms /PLOT EIGEN, /ROTATION VARIMAX and so on. A phrase that begins with / is a **subcommand**. Subcommands are requests for optional extras: they are the written equivalent of pressing those special buttons at the bottom of the original dialog box.

Now select the whole of the written FACTOR command by emboldening the entire contents of the syntax window. Press the **Run** button ▦ in the toolbar above the syntax window. This has the effect of re-running the entire factor analysis. Inspect the contents of the output window to confirm that this is true.

To save this syntax file, select
File
  Save SPSS Syntax

to obtain the **Save Syntax** dialog box (Figure 9).

Chapter 15 - Factor Analysis

Figure 9.
The Save SPSS Syntax dialog box

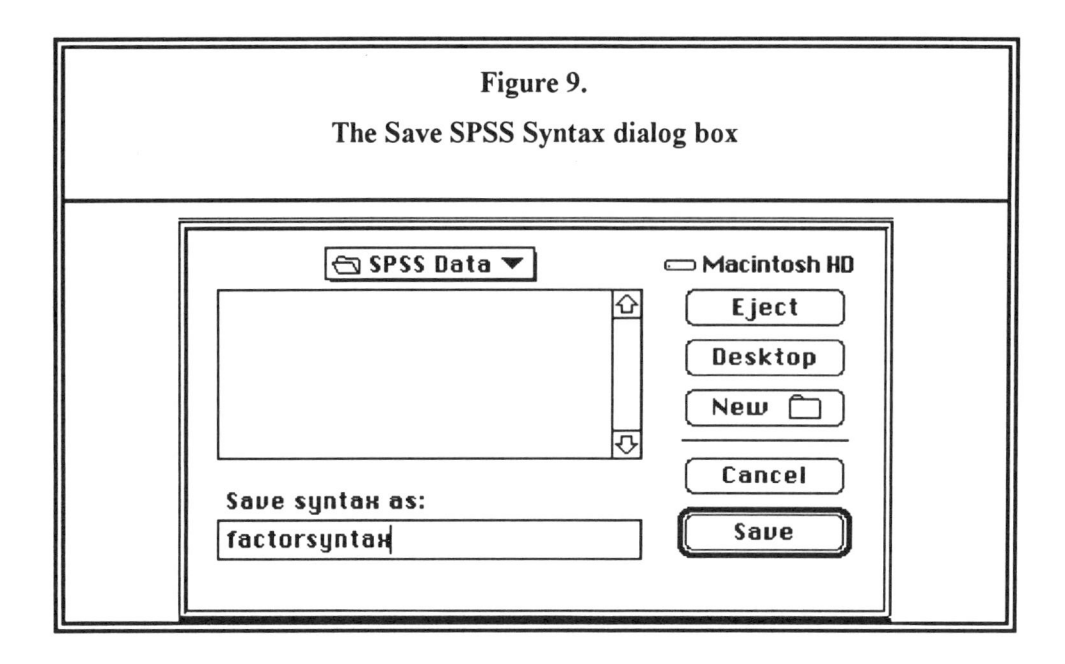

Select the appropriate target folder from the pop-up menu at the top of the dialog box and choose an appropriate name such as *factorsyntax* and click on **Save**. Close the syntax window.

The foregoing factor analysis can now be run very quickly indeed.

- Clear the output window by selecting its entire contents and pressing **Delete**.
- Select
  File
    New

  to obtain the **New** window (Figure 10).

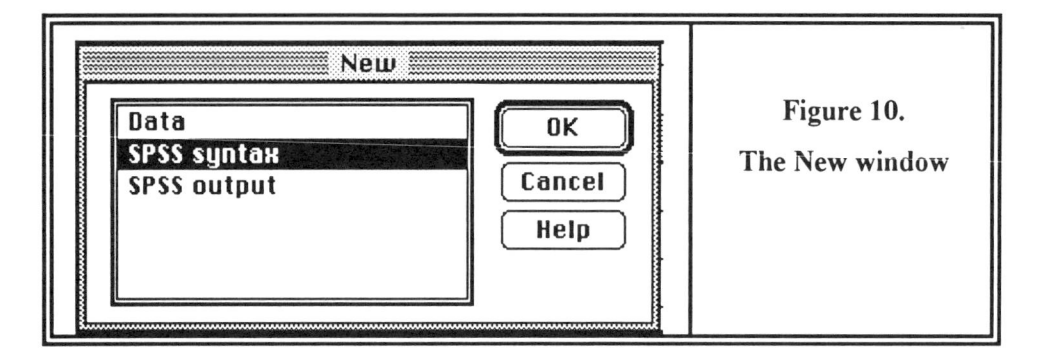

Figure 10.
The New window

- Click on **SPSS Syntax** to open the **syntax window**. The syntax window will be empty.
- Now choose
  File
    Open

  to obtain the **Open File** dialog box (Figure 11).

Figure 11.
The Open File dialog box

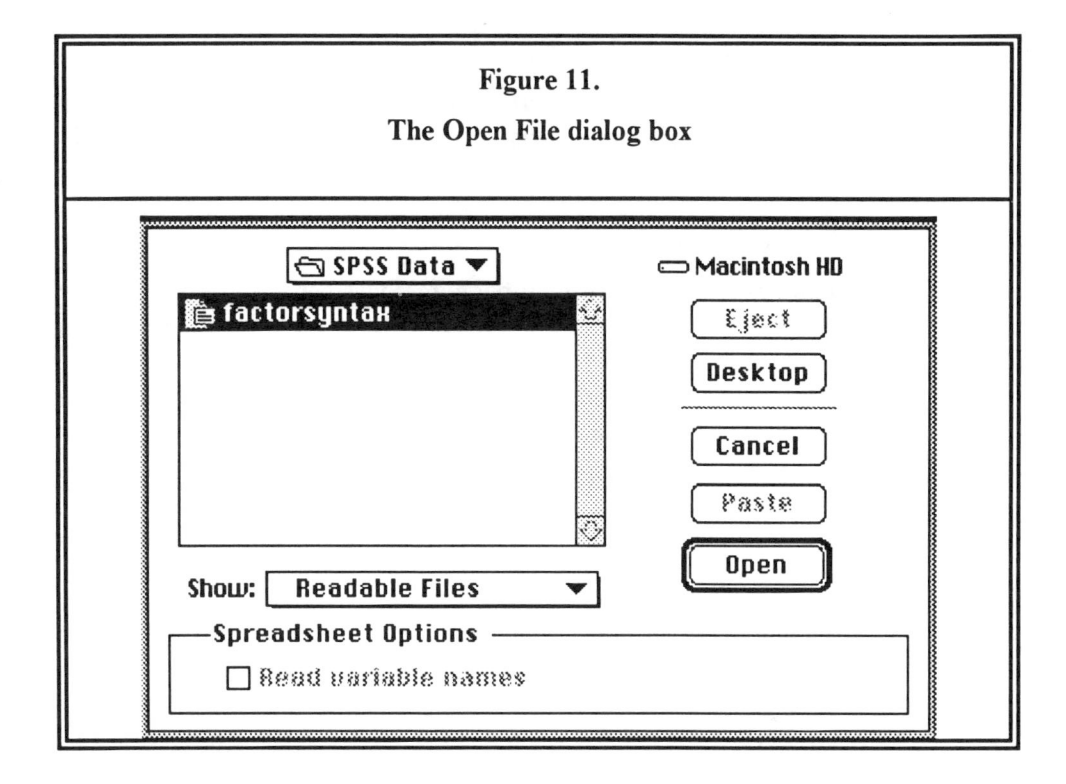

- Use the pop-up menu at the top to select the correct source folder. Choose the file *factorsyntax* and click on **Open**. The FACTOR command will appear in the syntax window once again.
- Now, one need only embolden the command in the window and press the **Run** button ▨ to obtain the complete factor analysis that we have just described.

It is easy to see that with another data set comprising scores on a different battery of tests or to run the same analysis with a different data set, it would be easy to edit the FACTOR command by changing the variable names and other specifications to match the new data in the **Data Editor** window. Inevitably, the experienced user of SPSS builds up a library of written commands, because it is quicker to carry out the analysis by editing the display in the syntax window than go through all the dialog and subdialog boxes again.

15.3.2 Using a correlation matrix as input for factor analysis

Historically, SPSS (like several other major statistical packages) was designed to respond to the user's written commands: the graphical interface is a comparatively recent development. The translation, moreover, is as yet incomplete: there are some routines that are available on older mainframe versions of SPSS, but cannot yet be accessed in the graphical interface. Ultimately, to harness the full power of SPSS, one needs to use the command language (SPSS syntax).

Chapter 15 - Factor Analysis

Factor analysis from a correlation matrix

So far we have been considering the statistical analysis of *raw scores*, that is, data sets comprising original measurements or observations, upon which no statistical manipulations have been carried out. In the present, factor analytic context, for example, our starting point has been a data set comprising the participants' scores on a set of tests.

Sometimes, however, it may be more convenient to use correlations (rather than raw scores) as the input for a factor analysis: the user may already have an R-matrix and wish to start at that point, rather than going back to the raw data. Unfortunately this cannot be done with dialog boxes: the user must resort to SPSS syntax. The procedure involves two stages:

(1) preparing the correlation matrix in a suitable format;

(2) commanding SPSS to read in the matrix and run the factor analysis.

Preparation of the correlation matrix

- Choose
  File
   New

  to obtain the **New** Dialog box and select **SPSS Syntax** in the usual way.

Figure 12 shows the correct syntax of the commands needed for the entry of a correlation matrix into SPSS.

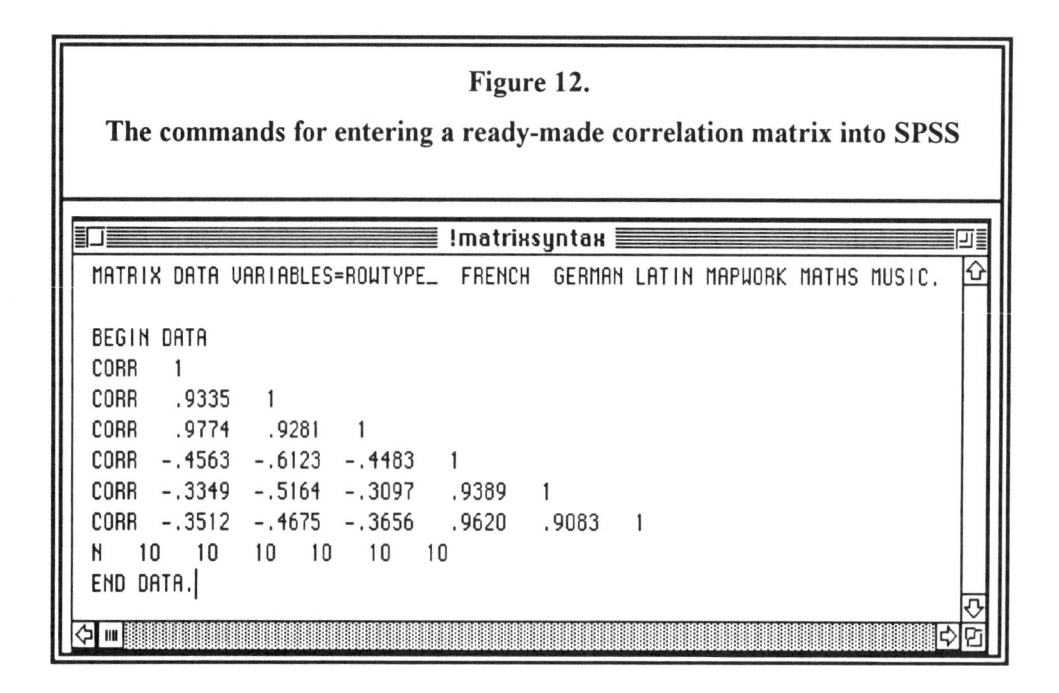

Figure 12.

The commands for entering a ready-made correlation matrix into SPSS

```
MATRIX DATA VARIABLES=ROWTYPE_  FRENCH  GERMAN  LATIN  MAPWORK  MATHS  MUSIC.

BEGIN DATA
CORR    1
CORR    .9335   1
CORR    .9774   .9281   1
CORR   -.4563  -.6123  -.4483   1
CORR   -.3349  -.5164  -.3097   .9389   1
CORR   -.3512  -.4675  -.3656   .9620   .9083   1
N       10      10      10      10      10      10
END DATA.
```

The first command is MATRIX DATA, whose purpose is to tell SPSS to prepare to receive data in the form of a matrix whose dimensions are specified by the number of variables in the list. Like all commands, it must end in a full stop. Note the term ROWTYPE_ . which is a special string variable used to identify the type of data for each record (row).

Chapter 15 - Factor Analysis

Next comes the DATA command: first there is BEGIN DATA; then come the data themselves; and the command ends with 'END DATA.'. *Note the full stop at the end of the command: this is absolutely essential.*

Underneath BEGIN DATA come the data themselves. The first six rows begin with the word CORR, which tells SPSS that the data are in the form of correlation coefficients. The final (7th) row begins with N, which is a count of the of the number of data points in each column. The terms CORR and N are instances of the generic term ROWTYPE_ which appeared in the MATRIX DATA command.

The default structure of a correlation matrix is a lower triangular matrix. If an upper triangular or rectangular matrix were to be input, an additional /FORMAT subcommand would be required. The value of *N* is not needed for a basic factor analysis, but it is needed for tests of significance and for assessing the sampling adequacy of the data. The correlation matrix and value of *N* are then entered (preceded in each row with *CORR* or *N*, as appropriate) between the usual *BEGIN DATA* and *END DATA* commands.

Run the **Matrix Data** command by dragging the cursor over all the syntax in Figure 12 to highlight the entire command, and clicking on ▨ icon in the toolbar at the top of the syntax window. If all is well, no error messages should appear in the **Output** window. The matrix of correlations and the vector of counts can be inspected in the **Data Editor** window by clicking on the **Window** menu and selecting **untitled data**. Part of the **Data Editor** window is shown in Figure 13.

Figure 13.
Part of the data set in the Data Editor window after running the Matrix Data commands

	rowtype_	varname_	french	german	latin	mapwork
1	N		10.0000	10.0000	10.0000	10.0000
2	CORR	FRENCH	1.0000	.9335	.9774	-.4563
3	CORR	GERMAN	.9335	1.0000	.9281	-.6123
4	CORR	LATIN	.9774	.9281	1.0000	-.4483
5	CORR	MAPWORK	-.4563	-.6123	-.4483	1.0000
6	CORR	MATHS	-.3349	-.5164	-.3097	.9389
7	CORR	MUSIC	-.3512	-.4675	-.3656	.9620

Preparation of the factor analysis command

Return to the syntax window and type the FACTOR command as shown in Figure 14.

Notice the identification of the source of the matrix in the /*MATRIX =IN* subcommand is given as (*CORR=**). This shows that it is a correlation matrix (and not, say, a factor matrix), and that it is in the current data file (represented by *) as shown in the **Data Editor** window. The /*PRINT* options are those selected in the **Descriptives** dialog box, the /*PLOT* option is that selected in the **Extraction** dialog box, and the /*ROTATION* option was chosen in the **Rotation** dialog box.

Run the **Factor** command by highlighting the whole command with the cursor and then clicking on the ▨ icon in the toolbar at the top of the syntax window. The output listing for the factor analysis will be identical with that previously described.

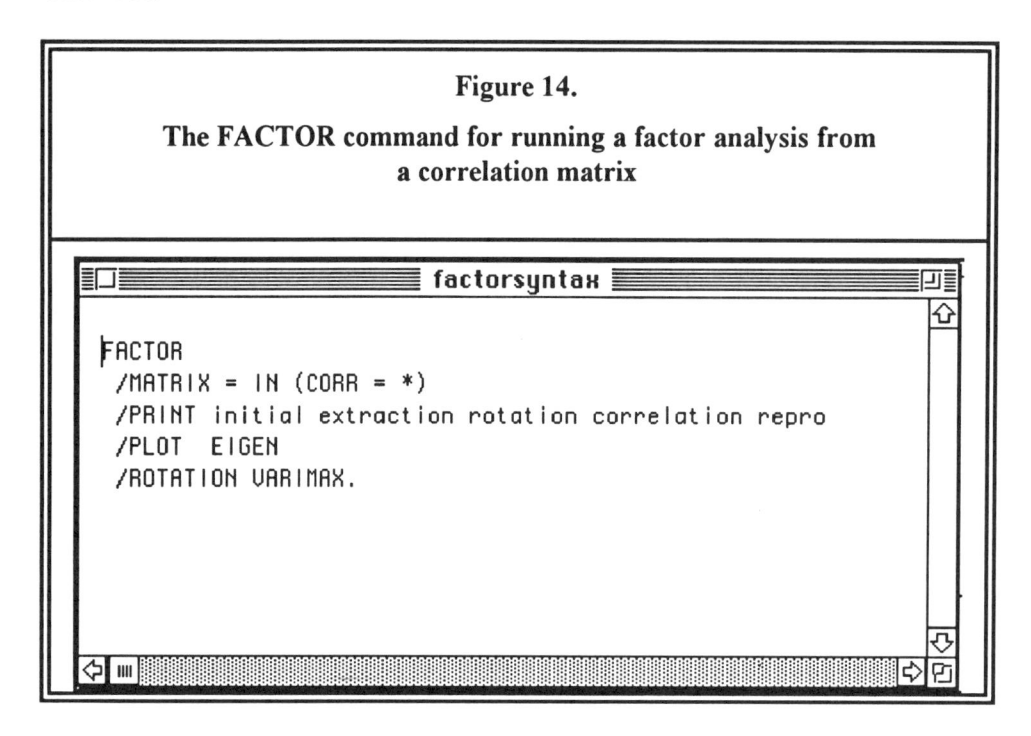

Figure 14.

The FACTOR command for running a factor analysis from a correlation matrix

```
FACTOR
 /MATRIX = IN (CORR = *)
 /PRINT initial extraction rotation correlation repro
 /PLOT  EIGEN
 /ROTATION VARIMAX.
```

15.3.3 Progressing with SPSS syntax

We think that the best way of learning SPSS syntax in a graphics environment like MACOS is by pasting the minimal basic commands into the **syntax window** from the appropriate dialog boxes in the manner described, and observing how these become more elaborate when extra options are chosen from the subdialog boxes. We recommend this as a very effective preparation for the standard textbooks on SPSS syntax.

The more experienced user will find it helpful, when writing a command in SPSS command language, to access the **Syntax Help** window by writing the command in the syntax window and pressing the icon ▨ in the toolbar. This will produce a syntax map of the command in the syntax window. Optional subcommands are shown in square brackets. Relevant parts can either be typed in the syntax window or, if desired, the whole block of syntax can be copied over for editing from the help window to the syntax window using **Copy** and **Paste** in the usual way. We do not recommend that you follow this procedure until you have already acquired some experience with SPSS syntax in the way we have described.

Chapter 15 - Factor Analysis

EXERCISE 24

FACTOR ANALYSIS

BEFORE YOU START

Before proceeding with this practical, please read Chapter 15.

THE PROJECT

A personality study

Ten subjects are given a battery of personality tests, comprising the following items: Anxiety; Agoraphobia; Arachnophobia; Extraversion; Adventure; Sociability. The purpose of this project is to ascertain whether the correlations among the six variables can be accounted for in terms of comparatively few latent variables, or factors (see Chapter 15).

Preparing the data set

The data are shown in Table 1. Enter these scores into the Data Editor in the usual way.

\multicolumn{7}{c	}{Table 1. The questionnaire data}
Participant	Anxiety	Agora	Arachno	Advent	Extrav	Sociab
1	71	68	80	44	54	52
2	39	30	41	77	90	80
3	46	55	45	50	46	48
4	33	33	39	57	64	62
5	74	75	90	45	55	48
6	39	47	48	91	87	91
7	66	70	69	54	44	48
8	33	40	36	31	37	36
9	85	75	93	45	50	42
10	45	35	44	70	66	78

Procedure for the factor analysis of the raw data

Having entered the data into the Data Editor, follow the procedure described in Section 15.2.1.

Interpretation of the results

Examine the correlation matrix in the output listing. Is there evident any pattern that would suggest that the R-matrix might be accounted for in terms of relatively few factors? Examine the remainder of the output listing in the manner outlined in Section 15.2.2, considering the scree plot, the unrotated F-matrix, the residuals and the final rotated matrix. How might the patterns among the correlations in the R-matrix be explained psychologically?

Procedure for the factor analysis of the correlation matrix

Following the procedure described in Section 15.3.2, type the appropriate commands and the lower triangular version of the R-matrix into the syntax window. Include the following items.
- The MATRIX DATA VARIABLES command with the appropriate variable names (including ROWTYPE_)
- A BEGIN DATA command
- Rows of correlation coefficients (each preceded by CORR)
- A row indicating the size of n (preceded by N and then the size of n repeated for as many variables as you have)
- An END DATA command concluding with a period (.)

When the data syntax is complete, run the factor analysis by dragging the cursor over all the syntax and then clicking on . The Data Editor window should now appear similar to that shown in Chapter 15, Figure 13.

If all is well, proceed to prepare the FACTOR command by studying the one shown in Chapter 15, Figure 14. Run the factor analysis by selecting the command and clicking on the Run button in the same way as described above. Confirm that the results of the analysis are the same as those obtained when you started from the raw scores.

Written summary of the results of the factor analysis

- **Construct your own table from the rotated factor matrix in the listing, showing the loadings of each of the variables on the two factors that have emerged from the analysis. State clearly whether there is a tendency for different groups of variables to load upon different factors.**

REFERENCES

Anscombe, F. J. (1973). Graphs in statistical analysis. *American Statistician, 27,* 17-21.

Bentler, P. M. (1983). *EQS structural equations program manual.* Los Angeles, CA: BMDP Statistical Sofware.

Cohen, J., & Cohen, P. (1983). *Applied multiple regression/correlation analysis for the behavioral sciences.* (2nd ed.). Hillsdale, N. J.: Lawrence Erlbaum.

Darlington, R. B. (1968). Multiple regression in psychological research and practice. *Psychological Bulletin, 69,* 161-182.

Delucchi, K. L. (1983). The use and misuse of chi-square: Lewis and Burke revisited. *Psychological Bulletin, 94,* 166-176.

Di Nucci, D., Castro, E., Abemathy, E., Blattner, D., Guglielmo, C., Kadyk, J., Norr, H., & Weibel, R. (1994). *The Macintosh bible.* (5th ed.). Berkeley, CA: Peachpit Press.

Everitt, B. S. (1977). *The analysis of contingency tables.* London: Chapman and Hall.

Gravetter, F. J., & Wallnau, L. B. (1996). *Statistics for the behavioral sciences: A first course for students of psychology and education.* (4th ed.). St. Paul: West.

Howell, D. C. (1997). *Statistical methods for psychology.* (4th ed.). Belmont, CA: Duxbury.

Jöreskog, K. G., & Sörbom, D. (1989). *Lisrel 7: A guide to the program and applications.* Chicago: SPSS Inc.

Keppel, G. (1973). *Design and analysis: A researcher's handbook.* Englewood Cliffs, NJ: Prentice-Hall, Inc.

Kerlinger, F. N. (1986). *Foundations of behavioral research.* (3rd ed.). New York: Holt, Rinehart & Winston.

Kim, J., & Mueller, C. W. (1978a). *Introduction to factor analysis: What it is and how to do it.* Sage University paper series on quantitative applications in the social sciences, 07-013. Newbury Park, CA: Sage.

Kim, J., & Mueller, C. W. (1978b). *Factor analysis: Statistical methods and practical issues.* Sage University paper series on quantitative applications in the social sciences, 07-014. Newbury Park, CA: Sage.

Kinnear, P.R., & Gray, C.D. (1992). *SPSS/PC+ made simple.* Hove (UK): Lawrence Erlbaum Associates.

Kinnear, P.R., & Gray, C.D. (1994). *SPSS for Windows made simple.* Hove (UK): Psychology Press.

Kinnear, P.R., & Gray, C.D. (1997). *SPSS for Windows made simple.* (2nd ed.) Hove (UK): Psychology Press.

Kirk, R. E. (1982). *Experimental design: Procedures for the behavioral sciences.* (2nd ed.). Belmont: Brooks/Cole.

Lewis, D., & Burke, C. J. (1949). The use and misuse of the chi-square test. *Psychological Bulletin, 46,* 433-489.

Lovie, P. (1991). Regression diagnostics: A rough guide to safer regression. In P. Lovie & A. D. Lovie, *New developments in statistics for psychology and the social sciences.* London and New York: The British Psychological Society and Routledge.

Maxwell, A. E. W. (1977). *Multivariate analysis in behavioural research.* London: Chapman & Hall.

Neave, H.R. & Worthington, P.L. (1988). *Distribution-free tests.* London: Unwin Hyman.

Reynolds, H. T. (1984). *The analysis of nominal data.* (2nd ed.). Sage University paper series on quantitative applications in the social sciences, 07-007. Newbury Park, CA: Sage.

References

Siegel, S., & Castellan, N. J. (1988). *Nonparametric statistics for the behavioral sciences.* (2nd ed.). New York: McGraw-Hill.

Tabachnick, B. G., & Fidell, L. S. (1996). *Using multivariate statistics.* (3rd ed.). New York: Harper and Row.

Upton, G. J. G. (1978). *The analysis of cross-tabulated data.* Chichester: John Wiley.

Upton, G. J. G. (1986). Cross-classified data. In A. D. Lovie (Ed.), *New developments in statistics for psychology and the social sciences.* London and New York: The British Psychological Society and Methuen.

Winer, B. J., Brown, D. R., & Michels, K. M. (1991). *Statistical principles in experimental design.* (3rd ed.). New York: McGraw-Hill.

INDEX

A
Adjusted R Squared *284*
Alias *25*
    creating one *25*
    transferring to the Apple menu *27*
Alternate [Alt] key *7*
Alternative hypothesis *148*
Analysis of variance - see ANOVA
ANOVA *171*
    completely randomised *173*
    completely randomised factorial *188*
    mixed *236*
    one-way (see completely randomised)
    repeated measures *211*
    within subjects (see repeated measures)
ANOVA (menu items)
    One-Way ANOVA *174*
    Simple Factorial *193*
    Repeated Measures *211*
Anscombe *271*
Apple extended keyboard *6*
Apple Guide *15*
Apple keyboard *6*
Apple menu *26*
Apple Menu Items folder *27*
Apple motif *8*
Application menu *12*
Arrow keys *7*
Association in interval, ordinal and nominal data *139*

B
Backspace [←] key *8*
Back up *3*
Balloon help *15*
Bar graph (or bar chart) *85, 93*
    simple *85*
    clustered *99*
    with error bars *103*
Bar spacing *216*
Basic mouse operations *13*
Beta weights *288*
Between subjects
    factors *38*
    experimental designs *38*
Binomial test *168*
Bivariate correlations (see Correlation)
Bonferroni method *221*

Booting up *10*
Bootstrapping *10*
Boxplot *96*
Boxplot, editing of a *215*

C
Capitalising upon chance *201*
Capitals lock [Caps Lock] key *7*
Carousel window (Chart Carousel window) *85*
carry-over effects *211*
Cases:
    adding additional cases *73*
    inserting *52*
    listing *62*
    selection of *66*
    weighting of *68*
Categorial data *129*
Causal modelling (path analysis) *339*
Cell editor *30*
Central processing *2*
Chart Aspect Ratio *216*
Charts (see Graphs)
Chart Carousel window *97*
Chart Editor menus *97*
Chi-square *264*
    cautions and caveats *265*
    goodness-of-fit test *124*
Clicking (on an icon) *14*
Click-and-drag mouse operation *14*
Clustered bar charts (see Bar graph)
Cochran's Q test *224*
Coding variable (see Grouping variable)
Coefficient of determination (R Squared) *284*
Command language *340*
Command key *8*
Common factor variance *344*
Compact disk (CD) *3*
Compute procedure *108*
Conditional expressions *67*
Confidence interval *154*
Confirmatory factor analysis *338*
Confounding *211*
Conservative F test *220*
Contingency table *68*
Control (in research) *37*
Control [Ctrl] key *8*
Control panels *17, 21*

359

Copying files *31*
Copying material in the Data Editor *52*
Correlation coefficient *138*
Correlational (versus experimental) research *36*
Correlation matrix (R-matrix) *336*
 as input for factor analysis *352*
Correlations procedure *258*
Corruption *3*
Counterbalancing *211*
Covariance, heterogeneity of *212*
Covariate *194*
Cramér's V *265*
Crashing *10*
Crosstabulation *264*
Crosstabs procedure *86*
Customising the Apple menu *27*
Cursor (insertion point) *6*
Cursor [←↑→↓] keys (see Arrow keys)
Cut command *53*

D
Data, nominal, ordinal and interval *129*
Data drop-down menu
Data Editor window *28*, *43*
Data menu *266*
Date and Time control panels *27*
Decimal places:
 setting with Preferences *44*
 setting with Type *56*
Define Labels *47*
Define Variable *29*
Define variable type *56*
Delete [Del] key *8*
Deleting:
 columns & rows from the Data Editor *52*
 a file or folder *17*
Dependent and independent variables *37*
Descriptives procedure *87*
Desktop *12*
Dialog box *10*
Directory dialog box *58*
Discriminant analysis procedure *323*
Discriminant function *320*
Disk cache *22*
Disks & disk drives *3*
Disks, floppy, hard and compact *3*
Display Order for Variable Lists *44*

E
EDA (Exploratory Data Analysis) *78*
Editing
 data *51*
 graph or bar chart *97*, *101*
 SPSS output
Eigenvalue *334*
Ejecting a floppy disk *17*
Emptying the Wastebasket *17*
Enter/Return [↵] key *8*
Entering data into SPSS *41*
Error bar chart *102*
Error bars in bar charts *103*
Escape [Esc] key *8*
EXCEL spreadsheet *59*
Exit command (see Quitting SPSS)
Expected frequencies *269*
Experimental hypothesis *148*
Experimental (versus correlational) research *37*
Exploratory data analysis (EDA) *78*
Exploratory factor analysis *338*
Explore procedure *87*
Exporting data (see Importing and exporting data)
Extraneous variables *37*

F
Factor
 in experimental design *37*
 in factor analysis *336*
Factor (in ANOVA) *37*
 between subjects *38*
 repeated measures *38*
 treatment *37*
 subject *37*
 within subjects *38*
Factor (in factor analysis) *336*
 extraction *338*
 rotation *338*
 scree plot *345*
 with correlations as input *351*
 with raw data as input *340*
Factor analysis procedure *353*
Factorial ANOVA *193*
Factor matrix, unrotated and rotated *346*
File *5*
File information *63*
File splitting *70*
File menu *22*
File names, difference between MACOS and Windows *5*

Filter 66
Find command 23
Floppy disk 3
Folder 5
F-matrix (factor matrix)
    unrotated 338
    rotated 338
Formatting disks 3
F-ratio 172
Frequencies procedure 83
Friedman test 222
Full variable names (in SPSS) 48
Function keys 8

G
Goodman & Kruskal's lambda 265
Graphical User Interface (see GUI) 12
Graphs menu 82
Graphs:
    bar 85
    boxplot 96
    editing 97, 115
    histogram 89
    line 122
    pie 105
    scatterplot 107
Greenhouse-Geisser test 219
Grouping (coding) variable 42
GUI interface (see Graphical User
    Interface)
Guide menu 12

H
Hanging up 9
Hard copy 3
Hard disk 3
Help drop-down menu in SPSS 145
Hierarchical loglinear model 305
Histograms 89
Homogeneity of covariance 212
    Mauchly test 212
Homogeneity of variance 178
Hypothesis, scientific 36
Hypothesis, statistical 148
    alternative 148
    null 148

I
Icons 4
    file and folder 19
    naming of 14
Importing and exporting data 60

Independent and related samples 130
Independent samples t-test 149
Independent-Samples T Test procedure 155
Independent variable 37
Initialising a disk (see Formatting)
Inserting additional cases and variables 52
Insertion point (cursor) 6
Interaction 189
Interaction graph 197
Interface 4
Interval data 129
Inverse video 51
Items found window 23

K
Kendall's tau correlations (tau-a, tau-b,
    tau-c) 262
Keyboard 6
Key combinations 24
Kolmogorov-Smirnov test 137
Kruskal-Wallis test (k-sample median test)
    180

L
Label menu 14
Lambda, Wilks' 321
Latent root (see Eigenvalue)
Latent variables 336
Layering in Compare Means 92
Level (of a factor in ANOVA) 37
Levene's test of homogeneity of variance
    178
License, for SPSS 28
Light pen 2
Likelihood ratio (L.R.) chi-square 305
Linear association 254
Line graph 106
List Cases procedure 61
Loading (in factor analysis) 336
Logging in and logging out of a network
    10
Loglinear analysis 304
    comparison with ANOVA 303
    small expected frequencies 305
    total independence model 315
Loglinear procedure 308
Lower triangular matrix 344

M
Macintosh Hard Disk (HD) 17
Macintosh HD window 18
Macintosh keyboard 5

Index

Macintosh Operating System *12*
Macintosh tutorial *15*
MACOS (see Macintosh Operating System)
McNemar test *132*
Main effect in ANOVA *188*
Mainframe (computer) *3*
Make Alias command *27*
Mann-Whitney test *159*
MANOVA (multivariate analysis of variance) *141*
Marginal means *188*
Matrix data command *353*
Mauchly sphericity test (homogeneity of covariance) *212*
McNemar test *135, 158*
Means procedure *87*
   (see also Compare Means, Descriptives and Explore procedures)
Memory control panel *20*
Menu bar *12*
Merging files *73*
Missing values *56*
Mixed (split-plot) designs *40*
Mouse operations *13*
   clicking *14*
   click-and-drag operations *14*
   shapes of screen pointer *13*
Multicollinearity *337*
Multiple comparisons, the problem *172*
   (see Tukey's HSD test; Bonferroni method)
Multiple correlation coefficient R *279*
Multiple regression *278*
   beta weights *290*
   procedure *289*
   simultaneous *289*
   stepwise *291*
Multivariate analysis of variance (MANOVA) *141*
Multivariate statistics *141*
Multiway contingency tables *303*

N
Network *10*
New folder *16*
Nominal data *129*
Nonparametric tests *133*
   (see also Binomial test, Chi-square test, Cochran Q test, Friedman test, Kruskal-Wallis test, McNemar test, Mann-Whitney test, Sign test, Wilcoxon test)
Null hypothesis *148*
Number pad *7*
Numeric variables *47*

O
One-factor experiment *171*
   between subjects *39, 171*
   within subjects (repeated measures) *39*
One-sample tests *136*
   binomial *168*
   chi-square *124*
   t-test *168*
One-way analysis of variance *173*
One-way ANOVA procedure *173*
Operating system *4*
Operating systems (MACOS, DOS, Windows, UNIX) *4*
Option key *9*
Order effects *211*
Ordinal data 129
Orthogonal factors (in factor analysis) *346*
Outliers, effect of *167*
Output window and output listing *85*

P
p-value (tail probability) *148*
Paired data (related samples) *149*
Paired-Samples T Test procedure *152*
Parametric and nonparametric tests *133*
   (see also Nonparametric tests)
Partial regression coefficients *278*
Paste *52*
PC (Personal Computer) *4*
PC clone *4*
Pearson correlation *255*
Percentiles (quantiles) *88*
Per family type 1 error rate *171, 201*
Phi coefficient *265*
Pie chart *104*
Platform *3*
Point-biserial correlation *261*
Pointer, screen *13*
Pooled (independent) t-test *149*
Pop-up menu *58*
Portable (SPSS) data *59*
Positioning a window *19*
Post hoc comparisons (see Multiple comparisons)
Power (of a statistical test) *149*
Power key *9*

Index

Powerbook *8*
Powermac *12*
Preferences dialog box *44*
Principal components *337*
Principal diagonal *344*
Principal factors *337*
Printing in SPSS *64*
Program *4*
p-value (tail probability) *148*

Q
q (Studentized range statistic) *179*
Qualitative & quantitative variables *129*
Quartiles *88*
Quitting SPSS *31*

R
R (multiple correlation coefficient) *279*
R Squared *284*
Radio button *56*
RAM (Random Access Memory) *27*
Rank correlation (see Spearman's rho and Kendall's tau)
Reboot *10*
    hard *10*
    soft *10*
Recode procedure *111*
Recording tape *3*
Regression constant *278*
Regression, simple and multiple *278*
Regression
    diagnostics *279*
    line *278*
    residuals *279*
Regression procedure
    simple *280*
    multiple *289*
Related samples *130*
Repeated measures (see Within subjects)
Reproduced correlation matrix (in factor analysis) *346*
Residuals (in regression) *279*
Retrieving a file *57*
Return/Enter [↵] key *9*
R-matrix (see Correlation matrix)
Rotated factor matrix *347*
Rotation (of factors) *338*
Run button *349*
Runs test *137*

S
Samples
    independent & related *130*
Save procedure *30*
Save As procedure *30*
    dialog box *30*
Save Data As dialog box *58*
Saving a file to a floppy disk *31*
Saving a file from floppy disk to the Mac *32*
Saving data in SPSS *57*
Scatterplot, importance of *256*
Scatterplot procedure *107*
    clustered *297*
    with regression line *295*
Scree plot *345*
Screen pointer *13*
Scroll bar *20*
Select Cases procedure *66*
Separate-variance t-test *149*
Setting decimal places
    using Preferences *44*
    using Type *56*
Shift [⇧] key *6*
Short-cuts (see Key combinations)
Shut Down *27*
Sign test *158*
Significance, statistical *148*
Simple Factorial ANOVA procedure *193*
Simple main effects (ANOVA) *189*
Simple regression *278*
    procedure for *280*
Simple structure (in factor analysis) *338*
Singularity (of R-matrix) *337*
Size box *20*
Space bar *6*
Spearman's rho (rank correlation) *262*
Special menu *14*
Sphericity (see homogeneity of covariance)
Splitting files *70*
Split-plot (mixed) factorial designs *40*
SPSS (Statistical Package for the Social Sciences) *4*
SPSS for Macintosh *4*
Startup disk *13*
Statistical model *80*
Statistics, descriptive and confirmatory *78*
Statistics drop-down menu *81*
Stem-and-leaf display *94*
Stepwise method in multiple regression *291*
String variables *55*
    short and long *55*
Structural equation modelling *338*

Index

Studentized range statistic (q) *179*
Subject variables *37*
Substantive model of causation (in regression) *294*
Summarize menu
    Crosstabs *83*
    Frequencies *83*
Syntax, SPSS *348*
Syntax window *348*
System folder *20*
System software *13*

T
Tabulation (Tab) key *9*
Tail probability (p-value) *148*
Title bar *19*
Toggle keys *7*
Trackball *2*
Trackpad *2*
Transposing data *120*
t-test
    independent samples *155*
    one-sample *136*
    paired samples *152*
    pooled variance *149*
    separate variance *149*
Tukey's HSD test *179*

U
Univariate statistics *141*
Unplanned multiple comparisons (post hoc tests) *221*
Unrotated factor matrix *338*
User-missing values *56*
Utilities menu *51*

V
Value labelling *48*
Variable *36*
Variance, homogeneity of *149*
Varimax method of factor rotation *343*
View
    by Date *19*
    by Icon *19*
    by Name *19*
View menu *14, 18*

W
Wastebasket *13*
Weight Cases procedure *68*
Wilcoxon paired samples test *158*
Wilks' lambda statistic *322*
Window, basic operations with *19*
Windows (operating system)
    conventions for file naming *5*
Within subjects experiments,
    advantages and disadvantages *210*
Within subjects
    design *38*
    factors *38*
Word *5*
Wrist-watch icon *12*

Z
Zoom box *19*

READER'S NOTES

Notes

Notes

Notes

Notes

Notes